UNIX® Shells
by Example
Fourth Edition

UNIX® Shells
by Example
Fourth Edition

Ellie Quigley

PRENTICE
HALL
PTR

Prentice Hall Professional Technical Reference
Upper Saddle River, NJ 07458
www.phptr.com

Library of Congress Cataloging-in-Publication Data
Quigley, Ellie.
  UNIX shells by example / Ellie Quigley.—4th ed.
    p. cm.
  Includes index.
  ISBN 0-13-147572-X (alk. paper)
   1. UNIX (Computer file)   2. UNIX Shells.   I. Title.

QA76.76.O63 Q54 2004
005.4'32—dc22

                          2004051960

Acquisitions: *Mark L. Taub, Publishing Partner*
Editorial Assistant: *Noreen Regina*
Marketing Manager: *Robin O'Brien*

Prentice Hall offers excellent discounts on this book when ordered in quantity for bulk purchases or special sales. For more information, please contact: U.S. Corporate and Government Sales, 1-800-382-3419, corpsales@pearsontechgroup.com. For sales outside of the U.S., please contact: International Sales, international@pearsoned.com.

Printed in the United States of America

ISBN 0-13-147572-X
1 2 3 4 5 6 7 8 9 10—CRS—0807060504
1st Printing, September 2004

Pearson Education Ltd.
Pearson Education Australia Pty., Limited
Pearson Education South Asia Pte. Ltd.
Pearson Education Asia Ltd.
Pearson Education Canada, Ltd.
Pearson Educación de Mexico, S.A. de C.V.
Pearson Education—Japan
Pearson Malaysia S.D.N. B.H.D.

~ To My Father ~

Contents at a Glance

Contents

14 Programming the Bash Shell   865

Preface

Playing the "shell" game is a lot of fun. This book was written to make your learning experience both fun and profitable. Since the first edition was published, many of you who have been helped by my book have contacted me, telling me that the book made you realize that shell programming doesn't need to be difficult at all! Learning by example makes it easy and fun. In fact, because of such positive feedback, I have been asked by Prentice Hall to produce this fourth edition of *UNIX® Shells by Example* for UNIX and Linux users, programmers, and administrators. Along with updated material throughout, it includes three completely new chapters, with full coverage of the GNU tools for those of you who use Linux. With the meteoric rise of Linux popularity, it seemed like a good time to combine the best of *Linux Shells by Example* with *UNIX® Shells by Example* and produce a single volume that touches on all the various aspects of the UNIX/Linux shell world.

The new chapters include Chapter 2, "Shell Programming QuickStart," an introductory jump-start for programmers who want a quick survey of the shell programming constructs and how they differ; Chapter 15, "Debugging Shell Scripts," which gives you an example of an error message, what caused it, and how to fix it; and Chapter 16, "The System Administrator and the Shell," which demonstrates how the shell is used by system administrators, from system boot-up to shutdown.

Writing *UNIX® Shells by Example* was the culmination of 21 years of teaching and developing classes for the various shells and UNIX/Linux utilities most heavily used by shell programmers. The course notes I developed have been used by the University of California, Santa Cruz; the University of California, Davis; Sun Microsystems; Apple Computer; Xilinx; National Semiconductor; LSI Logic; De Anza College; and numerous vendors throughout the world. Depending upon the requirements of my client, I normally teach one shell at a time rather than all of them at once. To accommodate the needs of so many clients, I developed separate materials for each of the respective UNIX/Linux shells and tools.

Whether I am teaching "Grep, Sed, and Awk," "Bourne Shell for the System Administrator," "The Interactive Korn Shell," or "Bash Programming," one student always asks, "What book can I get that covers all the shells and the important utilities such as *grep*, *sed*, and *awk*? How does *awk* differ from *gawk*? Will this work if I'm using Linux or is this just for Solaris? Should I get the *awk* book, or should I get a book on *grep* and *sed*? Is there one book that really covers it all? I don't want to buy three or four books in order to become a shell programmer."

In response, I could recommend a number of excellent books covering these topics separately, and some UNIX and Linux books that attempt to do it all, but the students want one book with everything, and not just a quick survey. They want the tools, regular expressions, all the major shells, quoting rules, a comparison of the shells, exercises, and so forth, all in one book. *This is that book.*

As I wrote it, I thought about how I teach the classes and organized the chapters in the same format. In the shell programming classes, the first topic is always an introduction to what the shell is and how it works. Then we talk about the utilities such as *grep*, *sed*, and *awk*—the most important tools in the shell programmer's toolbox. When learning about the shell, it is presented first as an interactive program where everything can be accomplished at the command line, and then as a programming language where the programming constructs are described and demonstrated in shell scripts. (Since the C and TC shells are almost identical as programming languages, there are separate chapters describing interactive use, but only one chapter discussing programming constructs.)

It's one thing to write a script, but yet another to debug it. I have been working with the shells for so long, that I can recognize bugs in a program almost before they happen! But these bugs are hard to find until you get used to the error messages and what they mean. I added a chapter on debugging to help you understand what the often cryptic error messages mean and how to fix them. Since the diagnostics for the shells may differ, each shell is presented with the most common error messages and what caused them.

Many students take a shell course as a step toward learning system administration. Susan Barr, a teaching colleague of mine who teaches system administration and shell programming, offered to share her extensive knowledge and write a chapter to describe how the system administrator uses the shell (Chapter 16, "The System Administrator and the Shell").

Having always found that simple examples are easier for quick comprehension, each concept is captured in a small example followed by the output and an explanation of each line of the program. This method has proven to be very popular with those who learned Perl programming from my first book, *Perl by Example*, or JavaScript from *Java-Script™ by Example*, and with those who learned to write shell programs from *UNIX®️ Shells by Example*.

Another aid to comprehension is that the five shells are discussed in parallel. If, for example, you're working in one shell but want to see how redirection is performed in another shell, you will find a parallel discussion of that topic presented in each of the other shell chapters.

It can be a nuisance to shuffle among several books or the *man* pages when all you want is enough information about a particular command to jog your memory on how a particular command works. To save you time, Appendix A contains a list of useful UNIX and Linux commands, their syntax, and definitions. Examples and explanations are provided for the more robust and often-used commands.

The comparison table in Appendix B will help you keep the different shells straight, especially when you port scripts from one shell to another, and serves as a quick syntax check when all you need is a reminder of how the construct works.

I think you'll find this book a valuable tutorial and reference. The objective is to explain through example and keep things simple so that you have fun learning and save time. Since the book replicates what I say in my classes, I am confident that you will be a productive shell programmer in a short amount of time. Everything you need is right here at your fingertips. Playing the shell game is fun . . . You'll see!

Ellie Quigley (lequig@aol.com)

ACKNOWLEDGMENTS

A special acknowledgment goes to Susan Barr, my friend and colleague, for contributing her expertise on system administration and providing a new chapter for this edition. Susan spent hours testing examples for the many flavors of UNIX and Linux, and also took extra time to correct typos and any errors she found in the third edition. Since she has used *UNIX® Shells by Example* in the classes she teaches, Susan was able to provide invaluable advice for this new edition. Thank you Susan!

I would also like to thank and acknowledge the following people, without whose help this book would not have been published: Mark Taub, my acquisitions editor; Vanessa Moore, my production editor, the best of the best in her field, whose creativity, energy, and style make the book a nice book; Jim A. Lola (author and Principal Systems and Storage Consultant, Life Sciences Consulting Partners), Mark Halegua, and Lawrence Hargett for reviewing, critiqing, and editing the new material. Finally, I would like to thank all my students for their continued support and feedback. They learned with me how to play the shell game. Without them, this book never would have happened.

chapter

1

Introduction to UNIX/Linux Shells

1.1 What Is UNIX? What Is Linux? A Little History

When learning about the shells, you will find they are often associated with different versions of the UNIX/Linux operating systems. For example, the Bourne and Korn shells are associated with AT&T UNIX, the C shell with Berkeley UNIX, and the Bash shell with Linux. Before delving into the particulars of the shells, this section is provided to give you a little background information about the operating systems on which they reside.

1.1.1 A Little Bit About UNIX

UNIX is a multiuser, multitasking operating system initiated by Ken Thompson in 1969 at AT&T Bell Labs. UNIX was designed to allow a large number of programmers to access the computer at the same time, sharing its resources. It was to be simple and powerful, versatile and portable. It could run on computer systems ranging from microcomputers to super minicomputers and mainframes.

At the heart of UNIX is the kernel, a program loaded when the system boots. The kernel talks to the hardware and devices, schedules tasks, and manages memory and storage. Due to the spartan nature of UNIX, a large number of small simple tools and utilities were developed, and because these tools (commands) could be easily combined to perform a variety of larger tasks, UNIX quickly gained popularity. One of the most important utilities developed was the shell, a program that allows the user to communicate with the operating system. This book explores the features of the most prominent shells available today.

1

At first UNIX was adopted, at nominal cost, by scientific research institutions and universities and later spread to computer companies, government bodies, and manufacturing industries. In 1973, the U.S. Defense Advanced Research Projects Agency (DARPA) initiated a research program to develop a way to link computers together transparently across multiple networks using UNIX. This project, and the system of networks that emerged from the research, resulted in the birth of the Internet!

By the late 1970s many of the students who had pioneered and experimented with UNIX in college were now working in industry and demanded a switch to UNIX, claiming that it was the most suitable operating system for a sophisticated programming environment. Soon a large number of vendors, large and small, started marketing their own versions of UNIX, optimizing it for their individual computer architectures. The two most prominent versions of UNIX were System V from AT&T and BSD UNIX, which was derived from AT&T's version and developed at the University of California, Berkeley, in the early 1980s.

(To see a chart of the many different versions of UNIX, over 80 flavors, see www.ugu.com/sui/ugu/show?ugu.flavors.) With so many versions of UNIX, applications and tools running on one system often could not run on another without considerable time and energy spent in making them compatible. This lack of uniformity fueled the rhetoric of competing vendors to abandon UNIX and stay with the older, non-UNIX proprietary systems, such as VMS, that had proven to be more consistent and reliable.

It was time to standardize UNIX. A group of vendors got together and started the concept of "open systems," whereby those participating would agree to conform to certain standards and specifications. UNIX was chosen as the basis for the new concept. A company called X/Open was formed to define the open systems platform, and many organizations began using X/Open as a basis for system design. X/Open is now a part of The Open Group and continues to develop a Single UNIX Specification.

In early 1993, AT&T sold its UNIX System Laboratories to Novell. In 1995 Novell transferred the rights to the UNIX trademark and the specification (which subsequently became the Single UNIX Specification) to The Open Group (at the time X/Open), and sold SCO the UNIX system source code. Today UNIX-based systems are sold by a number of companies. The systems include Solaris from Sun Microsystems, HP-UX and Tru64 UNIX from Hewlett-Packard, and AIX from IBM. In addition there are many freely available UNIX and UNIX-compatible implementations, such as Linux, FreeBSD, and NetBSD.

1.1.2 Why Linux?

In 1991, Linus Torvalds, a Finnish college student, developed a UNIX-compatible operating system kernel at the University of Helsinki, Finland. It was designed to be UNIX on a PC. Although Linux mimics UNIX System V and BSD UNIX, it is not derived from licensed source code.
Rather, it was developed independently by a group of developers from all over the world who were informally allied through the Internet.

For many, Linux offers an alternative to proprietary UNIX and Windows operating systems, and a large Linux culture has evolved sponsoring consortiums, conventions, expos, newsgroups, and publications in a new revolution to rival Windows' dominance in the PC world. With the help of many system programmers and developers, Linux has grown into today's full-fledged UNIX-compatible operating system, with upward of 20 million users. The current full-featured version is 2.6 (released December 2003) and development continues. Linux is distributed by a number of commercial and noncommercial organizations that provide enhancement to the kernel of the operating system, some examples being Red Hat, Slackware, Mandrake, Turbo, and SuSE Linux.

You may have noticed a penguin associated with Linux. The penguin is the official Linux mascot, called Tux, selected by Linus Torvalds to represent the image he associates with the operating system.

The Free Software Foundation.   In 1992, the Free Software Foundation added its GNU (GNU is a recursive acronym "GNU's Not UNIX") software to the Linux kernel to make a complete operating system, and licensed the Linux source code under its General Public License, making it freely available to everyone. Hundreds of GNU utilities were provided by the Free Software Foundation, including improvements to the standard UNIX Bourne shell.

The GNU tools, such as grep, sed, and gawk, are similar to their UNIX namesakes, but have also been improved and designed for POSIX[1] compliancy. When you install Linux, you will have access to the GNU shells and tools, not the standard UNIX shells and tools. And if you are using a traditional UNIX system, such as Sun's Solaris 5.9, you will also have access to many of these tools, including the GNU shells.

1.2 Definition and Function of a Shell

The shell is a special program used as an interface between the user and the heart of the UNIX/Linux operating system, a program called the *kernel*, as shown in Figure 1.1. The kernel is loaded into memory at boot-up time and manages the system until shutdown. It creates and controls processes, and manages memory, file systems, communications, and so forth. All other programs, including shell programs, reside on the disk. The kernel loads those programs into memory, executes them, and cleans up the system when they terminate. The shell is a utility program that starts up when you log on. It allows users to interact with the kernel by interpreting commands that are typed either at the command line or in a script file.

When you log on, an interactive shell starts up and prompts you for input. After you type a command, it is the responsibility of the shell to (a) parse the command line; (b) handle wildcards, redirection, pipes, and job control; and (c) search for the command,

---

1. The requirements for shell functionality are defined by the POSIX (Portable Operating System Interface) standard, POSIX 1003.2.

and if found, execute that command. When you first learn UNIX/Linux, you spend most of your time executing commands from the prompt. You use the shell interactively.

If you type the same set of commands on a regular basis, you may want to automate those tasks. This can be done by putting the commands in a file, called a *script file*, and then executing the file. A shell script works much like a batch file: A list of UNIX/Linux commands is typed into a file, and then the file is executed. More sophisticated scripts contain programming constructs for making decisions, looping, file testing, and so forth. Writing scripts not only requires learning programming constructs and techniques, but also assumes that you have a good understanding of UNIX/Linux utilities and how they work. There are some utilities, such as grep, sed, and awk, that are extremely powerful tools used in scripts for the manipulation of command output and files. After you have become familiar with these tools and the programming constructs for your particular shell, you will be ready to start writing useful scripts. When executing commands from within a script, you are using the shell as a programming language.

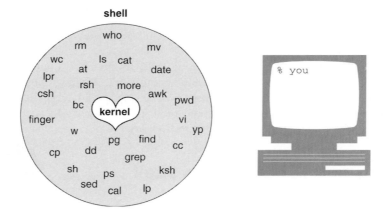

Figure 1.1 The kernel, the shell, and you.

1.2.1 The UNIX Shells

The three prominent and supported shells on most UNIX systems are the *Bourne* shell (AT&T shell), the *C* shell (Berkeley shell), and the *Korn* shell (a superset of the Bourne shell). All three of these behave pretty much the same way when running interactively, but have some differences in syntax and efficiency when used as scripting languages.

The Bourne shell (sh) is the standard UNIX shell, and is used to administer the system. Most of the system adBministration scripts, such as the rc start and stop scripts and shutdown are Bourne shell scripts; this is the shell commonly used by the administrator when running as root. This shell was written at AT&T and is known for being concise, compact, and fast. The default Bourne shell prompt is the dollar sign ($).

The C shell (csh) was developed at Berkeley and added a number of features, such as command-line history, aliasing, built-in arithmetic, filename completion, and job control.

The C shell has been favored over the Bourne shell by users running the shell interactively, but administrators prefer the Bourne shell for scripting, because Bourne shell scripts are simpler and faster than the same scripts written in C shell. The default C shell prompt is the percent sign (%).

The Korn shell is a superset of the Bourne shell written by David Korn at AT&T. A number of features were added to this shell above and beyond the enhancements of the C shell. Korn shell features include an editable history, aliases, functions, regular expression wildcards, built-in arithmetic, job control, coprocessing, and special debugging features. The Bourne shell is almost completely upward-compatible with the Korn shell, so older Bourne shell programs will run fine in this shell. Novell extended the new version of the Korn shell (ksh93) to enable X Windows programming for their desktop, dtksh. Dtksh is a standard part of CDE, the Common Desktop Environment supported by most major UNIX system hardware vendors. The public domain version of the Korn shell (packages.debian.org/stable/shells/pdksh), called pdksh, is also available for multiple platforms, including Linux. Korn shell for Windows is found at www.wipro.com/uwin. The default Korn shell prompt is the dollar sign ($).

1.2.2 The Linux Shells

When you install Linux, you will have access to the GNU shells and tools, not the standard UNIX shells and tools. The GNU Bourne Again shell—Bash, the Linux default shell—is an enhanced Bourne shell, not only at the programming level, but also when used interactively, allowing the user to tailor his working environment and create shortcuts to improve efficiency. This shell is one of the most popular shells used by UNIX and Linux users today, and can be downloaded from www.gnu.org/software/bash/bash.html. The default Bash prompt is the dollar sign ($).

Another prominent shell used by Linux users is the TC shell, a compatible offshoot of the UNIX C shell, but with many additional features.[2] See www.tcsh.org/MostRecent-Release. The default C shell prompt is the greater-than sign (>).

The Z shell is yet another Linux shell that incorporates a number of features from the Bourne Again shell, the TC shell, and the Korn shell. See sourceforge.net/projects/zsh/.

The Public Domain Korn shell (pdksh), a Korn shell clone, is also available, and for a fee, an AT&T Korn shell license can be obtained. The default Public Domain Korn shell prompt is a dollar sign ($).

To see what shells are available under your version of Linux, look in the file /etc/shell, as shown in Example 1.1.

---

2. Although often called the "Linux" shells, bash (Bourne Again shell) and tcsh (TC shell) are freely available and can be compiled on any UNIX system; in fact, the shells are now bundled with Solaris 8+, Sun's UNIX operating system.

EXAMPLE 1.1

```
$ cat /etc/shell
/bin/bash
/bin/sh
/bin/ash
/bin/bsh
/bin/tcsh
/bin/csh
/bin/ksh
/bin/zsh
```

EXPLANATION

The /etc/shell (Linux) file contains a list of all shell programs available on your version of Linux. The most popular versions are bash (Bourne Again shell), tcsh (TC shell), and ksh (Korn shell).

What Is POSIX?   In order to provide software standards for different operating systems and their programs, the POSIX standard (also referred to as the Open Systems Standards) evolved, consisting of participants from the Institute of Electrical and Electronics Engineering (IEEE) and the International Organization for Standardization (ISO). Their goal was to supply standards that would promote application portability across different platforms, to provide a UNIX-like computing environment; thus, new software written on one machine would compile and run on another machine with different hardware. For example, a program written for a BSD UNIX machine would also run on Solaris, Linux, and HP-UX machines. In 1988 the first standard was adopted, called POSIX 1003.1. Its purpose was to provide a C language standard. In 1992, the POSIX group established standards for the shell and utilities to define the terms for developing portable shell scripts, called the IEEE 1003.2 POSIX shell standard and general utility programs. Although there is no strict enforcement of these standards, most UNIX vendors try to comply with the POSIX standard. The term "POSIX compliancy," when discussing shells and their general UNIX utilities, is an attempt to comply with the standards presented by the POSIX committee, when writing new utilities or adding enhancements to the existing ones. For example, the Bourne Again shell is a shell that is almost 100% compliant and gawk is a user utility that can operate in strict POSIX mode.

1.3   History of the Shell

The first significant, standard UNIX shell was introduced in V7 (seventh edition of AT&T) UNIX in late 1979, and was named after its creator, Stephen Bourne. The Bourne shell as a programming language is based on a language called Algol, and was primarily used to automate system administration tasks. Although popular for its simplicity and speed, it lacks many of the features for interactive use, such as history, aliasing, and job control.

The C shell, developed at the University of California, Berkeley, in the late 1970s, was released as part of BSD UNIX. The shell, written primarily by Bill Joy, offered a number of additional features not provided in the standard Bourne shell. The C shell is based on the C programming language, and when used as a programming language, it shares a similar syntax. It also offers enhancements for interactive use, such as command-line history, aliases, and job control. Because the shell was designed on a large machine and a number of additional features were added, the C shell has a tendency to be slow on small machines and sluggish even on large machines when compared with the Bourne shell.

With both the Bourne shell and the C shell available, the UNIX user now had a choice, and conflicts arose over which was the better shell. To provide the best of both worlds, David Korn, from AT&T, invented the Korn shell in the mid-1980s. It was released in 1986 and officially became part of the SVR4 distribution of UNIX in 1988. The Korn shell, really a superset of the Bourne shell, runs not only on UNIX/Linux systems, but also on OS/2, VMS, and DOS. It provides upward compatibility with the Bourne shell, adds many of the popular features of the C shell, and is fast and efficient. The Korn shell has gone through a number of revisions. The most widely used version of the Korn shell is the 1988 version, although the 1993 version has gained popularity. Linux users may find they are running the free version of the Korn shell, called the Public Domain Korn shell, or simply pdksh, a clone of David Korn's 1988 shell. It is free and portable and currently work is underway to make it fully compatible with its namesake, Korn shell, and to make it POSIX compliant. Also available is the Z shell (zsh), another Korn shell clone with TC shell features, written by Paul Falsted, and freely available at a number of Web sites.

With the advent of Linux, the Bourne Again shell (bash) gained popularity as a super Bourne shell. The Bourne Again shell was developed in 1988 by Brian Fox of the Free Software Foundation under the GNU copyright license and is the default shell for the Linux operating system. It was intended to conform to the IEEE POSIX P1003.2/ISO 9945.2 Shell and Tools standard. The Bourne Again shell also offers a number of new features (both at the interactive and programming level) missing in the original Bourne shell (yet Bourne shell scripts will still run unmodified). It also incorporates the most useful features of both the C shell and Korn shell. It's big. The improvements over Bourne shell are command-line history and editing, directory stacks, job control, functions, aliases, arrays, integer arithmetic (in any base from 2 to 64), and Korn shell features such as extended metacharacters, select loops for creating menus, the let command, and more.

What is the TC shell? The TC shell is an expanded, completely compatible version of the C shell. Some of the new features are command-line editing (emacs and vi), scrolling the history list, advanced filename, variable, and command completion, spelling correction, job scheduling, automatic locking and logout, time stamps in the history list, and more. It's also big. People often ask, "What does the 'T' in TC shell stand for?" A little history is involved. Back in 1976, DEC announced and shipped a new virtual memory operating system called TOPS-20, based on TENEX, an operating system used by researchers at that time all around the country. One of the most favored features among TOPS-20 users, and one most identified with TOPS-20 itself, was "escape recognition," also called command completion. With this, the user can often get the system to, in effect, type most of a command or symbolic name by pressing the Esc key. The creator of the TC shell was impressed by this and several other features of TENEX/TOPS-20, and created a version of csh that mimicked them called the TENEX C shell, or simply TC shell, tc-shell, or tcsh. Hence, the "T" in TC shell. See info.astrian.net/doc/tcsh/copyright for more information on tcsh.

1.3.1   Uses of the Shell

When running interactively, one of the major functions of a shell is to interpret commands entered at the command-line prompt. The shell parses the command line, breaking it into words (called *tokens*) separated by whitespace, which consists of tabs, spaces, or a newline. If the words contain special metacharacters, the shell evaluates them. The shell handles file I/O and background processing. After the command line has been processed, the shell searches for the command and starts its execution.

Another important function of the shell is to customize the user's environment, normally done in shell initialization files. These files contain definitions for setting terminal keys and window characteristics; setting variables that define the search path, permissions, prompts, and the terminal type; and setting variables that are required for specific applications such as window managers, text-processing programs, and libraries for programming languages. The Korn/Bash shells and C/TC shells also provide further customization with the addition of history, aliases, and built-in variables set to protect the user from clobbering files, or inadvertently logging out, or to notify the user when a job has completed.

The shell can also be used as an interpreted programming language. Shell programs, also called scripts, consist of commands listed in a file. The programs are created in an editor (although online scripting is permitted). They consist of UNIX/Linux commands interspersed with fundamental programming constructs such as variable assignment, conditional tests, and loops. You do not have to compile shell scripts. The shell interprets each line of the script as if it had been entered from the keyboard. Because the shell is responsible for interpreting commands, it is necessary for the user to have an understanding of what those commands are. See Appendix A for a list of useful UNIX and Linux commands.

1.3.2   Responsibilities of the Shell

The shell is ultimately responsible for making sure that any commands typed at the prompt get executed properly. Included in those responsibilities are:

1. Reading input and parsing the command line
2. Evaluating special characters, such as wildcards and the history character
3. Setting up pipes, redirection, and background processing
4. Handling signals
5. Setting up programs for execution

Each of these topics is discussed in detail as it pertains to a particular shell.

1.4   **System Startup and the Login Shell**

When you start up your system, the first process called is init. Each process has a process identification number associated with it, called the PID. Because init is the first process, its PID is 1. The init process initializes the system and then starts other processes to open terminal lines and set up the standard input (stdin), standard output (stdout), and standard error (stderr), which are all associated with the terminal. The standard input normally comes from the keyboard; the standard output and standard error go to the screen. At this point, a login prompt would appear on your terminal.

After you type your login name, you will be prompted for a password. The /bin/login program then verifies your identity by checking the first field in the passwd file. If your username is there, the next step is to run the password you typed through an encryption program to determine if it is indeed the correct password. Once your password is verified, the login program sets up an initial environment consisting of variables that define the working environment that will be passed on to the shell. The HOME, SHELL, USER, and LOGNAME variables are assigned values extracted from information in the passwd file. The HOME variable is assigned your home directory, and the SHELL variable is assigned the name of the login shell, which is the last entry in the passwd file. The USER and/or LOGNAME variables are assigned your login name. A search path variable is set so that commonly used utilities may be found in specified directories. When login has finished, it will execute the program found in the last entry of the passwd file. Normally, this program is a shell. If the last entry in the passwd file is /bin/csh, the C shell program is executed. If the last entry in the passwd file is /bin/bash or is null, the Bash shell starts up. If the last entry is /bin/ksh or /bin/pdksh, the Korn shell is executed. This shell is called the *login shell*.

After the shell starts up, it checks for any systemwide initialization files set up by the system administrator and then checks your home directory to see if there are any shell-specific initialization files there. If any of these files exist, they are executed. The initialization files are used to further customize the user environment. At this point you may start up a windowing environment such as CDE, OpenWindows, or Gnome. A virtual desktop will appear and depending on the configuration, a console and some pseudo terminals displaying a shell prompt. The shell is now waiting for your input.

1.4.1   **Parsing the Command Line**

When you type a command at the prompt, the shell reads a line of input and parses the command line, breaking the line into words, called tokens. Tokens are separated by spaces and tabs and the command line is terminated by a newline.[3] The shell then checks to see whether the first word is a built-in command or an executable program located somewhere on the disk. If it is built-in, the shell will execute the command internally. Otherwise, the shell will search the directories listed in the path variable to find out where the program resides. If the command is found, the shell will fork a new process and then execute the program. The shell will sleep (or wait) until the program

---

3. The process of breaking the line up into tokens is called *lexical analysis*.

finishes execution and then, if necessary, will report the status of the exiting program. A prompt will appear and the whole process will start again. The order of processing the command line is as follows:

1. History substitution is performed (if applicable).
2. Command line is broken up into tokens, or words.
3. History is updated (if applicable).
4. Quotes are processed.
5. Alias substitution and functions are defined (if applicable).
6. Redirection, background, and pipes are set up.
7. Variable substitution ($user, $name, etc.) is performed.
8. Command substitution (echo "Today is `date`") is performed.
9. Filename substitution, called *globbing* (cat abc.??, rm *.c, etc.) is performed.
10. Command is executed.

1.4.2 Types of Commands

When a command is executed, it is an alias, a function, a built-in command, or an executable program residing on disk. Aliases are abbreviations (nicknames) for existing commands and apply to the C, TC, Bash, and Korn shells. Functions apply to the Bourne (introduced with AT&T System V, Release 2.0), Bash, and Korn shells. They are groups of commands organized as separate routines. Aliases and functions are defined within the shell's memory. Built-in commands are internal routines in the shell, and executable programs reside on disk. The shell uses the path variable to locate the executable programs on disk and forks a child process before the command can be executed. This takes time. When the shell is ready to execute the command, it evaluates command types in the following order[4]:

1. Aliases
2. Keywords
3. Functions
4. Built-in commands
5. Executable programs

If, for example, the command is xyz the shell will check to see if xyz is an alias. If not, is it a built-in command or a function? If neither of those, it must be an executable program residing on the disk. In order to execute the command, the shell must then search the path to find out where the command is located in the directory structure in order to execute it. This process is illustrated in Figure 1.2.

---

4. Numbers 3 and 4 are reversed for Bourne and Korn(88) shells. Number 3 does not apply for C and TC shells.

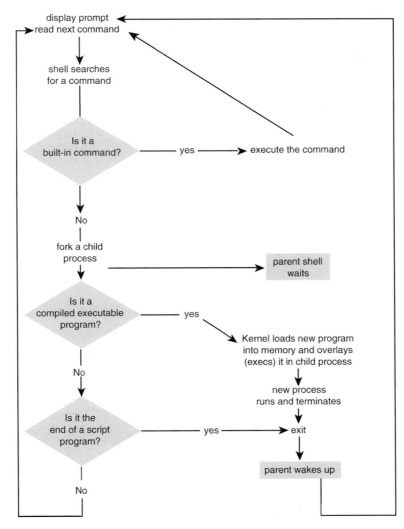

Figure 1.2 The shell and command execution.

1.5 Processes and the Shell

A process is a program in execution and can be identified by its unique PID number. The kernel controls and manages processes. A process consists of the executable program, its data and stack, program and stack pointer, registers, and all the information needed for the program to run. The shell is a special program that starts when you have completed the login process. Once started, the shell is a process. The shell belongs to a process group identified by the group's PID. Only one process group has control of the terminal at a time and is said to be running in the foreground. When you log on, your shell is in control of the terminal and waits for you to type a command at the prompt.

When you log on, your system may go directly into a graphical user interface (GUI) or start up in a terminal with a shell prompt. If you are using Linux, the shell normally starts up another process to launch the X Window System. After X Windows starts, a window manager process (twm, fvwm, etc.) is executed, providing a virtual desktop.[5] Then, from a pop-up menu, you can start up a number of other processes, such as xterm (gets a terminal), xman (provides manual pages), or emacs (starts a text editor). If you are using UNIX, the GUI may be CDE, KDE, or OpenWindows. Once started, you will have a virtual desktop consisting of a number of smaller windows, including a console and a number of terminals, each displaying a shell prompt.

Multiple processes are running and monitored by the Linux/UNIX kernel, allocating each of the processes a little slice of the CPU in a way that is unnoticeable to the user.

1.5.1   What Processes Are Running?

The ps Command.   The ps command with its many options displays a list of the processes currently running in a number of formats. Example 1.2 shows all processes that are running by users on a Linux system. (See Appendix A for ps and its options.)

EXAMPLE 1.2

```
$ ps aux  (BSD/Linux ps)  (use ps -ef for SVR4)
USER   PID  %CPU %MEM   SIZE   RSS TTY STAT   START TIME  COMMAND
ellie  456  0.0  1.3   1268   840  1   S     13:23 0:00  -bash
ellie  476  0.0  1.0   1200   648  1   S     13:23 0:00  sh /usr/X11R6/bin/sta
ellie  478  0.0  1.0   2028   676  1   S     13:23 0:00  xinit /home/ellie/.xi
ellie  480  0.0  1.6   1852  1068  1   S     13:23 0:00  fvwm2
ellie  483  0.0  1.3   1660   856  1   S     13:23 0:00  /usr/X11R6/lib/X11/fv
ellie  484  0.0  1.3   1696   868  1   S     13:23 0:00  /usr/X11R6/lib/X11/fv
ellie  487  0.0  2.0   2348  1304  1   S     13:23 0:00  xclock -bg #c0c0c0 -p
ellie  488  0.0  1.1   1620   724  1   S     13:23 0:00  /usr/X11R6/lib/X11/fv
ellie  489  0.0  2.0   2364  1344  1   S     13:23 0:00  xload -nolabel -bg gr
ellie  495  0.0  1.3   1272   848  p0  S     13:24 0:00  -bash
ellie  797  0.0  0.7    852   484  p0  R     14:03 0:00  ps au
root   457  0.0  0.4    724   296  2   S     13:23 0:00  /sbin/mingetty tty2
root   458  0.0  0.4    724   296  3   S     13:23 0:00  /sbin/mingetty tty3
root   459  0.0  0.4    724   296  4   S     13:23 0:00  /sbin/mingetty tty4
root   460  0.0  0.4    724   296  5   S     13:23 0:00  /sbin/mingetty tty5
root   461  0.0  0.4    724   296  6   S     13:23 0:00  /sbin/mingetty tty6
root   479  0.0  4.5  12092  2896  1   S     13:23 0:01  X :0
root   494  0.0  2.5   2768  1632  1   S     13:24 0:00  nxterm -ls -sb -fn
```

---

5. A number of desktop environments come with Linux, including Gnome, KDE, X, and so on.

The `pstree`/`ptree` Command.   Another way to see what processes are running and
what processes are child processes is to use the `pstree` (Linux) or `ptree` (Solaris) command. The `pstree` command displays all processes as a tree with its root being the first
process that runs, called `init`. If a user name is specified, then that user's processes are
at the root of the tree. If a process spawns more than one process of the same name,
`pstree` visually merges the identical branches by putting them in square brackets and prefixing them with the number of times the processes are repeated. To illustrate, in Example 1.3 the `httpd` server process has started up 10 child processes. (See Appendix A for a
list of `pstree` options.)

EXAMPLE 1.3

```
pstree
init---4*[getty]
init-+-atd
     |-bash---startx---xinit-+-X
     |                       `-fvwm2-+-FvwmButtons
     |                               |-FvwmPager
     |                               `-FvwmTaskBar
     |-cardmgr
     |-crond
     |-gpm
     |-httpd---10*[httpd]
     |-ifup-ppp---pppd---chat
     |-inetd
     |-kerneld
     |-kflushd
     |-klogd
     |-kswapd
     |-lpd
     |-2*[md_thread]
     |-5*[mingetty]
     |         |-nmbd
     |-nxterm---bash---tcsh---pstree
     |-portmap
     |-sendmail
     |-smbd
     |-syslogd
     |-update
     |-xclock
     `-xload
```

1.5.2 What Are System Calls?

The shell can spawn other processes. In fact, when you enter a command at the prompt or from a shell script, the shell has the responsibility of finding the command either in its internal code (built-in) or on the disk and then arranging for the command to be executed. This is done with calls to the kernel, called *system calls*. A system call is a request for kernel services and is the only way a process can access the system's hardware. There are a number of system calls that allow processes to be created, executed, and terminated. (The shell provides other services from the kernel when it performs redirection and piping, command substitution, and the execution of user commands.)

   The system calls used by the shell to cause new processes to run are discussed in the following sections. See Figure 1.4 on page 17.

1.5.3 Creating Processes

The fork System Call.   A process is created in UNIX with the fork system call. The fork system call creates a duplicate of the calling process. The new process is called the *child* and the process that created it is called the *parent*. The child process starts running right after the call to fork, and both processes initially share the CPU. The child process has a copy of the parent's environment, open files, real and user identifications, umask, current working directory, and signals.

   When you type a command, the shell parses the command line and determines whether the first word is a built-in command or an executable command that resides out on the disk. If the command is built-in, the shell handles it, but if on the disk, the shell invokes the fork system call to make a copy of itself (Figure 1.3). Its child will search the path to find the command, as well as set up the file descriptors for redirection, pipes, command substitution, and background processing. While the child shell works, the parent normally sleeps. (See "The wait System Call" below.)

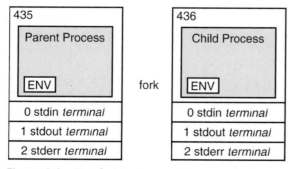

Figure 1.3 The fork system call.

The `wait` System Call.   The parent shell is programmed to go to sleep (wait) while the child takes care of details such as handling redirection, pipes, and background processing. The `wait` system call causes the parent process to suspend until one of its children terminates. If `wait` is successful, it returns the PID of the child that died and the child's exit status. If the parent does not wait and the child exits, the child is put in a zombie state (suspended animation) and will stay in that state until either the parent calls `wait` or the parent dies.[6] If the parent dies before the child, the `init` process adopts any orphaned zombie process. The `wait` system call, then, is not just used to put a parent to sleep, but also to ensure that the process terminates properly.

The `exec` System Call.   After you enter a command at the terminal, the shell normally forks off a new shell process: the child process. As mentioned earlier, the child shell is responsible for causing the command you typed to be executed. It does this by calling the `exec` system call. Remember, the user command is really just an executable program. The shell searches the path for the new program. If it is found, the shell calls the `exec` system call with the name of the command as its argument. The kernel loads this new program into memory in place of the shell that called it. The child shell, then, is overlaid with the new program. The new program becomes the child process and starts executing. Although the new process has its own local variables, all environment variables, open files, signals, and the current working directory are passed to the new process. This process exits when it has finished, and the parent shell wakes up.

The `exit` System Call.   A new program can terminate at any time by executing the `exit` call. When a child process terminates, it sends a signal (`sigchild`) and waits for the parent to accept its exit status. The exit status is a number between 0 and 255. An exit status of zero indicates that the program executed successfully, and a nonzero exit status means that the program failed in some way.

For example, if the command `ls` had been typed at the command line, the parent shell would fork a child process and go to sleep. The child shell would then `exec` (overlay) the `ls` program in its place. The `ls` program would run in place of the child, inheriting all the environment variables, open files, user information, and state information. When the new process finished execution, it would exit and the parent shell would wake up. A prompt would appear on the screen, and the shell would wait for another command. If you are interested in knowing how a command exited, each shell has a special built-in variable that contains the exit status of the last command that terminated. (All of this will be explained in detail in the individual shell chapters.) See Example 1.4 for an example of exit status.

---

6. To remove zombie processes, the system must be rebooted.

EXAMPLE 1.4

```
(C/TC Shell)
1   % cp filex filey
    % echo $status
    0
2   % cp xyz
    Usage: cp [-ip] f1 f2; or: cp [-ipr] f1 ... fn d2
    % echo $status
    1


(Bourne, Bash, Korn Shells)
3   $ cp filex filey
    $ echo $?
    0
    $ cp xyz
    Usage: cp [-ip] f1 f2; or: cp [-ipr] f1 ... fn d2
    $ echo $?
    1
```

EXPLANATION

1   The cp (copy) command is entered at the C shell command-line prompt. After the command has made a copy of filex called filey, the program exits and the prompt appears. The csh status variable contains the exit status of the last command that was executed. If the status is zero, the cp program exited with success. If the exit status is nonzero, the cp program failed in some way.

2   When entering the cp command, the user failed to provide two filenames: the source and destination files. The cp program sent an error message to the screen and exited with a status of 1. That number is stored in the csh status variable. Any number other than zero indicates that the program failed.

3   The Bourne, Bash, and Korn shells process the cp command as the C shell did in the first two examples. The only difference is that the Bourne and Korn shells store the exit status in the ? variable, rather than the status variable.

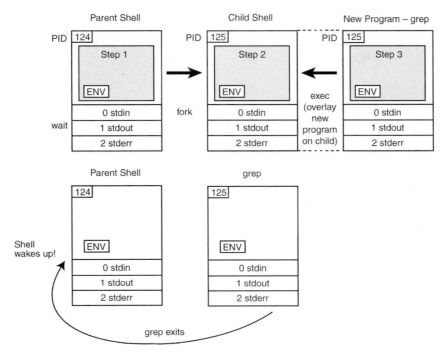

Figure 1.4 The fork, exec, wait, and exit system calls. See following Explanation.

EXPLANATION

1 The parent shell creates a copy of itself with the fork system call. The copy is called the child shell.

2 The child shell has a new PID and is a copy of its parent. It will share the CPU with the parent.

3 The kernel loads the grep program into memory and executes (exec) it in place of the child shell. The grep program inherits the open files and environment from the child.

4 The grep program exits, the kernel cleans up, and the parent is awakened.

Killing Processes.   A process can be terminated by using keystroke-generated signals like Ctrl-C or Ctrl-\, or by using the kill command. This command may be used for killing background jobs or, if your terminal is in a frozen, unresponsive state, to kill the process that is causing the problem. The kill command is a built-in shell command that terminates a process by its PID or, if using job control, by the number of the job. To find the PID number, the ps command is used. See Example 1.5.

EXAMPLE 1.5

```
1   $ sleep 60&
2   $ ps
    PID    TTY       TIME CMD
    27628 pts/7     0:00 sleep
    27619 pts/7     0:00 bash
    27629 pts/7     0:00 ps
3   $ kill 27628
4   $ ps
    PID    TTY       TIME CMD
    27631 pts/7     0:00 ps
    27619 pts/7     0:00 bash
    [1]+  Terminated                 sleep 60
```

EXPLANATION

1   The sleep command does nothing, just pauses for 60 seconds, and is running in the background due to the ampersand at the end of the command

2   The ps command displays the currently running processes for this user.

3   The kill command is a built-in shell command. It takes, as an argument, the PID of the process it will kill. The PID for the sleep command is entered.

4   The ps command demonstrates that the sleep command has been terminated.

1.6   The Environment and Inheritance

When you log on, the shell starts up and inherits a number of variables, I/O streams, and process characteristics from the /bin/login program that started it. In turn, if another shell is spawned (forked) from the login or parent shell, that child shell (subshell) will inherit certain characteristics from its parent. A subshell may be started for a number of reasons: for handling background processing, for handling groups of commands, or for executing scripts. The child shell inherits the environment of its parent. The environment consists of process permissions (who owns the process), the working directory, the file creation mask, special variables, open files, and signals.

1.6.1   Ownership and Permissions

When you log on, the shell is given an identity. It has a real user identification (UID), one or more real group identifications (GID), and an effective user identification and effective group identification (EUID and EGID). The EUID and EGID are initially the same as the real UID and GID. These ID numbers are found in the etc/passwd file and are used by the system to identify users and groups. The EUID and EGID determine what permissions a process has access to when reading, writing, or executing files. If the EUID of a process and the real UID of the owner of the file are the same, the process has the owner's access permissions for the file. If the EGID and real GID of a process are the same, the process has the owner's group privileges.

The real UID is the third entry in the /etc/passwd file. Its value is a positive integer that is associated with your login name. When you log on, the login shell is assigned the real UID and all processes spawned from the login shell inherit its permissions. Any process running with a UID of zero belongs to root (the superuser) and has root privileges. The real group identification, the GID, associates a group with your login name. It is found in the fourth field of the /etc/passwd file.

You can use the id command to see these values, as shown in Example 1.6.

EXAMPLE 1.6

```
1   $ id
    uid=502(ellie) gid=502(ellie)
```

The EUID and EGID can be changed to numbers assigned to a different owner. By changing the EUID (or EGID) to another owner, you can become the owner of a process that belongs to someone else. Programs that change the EUID or EGID to another owner are called setuid or setgid programs. The passwd program is an example of a setuid program that gives the user root privileges. This enables an ordinary user to change his password, and update the passwd file (accessible only to root) without calling for a system administrator. The user temporarily becomes the superuser, root, as long as the passwd program is running because his effective user ID is temporarily is set to root. Setuid programs are often sources for security holes. The shell allows you to create setuid scripts, and the shell itself may be a setuid program. (See Chapter 16, "The System Administrator and the Shell."

1.6.2   The File Creation Mask

When a file is created it is given a set of default permissions. These permissions are determined by the program creating the file. Child processes inherit a default mask from their parents. The user can change the mask for the shell by issuing the umask command at the prompt or by setting it in the shell's initialization files. The umask command is used to remove permissions from the existing mask.

Initially, the umask is 000, giving a directory 777 (rwxrwxrwx) permissions and a file 666 (rw-rw-rw-) permissions as the default. On most systems, the umask is assigned a value of 022 by the /bin/login program or the /etc/profile initialization file.

The umask value is subtracted from the default settings for both the directory and file permissions as follows:

```
 777 (Directory)           666 (File)
-022 (umask value)        -022 (umask value)
 -------                   ---------
 755                       644
Result: drwxr-xr-x        -rw-r--r--
```

After the umask is set, all directories and files created by this process are assigned the new default permissions. In this example, directories will be given read, write, and execute for the owner; read and execute for the group; and read and execute for the rest of the world (others). Any files created will be assigned read and write for the owner, and read for the group and others. To change permissions on individual directories and permissions, the chmod command is used.

1.6.3   Changing Permissions and Ownership

The chmod Command.   The chmod command changes permissions on files and directories. Every UNIX/Linux file has a set of permissions associated with it to control who can read, write, or execute the file. There is one owner for every UNIX/Linux file and only the owner or the superuser can change the permissions on a file or directory. A group may have a number of members, and the owner of the file may change the group permissions on a file so that the group can enjoy special privileges. To see what permissions a file has, type at the shell prompt:

ls -l *filename*

A total of nine bits constitutes the permissions on a file. The first set of three bits controls the permissions of the owner of the file, the second set controls the permissions of the group, and the last set controls the permissions for everyone else. The permissions are stored in the mode field of the file's inode. The user must own the files to change permissions on them.[7]

Table 1.1 illustrates the eight possible combinations of numbers used for changing permissions.

Table 1.1   Permission Modes

Decimal	Binary	Permissions
0	000	none
1	001	--x
2	010	-w-
3	011	-wx
4	100	r--
5	101	r-x
6	110	rw-
7	111	rwx

The symbolic notation for chmod is as follows:
r = read; w = write; x = execute; u = user; g = group; o = others; a = all.

---

7. The caller's EUID must match the owner's UID of the file, or the owner must be superuser.

EXAMPLE 1.7

```
1    $ chmod 755 file
     $ ls -l file
     -rwxr-xr-x 1 ellie  0 Mar  7 12:52 file
2    $ chmod g+w file
     $ ls -l file
     -rwxrwxr-x  1 ellie  0 Mar 7 12:54 file
3    $ chmod go-rx file
     $ ls -l file
     -rwx-w---- 1 ellie  0 Mar 7 12:56 file
4    $ chmod a=r file
     $ ls -l file
     -r--r--r-- 1 ellie  0 Mar 7 12:59 file
```

EXPLANATION

1   The first argument is the octal value 755. It turns on rwx for the user, r and x for the group, and others for file.

2   In the symbolic form of chmod, write permission is added to the group.

3   In the symbolic form of chmod, read and execute permissions are subtracted from the group and others.

4   In the symbolic form of chmod, all are given only read permission. The = sign causes all permissions to be reset to the new value.

The chown Command.   The chown command changes the owner and group on files and directories. If using Linux, only the superuser, root, can change ownership. If using UNIX, the owner of the file or the superuser can change the ownership. To see the usage and options for chown, check the man pages (UNIX) or use the chown command with the --help (Linux) option as shown in Example 1.8. Example 1.9 demonstrates how to use chown.

EXAMPLE 1.8

```
(The Command Line)
# chown --help
Usage: chown [OPTION]... OWNER[.[GROUP]] FILE...
  or:  chown [OPTION]... .[GROUP] FILE...
Change the owner and/or group of each FILE to OWNER and/or GROUP.

  -c, --changes         be verbose whenever change occurs
  -h, --no-dereference  affect symbolic links instead of any referenced file
                        (available only on systems with lchown system call)
```

EXAMPLE 1.8 (CONTINUED)

```
 -f, --silent, --quiet  suppress most error messages
 -R, --recursive        operate on files and directories recursively
 -v, --verbose          explain what is being done
     --help             display this help and exit
     --version          output version information and exit
```

Owner is unchanged if missing. Group is unchanged if missing, but changed to login group if implied by a period. A colon may replace the period.

Report bugs to fileutils-bugs@gnu.ai.mit.edu

EXAMPLE 1.9

```
(The Command Line)
1   $ ls -l filetest
    -rw-rw-r--  1 ellie    ellie       0 Jan 10 12:19 filetest
2   $ chown root filetest
    chown: filetest: Operation not permitted
3   $ su root
    Password:
4   # ls -l filetest
    -rw-rw-r--  1 ellie    ellie       0 Jan 10 12:19 filetest
5   # chown root filetest
6   # ls -l filetest
    -rw-rw-r--  1 root     ellie       0 Jan 10 12:19 filetest
7   # chown root:root filetest
8   # ls -l filetest
    -rw-rw-r--  1 root     root        0 Jan 10 12:19 filetest
```

EXPLANATION

1   The user and group ownership of filetest is ellie.

2   The chown command will only work if you are the superuser, i.e., user root.

3   The user changes identity to root with the su command.

4   The listing shows that user and group are ellie for filetest.

5   Only the superuser can change the ownership of files and directories. Ownership of filetest is changed to root with the chown command. Group ownership is still ellie.

6   Output of ls shows that root now owns filetest.

7   The colon (or a dot) is used to indicate that owner root will now change the group ownership to root. The group name is listed after the colon. There can be no spaces.

8   The user and group ownership for filetest now belongs to root.

1.6.4 The Working Directory

When you log on, you are given a working directory within the file system, called the *home directory*. The working directory is inherited by processes spawned from this shell. Any child process of this shell can change its own working directory, but the change will have no effect on the parent shell.

The cd command, used to change the working directory, is a shell built-in command. Each shell has its own copy of cd. A built-in command is executed directly by the shell as part of the shell's code; the shell does not perform the fork and exec system calls when executing built-in commands. If another shell (script) is forked from the parent shell, and the cd command is issued in the child shell, the directory will be changed in the child shell. When the child exits, the parent shell will be in the same directory it was in before the child started.

EXAMPLE 1.10

```
1   > cd /
2   > pwd
    /
3   > bash
4   $ cd /home
5   $ pwd
    /home
6   $ exit
7   > pwd
    /
    >
```

EXPLANATION

1   The > prompt is a TC shell prompt. The cd command changes the directory to /. The cd command is built into the shell's internal code.

2   The pwd command displays the present working directory, /.

3   The bash shell is started.

4   The cd command changes the directory to /home. The dollar sign ($) is the Bash prompt.

5   The pwd command displays the present working directory, /home.

6   The Bash shell is exited, returning to the TC shell.

7   In the TC shell, the present working directory is still /. Each shell has its own copy of cd.

1.6.5 Variables

The shell can define two types of variables: local and environment. The variables contain information used for customizing the shell, and information required by other processes so that they will function properly. Local variables are private to the shell in which they are created and not passed on to any processes spawned from that shell. The built-in set command will display local variables for C shell and TC shell, and both local and environment variables for Bourne, Bash, and Korn shells. Environment variables, on the other hand, are passed from parent to child process, from child to grandchild, and so on. Some of the environment variables are inherited by the login shell from the /bin/login program. Others are created in the user initialization files, in scripts, or at the command line. If an environment variable is set in the child shell, it is not passed back to the parent. The shell env command will display the environment variables. Example 1.11 lists environment variables for a user running Solaris 5.9 with the Bash shell.

EXAMPLE 1.11

```
$ env
PWD=/home/ellie
TZ=US/Pacific
PAGER=less
HOSTNAME=artemis
LD_LIBRARY_PATH=/lib:/usr/lib:/usr/local/lib:/usr/dt/lib:/usr/openwin/lib
MANPATH=/usr/local/man:/usr/man:/usr/openwin/man:/opt/httpd/man
USER=ellie
MACHTYPE=sparc-sun-solaris2.9
TCL_LIBRARY=/usr/local/lib/tcl8.0
EDITOR=vi
LOGNAME=ellie
SHLVL=1
SHELL=/bin/bash
HOSTTYPE=sparc
OSTYPE=solaris2.9
HOME=/home/ellie
TERM=xterm
TK_LIBRARY=/usr/local/lib/tk8.0
PATH=/bin:/usr/bin:/usr/local/bin:/usr/local/etc:/usr/ccs/bin:/usr/etc:/usr/ucb:/usr/
    local/X11:/usr/openwin/bin:/etc:.
SSH_TTY=/dev/pts/10
_=/bin/env
```

1.6.6   Redirection and Pipes

File Descriptors.   All I/O, including files, pipes, and sockets, is handled by the kernel via a mechanism called the *file descriptor*. A file descriptor is a small unsigned integer, an index into a file-descriptor table maintained by the kernel and used by the kernel to reference open files and I/O streams. Each process inherits its own file-descriptor table from its parent. The first three file descriptors, 0, 1, and 2, are assigned to your terminal. File descriptor 0 is standard input (stdin), 1 is standard output (stdout), and 2 is standard error (stderr). When you open a file, the next available descriptor is 3, and it will be assigned to the new file. If all the available file descriptors are in use,[8] a new file cannot be opened.

Redirection. When a file descriptor is assigned to something other than a terminal, it is called *I/O redirection*. The shell performs redirection of output to a file by closing the standard output file descriptor, 1 (the terminal), and then assigning that descriptor to the file (see Figure 1.5). When redirecting standard input, the shell closes file descriptor 0 (the terminal) and assigns that descriptor to a file (see Figure 1.6). The Bourne, Bash, and Korn shells handle errors by assigning a file to file descriptor 2 (see Figure 1.7). The C and TC shells, on the other hand, go through a more complicated process to do the same thing (see Figure 1.8).

EXAMPLE 1.12

```
1    $ who > file
2    $ cat file1 file2 >> file3
3    $ mail tom < file
4    $ find / -name file -print 2> errors
5    % ( find / -name file -print > /dev/tty) >& errors
```

EXPLANATION

1   The output of the who command is redirected from the terminal to file. (All shells redirect output in this way.)

2   The output from the cat command (concatenate file1 and file2) is appended to file3. (All shells redirect and append output in this way.)

3   The input of file is redirected to the mail program; that is, user tom will be sent the contents of file. (All shells redirect input in this way.)

4   Any errors from the find command are redirected to errors. Output goes to the terminal. (The Bourne, Bash, and Korn shells redirect errors this way.)

5   Any errors from the find command are redirected to errors. Output is sent to the terminal. (The C and TC shells redirect errors this way. % is the C shell prompt.)

---

8. See the built-in commands limit and ulimit.

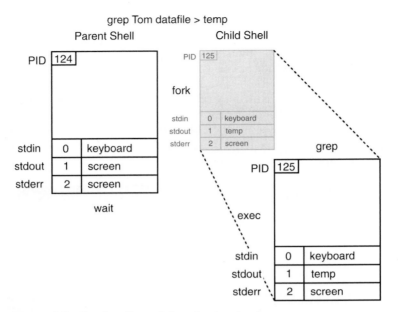

Figure 1.5 Redirection of standard output.

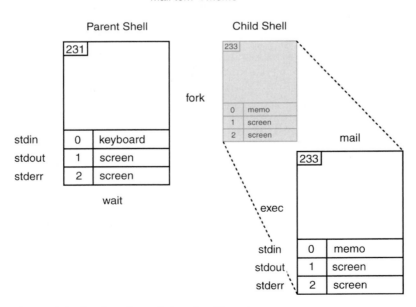

Figure 1.6 Redirection of standard input.

find . -name filex 2> errors

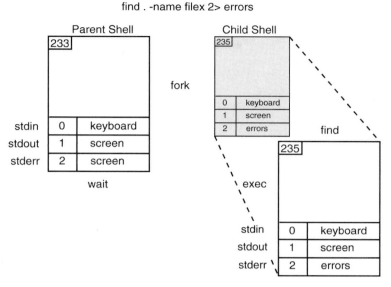

Figure 1.7   Redirection of standard error (Bourne, Bash, and Korn shells).

(find . -name filex > /dev/tty) >&errors

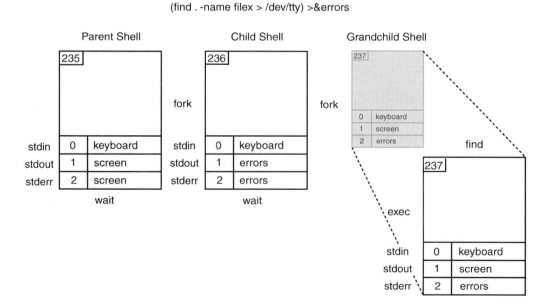

Figure 1.8   Redirection of standard error (C and TC shells).

Pipes.   A pipe is the oldest form of UNIX interprocess communication. A pipe allows processes to communicate with each other. It is a mechanism whereby the output of one command is sent as input to another command, with the limitation that data can only flow in one direction, normally between a parent and a child. The shell implements pipes by closing and opening file descriptors; however, instead of assigning the descriptors to a file, it assigns them to a pipe descriptor created with the pipe system call. After the parent creates the pipe file descriptors, it forks a child process for each command in the pipeline. By having each process manipulate the pipe descriptors, one will write to the pipe and the other will read from it.

To simplify things, a pipe is merely a kernel buffer from which both processes can share data, thus eliminating the need for intermediate temporary files. The output of one command is sent to the buffer, and when the buffer is full or the command has terminated, the command on the right-hand side of the pipe reads from the buffer. The kernel synchronizes the activities so that one process waits while the other reads from or writes to the buffer.

The syntax of the pipe command is

```
who | wc
```

In order to accomplish the same thing without a pipe, it would take three steps:

```
who > tempfile
wc tempfile
rm tempfile
```

With the pipe, the shell sends the output of the who command as input to the wc command; that is, the command on the left-hand side of the pipe *writes* to the pipe and the command on the right-hand side of the pipe *reads* from it (see Figure 1.9). You can tell if a command is a writer if it normally sends output to the screen when run at the command line. The ls, ps, and date commands are examples of writers. A reader is a command that waits for input from a file or from the keyboard or from a pipe. The sort, wc, and cat commands are examples of readers.

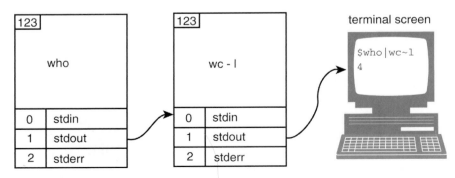

Figure 1.9   The pipe.

Figures 1.10 through 1.14 illustrate the steps for implementing the pipe.

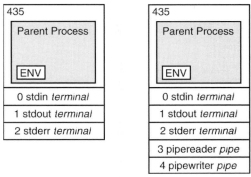

Figure 1.10   The parent calls the `pipe` system call for setting up a pipeline.

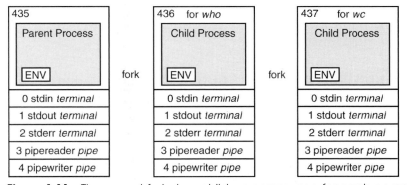

Figure 1.11   The parent forks two child processes, one for each command in the pipeline.

Child for who

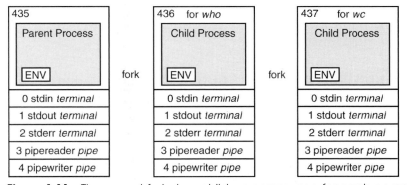

Figure 1.12   The first child is prepared to write to the pipe.

Child for wc

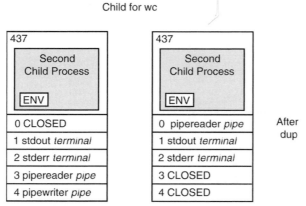

437		437	
Second **Child Process**		**Second** **Child Process**	
ENV		ENV	
0 CLOSED		0 pipereader *pipe*	After
1 stdout *terminal*		1 stdout *terminal*	dup
2 stderr *terminal*		2 stderr *terminal*	
3 pipereader *pipe*		3 CLOSED	
4 pipewriter *pipe*		4 CLOSED	

Figure 1.13   The second child is prepared to read input from the pipe.

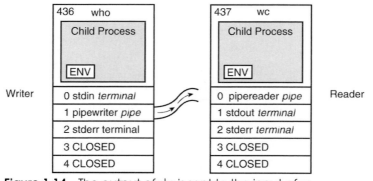

Writer

Reader

Figure 1.14   The output of who is sent to the input of wc.

1.6.7 The Shell and Signals

A signal sends a message to a process and normally causes the process to terminate, usually due to some unexpected event such as a hangup, bus error, or power failure, or by a program error such as illegal division by zero or an invalid memory reference. Signals can also be sent to a process by pressing certain key sequences. For example, you can send or deliver signals to a process by pressing the Break, Delete, Quit, or Stop keys, and all processes sharing the terminal are affected by the signal sent. You can kill a process with the kill command. By default, most signals terminate the program. Each process can take an action in response to a given signal:

1. The signal can be ignored.
2. The process can be stopped.
3. The process can be continued.
4. The signal can be caught by a function defined in the program.

The Bourne, Bash, and Korn shells allow you to handle signals coming into your program, (see "Trapping Signals" on page 378 for programming in the Bourne shell; "Trapping Signals" on page 716 for programming in the Korn shell; and "Trapping Signals" on page 935 for programing in the Bash shell) either by ignoring the signal, by specifying some action to be taken when a specified signal arrives, or by resetting the signal back to its default action. The C and TC shells are limited to handling ^C (Ctrl-C), the interrupt character.

Table 1.2 lists the standard signals that a process can use.

Table 1.2   Standard Signals[a]

Number	Name	Description	Action
0	EXIT	Shell exits	Termination
1	SIGHUP	Terminal has disconnected	Termination
2	SIGINT	User presses Ctrl-C	Termination
3	SIGQUIT	User presses Ctrl-\	Termination
4	SIGILL	Illegal hardware instruction	Program error
5	SIGTRAP	Produced by debugger	Program error
8	SIGFPE	Arithmetic error; e.g., division by zero	Program error
9	SIGKILL	Cannot be caught or ignored	Termination
10	SIGUSR1	Application-defined signal for user	
11	SIGSEGV	Invalid memory references	Program error
12	SIGUSR2	Application-defined signal for user	
13	SIGPIPE	Broken pipe connection	Operator error
14	SIGALRM	Timeout	Alarm sent
15	SIGTERM	Termination of a program	Termination
17	SIGCHLD	Child process has stopped or died	Ignored
18	SIGCONT	Starts a stopped job; can't be handled or ignored	Continue if stopped
19	SIGSTOP	Stops a job; can't be handled or ignored	Stops the process
20	SIGSTP	Interactive stop; user presses Ctrl-Z	Stops the process
21	SIGTTIN	Background job is trying to read from the controlling terminal	Stops the process
22	SIGTTOU	Background job is trying to write to the controlling terminal	Stops the process

a.   See your specific system manual. For a complete list of UNIX signals and their meanings, also go to www.cybermagician.co.uk/technet/unixsignals.htm. For Linux signals, go to www.comptechdoc.org/os/linux/programming/linux_pgsignals.html.

1.7 Executing Commands from Scripts

When the shell is used as a programming language, commands and shell control constructs are typed in an editor and saved to a file, called a script. The lines from the file are read and executed one at a time by the shell. These programs are interpreted, not compiled. Compiled programs are converted into machine language before they are executed. Therefore, shell programs are usually slower than binary executables, but they are easier to write and are used mainly for automating simple tasks. Shell programs can also be written interactively at the command line, and for very simple tasks, this is the quickest way. However, for more complex scripting, it is easier to write scripts in an editor (unless you are a really great typist). The following script can be executed by any shell to output the same results. Figure 1.15 and its following explanation illustrate the creation of a script called doit and how it fits in with already existing UNIX programs/utilities/commands.

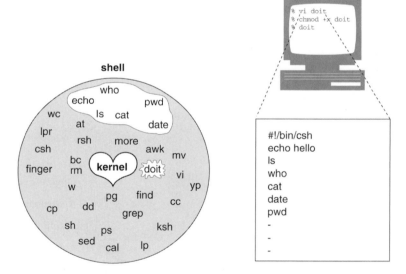

Figure 1.15 Creating a generic shell script.

1 Go into your favorite editor and type in a set of UNIX/Linux commands, one per line. Indicate what shell you want by placing the pathname of the shell after the #! on the first line. This program is being executed by the C shell and it is named doit.

2 Save your file and turn on the execute permissions so that you can run it.

3 Execute your program just as you would any other UNIX/Linux command.

chapter

2

Shell Programming QuickStart

2.1 Taking a Peek at Shell Scripts

If you read, write, or maintain programs, the following samples will give you a quick overview of the construction and style of a shell script and introduce you to some of the constructs and syntax found in these programs. *Note: If you are not familiar with programming, skip this chapter and go to Chapter 3.* When you have finished learning how to write scripts, you may want to return to this chapter for a quick reference to refresh your memory.

The C shell and TC shell emulate the C language syntax whereas the Bourne shell is based on an older programming language called Algol.

The Bash and Korn shells tend to be a combination of both the Bourne and C shells, although these shells originated from the Bourne shell.

To illustrate the differences in the shells, four sample programs are provided, one for each shell (the C and TC shells are presented together here). Above each program, a list of basic constructs are described for the shell being examined.

2.2 Sample Scripts: Comparing the Major Shells

At the end of each section pertaining to a specific shell, you will find a small program to illustrate how to write a complete script. At first glance, the programs for each shell look very similar. They are. And they all do the same thing. The main difference is the syntax. After you have worked with these shells for some time, you will quickly adapt to the differences and start formulating your own opinions about which shell is your favorite. A detailed comparison of differences among the C/TC, Bourne, Bash, and Korn shells is found in Appendix B.

Before Getting Started.   You must have a good handle on UNIX/Linux commands. If you do not know the basic commands, you cannot do much with shell programming. The next three chapters will teach you how to use some of the major UNIX/Linux commands, and Appendix A in the back of the book, gives you a list of the most common commands (also called utilities).

The Purpose.   The sample scripts provided at the end of each section send a mail message to a list of users, inviting each of them to a party. The place and time of the party are set in variables. The list of guests is selected from a file called guests. The existence of the guest file is checked and if it does not exist, the program will exit. A list of foods is stored in a word list (array). A loop is used to iterate through the list of guests. Each user will receive an e-mail invitation telling him or her the time and place of the party and asking him or her to bring an item from the food list. A conditional is used to check for a user named root, and if he is on the guest list, he will be excluded; that is, he will not be sent an e-mail invitation. The loop will continue until the guest list is empty. Each time through the loop, a food item is removed from the list, so that each guest will be asked to bring a different food. If, however, there are more users than foods, the list is reset. This is handled with a standard loop control statement.

2.3   The C and TC Shell Syntax and Constructs

The basic C and TC shell syntax and constructs are listed in Table 2.1.

Table 2.1   C and TC Shell Syntax and Constructs

The shbang line	The "shbang" line is the very first line of the script and lets the kernel know what shell will be interpreting the lines in the script. The shbang line consists of a hash mark #, an exclamation point ! (called a bang), followed by the full pathname of the shell, and any shell options. Any other lines beginning with a # are used as comments.
	EXAMPLE
	`#!/bin/csh or #!/bin/tcsh`
Comments	Comments are descriptive material preceded by a # sign; they are not executable statements. They are in effect until the end of a line and can be started anywhere on the line.
	EXAMPLE
	`# This is a comment`

Table 2.1   C and TC Shell Syntax and Constructs (continued)

Wildcards	There are some characters that are evaluated by the shell in a special way. They are called shell metacharacters or "wildcards." These characters are neither numbers nor letters. For example, the *, ?, and [ ] are used for filename expansion. The ! is the history character, the < , > , >> , <&, and | symbols are used for standard I/O redirection and pipes. To prevent these characters from being interpreted by the shell they must be quoted with a backslash or quote marks.

EXAMPLE

```
rm *; ls ??;  cat file[1-3]; !!
echo "How are you?"
echo Oh boy\!
```

Displaying output	To print output to the screen, the echo command is used. Wildcards must be escaped with either a backslash or matching quotes.

EXAMPLE

```
echo "Hello to you\!"
```

Local variables	Local variables are in scope for the current shell. When a script ends or the shell exits, they are no longer available; i.e., they go out of scope. Local variables are set and assigned values.

EXAMPLE

```
set variable_name = value
set name = "Tom Jones"
```

Global variables	Global variables are called environment variables. They are set for the currently running shell and are available to any process spawned from that shell. They go out of scope when the script ends or the shell where they are defined exits.

EXAMPLE

```
setenv  VARIABLE_NAME  value
setenv PRINTER Shakespeare
```

Extracting values from variables	To extract the value from variables, a dollar sign is used.

EXAMPLE

```
echo $variable_name
echo $name
echo $PRINTER
```

Reading user input	The special variable $< reads a line of input from the user and assigns it to a variable.

EXAMPLE

```
echo "What is your name?"
set name = $<
```

Table 2.1   C and TC Shell Syntax and Constructs (continued)

Arguments	Arguments can be passed to a script from the command line. Two methods can be used to receive their values from within the script: positional parameters and the argv array.

> **EXAMPLE**
>
> ```
> % scriptname arg1 arg2 arg3 ...
> ```
>
> Using positional parameters:
>
> ```
> echo $1 $2 $3                          arg1 is assigned to $1, arg2 to $2, etc.
> echo $*                                all the arguments
> ```
>
> Using the argv array:
>
> ```
> echo $argv[1] $argv[2] $argv[3]
> echo $argv[*]                          all the arguments
> echo $#argv                            the number of arguments
> ```

Arrays	An array is a list of words separated by whitespace. The list is enclosed in a set of parentheses.
	The built-in shift command shifts off the left-hand word in the list.
	Unlike C, the individual words are accessed by index values, which start at 1 rather than 0.

> **EXAMPLE**
>
> ```
> set word_list = ( word1 word2 word3 )
>
> set names = ( Tom Dick Harry Fred )
> shift names                           removes Tom from the list
>
> echo $word_list[1]                    displays first element of the list
> echo $word_list[2]                    displays second element of the list
> echo $word_list or $word_list[*]      displays all elements of the list
> echo $names[1]
> echo $names[2]
> echo $names[3]
> echo $names or echo $names[*]
> ```

Command substitution	To assign the output of a UNIX/Linux command to a variable, or use the output of a command in a string, the command is enclosed in backquotes.

> **EXAMPLE**
>
> ```
> set variable_name=`command`
> echo $variable_name
>
> set now = `date`                      The command in backquotes is executed and its output
> echo $now                             is assigned to the variable now
> echo "Today is `date`"                The output of the date command is inserted in the string
> ```

Table 2.1   C and TC Shell Syntax and Constructs (continued)

Arithmetic	Variables that will hold the results of an arithmetic computation must be preceded by an @ symbol and a space. Only integer arithmetic is provided by this shell.

EXAMPLE

```
@ n = 5 + 5
echo $n
```

Operators	The C and TC shells support operators for testing strings and numbers similar to those found in the C language.

EXAMPLE

Equality:
```
==
!=
```

Relational:
>	*greater than*
>=	*greater than or equal to*
<	*less than*
<=	*less than or equal to*

Logical:
&&	*and*
||	*or*
!	*not*

Conditional statements	The if construct is followed by an expression enclosed in parentheses. The operators are similar to C operators. The then keyword is placed after the closing parentheses. An if must end with an endif. An alternative to if/else if is the switch statement.

EXAMPLE

The if construct is:
```
if ( expression ) then
   block of statements
endif
```

The if/else construct is:
```
if ( expression ) then
   block of statements
else
   block of statements
endif
```

The if/else/else if construct is:
```
if ( expression ) then
   block of statements
else if ( expression ) then
   block of statements
else if ( expression ) then
   block of statements
else
   block of statements
endif
```

Table 2.1   C and TC Shell Syntax and Constructs (continued)

Conditional statements *(continued)*	The switch construct is:
	```switch variable_name```
	`    case constant1:`
	`        statements`
	`    case constant2:`
	`        statements`
	`    case constant3:`
	`        statements`
	`    default:`
	`        statements`
	`endsw`
		```switch ("$color")```
		`    case blue:`
		`        echo $color is blue`
		`        breaksw`
		`    case green:`
		`        echo $color is green`
		`        breaksw`
		`    case red:`
		`    case orange:`
		`        echo $color is red or orange`
		`        breaksw`
		`    default:`
		`        echo "Not a valid color"`
		`endsw`

Loops

There are two types of loops; the `while` and `foreach` loop.

The `while` loop is followed by an expression enclosed in parentheses, a block of statements, and terminated with the end keyword. As long as the expression is true, the looping continues.

The foreach loop is followed by a variable name and a list of words enclosed in parentheses, a block of statements, and terminates with the end keyword. The foreach loop iterates through a list of words, processing a word and then shifting it off, then moving to the next word. When all words have been shifted from the list, it ends.

The loop control commands are `break` and `continue`.

EXAMPLE

```
while ( expression )
   block of statements
end

foreach variable ( word list )
   block of statements
end
-----------------------------
foreach color (red green blue)
   echo $color
end
```

File testing

The C shell has a built-in set of options for testing attributes of files, such as whether it is a directory, a plain file (not a directory), a readable file, and so forth. For other types of file tests, the UNIX test command is used. See Example 2.1 for a demonstration.

Table 2.1   C and TC Shell Syntax and Constructs (continued)

File testing (continued)	EXAMPLE	
	-r	*Current user can read the file*
	-w	*Current user can write to the file*
	-x	*Current user can execute the file*
	-e	*File exists*
	-o	*Current user owns the file*
	-z	*File is zero length*
	-d	*File is a directory*
	-f	*File is a plain file*

EXAMPLE 2.1

```
    #!/bin/csh -f
1   if ( -e file ) then
        echo file exists
    endif

2   if ( -d file ) then
        echo file is a directory
    endif

3   if ( ! -z file ) then
        echo file is not of zero length
    endif

4   if ( -r file && -w file ) then
        echo file is readable and writable
    endif
```

2.3.1 The C/TC Shell Script

The program in Example 2.2 is an example of a C shell/TC shell script. The program contains many of the constructs discussed in Table 2.1.

EXAMPLE 2.2

```
1   #!/bin/csh -f
2   # The Party Program--Invitations to friends from the "guest" file
3   set guestfile = ~/shell/guests
4   if ( ! -e "$guestfile" ) then
        echo "$guestfile:t non-existent"
        exit 1
5   endif
6   setenv PLACE "Sarotini's"
```

EXAMPLE 2.2 (CONTINUED)

```
7    @ Time = `date +%H` + 1
8    set food = ( cheese crackers shrimp drinks "hot dogs" sandwiches )
9    foreach person ( `cat $guestfile` )
10       if ( $person =~ root ) continue
11       mail -v -s "Party" $person << FINIS   # Start of here document
         Hi $person! Please join me at $PLACE for a party!
         Meet me at $Time o'clock.
         I'll bring the ice cream. Would you please bring $food[1] and
         anything else you would like to eat? Let me know if you can
         make it. Hope to see you soon.
             Your pal,
             ellie@`hostname`        # or `uname -n`
12   FINIS
13       shift food
14       if ( $#food ==  0 ) then
             set food = ( cheese crackers shrimp drinks "hot dogs"
                          sandwiches )
         endif
15   end

     echo "Bye..."
```

EXPLANATION

1   This line lets the kernel know that you are running a C shell script. The -f option is a fast startup. It says, "Do not execute the .cshrc file," an initialization file that is automatically executed every time a new csh program is started.

2   This is a comment. It is ignored by the shell, but important for anyone trying to understand what the script is doing.

3   The variable guestfile is set to the full pathname of a file called guests.

4   This line reads: If the file guests does not exist, then print to the screen "guests non-existent" and exit from the script with an exit status of 1 to indicate that something went wrong in the program.

5   This marks the end of the statements based on the if condition.

6   Variables are assigned the values for the place and time. The PLACE variable is an environment variable.

7   The Time variable is a local variable. The @ symbol tells the C shell to perform its built-in arithmetic; that is, add 1 to the Time variable after extracting the hour from the date command. The Time variable is spelled with an uppercase T to prevent the C shell from confusing it with one of its reserved words, time.

8   The food array is created. It consists of a list of words separated by whitespace. Each word is an element of the food array.

9   The foreach loop consists of a list, created by using command substitution, `cat $guestfile`. The output of the cat command will create a list of guests from a file. For each person on the guest list, except the user root, a mail message will be created inviting the person to a party at a given place and time, and asking him or her to bring one of the foods on the list.

10   The condition tests to see if the value of the variable, person, matches the word root. If it does, the continue statement causes control to go immediately back to the top of the loop (rather than executing any further statements). The next word on the list will be then be processed by the foreach.

11   The mail message is created in what is called a here document. All text from the user-defined word FINIS to the final FINIS will be sent to the mail program. The foreach loop shifts through the list of names, performing all of the instructions from the foreach to the keyword end.

12   FINIS is a user-defined terminator that ends the here document, which consists of the body of an e-mail message.

13   After a message has been sent, the food list is shifted to the left with the shift command, so that the next person on the guest list will get the next food item on the list.

14   If the food list is empty, it will be reset to ensure that any additional guests will be instructed to bring a food item.

15   This marks the end of the looping statements.

2.4   The Bourne Shell Syntax and Constructs

The basic Bourne shell syntax and constructs are listed in Table 2.2.

Table 2.2   Bourne Shell Syntax and Constructs

The shbang line	The "shbang" line is the very first line of the script and lets the kernel know what shell will be interpreting the lines in the script. The shbang line consists of a #! followed by the full pathname to the shell, and can be followed by options to control the behavior of the shell.
	EXAMPLE
	`#!/bin/sh`
Comments	Comments are descriptive material preceded by a # sign. They are in effect until the end of a line and can be started anywhere on the line.
	EXAMPLE
	`# this text is not` `# interpreted by the shell`

Table 2.2   Bourne Shell Syntax and Constructs (continued)

Wildcards	There are some characters that are evaluated by the shell in a special way. They are called shell metacharacters or "wildcards." These characters are neither numbers nor letters. For example, the *, ?, and [ ] are used for filename expansion. The <, >, 2>, >>, and | symbols are used for standard I/O redirection and pipes. To prevent these characters from being interpreted by the shell they must be quoted.

EXAMPLE

Filename expansion:
```
rm *;  ls ??;  cat file[1-3];
```

Quotes protect metacharacter:
```
echo "How are you?"
```

Displaying output	To print output to the screen, the echo command is used. Wildcards must be escaped with either a backslash or matching quotes.

EXAMPLE

```
echo "What is your name?"
```

Local variables	Local variables are in scope for the current shell. When a script ends, they are no longer available; i.e., they go out of scope. Local variables are set and assigned values.

EXAMPLE

```
variable_name=value
name="John Doe"
x=5
```

Global variables	Global variables are called environment variables. They are set for the currently running shell and any process spawned from that shell. They go out of scope when the script ends.

EXAMPLE

```
VARIABLE_NAME=value
export VARIABLE_NAME

PATH=/bin:/usr/bin:.
export PATH
```

Extracting values from variables	To extract the value from variables, a dollar sign is used.

EXAMPLE

```
echo $variable_name
echo $name
echo $PATH
```

Table 2.2   Bourne Shell Syntax and Constructs (continued)

Reading user input	The read command takes a line of input from the user and assigns it to a variable(s) on the right-hand side. The read command can accept muliple variable names. Each variable will be assigned a word.

EXAMPLE

```
echo "What is your name?"
read name
read name1 name2 ...
```

Arguments (positional parameters)	Arguments can be passed to a script from the command line. Positional parameters are used to receive their values from within the script.

EXAMPLE

At the command line:
```
$ scriptname arg1 arg2 arg3 ...
```

In a script:
```
echo $1 $2 $3          Positional parameters
echo $*                All the positional paramters
echo $#                The number of positional parameters
```

Arrays (positional parameters)	The Bourne shell does support an array, but a word list can be created by using positional parameters. A list of words follows the built-in set command, and the words are accessed by position. Up to nine positions are allowed. The built-in shift command shifts off the first word on the left-hand side of the list. The individual words are accessed by position values starting at 1.

EXAMPLE

```
set word1 word2 word3
echo $1 $2 $3                  Displays word1, word2, and word3

set apples peaches plums
shift                         Shifts off apples
echo $1                       Displays first element of the list
echo $2                       Displays second element of the list
echo $*                       Displays all elements of the list
```

Command substitution	To assign the output of a UNIX/Linux command to a variable, or use the output of a command in a string, backquotes are used.

EXAMPLE

```
variable_name=`command`
echo $variable_name

now=`date`
echo $now
echo "Today is `date`"
```

Table 2.2 Bourne Shell Syntax and Constructs (continued)

Arithmetic	The Bourne shell does not support arithmetic. UNIX/Linux commands must be used to perform calculations.

> **EXAMPLE**
>
> ```
> n=`expr 5 + 5`
> echo $n
> ```

Operators	The Bourne shell uses the built-in test command operators to test numbers and strings.

> **EXAMPLE**
>
> Equality:
> | | |
> |---|---|
> | = | *string* |
> | != | *string* |
> | -eq | *number* |
> | -ne | *number* |
>
> Logical:
> | | |
> |---|---|
> | -a | *and* |
> | -o | *or* |
> | ! | *not* |
>
> Relational:
> | | |
> |---|---|
> | -gt | *greater than* |
> | -ge | *greater than, equal to* |
> | -lt | *less than* |
> | -le | *less than, equal to* |

Conditional statements	The if construct is followed by a command. If an expression is to be tested, it is enclosed in square brackets. The then keyword is placed after the closing parenthesis. An if must end with a fi.

> **EXAMPLE**
>
> The if construct is:
> ```
> if command
> then
>    block of statements
> fi
>
> if [ expression ]
> then
>    block of statements
> fi
> ```
>
> The if/else construct is:
> ```
> if [ expression ]
> then
>    block of statements
> else
>    block of statements
> fi
> ```

Table 2.2 Bourne Shell Syntax and Constructs (continued)

Conditional statements (continued)	The if/else/else if construct is: ```if command```	The case command construct is: ```case variable_name in```

<table>
<tr>
<td>
Conditional
statements
(continued)
</td>
<td>

```
The if/else/else if construct is:
if  command
then
    block of statements
elif  command
then
    block of statements
elif  command
then
    block of statements
else
    block of statements
fi
```

```
if  [ expression ]
then
    block of statements
elif  [  expression ]
then
    block of statements
elif  [  expression ]
then
    block of statements
else
    block of statements
fi
```
</td>
<td>

```
The case command construct is:
case variable_name in
    pattern1)
        statements
        ;;
    pattern2)
        statements
        ;;
    pattern3)
        ;;
    *) default value
        ;;
esac
```

```
case "$color" in
    blue)
        echo $color is blue
        ;;
    green)
        echo $color is green
        ;;
    red|orange)
        echo $color is red or orange
        ;;
    *) echo "Not a color" # default
esac
```
</td>
</tr>
</table>

Loops	There are three types of loops: `while`, `until` and `for`.

The `while` loop is followed by a command or an expression enclosed in square brackets, a do keyword, a block of statements, and terminated with the done keyword. As long as the expression is true, the body of statements between do and done will be executed.

The `until` loop is just like the `while` loop, except the body of the loop will be executed as long as the expression is false.

The for loop used to iterate through a list of words, processing a word and then shifting it off, to process the next word. When all words have been shifted from the list, it ends. The for loop is followed by a variable name, the `in` keyword, and a list of words then a block of statements, and terminates with the done keyword.
The loop control commands are break and continue.

EXAMPLE

```
while command
do
    block of statements
done

while [ expression ]
do
    block of statements
done
```

Table 2.2   Bourne Shell Syntax and Constructs (continued)

Loops (*continued*)	``` until command do block of statements done until [expression] do block of statements done ```	``` for variable in word1 word2 word3 ... do block of statements done ```
File testing	The Bourne shell uses the test command to evaluate conditional expressions and has a built-in set of options for testing attributes of files, such as whether it is a directory, a plain file (not a directory), a readable file, and so forth. See Example 2.3.	

EXAMPLE

-d   *File is a directory*
-f   *File exists and is not a directory*
-r   *Current user can read the file*
-s   *File is of nonzero size*
-w   *Current user can write to the file*
-x   *Current user can execute the file*

EXAMPLE   2.3

```
   #!/bin/sh
1  if [ -f file ]
   then
         echo file exists
   fi

2  if [ -d file ]
   then
         echo file is a directory
   fi

3  if [ -s file ]
   then
         echo file is not of zero length
   fi

4  if [ -r file -a -w file ]
   then
         echo file is readable and writable
   fi
```

Table 2.2   Bourne Shell Syntax and Constructs (continued)

Functions	Functions allow you to define a section of shell code and give it a name. The Bourne shell introduced the concept of functions. The C and TC shells do not have functions.

EXAMPLE

```
function_name() {
   block of code
}


----------------------


lister() {
   echo Your present working directory is `pwd`
   echo Your files are:
   ls
}
```

2.4.1   The Bourne Shell Script

EXAMPLE 2.4

```
1    #!/bin/sh
2    # The Party Program--Invitations to friends from the "guest" file
3    guestfile=/home/jody/ellie/shell/guests
4    if [ ! -f "$guestfile" ]
5    then
6          echo "`basename $guestfile` non-existent"
7          exit 1
8    fi
9    PLACE="Sarotini's"; export PLACE
10   Time=`date +%H`
     Time=`expr $Time + 1`
11   set cheese crackers shrimp drinks "hot dogs" sandwiches
12   for person in `cat $guestfile`
     do
13        if [ $person =~ root ]
          then
14             continue
15        else
16        #    mail -v -s "Party" $person <<- FINIS
```

EXAMPLE 2.4 (CONTINUED)

```
17          cat <<-FINIS
            Hi ${person}! Please join me at $PLACE for a party!
            Meet me at $Time o'clock.
            I'll bring the ice cream. Would you please bring $1 and
            anything else you would like to eat? Let me know if you
            can make it. Hope to see you soon.
                Your pal,
                ellie@`hostname`
            FINIS
18          shift
19          if [ $# -eq 0 ]
            then
20              set cheese crackers shrimp drinks "hot dogs" sandwiches
            fi
      fi
21  done
    echo "Bye..."
```

EXPLANATION

1   This line lets the kernel know that you are running a Bourne shell script.

2   This is a comment. It is ignored by the shell, but important for anyone trying to understand what the script is doing.

3   The variable guestfile is set to the full pathname of a file called guests.

4   This line reads: If the file guests does not exist, then print to the screen "guests non-existent" and exit from the script.

5   The then is usually on a line by itself, or on the same line as the if statement if it is preceded by a semicolon.

6   The UNIX basename command removes all but the filename in a search path. Because the command is enclosed in backquotes, command substitution will be performed and the output displayed by the echo command.

7   If the file does not exist, the program will exit. An exit with a value of 1 indicates that there was a failure in the program.

8   The fi keyword marks the end of the block of if statements.

9   Variables are assigned the values for the place and time. PLACE is an environment variable, because after it is set, it is exported.

10 The value in the Time variable is the result of command substitution; i.e., the output of the date +%H command (the current hour) will be assigned to Time.

11 The list of foods to bring is assigned to special variables (positional parameters) with the set command.

12 The for loop is entered. It loops through until each person listed in the guest file has been processed.

13   If the variable person matches the name of the user root, loop control will go to the top of the for loop and process the next person on the list. The user root will not get an invitation.

14   The continue statement causes loop control to start at line 12, rather than continuing to line 16.

15   The block of statements under else are executed if line 13 is not true.

16   The mail message is sent when this line is uncommented. It is a good idea to comment this line until the program has been thoroughly debugged, otherwise the e-mail will be sent to the same people every time the script is tested.

17   The next statement, using the cat command with the here document, allows the script to be tested by sending output to the screen that would normally be sent through the mail when line 7 is uncommented.

18   After a message has been sent, the food list is shifted so that the next person will get the next food on the list. If there are more people than foods, the food list will be reset, ensuring that each person is assigned a food.

19   The value of $# is the number of postional parameters left. If that number is 0, the food list is empty.

20   The food list is reset.

21   The done keyword marks the end of the block of statements in the body of the for loop.

2.5   The Korn Shell Constructs

The Korn and Bash shells are very similar. The following constructs will work for both shells. To see all the subtle variations, see the individual chapters for these shells.

Table 2.3   Korn Shell Syntax and Constructs

The shbang line	The "shbang" line is the very first line of the script and lets the kernel know what shell will be interpreting the lines in the script. The shbang line consists of a #! followed by the full pathname to the shell, and can be followed by options to control the behavior of the shell. **EXAMPLE** `#!/bin/ksh`
Comments	Comments are descriptive material preceded by a # sign. They are in effect until the end of a line and can be started anywhere on the line. **EXAMPLE** `# This program will test some files`

Table 2.3   Korn Shell Syntax and Constructs (continued)

Wildcards	There are some characters that are evaluated by the shell in a special way. They are called shell metacharacters or "wildcards." These characters are neither numbers nor letters. For example, the *, ?, and [ ] are used for filename expansion. The <, >, 2>, >>, and | symbols are used for standard I/O redirection and pipes. To prevent these characters from being interpreted by the shell they must be quoted.

EXAMPLE

```
rm *; ls ??;  cat file[1-3];
echo "How are you?"
```

Displaying output	To print output to the screen, the echo command can be used. Wildcards must be escaped with either a backslash or matching quotes. Korn shell also provides a built-in print function to replace the echo command.

EXAMPLE

```
echo "Who are you?"
print "How are you?"
```

Local variables	Local variables are in scope for the current shell. When a script ends or the shell exits, they are no longer available; i.e., they go out of scope. The typeset built-in command can also be used to declare variables. Local variables are set and assigned values.

EXAMPLE

```
variable_name=value
typeset variable_name=value
name="John Doe"
x=5
```

Global variables	Global variables are called environment variables. They are set for the currently running shell and any process spawned from that shell. They go out of scope when the script ends or the shell where they were defined exits.

EXAMPLE

```
export VARIABLE_NAME =value
export PATH=/bin:/usr/bin:.
```

Extracting values from variables	To extract the value from variables, a dollar sign is used.

EXAMPLE

```
echo $variable_name
echo $name
echo $PATH
```

Reading user input	The user will be asked to enter input. The read command is used to accept a line of input. Multiple arguments to read will cause a line to be broken into words, and each word will be assigned to the named variable. The Korn shell allows the prompt and read command to be combined.

Table 2.3 Korn Shell Syntax and Constructs (continued)

Reading user input *(continued)*	**EXAMPLE**
	
	 `read name?"What is your name?"` *The prompt is in quotes. After it is displayed, the*
	 `print -n "What is your name?"` *read command waits for user input*
	 `read name`
	 `read name1 name2 ...`

Arguments

Arguments can be passed to a script from the command line. Positional parameters are used to receive their values from within the script.

> **EXAMPLE**
>
> At the command line:
> `$ scriptname arg1 arg2 arg3 ...`
>
> In a script:
> `echo $1 $2 $3`   *Positional parameters, $1 is assigned arg1, $2 is assigned arg2, ...*
> `echo $*`   *All the positional paramters*
> `echo $#`   *The number of positional parameters*

Arrays

The Bourne shell utilizes positional parameters to create a word list. In addition to positional parameters, the Korn shell also supports an array syntax whereby the elements are accessed with a subscript, starting at 0. Korn shell arrays are created with the `set -A` command.

> **EXAMPLE**
>
> `set apples pears peaches`   *Positional parameters*
> `print $1 $2 $3`   *$1 is apples, $2 is pears, $3 is peaches*
> `set -A array_name word1 word2 word3 ...`   *Array*
> `set -A fruit apples pears plums`
> `print ${fruit[0]}`   *Prints* apples
> `${fruit[1]} = oranges`   *Assign a new value*

Arithmetic

The Korn shell supports integer arithmetic. The typeset `-i` command will declare an integer type variable. Integer arithmetic can be performed on variables declared this way. Otherwise, the `(( ))` syntax (`let` command) is used for arithmetic operations.

> **EXAMPLE**
>
> `typeset -i variable_name`   *Declare integer*
>
> `typeset -i  num`   *num is declared as an integer*
> `num=5+4`
> `print $num`   *Prints 9*
>
> `(( n=5 + 5 ))`   *The* let *command*
> `print $n`   *Prints 10*

Table 2.3   Korn Shell Syntax and Constructs (continued)

Command substitution	Like the C/TC shells and the Bourne shell, the output of a UNIX/Linux command can be assigned to a variable, or used as the output of a command in a string, by enclosing the command in backquotes. The Korn shell also provides a new syntax. Instead of placing the command between backquotes, it is enclosed in a set of parentheses, preceded by a dollar sign.

> **EXAMPLE**
>
> ```
> variable_name=`command`
> variable_name=$( command )
> echo $variable_name
>
> echo "Today is `date`"
> echo "Today is $(date)"
> ```

Operators	The Korn shell uses the built-in test command operators to test numbers and strings, similar to C language operators.

> **EXAMPLE**
>
> | Equality: | | | Relational: | | |
> |---|---|---|---|---|---|
> | = | *string, equal to* | | > | *greater than* | |
> | != | *string, not equal to* | | >= | *greater than, equal to* | |
> | == | *number, equal to* | | < | *less than* | |
> | != | *number, not equal to* | | <= | *less than, equal to* | |
>
> Logical:
> && *and*
> || *or*
> ! *not*

Conditional statements	The if construct is followed by an expression enclosed in parentheses. The operators are similar to C operators. The then keyword is placed after the closing parenthesis. An if must end with a fi. The new test command [[ ]] is now used to allow pattern matching in conditional expressions. The old test command [ ] is still available for backward compatibility with the Bourne shell. The case command is an alternative to if/else.

> **EXAMPLE**
>
> ```
> The if construct is:                       -----------------------------
> if command                                 if (( numeric expression ))
> then                                       then
>    block of statements                        block of statements
> fi                                         fi
> -----------------------------
> if [[ string expression ]]
> then
>    block of statements
> fi
> ```

Table 2.3   Korn Shell Syntax and Constructs (continued)

Conditional statements (*continued*)	The if/else construct is:	The if/else/else if construct is:

<table>
<tr>
<td valign="top">Conditional
statements
(continued)</td>
<td valign="top">

The if/else construct is:
```
if command
then
   block of statements
else
   block of statements
fi
------------------------
if [[ expression ]]
then
   block of statements
else
   block of statements
fi
--------------------------
if (( numeric expression  ))
then
   block of statements
else
   block of statements
fi


The case construct is:
case variable_name in
   pattern1)
      statements
         ;;
   pattern2)
      statements
         ;;
   pattern3)
         ;;
esac
------------------------
case "$color" in
   blue)
      echo $color is blue
         ;;
   green)
      echo $color is green
         ;;
   red|orange)
      echo $color is red or orange
         ;;
esac
```
</td>
<td valign="top">

The if/else/else if construct is:
```
if  command
then
   block of statements
elif  command
then
   block of statements
elif  command
then
   block of statements
else
   block of statements
fi
--------------------------
if [[ string expression ]]
then
   block of statements
elif  [[  string expression ]]
then
   block of statements
elif  [[  string expression ]]
then
   block of statements
else
   block of statements
fi
--------------------------
if (( numeric expression ))
then
   block of statements
elif  ((  numeric expression ))
then
   block of statements
elif  ((  numeric expression ))
then
   block of statements
else
   block of statements
fi
```
</td>
</tr>
</table>

Table 2.3   Korn Shell Syntax and Constructs (continued)

Loops	There are four types of loops: while, until, for, and select.

The while loop is followed by an expression enclosed in square brackets, a do keyword, a block of statements, and terminated with the done keyword. As long as the expression is true, the body of statements between do and done will be executed.

The until loop is just like the while loop, except the body of the loop will be executed as long as the expression is false.

The for loop is used to iterate through a list of words, processing a word and then shifting it off, to process the next word. When all words have been shifted from the list, it ends.

The select loop is used to provide a prompt (PS3 variable) and a menu of numbered items from which the user inputs a selection The input will be stored in the special built-in REPLY variable. The select loop is normally used with the case command.

The loop control commands are break and continue. The break command allows control to exit the loop before reaching the end of it; the continue command allows control to return to the looping expression before reaching the end.

EXAMPLE

```
while command
do
    block of statements
done
-----------------------------
while [[ string expression ]]
do
    block of statements
done
-----------------------------
while (( numeric expression ))
do
    block of statements
done


until command
do
    block of statements
done
-----------------------------
until [[ string expression ]]
do
    block of statements
done
-----------------------------
until (( numeric expression ))
do
    block of statements
done
```

```
for variable in word_list
do
    block of statements
done
-----------------------------
for name in Tom Dick Harry
do
    print "Hi $name"
done


select variable in word_list
do
    block of statements
done
-----------------------------
PS3="Select an item from the menu"
for item in blue red green
    echo $item
done
```

Shows menu:
  1) blue
  2) red
  3) green

Table 2.3   Korn Shell Syntax and Constructs (continued)

File testing	The Korn shell uses the test command to evaluate conditional expressions and has a built-in set of options for testing attributes of files, such as whether it is a directory, a plain file (not a directory), a readable file, and so forth. See Example 2.5.

EXAMPLE

```
-d        File is a directory
-a        File exists and is not a directory
-r        Current user can read the file
-s        File is of nonzero size
-w        Current user can write to the file
-x        Current user can execute the file
```

EXAMPLE   2.5

```
    #!/bin/sh
1   if [ -a file ]
    then
          echo file exists
    fi

2   if [ -d file ]
    then
          echo file is a directory
    fi

3   if [ -s file ]
    then
          echo file is not of zero length
    fi

4   if [ -r file -a -w file ]
    then
          echo file is readable and writable
    fi
```

Functions	Functions allow you to define a section of shell code and give it a name. There are two formats: one from the Bourne shell, and the Korn shell version that uses the function keyword.

EXAMPLE

```
function_name() {
   block of code
}

function function_name {
   block of code
}
-------------------------
```

Table 2.3   Korn Shell Syntax and Constructs (continued)

| Functions *(continued)* | ```
function lister {
    echo Your present working directory is `pwd`
    echo Your files are:
    ls
}
``` |
|---|---|

2.5.1 The Korn Shell Script

EXAMPLE   2.6

```
1   #!/bin/ksh
2   # The Party Program--Invitations to friends from the "guest" file
3   guestfile=~/shell/guests
4   if [[ ! -a "$guestfile" ]]
    then
        print "${guestfile##*/} non-existent"
        exit 1
    fi
5   export PLACE="Sarotini's"
6   (( Time=$(date +%H) + 1 ))
7   set -A foods cheese crackers shrimp drinks "hot dogs" sandwiches
8   typeset -i n=0
9   for person in $(< $guestfile)
    do
10      if  [[ $person = root ]]
        then
            continue
        else
            # Start of here document
11          mail -v -s "Party" $person <<- FINIS
            Hi ${person}! Please join me at $PLACE for a party!
            Meet me at $Time o'clock.
            I'll bring the ice cream. Would you please bring
            ${foods[$n]} and anything else you would like to eat? Let
            me know if you can make it.
                    Hope to see you soon.
                            Your pal,
                            ellie@`hostname`
            FINIS
12          n=n+1
```
```

EXAMPLE   2.6 (CONTINUED)

```
13              if (( ${#foods[*]} == $n ))
                then
14                  set -A foods cheese crackers shrimp drinks "hot dogs"
                    sandwiches
                fi
        fi
15  done
    print "Bye..."
```

EXPLANATION

1   This line lets the kernel know that you are running a Korn shell script.

2   This is a comment. It is ignored by the shell, but important for anyone trying to understand what the script is doing.

3   The variable guestfile is set to the full pathname of a file called guests.

4   This line reads: If the file guests does not exist, then print to the screen "guests non-existent" and exit from the script.

5   An environment variable is assigned a value and exported (made available to sub-shells).

6   The output of the UNIX/Linux command, the hour of the day, is assigned to the variable called Time. Variables are assigned the values for the place and time.

7   The list of foods to bring is assigned to an array called foods with the set -A command. Each item on the list can be accessed with an index starting at 0.

8   The typeset -i command is used to create an integer value.

9   For each person on the guest list a mail message will be created inviting the person to a party at a given place and time, and assigning a food from the list to bring.

10   The condition tests for the user root. If the user is root, control will go back to the top of the loop and assign the next user in the guest list to the variable, person.

11   The mail message is sent. The message body is contained in a here document.

12   The variable n is incremented by 1.

13   If the number of elements in the array is equal to the value of the variable, then the end of the array has been reached.

14   This marks the end of the looping statements.

2.6   The Bash Shell Constructs

The Korn and Bash shells are very similar, but there are some differences. The Bash constructs are listed in Table 2.4.

Table 2.4   Bash Shell Syntax and Constructs

The shbang line	The "shbang" line is the very first line of the script and lets the kernel know what shell will be interpreting the lines in the script. The shbang line consists of a #! followed by the full pathname to the shell, and can be followed by options to control the behavior of the shell.
	EXAMPLE
	```#!/bin/bash```
Comments	Comments are descriptive material preceded by a # sign. They are in effect until the end of a line and can be started anywhere on the line.
	EXAMPLE
	```# This is a comment```
Wildcards	There are some characters that are evaluated by the shell in a special way. They are called shell metacharacters or "wildcards." These characters are neither numbers or letters. For example, the *, ?, and [ ] are used for filename expansion. The <, >, 2>, >>, and | symbols are used for standard I/O redirection and pipes. To prevent these characters from being interpreted by the shell they must be quoted.
	EXAMPLE
	```rm *; ls ??; cat file[1-3];``` ```echo "How are you?"```
Displaying output	To print output to the screen, the echo command is used. Wildcards must be escaped with either a backslash or matching quotes.
	EXAMPLE
	```echo "How are you?"```
Local variables	Local variables are in scope for the current shell. When a script ends, they are no longer available; i.e., they go out of scope. Local variables can also be defined with the built-in declare function. Local variables are set and assigned values.
	EXAMPLE

	```variable_name=value```
	```declare variable_name=value```
	
	```name="John Doe"```
	```x=5```

Table 2.4 Bash Shell Syntax and Constructs (continued)

Global variables	Global variables are called environment variables and are created with the export built-in command. They are set for the currently running shell and any process spawned from that shell. They go out of scope when the script ends.
	The built-in declare function with the -x option also sets an environment variable and marks it for export.

> **EXAMPLE**
>
> ```
> export VARIABLE_NAME=value
> declare -x VARIABLE_NAME=value
> export PATH=/bin:/usr/bin:.
> ```

Extracting values from variables	To extract the value from variables, a dollar sign is used.

> **EXAMPLE**
>
> ```
> echo $variable_name
> echo $name
> echo $PATH
> ```

Reading user input	The user will be asked to enter input. The read command is used to accept a line of input. Multiple arguments to read will cause a line to be broken into words, and each word will be assigned to the named variable.

> **EXAMPLE**
>
> ```
> echo "What is your name?"
> read name
> read name1 name2 ...
> ```

Arguments	Arguments can be passed to a script from the command line. Positional parameters are used to receive their values from within the script.

> **EXAMPLE**
>
> At the command line:
> ```
> $ scriptname arg1 arg2 arg3 ...
> ```
>
> In a script:
> ```
> echo $1 $2 $3          Positional parameters
> echo $*                All the positional paramters
> echo $#                The number of positional parameters
> ```

Arrays	The Bourne shell utilizes positional parameters to create a word list. In addition to positional parameters, the Bash shell supports an array syntax whereby the elements are accessed with a subscript, starting at 0. Bash shell arrays are created with the declare -a command.

Table 2.4   Bash Shell Syntax and Constructs (continued)

Arrays (*continued*)	**EXAMPLE**
	
	```set apples pears peaches (positional parameters)```
	```echo $1 $2 $3```
	
	```declare -a array_name=(word1 word2 word3 ...)```
	```declare -a fruit=(apples pears plums)```
	```echo ${fruit[0]}```

Command substitution	Like the C/TC shells and the Bourne shell, the output of a UNIX/Linux command can be assigned to a variable, or used as the output of a command in a string, by enclosing the command in backquotes. The Bash shell also provides a new syntax. Instead of placing the command between backquotes, it is enclosed in a set of parentheses, preceded by a dollar sign.
	
	EXAMPLE
	
	```variable_name=`command` ```
	```variable_name=$(command)```
	```echo $variable_name```
	
	```echo "Today is `date`"```
	```echo "Today is $(date)"```

Arithmetic	The Bash shells support integer arithmetic. The ```declare -i``` command will declare an integer type variable.The Korn shell's typeset command can also be use for backward compatibility. Integer arithmetic can be performed on variables declared this way. Otherwise the (( )) (let command) syntax is used for arithmetic operations.
	
	EXAMPLE
	
	```declare -i variable_name``` *used for* bash
	```typeset -i variable_name``` *can be used to be compatible with* ksh
	
	```((n=5 + 5))```
	```echo $n```

Operators	The Bash shell uses the built-in test command operators to test numbers and strings, similar to C language operators. **EXAMPLE** Equality: Logical: == *equal to* && *and* != *not equal to* || *or* ! *not* Relational: > *greater than* >= *greater than, equal to* < *less than* <= *less than, equal to*

Table 2.4 Bash Shell Syntax and Constructs (continued)

Conditional statements	The if construct is followed by an expression enclosed in parentheses. The operators are similar to C operators. The then keyword is placed after the closing paren. An if must end with an endif. The new [[ ]] test command is now used to allow pattern matching in conditional expressions. The old [ ] test command is still available for backward compatibility with the Bourne shell. The case command is an alternative to if/else.

EXAMPLE

The if construct is:
```
if command
then
   block of statements
fi

if [[ expression ]]
then
   block of statements
fi

if (( numeric expression ))
then
   block of statements
else
   block of statements
 fi
```

The if/else construct is:
```
if command
then
   block of statements
else
   block of statements
fi

if [[ expression ]]
then
   block of statements
else
   block of statements
fi

if (( numeric expression ))
then
   block of statements
else
   block of statements
fi
```

The if/else/else if construct is:
```
if command
then
   block of statements
elif command
then
   block of statements
else if command
then
   block of statements
else
   block of statements
fi
-------------------------
if [[ expression ]]
then
   block of statements
elif [[ expression ]]
then
   block of statements
else if [[ expression ]]
then
   block of statements
else
   block of statements
fi
-------------------------
if (( numeric expression ))
then
   block of statements
elif (( numeric expression ))
then
   block of statements
else if ((numeric expression))
then
   block of statements
else
   block of statements
fi
```

Table 2.4   Bash Shell Syntax and Constructs (continued)

Conditional statements (*continued*)	The case construct is: ```case variable_name in pattern1) statements ;; pattern2) statements ;; pattern3) ;;esaccase "$color" in blue) echo $color is blue ;; green) echo $color is green ;; red|orange) echo $color is red or orange ;; *) echo "Not a matach" ;;esac```
Loops	There are four types of loops: `while`, `until`, `for`, and `select`.
	The `while` loop is followed by an expression enclosed in square brackets, a `do` keyword, a block of statements, and terminated with the `done` keyword. As long as the expression is true, the body of statements between `do` and `done` will be executed. The compound test operator `[[ ]]` is new with Bash, and the old-style test operator `[ ]` can still be used to evaluate conditional expressions for backward compatibility with the Bourne shell.
	The `until` loop is just like the `while` loop, except the body of the loop will be executed as long as the expression is false.
	The `for` loop is used to iterate through a list of words, processing a word and then shifting it off, to process the next word. When all words have been shifted from the list, it ends. The `for` loop is followed by a variable name, the `in` keyword, a list of words, then a block of statements, and terminates with the `done` keyword.
	The `select` loop is used to provide a prompt and a menu of numbered items from which the user inputs a selection. The input will be stored in the special built-in `REPLY` variable. The `select` loop is normally used with the `case` command.
	The loop control commands are `break` and `continue`. The `break` command allows control to exit the loop before reaching the end of it, and the `continue` command allows control to return to the looping expression before reaching the end.

Table 2.4   Bash Shell Syntax and Constructs (continued)

Loops *(continued)*	**EXAMPLE**

```
while command                      until command
do                                 do
   block of statements                block of statements
done                               done
-------------------------          -------------------------
while [[ string expression ]]      until [[ string expression ]]
do                                 do
   block of statements                block of statements
done                               done
-------------------------          -------------------------
while (( numeric expression ))     until (( numeric expression ))
do                                 do
   block of statements                block of statements
done                               done



for variable in word_list         select variable in word_list
do                                 do
   block of statements                block of statements
done                               done
-------------------------          -------------------------
for color in red green blue        PS3="Select an item from the menu"
do                                 do item in blue red green    Shows menu:
   echo $color                        echo $item                     1) blue
done                               done                               2) red
                                                                      3) green
```

Functions	Functions allow you to define a section of shell code and give it a name. There are two formats, one from the Bourne shell, and the Bash version that uses the `function` keyword.

EXAMPLE

```
function_name() {
   block of code
}

function  function_name {
   block of code
}
-------------------------
function  lister {
   echo Your present working directory is `pwd`
   echo Your files are:
   ls
}
```

2.6.1 The Bash Shell Script

EXAMPLE 2.7

```
1    #!/bin/bash
     # GNU bash versions 2.x
2    # The Party Program--Invitations to friends from the "guest" file
3    guestfile=~/shell/guests
4    if [[ ! -e "$guestfile" ]]
     then
5        printf "${guestfile##*/} non-existent"
         exit 1
     fi
6    export PLACE="Sarotini's"
7    (( Time=$(date +%H) + 1 ))
8    declare -a foods=(cheese crackers shrimp drinks `"hot dogs"` sandwiches)
9    declare -i  n=0
10   for person in $(cat $guestfile)
     do
11       if  [[ $person == root ]]
         then
             continue
         else
             # Start of here document
12           mail -v -s "Party" $person <<- FINIS
             Hi $person! Please join me at $PLACE for a party!
             Meet me at $Time o'clock.
             I'll bring the ice cream. Would you please bring
             ${foods[$n] and anything else you would like to eat?
             Let me know if you can make it.
                     Hope to see you soon.
                         Your pal,
                         ellie@$(hostname)
             FINIS
13           n=n+1
14           if (( ${#foods[*]} ==  $n ))
             then
15               declare -a foods=(cheese crackers shrimp drinks `"hot dogs"`
                                         sandwiches)
16               n=0
             fi
         fi
17   done
     printf "Bye..."
```

EXPLANATION

1   This line lets the kernel know that you are running a Bash shell script.

2   This is a comment. It is ignored by the shell, but important for anyone trying to understand what the script is doing.

3   The variable guestfile is set to the full pathname of a file called guests.

4   This line reads: If the file guests does not exist, then print to the screen "guests non-existent" and exit from the script.

5   The built-in printf function dipslays only the filename (pattern matching) and the string "non-existent".

6   An environment (global) variable is assigned and exported.

7   A numeric expression uses the output of the UNIX/Linux date command to get the current hour. The hour is assigned to the variable, Time.

8   A Bash array, foods, is defined (declare -a) with a list of elements.

9   An integer, n, is defined with an initial value of zero.

10   For each person on the guest list, except the user root, a mail message will be created inviting the person to a party at a given place and time, and assigning a food from the list to bring.

11   If the value in $person is root, control goes back to the top of the for loop and starts at the next person on the list.

12   The mail message is sent. The message body is contained in a here document.

13   The integer, n, is incremented by 1.

14   If the number of foods is equal to the value of the last number in the array index, the list is empty.

15   The array called foods is reassigned values. After a message has been sent, the food list is shifted so that the next person will get the next food on the list. If there are more people than foods, the food list will be reset, ensuring that each person is assigned a food.

16   The variable n, which will serve as the array index, is reset back to zero.

17   This marks the end of the looping statements.

chapter
3

Regular Expressions and Pattern Matching

There are hundreds of UNIX/Linux utilities available, and many of them are everyday commands such as `ls`, `pwd`, `who`, and `vi`. Just as there are essential tools that a carpenter uses, there are also essential tools the shell programmer needs to write meaningful and efficient scripts. The three major utilities that will be discussed in detail here are `grep`, `sed`, and `awk`. These programs are the most important UNIX/Linux tools available for manipulating text, output from a pipe, or standard input. In fact, `sed` and `awk` are often used as scripting languages by themselves. Before you fully appreciate the power of `grep`, `sed`, and `awk`, you must have a good foundation on the use of regular expressions and regular expression metacharacters. A complete list of useful UNIX/Linux utilities is found in Appendix A of this book.

3.1 Regular Expressions

3.1.1 Definition and Example

For users already familiar with the concept of regular expression metacharacters, this section may be bypassed. However, this preliminary material is crucial to understanding the variety of ways in which `grep`, `sed`, and `awk` are used to display and manipulate data.

What is a regular expression? A regular expression[1] is just a pattern of characters used to match the same characters in a search. In most programs, a regular expression is enclosed in forward slashes; for example, /love/ is a regular expression delimited by forward slashes, and the pattern love will be matched any time the same pattern is found in the line being searched. What makes regular expressions interesting is that they can be controlled by special metacharacters. If you are new to the idea of regular expressions, let us look at an example that will help you understand what this whole concept

---

1. If you receive an error message that contains the string RE, there is a problem with the regular expression you are using in the program.

is about. Suppose that you are working in the vi editor on an e-mail message to your friend. It looks like this:

% vi letter

```
-----------------------------------------------------------------
Hi tom,
I think I failed my anatomy test yesterday. I had a terrible
stomachache. I ate too many fried green tomatoes.
Anyway, Tom, I need your help. I'd like to make the test up
tomorrow, but don't know where to begin studying. Do you
think you could help me? After work, about 7 PM, come to
my place and I'll treat you to pizza in return for your help. Thanks.
    Your pal,
    guy@phantom
~
~
~
~

-----------------------------------------------------------------
```

Now, suppose you find out that Tom never took the test either, but David did. You also notice that in the greeting, you spelled Tom with a lowercase t. So you decide to make a global substitution to replace all occurrences of tom with David, as follows:

% vi letter

```
-----------------------------------------------------------------
Hi David,
I think I failed my anaDavidy test yesterday. I had a terrible
sDavidachache. I think I ate too many fried green Davidatoes.
Anyway, Tom, I need your help. I'd like to make the test up
Davidorrow, but don't know where to begin studying. Do you
think you could help me? After work, about 7 PM, come to
my place and I'll treat you to pizza in return for your help. Thanks.
    Your pal,
    guy@phanDavid
~
~
~
-->   :1,$s/tom/David/g
-----------------------------------------------------------------
```

The regular expression in the search string is tom. The replacement string is David. The vi command reads "for lines 1 to the end of the file ($), substitute tom everywhere it is found on each line and replace it with David." Hardly what you want! And one of the occurrences of Tom was untouched because you only asked for tom, not Tom, to be replaced with David. So what to do? Enter the regular expression metacharacters.

3.1.2   Regular Expression Metacharacters

Metacharacters are characters that represent something other than themselves. The two types of metacharacters that you will learn about in this book are shell metacharacters and regular expression metacharacters. They serve different purposes. Shell metacharacters are evaluated by the UNIX/Linux shell. For example, when you use the command: rm *, the asterisk is a shell metacharacter, called a wildcard, and is evaluated by the shell to mean "Match on all filenames in the current working directory." The shell metacharacters are described for the shells in their respective chapters.

Regular expression metacharacters are evaluated by the programs that perform pattern matching, such as vi, grep, sed, and awk.[2] They are special characters that allow you to delimit a pattern in some way so that you can control what substitutions will take place. There are metacharacters to anchor a word to the beginning or end of a line. There are metacharacters that allow you to specify any characters, or some number of characters, to find both upper- and lowercase characters, digits only, and so forth. For example, to change the name tom or Tom to David, the following vi command would have done the job:

:1,$s/\<[Tt]om\>/David/g

This command reads, "From the first line to the last line of the file (1,$), substitute (s) the word Tom or tom with David," and the g flag says to do this globally (i.e., make the substitution if it occurs more than once on the same line). The regular expression metacharacters are \< and \> for beginning and end of a word, and the pair of brackets, [Tt], match for one of the characters enclosed within them (in this case, for either T or t). There are five basic metacharacters that all UNIX/Linux pattern-matching utilities recognize. Table 3.1 presents regular expression metacharacters that can be used in all versions of vi, ex, grep, egrep, sed, and awk. Additional metacharacters are described for each of the utilities where applicable.

Table 3.1   Regular Expression Metacharacters

Metacharacter	Function	Example	What It Matches
^	Beginning-of-line anchor	/^love/	Matches all lines beginning with love
$	End-of-line anchor	/love$/	Matches all lines ending with love
.	Matches one character	/l..e/	Matches lines containing an l, followed by two characters, followed by an e
*	Matches zero or more of the preceding characters	/ *love/	Matches lines with zero or more spaces, followed by the pattern love

---

2. The Korn and Bash shells now support pattern-matching metacharacters similar to the regular expression metacharacters described for grep, sed, and awk.

Table 3.1 Regular Expression Metacharacters (continued)

Metacharacter	Function	Example	What It Matches
[ ]	Matches one in the set	/[Ll]ove/	Matches lines containing love or Love
[x-y]	Matches one character within a range in the set	/[A-Z]ove/	Matches letters from A through Z followed by ove
[^]	Matches one character not in the set	/[^A-Z]/	Matches any character not in the range between A and Z
\	Used to escape a metacharacter	/love\./	Matches lines containing love, followed by a literal period; Normally the period matches one of any character

Additional Metacharacters Supported by Many UNIX/Linux Programs That Use RE Metacharacters

Metacharacter	Function	Example	What It Matches
\<	Beginning-of-word anchor	/\<love/	Matches lines containing a word that begins with love (supported by vi and grep)
\>	End-of-word anchor	/love\>/	Matches lines containing a word that ends with love (supported by vi and grep)
\(..\)	Tags match characters to be used later	/\(love\)able \1er/	May use up to nine tags, starting with the first tag at the leftmost part of the pattern. For example, the pattern love is saved as tag 1, to be referenced later as \1. In this example, the search pattern consists of lovable followed by lover (supported by sed, vi, and grep)
x\{m\} or x\{m,\} or x\{m,n\}	Repetition of character x, m times, at least m times, at least m and not more than n times[a]	o\{5,10\}	Matches if line contains between 5 and 10 consecutive occurrences of the letter o (supported by vi and grep)

a. Not dependable on all versions of UNIX/Linux or all pattern-matching utilities; usually works with vi and grep.

Assuming that you know how the vi editor works, each metacharacter is described in terms of the vi search string. In the following examples, characters are highlighted to demonstrate what vi will find in its search.

EXAMPLE 3.1

(A simple regular expression search)
```
% vi picnic
----------------------------------------------------------------
I had a **love**ly time on our little picnic.
Lovers were all around us. It is springtime. Oh
**love**, how much I adore you. Do you know
the extent of my **love**? Oh, by the way, I think
I lost my g**love**s somewhere out in that field of
c**love**r. Did you see them?  I can only hope **love**
is forever. I live for you. It's hard to get back in the
groove.
~
~
~
/love/
----------------------------------------------------------------
```

EXPLANATION

The regular expression is love. The pattern love is found by itself and as part of other words, such as lovely, gloves, and clover.

EXAMPLE 3.2

(The beginning-of-line anchor (^))
```
% vi picnic
----------------------------------------------------------------
I had a lovely time on our little picnic.
Lovers were all around us. It is springtime. Oh
**love**, how much I adore you. Do you know
the extent of my love? Oh, by the way, I think
I lost my gloves somewhere out in that field of
clover. Did you see them? I can only hope love
is forever. I live for you. It's hard to get back in the
groove.
~
~
~
/^love/
----------------------------------------------------------------
```

EXPLANATION

The caret (^) is called the beginning-of-line anchor. Vi will find only those lines where the regular expression love is matched at the beginning of the line, i.e., love is the first set of characters on the line; it cannot be preceded by even one space.

EXAMPLE 3.3

```
(The end-of-line anchor ($))
% vi picnic
----------------------------------------------------------------
I had a lovely time on our little picnic.
Lovers were all around us. It is springtime. Oh
love, how much I adore you. Do you know
the extent of my love? Oh, by the way, I think
I lost my gloves somewhere out in that field of
clover. Did you see them? I can only hope love
is forever. I live for you. It's hard to get back in the
groove.
~
~
~
/love$/
----------------------------------------------------------------
```

EXPLANATION

The dollar sign ($) is called the end-of-line anchor. Vi will find only those lines where the regular expression love is matched at the end of the line, i.e., love is the last set of characters on the line and is directly followed by a newline.

EXAMPLE 3.4

```
(Any Single Character (.))
% vi picnic
----------------------------------------------------------------
I had a lovely time on our little picnic.
Lovers were all around us. It is springtime. Oh
love, how much I adore you. Do you know
the extent of my love? Oh, by the way, I think
I lost my gloves somewhere out in that field of
clover. Did you see them? I can only hope love
is forever. I live for you. It's hard to get back in the
groove.
~
~
~
/l.ve/
----------------------------------------------------------------
```

EXPLANATION

The dot (.) matches any one character, except the newline. Vi will find those lines where the regular expression consists of an l, followed by any single character, followed by a v and an e. It finds combinations of love and live.

EXAMPLE 3.5

```
(Zero or more of the preceding character (*))
% vi picnic
-----------------------------------------------------------------
I had a lovely time on our little picnic.
Lovers were all around us. It is springtime. Oh
love, how much I adore you. Do you know
the extent of my love? Oh, by the way, I think
I lost my gloves somewhere out in that field of
clover. Did you see them? I can only hope love
is forever. I live for you. It's hard to get back in the
groove.
~
~
~
/o*ve/
-----------------------------------------------------------------
```

EXPLANATION

The asterisk (*) matches zero or more of the preceding character.[a] It is as though the asterisk were glued to the character directly before it and controls only that character. In this case, the asterisk is glued to the letter o. It matches for only the letter o and as many consecutive occurrences of the letter o as there are in the pattern, even no occurrences of o at all. Vi searches for zero or more occurrences of the letter o followed by a v and an e, finding love, loooove, lve, and so forth.

a. Do not confuse this metacharacter with the shell wildcard (*). They are totally different. The shell asterisk matches for zero or more of any character, whereas the regular expression asterisk matches for zero or more of the preceding character.

EXAMPLE 3.6

```
(A set of characters ([]))
% vi picnic
-----------------------------------------------------------------
I had a lovely time on our little picnic.
Lovers were all around us. It is springtime. Oh
love, how much I adore you. Do you know
the extent of my love? Oh, by the way, I think
I lost my gloves somewhere out in that field of
clover. Did you see them? I can only hope love
is forever. I live for you. It's hard to get back in the
groove.
~
~
~
/[Ll]ove/
-----------------------------------------------------------------
```

EXPLANATION

The square brackets match for one of a set of characters. Vi will search for the regular expression containing either an uppercase or lowercase l followed by an o, v, and e.

EXAMPLE 3.7

```
(A range of characters ( [ - ] ))
% vi picnic
-----------------------------------------------------------------
I had a lovely time on our little picnic.
Lovers were all around us. It is springtime. Oh
love, how much I adore you. Do you know
the extent of my love? Oh, by the way, I think
I lost my gloves somewhere out in that field of
clover. Did you see them? I can only hope love
is forever. I live for you. It's hard to get back in the
groove.
~
~
~
/ove[a-z]/
-----------------------------------------------------------------
```

EXPLANATION

The dash between characters enclosed in square brackets matches one character in a range of characters. Vi will search for the regular expression containing an o, v, and e, followed by any character in the ASCII range between a and z. Since this is an ASCII range, the range cannot be represented as [z-a].

EXAMPLE 3.8

```
(Not one of the characters in the set ([^]))
% vi picnic
-----------------------------------------------------------------
I had a lovely time on our little picnic.
Lovers were all around us. It is springtime. Oh
love, how much I adore you. Do you know
the extent of my love? Oh, by the way, I think
I lost my gloves somewhere out in that field of
clover. Did you see them? I can only hope love
is forever. I live for you. It's hard to get back in the
groove.
~
~
~
/ove[^a-zA-Z0-9]/
-----------------------------------------------------------------
```

The caret inside square brackets is a negation metacharacter. Vi will search for the regular expression containing an o, v, and e, followed by any character *not* in the ASCII range between a and z, *not* in the range between A and Z, and *not* a digit between 0 and 9. For example, it will find ove followed by a comma, a space, a period, and so on, because those characters are *not* in the set.

3.2 Combining Regular Expression Metacharacters

Now that basic regular expression metacharacters have been explained, they can be combined into more complex expressions. Each of the regular expression examples enclosed in forward slashes is the search string and is matched against each line in the text file.

EXAMPLE 3.9

Note: The line numbers are NOT part of the text file. The vertical bars mark the left and right margins.

```
--------------------------------------------------------------
1  |Christian Scott lives here and will put on a Christmas party.|
2  |There are around 30 to 35 people invited.                   |
3  |They are:                                                    |
4  |                                                        Tom|
5  |Dan                                                          |
6  |   Rhonda Savage                                             |
7  |Nicky and Kimberly.                                          |
8  |Steve, Suzanne, Ginger and Larry.                           |
   --------------------------------------------------------------
```

EXPLANATION

a /^[A-Z]..$/   Will find all lines beginning with a capital letter, followed by two of any character, followed by a newline. Will find Dan on line 5.

b /^[A-Z][a-z]*3[0-5]/   Will find all lines beginning with an uppercase letter, followed by zero or more lowercase letters or spaces, followed by the number 3 and another number between 0 and 5. Will find line 2.

c /[a-z]*\./   Will find lines containing zero or more lowercase letters, followed by a literal period. Will find lines 1, 2, 7, and 8.

d /^ *[A-Z][a-z][a-z]$/   Will find a line that begins with zero or more spaces (tabs do not count as spaces), followed by an uppercase letter, two lowercase letters, and a newline. Will find Tom on line 4 and Dan on line 5.

e /^[A-Za-z]*[^,][A-Za-z]*$/   Will find a line that begins with zero or more uppercase and/or lowercase letters, followed by a noncomma, followed by zero or more upper- or lowercase letters and a newline. Will find line 5.

3.2.1 More Regular Expression Metacharacters

The following metacharacters are not necessarily portable across all utilities using regular expressions, but can be used in the vi editor and some versions of sed and grep. There is an extended set of metacharacters available with egrep and awk, which will be discussed in later sections.

EXAMPLE 3.10

```
        (Beginning-of-word (\<) and end-of-word (\>) anchors)
        % vi textfile
        -------------------------------------------------------------
        Unusual occurrences happened at the fair.
  --> Patty won fourth place in the 50 yard dash square and fair.
        Occurrences like this are rare.
        The winning ticket is 55222.
        The ticket I got is 54333 and Dee got 55544.
        Guy fell down while running around the south bend in his last event.
        ~
        ~
        ~
        /\<fourth\>/
        -------------------------------------------------------------
```

EXPLANATION

Will find the word fourth on each line. The \< is the beginning-of-word anchor and the \ > is the end-of-word anchor. A word can be separated by spaces, end in punctuation, start at the beginning of a line, end at the end of a line, and so forth.

EXAMPLE 3.11

```
        % vi textfile
        -------------------------------------------------------------
        Unusual occurrences happened at the fair.
  --> Patty won fourth place in the 50 yard dash square and fair.
        Occurrences like this are rare.
        The winning ticket is 55222.
        The ticket I got is 54333 and Dee got 55544.
  --> Guy fell down while running around the south bend in his last event.
        ~
        ~
        ~
        /\<f.*th\>/
        -------------------------------------------------------------
```

EXPLANATION

Will find any word (or group of words) beginning with an f, followed by zero or more of any character (.*), and a string ending with th.

EXAMPLE 3.12

```
(Remembered patterns \( and \))
    % vi textfile (Before substitution)
    -------------------------------------------------------------
    Unusual occurences happened at the fair.
    Patty won fourth place in the 50 yard dash square and fair.
    Occurences like this are rare.
    The winning ticket is 55222.
    The ticket I got is 54333 and Dee got 55544.
    Guy fell down while running around the south bend in his last event.
    ~
    ~
    ~
1   :1,$s/\([0o]ccur\)ence/\1rence/
    -------------------------------------------------------------


    % vi textfile (After substitution)
    ----------------------------------------------
--> Unusual occurrences happened at the fair.
    Patty won fourth place in the 50 yard dash square and fair.
--> Occurrences like this are rare.
    The winning ticket is 55222.
    The ticket I got is 54333 and Dee got 55544.
    Guy fell down while running around the south bend in his last event.
    ~
    ~
    ~
    -------------------------------------------------------------
```

EXPLANATION

1 The editor searches for the entire string occurence (intentionally misspelled) or Occurrence and if found, the pattern portion enclosed in parentheses is tagged (i.e., either occur or Occur is tagged). Because this is the first pattern tagged, it is called tag 1. The pattern is stored in a memory register called register 1. On the replacement side, the contents of the register are replaced for \1 and the rest of the word, rence, is appended to it. We started with occurence and ended up with occurrence. See Figure 3.1.

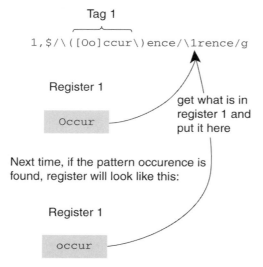

Tag 1

1,$/\([Oo]ccur\)ence/\1rence/g

Register 1

Occur

get what is in
register 1 and
put it here

Next time, if the pattern occurence is
found, register will look like this:

Register 1

occur

Figure 3.1 Remembered patterns and tags.

EXAMPLE 3.13

```
      % vi textfile (Before substitution)
      ------------------------------------------------------------
      Unusual occurrences happened at the fair.
      Patty won fourth place in the 50 yard dash square and fair.
      Occurrences like this are rare.
      The winning ticket is 55222.
      The ticket I got is 54333 and Dee got 55544.
      Guy fell down while running around the south bend in his last event.
      ~
      ~
      ~
   1  :s/\(square\) and \(fair\)/\2 and \1/
      ------------------------------------------------------------

      % vi textfile (After substitution)
      ------------------------------------------------------------
      Unusual occurrences happened at the fair.
-->   Patty won fourth place in the 50 yard dash fair and square.
      Occurrences like this are rare.
      The winning ticket is 55222.
      The ticket I got is 54333 and Dee got 55544.
      Guy fell down while running around the south bend in his last event.
      ~
      ~
      ~
      ------------------------------------------------------------
```

EXPLANATION

1   The editor searches for the regular expression square and fair, and tags square as 1 and fair as 2. On the replacement side, the contents of register 2 are substituted for \2 and the contents of register 1 are substituted for \1. See Figure 3.2.

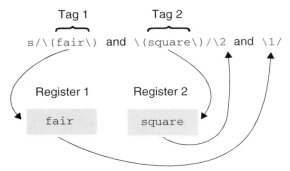

Figure 3.2   Using more than one tag.

EXAMPLE 3.14

```
(Repetition of patterns ( \{n\} ))
    % vi textfile
    ---------------------------------------------
    Unusual occurrences happened at the fair.
    Patty won fourth place in the 50 yard dash square and fair.
    Occurrences like this are rare.
--> The winning ticket is 55222.
    The ticket I got is 54333 and Dee got 55544.
    Guy fell down while running around the south bend in his last
    event.
    ~
    ~
    ~
    ~
1   /5\{2\}2\{3\}\./
    ---------------------------------------------------------------
```

EXPLANATION

1   Searches for lines containing two occurrences of the number 5, followed by three occurrences of the number 2, followed by a literal period.

chapter
4

The grep **Family**

The grep family consists of the commands grep, egrep, and fgrep. The grep command globally searches for regular expressions in files and prints all lines that contain the expression. The egrep and fgrep commands are simply variants of grep. The egrep command is an extended grep, supporting more regular expression metacharacters. The fgrep command, called *fixed* grep, and sometimes *fast* grep, treats all characters as literals; that is, regular expression metacharacters aren't special—they match themselves. The Free Software Foundation provides a free version of grep, called GNU grep. These versions of grep are the ones used on Linux systems, and can be found in /usr/xpg4/bin on Sun's Solaris OS. The GNU version of grep has extended the basic regular expression metacharacter set, added POSIX compliancy, and included a number of new command-line options. They also provide a recursive grep called rgrep for descending entire directory trees.

4.1   The grep **Command**

4.1.1   The Meaning of grep

The name grep can be traced back to the ex editor. If you invoked that editor and wanted to search for a string, you would type at the ex prompt:

: /pattern/p

   The first line containing the string pattern would be printed as "p" by the print command. If you wanted all the lines that contained pattern to be printed, you would type:

: g/pattern/p

When g precedes pattern, it means "all lines in the file," or "perform a global substitution."

Because the search pattern is called a *regular expression*, we can substitute RE for pattern and the command reads

: g/RE/p

And there you have it: the meaning of grep and the origin of its name. It means "globally search for the regular expression (RE) and print out the line." The nice part of using grep is that you do not have to invoke an editor to perform a search, and you do not need to enclose the regular expression in forward slashes. It is much faster than using ex or vi.

4.1.2 How grep Works

The grep command searches for a pattern of characters in a file or multiple files. If the pattern contains whitespace, it must be quoted. The pattern is either a quoted string or a single word,[1] and all other words following it are treated as filenames. Grep sends its output to the screen and does not change or affect the input file in any way.

FORMAT

    grep word filename filename

EXAMPLE 4.1

    grep Tom /etc/passwd

EXPLANATION

Grep will search for the pattern Tom in a file called /etc/passwd. If successful, the line from the file will appear on the screen; if the pattern is not found, there will be no output at all; and if the file is not a legitimate file, an error will be sent to the screen. If the pattern is found, grep returns an exit status of 0, indicating success; if the pattern is not found, the exit status returned is 1; and if the file is not found, the exit status is 2.

The grep program can get its input from a standard input or a pipe, as well as from files. If you forget to name a file, grep will assume it is getting input from standard input, the keyboard, and will stop until you type something. If coming from a pipe, the output of a command will be piped as input to the grep command, and if a desired pattern is matched, grep will print the output to the screen.

---

1. A word is also called a token.

EXAMPLE 4.2

```
ps -ef | grep root
```

EXPLANATION

The output of the ps command (ps -ef displays all processes running on this system) is sent to grep and all lines containing root are printed.

4.1.3 Metacharacters

A metacharacter is a character that represents something other than itself. ∧ and $ are examples of metacharacters.

The grep command supports a number of regular expression metacharacters (see Table 4.1) to help further define the search pattern. It also provides a number of options (see Table 4.2) to modify the way it does its search or displays lines. For example, you can provide options to turn off case sensitivity, display line numbers, display errors only, and so on.

EXAMPLE 4.3

```
grep -n '∧jack:' /etc/passwd
```

EXPLANATION

Grep searches the /etc/passwd file for jack; if jack is at the beginning of a line, grep prints out the number of the line on which jack was found and where in the line jack was found.

Table 4.1 grep's Regular Expression Metacharacters

Metacharacter	Function	Example	What It Matches
∧	Beginning-of-line anchor	'∧love'	Matches all lines beginning with love.
$	End-of-line anchor	'love$'	Matches all lines ending with love.
.	Matches one character	'l..e'	Matches lines containing an l, followed by two characters, followed by an e.
*	Matches zero or more characters preceding the asterisk	' *love'	Matches lines with zero or more spaces, followed by the pattern love.
[ ]	Matches one character in the set	'[Ll]ove'	Matches lines containing love or Love.

Table 4.1 grep's Regular Expression Metacharacters (continued)

Metacharacter	Function	Example	What It Matches
[^]	Matches one character not in the set	'[^A-K]ove'	Matches lines *not* containing a character in the range A through K, followed by ove.
\<	Beginning-of-word anchor	'\<love'	Matches lines containing a word that begins with love.
\>	End-of-word anchor	'love\>'	Matches lines containing a word that ends with love.
\(..\)	Tags matched characters	'\(love\)ing'	Tags marked portion in a register to be remembered later as number 1. To reference later, use \1 to repeat the pattern. May use up to nine tags, starting with the first tag at the leftmost part of the pattern. For example, the pattern love is saved in register 1 to be referenced later as \1.
x\{m\} x\{m,\} x\{m,n\}ª	Repetition of character x: m times, at least m times, or between m and n times	'o\{5\}' 'o\{5,\}' 'o\{5,10\}'	Matches if line has 5 occurences of o, at least 5 occurences of o, or between 5 and 10 occurrences of o.

a. The \{ \} metacharacters are not supported on all versions of UNIX or all pattern-matching utilities; they usually work with vi and grep.

Table 4.2 grep's Options

Option	What It Does
-b	Precedes each line by the block number on which it was found. This is sometimes useful in locating disk block numbers by context.
-c	Displays a count of matching lines rather than displaying the lines that match.
-h	Does not display filenames.
-i	Ignores the case of letters in comparisons (i.e., upper- and lowercase are considered identical).
-l	Lists only the names of files with matching lines (once), separated by newline characters.
-n	Precedes each line by its relative line number in the file.
-s	Works silently, that is, displays nothing except error messages. This is useful for checking the exit status.
-v	Inverts the search to display only lines that do not match.
-w	Searches for the expression as a word, as if surrounded by \< and \>. This applies to grep only. (Not all versions of grep support this feature; e.g., SCO UNIX does not.)

4.1.4   grep and Exit Status

The grep command is very useful in shell scripts, because it always returns an exit status to indicate whether it was able to locate the pattern or the file you were looking for. If the pattern is found, grep returns an exit status of 0, indicating success; if grep cannot find the pattern, it returns 1 as its exit status; and if the file cannot be found, grep returns an exit status of 2. (Other UNIX utilities that search for patterns, such as sed and awk, do not use the exit status to indicate the success or failure of locating a pattern; they report failure only if there is a syntax error in a command.)

In the following example, john is not found in the /etc/passwd file.

EXAMPLE 4.4

```
1   % grep 'john' /etc/passwd        # john is not in the passwd file
2   % echo $status        (csh)
    1


    or


2   $ echo $?            (sh, ksh)
    1
```

EXPLANATION

1   Grep searches for john in the /etc/passwd file, and if successful, grep exits with a status of 0. If john is not found in the file, grep exits with 1. If the file is not found, an exit status of 2 is returned.

2   The C shell variable, status, and the Bourne/Korn shell variable, ?, are assigned the exit status of the last command that was executed.

4.2   grep **Examples with Regular Expressions**

The following datafile, used for the examples in this section, is repeated periodically for your convenience.

% **cat datafile**						
northwest	NW	Charles Main	3.0	.98	3	34
western	WE	Sharon Gray	5.3	.97	5	23
southwest	SW	Lewis Dalsass	2.7	.8	2	18
southern	SO	Suan Chin	5.1	.95	4	15
southeast	SE	Patricia Hemenway	4.0	.7	4	17
eastern	EA	TB Savage	4.4	.84	5	20
northeast	NE	AM Main Jr.	5.1	.94	3	13
north	NO	Margot Weber	4.5	.89	5	9
central	CT	Ann Stephens	5.7	.94	5	13

EXAMPLE 4.5

```
% grep NW datafile
northwest          NW        Charles Main        3.0  .98   3    34
```

EXPLANATION

Prints all lines containing the regular expression NW in a file called datafile.

EXAMPLE 4.6

```
% grep NW d*
datafile: northwest  NW     Charles Main        3.0  .98   3    34
db: northwest        NW     Joel Craig          30   40    5    123
```

EXPLANATION

Prints all lines containing the regular expression NW in all files starting with a d. The shell expands d* to all files that begin with a d. In this case, the filenames retrieved are db and datafile.

EXAMPLE 4.7

```
% grep '^n' datafile
northwest          NW        Charles Main        3.0  .98   3    34
northeast          NE        AM Main Jr.         5.1  .94   3    13
north              NO        Margot Weber        4.5  .89   5    9
```

EXPLANATION

Prints all lines beginning with an n. The caret (^) is the beginning-of-line anchor.

EXAMPLE 4.8

```
% grep '4$' datafile
northwest          NW        Charles Main        3.0   .98   3   34
```

EXPLANATION

Prints all lines ending with a 4. The dollar sign ($) is the end-of-line anchor.

EXAMPLE 4.9

```
% grep TB Savage datafile
grep: Savage: No such file or directory
datafile: eastern     EA       TB Savage        4.4   .84   5   20
```

EXPLANATION

Because the first argument is the pattern and all of the remaining arguments are file-names, grep will search for TB in a file called Savage and a file called datafile. To search for TB Savage, see the next example.

EXAMPLE 4.10

```
% grep 'TB Savage' datafile
eastern            EA        TB Savage           4.4   .84   5   20
```

EXPLANATION

Prints all lines containing the pattern TB Savage. Without quotes (in this example, ei-ther single or double quotes will do), the whitespace between TB and Savage would cause grep to search for TB in a file called Savage and a file called datafile, as in the pre-vious example.

EXAMPLE 4.11

```
% grep '5\..' datafile
western            WE        Sharon Gray         5.3   .97   5   23
southern           SO        Suan Chin           5.1   .95   4   15
northeast          NE        AM Main Jr.         5.1   .94   3   13
central            CT        Ann Stephens        5.7   .94   5   13
```

EXPLANATION

Prints a line containing the number 5, followed by a literal period and any single char-acter. The "dot" metacharacter represents a single character, unless it is escaped with a backslash. When escaped, the character is no longer a special metacharacter, but rep-resents itself, a literal period.

```
% cat datafile
northwest      NW      Charles Main          3.0    .98    3    34
western        WE      Sharon Gray           5.3    .97    5    23
southwest      SW      Lewis Dalsass         2.7    .8     2    18
southern       SO      Suan Chin             5.1    .95    4    15
southeast      SE      Patricia Hemenway     4.0    .7     4    17
eastern        EA      TB Savage             4.4    .84    5    20
northeast      NE      AM Main Jr.           5.1    .94    3    13
north          NO      Margot Weber          4.5    .89    5     9
central        CT      Ann Stephens          5.7    .94    5    13
```

EXAMPLE 4.12

```
% grep '\.5' datafile
north                  NO      Margot Weber          4.5    .89    5    9
```

EXPLANATION

Prints any line containing the expression .5.

EXAMPLE 4.13

```
% grep '^[we]' datafile
western        WE      Sharon Gray           5.3    .97    5    23
eastern        EA      TB Savage             4.4    .84    5    20
```

EXPLANATION

Prints lines beginning with either a w or an e. The caret (^) is the beginning-of-line anchor, and either one of the characters in the brackets will be matched.

EXAMPLE 4.14

```
% grep '[^0-9]' datafile
northwest      NW      Charles Main          3.0    .98    3    34
western        WE      Sharon Gray           5.3    .97    5    23
southwest      SW      Lewis Dalsass         2.7    .8     2    18
southern       SO      Suan Chin             5.1    .95    4    15
southeast      SE      Patricia Hemenway     4.0    .7     4    17
eastern        EA      TB Savage             4.4    .84    5    20
northeast      NE      AM Main Jr.           5.1    .94    3    13
north          NO      Margot Weber          4.5    .89    5     9
central        CT      Ann Stephens          5.7    .94    5    13
```

EXPLANATION

Prints all lines containing one nondigit. Because all lines have at least one nondigit, all lines are printed. (See the -v option in Table 4.2 on page 84.)

EXAMPLE   4.15

```
% grep '[A-Z][A-Z] [A-Z]' datafile
eastern        EA     TB Savage        4.4   .84   5    20
northeast      NE     AM Main Jr.      5.1   .94   3    13
```

EXPLANATION

Prints all lines containing two capital letters followed by a space and a capital letter; e.g., TB Savage and AM Main.

EXAMPLE   4.16

```
% grep 'ss* ' datafile
northwest      NW     Charles Main     3.0   .98   3    34
southwest      SW     Lewis Dalsass    2.7   .8    2    18
```

EXPLANATION

Prints all lines containing an s followed by zero or more consecutive occurrences of the letter s and a space. Finds Charles and Dalsass.

EXAMPLE   4.17

```
% grep '[a-z]\{9\}' datafile
northwest      NW     Charles Main       3.0   .98   3    34
southwest      SW     Lewis Dalsass      2.7   .8    2    18
southeast      SE     Patricia Hemenway  4.0   .7    4    17
northeast      NE     AM Main Jr.        5.1   .94   3    13
```

EXPLANATION

Prints all lines where there are at least nine consecutive lowercase letters, for example, northwest, southwest, southeast, and northeast.

EXAMPLE   4.18

```
% grep '\(3\)\.[0-9].*\1    *\1' datafile
northwest      NW     Charles Main     3.0   .98   3    34
```

EXPLANATION

Prints the line if it contains a 3 followed by a period and another number, followed by any number of characters (.*), another 3 (originally tagged), any number of tabs, and another 3. Because the 3 was enclosed in parentheses, \(3\), it can be later referenced with \1. \1 means that this was the first expression to be tagged with the \(\) pair.

```
% cat datafile
northwest       NW      Charles Main         3.0    .98    3    34
western         WE      Sharon Gray          5.3    .97    5    23
southwest       SW      Lewis Dalsass        2.7    .8     2    18
southern        SO      Suan Chin            5.1    .95    4    15
southeast       SE      Patricia Hemenway    4.0    .7     4    17
eastern         EA      TB Savage            4.4    .84    5    20
northeast       NE      AM Main Jr.          5.1    .94    3    13
north           NO      Margot Weber         4.5    .89    5     9
central         CT      Ann Stephens         5.7    .94    5    13
```

EXAMPLE 4.19

```
% grep '\<north' datafile
northwest       NW      Charles Main         3.0    .98    3    34
northeast       NE      AM Main Jr.          5.1    .94    3    13
north           NO      Margot Weber         4.5    .89    5     9
```

EXPLANATION

Prints all lines containing a word starting with north. The \< is the beginning-of-word anchor.

EXAMPLE 4.20

```
% grep '\<north\>' datafile
north           NO      Margot Weber         4.5    .89    5     9
```

EXPLANATION

Prints the line if it contains the word north. The \< is the beginning-of-word anchor, and the \> is the end-of-word anchor.

EXAMPLE 4.21

```
% grep '\<[a-z].*n\>' datafile
northwest       NW      Charles Main         3.0    .98    3    34
western         WE      Sharon Gray          5.3    .97    5    23
southern        SO      Suan Chin            5.1    .95    4    15
eastern         EA      TB Savage            4.4    .84    5    20
northeast       NE      AM Main Jr.          5.1    .94    3    13
central         CT      Ann Stephens         5.7    .94    5    13
```

EXPLANATION

Prints all lines containing a word starting with a lowercase letter, followed by any number of characters, and a word ending in n. Watch the .* symbol. It means any character, including whitespace.

4.3 grep with Options

The grep command has a number of options that control its behavior. Not all versions of UNIX support exactly the same options, so be sure to check your man pages for a complete list.

The following datafile, used for the examples in this section, is repeated periodically for your convenience.

% cat datafile

northwest	NW	Charles Main	3.0	.98	3	34
western	WE	Sharon Gray	5.3	.97	5	23
southwest	SW	Lewis Dalsass	2.7	.8	2	18
southern	SO	Suan Chin	5.1	.95	4	15
southeast	SE	Patricia Hemenway	4.0	.7	4	17
eastern	EA	TB Savage	4.4	.84	5	20
northeast	NE	AM Main Jr.	5.1	.94	3	13
north	NO	Margot Weber	4.5	.89	5	9
central	CT	Ann Stephens	5.7	.94	5	13

EXAMPLE 4.22

```
% grep -n '^south' datafile
3:southwest       SW    Lewis Dalsass       2.7   .8    2   18
4:southern        SO    Suan Chin           5.1   .95   4   15
5:southeast       SE    Patricia Hemenway   4.0   .7    4   17
```

EXPLANATION

The -n option precedes each line with the number of the line where the pattern was found, followed by the line.

EXAMPLE 4.23

```
% grep -i 'pat' datafile
southeast           SE    Patricia Hemenway   4.0   .7    4   17
```

EXPLANATION

The -i option turns off case sensitivity. It does not matter if the expression pat contains any combination of upper- or lowercase letters.

```
% cat datafile
```

northwest	NW	Charles Main	3.0	.98	3	34
western	WE	Sharon Gray	5.3	.97	5	23
southwest	SW	Lewis Dalsass	2.7	.8	2	18
southern	SO	Suan Chin	5.1	.95	4	15
southeast	SE	Patricia Hemenway	4.0	.7	4	17
eastern	EA	TB Savage	4.4	.84	5	20
northeast	NE	AM Main Jr.	5.1	.94	3	13
north	NO	Margot Weber	4.5	.89	5	9
central	CT	Ann Stephens	5.7	.94	5	13

EXAMPLE 4.24

```
% grep -v 'Suan Chin' datafile
```

northwest	NW	Charles Main	3.0	.98	3	34
western	WE	Sharon Gray	5.3	.97	5	23
southwest	SW	Lewis Dalsass	2.7	.8	2	18
southeast	SE	Patricia Hemenway	4.0	.7	4	17
eastern	EA	TB Savage	4.4	.84	5	20
northeast	NE	AM Main Jr.	5.1	.94	3	13
north	NO	Margot Weber	4.5	.89	5	9
central	CT	Ann Stephens	5.7	.94	5	13

EXPLANATION

Here, the -v option prints all lines *not* containing the pattern Suan Chin. This option is used when deleting a specific entry from the input file. To really remove the entry, you would redirect the output of grep to a temporary file, and then change the name of the temporary file back to the name of the original file as shown here:

```
grep -v 'Suan Chin' datafile > temp
mv temp datafile
```

Remember that you must use a temporary file when redirecting the output from datafile. If you redirect from datafile to datafile, the shell will "clobber" the datafile. (See "Redirection" on page 25.)

EXAMPLE 4.25

```
% grep -l 'SE' *
datafile
datebook
```

EXPLANATION

The -l option causes grep to print out only the filenames where the pattern is found instead of the line of text.

EXAMPLE 4.26

```
% grep -c 'west' datafile
3
```

EXPLANATION

The -c option causes grep to print the number of lines where the pattern was found. This does not mean the number of occurrences of the pattern. For example, if west is found three times on a line, it only counts the line once.

EXAMPLE 4.27

```
% grep  -w 'north' datafile
north              NO      Margot Weber        4.5   .89   5   9
```

EXPLANATION

The -w option causes grep to find the pattern only if it is a word,[a] not part of a word. Only the line containing the word north is printed, not northwest, northeast, etc.

a. A word is a sequence of alphanumeric characters starting at the beginning of a line or preceded by whitespace and ending in whitespace, punctuation, or a newline.

EXAMPLE 4.28

```
% echo $LOGNAME
lewis

% grep -i "$LOGNAME" datafile
southwest          SW      Lewis Dalsass       2.7   .8    2   18
```

EXPLANATION

The value of the shell ENV variable, LOGNAME, is printed. It contains the user's login name. If the variable is enclosed in double quotes, it will still be expanded by the shell, and in case there is more than one word assigned to the variable, whitespace is shielded from shell interpretation. If single quotes are used, variable substitution does not take place; that is, $LOGNAME is printed.

4.4   grep **with Pipes**

Instead of taking its input from a file, grep often gets its input from a pipe.

EXAMPLE 4.29

```
% ls -l
drwxrwxrwx  2  ellie      2441 Jan 6 12:34    dir1
-rw-r--r--  1  ellie      1538 Jan 2 15:50    file1
-rw-r--r--  1  ellie      1539 Jan 3 13:36    file2
drwxrwxrwx  2  ellie      2341 Jan 6 12:34    grades

% ls -l | grep '^d'
drwxrwxrwx  2  ellie      2441 Jan 6 12:34    dir1
drwxrwxrwx  2  ellie      2341 Jan 6 12:34    grades
```

EXPLANATION

The output of the ls command is piped to grep. All lines of output that begin with a d are printed; that is, all directories are printed.

4.4.1   grep Review

Table 4.3 contains examples of grep commands and what they do.

Table 4.3   Review of grep

Command	What It Does
grep '\<Tom\>' file	Prints lines containing the word Tom.
grep 'Tom Savage' file	Prints lines containing Tom Savage.
grep '^Tommy' file	Prints lines if Tommy is at the beginning of the line.
grep '\.bak$' file	Prints lines ending in .bak. Single quotes protect the dollar sign ($) from interpretation.
grep '[Pp]yramid' *	Prints lines from all files containing pyramid or Pyramid in the current working directory.
grep '[A-Z]' file	Prints lines containing at least one capital letter.
grep '[0-9]' file	Prints lines containing at least one number.
grep '[A-Z]...[0-9]' file	Prints lines containing five-character patterns starting with a capital letter and ending with a number.
grep -w '[tT]est' files	Prints lines with the word Test and/or test.

Table 4.3   Review of grep (continued)

Command	What It Does
grep -s 'Mark Todd' file	Finds lines containing Mark Todd, but does not print the lines. Can be used when checking grep's exit status.
grep -v 'Mary' file	Prints all lines not containing Mary.
grep -i 'sam' file	Prints all lines containing sam, regardless of case (e.g., SAM, sam, SaM, sAm).
grep -l 'Dear Boss' *	Lists all filenames containing Dear Boss.
grep -n 'Tom' file	Precedes matching lines with line numbers.
grep "$name" file	Expands the value of variable name and prints lines containing that value. Must use double quotes.
grep '$5' file	Prints lines containing literal $5. Must use single quotes.
ps -ef| grep '^ *user1'	Pipes output of ps -ef to grep, searching for user1 at the beginning of a line, even if it is preceded by zero or more spaces.

4.5   egrep (Extended grep)

The main advantage of using egrep is that additional regular expression metacharacters (see Table 4.4) have been added to the set provided by grep. The \(\) and \{ \}, however, are not allowed. (See GNU grep -E if using Linux.)

Table 4.4   egrep's Regular Expression Metacharacters

Metacharacter	Function	Example	What It Matches
^	Beginning-of-line anchor	'^love'	Matches all lines beginning with love.
$	End-of-line anchor	'love$'	Matches all lines ending with love.
.	Matches one character	'l..e'	Matches lines containing an l, followed by two characters, followed by an e.
*	Matches zero or more of the characters preceding the asterisk	' *love'	Matches lines with zero or more spaces followed by the pattern love.
[ ]	Matches one character in the set	'[Ll]ove'	Matches lines containing love or Love.

Table 4.4 egrep's Regular Expression Metacharacters (continued)

Metacharacter	Function	Example	What It Matches
[^]	Matches one character not in the set	'[^A-KM-Z]ove'	Matches lines not containing A through K or M through Z, followed by ove.

New with egrep

Metacharacter	Function	Example	What It Matches
+	Matches one or more of the characters preceding the + sign	'[a-z]+ove'	Matches one or more lowercase letters, followed by ove. Would find move, approve, love, behoove, etc.
?	Matches zero or one of the preceding characters	'lo?ve'	Matches for an l followed by either one or not any occurrences of the letter o. Would find love or lve.
a|b	Matches either a or b	'love|hate'	Matches for either expression, love or hate.
()	Groups characters	'love(able|ly)' '(ov)+'	Matches for lovable or lovely. Matches for one or more occurrences of ov.

4.5.1   egrep Examples

The following examples illustrate only the way the new extended set of regular expression metacharacters is used with egrep. The grep examples presented earlier illustrate the use of the standard metacharacters, which behave the same way with egrep. Egrep also uses the same options at the command line as grep.

The following datafile is used in the examples in this section.

```
% cat datafile
northwest    NW    Charles Main        3.0    .98    3    34
western      WE    Sharon Gray         5.3    .97    5    23
southwest    SW    Lewis Dalsass       2.7    .8     2    18
southern     SO    Suan Chin           5.1    .95    4    15
southeast    SE    Patricia Hemenway   4.0    .7     4    17
eastern      EA    TB Savage           4.4    .84    5    20
northeast    NE    AM Main Jr.         5.1    .94    3    13
north        NO    Margot Weber        4.5    .89    5     9
central      CT    Ann Stephens        5.7    .94    5    13
```

EXAMPLE 4.30

```
% egrep 'NW|EA' datafile
northwest        NW      Charles Main      3.0   .98   3   34
eastern          EA      TB Savage         4.4   .84   5   20
```

EXPLANATION

Prints the line if it contains either the expression NW or the expression EA.

EXAMPLE 4.31

```
% egrep '3+' datafile
northwest        NW      Charles Main      3.0   .98   3   34
western          WE      Sharon Gray       5.3   .97   5   23
northeast        NE      AM Main Jr.       5.1   .94   3   13
central          CT      Ann Stephens      5.7   .94   5   13
```

EXPLANATION

Prints all lines containing one or more occurrences of the number 3; e.g., 3, 33, 33333333.

EXAMPLE 4.32

```
% egrep '2\.?[0-9]' datafile
western          WE      Sharon Gray       5.3   .97   5   23
southwest        SW      Lewis Dalsass     2.7   .8    2   18
eastern          EA      TB Savage         4.4   .84   5   20
```

EXPLANATION

Prints all lines containing a 2, followed by one period or no period at all, followed by a number; e.g., matches 2.5, 25, 29, 2.3, etc.

EXAMPLE 4.33

```
% egrep '(no)+' datafile
northwest        NW      Charles Main      3.0   .98   3   34
northeast        NE      AM Main Jr.       5.1   .94   3   13
north            NO      Margot Weber      4.5   .89   5   9
```

EXPLANATION

Prints lines containing one or more consecutive occurrences of the pattern group no; e.g., no, nono, nonononono, etc.

EXAMPLE 4.34

```
% egrep 'S(h|u)' datafile
western          WE      Sharon Gray        5.3   .97   5   23
southern         SO      Suan Chin          5.1   .95   4   15
```

EXPLANATION

Prints all lines containing S, followed by either h or u; e.g., **Sh**aron or **Su**an.

EXAMPLE 4.35

```
% egrep 'Sh|u' datafile
western          WE      Sharon Gray        5.3   .97   5   23
southern         SO      Suan Chin          5.1   .95   4   15
southwest        SW      Lewis Dalsass      2.7   .8    2   18
southeast        SE      Patricia Hemenway  4.0   .7    4   17
```

EXPLANATION

Prints all lines containing the expression Sh or u; e.g., **Sh**aron or so**u**thern.

4.5.2   egrep Review

Table 4.5 contains examples of egrep commands and what they do.

Table 4.5   Review of egrep

Command	What It Does
egrep '^ +' file	Prints lines beginning with one or more spaces.
egrep '^ *' file	Prints lines beginning with zero or more spaces.[a]
egrep '(Tom|Dan) Savage' file	Prints lines containing Tom Savage or Dan Savage.
egrep '(ab)+' file	Prints lines with one or more occurrences of ab.
egrep '^X[0-9]?' file	Prints lines beginning with X followed by zero or one single digit.
egrep 'fun\.$' *	Prints lines ending in fun. from all files.[a]
egrep '[A-Z]+' file	Prints lines containing one or more capital letters.
egrep '[0-9]' file	Prints lines containing a number.[a]

Table 4.5 Review of egrep (continued)

Command	What It Does
egrep '[A-Z]...[0-9]' file	Prints lines containing five-character patterns starting with a capital letter, followed by three of any character, and ending with a number.[a]
egrep '[tT]est' files	Prints lines with Test and/or test.[a]
egrep '(Susan|Jean) Doe' file	Prints lines containing Susan Doe or Jean Doe.
egrep -v 'Mary' file	Prints all lines *not* containing Mary.[a]
egrep -i 'sam' file	Prints all lines containing sam, regardless of case (e.g., SAM, sam, SaM, sAm).[a]
egrep -l 'Dear Boss' *	Lists all filenames containing Dear Boss.[a]
egrep -n 'Tom' file	Precedes matching lines with line numbers.[a]
egrep -s "$name" file	Expands variable name, finds it, but prints nothing. Can be used to check the exit status of egrep.[a] (s stands for silent)

a. egrep and grep handle this pattern in the same way.

4.6 fgrep (Fixed grep or Fast grep)

The fgrep command behaves like grep, but does not recognize any regular expression metacharacters as being special. All characters represent only themselves. A caret is simply a caret, a dollar sign is a dollar sign, and so forth. (See GNU grep -F if using Linux.)

EXAMPLE 4.36

```
fgrep '[A-Z]****[0-9]..$5.00'  file
```

EXPLANATION

Finds all lines in the file containing the literal string [A-Z]****[0-9]..$5.00. All characters are treated as themselves. There are no special characters.

4.7 Linux and GNU grep

Linux uses the GNU version of grep, which in functionality is much the same as grep, only better. In addition to POSIX character classes (see Table 4.7 and Table 4.8), there are a number of new options, including -G, -E, -F, and -P that allow you to use regular grep for everything, and still get the functionality of both egrep and fgrep.[2]

4.7.1 Basic and Extended Regular Expressions

The GNU grep command supports the same regular expression metacharacters (see Table 4.7) as the UNIX grep and then some (see Table 4.8), to modify the way it does its search or displays lines. For example, you can provide options to turn off case sensitivity, display line numbers, display filenames, and so on.

There are two versions of regular expression metacharacters: *basic* and *extended*. The regular version of GNU grep (also grep -G) uses the basic set (see Table 4.7), and egrep (or grep -E) uses the extended set (Table 4.8). With GNU grep, both sets are available. The *basic set* consists of

^, $, ., *, [ ], [^], \< \>, and \(\)

In addition, GNU grep recognizes \b, \w, and \W, as well as a new class of POSIX metacharacters (see Table 4.9).

With the -E option to GNU grep, the extended (egrep) set is available, but even without the -E option, regular grep, the default, can use the extended set of metacharacters, provided that the metacharacters are preceded with a backslash.[3] For example, the *extended set* of metacharacters is

?, +, { }, |, ( )

The extended set of metacharacters have no special meaning to regular grep, unless they are backslashed, as follows:

\?, \+, \{, \|, \(, \)

The format for using the GNU grep is shown in Table 4.6.

---

2. To use grep recursively, see Appendix A for GNU rgrep and xargs.

3. In any version of grep, a metacharacter can be quoted with a backslash to turn off its special meaning.

Table 4.6 GNU grep

Format	What It Understands
grep 'pattern' filename(s)	Basic RE metacharacters (the default)
grep -G 'pattern' filename(s)	Same as above; the default
grep -E 'pattern' filename(s)	Extended RE metacharacters
grep -F 'pattern' filename	No RE metacharacters
grep -P 'pattern' filename	Interpret the pattern as a Perl RE

Table 4.7 The Basic Set—GNU grep's Regular Expression Metacharacters

Metacharacter	Function	Example	What It Matches
^	Beginning-of-line anchor	^love	Matches all lines beginning with love.
$	End-of-line anchor	love$	Matches all lines ending with love.
.	Matches one character	l..e	Matches lines containing an l, followed by two characters, followed by an e.
*	Matches zero or more characters	*love	Matches lines with zero or more spaces, of the preceding characters followed by the pattern love.
[ ]	Matches one character in the set	[Ll]ove	Matches lines containing love or Love.
[^]	Matches one character not in the set	[^A-K]ove	Matches lines not containing A through K followed by ove.
\\<[a]	Beginning-of-word anchor	\\<love	Matches lines containing a word that begins with love.
\\>	End-of-word anchor	love\\>	Matches lines containing a word that ends with love.
\\(..\\)[b]	Tags matched characters	\\(love\\)able	Tags marked portion in a register to be remembered later as number 1. To reference later, use \\1 to repeat the pattern. May use up to nine tags, starting with the first tag at the leftmost part of the pattern. For example, the pattern love is saved in register 1 to be referenced later as \\1.
x\\{m\\} x\\{m,\\} x\\{m,n\\}[c]	Repetition of character x: m times, at least m times, or between m and n times	o\\{5\\} o\\{5,\\} o\\{5,10\\}	Matches if line has 5 occurrences of o, at least 5 occurrences of o, or between 5 and 10 occurrences of o.

Table 4.7 The Basic Set—GNU grep's Regular Expression Metacharacters (continued)

Metacharacter	Function	Example	What It Matches
\w	Alphanumeric word character; [a-zA-Z0-9_]	l\w*e	Matches an l followed by zero more word characters, and an e.
\W	Nonalphanumeric word character; [^a-zA-Z0-9_]	love\W+	Matches love followed by one or more nonword characters (., ?, etc.).
\b	Word boundary	\blove\b	Matches only the word love.

a. Won't work unless backslashed, even with grep -E and GNU egrep; work with UNIX egrep at all.
b. These metacharacters are really part of the extended set, but are placed here because they work with UNIX grep and GNU regular grep, if backslashed. They do not work with UNIX egrep at all.
c. The \{ \} metacharacters are not supported on all versions of UNIX or all pattern-matching utilities; they usually work with vi and grep. They don't work with UNIX egrep at all.

Table 4.8 The Extended Set—Used with egrep and grep -E

Metacharacter	Function	Example	What It Matches
+	Matches one or more of the preceding characters	[a-z]+ove	Matches one or more lowercase letters, followed by ove. Would find move, approve, love, behoove, etc.
?	Matches zero or one of the preceding characters	lo?ve	Matches for an l followed by either one or not any o's at all. Would find love or lve.
a|b|c	Matches either a or b or c	love|hate	Matches for either expression, love or hate.
()	Groups characters	love(able|rs) (ov)+	Matches for loveable or lovers. Matches for one or more occurrences of ov.
(..) (...) \1 \2[a]	Tags matched characters	\(love\)ing	Tags marked portion in a register to be remembered later as number 1. To reference later, use \1 to repeat the pattern. May use up to nine tags, starting with the first tag at the leftmost part of the pattern. For example, the pattern love is saved in register 1 to be referenced later as \1.
x{m} x{m,} x{m,n}[b]	Repetition of character x: m times, at least m times, or between m and n times	o\{5\} o\{5,\} o\{5,10\}	Matches if line has 5 occurrences of o, at least 5 occurrences of o, or between 5 and 10 occurrences of o.

a. Tags and back references do not work with UNIX egrep.
b. The \{ \} metacharacters are not supported on all versions of UNIX or all pattern-matching utilities; they usually work with vi and grep. They do not work with UNIX egrep at all.

The POSIX Class.   POSIX (the Portable Operating System Interface) is an industry standard to ensure that programs are portable across operating systems. In order to be portable, POSIX recognizes that different countries or locales may differ in the way they encode characters, represent currency, and how times and dates are represented. To handle different types of characters, POSIX added to the basic and extended regular expressions the bracketed character class of characters shown in Table 4.9.

The class, for example, [:alnum:] is another way of saying A–Za–z0–9. To use this class, it must be enclosed in another set of brackets for it to be recognized as a regular expression. For example, A–Za–z0–9, by itself, is not a regular expression, but [A–Za–z0–9] is. Likewise, [:alnum:] should be written [[:alnum:]]. The difference between using the first form, [A–Za–z0–9] and the bracketed form, [[:alnum:]] is that the first form is dependent on ASCII character encoding, whereas the second form allows characters from other languages to be represented in the class, such as Swedish rings and German umlauts.

Table 4.9   The Bracketed Character Class

Bracket Class	Meaning
[:alnum:]	Alphanumeric characters
[:alpha:]	Alphabetic characters
[:cntrl:]	Control characters
[:digit:]	Numeric characters
[:graph:]	Nonblank characters (not spaces, control characters, etc.)
[:lower:]	Lowercase letters
[:print:]	Like [:graph:], but includes the space character
[:punct:]	Punctuation characters
[:space:]	All whitespace characters (newlines, spaces, tabs)
[:upper:]	Uppercase letters
[:xdigit:]	Allows digits in a hexadecimal number (0–9a–fA–F)

EXAMPLE 4.37

```
1   % grep '[[:space:]]\.[[:digit:]]][[:space:]]' datafile
    southwest   SW    Lewis Dalsass       2.7    .8   2    18
    southeast   SE    Patricia Hemenway   4.0    .7   4    17

2   % grep -E '[[:space:]]\.[[:digit:]]][[:space:]]' datafile
    southwest   SW    Lewis Dalsass       2.7    .8   2    18
    southeast   SE    Patricia Hemenway   4.0    .7   4    17
```

EXAMPLE 4.37 (CONTINUED)

```
3   % egrep '[[:space:]]\.[[:digit:]][[:space:]]' datafile
    southwest   SW    Lewis Dalsass        2.7    .8   2   18
    southeast   SE    Patricia Hemenway    4.0    .7   4   17
```

EXPLANATION

1, 2, 3 For all Linux variants of grep (other than fgrep), the POSIX bracketed class set is supported. In each of these examples, grep will search for a space character, a literal period, a digit [0-9], and another space character.

4.8   GNU Basic grep (grep -G) with Regular Expressions

Basic grep interprets its patterns as basic regular expressions. All of the examples for UNIX basic grep in this section also apply to the GNU version of basic grep, also grep -G or grep '--basic-regexp'.

The metacharacters used in the examples below are not found in the basic UNIX grep. The examples in this section use the following datafile.

% **cat datafile**						
northwest	NW	Charles Main	3.0	.98	3	34
western	WE	Sharon Gray	5.3	.97	5	23
southwest	SW	Lewis Dalsass	2.7	.8	2	18
southern	SO	Suan Chin	5.1	.95	4	15
southeast	SE	Patricia Hemenway	4.0	.7	4	17
eastern	EA	TB Savage	4.4	.84	5	20
northeast	NE	AM Main Jr.	5.1	.94	3	13
north	NO	Margot Weber	4.5	.89	5	9
central	CT	Ann Stephens	5.7	.94	5	13

EXAMPLE 4.38

```
% grep NW datafile   or
% grep -G NW datafile
northwest            NW         Charles Main        3.0   .98   3     34
```

EXPLANATION

Prints all lines containing the regular expression NW in a file called datafile.

EXAMPLE 4.39

```
% grep '^n\w*\W' datafile
northwest        NW      Charles Main      3.0   .98   3    34
northeast        NE      AM Main Jr.       5.1   .94   3    13
```

EXPLANATION

Prints any line starting with an n, followed by zero or more alphanumeric word characters [a-zA-Z0-9_], followed by a nonalphanumeric word character [^a-zA-Z0-9_]. \w and \W are standard word metacharacters for GNU variants of grep.

EXAMPLE 4.40

```
% grep '\bnorth\b' datafile
north            NO      Margot Weber      4.5   .89   5    9
```

EXPLANATION

Prints the line if it contains the word north. The \b is a word boundary. It can be used instead of the word anchors (\< \>) on all GNU variants of grep.

4.9 grep –E or egrep (GNU Extended grep)

The main advantage of using extended grep is that additional regular expression metacharacters (see Table 4.10) have been added to the basic set. With the -E extension, GNU grep allows the use of these new metacharacters.

Table 4.10 egrep's Regular Expression Metacharacters

Metacharacter	Function	Example	What It Matches
^	Beginning-of-line anchor	^love	Matches all lines beginning with love.
$	End-of-line anchor	love$	Matches all lines ending with love.
.	Matches one character	l..e	Matches lines containing an l, followed by two characters, followed by an e.
*	Matches zero or more characters	*love	Matches lines with zero or more spaces, of the preceding characters followed by the pattern love.
[ ]	Matches one character in the set	[Ll]ove	Matches lines containing love or Love.

Table 4.10 egrep's Regular Expression Metacharacters (continued)

Metacharacter	Function	Example	What It Matches
[^]	Matches one character not in the set	[^A-KM-Z]ove	Matches lines not containing A through K or M through Z, followed by ove.

New with grep -E or egrep

Metacharacter	Function	Example	What It Matches
+	Matches one or more of the preceding characters	[a-z]+ove	Matches one or more lowercase letters, followed by ove. Would find move, approve, love, behoove, etc.
?	Matches zero or one of the preceding characters	lo?ve	Matches for an l followed by either one or not any o's at all. Would find love or lve.
a|b	Matches either a or b	love|hate	Matches for either expression, love or hate.
()	Groups characters	love(able|ly) (ov)+	Matches for loveable or lovely. Matches for one or more occurrences of ov.
x{m} x{m,} x{m,n}[a]	Repetition of character x: m times, at least m times, or between m and n times	o\{5} o\{5,} o\{5,10}	Matches if line has 5 occurrences of o at least 5 occurrences of o, or between 5 and 10 occurrences of o.
\w	Alphanumeric word character; [a-zA-Z0-9_]	l\w*e	Matches an l followed by zero more word characters, and an e.
\W	Nonalphanumeric word character; [^a-zA-Z0-9_]	\W\w*	Matches a non-word (\W) character followed by zero or more word characters (\w).
\b	Word boundary	\blove\b	Matches only the word love.

a. The { } metacharacters are not supported on all versions of UNIX or all pattern-matching utilities; they usually work with vi and grep. They don't work with UNIX egrep at all.

4.9.1 grep -E and egrep Examples

The following examples illustrate the way the extended set of regular expression metacharacters are used with grep -E and egrep. The grep examples presented earlier illustrate the use of the standard metacharacters, also recognized by egrep. With basic GNU grep (grep -G), it is possible to use any of the additional metacharacters, provided that each of the special metacharacters is preceded by a backslash.

The following examples show all three variants of grep to accomplish the same task.

The examples in this section use the following datafile, repeated periodically for your convenience.

% **cat datafile**						
northwest	NW	Charles Main	3.0	.98	3	34
western	WE	Sharon Gray	5.3	.97	5	23
southwest	SW	Lewis Dalsass	2.7	.8	2	18
southern	SO	Suan Chin	5.1	.95	4	15
southeast	SE	Patricia Hemenway	4.0	.7	4	17
eastern	EA	TB Savage	4.4	.84	5	20
northeast	NE	AM Main Jr.	5.1	.94	3	13
north	NO	Margot Weber	4.5	.89	5	9
central	CT	Ann Stephens	5.7	.94	5	13

EXAMPLE 4.41

```
1  % egrep 'NW|EA' datafile
   northwest      NW      Charles Main      3.0    .98    3    34
   eastern        EA      TB Savage         4.4    .84    5    20

2  % grep -E 'NW|EA' datafile
   northwest      NW      Charles Main      3.0    .98    3    34
   eastern        EA      TB Savage         4.4    .84    5    20

3  % grep 'NW|EA' datafile

4  % grep 'NW\|EA' datafile
   northwest      NW      Charles Main      3.0    .98    3    34
   eastern        EA      TB Savage         4.4    .84    5    20
```

EXPLANATION

1 Prints the line if it contains either the expression NW or the expression EA. In this example, egrep is used. If you do not have the GNU version of grep, use egrep.

2 In this example, the GNU grep is used with the -E option to include the extended metacharacters. Same as egrep.

3 Regular grep does not normally support extended regular expressions; the vertical bar is an extended regular expression metacharacter used for alternation. Regular grep doesn't recognize it and searches for the explicit pattern 'NW|EA'. Nothing matches; nothing prints.

4 With GNU regular grep (grep -G), if the metacharacter is preceded by a backslash it will be interpreted as an extended regular expression just as with egrep and grep -E.

```
% cat datafile
northwest      NW      Charles Main         3.0     .98     3       34
western        WE      Sharon Gray          53      .97     5       23
southwest      SW      Lewis Dalsass        2.7     .8      2       18
southern       SO      Suan Chin            5.1     .95     4       15
southeast      SE      Patricia Hemenway    4.0     .7      4       17
eastern        EA      TB Savage            4.4     .84     5       20
northeast      NE      AM Main Jr.          5.1     .94     3       13
north          NO      Margot Weber         4.5     .89     5       9
central        CT      Ann Stephens         5.7     .94     5       13
```

EXAMPLE 4.42

```
% egrep '3+' datafile
% grep -E '3+' datafile
% grep '3\+' datafile
northwest      NW      Charles Main    3.0     .98     3       34
western        WE      Sharon Gray     5.3     .97     5       23
northeast      NE      AM Main Jr.     5.1     .94     3       13
central        CT      Ann Stephens    5.7     .94     5       13
```

EXPLANATION
Prints all lines containing one or more 3s.

EXAMPLE 4.43

```
% egrep '2\.?[0-9]' datafile
% grep -E '2\.?[0-9]' datafile
% grep '2\.\?[0-9]' datafile
western        WE      Sharon Gray     5.3     .97     5       23
southwest      SW      Lewis Dalsass   2.7     .8      2       18
eastern        EA      TB Savage       4.4     .84     5       20
```

EXPLANATION
Prints all lines containing a 2, followed by zero or one period, followed by a number in the range between 0 and 9.

EXAMPLE 4.44

```
% egrep '(no)+' datafile
% grep -E '(no)+' datafile
% grep '\(no\)\+' datafile
northwest      NW      Charles Main    3.0     .98     3       34
northeast      NE      AM Main Jr.     5.1     .94     3       13
north          NO      Margot Weber    4.5     .89     5       9
```

EXPLANATION

Prints lines containing one or more occurrences of the pattern group no.

EXAMPLE 4.45

```
% grep -E '\w+\W+[ABC]' datafile
```
northwest	NW	Charles Main	3.0	.98	3	34
southern	SO	Suan Chin	5.1	.95	4	15
northeast	NE	AM Main Jr.	5.1	.94	3	13
central	CT	Ann Stephens	5.7	.94	5	13

EXPLANATION

Prints all lines containing one or more alphanumeric word characters (\w+), followed by one or more nonalphanumeric word characters (\W+), followed by one letter in the set ABC.

EXAMPLE 4.46

```
% egrep 'S(h|u)' datafile
% grep -E 'S(h|u)' datafile
% grep 'S\(h\|u\)' datafile
```
| western | WE | Sharon Gray | 5.3 | .97 | 5 | 23 |
| southern | SO | Suan Chin | 5.1 | .95 | 4 | 15 |

EXPLANATION

Prints all lines containing S, followed by either h or u; i.e., Sh or Su.

EXAMPLE 4.47

```
% egrep 'Sh|u' datafile
% grep -E 'Sh|u' datafile
% grep 'Sh\|u' datafile
```
western	WE	Sharon Gray	5.3	.97	5	23
southern	SO	Suan Chin	5.1	.95	4	15
southwest	SW	Lewis Dalsass	2.7	.8	2	18
southeast	SE	Patricia Hemenway	4.0	.7	4	17

EXPLANATION

Prints all lines containing the expression Sh or u.

4.9.2 Anomalies with Regular and Extended Variants of grep

The variants of GNU grep supported by Linux are almost, but not the same, as their UNIX namesakes. For example, the version of egrep, found in Solaris or BSD UNIX, does not support three metacharacter sets: \{ \}for repetition, \(\) for tagging characters, and \< \>, the word anchors. Under Linux, these metacharacters are available with grep and grep -E, but egrep does not recognize \< \>. The following examples illustrate these differences, just in case you are running bash or tcsh under a UNIX system other than Linux, and you want to use grep and its family in your shell scripts.

The examples in this section use the following datafile, repeated periodically for your convenience.

% **cat datafile**						
northwest	NW	Charles Main	3.0	.98	3	34
western	WE	Sharon Gray	53	.97	5	23
southwest	SW	Lewis Dalsass	2.7	.8	2	18
southern	SO	Suan Chin	5.1	.95	4	15
southeast	SE	Patricia Hemenway	4.0	.7	4	17
eastern	EA	TB Savage	4.4	.84	5	20
northeast	NE	AM Main Jr.	5.1	.94	3	13
north	NO	Margot Weber	4.5	.89	5	9
central	CT	Ann Stephens	5.7	.94	5	13

EXAMPLE 4.48

```
(Linux GNU grep)
1   % grep '<north>' datafile     # Must use backslashes

2   % grep '\<north\>' datafile
    north            NO        Margot Weber          4.5   .89   5    9

3   % grep -E '\<north\>' datafile
    north            NO        Margot Weber          4.5   .89   5    9

4   % egrep '\<north\>' datafile
    north            NO        Margot Weber          4.5   .89   5    9

(Solaris egrep)
5   % egrep '\<north\>' datafile
    <no output; not recognized>
```

EXPLANATION

1. No matter what variant of grep is being used, the word anchor metacharacters, < >, must be preceded by a backslash.
2. This time, grep searches for a word that begins and ends with north. \< represents the beginning-of-word anchor and \> represents the end-of-word anchor.
3. Grep with the -E option also recognizes the word anchors.
4. The GNU form of egrep recognizes the word anchors.
5. When using Solaris (SVR4), egrep does not recognize word anchors as regular expression metacharacters.

EXAMPLE 4.49

(Linux GNU grep)
1. `% grep 'w(es)t.*\1' datafile`
   grep: Invalid back reference

2. `% grep 'w\(es\)t.*\1' datafile`
   northwest   NW   Charles Main   3.0   .98   3   34

3. `% grep -E 'w(es)t.*\1' datafile`
   northwest   NW   Charles Main   3.0   .98   3   34

4. `% egrep 'w(es)t.*\1' datafile`
   northwest   NW   Charles Main   3.0   .98   3   34

(Solaris egrep)
5. `% egrep 'w(es)t.*\1' datafile`
   <no output; not recognized>

EXPLANATION

1. When using regular grep, the ( ) extended metacharacters must be backslashed or an error occurs.
2. If the regular expression, w\(es\)t, is matched, the pattern, es, is saved and stored in memory register 1. The expression reads: if west is found, tag and save es, search for any number of characters (.*) after it, followed by es (\1) again, and print the line. The es in Charles is matched by the backreference.
3. This is the same as the previous example, except that grep with the -E switch does not precede the ( ) with backslashes.
4. The GNU egrep also uses the extended metacharacters, ( ), without backslashes.
5. With Solaris, egrep doesn't recognize any form of tagging and backreferencing.

```
% cat datafile
```

northwest	NW	Charles Main	3.0	.98	3	34
western	WE	Sharon Gray	5.3	.97	5	23
southwest	SW	Lewis Dalsass	2.7	.8	2	18
southern	SO	Suan Chin	5.1	.95	4	15
southeast	SE	Patricia Hemenway	4.0	.7	4	17
eastern	EA	TB Savage	4.4	.84	5	20
northeast	NE	AM Main Jr.	5.1	.94	3	13
north	NO	Margot Weber	4.5	.89	5	9
central	CT	Ann Stephens	5.7	.94	5	13

EXAMPLE 4.50

```
(Linux GNU grep)
1 % grep '\.[0-9]\{2\}[^0-9]' datafile
```

northwest	NW	Charles Main	3.0	.98	3	34
western	WE	Sharon Gray	5.3	.97	5	23
southern	SO	Suan Chin	5.1	.95	4	15
eastern	EA	TB Savage	4.4	.84	5	20
northeast	NE	AM Main Jr.	5.1	.94	3	13
north	NO	Margot Weber	4.5	.89	5	9
central	CT	Ann Stephens	5.7	.94	5	13

```
2 % grep -E '\.[0-9]{2}[^0-9]' datafile
```

northwest	NW	Charles Main	3.0	.98	3	34
western	WE	Sharon Gray	5.3	.97	5	23
southern	SO	Suan Chin	5.1	.95	4	15
eastern	EA	TB Savage	4.4	.84	5	20
northeast	NE	AM Main Jr.	5.1	.94	3	13
north	NO	Margot Weber	4.5	.89	5	9
central	CT	Ann Stephens	5.7	.94	5	13

```
3 % egrep  '\.[0-9]{2}[^0-9]' datafile
```

northwest	NW	Charles Main	3.0	.98	3	34
western	WE	Sharon Gray	5.3	.97	5	23
southern	SO	Suan Chin	5.1	.95	4	15
eastern	EA	TB Savage	4.4	.84	5	20
northeast	NE	AM Main Jr.	5.1	.94	3	13
north	NO	Margot Weber	4.5	.89	5	9
central	CT	Ann Stephens	5.7	.94	5	13

```
(Solaris egrep)
4 % egrep  '\.[0-9]{2}[^0-9]' datafile
  <no output; not recognized with or without backslashes>
```

EXPLANATION

1   The extended metacharacters, { }, are used for repetition. The GNU and UNIX versions of regular grep do not evaluate this extended metacharacter set unless the curly braces are preceded by backslashes. The whole expression reads: search for a literal period \., followed by a number between 0 and 9, [0-9], if the pattern is repeated exactly two times, \{2\}, followed by a nondigit [^0-9].

2   With extended grep, grep -E, the repetition metacharacters, {2}, do not need to be preceded with backslashes as in the previous example.

3   Because GNU egrep and grep -E are functionally the same, this command produces the same output as the previous example.

4   This is the standard UNIX version of egrep. It does not recognize the curly braces as an extended metacharacter set either with or without backslashes.

4.10 Fixed grep (grep -F and fgrep)

The fgrep command behaves like grep, but does not recognize any regular expression metacharacters as being special. All characters represent only themselves. A caret is simply a caret, a dollar sign is a dollar sign, and so forth. With the -F option, GNU grep behaves exactly the same as fgrep.

EXAMPLE 4.51

```
% fgrep '[A-Z]****[0-9]..$5.00' file      or
% grep -F '[A-Z]****[0-9]..$5.00' file
```

EXPLANATION

Finds all lines in the file containing the literal string [A-Z]****[0-9]..$5.00. All characters are treated as themselves. There are no special characters.

4.11 Recursive grep (rgrep, grep -R)

Unlike the members of the grep family, Linux's rgrep can recursively descend a directory tree. Rgrep has a number of command-line options and supports the same metacharacters as regular grep (grep -R). See Appendix A for a complete description of rgrep, or type rgrep-? for online help (not supported on regular versions of UNIX).

EXAMPLE 4.52

```
% grep -r 'Tom' ./dir
% rgrep 'Tom' ./dir
```

EXPLANATION

Searches recursively for all files containing Tom starting from under the ./dir directory.

4.12 GNU grep with Options

The grep command has a number of options that control its behavior. The GNU version of grep added a number of new options and alternative ways to use the options. The GNU grep options work with all the different variants of grep, including grep −G, −E, and −F, as shown in Table 4.11.

Table 4.11   GNU grep Options for All Variants (-G, -E, and -F)

Option	What It Does
-#- (# is a symbol used to represent an integer value)	Matches will be printed with # lines of leading and trailing context; i.e., grep -2 pattern filename will cause grep to print the matched line with the two lines before and after it.
-A #, --after-context=#	Print # lines of trailing context after matching lines; i.e, the matched line and the specified # lines after it.
-B #, --before-context=#	Print # lines of leading context before matching lines; i.e., the matched lines and the specified # lines before it.
-C #, --context=#	Equivalent to -2. Prints the two lines before and after the matched line.
-V, --version	Displays the version information about grep that should be included in all bug reports.
-a, --text, --binary-files=text	Processes binary files as text files.
-b, --byte-offset	Displays the byte offset before each line of output.
-c, --count	Prints a count of matching lines for each input file. With the -v prints a count of nonmatching lines.
-D action, --devices=action	If the input file is a device such as a socket or pipe, action is read from the device by default just as thought it were a normal file. If action is skip, the device will be silently skipped over.
-e PATTERN, --regexp=PATTERN	Use PATTERN literally as the pattern; useful to protect patterns beginning with -.
-f FILE, --file=FILE	Obtain patterns from FILE, one per line. The empty file contains zero patterns, and therefore matches nothing.
--help--	Display a usage message summarizing grep's command-line options and bug reporting address, then exit.
-h, --no-filename	Suppress the prefixing of filenames on output when multiple files are searched.
-i, --ignore-case	Ignore case distinctions in both the pattern and the input files.

Table 4.11   GNU grep Options for All Variants (-G, -E, and -F) (continued)

Option	*What It Does*
-L, --files-without-match	Print just the names of all files where the pattern does not match.
-l, --files-with-matches	Print just the names of all files where the pattern does match.
-m #, --max-count-#	Stop reading a file after specified number (#) of matching lines if the file is standard input or a regular file.
-n, --line-number	Prefix each line of output with the line number where the match occurred.
-q, --quiet	Suppress normal output. Can be used instead of -n.
-r, -R, --recursive, --directories=recurse	For directories listed, reads and processes all files in those directories recursively; i.e., all directories from that directory down the tree.
-s, --silent	Suppress error messages about nonexistent or unreadable files.
-v, --revert-match	Invert the sense of matching, to select nonmatch in lines.
-w, --word-regexp	Select only those lines containing matches that are words. Matches are for strings containing letters, digits, and the underscore, on word boundaries.
-x, --line-regexp	Select only those matches that exactly match the whole line.
-y	Obsolete synonym for -i.
-U, --binary	Treat the file(s) as binary. This option is only supported on MS-DOS and MS-Windows.
-u, --unix-byte-offsets	Report UNIX-style byte offsets. This option has no effect unless -b option is also used; it is only supported on MS-DOS and MS-Windows.
-Z, --null	Places the ASCII null character at the end of filenames, instead of a newline.

4.13 grep with Options (UNIX and GNU)

The grep command has a number of options that control its behavior. Not all versions of UNIX support exactly the same options, so be sure to check your man pages for a complete list.

The examples in this section use the following datafile, which is repeated periodically for your convenience.

% **cat datafile**						
northwest	NW	Charles Main	3.0	.98	3	34
western	WE	Sharon Gray	5.3	.97	5	23
southwest	SW	Lewis Dalsass	2.7	.8	2	18
southern	SO	Suan Chin	5.1	.95	4	15
southeast	SE	Patricia Hemenway	4.0	.7	4	17
eastern	EA	TB Savage	4.4	.84	5	20
northeast	NE	AM Main Jr.	5.1	.94	3	13
north	NO	Margot Weber	4.5	.89	5	9
central	CT	Ann Stephens	5.7	.94	5	13

EXAMPLE 4.53

```
% grep -n '^south' datafile
3:southwest      SW      Lewis Dalsass       2.7   .8    2    18
4:southern       SO      Suan Chin           5.1   .95   4    15
5:southeast      SE      Patricia Hemenway   4.0   .7    4    17
```

EXPLANATION

The -n option precedes each line with the number of the line where the pattern was found, followed by the line.

EXAMPLE 4.54

```
% grep -i 'pat' datafile
southeast        SE      Patricia Hemenway      4.0  .7    4    17
```

EXPLANATION

The –i option turns off case sensitivity. It does not matter if the expression pat contains any combination of upper- or lowercase letters.

EXAMPLE 4.55

```
% grep -v 'Suan Chin' datafile
northwest        NW      Charles Main           3.0   .98   3   34
western          WE      Sharon Gray            5.3   .97   5   23
southwest        SW      Lewis Dalsass          2.7   .8    2   18
southeast        SE      Patricia Hemenway      4.0   .7    4   17
eastern          EA      TB Savage              4.4   .84   5   20
northeast        NE      AM Main Jr.            5.1   .94   3   13
north            NO      Margot Weber           4.5   .89   5   9
central          CT      Ann Stephens           5.7   .94   5   13
```

EXPLANATION

Here, the -v option prints all lines *not* containing the pattern Suan Chin. This option is used when deleting a specific entry from the input file. To really remove the entry, you would redirect the output of grep to a temporary file, and then change the name of the temporary file back to the name of the original file as shown here:

```
grep -v 'Suan Chin' datafile > temp
mv temp datafile
```

Remember that you must use a temporary file when redirecting the output from datafile. If you redirect from datafile to datafile, the shell will "clobber" the datafile. (See "Redirection" on page 25.)

EXAMPLE 4.56

```
% grep -l 'SE' *
datafile
datebook
```

EXPLANATION

The -l option causes grep to print out only the filenames where the pattern is found instead of the line of text.

EXAMPLE 4.57

```
% grep -c 'west' datafile
3
```

EXPLANATION

The -c option causes grep to print the number of lines where the pattern was found. This does not mean the number of occurrences of the pattern. For example, if west is found three times on a line, it only counts the line once.

```
% cat datafile
northwest    NW    Charles Main        3.0    .98    3    34
western      WE    Sharon Gray         5.3    .97    5    23
southwest    SW    Lewis Dalsass       2.7    .8     2    18
southern     SO    Suan Chin           5.1    .95    4    15
southeast    SE    Patricia Hemenway   4.0    .7     4    17
eastern      EA    TB Savage           4.4    .84    5    20
northeast    NE    AM Main Jr.         5.1    .94    3    13
north        NO    Margot Weber        4.5    .89    5    9
central      CT    Ann Stephens        5.7    .94    5    13
```

EXAMPLE 4.58

```
% grep -w 'north' datafile
north        NO    Margot Weber        4.5    .89    5    9
```

EXPLANATION

The -w option causes grep to find the pattern only if it is a word,[a] not part of a word. Only the line containing the word north is printed, not northwest, northeast, etc.

a. A word is a sequence of alphanumeric characters starting at the beginning of a line or preceded by whitespace and ending in whitespace, punctuation, or a newline.

EXAMPLE 4.59

```
% echo $LOGNAME
lewis
% grep -i "$LOGNAME" datafile
southwest        SW      Lewis Dalsass        2.7    .8     2     18
```

EXPLANATION

The value of the shell ENV variable, LOGNAME, is printed. It contains the user's login name. If the variable is enclosed in double quotes, it will still be expanded by the shell, and in case there is more than one word assigned to the variable, whitespace is shielded from shell interpretation. If single quotes are used, variable substitution does not take place; that is, $LOGNAME is printed.

4.13.1　GNU grep Options Examples

In addition to the options provided with UNIX grep, the GNU version provides options that further refine the output resulting from pattern searches.

The examples in this section use the following datafile, repeated periodically for your convenience.

```
% cat datafile
northwest      NW      Charles Main          3.0     .98     3     34
western        WE      Sharon Gray           5.3     .97     5     23
southwest      SW      Lewis Dalsass         2.7     .8      2     18
southern       SO      Suan Chin             5.1     .95     4     15
southeast      SE      Patricia Hemenway     4.0     .7      4     17
eastern        EA      TB Savage             4.4     .84     5     20
northeast      NE      AM Main Jr.           5.1     .94     3     13
north          NO      Margot Weber          4.5     .89     5     9
central        CT      Ann Stephens          5.7     .94     5     13
```

EXAMPLE 4.60

```
% grep -V
grep (GNU grep) 2.2
```

```
Copyright (C) 1988, 92, 93, 94, 95, 96, 97 Free Software Foundation, Inc. This is free
software; see the source for copying conditions. There is NO warranty; not even for MER-
CHANTABILITY or FITNESS FOR A PARTICULAR PURPOSE.
```

EXPLANATION

With the –V option, grep's version and copyright information are listed. The version information should be included with any bug reports sent to the GNU Foundation.

EXAMPLE 4.61

```
1   % grep -2 Patricia datafile
    southwest      SW      Lewis Dalsass         2.7     .8      2     18
    southern       SO      Suan Chin             5.1     .95     4     15
    southeast      SE      Patricia Hemenway     4.0     .7      4     17
    eastern        EA      TB Savage             4.4     .84     5     20
    northeast      NE      AM Main Jr.           5.1     .94     3     13

2   % grep -C Patricia datafile
    southwest      SW      Lewis Dalsass         2.7     .8      2     18
    southern       SO      Suan Chin             5.1     .95     4     15
    southeast      SE      Patricia Hemenway     4.0     .7      4     17
    eastern        EA      TB Savage             4.4     .84     5     20
    northeast      NE      AM Main Jr.           5.1     .94     3     13
```

EXPLANATION

1   After a line matching Patricia is found, grep displays that line and the two lines before and after it.

2   The –C option is the same as –2.

```
% cat datafile
northwest      NW      Charles Main        3.0     .98     3       34
western        WE      Sharon Gray         5.3     .97     5       23
southwest      SW      Lewis Dalsass       2.7     .8      2       18
southern       SO      Suan Chin           5.1     .95     4       15
southeast      SE      Patricia Hemenway   4.0     .7      4       17
eastern        EA      TB Savage           4.4     .84     5       20
northeast      NE      AM Main Jr.         5.1     .94     3       13
north          NO      Margot Weber        4.5     .89     5       9
central        CT      Ann Stephens        5.7     .94     5       13
```

EXAMPLE 4.62

```
% grep -A 2 Patricia datafile
southeast      SE      Patricia Hemenway   4.0     .7      4       17
eastern        EA      TB Savage           4.4     .84     5       20
northeast      NE      AM Main Jr.         5.1     .94     3       13
```

EXPLANATION

After a line matching Patricia is found, grep displays that line and the two lines after it.

EXAMPLE 4.63

```
% grep -B 2 Patricia datafile
southwest      SW      Lewis Dalsass       2.7     .8      2       18
southern       SO      Suan Chin           5.1     .95     4       15
southeast      SE      Patricia Hemenway   4.0     .7      4       17
```

EXPLANATION

After a line matching Patricia is found, grep displays that line and the two lines before (preceding) it.

EXAMPLE 4.64

```
% grep -b '[abc]' datafile
0:northwest      NW      Charles Main        3.0     .98     3       34
39:western       WE      Sharon Gray         5.3     .97     5       23
76:southwest     SW      Lewis Dalsass       2.7     .8      2       18
115:southern     SO      Suan Chin           5.1     .95     4       15
150:southeast    SE      Patricia Hemenway   4.0     .7      4       17
193:eastern      EA      TB Savage           4.4     .84     5       20
228:northeast    NE      AM Main Jr.         5.1     .94     3       13
266:north        NO      Margot Weber        4.5     .89     5       9
301:central      CT      Ann Stephens        5.7     .94     5       13
```

EXPLANATION

With the -b option, grep prints the byte offset from the input file before each line of output.

Instead of using the datafile for these next two examples, we'll use a file called negative to demonstrate the -e and -x options.

% **cat negative**
-40 is cold.
This is line 1.
This is line 2.5
-alF are options to the ls command

EXAMPLE 4.65

1   % **grep -e '-alF' negative**
     -alF are options to the ls command

2   % **grep --regexp=-40 negative**
     -40 is cold.

EXPLANATION

1   With the -e option, grep treats all characters in the pattern equally, so that leading dashes are not mistaken for options.
2   The alternate way to represent -e is --regexp=pattern, where pattern is the regular expression; in this example the regular expression is -40.

EXAMPLE 4.66

% **grep -x -e '-40 is cold.' negative**
-40 is cold.

EXPLANATION

With the -x option, grep will not match a line unless the search pattern is identical to the entire line. The -e is used to allow a dash as the first character in the search string.

The remaining examples in this section use the following datafile.

% **cat datafile**						
northwest	NW	Charles Main	3.0	.98	3	34
western	WE	Sharon Gray	5.3	.97	5	23
southwest	SW	Lewis Dalsass	2.7	.8	2	18
southern	SO	Suan Chin	5.1	.95	4	15
southeast	SE	Patricia Hemenway	4.0	.7	4	17
eastern	EA	TB Savage	4.4	.84	5	20
northeast	NE	AM Main Jr.	5.1	.94	3	13
north	NO	Margot Weber	4.5	.89	5	9
central	CT	Ann Stephens	5.7	.94	5	13

EXAMPLE 4.67

```
1   % cat repatterns
    western
    north

2   % grep -f repatterns datafile
    northwest    NW    Charles Main    3.0   .98   5   34
    western      WE    Sharon Gray     5.3   .97   5   23
    northeast    NE    AM Main Jr.     5.1   .94   3   13
    north        NO    Margot Weber    4.5   .89   5   9
```

EXPLANATION

1   The file repatterns is displayed. It contains grep's search patterns that will be matched against lines in an input file. Western and north are the patterns grep will use in its search.

2   With the –f option followed by a filename (in this example, repatterns), grep will get its search patterns from that file and match them against lines in datafile. Grep searched for and printed all lines containing patterns western and north.

EXAMPLE 4.68

```
1   % grep '[0-9]' datafile db
    datafile:northwest NW    Charles Main       3.0   .98   3   34
    datafile:western WE      Sharon Gray        5.3   .97   5   23
    datafile:southwest SW    Lewis Dalsass      2.7   .8    2   18
    datafile:southern SO     Suan Chin          5.1   .95   4   15
    datafile:southeast SE    Patricia Hemenway  4.0   .7    4   17
    datafile:eastern EA      TB Savage          4.4   .84   5   20
    datafile:northeast NE    AM Main Jr.        5.1   .94   3   13
    datafile:north NO        Margot Weber       4.5   .89   5   9
    datafile:central CT      Ann Stephens       5.7   .94   5   13
    db:123
```

EXAMPLE 4.68 (CONTINUED)

2 `% grep -h '[0-9]' datafle db`

northwest	NW	Charles Main	3.0	.98	3	34
western	WE	Sharon Gray	5.3	.97	5	23
southwest	SW	Lewis Dalsass	2.7	.8	2	18
southern	SO	Suan Chin	5.1	.95	4	15
southeast	SE	Patricia Hemenway	4.0	.7	4	17
eastern	EA	TB Savage	4.4	.84	5	20
northeast	NE	AM Main Jr.	5.1	.94	3	13
north	NO	Margot Weber	4.5	.89	5	9
central	CT	Ann Stephens	5.7	.94	5	13

123

EXPLANATION

1 If more than one file is listed, grep prepends each line of its output with the file-name. Filenames are datafile and db.

2 With the -h option, grep suppresses the header information; i.e., does not print the filenames.

EXAMPLE 4.69

```
% grep -q Charles datafile      or
% grep --quiet Charles datafile
% echo $status
0
```

EXPLANATION

The quiet option suppresses any output from grep. It is used when the exit status is all that is needed. If the exit status is zero, grep found the pattern.

LAB 1: grep EXERCISE

(Refer to the file called datebook on the CD.)

Steve Blenheim:238-923-7366:95 Latham Lane, Easton, PA 83755:11/12/56:20300
Betty Boop:245-836-8357:635 Cutesy Lane, Hollywood, CA 91464:6/23/23:14500
Igor Chevsky:385-375-8395:3567 Populus Place, Caldwell, NJ 23875:6/18/68:23400
Norma Corder:397-857-2735:74 Pine Street, Dearborn, MI 23874:3/28/45:245700
Jennifer Cowan:548-834-2348:583 Laurel Ave., Kingsville, TX 83745:10/1/35:58900
Jon DeLoach:408-253-3122:123 Park St., San Jose, CA 04086:7/25/53:85100
Karen Evich:284-758-2857:23 Edgecliff Place, Lincoln, NB 92743:7/25/53:85100
Karen Evich:284-758-2867:23 Edgecliff Place, Lincoln, NB 92743:11/3/35:58200
Karen Evich:284-758-2867:23 Edgecliff Place, Lincoln, NB 92743:11/3/35:58200
Fred Fardbarkle:674-843-1385:20 Parak Lane, Duluth, MN 23850:4/12/23:780900
Fred Fardbarkle:674-843-1385:20 Parak Lane, Duluth, MN 23850:4/12/23:780900
Lori Gortz:327-832-5728:3465 Mirlo Street, Peabody, MA 34756:10/2/65:35200
Paco Gutierrez:835-365-1284:454 Easy Street, Decatur, IL 75732:2/28/53:123500
Ephram Hardy:293-259-5395:235 CarltonLane, Joliet, IL 73858:8/12/20:56700
James Ikeda:834-938-8376:23445 Aster Ave., Allentown, NJ 83745:12/1/38:45000
Barbara Kertz:385-573-8326:832 Ponce Drive, Gary, IN 83756:12/1/46:268500
Lesley Kirstin:408-456-1234:4 Harvard Square, Boston, MA 02133:4/22/62:52600
William Kopf:846-836-2837:6937 Ware Road, Milton, PA 93756:9/21/46:43500
Sir Lancelot:837-835-8257:474 Camelot Boulevard, Bath, WY 28356:5/13/69:24500
Jesse Neal:408-233-8971:45 Rose Terrace, San Francisco, CA 92303:2/3/36:25000
Zippy Pinhead:834-823-8319:2356 Bizarro Ave., Farmount, IL 84357:1/1/67:89500
Arthur Putie:923-835-8745:23 Wimp Lane, Kensington, DL 38758:8/31/69:126000
Popeye Sailor:156-454-3322:945 Bluto Street, Anywhere, USA 29358:3/19/35:22350
Jose Santiago:385-898-8357:38 Fife Way, Abilene, TX 39673:1/5/58:95600
Tommy Savage:408-724-0140:1222 Oxbow Court, Sunnyvale, CA 94087:5/19/66:34200
Yukio Takeshida:387-827-1095:13 Uno Lane, Ashville, NC 23556:7/1/29:57000
Vinh Tranh:438-910-7449:8235 Maple Street, Wilmington, VM 29085:9/23/63:68900

1. Print all lines containing the string San.

2. Print all lines where the person's first name starts with J.

3. Print all lines ending in 700.

4. Print all lines that don't contain 834.

5. Print all lines where birthdays are in December.

6. Print all lines where the phone number is in the 408 area code.

7. Print all lines containing an uppercase letter, followed by four lowercase letters, a comma, a space, and one uppercase letter.

8. Print lines where the last name begins with K or k.

9. Print lines preceded by a line number where the salary is a six-figure number.

10. Print lines containing Lincoln or lincoln (remember that grep is insensitive to case).

5

sed, the
Streamlined Editor

5.1 What Is sed?

Sed is a streamlined, noninteractive editor. It allows you to perform the same kind of editing tasks used in the vi and ex editors. Instead of working interactively with the editor, the sed program lets you type your editing commands at the command line, name the file, and then see the output of the editing command on the screen. The sed editor is nondestructive. It does not change your file unless you save the output with shell redirection. All lines are printed to the screen by default.

The sed editor is useful in shell scripts, where using interactive editors such as vi or ex would require the user of the script to have familiarity with the editor and would expose the user to making unwanted modifications to the open file. You can also put sed commands in a file called a sed script, if you need to perform multiple edits or do not like worrying about quoting the sed commands at the shell command line.[1]

5.2 Versions of sed

Linux uses the GNU version of sed, copyrighted by the Free Software Foundation. This version is almost identical to the sed provided by standard UNIX distributions.

---

1. Remember, the shell will try to evaluate any metacharacters or whitespace when a command is typed at the command line; any characters in the sed command that could be interpreted by the shell must be quoted.

EXAMPLE 5.1

```
% sed -V   or  sed --version
GNU sed version 3.02

Copyright (C) 1998 Free Software Foundation, Inc.
This is free software; see the source for copying conditions.
There is NO warranty; not even for MERCHANTABILITY or FITNESS FOR A
PARTICULAR PURPOSE, to the extent permitted by law.
```

5.3   How Does sed Work?

The sed editor processes a file (or input) one line at a time and sends its output to the screen. Its commands are those you may recognize from the vi and ed/ex editors. Sed stores the line it is currently processing in a temporary buffer called a *pattern space* or *temporary buffer*. Once sed is finished processing the line in the pattern space (i.e., executing sed commands on that line), the line in the pattern space is sent to the screen (unless the command was to delete the line or suppress its printing). After the line has been processed, it is removed from the pattern space and the next line is then read into the pattern space, processed, and displayed. Sed ends when the last line of the input file has been processed. By storing each line in a temporary buffer and performing edits on that line, the original file is never altered or destroyed.

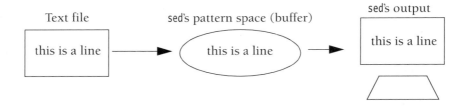

5.4   Regular Expressions

Sed, like grep, searches for patterns in files using regular expressions (REs) and a variety of metacharacters shown in Table 5.3 on page 132. Regular expressions are patterns of characters enclosed in forward slashes for searches and substitutions.

```
sed -n '/RE/p' filename
sed -n '/love/p' filename

sed -n 's/RE/replacement string/' filename
sed -n 's/love/like/' filename
```

To change the regular expression delimiter, some character, say c, is preceded by a backslash, followed by the regular expression, and that character; for example,

```
sed -n '/love/p' filename
```

prints all lines containing love.

To change the delimiter:

```
sed -n '\cREcp' filename
```

where c represents the character to delimit the regular expression (RE) in place of forward slashes.

EXAMPLE 5.2

```
1    % sed -n '/12\/10\/04/p' datafile
2    % sed -n '\x12/10/04xp' datafile        # sed lets you change the delimiter
```

EXPLANATION

1   When forward slashes are part of the regular expression, they must be back-slashed so they won't be confused with the forward slashes that delimit it.

2   The forward slashes are replaced by the letter x. This makes it easier when the regular expression contains forward slashes.

If you recall, the grep command returns a zero exit status if a pattern is found in a file, and 1 if it is not found. The exit status of the sed command, however, will be zero, whether or not the pattern being searched for is found. The only time the exit status will be nonzero is when the command contains a syntax error. (See "Error Messages and Exit Status" on page 131.) In the following example, both grep and sed search for the regular expression, John, in a file.

Regular expressions can also be made part of an address as shown in "Addressing" on page 128.

EXAMPLE 5.3

```
1    % grep 'John' datafile        # grep searches for John
2    % echo $status
     1

3    % sed -n '/John/p' datafile    # sed searches for John
4    % echo $status
     0
```

EXPLANATION

1   With grep, the regular expression John is not enclosed in a delimiter.

2   The exit status of the grep command is zero if the pattern John was found, and non-zero if not.

3   The sed command will print all lines containing the RE pattern, John.

4   Even though the pattern John is not found in the file, the exit status is zero because the syntax was okay.

5.5 Addressing

You can use addressing to decide which lines you want to edit. The addresses can be in the form of decimal numbers or regular expressions (also called context addresses), or a combination of both. Without specifying an address, sed processes all lines of the input file.

When an address consists of a number, the number represents a line number. A dollar sign can be used to represent the last line of the input file. If a comma separates two line numbers, the addresses that will be processed are within that range of lines, including the first and last line in the range. The range may be numbers, regular expressions, or a combination of numbers and regular expressions.

Sed commands tell sed what to do with the line: print it, remove it, change it, and so forth.

FORMAT

```
sed 'command' filename(s)
```

EXAMPLE 5.4

```
1    sed '1,3d' myfile
2    sed -n '/[Jj]ohn/p' datafile
```

EXPLANATION

1   Lines 1 through 3 of myfile are deleted.

2   Only lines matching the pattern John or john in myfile are printed.

5.6 Commands and Options

Sed commands tell sed how to process each line of input specified by an address. If an address is not given, sed processes every line of input. (The % is the csh prompt.) See Table 5.1 for a list of sed commands and what they do, and see Table 5.2 for a list of options and how they control sed's behavior.

Table 5.1 sed Commands

Command	Function
a\	Appends one or more lines of text to the current line
c\	Changes (replaces) text in the current line with new text
d	Deletes lines
i\	Inserts text above the current line
h	Copies the contents of the pattern space to a holding buffer
H	Appends the contents of the pattern space to a holding buffer
g	Gets what is in the holding buffer and copies it into the pattern buffer, overwriting what was there
G	Gets what is in the holding buffer and copies it into the pattern buffer, appending to what was there
l	Lists nonprinting characters
p	Prints lines
n	Reads the next input line and starts processing the newline with the next command rather than the first command
q	Quits or exits sed
r	Reads lines from a file
!	Applies the command to all lines *except* the selected ones
s	Substitutes one string for another

Substitution Flags

g	Globally substitutes on a line
p	Prints lines
w	Writes lines out to a file
x	Exchanges contents of the holding buffer with the pattern space
y	Translates one character to another (cannot use regular expression metacharacters with y)

Table 5.2   sed Options

Options	Function
-e	Allows multiple edits
-f	Precedes a sed script filename
-n	Suppresses default output

   When multiple commands are used or addresses need to be nested within a range of addresses, the commands are enclosed in curly braces and each command is either on a separate line or terminated with semicolons.
   The exclamation point (!) can be used to negate a command. For example,

```
sed '/Tom/d' file
```

tells sed to delete all lines containing the pattern Tom, whereas

```
sed '/Tom/!d' file  (sh, ksh, bash)
sed '/Tom/\!d' file  (csh, tcsh)
```

tells sed to delete lines *not* containing Tom.

   The sed options are -e, -f, and, -n. The -e is used for multiple edits at the command line, the -f precedes a sed script filename, and the -n suppresses printing output.

5.6.1   How to Modify a File with sed

Sed is a nondestructive editor. It will display the edits you make on your screen, but it will not change the file you are editing. To really reflect the edits in the file, you must redirect the output to another file, and then rename the orginal file.

EXAMPLE 5.5

```
1   % sed '1,3d' filex >  temp
2   % mv temp filex
```

EXPLANATION

1   Lines 1 through 3 of myfile are deleted. Instead of displaying the remaining lines on the screen, they are redirected to a file called temp. (Make sure the file where you are sending your output, in this case temp, is an empty file. Otherwise the redirection will cause it to be clobbered.)

2   The mv command will overwrite filex with the contents of temp.

5.6.2   GNU sed Options

Example 5.6 lists additional options provided by GNU sed, and how they control sed's behavior. With the -h option, sed displays a list of its command-line options and a short description of what each one does.

EXAMPLE 5.6

```
% sed -h
Usage: sed [OPTION]... {script-only-if-no-other-script} [input-file]...

  -n, --quiet, --silent
                suppress automatic printing of pattern space
  -e script, --expression=script
                add the script to the commands to be executed
  -f script-file, --file=script-file
                add the contents of script-file to the commands to be executed
  --help        display this help and exit
  -V, --version output version information and exit
```

EXPLANATION

If an -e, --expression, -f, or --file option is not given, then the first nonoption argument is taken as a sed script to be interpreted. All remaining arguments are names of input files; if no input files are specified, then the standard input is read.

5.7   Error Messages and Exit Status

When sed encounters a syntax error, it sends a pretty straightforward error message to standard error, but if it cannot figure out what you did wrong, sed gets "garbled," which we could guess means confused. If the syntax is error-free, the exit status that sed returns to the shell is a zero for success and a nonzero integer for failure.[2]

EXAMPLE 5.7

```
1   % sed '1,3v ' file
    sed: Unrecognized command: 1,3v
    % echo $status              # use echo $? if using Korn or Bourne shell
    2

2   % sed '/^John' file
    sed: Illegal or missing delimiter: /^John
```

---

2. For a complete list of diagnostics, see the man page for sed.

EXAMPLE 5.7 (CONTINUED)

3 % **sed 's/134345/g' file**
   sed: Ending delimiter missing on substitution: s/134345/g

EXPLANATION

1 The v command is unrecognized by sed. The exit status was 2, indicating that sed exited with a syntax problem.
2 The pattern /^John is missing the closing forward slash.
3 The substitution command, s, contains the search string but not the replacement string.

5.8   Metacharacters

Like grep, sed supports a number of special metacharacters to control pattern searching. See Table 5.3.

Table 5.3   sed's Regular Expression Metacharacters

Metacharacter	Function	Example	What It Matches
^	Beginning-of-line anchor	/^love/	Matches all lines beginning with love.
$	End-of-line anchor	/love$/	Matches all lines ending with love.
.	Matches one character, but not the newline character	/l..e/	Matches lines containing an l, followed by two characters, followed by an e.
*	Matches zero or more characters	/ *love/	Matches lines with zero or more spaces, followed by the pattern love.
[ ]	Matches one character in the set	/[Ll]ove/	Matches lines containing love or Love.
[^]	Matches one character not in the set	/[^A-KM-Z]ove/	Matches lines not containing A through K or M through Z followed by ove.
\(..\)	Saves matched characters	s/\(love\)able/\1er/	Tags marked portion and saves it as tag number 1. To reference later, use \1 to reference the pattern. May use up to nine tags, starting with the first tag at the leftmost part of the pattern. For example, love is saved in register 1 and remembered in the replacement string. lovable is replaced with lover.

Table 5.3   sed's Regular Expression Metacharacters (continued)

Metacharacter	Function	Example	What It Matches
&	Saves search string so it can be remembered in the replacement string	s/love/**&**/	The ampersand represents the search string. The string love will be replaced with itself surrounded by asterisks; i.e., love will become **love**.
\<	Beginning-of-word anchor	/\<love/	Matches lines containing a word that begins with *love*.
\>	End-of-word anchor	/love\>/	Matches lines containing a word that ends with *love*.
x\{m\} x\{m,\} x\{m,n\} [a]	Repetition of character x: m times, at least m times, or between m and n times	/o\{5\}/ /o\{5,\}/ /o\{5,10\}/	Matches if line has: 5 occurrences of o, at least 5 occurrences of o, or between 5 and 10 occurrences of o.

a.   Not dependable on all versions of UNIX or all pattern-matching utilities; usually works with vi and grep.

5.9   sed **Examples**

The following examples show you how to use sed, its options, commands, and regular expressions. Remember that sed is non-destructive; that is the file that sed is editing will not be modified unless its output is redirected, as shown in Example 5.6.

The examples in the following sections use the following datafile, repeated periodically for your convenience.

```
% cat datafile
northwest       NW      Charles Main        3.0     .98     3     34
western         WE      Sharon Gray         5.3     .97     5     23
southwest       SW      Lewis Dalsass       2.7     .8      2     18
southern        SO      Suan Chin           5.1     .95     4     15
southeast       SE      Patricia Hemenway   4.0     .7      4     17
eastern         EA      TB Savage           4.4     .84     5     20
northeast       NE      AM Main Jr.         5.1     .94     3     13
north           NO      Margot Weber        4.5     .89     5      9
central         CT      Ann Stephens        5.7     .94     5     13
```

5.9.1 Printing: The p Command

The p command is the *print* command. It is used to display the contents of the pattern buffer. Because, by default, sed prints lines to the screen, the -n option is used to suppress default printing. With the -n option and the p command together, selected text can be printed.

EXAMPLE 5.8

```
% sed '/north/p' datafile
```

northwest	NW	Charles Main	3.0	.98	3	34
northwest	NW ·	Charles Main	3.0	.98	3	34
western	WE	Sharon Gray	5.3	.97	5	23
southwest	SW	Lewis Dalsass	2.7	.8	2	18
southern	SO	Suan Chin	5.1	.95	4	15
southeast	SE	Patricia Hemenway	4.0	.7	4	17
eastern	EA	TB Savage	4.4	.84	5	20
northeast	NE	AM Main Jr.	5.1	.94	3	13
northeast	NE	AM Main Jr.	5.1	.94	3	13
north	NO	Margot Weber	4.5	.89	5	9
north	NO	Margot Weber	4.5	.89	5	9
central	CT	Ann Stephens	5.7	.94	5	13

EXPLANATION

Prints all lines to standard output by default. If the pattern north is found, sed will print that line in addition to all the other lines.

EXAMPLE 5.9

```
% sed -n '/north/p' datafile
```

northwest	NW	Charles Main	3.0	.98	3	34
northeast	NE	AM Main Jr.	5.1	.94	3	13
north	NO	Margot Weber	4.5	.89	5	9

EXPLANATION

By default, sed prints the line currently in the pattern buffer. With the p command, sed is told to print the line again. The -n option suppresses the default behavior of sed. When used with the p command, the line in the pattern buffer is printed only once. Without the -n option, sed will print duplicate lines of output as shown in the preceding example. Only the lines containing the pattern north are printed when -n is used.

5.9.2 Deleting: The d Command

The d command is used to *delete* lines. After sed copies a line from a file and puts it into a pattern buffer, it executes any sed commands for that line, and finally, displays the contents of the pattern buffer to the screen. When the d command is issued, the line currently in the pattern buffer is removed, not displayed.

```
% cat datafile
northwest     NW     Charles Main          3.0   .98   3   34
western       WE     Sharon Gray           5.3   .97   5   23
southwest     SW     Lewis Dalsass         2.7   .8    2   18
southern      SO     Suan Chin             5.1   .95   4   15
southeast     SE     Patricia Hemenway     4.0   .7    4   17
eastern       EA     TB Savage             4.4   .84   5   20
northeast     NE     AM Main Jr.           5.1   .94   3   13
north         NO     Margot Weber          4.5   .89   5    9
central       CT     Ann Stephens          5.7   .94   5   13
```

EXAMPLE 5.10

```
% sed '3d' datafile
northwest     NW     Charles Main          3.0   .98   3   34
western       WE     Sharon Gray           5.3   .97   5   23
southern      SO     Suan Chin             5.1   .95   4   15
southeast     SE     Patricia Hemenway     4.0   .7    4   17
eastern       EA     TB Savage             4.4   .84   5   20
northeast     NE     AM Main Jr.           5.1   .94   3   13
north         NO     Margot Weber          4.5   .89   5    9
central       CT     Ann Stephens          5.7   .94   5   13
```

EXPLANATION

Deletes the third line. All other lines are printed to the screen, by default.

EXAMPLE 5.11

```
% sed '3,$d' datafile
northwest     NW     Charles Main          3.0   .98   3   34
western       WE     Sharon Gray           5.3   .97   5   23
```

EXPLANATION

The third line through the last line are deleted. The dollar sign ($) represents the last line of the file. The comma is called the *range operator*. The remaining lines are printed. In this example, the range of addresses starts at line 3 and ends at the last line, which is represented by the dollar sign ($).

EXAMPLE 5.12

```
% sed '$d' datafile
northwest        NW      Charles Main         3.0    .98    3    34
western          WE      Sharon Gray          5.3    .97    5    23
southwest        SW      Lewis Dalsass        2.7    .8     2    18
southern         SO      Suan Chin            5.1    .95    4    15
southeast        SE      Patricia Hemenway    4.0    .7     4    17
eastern          EA      TB Savage            4.4    .84    5    20
northeast        NE      AM Main Jr.          5.1    .94    3    13
north            NO      Margot Weber         4.5    .89    5    9
```

EXPLANATION

Deletes the last line. The dollar sign ($) represents the last line. The default is to print all of the lines except those affected by the d command.

EXAMPLE 5.13

```
% sed '/north/d' datafile
western          WE      Sharon Gray          5.3    .97    5    23
southwest        SW      Lewis Dalsass        2.7    .8     2    18
southern         SO      Suan Chin            5.1    .95    4    15
southeast        SE      Patricia Hemenway    4.0    .7     4    17
eastern          EA      TB Savage            4.4    .84    5    20
central          CT      Ann Stephens         5.7    .94    5    13
```

EXPLANATION

All lines containing the pattern north are deleted. The remaining lines are printed.

5.9.3 Substitution: The s Command

The s command is the *substitution* command. Substitution and replacement of text in files is accomplished with sed's s command. The text enclosed in the forward slashes after the s command is a regular expression, followed by the replacement text on the right-hand side. Replacements can be done globally across a line if the g flag is used.

% **cat datafile**						
northwest	NW	Charles Main	3.0	.98	3	34
western	WE	Sharon Gray	5.3	.97	5	23
southwest	SW	Lewis Dalsass	2.7	.8	2	18
southern	SO	Suan Chin	5.1	.95	4	15
southeast	SE	Patricia Hemenway	4.0	.7	4	17
eastern	EA	TB Savage	4.4	.84	5	20
northeast	NE	AM Main Jr.	5.1	.94	3	13
north	NO	Margot Weber	4.5	.89	5	9
central	CT	Ann Stephens	5.7	.94	5	13

EXAMPLE 5.14

% **sed 's/west/north/g' datafile**						
northnorth	NW	Charles Main	3.0	.98	3	34
northern	WE	Sharon Gray	5.3	.97	5	23
southnorth	SW	Lewis Dalsass	2.7	.8	2	18
southern	SO	Suan Chin	5.1	.95	4	15
southeast	SE	Patricia Hemenway	4.0	.7	4	17
eastern	EA	TB Savage	4.4	.84	5	20
northeast	NE	AM Main Jr.	5.1	.94	3	13
north	NO	Margot Weber	4.5	.89	5	9
central	CT	Ann Stephens	5.7	.94	5	13

EXPLANATION

The s command is for substitution. The g flag at the end of the command indicates that the substitution is global across the line; that is, if multiple occurrences of west are found, all of them will be replaced with north. Without the g command, only the first occurrence of west on each line would be replaced with north.

EXAMPLE 5.15

% **sed -n 's/^west/north/p' datafile**						
northern	WE	Sharon Gray	5.3	.97	5	23

EXPLANATION

The s command is for substitution. The -n option with the p flag at the end of the command tells sed to print only those lines where the substitution occurred; that is, if west is found at the beginning of the line and is replaced with north, just those lines are printed.

EXAMPLE 5.16

```
% sed 's/[0-9][0-9]$/&.5/' datafile
northwest          NW      Charles Main        3.0   .98    3    34.5
western            WE      Sharon Gray         5.3   .97    5    23.5
southwest          SW      Lewis Dalsass       2.7   .8     2    18.5
southern           SO      Suan Chin           5.1   .95    4    15.5
southeast          SE      Patricia Hemenway   4.0   .7     4    17.5
eastern            EA      TB Savage           4.4   .84    5    20.5
northeast          NE      AM Main Jr.         5.1   .94    3    13.5
north              NO      Margot Weber        4.5   .89    5    9
central            CT      Ann Stephens        5.7   .94    5    13.5
```

EXPLANATION

The ampersand[a] (&) in the replacement string represents exactly what was found in the search string. Each line that ends in two digits will be replaced by itself, and .5 will be appended to it.

a.   To represent a literal ampersand in the replacement string, it must be escaped: \&.

EXAMPLE 5.17

```
% sed -n 's/Hemenway/Jones/gp' datafile
southeast          SE      Patricia Jones      4.0   .7     4    17
```

EXPLANATION

All occurrences of Hemenway are replaced with Jones, and only the lines that changed are printed. The -n option combined with the p command suppresses the default output. The g stands for global substitution across the line.

EXAMPLE 5.18

```
% sed -n 's/\(Mar\)got/\1ianne/p' datafile
north              NO      Marianne Weber      4.5   .89    5    9
```

EXPLANATION

The pattern Mar is enclosed in parentheses and saved as tag 1 in a special register. It will be referenced in the replacement string as \1. Margot is then replaced with Marianne.

```
% cat datafile
northwest    NW    Charles Main         3.0    .98    3    34
western      WE    Sharon Gray          5.3    .97    5    23
southwest    SW    Lewis Dalsass        2.7    .8     2    18
southern     SO    Suan Chin            5.1    .95    4    15
southeast    SE    Patricia Hemenway    4.0    .7     4    17
eastern      EA    TB Savage            4.4    .84    5    20
northeast    NE    AM Main Jr.          5.1    .94    3    13
north        NO    Margot Weber         4.5    .89    5    9
central      CT    Ann Stephens         5.7    .94    5    13
```

EXAMPLE 5.19

```
% sed 's#3#88#g' datafile
northwest    NW    Charles Main         88.0   .98    88   884
western      WE    Sharon Gray          5.88   .97    5    288
southwest    SW    Lewis Dalsass        2.7    .8     2    18
southern     SO    Suan Chin            5.1    .95    4    15
southeast    SE    Patricia Hemenway    4.0    .7     4    17
eastern      EA    TB Savage            4.4    .84    5    20
northeast    NE    AM Main Jr.          5.1    .94    88   188
north        NO    Margot Weber         4.5    .89    5    9
central      CT    Ann Stephens         5.7    .94    5    188
```

EXPLANATION

The character after the s command is the delimiter between the search string and the replacement string. The delimiter character is a forward slash by default, but can be changed. Whatever character follows the s command (with the exception of the new-line character or backslash) is the new delimiter. This technique can be useful when searching for patterns containing a forward slash, such as pathnames or birthdays.

5.9.4 Range of Selected Lines: The Comma

A range of lines starts at one address in a file and ends at another address in the file. The address range can be line numbers (such as 5,10), regular expressions (such as /Dick/,/Joe/), or a combination of both (such as /north/,$). The range is inclusive—it consists of the line with the starting condition, all lines in between, and the line ending the condition of the range. If the ending condition is never reached, it ends when the file ends. If the ending condition is reached, and then the condition for starting again applies, the range starts over.

EXAMPLE 5.20

```
% sed -n '/west/,/east/p' datafile
```
➤ northwest	NW	Charles Main	3.0	.98	3	34
western	WE	Sharon Gray	5.3	.97	5	23
southwest	SW	Lewis Dalsass	2.7	.8	2	18
southern	SO	Suan Chin	5.1	.95	4	15
➤ southeast	SE	Patricia Hemenway	4.0	.7	4	17

EXPLANATION

All lines in the range of patterns between west and east are printed. If west were to appear on a line after east, the lines from west to the next east or to the end of file, which-
ever comes first, would be printed. The arrows mark the range.

EXAMPLE 5.21

```
% sed -n '5,/^northeast/p' datafile
```
southeast	SE	Patricia Hemenway	4.0	.7	4	17
eastern	EA	TB Savage	4.4	.84	5	20
northeast	NE	AM Main Jr.	5.1	.94	3	13

EXPLANATION

Prints the lines from line 5 through the first line that begins with northeast.

EXAMPLE 5.22

```
% sed '/west/,/east/s/$/**VACA**/' datafile
```
➤ northwest	NW	Charles Main	3.0	.98	3	34**VACA**
western	WE	Sharon Gray	5.3	.97	5	23**VACA**
southwest	SW	Lewis Dalsass	2.7	.8	2	18**VACA**
southern	SO	Suan Chin	5.1	.95	4	15**VACA**
➤ southeast	SE	Patricia Hemenway	4.0	.7	4	17**VACA**
eastern	EA	TB Savage	4.4	.84	5	20
northeast	NE	AM Main Jr.	5.1	.94	3	13
north	NO	Margot Weber	4.5	.89	5	9
central	CT	Ann Stephens	5.7	.94	5	13

EXPLANATION

For lines in the range between the patterns east and west, the end-of-line ($) is replaced
with the string **VACA**. The newline is moved over to the end of the new string. The
arrows mark the range.

5.9.5 Multiple Edits: The e Command

The -e command is the *edit* command, and is used if you have more than one editing command for sed to execute. All edits are applied to the line in the pattern buffer, before the next line is edited.

% **cat datafile**						
northwest	NW	Charles Main	3.0	.98	3	34
western	WE	Sharon Gray	5.3	.97	5	23
southwest	SW	Lewis Dalsass	2.7	.8	2	18
southern	SO	Suan Chin	5.1	.95	4	15
southeast	SE	Patricia Hemenway	4.0	.7	4	17
eastern	EA	TB Savage	4.4	.84	5	20
northeast	NE	AM Main Jr.	5.1	.94	3	13
north	NO	Margot Weber	4.5	.89	5	9
central	CT	Ann Stephens	5.7	.94	5	13

EXAMPLE 5.23

```
% sed -e '1,3d' -e 's/Hemenway/Jones/' datafile
southern        SO      Suan Chin       5.1    .95    4    15
southeast       SE      Patricia Jones  4.0    .7     4    17
eastern         EA      TB Savage       4.4    .84    5    20
northeast       NE      AM Main Jr.     5.1    .94    3    13
north           NO      Margot Weber    4.5    .89    5    9
central         CT      Ann Stephens    5.7    .94    5    13
```

EXPLANATION

The -e option allows multiple edits. The first edit removes lines 1 through 3. The second edit substitutes Hemenway with Jones. Because both edits are done on a per-line basis (i.e., both commands are executed on the current line in the pattern space), the order of the edits may affect the outcome. For example, if both commands had performed substitutions on the line, the first substitution could affect the second substitution.

5.9.6 Reading from Files: The r Command

The r command is the *read* command. It allows sed to load content from one text file into the current file at some specified location.

EXAMPLE 5.24

```
% cat newfile
                  ------------------------------------
                  | ***SUAN HAS LEFT THE COMPANY*** |
                  |_____|
% sed '/Suan/r newfile' datafile
northwest        NW        Charles Main          3.0    .98    3    34
western          WE        Sharon Gray           5.3    .97    5    23
southwest        SW        Lewis Dalsass         2.7    .8     2    18
southern         SO        Suan Chin             5.1    .95    4    15
                  ------------------------------------
                  | ***SUAN HAS LEFT THE COMPANY*** |
                  |_____|
southeast        SE        Patricia Hemenway     4.0    .7     4    17
eastern          EA        TB Savage             4.4    .84    5    20
northeast        NE        AM Main Jr.           5.1    .94    3    13
north            NO        Margot Weber          4.5    .89    5    9
central          CT        Ann Stephens          5.7    .94    5    13
```

EXPLANATION

The r command reads specified lines from a file. The contents of newfile are read into the input file datafile, after the line where the pattern Suan is matched. If Suan had appeared on more than one line, the contents of newfile would have been read in under each occurrence.

5.9.7   Writing to Files: The w Command

The w command is the *write* command. It allows sed to write lines from the current file ito another file.

EXAMPLE 5.25

```
% sed -n '/north/w newfile' datafile
cat newfile
northwest        NW        Charles Main          3.0    .98    3    34
northeast        NE        AM Main Jr.           5.1    .94    3    13
north            NO        Margot Weber          4.5    .89    5    9
```

EXPLANATION

The w command writes specified lines to a file. All lines containing the pattern north are written to a file called newfile.

5.9.8   Appending: The a Command

The a command is the *append* command. Appending causes new text to be placed *below* the current line in the file; that is, the line that was just read into the pattern buffer. Whether at the command line or in a sed script, the a command is followed by a backslash. If you are at the C/TC command line, two backslashes are required as shown in Example 5.26—one backslash is for sed's append command, and one is for line continuation. With C/TC the opening quote that starts the sed command must be terminated on the same line. The second backslash makes it possible to continue typing on the next line without an "Unmatched quote" error. (The Bourne and Bash shells do not require the second backslash because closing quotes do not have to be matched on the same line.) The line of text that will be appended is placed after the sed command on its own line. If additional lines are to be appended, each line must be terminated with a backslash, except the final line, which ends with the closing quote and filename. That line will not be terminated with a backslash.

% **cat datafile**							
northwest	NW	Charles Main	3.0	.98	3	34
western	WE	Sharon Gray	5.3	.97	5	23
southwest	SW	Lewis Dalsass	2.7	.8	2	18
southern	SO	Suan Chin	5.1	.95	4	15
southeast	SE	Patricia Hemenway	4.0	.7	4	17
eastern	EA	TB Savage	4.4	.84	5	20
northeast	NE	AM Main Jr.	5.1	.94	3	13
north	NO	Margot Weber	4.5	.89	5	9
central	CT	Ann Stephens	5.7	.94	5	13

EXAMPLE 5.26

```
% sed '/^north /a\\        # Use two backslashes only if the shell is C/TC
--->THE NORTH SALES DISTRICT HAS MOVED<---' datafile
northwest          NW       Charles Main         3.0   .98    3    34
western            WE       Sharon Gray          5.3   .97    5    23
southwest          SW       Lewis Dalsass        2.7   .8     2    18
southern           SO       Suan Chin            5.1   .95    4    15
southeast          SE       Patricia Hemenway    4.0   .7     4    17
eastern            EA       TB Savage            4.4   .84    5    20
northeast          NE       AM Main Jr.          5.1   .94    3    13
north              NO       Margot Weber         4.5   .89    5    9
--->THE NORTH SALES DISTRICT HAS MOVED<---
central            CT       Ann Stephens         5.7   .94    5    13
```

EXPLANATION

The a command is the append command. The string --->THE NORTH SALES DISTRICT HAS MOVED<--- is appended after lines beginning with the pattern north, when north is followed by a space. The text that will be appended must be on the line following the append command.

Sed requires a backslash after the a command. The second backslash is used by the C shell to escape the newline so that its closing quote can be on the next line.[a] If more than one line is appended, each line, except the last one, must also end with a backslash.

a.   The Bourne and Korn shells do not require the second backslash to escape the newline because they do not require quotes to be matched on the same line, only that they match.

5.9.9   Inserting: The i Command

The i command is the *insert* command. It is like the a command, but instead of placing text below the current line, it inserts new text *above* the current line in the file; that is, the line that was just read into the pattern buffer. Whether at the command line or in a sed script, the i command is followed by a backslash.

EXAMPLE 5.27

```
% sed '/eastern/i\\       # Use two backslashes for C/TC
NEW ENGLAND REGION\\

-----------------------------' datafile
northwest         NW      Charles Main        3.0   .98   3   34
western           WE      Sharon Gray         5.3   .97   5   23
southwest         SW      Lewis Dalsass       2.7   .8    2   18
southern          SO      Suan Chin           5.1   .95   4   15
southeast         SE      Patricia Hemenway   4.0   .7    4   17
NEW ENGLAND REGION

-----------------------------
eastern           EA      TB Savage           4.4   .84   5   20
northeast         NE      AM Main Jr.         5.1   .94   3   13
north             NO      Margot Weber        4.5   .89   5   9
central           CT      Ann Stephens        5.7   .94   5   13
```

EXPLANATION

The i command is the insert command. If the pattern eastern is matched, the i command causes the text following the backslash to be inserted above the line containing eastern. A backslash is required after each line to be inserted, except the last one. (The extra backslash is for the C shell.)

5.9.10 Changing: The c Command

The c command is the *change* command. It allows sed to modify or change existing text with new text. The old text is overwritten with the new.

% cat datafile

northwest	NW	Charles Main	3.0	.98	3	34
western	WE	Sharon Gray	5.3	.97	5	23
southwest	SW	Lewis Dalsass	2.7	.8	2	18
southern	SO	Suan Chin	5.1	.95	4	15
southeast	SE	Patricia Hemenway	4.0	.7	4	17
eastern	EA	TB Savage	4.4	.84	5	20
northeast	NE	AM Main Jr.	5.1	.94	3	13
north	NO	Margot Weber	4.5	.89	5	9
central	CT	Ann Stephens	5.7	.94	5	13

EXAMPLE 5.28

```
% sed '/eastern/c\\
    THE EASTERN REGION HAS BEEN TEMPORARILY CLOSED' datafile
northwest        NW      Charles Main        3.0     .98     3       34
western          WE      Sharon Gray         5.3     .97     5       23
southwest        SW      Lewis Dalsass       2.7     .8      2       18
southern         SO      Suan Chin           5.1     .95     4       15
southeast        SE      Patricia Hemenway   4.0     .7      4       17
    THE EASTERN REGION HAS BEEN TEMPORARILY CLOSED
northeast        NE      AM Main Jr.         5.1     .94     3       13
north            NO      Margot Weber        4.5     .89     5       9
central          CT      Ann Stephens        5.7     .94     5       13
```

EXPLANATION

The c command is the change command. It completely changes or modifies the current line in the pattern buffer. If the pattern eastern is matched, the c command causes the text following the backslash to replace the line containing eastern. A backslash is required after each line to be inserted, except the last one. (The extra backslash is for the C shell.)

5.9.11 Next: The n Command

The n command is the *next* command. It causes sed to get the next line from the input file, and read it into the pattern buffer. Any sed commands will be applied to the line immediately following the line that is being addressed.

EXAMPLE 5.29

```
% sed '/eastern/{ n; s/AM/Archie/; }' datafile
northwest    NW    Charles Main         3.0   .98   3   34
western      WE    Sharon Gray          5.3   .97   5   23
southwest    SW    Lewis Dalsass        2.7   .8    2   18
southern     SO    Suan Chin            5.1   .95   4   15
southeast    SE    Patricia Hemenway    4.0   .7    4   17
eastern      EA    TB Savage            4.4   .84   5   20
```
➤
```
northeast    NE    Archie Main Jr.      5.1   .94   3   13
north        NO    Margot Weber         4.5   .89   5   9
central      CT    Ann Stephens         5.7   .94   5   13
```

EXPLANATION

If the pattern eastern is matched on a line, the n command causes sed to get the next line of input (the line with AM Main Jr.), replace the pattern space with this line, substitute AM with Archie, print the line, and continue.

5.9.12   Transform: The y Command

The y command is the *transform* command. It is similar to the UNIX/Linux tr command. Characters are translated on a one-to-one, corresponding basis from those on the lefthand side to those on the right-hand side. For example, in the command y/abc/ABC/ any lowercase letter a will be transformed to an uppercase A, as will b to B, and c to C.

EXAMPLE 5.30

```
% sed '1,3y/abcdefghijklmnopqrstuvwxyz/ABCDEFGHIJKL
  MNOPQRSTUVWXYZ/'  datafile
```
➤
```
NORTHWEST    NW    CHARLES MAIN         3.0   .98   3   34
WESTERN      WE    SHARON GRAY          5.3   .97   5   23
```
➤
```
SOUTHWEST    SW    LEWIS DALSASS        2.7   .8    2   18
southern     SO    Suan Chin            5.1   .95   4   15
southeast    SE    Patricia Hemenway    4.0   .7    4   17
eastern      EA    TB Savage            4.4   .84   5   20
northeast    NE    AM Main Jr.          5.1   .94   3   13
north        NO    Margot Weber         4.5   .89   5   9
central      CT    Ann Stephens         5.7   .94   5   13
```

EXPLANATION

For lines 1 through 3, the y command translates all lowercase letters to uppercase letters. Regular expression metacharacters do not work with this command, and like the substitution delimiter, the forward slash can be changed to a different character.

5.9.13 Quit: The q Command

The q command is the *quit* command. It causes the sed program to exit without further processing.

% **cat datafile**						
northwest	NW	Charles Main	3.0	.98	3	34
western	WE	Sharon Gray	5.3	.97	5	23
southwest	SW	Lewis Dalsass	2.7	.8	2	18
southern	SO	Suan Chin	5.1	.95	4	15
southeast	SE	Patricia Hemenway	4.0	.7	4	17
eastern	EA	TB Savage	4.4	.84	5	20
northeast	NE	AM Main Jr.	5.1	.94	3	13
north	NO	Margot Weber	4.5	.89	5	9
central	CT	Ann Stephens	5.7	.94	5	13

EXAMPLE 5.31

% **sed '5q' datafile**						
northwest	NW	Charles Main	3.0	.98	3	34
western	WE	Sharon Gray	5.3	.97	5	23
southwest	SW	Lewis Dalsass	2.7	.8	2	18
southern	SO	Suan Chin	5.1	.95	4	15
southeast	SE	Patricia Hemenway	4.0	.7	4	17

EXPLANATION

After line 5 is printed, the q command causes the sed program to quit.

EXAMPLE 5.32

% **sed '/Lewis/{ s/Lewis/Joseph/;q; }' datafile**						
northwest	NW	Charles Main	3.0	.98	3	34
western	WE	Sharon Gray	5.3	.97	5	23
southwest	SW	Joseph Dalsass	2.7	.8	2	18

EXPLANATION

When the pattern Lewis is matched on a line, first the substitution command (s) replaces Lewis with Joseph, and then the q command causes the sed program to quit.

5.9.14 Holding and Getting: The h and g Commands

The h command is for *holding*; the g command is for *getting*. When a line is read in from a file, sed places it in the pattern buffer and executes commands on that line. There is an additional buffer called the holding buffer. (Both buffers can hold up to 8,192 bytes.) A line can be sent from the pattern buffer to a holding buffer with the h command, later to be retrieved with the g or G (get) command.

% cat datafile

northwest	NW	Charles Main	3.0	.98	3	34
western	WE	Sharon Gray	5.3	.97	5	23
southwest	SW	Lewis Dalsass	2.7	.8	2	18
southern	SO	Suan Chin	5.1	.95	4	15
southeast	SE	Patricia Hemenway	4.0	.7	4	17
eastern	EA	TB Savage	4.4	.84	5	20
northeast	NE	AM Main Jr.	5.1	.94	3	13
north	NO	Margot Weber	4.5	.89	5	9
central	CT	Ann Stephens	5.7	.94	5	13

EXAMPLE 5.33

```
% sed -e '/northeast/h'  -e '$G'  datafile
northwest      NW    Charles Main        3.0    .98    3    34
western        WE    Sharon Gray         5.3    .97    5    23
southwest      SW    Lewis Dalsass       2.7    .8     2    18
southern       SO    Suan Chin           5.1    .95    4    15
southeast      SE    Patricia Hemenway   4.0    .7     4    17
eastern        EA    TB Savage           4.4    .84    5    20
➤ northeast    NE    AM Main Jr.         5.1    .94    3    13
north          NO    Margot Weber        4.5    .89    5    9
central        CT    Ann Stephens        5.7    .94    5    13
➤ northeast    NE    AM Main Jr.         5.1    .94    3    13
```

EXPLANATION

As sed processes the file, each line is stored in a temporary buffer called the pattern space. Unless the line is deleted or suppressed from printing, the line will be printed to the screen after it is processed. The pattern space is then cleared and the next line of input is stored there for processing. In this example, after the line containing the pattern northeast is found, it is placed in the pattern space and the h command copies it and places it into another special buffer called the holding buffer. In the second sed instruction, when the last line is reached ($) the G command tells sed to get the line from the holding buffer and put it back in the pattern space buffer, appending it to the line that is currently stored there, in this case, the last line. Simply stated: Any line containing the pattern northeast will be copied and appended to the end of the file.

EXAMPLE 5.34

```
% sed -e '/WE/{h; d; }' -e '/CT/{G; }' datafile
```

northwest	NW	Charles Main	3.0	.98	3	34
southwest	SW	Lewis Dalsass	2.7	.8	2	18
southern	SO	Suan Chin	5.1	.95	4	15
southeast	SE	Patricia Hemenway	4.0	.7	4	17
eastern	EA	TB Savage	4.4	.84	5	20
northeast	NE	AM Main Jr.	5.1	.94	3	13
north	NO	Margot Weber	4.5	.89	5	9
central	CT	Ann Stephens	5.7	.94	5	13
➤ western	WE	Sharon Gray	5.3	.97	5	23

EXPLANATION

If the pattern WE is found on a line, the h command causes the line to be copied from the pattern space into a holding buffer, from which the line can be retrieved (G or g command) at a later time. In this example, the line where the pattern WE is found is stored in the pattern buffer first. The h command then puts a copy of the line in the holding buffer. The d command deletes the copy in the pattern buffer, so that it will not be displayed. The second command searches for CT in a line, and when it is found, sed gets (G) the line that was stored in the holding buffer and appends it to the line currently in the pattern space. Simply stated: The line containing WE is moved after the line containing CT. See also "Holding and Exchanging: The h and x Commands" on page 151.

EXAMPLE 5.35

```
% sed -e '/northeast/h'  -e '$g'  datafile
```

northwest	NW	Charles Main	3.0	.98	3	34
western	WE	Sharon Gray	5.3	.97	5	23
southwest	SW	Lewis Dalsass	2.7	.8	2	18
southern	SO	Suan Chin	5.1	.95	4	15
southeast	SE	Patricia Hemenway	4.0	.7	4	17
eastern	EA	TB Savage	4.4	.84	5	20
➤ northeast	NE	AM Main Jr.	5.1	.94	3	13
north	NO	Margot Weber	4.5	.89	5	9
➤ northeast	NE	AM Main Jr.	5.1	.94	3	13

EXPLANATION

As sed processes the file, each line is stored in a temporary buffer called the pattern space. Unless the line is deleted or suppressed from printing, the line will be printed to the screen after it is processed. The pattern space is then cleared and the next line of input is stored there for processing. In this example, after the line containing the pattern northeast is found, it is placed in the pattern space. The h command takes a copy of it and places it in another special buffer called the holding buffer. In the second sed instruction, when the last line is reached ($), the g command tells sed to get the line from the holding buffer and put it back in the pattern space buffer, replacing the line that is currently stored there, in this case, the last line. Simply stated: The line containing the pattern northeast is copied and moved to overwrite the last line in the file.

```
% cat datafile
northwest       NW      Charles Main            3.0     .98     3       34
western         WE      Sharon Gray             5.3     .97     5       23
southwest       SW      Lewis Dalsass           2.7     .8      2       18
southern        SO      Suan Chin               5.1     .95     4       15
southeast       SE      Patricia Hemenway       4.0     .7      4       17
eastern         EA      TB Savage               4.4     .84     5       20
northeast       NE      AM Main Jr.             5.1     .94     3       13
north           NO      Margot Weber            4.5     .89     5       9
central         CT      Ann Stephens            5.7     .94     5       13
```

EXAMPLE 5.36

```
% sed -e '/WE/{h; d; }' -e '/CT/{g; }' datafile
northwest       NW      Charles Main            3.0     .98     3       34
southwest       SW      Lewis Dalsass           2.7     .8      2       18
southern        SO      Suan Chin               5.1     .95     4       15
southeast       SE      Patricia Hemenway       4.0     .7      4       17
eastern         EA      TB Savage               4.4     .84     5       20
northeast       NE      AM Main Jr.             5.1     .94     3       13
north           NO      Margot Weber            4.5     .89     5       9
western         WE      Sharon Gray             5.3     .97     5       23
```

EXPLANATION

If the pattern WE is found, the h command copies the line into the holding buffer; the d command deletes the line in the pattern space. When the pattern CT is found, the g command gets the copy in the holding buffer and overwrites the line currently in the pattern space. Simply stated: Any line containing the pattern WE will be moved to overwrite lines containing CT. (See Figure 5.1.)

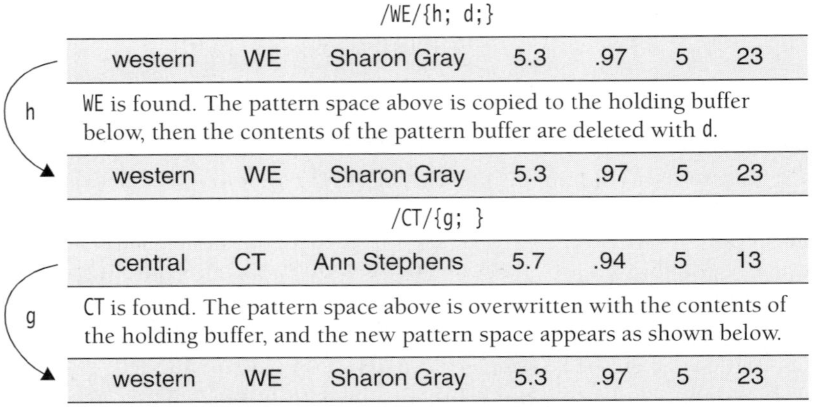

Figure 5.1   The pattern space and holding buffer. See Example 5.36.

5.9.15   Holding and Exchanging: The h and x Commands

The x command is the *exchange* command. It lets sed exchange the pattern in the holding buffer with what is currently in the pattern buffer.

```
% sed -e '/Patricia/h'  -e '/Margot/x' datafile
northwest       NW       Charles Main           3.0   .98   3    34
western         WE       Sharon Gray            5.3   .97   5    23
southwest       SW       Lewis Dalsass          2.7   .8    2    18
southern        SO       Suan Chin              5.1   .95   4    15
southeast       SE       Patricia Hemenway      4.0   .7    4    17
eastern         EA       TB Savage              4.4   .84   5    20
northeast       NE       AM Main Jr.            5.1   .94   3    13
southeast       SE       Patricia Hemenway      4.0   .7    4    17
central         CT       Ann Stephens           5.7   .94   5    13
```

The x command exchanges (swaps) the contents of the holding buffer with the current pattern space. When the line containing the pattern Patricia is found, it will be stored in the holding buffer. When the line containing Margot is found, the pattern space will be exchanged for the line in the holding buffer. Simply stated: The line containing Margot will be replaced with the line containing Patricia.

5.10 sed **Scripting**

A sed script is a list of sed commands in a file. To let sed know your commands are in a file, when invoking sed at the command line, use the -f option followed by the name of the sed script. Sed is very particular about the way you type lines into the script. There cannot be any trailing whitespace or text at the end of the command. If commands are not placed on a line by themselves, they must be terminated with a semicolon. A line from the input file is copied into the pattern buffer, and all commands in the sed script are executed on that line. After the line has been processed, the next line from the input file is placed in the pattern buffer, and all commands in the script are executed on that line. Sed gets "garbled" if your syntax is incorrect.

The nice thing about sed scripts is that you don't have to worry about the shell's interaction as you do when at the command line. Quotes are not needed to protect sed commands from interpretation by the shell and only one backslash is used in line continuation. In fact, you cannot use quotes in a sed script at all, unless they are part of a search pattern.

The examples in this section use the following datafile.

```
% cat datafile
northwest      NW      Charles Main        3.0   .98   3    34
western        WE      Sharon Gray         5.3   .97   5    23
southwest      SW      Lewis Dalsass       2.7   .8    2    18
southern       SO      Suan Chin           5.1   .95   4    15
southeast      SE      Patricia Hemenway   4.0   .7    4    17
eastern        EA      TB Savage           4.4   .84   5    20
northeast      NE      AM Main Jr.         5.1   .94   3    13
north          NO      Margot Weber        4.5   .89   5     9
central        CT      Ann Stephens        5.7   .94   5    13
```

5.10.1   sed Script Examples

EXAMPLE 5.38

```
% cat sedding1                   # Look at the contents of the sed script
1   # My first sed script by Jack Sprat
2   /Lewis/a\
3       Lewis is the TOP Salesperson for April!!\
        Lewis is moving to the southern district next month.\
4       CONGRATULATIONS!
5   /Margot/c\
        ******************\
        MARGOT HAS RETIRED\
        ******************
6   1i\
    EMPLOYEE DATABASE\
    --------------------
7   $d

% sed -f sedding1 datafile     # Execute the sed script commands; input file is datafile
EMPLOYEE DATABASE
--------------------
northwest        NW      Charles Main      3.0   .98   3    34
western          WE      Sharon Gray       5.3   .97   5    23
southwest        SW      Lewis Dalsass     2.7   .8    2    18
Lewis is the TOP Salesperson for April!!
Lewis is moving to the southern district next month.
CONGRATULATIONS!
```

EXAMPLE 5.38 (CONTINUED)

```
southern        SO    Suan Chin         5.1   .95   4   15
southeast       SE    Patricia Hemenway 4.0   .7    4   17
eastern         EA    TB Savage         4.4   .84   5   20
northeast       NE    AM Main Jr.       5.1   .94   3   13


*********************
MARGOT HAS RETIRED
*****************
```

EXPLANATION

1   This line is a comment. Comments must be on lines by themselves and start with a pound sign (#).

2   If a line contains the pattern Lewis, the next three lines are appended to that line.

3   Each line being appended, except the last one, is terminated with a backslash. The backslash must be followed immediately with a newline. If there is any trailing text, even one space after the newline, sed will complain.

4   The last line to be appended does not have the terminating backslash. This indicates to sed that this is the last line to be appended and that the next line is another command.

5   Any lines containing the pattern Margot will be replaced (c command) with the next three lines of text.

6   The next two lines will be inserted (i command) above line 1.

7   The last line ($) will be deleted.

EXAMPLE 5.39

```
% cat sedding2              # Look at the contents of the sed script
# This script demonstrates the use of curly braces to nest addresses
# and commands. Comments are preceded by a pound sign (#) and must
# be on a line by themselves. Commands are terminated with a newline
# or semicolon.  If there is any text after a command, even one
# space, you receive an error message:
#      sed: Extra text at end of command:

1   /western/, /southeast/{
        /^ *$/d
        /Suan/{ h; d; }
    }
2   /Ann/g
3   s/TB \(Savage\)/Thomas \1/
```

EXAMPLE   5.39 (CONTINUED)

```
4 % sed -f sedding2 datafile
northwest       NW      Charles Main          3.0   .98   3    34
western         WE      Sharon Gray           5.3   .97   5    23
southwest       SW      Lewis Dalsass         2.7   .8    2    18
southeast       SE      Patricia Hemenway     4.0   .7    4    17
eastern         EA      Thomas Savage         4.4   .84   5    20
northeast       NE      AM Main Jr.           5.1   .94   3    13
north           NO      Margot Weber          4.5   .89   5     9
southern        SO      Suan Chin             5.1   .95   4    15
```

EXPLANATION

1   In the range of lines starting at western and ending at southeast, blank lines are de-
    leted, and lines matching Suan are copied from the pattern buffer into the holding
    buffer, then deleted from the pattern buffer.

2   When the pattern Ann is matched, the g command copies the line in the holding
    buffer to the pattern buffer, overwriting what is in the pattern buffer.

3   All lines containing the pattern TB Savage are replaced with Thomas and the pattern
    that was tagged, Savage. In the search string, Savage is enclosed in escaped paren-
    theses, tagging the enclosed string so that it can be used again. It is tag number 1,
    referenced by \1.

4   Sed will get its commands from the file following the –f option, sedding2. The file
    that sed is editing is datafile.

5.10.2   sed Review

Table 5.4 lists sed commands and what they do.

Table 5.4   sed Review

Command	*What It Does*
sed -n '/sentimental/p' filex	Prints to the screen all lines containing sentimental. The file filex does not change. Without the -n option, all lines with sentimental will be printed twice.
sed '1,3d' filex > newfilex	Deletes lines 1, 2, and 3 from filex and saves changes in newfilex.
sed '/[Dd]aniel/d' filex	Deletes lines containing Daniel or daniel.
sed -n '15,20p' filex	Prints only lines 15 through 20.
sed '1,10s/Montana/MT/g' filex	Substitutes Montana with MT globally in lines 1 through 10.
sed '/March/\!d' filex (csh) sed '/March/!d' filex (sh)	Deletes all lines not containing March. (The backslash is used only in the csh to escape the history character.)

Table 5.4   sed Review (continued)

Command	What It Does
`sed '/report/s/5/8/' filex`	Changes the first occurrence of 5 to 8 on all lines containing report.
`sed 's/....//' filex`	Deletes the first four characters of each line.
`sed 's/...$//' filex`	Deletes the last three characters of each line.
`sed '/east/,/west/s/North/South/' filex`	For any lines falling in the range from east to west, substitutes North with South.
`sed -n '/Time off/w timefile' filex`	Writes all lines containing Time off to the file timefile.
`sed 's/\([Oo]ccur\)ence/\1rence/' file`	Substitutes either Occurence or occurence with Occurrence or occurrence.
`sed -n 'l' filex`	Prints all lines showing nonprinting characters as \nn, where nn is the octal value of the character, and showing tabs as >.

LAB 2: sed EXERCISE

(Refer to the file called datebook on the CD.)

Steve Blenheim:238-923-7366:95 Latham Lane, Easton, PA 83755:11/12/56:20300
Betty Boop:245-836-8357:635 Cutesy Lane, Hollywood, CA 91464:6/23/23:14500
Igor Chevsky:385-375-8395:3567 Populus Place, Caldwell, NJ 23875:6/18/68:23400
Norma Corder:397-857-2735:74 Pine Street, Dearborn, MI 23874:3/28/45:245700
Jennifer Cowan:548-834-2348:583 Laurel Ave., Kingsville, TX 83745:10/1/35:58900
Jon DeLoach:408-253-3122:123 Park St., San Jose, CA 04086:7/25/53:85100
Karen Evich:284-758-2857:23 Edgecliff Place, Lincoln, NB 92743:7/25/53:85100
Karen Evich:284-758-2867:23 Edgecliff Place, Lincoln, NB 92743:11/3/35:58200
Karen Evich:284-758-2867:23 Edgecliff Place, Lincoln, NB 92743:11/3/35:58200
Fred Fardbarkle:674-843-1385:20 Parak Lane, Duluth, MN 23850:4/12/23:780900
Fred Fardbarkle:674-843-1385:20 Parak Lane, Duluth, MN 23850:4/12/23:780900
Lori Gortz:327-832-5728:3465 Mirlo Street, Peabody, MA 34756:10/2/65:35200
Paco Gutierrez:835-365-1284:454 Easy Street, Decatur, IL 75732:2/28/53:123500
Ephram Hardy:293-259-5395:235 CarltonLane, Joliet, IL 73858:8/12/20:56700
James Ikeda:834-938-8376:23445 Aster Ave., Allentown, NJ 83745:12/1/38:45000
Barbara Kertz:385-573-8326:832 Ponce Drive, Gary, IN 83756:12/1/46:268500
Lesley Kirstin:408-456-1234:4 Harvard Square, Boston, MA 02133:4/22/62:52600
William Kopf:846-836-2837:6937 Ware Road, Milton, PA 93756:9/21/46:43500
Sir Lancelot:837-835-8257:474 Camelot Boulevard, Bath, WY 28356:5/13/69:24500
Jesse Neal:408-233-8971:45 Rose Terrace, San Francisco, CA 92303:2/3/36:25000
Zippy Pinhead:834-823-8319:2356 Bizarro Ave., Farmount, IL 84357:1/1/67:89500
Arthur Putie:923-835-8745:23 Wimp Lane, Kensington, DL 38758:8/31/69:126000
Popeye Sailor:156-454-3322:945 Bluto Street, Anywhere, USA 29358:3/19/35:22350
Jose Santiago:385-898-8357:38 Fife Way, Abilene, TX 39673:1/5/58:95600

Tommy Savage:408-724-0140:1222 Oxbow Court, Sunnyvale, CA 94087:5/19/66:34200
Yukio Takeshida:387-827-1095:13 Uno Lane, Ashville, NC 23556:7/1/29:57000
Vinh Tranh:438-910-7449:8235 Maple Street, Wilmington, VM 29085:9/23/63:68900

1. Change the name Jon to Jonathan.

2. Delete the first three lines.

3. Print lines 5 through 10.

4. Delete lines containing Lane.

5. Print all lines where the birthdays are in November or December.

6. Append three asterisks to the end of lines starting with Fred.

7. Replace the line containing Jose with JOSE HAS RETIRED.

8. Change Popeye's birthday to 11/14/46. Assume you don't know Popeye's original birthday. Use a regular expression to search for it.

9. Delete all blank lines.

10. Write a sed script that will

    a. Insert above the first line the title PERSONNEL FILE.

    b. Remove the salaries ending in 500.

    c. Print the contents of the file with the last names and first names reversed.

    d. Append at the end of the file THE END.

chapter

6

The awk **Utility**

6.1 What's awk? What's nawk? What's gawk?

Awk is a UNIX programming language used for manipulating data and generating reports. Nawk is a newer version of awk, and gawk is the GNU version used on Linux.

The data may come from standard input, one or more files, or as output from a process. Awk can be used at the command line for simple operations, or it can be written into programs for larger applications. Because awk can manipulate data, it is an indispensable tool used in shell scripts and for managing small databases.

Awk scans a file (or input) line by line, from the first to the last line, searching for lines that match a specified pattern and performing selected actions (enclosed in curly braces) on those lines. If there is a pattern with no specific action, all lines that match the pattern are displayed; if there is an action with no pattern, all input lines specified by the action are executed upon.

6.1.1 What Does awk Stand For?

Awk stands for the first initials in the last names of each of the authors of the language, Alfred Aho, Brian Kernighan, and Peter Weinberger. They could have called it wak or kaw, but for whatever reason, awk won out.

6.1.2 Which awk?

There are a number of versions of awk: old awk, new awk, GNU awk (gawk), POSIX awk, and others. Awk was originally written in 1977, and in 1985, the original implementation was improved so that awk could handle larger programs. Additional features included user-defined functions, dynamic regular expressions, processing multiple input files, and more. On most systems, the command is awk if using the old version, nawk if using the new version, and gawk if using the GNU version.[1]

---

1. On SCO UNIX, the new version is spelled awk, and on Linux, the GNU version is spelled gawk. This text pertains primarily to the new awk, nawk. The GNU implementation, gawk, is fully upward-compatible with nawk.

6.2   awk's Format

An awk program consists of the awk command, the program instructions enclosed in quotes (or in a file), and the name of the input file. If an input file is not specified, input comes from standard input (stdin), the keyboard.

Awk instructions consist of patterns, actions, or a combination of patterns and actions. A pattern is a statement consisting of an expression of some type. If you do not see the keyword if, but you *think* the word if when evaluating the expression, it is a pattern. Actions consist of one or more statements separated by semicolons or newlines and enclosed in curly braces. Patterns cannot be enclosed in curly braces, and consist of regular expressions enclosed in forward slashes or expressions consisting of one or more of the many operators provided by awk.

Awk commands can be typed at the command line or in awk script files. The input lines can come from files, pipes, or standard input.

6.2.1   Input from Files

In the following examples, the percent sign is a shell prompt. **Please take note:** In all examples where the command is nawk, use either awk or gawk if you are on an HP-UX flavor system or using Linux.

FORMAT

```
% nawk 'pattern' filename
% nawk '{action}' filename
% nawk 'pattern {action}' filename
```

Here is a sample file called employees:

EXAMPLE 6.1

```
% cat employees
Tom Jones        4424     5/12/66           543354
Mary Adams       5346     11/4/63           28765
Sally Chang      1654     7/22/54           650000
Billy Black      1683     9/23/44           336500

% nawk '/Mary/'  employees
Mary Adams       5346     11/4/63           28765
```

EXPLANATION

Nawk prints all lines that contain the pattern Mary.

EXAMPLE 6.2

```
% cat employees
Tom Jones       4424    5/12/66         543354
Mary Adams      5346    11/4/63         28765
Sally Chang     1654    7/22/54         650000
Billy Black     1683    9/23/44         336500

% nawk '{print $1}' employees
Tom
Mary
Sally
Billy
```

EXPLANATION

Nawk prints the first field of file employees, where the field starts at the left margin of the line and is delimited by whitespace.

EXAMPLE 6.3

```
% cat employees
Tom Jones       4424    5/12/66         543354
Mary Adams      5346    11/4/63         28765
Sally Chang     1654    7/22/54         650000
Billy Black     1683    9/23/44         336500

% nawk '/Sally/{print $1, $2}' employees
Sally Chang
```

EXPLANATION

Nawk prints the first and second fields of file employees, only if the line contains the pattern Sally. Remember, the field separator is whitespace.

6.2.2 Input from Commands

The output from a UNIX/Linux command or commands can be piped to awk for processing. Shell programs commonly use awk for manipulating commands.

FORMAT

```
% command | nawk 'pattern'
% command | nawk '{action}'
% command | nawk 'pattern {action}'
```

```
1   % df | nawk '$4 > 75000'
    /oracle   (/dev/dsk/c0t0d057 ):390780 blocks      105756 files
    /opt      (/dev/dsk/c0t0d058 ):1943994 blocks      49187 files

2   % rusers  | nawk '/root$/{print  $1}'
    owl
    crow
    bluebird
```

EXPLANATION

1   The df command reports the free disk space on file systems. The output of the df
     command is piped to nawk. If the fourth field is greater than 75,000 blocks, the line
     is printed.

2   The rusers command prints those logged on remote machines on the network.
     The output of the rusers command is piped to nawk as input. The first field is print-
     ed if the regular expression root is matched at the end of the line ($); that is, all
     machine names are printed where root is logged on.

6.3   How awk Works

Before getting into all the details of awk, let's look at how it does its job, step by step. We'll
look at a simple three-line file called names:

```
Tom Savage 100
Molly Lee 200
John Doe 300
```

The awk command follows:

```
% nawk '{print $1, $3}' names
```

1.   Awk takes a line of input (from a file or pipe) and puts the line into an internal
     variable called $0. Each line is also called a record and is terminated by a new-
     line, by default.

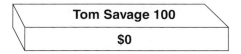

2.   Next, the line is broken into fields (words) separated by whitespace. Each field
     is stored in a numbered variable, starting with $1. There can be as many as 100
     fields.

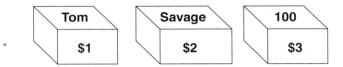

3. How does awk know that whitespace separates the fields? There is another internal variable, called FS, that designates the field separator. Initially, FS is assigned whitespace—tabs and spaces. If the fields are separated by another character, such as a colon or dash, you can change the value of FS to designate the new field separator. (See "Field Separators" on page 169.)

4. When awk prints the fields, it uses the print function as follows:

```
{print $1,$3}
```

And the output shows each field separated by a space, as

```
Tom 100
Molly 200
John 300
```

Awk provides the space in the output between Tom and 100 for you because there is a comma placed between $1 and $3. The comma is special. It is mapped to another internal variable, called the output field separator (OFS). The OFS is assigned a space as its default. The comma generates whatever character has been assigned to the OFS variable.

5. After awk displays its output, it gets the next line in the file and stores that in $0, overwriting what was there. It then breaks that line into fields, and processes it. This continues until all the lines in the file have been processed.

6.4 Formatting Output

6.4.1 The print Function

The action part of the awk command is enclosed in curly braces. If no action is specified and a pattern is matched, awk takes the default action, which is to print the lines that are matched to the screen. The print function is used to print simple output that does not require fancy formatting. For more sophisticated formatting, the printf or sprintf functions are used. If you are familiar with C, then you already know how printf and sprintf work.

The print function can also be explicitly used in the action part of awk as {print}. The print function accepts arguments as variables, computed values, or string constants. Strings must be enclosed in double quotes. Commas are used to separate the arguments; if commas are not provided, the arguments are concatenated together. The comma evaluates to the value of the OFS, which is by default a space.

The output of the print function can be redirected or piped to another program, and the output of another program can be piped to awk for printing. (See "Redirection" on page 25 and "Pipes" on page 28.)

EXAMPLE 6.5

```
% date
Wed Jul 28 22:23:16 PDT 2004

% date | nawk '{ print "Month: " $2 "\nYear: " , $6 }'
Month: Jul
Year: 2004
```

EXPLANATION

The output of the UNIX date command will be piped to nawk. The string Month: is printed, followed by the second field, the string containing the newline character (\n), and Year:, followed by the sixth field ($6).

Escape Sequences. Escape sequences are represented by a backslash and a letter or number. They can be used in strings to represent tabs, newlines, form feeds, and so forth (see Table 6.1).

Table 6.1   print Escape Sequences

Escape Sequence	Meaning
\b	Backspace
\f	Form feed
\n	Newline
\r	Carriage return
\t	Tab
\047	Octal value 47, a single quote
\c	c represents any other character, e.g., \

EXAMPLE 6.6

```
Tom Jones      4424    5/12/66    543354
Mary Adams     5346    11/4/63    28765
Sally Chang    1654    7/22/54    650000
Billy Black    1683  ' 9/23/44    336500

% nawk '/Sally/{print "\t\tHave a nice day, " $1, $2 "\!"}' employees
        Have a nice day, Sally Chang!
```

If the line contains the pattern Sally, the print function prints two tabs, the string Have a nice day, the first (where $1 is Sally) and second fields (where $2 is Chang), followed by a string containing an exclamation mark.

6.4.2 The OFMT Variable

When printing numbers, you may want to control the format of the number. Normally this would be done with the printf function, but the special awk variable, OFMT, can be set to control the printing of numbers when using the print function. It is set by default to %.6g—six significant digits to the right of the decimal are printed. (The following section describes how this value can be changed.)

```
% nawk 'BEGIN{OFMT="%.2f"; print 1.2456789, 12E-2}'
1.25  0.12
```

The OFMT variable is set so that floating-point numbers (f) will be printed with two numbers following the decimal point. The percent sign (%) indicates a format is being specified.

6.4.3 The printf Function

When printing output, you may want to specify the amount of space between fields so that columns line up neatly. Because the print function with tabs does not always guarantee the desired output, the printf function can be used for formatting fancy output.

The printf function returns a formatted string to standard output, like the printf statement in C. The printf statement consists of a quoted control string that may be embedded with format specifications and modifiers. The control string is followed by a comma and a list of comma-separated expressions that will be formatted according to the specifications stated in the control string. Unlike the print function, printf does not provide a newline. The escape sequence, \n, must be provided if a newline is desired.

For each percent sign and format specifier, there must be a corresponding argument. To print a literal percent sign, two percent signs must be used. See Table 6.2 for a list of printf conversion characters and Table 6.3 for printf modifiers. The format specifiers are preceded by a percent sign; see Table 6.4 for a list of printf format specifiers.

When an argument is printed, the place where the output is printed is called the *field*, and the *width* of the field is the number of characters contained in that field.

The pipe symbol (vertical bar) in the following examples, when part of the printf string, is part of the text and is used to indicate where the formatting begins and ends.

EXAMPLE 6.8

```
1   % echo "UNIX" | nawk ' {printf "|%-15s|\n", $1}'
    (Output)
    |UNIX           |

2   % echo "UNIX" | nawk '{ printf "|%15s|\n", $1}'
    (Output)
    |           UNIX|
```

EXPLANATION

1   The output of the echo command, UNIX, is piped to nawk. The printf function con-
     tains a control string. The percent sign alerts printf that it will be printing a 15-
     space, left-justified string enclosed in vertical bars and terminated with a newline.
     The dash after the percent sign indicates left justification. The control string is fol-
     lowed by a comma and $1. The string UNIX will be formatted according to the for-
     mat specification in the control string.

2   The string UNIX is printed in a right-justified, 15-space string, enclosed in vertical
     bars, and terminated with a newline.

EXAMPLE 6.9

```
% cat employees
Tom Jones       4424     5/12/66      543354
Mary Adams      5346     11/4/63      28765
Sally Chang     1654     7/22/54      650000
Billy Black     1683     9/23/44      336500

% nawk '{printf "The name is: %-15s ID is %8d\n", $1, $3}' employees
The name is Tom             ID is 4424
The name is Mary            ID is 5346
The name is Sally           ID is 1654
The name is Billy           ID is 1683
```

EXPLANATION

The string to be printed is enclosed in double quotes. The first format specifier is %-
15s. It has a corresponding argument, $1, positioned directly to the right of the comma
after the closing quote in the control string. The percent sign indicates a format specification: The dash means left justify, the 15s means 15-space string. At this spot, print
a left-justified, 15-space string followed by the string ID is and a number.

The %8d format specifies that the decimal (integer) value of $2 will be printed in its
place within the string. The number will be right justified and take up eight spaces.
Placing the quoted string and expressions within parentheses is optional.

Table 6.2 printf Conversion Characters

Conversion Character	Definition
c	Character
s	String
d	Decimal number
ld	Long decimal number
u	Unsigned decimal number
lu	Long unsigned decimal number
x	Hexadecimal number
lx	Long hexadecimal number
o	Octal number
lo	Long octal number
e	Floating-point number in scientific notation (*e*-notation)
f	Floating-point number
g	Floating-point number using either e or f conversion, whichever takes the least space

Table 6.3 printf Modifiers

Character	Definition
–	Left-justification modifier
#	Integers in octal format are displayed with a leading 0; integers in hexadecimal form are displayed with a leading 0*x*
+	For conversions using d, e, f, and g, integers are displayed with a numeric sign + or –
0	The displayed value is padded with zeros instead of whitespace

Table 6.4 printf Format Specifiers

Format Specifier	What It Does
Given x = 'A', y = 15, z = 2.3, and $1 = Bob Smith:	
%c	Prints a single ASCII character. printf("The character is %c.\n",x) prints: The character is A.
%d	Prints a decimal number. printf("The boy is %d years old.\n", y) prints: The boy is 15 years old.
%e	Prints the *e*-notation of a number. printf("z is %e.\n",z) prints: z is 2.3e+01.
%f	Prints a floating-point number. printf("z is %f.\n", 2.3 *2) prints: z is 4.600000.
%o	Prints the octal value of a number. printf("y is %o.\n", y) prints: z is 17.
%s	Prints a string of characters. printf("The name of the culprit is %s.\n", $1) prints: The name of the culprit is Bob Smith.
%x	Prints the hex value of a number. printf ("y is %x.\n", y) prints: x is f.

6.5   awk **Commands from Within a File**

If awk commands are placed in a file, the -f option is used with the name of the awk file, followed by the name of the input file to be processed. A record is read into awk's buffer and each of the commands in the awk file is tested and executed for that record. After awk has finished with the first record, it is discarded and the next record is read into the buffer, and so on. If an action is not controlled by a pattern, the default behavior is to print the entire record. If a pattern does not have an action associated with it, the default is to print the record where the pattern matches an input line.

EXAMPLE 6.10

```
(The Database)
    $1        $2        $3        $4          $5
    Tom       Jones     4424      5/12/66     543354
    Mary      Adams     5346      11/4/63     28765
    Sally     Chang     1654      7/22/54     650000
    Billy     Black     1683      9/23/44     336500


    % cat awkfile
1   /^Mary/{print "Hello Mary!"}
2   {print $1, $2, $3}

    % nawk -f awkfile employees
    Tom Jones 4424
    Hello Mary!
    Mary Adams 5346
    Sally Chang 1654
    Billy Black 1683
```

EXPLANATION

1   If the record begins with the regular expression Mary, the string Hello Mary! is print-
    ed. The action is controlled by the pattern preceding it. Fields are separated by
    whitespace.

2   The first, second, and third field of each record are printed. The action occurs for
    each line because there is not a pattern controlling the action.

6.6 Records and Fields

6.6.1 Records

Awk does not see input data as an endless string of characters, but sees it as having a format
or structure. By default, each line is called a *record* and is terminated with a newline.

The Record Separator.   By default, the output and input record separator (line separator) is a carriage return (newline), stored in the built-in awk variables ORS and RS,
respectively. The ORS and RS values can be changed, but only in a limited fashion.

The $0 Variable.   An entire record is referenced as $0 by awk. (When $0 is changed by
substitution or assignment, the value of NF, the number of fields, may be changed.) The
newline value is stored in awk's built-in variable RS, a carriage return by default.

EXAMPLE 6.11

```
% cat employees
Tom Jones       4424      5/12/66      543354
Mary Adams      5346      11/4/63      28765
Sally Chang     1654      7/22/54      650000
Billy Black     1683      9/23/44      336500

% nawk '{print $0}' employees
Tom Jones       4424      5/12/66      543354
Mary Adams      5346      11/4/63      28765
Sally Chang     1654      7/22/54      650000
Billy Black     1683      9/23/44      336500
```

EXPLANATION

The nawk variable $0 holds the current record. It is printed to the screen. By default, nawk would also print the record if the command were

```
% nawk '{print}' employees
```

The NR Variable.   The number of each record is stored in awk's built-in variable, NR. After a record has been processed, the value of NR is incremented by one.

EXAMPLE 6.12

```
% cat employees
Tom Jones       4424      5/12/66      543354
Mary Adams      5346      11/4/63      28765
Sally Chang     1654      7/22/54      650000
Billy Black     1683      9/23/44      336500

% nawk '{print NR, $0}' employees
1 Tom Jones     4424      5/12/66      543354
2 Mary Adams    5346      11/4/63      28765
3 Sally Chang   1654      7/22/54      650000
4 Billy Black   1683      9/23/44      336500
```

EXPLANATION

Each record, $0, is printed as it is stored in the file and is preceded with the number of the record, NR.

6.6.2 Fields

Each record consists of words called *fields* that, by default, are separated by whitespace (blank spaces or tabs). Each of these words is called a field, and awk keeps track of the number of fields in its built-in variable, NF. The value of NF can vary from line to line, and the limit is implementation-dependent, typically 100 fields per line. New fields can be created. The following example has four records (lines) and five fields (columns). Each record starts at the first field, represented as $1, then moves to the second field, $2, and so forth.

EXAMPLE 6.13

(Fields are represented by a dollar sign and the number of the field.)
(The Database)

```
$1         $2        $3       $4         $5
Tom        Jones     4424     5/12/66    543354
Mary       Adams     5346     11/4/63    28765
Sally      Chang     1654     7/22/54    650000
Billy      Black     1683     9/23/44    336500

% nawk '{print NR, $1, $2, $5}' employees
1 Tom Jones 543354
2 Mary Adams 28765
3 Sally Chang 650000
4 Billy Black 336500
```

EXPLANATION

Nawk will print the number of the record (NR), and the first, second, and fifth fields (columns) of each line in the file.

EXAMPLE 6.14

```
% nawk '{print $0, NF}' employees
Tom Jones      4444     5/12/66    543354     5
Mary Adams     5346     11/4/63    28765      5
Sally Chang    1654     7/22/54    650000     5
Billy Black    1683     9/23/44    336500     5
```

EXPLANATION

Nawk will print each record ($0) in the file, followed by the number of fields.

6.6.3 Field Separators

The Input Field Separator.   Awk's built-in variable, FS, holds the value of the input field separator. When the default value of FS is used, awk separates fields by spaces and/or tabs, stripping leading blanks and tabs. The value of FS can be changed by assigning a new value to it, either in a BEGIN statement or at the command line. For now, we will assign the new value at the command line. To change the value of FS at the command line, the -F option is used, followed by the character representing the new separator.

Changing the Field Separator at the Command Line. See Example 6.15 for a demonstration on how to change the input field separator at the command line using the -F option.

EXAMPLE 6.15

```
% cat employees
Tom Jones:4424:5/12/66:543354
Mary Adams:5346:11/4/63:28765
Sally Chang:1654:7/22/54:650000
Billy Black:1683:9/23/44:336500

% nawk -F: '/Tom Jones/{print $1, $2}'  employees2
Tom Jones   4424
```

EXPLANATION

The -F option is used to reassign the value of the input field separator at the command line. When a colon is placed directly after the -F option, nawk will look for colons to separate the fields in the employees file.

Using More Than One Field Separator. You may specify more than one input separator. If more than one character is used for the field separator, FS, then the string is a regular expression and is enclosed in square brackets. In the following example, the field separator is a space, colon, or tab. (The old version of awk did not support this feature.)

EXAMPLE 6.16

```
% nawk -F'[ :\t]'  '{print $1, $2, $3}' employees
Tom Jones 4424
Mary Adams 5346
Sally Chang 1654
Billy Black 1683
```

EXPLANATION

The -F option is followed by a regular expression enclosed in brackets. If a space, colon, or tab is encountered, nawk will use that character as a field separator. The expression is surrounded by quotes so that the shell will not pounce on the metacharacters for its own. (Remember that the shell uses brackets for filename expansion.)

The Output Field Separator. The default output field separator is a single space and is stored in awk's internal variable, OFS. In all of the examples thus far, we have used the print statement to send output to the screen. The comma that is used to separate fields in print statements evaluates to whatever the OFS has been set. If the default is used, the comma inserted between $1 and $2 will evaluate to a single space and the print function will print the fields with a space between them.

The fields are jammed together if a comma is not used to separate the fields. The OFS will not be evaluated unless the comma separates the fields. The OFS can be changed.

EXAMPLE 6.17

```
% cat employees2
Tom Jones:4424:5/12/66:543354
Mary Adams:5346:11/4/63:28765
Sally Chang:1654:7/22/54:650000
Billy Black:1683:9/23/44:336500

(The Command Line)
% nawk -F: '/Tom Jones/{print $1, $2, $3, $4}' employees2
Tom Jones   4424 5/12/66   543354
```

EXPLANATION

The output field separator, a space, is stored in nawk's OFS variable. The comma between the fields evaluates to whatever is stored in OFS. The fields are printed to standard output separated by a space.

EXAMPLE 6.18

```
% nawk -F: '/Tom Jones/{print $0}' employees2
Tom Jones:4424:5/12/66:543354
```

EXPLANATION

The $0 variable holds the current record exactly as it is found in the input file. The record will be printed as is.

6.7   Patterns and Actions

6.7.1   Patterns

Awk *patterns* control what actions awk will take on a line of input. A pattern consists of a regular expression, an expression resulting in a true or false condition, or a combination of these. The default action is to print each line where the expression results in a true condition. When reading a pattern expression, there is an implied if statement. When an if is implied, there can be no curly braces surrounding it. When the if is explicit, it becomes an action statement and the syntax is different. (See "Conditional Statements" on page 227.)

EXAMPLE 6.19

```
% cat employees
Tom Jones       4424     5/12/66      543354
Mary Adams      5346     11/4/63      28765
Sally Chang     1654     7/22/54      650000
Billy Black     1683     9/23/44      336500


(The Command Line)
1   nawk '/Tom/' employees
    Tom Jones       4424     5/12/66      543354

2   nawk '$3 < 4000' employees
    Sally Chang     1654     7/22/54      650000
    Billy Black     1683     9/23/44      336500
```

EXPLANATION

1   If the pattern Tom is matched in the input file, the record is printed. The default action is to print the line if no explicit action is specified. This is equivalent to
    `nawk '$0 ~ /Tom/{print $0}' employees`
2   If the third field is less than 4000, the record is printed.

6.7.2 Actions

Actions are statements enclosed within curly braces and separated by semicolons.[2] If a pattern precedes an action, the pattern dictates when the action will be performed. Actions can be simple statements or complex groups of statements. Statements are separated by semicolons, or by a newline if placed on their own line.

FORMAT

`{ action }`

EXAMPLE 6.20

`{ print $1, $2 }`

---

2. On some versions of awk, actions must be separated by semicolons or newlines, and the statements within the curly braces also must be separated by semicolons or newlines. SVR4's nawk requires the use of semicolons or newlines to separate statements within an action, but does not require the use of semicolons to separate actions; for example, the two actions that follow do not need a semicolon:
    `nawk '/Tom/{print "hi Tom"};{x=5}' file`

> ### EXPLANATION
>
> The action is to print fields 1 and 2.
>   Patterns can be associated with actions. Remember, actions are statements enclosed
> in curly braces. A pattern controls the action from the first open curly brace to the first
> closing curly brace. If an action follows a pattern, the first opening curly brace must
> be on the same line as the pattern. Patterns are *never* enclosed in curly braces.

> ### FORMAT
>
> ```
> pattern{ action statement; action statement; etc. }
>     or
> pattern{
>     action statement
>     action statement
> }
> ```

> ### EXAMPLE   6.21
>
> ```
> % nawk '/Tom/{print "Hello there, " $1}' employees
> Hello there, Tom
> ```

> ### EXPLANATION
>
> If the record contains the pattern Tom, the string Hello there, Tom will print.
>   A pattern with no action displays all lines matching the pattern. String-matching
> patterns contain regular expressions enclosed in forward slashes.

6.8   Regular Expressions

A *regular expression* to awk is a pattern that consists of characters enclosed in forward
slashes. Awk supports the use of regular expression metacharacters (same as egrep) to
modify the regular expression in some way. If a string in the input line is matched by the
regular expression, the resulting condition is true, and any actions associated with the
expression are executed. If no action is specified and an input line is matched by the regular expression, the record is printed. See Table 6.5.

> ### EXAMPLE   6.22
>
> ```
> % nawk '/Mary/' employees
> Mary Adams    5346    11/4/63    28765
> ```

> ### EXPLANATION
>
> All lines in the employees file containing the regular expression pattern Mary are
> displayed.

EXAMPLE 6.23

```
% nawk '/Mary/{print $1, $2}' employees
Mary Adams
```

EXPLANATION

The first and second fields of all lines in the employees file containing the regular expression pattern Mary are displayed.

Table 6.5 awk Regular Expression Metacharacters

Metacharacter	What It Does
^	Matches at the beginning of string
$	Matches at the end of string
.	Matches for a single character
*	Matches for zero or more of the preceding characters
+	Matches for one or more of the preceding characters
?	Matches for zero or one of the preceding characters
[ABC]	Matches for any one character in the set of characters A, B, or C
[^ABC]	Matches any one character not in the set of characters A, B, or C
[A-Z]	Matches for any one character in the range from A to Z
A|B	Matches either A or B
(AB)+	Matches one or more sets of AB; e.g., AB, ABAB, ABABAB
*	Matches for a literal asterisk
&	Used in the replacement string to represent what was found in the search string

The metacharacters listed in Table 6.6 are supported by most versions of grep and sed, but are not supported by any versions of awk.

Table 6.6 Metacharacters NOT supported

Metacharacter	Function
\< >/	Word anchors
\(\)	Backreferencing
\{ \}	Repetition

6.8.1 Matching on an Entire Line

A stand-alone regular expression matches for the pattern on an entire line and if no action is given, the entire line where the match occurred will be printed. The regular expression can be anchored to the beginning of the line with the ^ metacharacter.

EXAMPLE 6.24

```
% nawk '/^Mary/' employees
Mary Adams     5346     11/4/63     28765
```

EXPLANATION

All lines in the employees file that start with the regular expression Mary are displayed.

EXAMPLE 6.25

```
% nawk '/^[A-Z][a-z]+ /' employees
Tom Jones      4424     5/12/66     543354
Mary Adams     5346     11/4/63     28765
Sally Chang    1654     7/22/54     650000
Billy Black    1683     9/23/44     336500
```

EXPLANATION

All lines in the employees file beginning with an uppercase letter, followed by one or more lowercase letters, followed by a space, are displayed.

6.8.2 The match Operator

The match operator, the tilde (~), is used to match an expression within a record or field.

EXAMPLE 6.26

```
% cat employees
Tom Jones      4424     5/12/66     543354
Mary Adams     5346     11/4/63     28765
Sally Chang    1654     7/22/54     650000
Billy Black    1683     9/23/44     336500

% nawk '$1 ~ /[Bb]ill/' employees
Billy Black    1683     9/23/44     336500
```

EXPLANATION

Any lines matching Bill or bill in the first field are displayed.

EXAMPLE 6.27

```
% nawk '$1 !~ /ly$/' employees
Tom Jones      4424     5/12/66     543354
Mary Adams     5346     11/4/63     28765
```

EXPLANATION

Any lines not matching 1y, when 1y is at the end of the first field are displayed.

The POSIX Character Class. POSIX (the Portable Operating System Interface) is an industry standard to ensure that programs are portable across operating systems. In order to be portable, POSIX recognizes that different countries or locales may differ in the way characters are encoded, alphabets, the symbols used to represent currency, and how times and dates are represented. To handle different types of characters, POSIX added to the basic and extended regular expressions, the bracketed character class of characters shown in Table 6.7. Gawk supports this new character class of metacharacters, whereas awk and nawk do not.

The class, [:alnum:] is another way of saying A-Za-z0-9. To use this class, it must be enclosed in another set of brackets for it to be recognized as a regular expression. For example, A-Za-z0-9, by itself, is not a regular expression, but [A-Za-z0-9] is. Likewise, [:alnum:] should be written [[:alnum:]]. The difference between using the first form, [A-Za-z0-9] and the bracketed form, [[:alnum:]] is that the first form is dependent on ASCII character encoding, whereas the second form allows characters from other languages to be represented in the class, such as Swedish rings and German umlauts.

Table 6.7   Bracketed Character Class Added by POSIX

Bracket Class	Meaning
[:alnum:]	Alphanumeric characters
[:alpha:]	Alphabetic characters
[:cntrl:]	Control characters
[:digit:]	Numeric characters
[:graph:]	Nonblank characters (not spaces, control characters, etc.)
[:lower:]	Lowercase letters
[:print:]	Like [:graph:], but includes the space character
[:punct:]	Punctuation characters
[:space:]	All whitespace characters (newlines, spaces, tabs)
[:upper:]	Uppercase letters
[:xdigit:]	Allows digits in a hexadecimal number (0-9a-fA-F)

EXAMPLE 6.28

```
% gawk '/[[:lower:]]+g[[:space:]]+[[:digit:]]/' employees
Sally Chang 1654 7/22/54 650000
```

EXPLANATION

Gawk searches for one or more lowercase letters, followed by a g, followed by one or more spaces, followed by a digit. (If you are a Linux user, awk is linked to gawk, making both awk and gawk valid commands.)

6.9 awk **Commands in a Script File**

When you have multiple awk pattern/action statements, it is often much easier to put the statements in a script. The script is a file containing awk comments and statements. If statements and actions are on the same line, they are separated by semicolons. If statements are on separate lines, semicolons are not necessary. If an action follows a pattern, the opening curly brace must be on the same line as the pattern. Comments are preceded by a pound (#) sign.

EXAMPLE 6.29

```
% cat employees
Tom Jones:4424:5/12/66:54335
Mary Adams:5346:11/4/63:28765
Billy Black:1683:9/23/44:336500
Sally Chang:1654:7/22/54:65000
Jose Tomas:1683:9/23/44:33650

(The Awk Script)
% cat info
1    # My first awk script by Jack Sprat
     # Script name: info; Date: February 28, 2004
2    /Tom/{print  "Tom's birthday is "$3}
3    /Mary/{print NR, $0}
4    /^Sally/{print "Hi Sally. "  $1 " has a salary of  $" $4 "."}
     # End of info script

(The Command Line)
5    % nawk -F: -f info employees2
     Tom's birthday is 5/12/66
     2 Mary Adams:5346:11/4/63:28765
     Hi Sally. Sally Chang has a salary of $65000.
```

EXPLANATION

1   These are comment lines.

2   If the regular expression Tom is matched against an input line, the string Tom's birthday is and the value of the third field ($3) are printed.

EXPLANATION (CONTINUED)

3   If the regular expression Mary is matched against an input line, the action block prints NR, the number of the current record, and the record.

4   If the regular expression Sally is found at the beginning of the input line, the string Hi Sally. is printed, followed by the value of the first field ($1), the string has a salary of $, and the value of the fourth field ($4).

5   The nawk command is followed by the -F: option, specifying the colon to be the field separator. The -f option is followed by the name of the awk script. Awk will read instructions from the info file. The input file, employees2, is next.

6.10 Review

The examples in this section use the following sample database, called datafile, repeated periodically for your convenience. In the database, the input field separator, FS, is whitespace, the default. The number of fields, NF, is 8. The number may vary from line to line, but in this file, the number of fields is fixed. The record separator, RS, is the newline, which separates each line of the file. Awk keeps track of the number of each record in the NR variable. The output field separator, OFS, is a space. If a comma is used to separate fields, when the line is printed, each field printed will be separated by a space.

```
% cat datafile
northwest      NW    Joel Craig        3.0    .98    3    4
western        WE    Sharon Kelly      5.3    .97    5    23
southwest      SW    Chris Foster      2.7    .8     2    18
southern       SO    May Chin          5.1    .95    4    15
southeast      SE    Derek Johnson     4.0    .7     4    17
eastern        EA    Susan Beal        4.4    .84    5    20
northeast      NE    TJ Nichols        5.1    .94    3    13
north          NO    Val Shultz        4.5    .89    5    9
central        CT    Sheri Watson      5.7    .94    5    13
```

6.10.1   Simple Pattern Matching

EXAMPLE 6.30

```
nawk '/west/'  datafile
northwest      NW    Joel Craig        3.0    .98    3    4
western        WE    Sharon Kelly      5.3    .97    5    23
southwest      SW    Chris Foster      2.7    .8     2    18
```

EXPLANATION

All lines containing the pattern west are printed.

EXAMPLE 6.31

```
nawk '/^north/' datafile
```
northwest	NW	Joel Craig	3.0	.98	3	4
northeast	NE	TJ Nichols	5.1	.94	3	13
north	NO	Val Shultz	4.5	.89	5	9

EXPLANATION
All lines beginning with the pattern north are printed.

EXAMPLE 6.32

```
nawk '/^(no|so)/' datafile
```
northwest	NW	Joel Craig	3.0	.98	3	4
southwest	SW	Chris Foster	2.7	.8	2	18
southern	SO	May Chin	5.1	.95	4	15
southeast	SE	Derek Johnson	4.0	.7	4	17
northeast	NE	TJ Nichols	5.1	.94	3	13
north	NO	Val Shultz	4.5	.89	5	9

EXPLANATION
All lines beginning with the pattern no or so are printed.

6.10.2 Simple Actions

EXAMPLE 6.33

```
nawk '{print $3, $2}' datafile
Joel NW
Sharon WE
Chris SW
May SO
Derek SE
Susan EA
TJ NE
Val NO
Sheri CT
```

EXPLANATION
The output field separator, OFS, is a space by default. The comma between $3 and $2 is translated to the value of the OFS. The third field is printed, followed by a space and the second field.

% cat datafile						
northwest	NW	Joel Craig	3.0	.98	3	4
western	WE	Sharon Kelly	5.3	.97	5	23
southwest	SW	Chris Foster	2.7	.8	2	18
southern	SO	May Chin	5.1	.95	4	15
southeast	SE	Derek Johnson	4.0	.7	4	17
eastern	EA	Susan Beal	4.4	.84	5	20
northeast	NE	TJ Nichols	5.1	.94	3	13
north	NO	Val Shultz	4.5	.89	5	9
central	CT	Sheri Watson	5.7	.94	5	13

EXAMPLE 6.34

```
nawk '{print $3 $2}' datafile
JoelNW
SharonWE
ChrisSW
MaySO
DerekSE
SusanEA
TJNE
ValNO
SheriCT
```

EXPLANATION

The third field is followed by the second field. Because the comma does not separate fields $3 and $2, the output is displayed without spaces between the fields.

EXAMPLE 6.35

```
nawk 'print $1' datafile
nawk: syntax error at source line 1
 context is
        >>> print <<< $1
nawk: bailing out at source line 1
```

EXPLANATION

This is the nawk (new awk) error message. Nawk error messages are much more verbose than those of the old awk. In this program, the curly braces are missing in the action statement.

EXAMPLE 6.36

```
awk 'print $1' datafile
awk: syntax error near line 1
awk: bailing out near line 1
```

EXPLANATION

This is the awk (old awk) error message. Old awk programs were difficult to debug because almost all errors produced this same message. The curly braces are missing in the action statement.

EXAMPLE 6.37

```
nawk '{print $0}' datafile
northwest      NW      Joel Craig        3.0   .98   3   4
western        WE      Sharon Kelly      5.3   .97   5   23
southwest      SW      Chris Foster      2.7   .8    2   18
southern       SO      May Chin          5.1   .95   4   15
southeast      SE      Derek Johnson     4.0   .7    4   17
eastern        EA      Susan Beal        4.4   .84   5   20
northeast      NE      TJ Nichols        5.1   .94   3   13
north          NO      Val Shultz        4.5   .89   5   9
central        CT      Sheri Watson      5.7   .94   5   13
```

EXPLANATION

Each record is printed. $0 holds the current record.

EXAMPLE 6.38

```
nawk '{print "Number of fields: "NF}' datafile
Number of fields: 8
Number of fields: 8
Number of fields: 8
Number of fields: 8
Number of fields: 8
Number of fields: 8
Number of fields: 8
Number of fields: 8
Number of fields: 8
```

EXPLANATION

There are 8 fields in each record. The built-in awk variable NF holds the number of fields and is reset for each record.

% **cat datafile**						
northwest	NW	Joel Craig	3.0	.98	3	4
western	WE	Sharon Kelly	5.3	.97	5	23
southwest	SW	Chris Foster	2.7	.8	2	18
southern	SO	May Chin	5.1	.95	4	15
southeast	SE	Derek Johnson	4.0	.7	4	17
eastern	EA	Susan Beal	4.4	.84	5	20
northeast	NE	TJ Nichols	5.1	.94	3	13
north	NO	Val Shultz	4.5	.89	5	9
central	CT	Sheri Watson	5.7	.94	5	13

6.10.3 Regular Expressions in Pattern and Action Combinations

EXAMPLE 6.39

```
nawk '/northeast/{print $3, $2}' datafile
TJ NE
```

EXPLANATION

If the record contains (or matches) the pattern northeast, the third field, followed by the second field, is printed.

EXAMPLE 6.40

```
nawk '/E/' datafile
western          WE      Sharon Kelly      5.3    .97    5    23
southeast        SE      Derek Johnson     4.0    .7     4    17
eastern          EA      Susan Beal        4.4    .84    5    20
northeast        NE      TJ Nichols        5.1    .94    3    13
```

EXPLANATION

If the record contains an E, the entire record is printed.

EXAMPLE 6.41

```
nawk '/^[ns]/{print $1}' datafile
northwest
southwest
southern
southeast
northeast
north
```

EXPLANATION

If the record begins with an n or s, the first field is printed.

EXAMPLE 6.42

```
nawk '$5 ~ /\.[7-9]+/' datafile
southwest          SW        Chris Foster        2.7    .8     2     18
central            CT        Sheri Watson        5.7    .94    5     13
```

EXPLANATION

If the fifth field ($5) contains a literal period, followed by one or more numbers between 7 and 9, the record is printed.

EXAMPLE 6.43

```
nawk '$2 !~ /E/{print $1, $2}' datafile
northwest NW
southwest SW
southern SO
north NO
central CT
```

EXPLANATION

If the second field does not contain the pattern E, the first field followed by the second field ($1, $2) is printed.

EXAMPLE 6.44

```
nawk '$3 ~ /^Joel/{print $3 " is a nice guy."}' datafile
Joel is a nice guy.
```

EXPLANATION

If the third field ($3) begins with the pattern Joel, the third field followed by the string is a nice guy. is printed. Note that a space is included in the string if it is to be printed.

EXAMPLE 6.45

```
nawk '$8 ~ /[0-9][0-9]$/{print $8}' datafile
23
18
15
17
20
13
13
```

EXPLANATION

If the eighth field ($8) ends in two digits, it is printed.

```
% cat datafile
northwest      NW      Joel Craig           3.0    .98    3    4
western        WE      Sharon Kelly         5.3    .97    5    23
southwest      SW      Chris Foster         2.7    .8     2    18
southern       SO      May Chin             5.1    .95    4    15
southeast      SE      Derek Johnson        4.0    .7     4    17
eastern        EA      Susan Beal           4.4    .84    5    20
northeast      NE      TJ Nichols           5.1    .94    3    13
north          NO      Val Shultz           4.5    .89    5    9
central       ,CT      Sheri Watson         5.7    .94    5    13
```

EXAMPLE 6.46

```
nawk '$4 ~ /Chin$/{print "The price is $" $8 "."}' datafile
The price is $15.
```

EXPLANATION

If the fourth field ($4) ends with Chin, the string enclosed in double quotes ("The price is $"), the eighth field ($8), and the string containing a period are printed.

EXAMPLE 6.47

```
nawk '/TJ/{print $0}' datafile
northeast          NE        TJ Nichols          5.1    .94    3    13
```

EXPLANATION

If the record contains the pattern TJ, $0 (the record) is printed.

6.10.4 Input Field Separators

Use the following datafile2 for Examples 6.48 through 6.52.

```
% cat datafile2
Joel Craig:northwest:NW:3.0:.98:3:4
Sharon Kelly:western:WE:5.3:.97:5:23
Chris Foster:southwest:SW:2.7:.8:2:18
May Chin:southern:SO:5.1:.95:4:15
Derek Johnson:southeast:SE:4.0:.7:4:17
Susan Beal:eastern:EA:4.4:.84:5:20
TJ Nichols:northeast:NE:5.1:.94:3:13
Val Shultz:north:NO:4.5:.89:5:9
Sheri Watson:central:CT:5.7:.94:5:13
```

EXAMPLE 6.48

```
nawk '{print $1}' datafile2
```
```
Joel
Sharon
Chris
May
Derek
Susan
TJ
Val
Sheri
```

EXPLANATION

The default input field separator is whitespace. The first field ($1) is printed.

EXAMPLE 6.49

```
nawk -F: '{print $1}' datafile2
```
```
Joel Craig
Sharon Kelly
Chris Foster
    <more output here>
Val Shultz
Sheri Watson
```

EXPLANATION

The –F option specifies the colon as the input field separator. The first field ($1) is printed.

EXAMPLE 6.50

```
nawk '{print "Number of fields: "NF}' datafile2
```
```
Number of fields: 2
Number of fields: 2
Number of fields: 2
    <more of the same output here>
Number of fields: 2
Number of fields: 2
```

EXPLANATION

Because the field separator is the default (whitespace), the number of fields for each record is 2. The only space is between the first and last name.

EXAMPLE 6.51

```
nawk -F: '{print "Number of fields: "NF}' datafile2
```
Number of fields: 7
Number of fields: 7
Number of fields: 7
    <more of the same output here>
Number of fields: 7
Number of fields: 7

EXPLANATION

Because the field separator is a colon, the number of fields in each record is 7.

EXAMPLE 6.52

```
nawk -F"[ :]" '{print $1, $2}' datafile2
```
Joel Craig northwest
Sharon Kelly western
Chris Foster southwest
May Chin southern
Derek Johnson southeast
Susan Beal eastern
TJ Nichols northeast
Val Shultz north
Sheri Watson central

EXPLANATION

Multiple field separators can be specified with nawk as a regular expression. Either a space or a colon will be designated as a field separator. The first and second fields ($1, $2) are printed. (The square brackets must be quoted to prevent the shell from trying to interpret them as shell metacharacters.)

6.10.5 awk Scripting

The following datafile is used for the next example.

% **cat datafile**						
northwest	NW	Joel Craig	3.0	.98	3	4
western	WE	Sharon Kelly	5.3	.97	5	23
southwest	SW	Chris Foster	2.7	.8	2	18
southern	SO	May Chin	5.1	.95	4	15
southeast	SE	Derek Johnson	4.0	.7	4	17
eastern	EA	Susan Beal	4.4	.84	5	20
northeast	NE	TJ Nichols	5.1	.94	3	13
north	NO	Val Shultz	4.5	.89	5	9
central	CT	Sheri Watson	5.7	.94	5	13

EXAMPLE 6.53

```
cat nawk.scl
# This is a comment
# This is my first nawk script
1    /^north/{print $1, $2, $3}
2    /^south/{print "The " $1 " district."}


3    nawk -f nawk.scl datafile
     northwest NW Joel
     The southwest district.
     The southern district.
     The southeast district.
     northeast NE TJ
     north NO Val
```

EXPLANATION

1   If the record begins with the pattern north, the first, second, and third fields ($1, $2, $3) are printed.

2   If the record begins with the pattern south, the string The, followed by the value of the first field ($1), and the string district. are printed.

3   The -f option precedes the name of the nawk script file, followed by the input file that is to be processed.

LAB 3: awk EXERCISE

(Refer to the database called lab3.data on the CD.)

Mike Harrington:(510) 548-1278:250:100:175
Christian Dobbins:(408) 538-2358:155:90:201
Susan Dalsass:(206) 654-6279:250:60:50
Archie McNichol:(206) 548-1348:250:100:175
Jody Savage:(206) 548-1278:15:188:150
Guy Quigley:(916) 343-6410:250:100:175
Dan Savage:(406) 298-7744:450:300:275
Nancy McNeil:(206) 548-1278:250:80:75
John Goldenrod:(916) 348-4278:250:100:175
Chet Main:(510) 548-5258:50:95:135
Tom Savage:(408) 926-3456:250:168:200
Elizabeth Stachelin:(916) 440-1763:175:75:300

The database contains the names, phone numbers, and money contributions to the party campaign for the past three months.

1. Print all the phone numbers.

2. Print Dan's phone number.

3. Print Susan's name and phone number.

4. Print all last names beginning with D.

5. Print all first names beginning with either a C or E.

6. Print all first names containing only four characters.

7. Print the first names of all those in the 916 area code.

8. Print Mike's campaign contributions. Each value should be printed with a leading dollar sign; e.g., $250 $100 $175.

9. Print last names followed by a comma and the first name.

10. Write an awk script called facts that

    a. Prints full names and phone numbers for the Savages.

    b. Prints Chet's contributions.

    c. Prints all those who contributed $250 the first month.

6.11 Comparison Expressions

Comparison expressions match lines where the action is performed only if a certain condition is true. These expressions use relational operators and are used to compare numbers or strings.

6.11.1   Relational and Equality Operators

Table 6.8 provides a list of the relational operators. The value of the expression is 1 if the expression evaluates true, and 0 if false.

Table 6.8   Relational Operators

Operator	Meaning	Example
<	Less than	x < y
<=	Less than or equal to	x <= y
==	Equal to	x == y
!=	Not equal to	x != y
>=	Greater than or equal to	x >= y
>	Greater than	x > y

Table 6.8 Relational Operators (continued)

Operator	Meaning	Example
~	Matched by regular expression	x ~ /y/
!~	Not matched by regular expression	x !~ /y/

EXAMPLE 6.54

```
(The Database)
% cat employees
    Tom Jones       4423    5/12/66             543354
    Mary Adams      5346    11/4/63             28765
    Sally Chang     1654    7/22/54             650000
    Billy Black     1683    9/23/44             336500

(The Command Line)
1   % awk '$3 == 5346' employees
    Mary Adams      5346    11/4/63             28765

2   % awk '$3 > 5000{print $1} ' employees
    Mary

3   % awk '$2 ~ /Adam/ ' employees
    Mary Adams      5346    11/4/63             28765

4   % awk '$2 !~ /Adam/ ' employees
    Tom Jones       4423    5/12/66             543354
    Sally Chang     1654    7/22/54             650000
    Billy Black     1683    9/23/44             336500
```

EXPLANATION

1 If the third field is exactly equal to 5346, the condition is true and awk will perform the default action—print the line. When an if condition is implied, it is a conditional pattern test.

2 If the third field is greater than 5000, awk prints the first field.

3 If the second field matches or contains the regular expression Adam, the record is printed.

4 If the second field does not match or does not contain the regular expression Adam, the record is printed. If an expression is a numeric value and is being compared with a string value with an operator that requires a numeric comparison, the string value will be converted to a numeric value. If the operator requires a string value, the numeric value will be converted to a string value.

6.11.2 Conditional Expressions

A conditional expression uses two symbols, the question mark and the colon, to evaluate expressions. It is really just a short way to achieve the same result as doing an if/else statement. The general format is as follows:

FORMAT

```
conditional expression1 ? expression2 : expression3
```

This produces the same result as the if/else shown here. (A complete discussion of the if/else construct is given later.)

```
{
if (expression1)
        expression2
else
        expression3
}
```

EXAMPLE 6.55

```
% awk '{max=($1 > $2) ? $1 : $2; print max}' filename
```

EXPLANATION

If the first field is greater than the second field, the value of the expression after the question mark is assigned to max; otherwise the value of the expression after the colon is assigned to max. This is comparable to

```
if ($1 > $2 )
        max=$1
else
        max=$2
```

6.11.3 Computation

Computation can be performed within patterns. Awk (all versions) performs all arithmetic in floating point. The arithmetic operators are provided in Table 6.9.

EXAMPLE 6.56

```
% awk '$3 * $4 > 500' filename
```

EXPLANATION

Awk will multiply the third field ($3) by the fourth field ($4), and if the result is greater than 500, it will display those lines. (Filename is assumed to be a file containing the input.)

Table 6.9 Arithmetic Operators

Operator	Meaning	Example
+	Add	x + y
-	Subtract	x - y
*	Multiply	x * y
/	Divide	x / y
%	Modulus	x % y
^	Exponentiation	x ^ y

6.11.4 Logical Operators and Compound Patterns

Logical operators test whether an expression or pattern is true or false. With the &&, logical AND operator, if both expressions are true, the entire expression is true. If one expression is false, the whole expression is false. With ||, the logical OR operator, only one expression or pattern must evaluate to true to make the whole expression true. If both expressions are false, the entire expression is false.

Compound patterns are expressions that combine patterns with logical operators (see Table 6.10). An expression is evaluated from left to right.

Table 6.10 Logical Operators

Operator	Meaning	Example
&&	Logical AND	a && b
||	Logical OR	a || b
!	NOT	! a

EXAMPLE 6.57

```
% awk '$2 > 5 && $2 <= 15' filename
```

EXPLANATION

Awk will display those lines that match both conditions; that is, where the second field ($2) is greater than 5 AND the second field ($2) is also less than or equal to 15. With the && operator, *both* conditions must be true. (Filename is assumed to be a file containing the input.)

EXAMPLE 6.58

```
% awk '$3 == 100 || $4 > 50' filename
```

EXPLANATION

Awk will display those lines that match one of the conditions; that is, where the third field is equal to 100 OR the fourth field is greater than 50. With the || operator, only one of the conditions must be true. (Filename is assumed to be a file containing the input.)

EXAMPLE 6.59

```
% awk '!($2 < 100 && $3 < 20)' filename
```

EXPLANATION

If both conditions are true, awk will negate the expression and display those lines—so the lines displayed will have one or both conditions false. The unary ! operator negates the result of the condition so that if the expression yields a true condition, the NOT will make it false, and vice versa. (Filename is assumed to be a file containing the input.)

6.11.5   Range Patterns

Range patterns match from the first occurrence of one pattern to the first occurrence of the second pattern, then match for the next occurrence of the first pattern to the next occurrence of the second pattern, and so on. If the first pattern is matched and the second pattern is not found, awk will display all lines to the end of the file.

EXAMPLE 6.60

```
% awk '/Tom/,/Suzanne/' filename
```

EXPLANATION

Awk will display all lines, inclusive, that range between the first occurrence of Tom and the first occurrence of Suzanne. If Suzanne is not found, awk will continue processing lines until the end of the file. If, after the range between Tom and Suzanne is printed, Tom appears again, awk will start displaying lines until another Suzanne is found or the file ends.

6.11.6   A Data Validation Program

Using the awk commands discussed so far, the password-checking program from the book *The AWK Programming Language*[3] illustrates how the data in a file can be validated.

---

3. Aho, Weinberger, and Kernighan, *The Awk Programming Language* (Boston: Addison-Wesley, 1988).

EXAMPLE 6.61

(The Password Database)
1 % **cat /etc/passwd**
tooth:pwHfudo.eC9sM:476:40:Contract Admin.:/home/rickenbacker/tooth:/bin/csh
lisam:9JY7OuS2f3lHY:4467:40:Lisa M. Spencer:/home/fortune1/lisam:/bin/csh
goode:v7Ww.nWJCeSIQ:32555:60:Goodwill Guest User:/usr/goodwill:/bin/csh
bonzo:eTZbu6M2jM7VA:5101:911: SSTOOL Log account :/home/sun4/bonzo:/bin/csh
info:mKZsrioPtW9hA:611:41:Terri Stern:/home/chewie/info:/bin/csh
cnc:IN1IVqVj1bVv2:10209:41:Charles Carnell:/home/christine/cnc:/bin/csh
bee:*:347:40:Contract Temp.:/home/chanel5/bee:/bin/csh
friedman:oyuIiKoFTV0TE:3561:50:Jay Friedman:/home/ibanez/friedman:/bin/csh
chambers:Rw7R1k77yUY4.:592:40:Carol Chambers:/usr/callisto2/chambers:/bin/csh
gregc:nkLulOg:7777:30:Greg Champlin FE Chicago
ramona:gbDQLdDBeRc46:16660:68:RamonaLeininge MWA CustomerService Rep:/home/forsh:

(The Awk Commands)
2   % **cat /etc/passwd | awk -F: '**
3   **NF != 7{**
4   **printf("line %d, does not have 7 fields: %s\n",NR,$0)} **
5   **$1 !~ /[A-Za-z0-9]/{printf("line %d, nonalphanumeric user id: %s\n",NR,$0)} **
6   **$2 == "*" {printf("line %d, no password: %s\n",NR,$0)} '**

(The Output)
line 7, no password: bee::347:40:Contract Temp.:/home/chanel5/bee:/bin/csh*
line 10, does not have 7 fields: gregc:nk2EYi7kLulOg:7777:30:Greg Champlin
FE Chicago
line 11, does not have 7 fields: ramona:gbDQLdDBeRc46:16660:68:Ramona
Leininger MWA Customer Service Rep:/home/forsh:

EXPLANATION

1   The contents of the /etc/passwd file are displayed.

2   The cat program sends its output to awk. Awk's field separator is a colon.

3   If the number of fields (NF) is not equal to 7, the following action block is executed.

4   The printf function prints the string line <number>, does not have 7 fields followed by the number of the current record (NR) and the record itself ($0).

5   If the first field ($1) does not contain any alphanumeric characters, the printf function prints the string nonalphanumeric user id, followed by the number of the record and the record itself.

6   If the second field ($2) equals an asterisk, the string no password is printed, followed by the number of the record and the record itself.

6.12 Review

The examples in this section use the following sample database, called datafile, repeated periodically for your convenience.

% **cat datafile**						
northwest	NW	Joel Craig	3.0	.98	3	4
western	WE	Sharon Kelly	5.3	.97	5	23
southwest	SW	Chris Foster	2.7	.8	2	18
southern	SO	May Chin	5.1	.95	4	15
southeast	SE	Derek Johnson	4.0	.7	4	17
eastern	EA	Susan Beal	4.4	.84	5	20
northeast	NE	TJ Nichols	5.1	.94	3	13
north	NO	Val Shultz	4.5	.89	5	9
central	CT	Sheri Watson	5.7	.94	5	13

6.12.1   Equality Testing

EXAMPLE 6.62

```
% awk '$7 == 5' datafile
```
western	WE	Sharon Kelly	5.3	.97	5	23
eastern	EA	Susan Beal	4.4	.84	5	20
north	NO	Val Shultz	4.5	.89	5	9
central	CT	Sheri Watson	5.7	.94	5	13

EXPLANATION

If the seventh field ($7) is equal to the number 5, the record is printed.

EXAMPLE 6.63

```
% awk '$2 == "CT"{print $1, $2}' datafile
```
central		CT

EXPLANATION

If the second field is equal to the string CT, fields one and two ($1, $2) are printed. Strings must be quoted.

EXAMPLE 6.64

```
% awk '$7 != 5' datafile
```
northwest	NW	Joel Craig	3.0	.98	3	4
southwest	SW	Chris Foster	2.7	.8	2	18
southern	SO	May Chin	5.1	.95	4	15
southeast	SE	Derek Johnson	4.0	.7	4	17
northeast	NE	TJ Nichols	5.1	.94	3	13

If the seventh field ($7) is not equal to the number 5, the record is printed.

6.12.2 Relational Operators

```
% awk '$7 < 5 {print $4, $7}' datafile
Craig 3
Foster 2
Chin 4
Johnson 4
Nichols 3
```

If the seventh field ($7) is less than 5, fields 4 and 7 are printed.

```
% awk '$6 > .9 {print $1, $6}' datafile
northwest .98
western .97
southern .95
northeast .94
central .94
```

If the sixth field ($6) is greater than .9, fields 1 and 6 are printed.

```
% awk '$8 <= 17 { print $8}' datafile
4
15
17
13
9
13
```

If the eighth field ($8) is less than or equal to 17, it is printed.

```
% cat datafile
northwest    NW    Joel Craig        3.0    .98    3    4
western      WE    Sharon Kelly      5.3    .97    5    23
southwest    SW    Chris Foster      2.7    .8     2    18
southern     SO    May Chin          5.1    .95    4    15
southeast    SE    Derek Johnson     4.0    .7     4    17
eastern      EA    Susan Beal        4.4    .84    5    20
northeast    NE    TJ Nichols        5.1    .94    3    13
north        NO    Val Shultz        4.5    .89    5    9
central      CT    Sheri Watson      5.7    .94    5    13
```

EXAMPLE 6.68

```
% awk '$8 >= 17 {print $8}' datafile
23
18
17
20
```

EXPLANATION

If the eighth field ($8) is greater than or equal to 17, the eighth field is printed.

6.12.3 Logical Operators (&&, ||)

EXAMPLE 6.69

```
% awk '$8 > 10 && $8 < 17' datafile
southern     SO    May Chin          5.1    .95    4    15
northeast    NE    TJ Nichols        5.1    .94    3    13
central      CT    Sheri Watson      5.7    .94    5    13
```

EXPLANATION

If the eighth field ($8) is greater than 10 AND less than 17, the record is printed. The record will be printed only if both expressions are true.

EXAMPLE 6.70

```
% awk '$2 == "NW" || $1 ~ /south/{print $1, $2}' datafile
northwest NW
southwest SW
southern SO
southeast SE
```

EXPLANATION

If the second field ($2) is equal to the string NW OR the first field ($1) contains the pattern south, the first and second fields ($1, $2) are printed. The record will be printed if only one of the expressions is true.

6.12.4 Logical NOT Operator (!)

EXAMPLE 6.71

```
% awk '!($8 == 13){print $8}' datafile
4
23
18
15
17
20
9
```

EXPLANATION

If the eighth field ($8) is equal to 13, the ! (NOT operator) NOTs the expression and prints the eighth field ($8). The ! is a unary negation operator.

6.12.5 Arithmetic Operators

EXAMPLE 6.72

```
% awk '/southern/{print $5 + 10}' datafile
15.1
```

EXPLANATION

If the record contains the regular expression southern, 10 is added to the value of the fifth field ($5) and printed. Note that the number prints in floating point.

EXAMPLE 6.73

```
% awk '/southern/{print $8 + 10}' datafile
25
```

EXPLANATION

If the record contains the regular expression southern, 10 is added to the value of the eighth field ($8) and printed. Note that the number prints in decimal.

```
% cat datafile
```

northwest	NW	Joel Craig	3.0	.98	3	4
western	WE	Sharon Kelly	5.3	.97	5	23
southwest	SW	Chris Foster	2.7	.8	2	18
southern	SO	May Chin	5.1	.95	4	15
southeast	SE	Derek Johnson	4.0	.7	4	17
eastern	EA	Susan Beal	4.4	.84	5	20
northeast	NE	TJ Nichols	5.1	.94	3	13
north	NO	Val Shultz	4.5	.89	5	9
central	CT	Sheri Watson	5.7	.94	5	13

EXAMPLE   6.74

```
% awk '/southern/{print $5 + 10.56}' datafile
15.66
```

EXPLANATION

If the record contains the regular expression southern, 10.56 is added to the value of the fifth field ($5) and printed.

EXAMPLE   6.75

```
% awk '/southern/{print $8 - 10}' datafile
5
```

EXPLANATION

If the record contains the regular expression southern, 10 is subtracted from the value of the eighth field ($8) and printed.

EXAMPLE   6.76

```
% awk '/southern/{print $8 / 2}' datafile
7.5
```

EXPLANATION

If the record contains the regular expression southern, the value of the eighth field ($8) is divided by 2 and printed.

EXAMPLE 6.77

```
% awk '/northeast/{print $8 / 3}' datafile
4.33333
```

EXPLANATION

If the record contains the regular expression northeast, the value of the eighth field ($8) is divided by 3 and printed. The precision is five places to the right of the decimal point.

EXAMPLE 6.78

```
% awk '/southern/{print $8 * 2}' datafile
30
```

EXPLANATION

If the record contains the regular expression southern, the eighth field ($8) is multiplied by 2 and printed.

EXAMPLE 6.79

```
% awk '/northeast/ {print $8 % 3}' datafile
1
```

EXPLANATION

If the record contains the regular expression northeast, the eighth field ($8) is divided by 3 and the remainder (modulus) is printed.

EXAMPLE 6.80

```
% awk '$3 ~ /^Susan/\
{print "Percentage: "$6 + .2 " Volume: " $8}' datafile
Percentage: 1.04 Volume: 20
```

EXPLANATION

If the third field ($3) begins with the regular expression Susan, the print function prints the result of the calculations and the strings in double quotes.

% **cat datafile**						
northwest	NW	Joel Craig	3.0	.98	3	4
western	WE	Sharon Kelly	5.3	.97	5	23
southwest	SW	Chris Foster	2.7	.8	2	18
southern	SO	May Chin	5.1	.95	4	15
southeast	SE	Derek Johnson	4.0	.7	4	17
eastern	EA	Susan Beal	4.4	.84	5	20
northeast	NE	TJ Nichols	5.1	.94	3	13
north	NO	Val Shultz	4.5	.89	5	9
central	CT	Sheri Watson	5.7	.94	5	13

6.12.6 Range Operator

EXAMPLE 6.81

```
% awk '/^western/,/^eastern/' datafile
western      WE    Sharon Kelly     5.3   .97   5    23
southwest    SW    Chris Foster     2.7   .8    2    18
southern     SO    May Chin         5.1   .95   4    15
southeast    SE    Derek Johnson    4.0   .7    4    17
eastern      EA    Susan Beal       4.4   .84   5    20
```

EXPLANATION

All records within the range beginning with the regular expression western are printed until a record beginning with the expression eastern is found. Records will start being printed again if the pattern western is found and will continue to print until eastern or the end of the file is reached.

6.12.7 Conditional Operator

EXAMPLE 6.82

```
% awk '{print ($7 > 4 ? "high "$7 : "low "$7)}' datafile
low 3
high 5
low 2
low 4
low 4
high 5
low 3
high 5
high 5
```

If the seventh field ($7) is greater than 4, the print function gets the value of the expression after the question mark (the string high and the seventh field); else the print function gets the value of the expression after the colon (the string low and the value of the seventh field).

6.12.8 Assignment Operators

EXAMPLE 6.83

```
% awk '$3 == "Chris"{ $3 = "Christian"; print}' datafile
southwest SW Christian Foster 2.7 .8 2 18
```

EXPLANATION

If the third field ($3) is equal to the string Chris, the action is to assign Christian to the third field ($3) and print the record. The double equal tests its operands for equality, whereas the single equal is used for assignment.

EXAMPLE 6.84

```
% awk '/Derek/{$8 += 12; print $8}' datafile
29
```

EXPLANATION

If the regular expression Derek is found, 12 is added and assigned to (+=), the eighth field ($8), and that value is printed. Another way to write this is $8 = $8 + 12.

EXAMPLE 6.85

```
% awk '{$7 %= 3; print $7}' datafile
0
2
2
1
1
2
0
2
2
```

EXPLANATION

For each record, the seventh field ($7) is divided by 3, and the remainder of that division (modulus) is assigned to the seventh field and printed.

LAB 4: awk EXERCISE

(Refer to the database called lab4.data on the CD.)

Mike Harrington:(510) 548-1278:250:100:175
Christian Dobbins:(408) 538-2358:155:90:201
Susan Dalsass:(206) 654-6279:250:60:50
Archie McNichol:(206) 548-1348:250:100:175
Jody Savage:(206) 548-1278:15:188:150
Guy Quigley:(916) 343-6410:250:100:175
Dan Savage:(406) 298-7744:450:300:275
Nancy McNeil:(206) 548-1278:250:80:75
John Goldenrod:(916) 348-4278:250:100:175
Chet Main:(510) 548-5258:50:95:135
Tom Savage:(408) 926-3456:250:168:200
Elizabeth Stachelin:(916) 440-1763:175:75:300

The database contains the names, phone numbers, and money contributions to the party campaign for the past three months.

1. Print the first and last names of those who contributed more than $100 in the second month.

2. Print the names and phone numbers of those who contributed less than $85 in the last month.

3. Print the names of those who contributed between $75 and $150 in the first month.

4. Print the names of those who contributed less than $800 over the three-month period.

5. Print the names and addresses of those with an average monthly contribution greater than $200.

6. Print the first name of those not in the 916 area code.

7. Print each record preceded by the number of the record.

8. Print the name and total contribution of each person.

9. Add $10 to Chet's second contribution.

10. Change Nancy McNeil's name to Louise McInnes.

6.13 Variables

6.13.1 Numeric and String Constants

Numeric constants can be represented as integers, such as 243; floating-point numbers, such as 3.14; or numbers using scientific notation, such as .723E-1 or 3.4e7. Strings, such as Hello world, are enclosed in double quotes.

Initialization and Type Coercion.   Just mentioning a variable in your awk program causes it to exist. A variable can be a string, a number, or both. When it is set, it becomes the type of the expression on the right-hand side of the equal sign.

Uninitialized variables have the value zero or the value " ", depending on the context in which they are used.

```
name = "Nancy"    name is a string

x++               x is a number;
                  x is initialized to zero and incremented by 1

number = 35       number is a number
```

To coerce a string to be a number:

```
name + 0
```

To coerce a number to be a string:

```
number " "
```

All fields and array elements created by the split function are considered strings, unless they contain only a numeric value. If a field or array element is null, it has the string value of null. An empty line is also considered to be a null string.

6.13.2 User-Defined Variables

User-defined variables consist of letters, digits, and underscores, and cannot begin with a digit. Variables in awk are not declared. Awk infers data type by the context of the variable in the expression. If the variable is not initialized, awk initializes string variables to null and numeric variables to zero. If necessary, awk will convert a string variable to a numeric variable, and vice versa. Variables are assigned values with awk's assignment operators. See Table 6.11.

Table 6.11   Assignment Operators

Operator	Meaning	Equivalence
=	$a = 5$	$a = 5$
+=	$a = a + 5$	$a += 5$
−=	$a = a − 5$	$a −= 5$
*=	$a = a * 5$	$a *= 5$
/=	$a = a / 5$	$a /= 5$
%=	$a = a \% 5$	$a \%= 5$
^=	$a = a \wedge 5$	$a \wedge= 5$

The simplest assignment takes the result of an expression and assigns it to a variable.

FORMAT

```
variable = expression
```

EXAMPLE   6.86

```
% nawk '$1 ~ /Tom/ {wage = $2 * $3; print wage}'  filename
```

EXPLANATION

Awk will scan the first field for Tom and when there is a match, it will multiply the value of the second field by the value of the third field and assign the result to the user-defined variable wage. Because the multiplication operation is arithmetic, awk assigns wage an initial value of zero. (The % is the shell prompt and filename is an input file.)

Increment and Decrement Operators.   To add one to an operand, the *increment operator* is used. The expression x++ is equivalent to x = x + 1. Similarly, the *decrement operator* subtracts one from its operand. The expression x-- is equivalent to x = x - 1. This notation is useful in looping operations when you simply want to increment or decrement a counter. You can use the increment and decrement operators either preceding the operator, as in ++x, or after the operator, as in x++. If these expressions are used in assignment statements, their placement will make a difference in the result of the operation.

```
{x = 1;  y = x++ ; print x, y}
```

The ++ here is called a *post-increment operator*; y is assigned the value of 1, and then x is increased by 1, so that when all is said and done, y will equal 1, and x will equal 2.

```
{x = 1; y = ++x;  print x, y}
```

The ++ here is called a *pre-increment operator*; x is incremented first, and the value of two is assigned to y, so that when this statement is finished, y will equal 2, and x will equal 2.

User-Defined Variables at the Command Line. A variable can be assigned a value at the command line and passed into an awk script. For more on processing arguments and ARGV, see "Processing Command Arguments (nawk)" on page 239.

EXAMPLE 6.87

```
nawk -F: -f awkscript    month=4  year=2004 filename
```

EXPLANATION

The user-defined variables month and year are assigned the values 4 and 2004, respectively. In the awk script, these variables may be used as though they were created in the script. Note: If filename precedes the arguments, the variables will not be available in the BEGIN statements. (See "BEGIN Patterns" on page 208.)

The -v Option (nawk). The -v option provided by nawk allows command-line arguments to be processed within a BEGIN statement. For each argument passed at the command line, there must be a -v option preceding it.

Field Variables. Field variables can be used like user-defined variables, except they reference fields. New fields can be created by assignment. A field value that is referenced and has no value will be assigned the null string. If a field value is changed, the $0 variable is recomputed using the current value of OFS as a field separator. The number of fields allowed is usually limited to 100.

EXAMPLE 6.88

```
% nawk ' { $5 = 1000 * $3 / $2;  print } ' filename
```

EXPLANATION

If $5 does not exist, nawk will create it and assign the result of the expression 1000 * $3 / $2 to the fifth field ($5). If the fifth field exists, the result will be assigned to it, overwriting what is there.

EXAMPLE 6.89

```
% nawk ' $4 == "CA" { $4 = "California"; print}' filename
```

EXPLANATION

If the fourth field ($4) is equal to the string CA, nawk will reassign the fourth field to California. The double quotes are essential. Without them, the strings become user-defined variables with an initial value of null.

Built-In Variables. Built-in variables have uppercase names. They can be used in expressions and can be reset. See Table 6.12 for a list of built-in variables.

Table 6.12   Built-In Variables

Variable Name	Contents
ARGC	Number of command-line argument
ARGIND	Index in ARGV of the current file being processed from the command line (gawk only)
ARGV	Array of command-line arguments
CONVFMT	Conversion format for numbers, %.6g, by default (gawk only)
ENVIRON	An array containing the values of the current environment variables passed in from the shell
ERRNO	Contains a string describing a system error occurring from redirection when reading from the getline function or when using the close function (gawk only)
FIELDWIDTHS	A whitespace-separated list of fieldwidths used instead of FS when splitting records of fixed fieldwidth (gawk only)
FILENAME	Name of current input file
FNR	Record number in current file
FS	The input field separator, by default a space
IGNORECASE	Turns off case sensitivity in regular expressions and string operations (gawk only)
NF	Number of fields in current record
NR	Number of records so far
OFMT	Output format for numbers
OFS	Output field separator
ORS	Output record separator
RLENGTH	Length of string matched by match function
RS	Input record separator

Table 6.12 Built-In Variables (continued)

Variable Name	Contents
RSTART	Offset of string matched by match function
RT	The record terminator; gawk sets it to the input text that matched the character or regex specified by RS
SUBSEP	Subscript separator

EXAMPLE 6.90

```
(The Employees Database)
% cat employees2
Tom Jones:4423:5/12/66:543354
Mary Adams:5346:11/4/63:28765
Sally Chang:1654:7/22/54:650000
Mary Black:1683:9/23/44:336500

(The Command Line)
% nawk  -F:  '$1 == "Mary Adams"{print NR, $1, $2, $NF}' employees2

(The Output)
2  Mary Adams 5346  28765
```

EXPLANATION

The -F option sets the field separator to a colon. The print function prints the record number, the first field, the second field, and the last field ($NF).

EXAMPLE 6.91

```
(The Employees Database)
% cat employees2
    Tom Jones:4423:5/12/66:543354
    Mary Adams:5346:11/4/63:28765
    Sally Chang:1654:7/22/54:650000
    Mary Black:1683:9/23/44:336500

(The Command Line)
% gawk  -F:  '{IGNORECASE=1}; \
  $1 == "mary adams"{print NR, $1, $2,$NF}' employees2


(The Output)
    2  Mary Adams 5346  28765
```

EXPLANATION

The –F option sets the field separator to a colon. The gawk built-in variable, IGNORECASE, when set to a nonzero value, turns off gawk's case-sensitivity when doing case-sensitive string and regular expression operations. The string mary adams will be matched, even though in the input file, her name is spelled Mary Adams. The print function prints the record number, the first field, the second field, and the last field ($NF).

6.13.3 BEGIN Patterns

The BEGIN pattern is followed by an action block that is executed *before* awk processes any lines from the input file. In fact, a BEGIN block can be tested without any input file, becuase awk does not start reading input until the BEGIN action block has completed. The BEGIN action is often used to change the value of the built-in variables, OFS, RS, FS, and so forth, to assign initial values to user-defined variables and to print headers or titles as part of the output.

EXAMPLE 6.92

```
% nawk 'BEGIN{FS=":"; OFS="\t"; ORS="\n\n"}{print $1,$2,$3}' file
```

EXPLANATION

Before the input file is processed, the field separator (FS) is set to a colon, the output field separator (OFS) to a tab, and the output record separator (ORS) to two newlines. If there are two or more statements in the action block, they should be separated with semicolons or placed on separate lines (use a backslash to escape the newline character if at the shell prompt).

EXAMPLE 6.93

```
% nawk 'BEGIN{print "MAKE YEAR"}'
MAKE YEAR
```

EXPLANATION

Awk will display MAKE YEAR. The print function is executed before awk opens the input file, and even though the input file has not been assigned, awk will still print MAKE and YEAR. When debugging awk scripts, you can test the BEGIN block actions before writing the rest of the program.

6.13.4 END Patterns

END patterns do not match any input lines, but execute any actions that are associated with the END pattern. END patterns are handled *after* all lines of input have been processed.

EXAMPLE 6.94

```
% nawk 'END{print "The number of records is " NR }' filename
The number of records is 4
```

EXPLANATION

The END block is executed after awk has finished processing the file. The value of NR is the number of the last record read.

EXAMPLE 6.95

```
% nawk '/Mary/{count++}END{print "Mary was found " count " times."}' employees
Mary was found 2 times.
```

EXPLANATION

For every input line from the file employees containing the pattern Mary, the user-defined variable, count, is incremented by 1. When all input lines have been read, the END block is executed to display the string Mary was found 2 times containing the final value of count.

6.14 Redirection and Pipes

6.14.1 Output Redirection

When redirecting output from within awk to a UNIX/Linux file, the shell redirection operators are used. The filename must be enclosed in double quotes. When the > symbol is used, the file is opened and truncated. Once the file is opened, it remains open until explicitly closed or the awk program terminates. Output from subsequent print statements to that file will be appended to the file.

The >> symbol is used to open the file, but does not clear it out; instead it simply appends to it.

EXAMPLE 6.96

```
% nawk '$4 >= 70 {print $1, $2  > "passing_file" }' filename
```

EXPLANATION

If the value of the fourth field is greater than or equal to 70, the first and second fields will be printed to the file passing_file.

6.14.2   Input Redirection (getline)

The getline Function.   The getline function is used to read input from the standard input, a pipe, or a file other than the current file being processed. It gets the next line of input and sets the NF, NR, and the FNR built-in variables. The getline function returns 1 if a record is found and 0 if EOF (end of file) is reached. If there is an error, such as failure to open a file, the getline function returns a value of –1.

EXAMPLE 6.97

```
% nawk 'BEGIN{ "date" | getline d; print d}' filename
Thu Jan 14 11:24:24 PST 2004
```

EXPLANATION

Will execute the UNIX/Linux date command, pipe the output to getline, assign it to the user-defined variable d, and then print d.

EXAMPLE 6.98

```
% nawk 'BEGIN{ "date " | getline d; split( d, mon) ; print mon[2]}' filename
Jan
```

EXPLANATION

Will execute the date command and pipe the output to getline. The getline function will read from the pipe and store the input in a user-defined variable, d. The split function will create an array called mon out of variable d and then the second element of the array mon will be printed.

EXAMPLE 6.99

```
% nawk 'BEGIN{while("ls" | getline) print}'
a.out
db
dbook
getdir
file
sortedf
```

EXPLANATION

Will send the output of the ls command to getline; for each iteration of the loop, getline will read one more line of the output from ls and then print it to the screen. An input file is not necessary, because the BEGIN block is processed before awk attempts to open input.

EXAMPLE 6.100

```
(The Command Line)
1   % nawk 'BEGIN{ printf "What is your name?" ;\
        getline name < "/dev/tty"}\
2   $1 ~ name {print "Found " name " on line ", NR "."}\
3   END{print "See ya, " name "."}' filename
```

```
(The Output)
What is your name? Ellie     < Waits for input from user >
Found Ellie on line 5.
See ya, Ellie.
```

EXPLANATION

1   Will print to the screen What is your name? and wait for user response; the getline function will accept input from the terminal (/dev/tty) until a newline is entered, and then store the input in the user-defined variable name.

2   If the first field matches the value assigned to name, the print function is executed.

3   The END statement prints out See ya, and then the value Ellie, stored in variable name, is displayed, followed by a period.

EXAMPLE 6.101

```
(The Command Line)
% nawk 'BEGIN{while (getline < "/etc/passwd"  > 0 )lc++; print lc}' file
```

```
(The Output)
16
```

EXPLANATION

Awk will read each line from the /etc/passwd file, increment lc until EOF is reached, then print the value of lc, which is the number of lines in the passwd file.

Note: The value returned by getline is –1 if the file does not exist. If the EOF is reached, the return value is 0, and if a line was read, the return value is 1. Therefore, the command

```
while ( getline < "/etc/junk")
```

would start an infinite loop if the file /etc/junk did not exist, because the return value of –1 yields a true condition.

6.15 Pipes

If you open a pipe in an awk program, you must close it before opening another one. The command on the right-hand side of the pipe symbol is enclosed in double quotes. Only one pipe can be open at a time.

EXAMPLE 6.102

```
(The Database)
% cat names
john smith
alice cheba
george goldberg
susan goldberg
tony tram
barbara nguyen
elizabeth lone
dan savage
eliza goldberg
john goldenrod

(The Command Line)
% nawk '{print $1, $2 | "sort -r +1 -2 +0 -1 "}' names

(The Output)
tony tram
john smith
dan savage
barbara nguyen
elizabeth lone
john goldenrod
susan goldberg
george goldberg
eliza goldberg
alice cheba
```

EXPLANATION

Awk will pipe the output of the print statement as input to the UNIX/Linux sort command, which does a reversed sort using the second field as the primary key and the first field as the secondary key (i.e., sort by last name in reverse). The UNIX/Linux command must be enclosed in double quotes. (See "sort" in Appendix A.)

6.15.1 Closing Files and Pipes

If you plan to use a file or pipe in an awk program again for reading or writing, you may want to close it first, because it remains open until the script ends. Once opened, the pipe remains open until awk exits. Therefore, statements in the END block will also be affected by the pipe. The first line in the END block closes the pipe.

EXAMPLE 6.103

```
(In Script)
1   { print $1, $2, $3 | " sort -r +1 -2 +0 -1"}
    END{
2   close("sort -r +1 -2 +0 -1")
    <rest of statements>  }
```

EXPLANATION

1   Awk pipes each line from the input file to the UNIX/Linux sort utility.

2   When the END block is reached, the pipe is closed. The string enclosed in double quotes must be identical to the pipe string where the pipe was initially opened.

The system Function.   The built-in system function takes a UNIX/Linux system command as its argument, executes the command, and returns the exit status to the awk program. It is similar to the C standard library function, also called system(). The UNIX/Linux command must be enclosed in double quotes.

FORMAT

```
system( "UNIX/Linux Command")
```

EXAMPLE 6.104

```
(In Script)
    {
1   system ( "cat" $1 )
2   system ( "clear" )
    }
```

EXPLANATION

1   The system function takes the UNIX/Linux cat command and the value of the first field in the input file as its arguments. The cat command takes the value of the first field, a filename, as its argument. The UNIX/Linux shell causes the cat command to be executed.

2   The system function takes the UNIX/Linux clear command as its argument. The shell executes the command, causing the screen to be cleared.

6.16 Review

The examples in this section, unless noted otherwise, use the following datafile, repeated periodically for your convenience.

% **cat datafile**						
northwest	NW	Joel Craig	3.0	.98	3	4
western	WE	Sharon Kelly	5.3	.97	5	23
southwest	SW	Chris Foster	2.7	.8	2	18
southern	SO	May Chin	5.1	.95	4	15
southeast	SE	Derek Johnson	4.0	.7	4	17
eastern	EA	Susan Beal	4.4	.84	5	20
northeast	NE	TJ Nichols	5.1	.94	3	13
north	NO	Val Shultz	4.5	.89	5	9
central	CT	Sheri Watson	5.7	.94	5	13

6.16.1   Increment and Decrement Operators

EXAMPLE 6.105

```
% nawk '/^north/{count += 1; print count}' datafile
1
2
3
```

EXPLANATION

If the record begins with the regular expression north, a user-defined variable, count, is created; count is incremented by 1 and its value is printed.

EXAMPLE 6.106

```
% nawk '/^north/{count++; print count}' datafile
1
2
3
```

EXPLANATION

The auto-increment operator increments the user-defined variable count by 1. The value of count is printed.

EXAMPLE 6.107

```
% nawk '{x = $7--; print "x = "x ", $7 = "$7}' datafile
x = 3, $7 = 2
x = 5, $7 = 4
x = 2, $7 = 1
x = 4, $7 = 3
x = 4, $7 = 3
x = 5, $7 = 4
x = 3, $7 = 2
x = 5, $7 = 4
x = 5, $7 = 4
```

EXPLANATION

After the value of the seventh field ($7) is assigned to the user-defined variable x, the auto-decrement operator decrements the seventh field by 1. The value of x and the seventh field are printed.

6.16.2   Built-In Variables

EXAMPLE 6.108

```
% nawk '/^north/{print "The record number is " NR}' datafile
The record number is 1
The record number is 7
The record number is 8
```

EXPLANATION

If the record begins with the regular expression north, the string The record number is and the value of NR (record number) are printed.

EXAMPLE 6.109

```
% nawk '{print NR, $0}' datafile
1 northwest      NW     Joel Craig       3.0   .98   3    4
2 western        WE     Sharon Kelly     5.3   .97   5    23
3 southwest      SW     Chris Foster     2.7   .8    2    18
4 southern       SO     May Chin         5.1   .95   4    15
5 southeast      SE     Derek Johnson    4.0   .7    4    17
6 eastern        EA     Susan Beal       4.4   .84   5    20
7 northeast      NE     TJ Nichols       5.1   .94   3    13
8 north          NO     Val Shultz       4.5   .89   5    9
9 central        CT     Sheri Watson     5.7   .94   5    13
```

EXPLANATION

The value of NR, the number of the current record, and the value of $0, the entire record, are printed.

```
% cat datafile
northwest      NW      Joel Craig           3.0    .98   3    4
western        WE      Sharon Kelly         5.3    .97   5    23
southwest      SW      Chris Foster         2.7    .8    2    18
southern       SO      May Chin             5.1    .95   4    15
southeast      SE      Derek Johnson        4.0    .7    4    17
eastern        EA      Susan Beal           4.4    .84   5    20
northeast      NE      TJ Nichols           5.1    .94   3    13
north          NO      Val Shultz           4.5    .89   5    9
central        CT      Sheri Watson         5.7    .94   5    13
```

EXAMPLE 6.110

```
% nawk 'NR==2,NR==5{print NR, $0}' datafile
2 western         WE      Sharon Kelly      5.3   .97   5      23
3 southwest       SW      Chris Foster      2.7   .8    2      18
4 southern        SO      May Chin          5.1   .95   4      15
5 southeast       SE      Derek Johnson     4.0   .7    4      17
```

EXPLANATION

If the value of NR is in the *range* between 2 and 5 (record numbers 2–5), the number of the record (NR) and the record ($0) are printed.

EXAMPLE 6.111

```
% nawk '/^north/{print NR, $1, $2, $NF, RS}' datafile
1 northwest NW 4

7 northeast NE 13

8 north NO 9
```

EXPLANATION

If the record begins with the regular expression north, the number of the record (NR), followed by the first field, the second field, the value of the last field (NF preceded by a dollar sign), and the value of RS (a newline) are printed. Because the print function generates a newline by default, RS will generate another newline, resulting in double spacing between records.

Use the following datafile2 for Examples 6.112 and 6.113.

% **cat datafile2**
Joel Craig:northwest:NW:3.0:.98:3:4
Sharon Kelly:western:WE:5.3:.97:5:23
Chris Foster:southwest:SW:2.7:.8:2:18
May Chin:southern:SO:5.1:.95:4:15
Derek Johnson:southeast:SE:4.0:.7:4:17
Susan Beal:eastern:EA:4.4:.84:5:20
TJ Nichols:northeast:NE:5.1:.94:3:13
Val Shultz:north:NO:4.5:.89:5:9
Sheri Watson:central:CT:5.7:.94:5:13

EXAMPLE 6.112

```
% nawk -F: 'NR == 5{print NF}' datafile2
7
```

EXPLANATION

The field separator is set to a colon at the command line with the -F option. If the number of the record (NR) is 5, the number of fields (NF) is printed.

EXAMPLE 6.113

```
% nawk 'BEGIN{OFMT="%.2f";print 1.2456789,12E-2}' datafile2
1.25 0.12
```

EXPLANATION

OFMT, the output format variable for the print function, is set so that floating-point numbers will be printed with a decimal-point precision of two digits. The numbers 1.23456789 and 12E-2 are printed in the new format.

```
% cat datafile
northwest     NW     Joel Craig         3.0    .98    3    4
western       WE     Sharon Kelly       5.3    .97    5    23
southwest     SW     Chris Foster       2.7    .8     2    18
southern      SO     May Chin           5.1    .95    4    15
southeast     SE     Derek Johnson      4.0    .7     4    17
eastern       EA     Susan Beal         4.4    .84    5    20
northeast     NE     TJ Nichols         5.1    .94    3    13
north         NO     Val Shultz         4.5    .89    5    9
central       CT     Sheri Watson       5.7    .94    5    13
```

EXAMPLE   6.114

```
% nawk '{$9 = $6 * $7; print $9}' datafile
2.94
4.85
1.6
3.8
2.8
4.2
2.82
4.45
4.7
```

EXPLANATION

The result of multiplying the sixth field ($6) and the seventh field ($7) is stored in a new field, $9, and printed. There were eight fields; now there are nine.

EXAMPLE   6.115

```
% nawk '{$10 = 100; print NF, $9, $0}' datafile
10   northwest    NW    Joel Craig      3.0   .98   3   4    100
10   western      WE    Sharon Kelly    5.3   .97   5   23   100
10   southwest    SW    Chris Foster    2.7   .8    2   18   100
10   southern     SO    May Chin        5.1   .95   4   15   100
10   southeast    SE    Derek Johnson   4.0   .7    4   17   100
10   eastern      EA    Susan Beal      4.4   .84   5   20   100
10   northeast    NE    TJ Nichols      5.1   .94   3   13   100
10   north        NO    Val Shultz      4.5   .89   5   9    100
10   central      CT    Sheri Watson    5.7   .94   5   13   100
```

EXPLANATION

A tenth field ($10) is assigned 100 for each record. This is a new field. The ninth field ($9) does not exist, so it will be considered a null field. The number of fields is printed (NF), followed by the value of $9, the null field, and the entire record ($0). The value of the tenth field is 100.

6.16.3 BEGIN Patterns

EXAMPLE 6.116

```
% nawk 'BEGIN{print "---------EMPLOYEES---------"}'
---------EMPLOYEES---------
```

EXPLANATION

The BEGIN pattern is followed by an action block. The action is to print out the string
---------EMPLOYEES--------- before opening the input file. Note that an input file has
not been provided and awk does not complain because any action preceded by BEGIN occurs first, even before awk looks for an input file.

EXAMPLE 6.117

```
% nawk 'BEGIN{print "\t\t---------EMPLOYEES-------\n"}\
  {print $0}' datafile
                      ---------EMPLOYEES-------
northwest     NW     Joel Craig      3.0    .98    3    4
western       WE     Sharon Kelly    5.3    .97    5    23
southwest     SW     Chris Foster    2.7    .8     2    18
southern      SO     May Chin        5.1    .95    4    15
southeast     SE     Derek Johnson   4.0    .7     4    17
eastern       EA     Susan Beal      4.4    .84    5    20
northeast     NE     TJ Nichols      5.1    .94    3    13
north         NO     Val Shultz      4.5    .89    5    9
central       CT     Sheri Watson    5.7    .94    5    13
```

EXPLANATION

The BEGIN action block is executed first. The title ---------EMPLOYEES------- is printed.
The second action block prints each record in the input file. When breaking lines, the
backslash is used to suppress the carriage return. Lines can be broken at a semicolon
or a curly brace.

The following datafile2 is used for Example 6.118.

% **cat datafile2**
Joel Craig:northwest:NW:3.0:.98:3:4
Sharon Kelly:western:WE:5.3:.97:5:23
Chris Foster:southwest:SW:2.7:.8:2:18
May Chin:southern:SO:5.1:.95:4:15
Derek Johnson:southeast:SE:4.0:.7:4:17
Susan Beal:eastern:EA:4.4:.84:5:20
TJ Nichols:northeast:NE:5.1:.94:3:13
Val Shultz:north:NO:4.5:.89:5:9
Sheri Watson:central:CT:5.7:.94:5:13

EXAMPLE 6.118

```
% nawk 'BEGIN{ FS=":";OFS="\t"};/^Sharon/{print $1, $2, $8 }' datafile2
Sharon Kelly     western     28
```

EXPLANATION

The BEGIN action block is used to initialize variables. The FS variable (field separator) is assigned a colon. The OFS variable (output field separator) is assigned a tab (\t). After processing the BEGIN action block, awk opens datafile2 and starts reading input from the file. If a record begins with the regular expression Sharon, the first, second, and eighth fields ($1, $2, $8) are printed. Each field in the output is separated by a tab.

6.16.4   END Patterns

The following datafile is used for Examples 6.119 and 6.120.

% **cat datafile**

northwest	*NW*	*Joel Craig*	*3.0*	*.98*	*3*	*4*
western	*WE*	*Sharon Kelly*	*5.3*	*.97*	*5*	*23*
southwest	*SW*	*Chris Foster*	*2.7*	*.8*	*2*	*18*
southern	*SO*	*May Chin*	*5.1*	*.95*	*4*	*15*
southeast	*SE*	*Derek Johnson*	*4.0*	*.7*	*4*	*17*
eastern	*EA*	*Susan Beal*	*4.4*	*.84*	*5*	*20*
northeast	*NE*	*TJ Nichols*	*5.1*	*.94*	*3*	*13*
north	*NO*	*Val Shultz*	*4.5*	*.89*	*5*	*9*
central	*CT*	*Sheri Watson*	*5.7*	*.94*	*5*	*13*

EXAMPLE 6.119

```
% nawk 'END{print "The total number of records is " NR}' datafile
The total number of records is 9
```

EXPLANATION

After awk has finished processing the input file, the statements in the END block are executed. The string The total number of records is is printed, followed by the value of NR, the number of the last record.

EXAMPLE 6.120

```
% nawk '/^north/{count++}END{print count}' datafile
3
```

EXPLANATION

If the record begins with the regular expression north, the user-defined variable count is incremented by one. When awk has finished processing the input file, the value stored in the variable count is printed.

6.16.5   awk Script with BEGIN and END

The following datafile2 is used for Example 6.121.

% **cat datafile2**
Joel Craig:northwest:NW:3.0:.98:3:4
Sharon Kelly:western:WE:5.3:.97:5:23
Chris Foster:southwest:SW:2.7:.8:2:18
May Chin:southern:SO:5.1:.95:4:15
Derek Johnson:southeast:SE:4.0:.7:4:17
Susan Beal:eastern:EA:4.4:.84:5:20
TJ Nichols:northeast:NE:5.1:.94:3:13
Val Shultz:north:NO:4.5:.89:5:9
Sheri Watson:central:CT:5.7:.94:5:13

EXAMPLE 6.121

```
    # Second awk script-- awk.sc2
1   BEGIN{ FS=":"
        print "  NAME\t\tDISTRICT\tQUANTITY"
        print "_____\n"
    }

2       {print $1"\t  " $3"\t\t" $7}
        {total+=$7}
        /north/{count++}

3   END{
        print "--------------------------------------------"
        print "The total quantity is " total
        print "The number of northern salespersons is " count "."
    }
```

(The Output)
4 % **nawk -f awk.sc2 datafile2**

```
    NAME DISTRICT  QUANTITY

    _____
    Joel Craig      NW      4
    Sharon Kelly    WE      23
    Chris Foster    SW      18
    May Chin        SO      15
    Derek Johnson   SE      17
    Susan Beal      EA      20
    TJ Nichols      NE      13
    Val Shultz      NO      9
    Sheri Watson    CT      13
    --------------------------------------------
    The total quantity is 132
    The number of northern salespersons is 3.
```

EXPLANATION

1   The BEGIN block is executed first. The field separator (FS) is set. Header output is printed.

2   The body of the awk script contains statements that are executed for each line of input coming from datafile2.

3   Statements in the END block are executed after the input file has been closed, i.e., before awk exits.

4   At the command line, the nawk program is executed. The -f option is followed by the script name, awk.sc2, and then by the input file, datafile2.

The remaining examples in this section use the following datafile, repeated periodically for your convenience.

% **cat datafile**							
northwest	NW	Joel Craig	3.0	.98	3	4
western	WE	Sharon Kelly	5.3	.97	5	23
southwest	SW	Chris Foster	2.7	.8	2	18
southern	SO	May Chin	5.1	.95	4	15
southeast	SE	Derek Johnson	4.0	.7	4	17
eastern	EA	Susan Beal	4.4	.84	5	20
northeast	NE	TJ Nichols	5.1	.94	3	13
north	NO	Val Shultz	4.5	.89	5	9
central	CT	Sheri Watson	5.7	.94	5	13

6.16.6 The printf Function

EXAMPLE 6.122

```
% nawk '{printf "$%6.2f\n",$6 * 100}' datafile
$ 98.00
$ 97.00
$ 80.00
$ 95.00
$ 70.00
$ 84.00
$ 94.00
$ 89.00
$ 94.00
```

EXPLANATION

The printf function formats a floating-point number to be right-justified (the default) with a total of 6 digits, one for the decimal point, and two for the decimal numbers to the right of the period. The number will be rounded up and printed.

```
% nawk '{printf "|%-15s|\n",$4}' datafile
|Craig|
|Kelly  |
|Foster |
|Chin   |
|Johnson|
|Beal |
|Nichols|
|Shultz|
|Watson|
```

EXPLANATION

A left-justified, 15-space string is printed. The fourth field ($4) is printed enclosed in vertical bars to illustrate the spacing.

6.16.7 Redirection and Pipes

```
% nawk '/north/{print $1, $3, $4 > "districts"}' datafile
% cat districts
northwest Joel Craig
northeast TJ Nichols
north Val Shultz
```

EXPLANATION

If the record contains the regular expression north, the first, third, and fourth fields ($1, $3, $4) are printed to an output file called districts. Once the file is opened, it remains open until closed or the program terminates. The filename "districts" must be enclosed in double quotes.

```
% nawk '/south/{print $1, $2, $3 >> "districts"}' datafile
% cat districts
southwest SW Chris
southern SO May
southeast SE Derek
```

EXPLANATION

If the record contains the pattern south, the first, second, and third fields ($1, $2, $3) are appended to the output file districts.

% **cat datafile**						
northwest	NW	Joel Craig	3.0	.98	3	4
western	WE	Sharon Kelly	5.3	.97	5	23
southwest	SW	Chris Foster	2.7	.8	2	18
southern	SO	May Chin	5.1	.95	4	15
southeast	SE	Derek Johnson	4.0	.7	4	17
eastern	EA	Susan Beal	4.4	.84	5	20
northeast	NE	TJ Nichols	5.1	.94	3	13
north	NO	Val Shultz	4.5	.89	5	9
central	CT	Sheri Watson	5.7	.94	5	13

6.16.8   Opening and Closing a Pipe

EXAMPLE   6.126

```
# awk script using pipes -- awk.sc3
1   BEGIN{
2       printf " %-22s%s\n", "NAME", "DISTRICT"
        print "------------------------------------"
3   }
4   /west/{count++}
5   {printf "%s %s\t\t%-15s\n", $3, $4, $1| "sort +1" }
6   END{
7       close "sort +1"
        printf "The number of sales persons in the western "
        printf "region is " count "."}
```

(The Output)
```
% nawk -f awk.sc3 datafile
1   NAME                    DISTRICT
2   -------------------------------------------------
3   Susan Beal              eastern
    May Chin                southern
    Joel Craig              northwest
    Chris Foster            southwest
    Derek Johnson           southeast
    Sharon Kelly            western
    TJ Nichols              northeast
    Val Shultz              north
    Sheri Watson            central
    The number of sales persons in the western region is 3.
```

EXPLANATION

1 The special BEGIN pattern is followed by an action block. The statements in this block are executed first, before awk processes the input file.

2 The printf function displays the string NAME as a 22-character, left-justified string, followed by the string DISTRICT, which is right-justified.

3 The BEGIN block ends.

4 Now awk will process the input file, one line at a time. If the pattern west is found, the action block is executed, i.e., the user-defined variable count is incremented by one. The first time awk encounters the count variable, it will be created and given an initial value of 0.

5 The printf function formats and sends its output to a pipe. After all of the output has been collected, it will be sent to the sort command.

6 The END block is started.

7 The pipe (sort +1) must be closed with exactly the same command that opened it; in this example, sort +1. Otherwise, the END statements will be sorted with the rest of the output.

LAB 5: nawk EXERCISE

(Refer to the database called lab5.data on the CD.)

Mike Harrington:(510) 548-1278:250:100:175
Christian Dobbins:(408) 538-2358:155:90:201
Susan Dalsass:(206) 654-6279:250:60:50
Archie McNichol:(206) 548-1348:250:100:175
Jody Savage:(206) 548-1278:15:188:150
Guy Quigley:(916) 343-6410:250:100:175
Dan Savage:(406) 298-7744:450:300:275
Nancy McNeil:(206) 548-1278:250:80:75
John Goldenrod:(916) 348-4278:250:100:175
Chet Main:(510) 548-5258:50:95:135
Tom Savage:(408) 926-3456:250:168:200
Elizabeth Stachelin:(916) 440-1763:175:75:300

The database contains the names, phone numbers, and money contributions to the party campaign for the past three months.

Write a nawk script to produce the following output:

```
% nawk -f nawk.sc db
```

```
                    ***CAMPAIGN 1998 CONTRIBUTIONS***
------------------------------------------------------------------------
NAME              PHONE           Jan |  Feb  |  Mar | Total Donated
------------------------------------------------------------------------
Mike Harrington   (510) 548-1278  250.00   100.00  175.00  525.00
Christian Dobbins (408) 538-2358  155.00    90.00  201.00  446.00
Susan Dalsass     (206) 654-6279  250.00    60.00   50.00  360.00
Archie McNichol   (206) 548-1348  250.00   100.00  175.00  525.00
Jody Savage       (206) 548-1278   15.00   188.00  150.00  353.00
Guy Quigley       (916) 343-6410  250.00   100.00  175.00  525.00
Dan Savage        (406) 298-7744  450.00   300.00  275.00 1025.00
Nancy McNeil      (206) 548-1278  250.00    80.00   75.00  405.00
John Goldenrod    (916) 348-4278  250.00   100.00  175.00  525.00
Chet Main         (510) 548-5258   50.00    95.00  135.00  280.00
Tom Savage        (408) 926-3456  250.00    68.00  200.00  618.00
Elizabeth Stachelin (916) 440-1763 175.00   75.00  300.00  550.00
------------------------------------------------------------------------
                            SUMMARY
------------------------------------------------------------------------
The campaign received a total of $6137.00 for this quarter.
The average donation for the 12 contributors was $511.42.
The highest contribution was $300.00.
The lowest contribution was $15.00.
```

6.17 Conditional Statements

The conditional statements in awk were borrowed from the C language. They are used to control the flow of the program in making decisions.

6.17.1 if Statements

Statements beginning with the if construct are action statements. With *conditional patterns*, the if is implied; with a conditional *action* statement, the if is explicitly stated, and followed by an expression enclosed in parentheses. If the expression evaluates true (nonzero or non-null), the statement or block of statements following the expression is executed. If there is more than one statement following the conditional expression, the statements are separated either by semicolons or a newline, and the group of statements must be enclosed in curly braces so that the statements are executed as a block.

FORMAT

```
if (expression) {
    statement; statement; ...
    }
```

EXAMPLE 6.127

```
1   % nawk '{if ( $6 > 50 ) print $1 "Too high"}' filename

2   % nawk '{if ($6 > 20 && $6  <= 50){safe++; print "OK"}}' filename
```

EXPLANATION

1   In the if action block, the expression is tested. If the value of the sixth field ($6) is greater than 50, the print statement is executed. Because the statement following the expression is a single statement, curly braces are not required. (filename represents the input file.)

2   In the if action block, the expression is tested. If the sixth field ($6) is greater than 20 *and* the sixth field is less than or equal to 50, the statements following the expression are executed as a block and must be enclosed in curly braces.

6.17.2   if/else Statements

The if/else statement allows a two-way decision. If the expression after the if keyword is true, the block of statements associated with that expression are executed. If the first expression evaluates to false or 0, the block of statements after the else keyword is executed. If multiple statements are to be included with the if or else, they must be blocked with curly braces.

FORMAT

```
{if (expression) {
    statement; statement; ...
    }
else{
    statement; statement; ...
    }
}
```

EXAMPLE 6.128

```
1   % nawk '{if( $6 > 50) print  $1 " Too high" ;\
        else print "Range is OK"}' filename
2   % nawk '{if ( $6 > 50 ) { count++; print $3 } \
        else { x+5; print $2 } }' filename
```

1   If the first expression is true, that is, the sixth field ($6) is greater than 50, the print function prints the first field and Too high; otherwise, the statement after the else, Range is OK, is printed.

2   If the first expression is true, that is, the sixth field ($6) is greater than 50, the block of statements is executed; otherwise, the block of statements after the else is executed. Note that the blocks are enclosed in curly braces.

6.17.3   if/else and else if Statements

The if/else and else if statements allow a multiway decision. If the expression following the keyword if is true, the block of statements associated with that expression is executed and control starts again after the last closing curly brace associated with the final else. Otherwise, control goes to the else if and that expression is tested. When the first else if condition is true, the statements following the expression are executed. If none of the conditional expressions test true, control goes to the else statements. The else is called the default action because if none of the other statements are true, the else block is executed.

FORMAT

```
{if (expression) {
    statement; statement; ...
    }
else if (expression){
    statement; statement; ...
    }
else if (expression){
    statement; statement; ...
    }
else{
    statement
    }
}
```

EXAMPLE 6.129

```
(In the Script)
1    {if ( $3 > 89 && $3 < 101 ) Agrade++
2    else if ( $3 > 79 ) Bgrade++
3    else if ( $3 > 69 ) Cgrade++
4    else if ( $3 > 59 ) Dgrade++
5    else Fgrade++
     }
     END{print "The number of failures is" Fgrade }
```

EXPLANATION

1   The if statement is an action and must be enclosed in curly braces. The expression is evaluated from left to right. If the first expression is false, the whole expression is false; if the first expression is true, the expression after the logical AND (&&) is evaluated. If it is true, the variable Agrade is incremented by 1.

2   If the first expression following the if keyword evaluates to false (0), the else if expression is tested. If it evaluates to true, the statement following the expression is executed; that is, if the third field ($3) is greater than 79, Bgrade is incremented by 1.

3   If the first two statements are false, the else if expression is tested, and if the third field ($3) is greater than 69, Cgrade is incremented.

4   If the first three statements are false, the else if expression is tested, and if the third field is greater than 59, Dgrade is incremented.

5   If none of the expressions tested above is true, the else block is executed. The curly brace ends the action block. Fgrade is incremented.

6.18 Loops

Loops are used to repeatedly execute the statements following the test expression if a condition is true. Loops are often used to iterate through the fields within a record and to loop through the elements of an array in the END block. Awk has three types of loops: while, for, and special-for, which will be discussed later when working with awk arrays.

6.18.1   while Loop

The first step in using a while loop is to set a variable to an initial value. The value is then tested in the while expression. If the expression evaluates to true (nonzero), the body of the loop is entered and the statements within that body are executed. If there is more than one statement within the body of the loop, those statements must be enclosed in curly braces. Before ending the loop block, the variable controlling the loop expression must be updated or the loop will continue forever. In the following example, the variable is reinitialized each time a new record is processed.

The do/while loop is similar to the while loop, except that the expression is not tested until the body of the loop is executed at least once.

EXAMPLE   6.130

```
% nawk '{ i  = 1; while ( i <= NF ) { print NF, $i ; i++ } }' filename
```

EXPLANATION

The variable i is initialized to 1; while i is less than or equal to the number of fields (NF) in the record, the print statement will be executed, then i will be incremented by 1. The expression will then be tested again, until the variable i is greater than the value of NF. The variable i is not reinitialized until awk starts processing the next record.

6.18.2 for Loop

The for loop and while loop are essentially the same, except the for loop requires three expressions within the parentheses: the initialization expression, the test expression, and the expression to update the variables within the test expression. In awk, the first statement within the parentheses of the for loop can perform only one initialization. (In C, you can have multiple initializations separated by commas.)

EXAMPLE 6.131

```
% nawk '{ for( i = 1; i <= NF; i++) print NF,$i }' filex
```

EXPLANATION

The variable i is initialized to 1 and tested to see whether it is less than or equal to the number of fields (NF) in the record. If so, the print function prints the value of NF and the value of $i (the $ preceding the i is the number of the ith field), then i is incremented by 1. (Frequently the for loop is used with arrays in an END action to loop through the elements of an array.) See "Arrays" on page 233.

6.18.3 Loop Control

break and continue Statements.   The break statement lets you break out of a loop if a certain condition is true. The continue statement causes the loop to skip any statements that follow if a certain condition is true, and returns control to the top of the loop, starting at the next iteration.

EXAMPLE 6.132

```
(In the Script)
1   {for ( x = 3; x <= NF; x++ )
         if ( $x < 0 ){ print "Bottomed out!"; break}
         # breaks out of for loop
    }

2   {for ( x = 3; x <= NF; x++ )
         if ( $x == 0 ) { print "Get next item"; continue}
         # starts next iteration of the for loop
    }
```

EXPLANATION

1   If the value of the field $x is less than 0, the break statement causes control to go to the statement after the closing curly brace of the loop body; i.e., it breaks out of the loop.

2   If the value of the field $x is equal to 0, the continue statement causes control to start at the top of the loop and start execution, in the third expression at the for loop at x++.

6.19 Program Control Statements

6.19.1   next Statement

The next statement gets the next line of input from the input file, restarting execution at the top of the awk script.

EXAMPLE 6.133

```
(In Script)
{ if ($1 ~ /Peter/){next}
   else {print}
}
```

EXPLANATION

If the first field contains Peter, awk skips over this line and gets the next line from the input file. The script resumes execution at the beginning.

6.19.2   exit Statement

The exit statement is used to terminate the awk program. It stops processing records, but does not skip over an END statement. If the exit statement is given a value between 0 and 255 as an argument—in the following example, it is exit (1)—this value can be printed at the command line to indicate success or failure by typing the following.

EXAMPLE 6.134

```
(In Script)
  {exit (1) }

(The Command Line)
% echo $status     (csh)
1

$ echo $?     (sh/ksh)
1
```

EXPLANATION

An exit status of 0 indicates success, and an exit value of nonzero indicates failure (a convention in UNIX). It is up to the programmer to provide the exit status in a program. The exit value returned in this example is 1.

6.20 Arrays

Arrays in awk are called *associative arrays* because the subscripts can be either numbers or strings. The subscript is often called the *key* and is associated with the value assigned to the corresponding array element. The keys and values are stored internally in a table where a hashing algorithm is applied to the value of the key in question. Due to the techniques used for hashing, the array elements are not stored in a sequential order, and when the contents of the array are displayed, they may not be in the order you expected.

An array, like a variable, is created by using it, and awk can infer whether it is used to store numbers or strings. Array elements are initialized with numeric value zero and string value null, depending on the context. You do not have to declare the size of an awk array. Awk arrays are used to collect information from records and may be used for accumulating totals, counting words, tracking the number of times a pattern occurred, and so forth.

6.20.1 Subscripts for Associative Arrays

Using Variables As Array Indexes.   [See Example 6.135 for a demonstration.

EXAMPLE 6.135

```
(The Input File)
% cat employees
Tom Jones         4424    5/12/66              543354
Mary Adams        5346    11/4/63              28765
Sally Chang       1654    7/22/54              650000
Billy Black       1683    9/23/44              336500

(The Command Line)
1   % nawk '{name[x++]=$2};END{for(i=0; i<NR; i++)\
      print i, name[i]}' employees
    0 Jones
    1 Adams
    2 Chang
    3 Black

2   % nawk '{id[NR]=$3};END{for(x = 1; x <= NR; x++)\
      print id[x]}' employees
    4424
    5346
    1654
    1683
```

EXPLANATION

1 The subscript in array name is a user-defined variable, x. The ++ indicates a numeric context. Awk initializes x to 0 and increments x by 1 *after* (post-increment operator) it is used. The value of the second field is assigned to each element of the name array. In the END block, the for loop is used to loop through the array, printing the value that was stored there, starting at subscript 0. Because the subscript is just a key, it does not have to start at 0. It can start at any value, either a number or a string.

2 The awk variable NR contains the number of the current record. By using NR as a subscript, the value of the third field is assigned to each element of the array for each record. At the end, the for loop will loop through the array, printing out the values that were stored there.

The Special-for Loop.   The special-for loop is used to read through an associative array in cases where the for loop is not practical; that is, when strings are used as subscripts or the subscripts are not consecutive numbers. The special-for loop uses the subscript as a key into the value associated with it.

FORMAT

```
{for(item in arrayname){
    print arrayname[item]
    }
}
```

EXAMPLE 6.136

```
(The Input File)
% cat db
1    Tom Jones
2    Mary Adams
3    Sally Chang
4    Billy Black
5    Tom Savage
6    Tom Chung
7    Reggie Steel
8    Tommy Tucker

(The Command Line, for Loop)
1    % nawk '/^Tom/{name[NR]=$1};\
        END{for( i = 1; i <= NR; i++ )print name[i]}' db
    Tom




    Tom
    Tom

    Tommy
```

EXAMPLE   6.136 (CONTINUED)

```
(The Command Line, Special-for Loop)
2    % nawk '/^Tom/{name[NR]=$1};\
        END{for(i in name){print name[i]}}' db
     Tom
     Tommy
     Tom
     Tom
```

EXPLANATION

1   If the regular expression Tom is matched against an input line, the name array is as-
    signed a value. The NR value, the number of the current record, will be used as an
    index in the name array. Each time Tom is matched on a line, the name array is assigned
    the value of $1, the first field. When the END block is reached, the name array consists
    of four elements: name[1], name[5], name[6], and name[8]. Therefore, when printing
    the values for the name array with the traditional for loop, the values for indexes 2,
    3, 4, and 7 are null.

2   The special-for loop iterates through the array, printing only values where there
    was a subscript associated with that value. The order of the printout is random
    because of the way the associative arrays are stored (hashed).

Using Strings As Array Subscripts.   A subscript may consist of a variable containing a string or literal string. If the string is a literal, it must be enclosed in double quotes.

EXAMPLE   6.137

```
(The Input File)
% cat datafile3
tom
mary
sean
tom
mary
mary
bob
mary
alex

(The Script)
     # awk.sc script
1    /tom/ { count["tom"]++ }
2    /mary/ { count["mary"]++ }
3    END{print "There are " count["tom"] " Toms in the file and
         " count["mary"]" Marys in the file."}
```

EXAMPLE 6.137 (CONTINUED)

(The Command Line)
```
% nawk -f awk.sc datafile3
There are 2 Toms in the file and 4 Marys in the file.
```

EXPLANATION

1   An array called count consists of two elements, count["tom"] and count["mary"]. The initial value of each of the array elements is 0. Every time tom is matched, the value of the array is incremented by 1.

2   The same procedure applies to count["mary"]. Note: Only one tom is recorded for each line, even if there are multiple occurrences on the line.

3   The END pattern prints the value stored in each of the array elements.

Figure 6.1   Using strings as subscripts in an array (Example 6.137).

Using Field Values As Array Subscripts.   Any expression can be used as a subscript in an array. Therefore, fields can be used. The program in Example 6.138 counts the frequency of all names appearing in the second field and introduces a new form of the for loop:

```
for( index_value in array ) statement
```

The for loop found in the END block of the previous example works as follows: The variable name is set to the index value of the count array. After each iteration of the for loop, the print action is performed, first printing the *value of the index*, and then the *value stored* in that element. (*The order of the printout is not guaranteed.*)

EXAMPLE 6.138

```
(The Input File)
% cat datafile4
4234  Tom    43
4567  Arch   45
2008  Eliza  65
4571  Tom    22
3298  Eliza  21
4622  Tom    53
2345  Mary   24
```

EXAMPLE 6.138 (CONTINUED)

```
(The Command Line)
% nawk '{count[$2]++}END{for(name in count)print name,count[name] }' datafile4
Tom 3
Arch 1
Eliza 2
Mary 1
```

EXPLANATION

The awk statement first will use the second field as an index in the count array. The index varies as the second field varies, thus the first index in the count array is Tom and the value stored in count["Tom"] is 1.

Next, count["Arch"] is set to 1, count["Eliza"] to 1, and count["Mary"] to 1. When awk finds the next occurrence of Tom in the second field, count["Tom"] is incremented, now containing the value 2. The same thing happens for each occurrence of Arch, Eliza, and Mary.

EXAMPLE 6.139

```
(The Input File)
% cat datafile4
4234  Tom    43
4567  Arch   45
2008  Eliza  65
4571  Tom    22
3298  Eliza  21
4622  Tom    53
2345  Mary   24

(The Command Line)
% nawk  '{dup[$2]++; if (dup[$2] > 1){name[$2]++ }}\
  END{print "The duplicates were"\
  for (i in name){print i, name[i]}}' datafile4

(The Output)
Tom 2
Eliza 2
```

EXPLANATION

The subscript for the dup array is the value in the second field, that is, the name of a person. The value stored there is initially zero, and it is incremented by one each time a new record is processed. If the name is a duplicate, the value stored for that subscript will go up to two, and so forth. If the value in the dup array is greater than one, a new array called name also uses the second field as a subscript and keeps track of the number of names greater than one.

Arrays and the split Function.   Awk's built-in split function allows you to split a string into words and store them in an array. You can define the field separator or use the value currently stored in FS.

FORMAT

```
split(string, array, field separator)
split (string, array)
```

EXAMPLE 6.140

```
(The Command Line)
% nawk BEGIN{ split( "3/15/2004", date, "/");\
   print "The month is " date[1] "and the year is "date[3]"} filename

(The Output)
The month is 3 and the year is 2004.
```

EXPLANATION

The string 3/15/2004 is stored in the array date, using the forward slash as the field separator. Now date[1] contains 3, date[2] contains 15, and date[3] contains 2004. The field separator is specified in the third argument; if not specified, the value of FS is used as the separator.

The delete Function.   The delete function removes an array element.

EXAMPLE 6.141

```
% nawk '{line[x++]=$2}END{for(x in line) delete(line[x])}' filename
```

EXPLANATION

The value assigned to the array line is the value of the second field. After all the records have been processed, the special-for loop will go through each element of the array, and the delete function will in turn remove each element.

Multidimensional Arrays (nawk).   Although awk does not officially support multidimensional arrays, a syntax is provided that gives the appearance of a multidimensional array. This is done by concatenating the indexes into a string separated by the value of a special built-in variable, SUBSEP. The SUBSEP variable contains the value "\034", an unprintable character that is so unusual that it is unlikely to be found as an index character. The expression matrix[2,8] is really the array matrix[2 SUBSEP 8], which evaluates to matrix["2\0348"]. The index becomes a unique string for an associative array.

EXAMPLE 6.142

```
(The Input File)
1 2 3 4 5
2 3 4 5 6
6 7 8 9 10

(The Script)
1    {nf=NF
2    for(x = 1; x <= NF; x++ ){
3        matrix[NR, x] = $x
         }
     }
4    END { for (x=1; x <= NR; x++ ){
         for (y = 1; y <= nf; y++ )
             printf "%d ", matrix[x,y]
     printf"\n"
         }
     }

(The Output)
1 2 3 4 5
2 3 4 5 6
6 7 8 9 10
```

EXPLANATION

1 The variable nf is assigned the value of NF, the number of fields. (This program assumes a fixed number of five fields per record.)

2 The for loop is entered, storing the number of each field on the line in the variable x.

3 The matrix array is a two-dimensional array. The two indexes, NR (number of the current record) and x, are assigned the value of each field.

4 In the END block, the two for loops are used to iterate through the matrix array, printing out the values stored there. This example does nothing more than demonstrate that multidimensional arrays can be simulated.

6.20.2 Processing Command Arguments (nawk)

ARGV.   Command-line arguments are available to nawk (the new version of awk) with the built-in array called ARGV. These arguments include the command nawk, but not any of the options passed to nawk. The index of the ARGV array starts at zero. (This works only for nawk.)

ARGC.   ARGC is a built-in variable that contains the number of command-line arguments.

EXAMPLE 6.143

```
(The Script)
# Scriptname: argvs
BEGIN{
    for ( i=0; i < ARGC; i++ ){
        printf("argv[%d] is %s\n", i, ARGV[i])
        }
    printf("The number of arguments, ARGC=%d\n", ARGC)
}


(The Output)
% nawk -f argvs datafile
argv[0] is nawk
argv[1] is datafile
The number of arguments, ARGC=2
```

EXPLANATION

In the for loop, i is set to zero, i is tested to see if it is less than the number of command-line arguments (ARGC), and the printf function displays each argument encountered, in turn. When all of the arguments have been processed, the last printf statement outputs the number of arguments, ARGC. The example demonstrates that nawk does not count command-line options as arguments.

EXAMPLE 6.144

```
(The Command Line)
% nawk -f argvs datafile "Peter Pan" 12
argv[0] is nawk
argv[1] is datafile
argv[2] is Peter Pan
argv[3] is 12
The number of arguments, ARGC=4
```

EXPLANATION

As in the last example, each of the arguments is printed. The nawk command is considered the first argument, whereas the -f option and script name, argvs, are excluded.

EXAMPLE 6.145

```
(The Datafile)
% cat datafile5
Tom Jones:123:03/14/56
Peter Pan:456:06/22/58
Joe Blow:145:12/12/78
Santa Ana:234:02/03/66
Ariel Jones:987:11/12/66

(The Script)
% cat arging.sc
# Scriptname: arging.sc
1    BEGIN{FS=":"; name=ARGV[2]
2    print "ARGV[2] is "ARGV[2]
     }
     $1 ~ name { print $0 }

(The Command Line)
% nawk -f arging.sc datafile5 "Peter Pan"
ARGV[2] is Peter Pan
Peter Pan:456:06/22/58
nawk: can't open Peter Pan
input record number 5, file Peter Pan
source line number 2
```

EXPLANATION

1   In the BEGIN block, the variable name is assigned the value of ARGV[2], Peter Pan.

2   Peter Pan is printed, but then nawk tries to open Peter Pan as an input file after it has processed and closed the datafile. Nawk treats arguments as input files.

EXAMPLE 6.146

```
(The Script)
% cat arging2.sc
BEGIN{FS=":"; name=ARGV[2]
    print "ARGV[2] is " ARGV[2]
    delete ARGV[2]
}
$1 ~ name { print $0 }

(The Command Line)
% nawk -f arging2.sc datafile "Peter Pan"
ARGV[2] is Peter Pan
Peter Pan:456:06/22/58
```

EXPLANATION

Nawk treats the elements of the ARGV array as input files; after an argument is used, it is shifted to the left and the next one is processed, until the ARGV array is empty. If the argument is deleted immediately after it is used, it will not be processed as the next input file.

6.21 awk **Built-In Functions**

6.21.1   String Functions

The sub and gsub Functions.   The sub function matches the regular expression for the largest and leftmost substring in the record, and then replaces that substring with the substitution string. If a target string is specified, the regular expression is matched for the largest and leftmost substring in the target string, and the substring is replaced with the substitution string. If a target string is not specified, the entire record is used.

FORMAT

```
sub (regular expression, substitution string);
sub (regular expression, substitution string, target string)
```

EXAMPLE   6.147

```
1 % nawk '{sub(/Mac/, "MacIntosh"); print}' filename
2 % nawk '{sub(/Mac/, "MacIntosh", $1); print}' filename
```

EXPLANATION

1   The first time the regular expression Mac is matched in the record ($0), it will be replaced with the string MacIntosh. The replacement is made only on the first occurrence of a match on the line. (See gsub for multiple occurrences.)

2   The first time the regular expression Mac is matched in the first field of the record, it will be replaced with the string MacIntosh. The replacement is made only on the first occurrence of a match on the line for the target string. The gsub function substitutes a regular expression with a string globally, that is, for every occurrence where the regular expression is matched in each record ($0).

FORMAT

```
gsub(regular expression, substitution string)
gsub(regular expression, substitution string, target string)
```

EXAMPLE 6.148

```
1  % nawk '{ gsub(/CA/, "California"); print }' datafile
2  % nawk '{ gsub(/[Tt]om/, "Thomas", $1 ); print }' filename
```

EXPLANATION

1   Everywhere the regular expression CA is found in the record ($0), it will be replaced with the string California.

2   Everywhere the regular expression Tom or tom is found in the first field, it will be replaced with the string Thomas.

The index Function.   The index function returns the first position where a substring is found in a string. Offset starts at position 1.

FORMAT

```
index(string, substring)
```

EXAMPLE 6.149

```
% nawk '{ print index("hollow", "low") }' filename
4
```

EXPLANATION

The number returned is the position where the substring low is found in hollow, with the offset starting at one.

The length Function.   The length function returns the number of characters in a string. Without an argument, the length function returns the number of characters in a record.

FORMAT

```
length ( string )
length
```

EXAMPLE 6.150

```
% nawk '{ print length("hello") }' filename
5
```

EXPLANATION

The length function returns the number of characters in the string hello.

The substr Function.   The substr function returns the substring of a string starting at a position where the first position is one. If the length of the substring is given, that part of the string is returned. If the specified length exceeds the actual string, the string is returned.

FORMAT

```
substr(string, starting position)
substr(string, starting position, length of string)
```

EXAMPLE   6.151

```
% nawk ' { print substr("Santa Claus", 7, 6 )} ' filename
Claus
```

EXPLANATION

In the string Santa Claus, print the substring starting at position 7 with a length of 6 characters.

The match Function.   The match function returns the index where the regular expression is found in the string, or zero if not found. The match function sets the built-in variable RSTART to the starting position of the substring within the string, and RLENGTH to the number of characters to the end of the substring. These variables can be used with the substr function to extract the pattern. (Works only with nawk.)

FORMAT

```
match(string, regular expression)
```

EXAMPLE   6.152

```
% nawk 'END{start=match("Good ole USA", /[A-Z]+$/); print start}'\
  filename
10
```

EXPLANATION

The regular expression /[A-Z]+$/ says search for consecutive uppercase letters at the end of the string. The substring USA is found starting at the tenth character of the string Good ole USA. If the string cannot be matched, 0 is returned.

```
1   % nawk 'END{start=match("Good ole USA", /[A-Z]+$/);\
      print RSTART, RLENGTH}' filename
    10 3
2   % nawk 'BEGIN{ line="Good ole USA"}; \
      END{ match( line, /[A-Z]+$/);\
      print substr(line, RSTART,RLENGTH)}' filename
    USA
```

EXPLANATION

1   The RSTART variable is set by the match function to the starting position of the regular expression matched. The RLENGTH variable is set to the length of the substring.

2   The substr function is used to find a substring in the variable line, and uses the RSTART and RLENGTH values (set by the match function) as the beginning position and length of the substring.

The split Function.   The split function splits a string into an array using whatever field separator is designated as the third parameter. If the third parameter is not provided, awk will use the current value of FS.

FORMAT

```
split (string, array, field separator)
split (string, array)
```

EXAMPLE 6.154

```
% awk 'BEGIN{split("12/25/2001",date,"/");print date[2]}' filename
25
```

EXPLANATION

The split function splits the string 12/25/2001 into an array, called date, using the forward slash as the separator. The array subscript starts at 1. The second element of the date array is printed.

The sprintf Function.   The sprintf function returns an expression in a specified format. It allows you to apply the format specifications of the printf function.

FORMAT

```
variable=sprintf("string with format specifiers ", expr1, expr2, ... , expr2)
```

EXAMPLE 6.155

```
% awk '{line = sprintf ( "%-15s %6.2f ", $1 , $3 ); print line}' filename
```

EXPLANATION

The first and third fields are formatted according to the printf specifications (a left-justified, 15-space string and a right-justified, 6-character floating-point number). The result is assigned to the user-defined variable line. See "The printf Function" on page 223.

6.22 Built-In Arithmetic Functions

Table 6.13 lists the built-in arithmetic functions, where x and y are arbitrary expressions.

Table 6.13 Arithmetic Functions

Function	Value Returned
atan2(x,y)	Arctangent of y/x in the range
cos(x)	Cosine of x (x in radians)
exp(x)	Exponential function *e* to the power of x
int(x)	Integer portion of x; truncated toward 0 when x > 0
log(x)	Natural (base *e*) logarithm of x
rand( )	Random number r, where 0 < r < 1
sin(x)	Sine of x (with x in radians)
sqrt(x)	Square root of x
srand(x)	x is a new seed for rand( )

6.22.1   Integer Function

The int function truncates any digits to the right of the decimal point to create a whole number. There is no rounding off.

EXAMPLE 6.156

```
1    % awk 'END{print 31/3}' filename
     10.3333
2    % awk 'END{print int(31/3)}' filename
     10
```

EXPLANATION

1   In the END block, the result of the division is to print a floating-point number.
2   In the END block, the int function causes the result of the division to be truncated at the decimal point. A whole number is displayed.

6.22.2   Random Number Generator

The rand Function.   The rand function generates a pseudorandom floating-point number greater than or equal to 0 and less than 1.

EXAMPLE 6.157

```
% nawk '{print rand()}' filename
0.513871
0.175726
0.308634

% nawk '{print rand()}' filename
0.513871
0.175726
0.308634
```

EXPLANATION

Each time the program runs, the same set of numbers is printed. The srand function can be used to seed the rand function with a new starting value. Otherwise, as in this example, the same sequence is repeated each time rand is called.

The srand Function.   The srand function without an argument uses the time of day to generate the seed for the rand function. Srand(x) uses x as the seed. Normally, x should vary during the run of the program.

EXAMPLE 6.158

```
% nawk 'BEGIN{srand()};{print rand()}' filename
0.508744
0.639485
0.657277

% nawk 'BEGIN{srand()};{print rand()}' filename
0.133518
0.324747
0.691794
```

EXPLANATION
The srand function sets a new seed for rand. The starting point is the time of day. Each
time rand is called, a new sequence of numbers is printed.

EXAMPLE 6.159

```
% nawk 'BEGIN{srand()};{print 1 + int(rand() * 25)}' filename
6
24
14
```

EXPLANATION
The srand function sets a new seed for rand. The starting point is the time of day. The
rand function selects a random number between 0 and 25 and casts it to an integer
value.

6.23 User-Defined Functions (nawk)

A user-defined function can be placed anywhere in the script that a pattern action rule can
be placed.

FORMAT

```
function name ( parameter, parameter, parameter, ... ) {
     statements
     return expression
(The return statement and expression are optional)
}
```

Variables are passed by value and are local to the function where they are used. Only copies of the variables are used. Arrays are passed by address or by reference, so array elements can be directly changed within the function. Any variable used within the function that has *not* been passed in the parameter list is considered a global variable; that is, it is visible to the entire nawk program, and if changed in the function, is changed throughout the program. The only way to provide local variables within a function is to include them in the parameter list. Such parameters are usually placed at the end of the list. If there is not a formal parameter provided in the function call, the parameter is initially set to null. The return statement returns control and possibly a value to the caller.

EXAMPLE   6.160

```
(The Command Line Display of grades File before Sort)
% cat  grades
44 55 66 22 77 99
100 22 77 99 33 66
55 66 100 99 88 45

(The Script)
% cat sorter.sc
      # Scriptname: sorter
      # It sorts numbers in ascending order
1     function sort ( scores, num_elements, temp, i, j ) {
          # temp, i, and j will be local and private,
          # with an initial value of null.
2         for( i = 2; i <= num_elements ; ++i ) {
3             for ( j = i; scores [j-1] > scores[j]; --j ){
                  temp = scores[j]
                  scores[j] = scores[j-1]
                  scores[j-1] = temp
              }
4         }
5     }
6     {for ( i = 1; i <= NF; i++)
          grades[i]=$i
7     sort(grades, NF)     # Two arguments are passed
8     for( j = 1; j <= NF; ++j )
          printf( "%d ", grades[j] )
          printf("\n")
      }

(After the Sort)
% nawk -f sorter.sc grades
22 44 55 66 77 99
22 33 66 77 99 100
45 55 66 88 99 100
```

EXPLANATION

1   The function called sort is defined. The function can be defined anywhere in the script. All variables, except those passed as parameters, are global in scope. If changed in the function, they will be changed throughout the nawk script. Arrays are passed by reference. Five formal arguments are enclosed within the parentheses. The array scores will be passed by reference, so that if any of the elements of the array are modified within the function, the original array will be modified. The variable num_elements is a local variable, a copy of the original. The variables temp, i, and j are local variables in the function.

2   The outer for loop will iterate through an array of numbers, as long as there are at least two numbers to compare.

3   The inner for loop will compare the current number with the previous number, scores[j -1]). If the previous array element is larger than the current one, temp will be assigned the value of the current array element, and the current array element will be assigned the value of the previous element.

4   The outer loop block ends.

5   This is the end of the function definition.

6   The first action block of the script starts here. The for loop iterates through each field of the current record, creating an array of numbers.

7   The sort function is called, passing the array of numbers from the current record and the number of fields in the current record.

8   When the sort function has completed, program control starts here. The for loop prints the elements in the sorted array.

6.24 Review

Unless otherwise noted, the examples in this section use the following datafile, repeated periodically for your convenience.

% **cat datafile**						
northwest	NW	Joel Craig	3.0	.98	3	4
western	WE	Sharon Kelly	5.3	.97	5	23
southwest	SW	Chris Foster	2.7	.8	2	18
southern	SO	May Chin	5.1	.95	4	15
southeast	SE	Derek Johnson	4.0	.7	4	17
eastern	EA	Susan Beal	4.4	.84	5	20
northeast	NE	TJ Nichols	5.1	.94	3	13
north	NO	Val Shultz	4.5	.89	5	9
central	CT	Sheri Watson	5.7	.94	5	13

EXAMPLE 6.161

```
% nawk '{if ( $8 > 15 ){ print $3 " has a high rating"}\
  else print $3 "---NOT A COMPETITOR---"}' datafile

Joel---NOT A COMPETITOR---
Sharon has a high rating
Chris has a high rating
May---NOT A COMPETITOR---
Derek has a high rating
Susan has a high rating
TJ---NOT A COMPETITOR---
Val---NOT A COMPETITOR---
Sheri---NOT A COMPETITOR---
```

EXPLANATION

The if statement is an action statement. If there is more than one statement following the expression, it must be enclosed in curly braces. (Curly braces are not required in this example, because there is only one statement following the expression.) The expression reads: if the eighth field is greater than 15, print the third field and the string has a high rating; else print the third field and ---NOT A COMPETITOR---.

EXAMPLE 6.162

```
% nawk '{i=1; while(i<=NF && NR < 2){print $i; i++}}' datafile
northwest
NW
Joel
Craig
3.0
.98
3
4
```

EXPLANATION

The user-defined variable i is assigned 1. The while loop is entered and the expression tested. If the expression evaluates true, the print statement is executed; the value of the ith field is printed. The value of i is printed, next the value is incremented by 1, and the loop is reentered. The loop expression will become false when the value of i is greater than NF and the value of NR is 2 or more. The variable i will not be reinitialized until the next record is entered.

```
% cat datafile
northwest      NW      Joel Craig          3.0    .98    3    4
western        WE      Sharon Kelly        5.3    .97    5    23
southwest      SW      Chris Foster        2.7    .8     2    18
southern       SO      May Chin            5.1    .95    4    15
southeast      SE      Derek Johnson       4.0    .7     4    17
eastern        EA      Susan Beal          4.4    .84    5    20
northeast      NE      TJ Nichols          5.1    .94    3    13
north          NO      Val Shultz          4.5    .89    5    9
central        CT      Sheri Watson        5.7    .94    5    13
```

EXAMPLE   6.163

```
% nawk '{ for( i=3 ; i <= NF && NR == 3 ; i++ ){ print $i }}' datafile
Chris
Foster
2.7
.8
2
18
```

EXPLANATION

This is similar to the while loop in functionality. The initialization, test, and loop control statements are all in one expression. The value of i (i = 3) is initialized once for the current record. The expression is then tested. If i is less than or equal to NF, and NR is equal to 3, the print block is executed. After the value of the ith field is printed, control is returned to the loop expression. The value of i is incremented and the test is repeated.

EXAMPLE   6.164

```
(The Command Line)
% cat nawk.sc4
# Awk script illustrating arrays
BEGIN{OFS="\t"}
{ list[NR] = $1 }     # The array is called list. The index is
                      # the number of the current record. The value of the
                      # first field is assigned to the array element.
END{ for( n = 1; n <= NR; n++){
        print list[n]}     # for loop is used to loop through the array.
}
```

EXAMPLE 6.164 (CONTINUED)

```
(The Command Line)
% nawk -f nawk.sc4 datafile
northwest
western
southwest
southern
southeast
eastern
northeast
north
central
```

EXPLANATION

The array, list, uses NR as an index value. Each time a line of input is processed, the first field is assigned to the list array. In the END block, the for loop iterates through each element of the array.

EXAMPLE 6.165

```
(The Command Line)
% cat nawk.sc5
# Awk script with special for loop
/north/{name[count++]=$3}
END{ print "The number living in a northern district: " count
     print "Their names are: "
     for ( i in name )       # Special nawk for loop is used to
         print name[i]        # iterate through the array.
}

% nawk -f nawk.sc5 datafile
The number living in a northern district: 3
Their names are:
Joel
TJ
Val
```

EXPLANATION

Each time the regular expression north appears on the line, the name array is assigned the value of the third field. The index count is incremented each time a new record is processed, thus producing another element in the array. In the END block, the special-for loop is used to iterate through the array.

% **cat datafile**						
northwest	NW	Joel Craig	3.0	.98	3	4
western	WE	Sharon Kelly	5.3	.97	5	23
southwest	SW	Chris Foster	2.7	.8	2	18
southern	SO	May Chin	5.1	.95	4	15
southeast	SE	Derek Johnson	4.0	.7	4	17
eastern	EA	Susan Beal	4.4	.84	5	20
northeast	NE	TJ Nichols	5.1	.94	3	13
north	NO	Val Shultz	4.5	.89	5	9
central	CT	Sheri Watson	5.7	.94	5	13

EXAMPLE 6.166

```
(The Command Line)
% cat nawk.sc6
# Awk and the special for loop
{region[$1]++}   # The index is the first field of each record
END{for(item in region){
        print region[item], item
    }
}

% nawk -f nawk.sc6 datafile
1 central
1 northwest
1 western
1 southeast
1 north
1 southern
1 northeast
1 southwest
1 eastern

% nawk -f nawk.sc6 datafile3
4 Mary
2 Tom
1 Alax
1 Bob
1 Sean
```

EXPLANATION

The region array uses the first field as an index. The value stored is the number of times each region was found. The END block uses the awk special-for loop to iterate through the array called region.

LAB 6: nawk EXERCISE

(Refer to the database called lab6.data on the CD.)

Mike Harrington:(510) 548-1278:250:100:175
Christian Dobbins:(408) 538-2358:155:90:201
Susan Dalsass:(206) 654-6279:250:60:50
Archie McNichol:(206) 548-1348:250:100:175
Jody Savage:(206) 548-1278:15:188:150
Guy Quigley:(916) 343-6410:250:100:175
Dan Savage:(406) 298-7744:450:300:275
Nancy McNeil:(206) 548-1278:250:80:75
John Goldenrod:(916) 348-4278:250:100:175
Chet Main:(510) 548-5258:50:95:135
Tom Savage:(408) 926-3456:250:168:200
Elizabeth Stachelin:(916) 440-1763:175:75:300

The database above contains the names, phone numbers, and money contributions to the party campaign for the past three months.

1. Write a nawk script that will produce the following report:

```
            ***FIRST QUARTERLY REPORT***
            ***CAMPAIGN 2004 CONTRIBUTIONS***
-------------------------------------------------------------------
   NAME              PHONE       Jan  |  Feb  |  Mar  | Total Donated
-------------------------------------------------------------------
Mike Harrington     (510) 548-1278  250.00  100.00  175.00   525.00
Christian Dobbins   (408) 538-2358  155.00   90.00  201.00   446.00
Susan Dalsass       (206) 654-6279  250.00   60.00   50.00   360.00
Archie McNichol     (206) 548-1348  250.00  100.00  175.00   525.00
Jody Savage         (206) 548-1278   15.00  188.00  150.00   353.00
Guy Quigley         (916) 343-6410  250.00  100.00  175.00   525.00
Dan Savage          (406) 298-7744  450.00  300.00  275.00  1025.00
Nancy McNeil        (206) 548-1278  250.00   80.00   75.00   405.00
John Goldenrod      (916) 348-4278  250.00  100.00  175.00   525.00
Chet Main           (510) 548-5258   50.00   95.00  135.00   280.00
Tom Savage          (408) 926-3456  250.00  168.00  200.00   618.00
Elizabeth Stachelin (916) 440-1763  175.00   75.00  300.00   550.00
-------------------------------------------------------------------
                              SUMMARY
-------------------------------------------------------------------
The campaign received a total of $6137.00 for this quarter.
The average donation for the 12 contributors was $511.42.
The highest total contribution was $1025.00 made by Dan Savage.
                    ***THANKS Dan***
The following people donated over $500 to the campaign.
They are eligible for the quarterly drawing!!
Listed are their names (sorted by last names) and phone numbers:
   John Goldenrod--(916) 348-4278
   Mike Harrington--(510) 548-1278
```

```
Archie McNichol--(206) 548-1348
Guy Quigley--(916) 343-6410
Dan Savage--(406) 298-7744
Tom Savage--(408) 926-3456
Elizabeth Stachelin--(916) 440-1763
    Thanks to all of you for your continued support!!
```

6.25 Odds and Ends

Some data (e.g., that read in from tape or from a spreadsheet) may not have obvious field separators but may instead have fixed-width columns. To preprocess this type of data, the substr function is useful.

6.25.1   Fixed Fields

In the following example, the fields are of a fixed width, but are not separated by a field separator. The substr function is used to create fields.

EXAMPLE 6.167

```
% cat fixed
031291ax5633(408)987-0124
021589bg2435(415)866-1345
122490de1237(916)933-1234
010187ax3458(408)264-2546
092491bd9923(415)134-8900
112990bg4567(803)234-1456
070489qr3455(415)899-1426

% nawk '{printf substr($0,1,6)" ";printf substr($0,7,6)" ";\
  print substr($0,13,length)}' fixed
031291  ax5633  (408)987-0124
021589  bg2435  (415)866-1345
122490  de1237  (916)933-1234
010187  ax3458  (408)264-2546
092491  bd9923  (415)134-8900
112990  bg4567  (803)234-1456
070489  qr3455  (415)899-1426
```

EXPLANATION

The first field is obtained by getting the substring of the entire record, starting at the first character, offset by 6 places. Next, a space is printed. The second field is obtained by getting the substring of the record, starting at position 7, offset by 6 places, followed by a space. The last field is obtained by getting the substring of the entire record, starting at position 13 to the position represented by the length of the line. (The length function returns the length of the current line, $0, if it does not have an argument.)

Empty Fields. If the data is stored in fixed-width fields, it is possible that some of the fields are empty. In the following example, the substr function is used to preserve the fields, regardless of whether they contain data.

```
1   % cat db
    xxx xxx
    xxx abc xxx
    xxx a   bbb
    xxx     xx

    % cat awkfix
    # Preserving empty fields. Field width is fixed.
    {
2   f[1]=substr($0,1,3)
3   f[2]=substr($0,5,3)
4   f[3]=substr($0,9,3)
5   line=sprintf("%-4s%-4s%-4s\n", f[1],f[2], f[3])
6   print line
    }
    % nawk -f awkfix db
    xxx xxx
    xxx abc xxx
    xxx a   bbb
    xxx     xx
```

EXPLANATION

1   The contents of the file db are printed. There are empty fields in the file.

2   The first element of the f array is assigned the substring of the record, starting at position 1 and offset by 3.

3   The second element of the f array is assigned the substring of the record, starting at position 5 and offset by 3.

4   The third element of the f array is assigned the substring of the record, starting at position 9 and offset by 3.

5   The elements of the array are assigned to the user-defined variable line after being formatted by the sprintf function.

6   The value of line is printed and the empty fields are preserved.

Numbers with $, Commas, or Other Characters. In the following example, the price field contains a dollar sign and comma. The script must eliminate these characters to add up the prices to get the total cost. This is done using the gsub function.

EXAMPLE 6.169

```
% cat vendor
access tech:gp237221:220:vax789:20/20:11/01/90:$1,043.00
alisa systems:bp262292:280:macintosh:new updates:06/30/91:$456.00
alisa systems:gp262345:260:vax8700:alisa talk:02/03/91:$1,598.50
apple computer:zx342567:240:macs:e-mail:06/25/90:$575.75
caci:gp262313:280:sparc station:network11.5:05/12/91:$1,250.75
datalogics:bp132455:260:microvax2:pagestation maint:07/01/90:$1,200.00
dec:zx354612:220:microvax2:vms sms:07/20/90:$1,350.00

% nawk -F: '{gsub(/\$/,"");gsub(/,/,""); cost +=$7};\

END{print "The total is $" cost}' vendor
$7474
```

EXPLANATION

The first gsub function globally substitutes the literal dollar sign (\$) with the null string, and the second gsub function substitutes commas with a null string. The user-defined cost variable is then totaled by adding the seventh field to cost and assigning the result back to cost. In the END block, the string The total is $ is printed, followed by the value of cost.[a]

a. For details on how commas are added back into the program, see Alfred V. Aho, Brian W. Kernighan, and Peter J. Weinberger, *The AWK Programming Language* (Boston: Addison-Wesley, 1988), p. 72.

6.25.2 Multiline Records

In the sample data files used so far, each record is on a line by itself. In the following sample datafile, called checkbook, the records are separated by blank lines and the fields are separated by newlines. To process this file, the record separator (RS) is assigned a value of null, and the field separator (FS) is assigned the newline.

EXAMPLE 6.170

```
(The Input File)
% cat checkbook
1/1/04
#125
-695.00
Mortgage

1/1/04
#126
-56.89
PG&E
```

EXAMPLE 6.170 (CONTINUED)

```
1/2/04
#127
-89.99
Safeway

1/3/04
+750.00
Paycheck

1/4/04
#128
-60.00
Visa
```

(The Script)

```
    % cat awkchecker
1   BEGIN{RS=""; FS="\n";ORS="\n\n"}
2   {print NR, $1,$2,$3,$4}
```

(The Output)

```
% nawk -f awkchecker checkbook
1 1/1/04 #125 -695.00 Mortgage

2 1/1/04 #126 -56.89 PG&E

3 1/2/04 #127 -89.99 Safeway

4 1/3/04 +750.00 Paycheck

5 1/4/04 #128 -60.00 Visa
```

EXPLANATION

1   In the BEGIN block, the record separator (RS) is assigned null, the field separator (FS) is assigned a newline, and the output record separator (ORS) is assigned two newlines. Now each line is a field and each output record is separated by two newlines.

2   The number of the record is printed, followed by each of the fields.

6.25.3   Generating Form Letters

The following example is modified from a program in *The AWK Programming Language*.[4] The tricky part of this is keeping track of what is actually being processed. The input file is called data.form. It contains just the data. Each field in the input file is separated by colons. The other file is called form.letter. It is the actual form that will be used to create the letter. This file is loaded into awk's memory with the getline function. Each line of the form letter is stored in an array. The program gets its data from data.form, and the letter is created by substituting real data for the special strings preceded by # and @ found in form.letter. A temporary variable, temp, holds the actual line that will be displayed after the data has been substituted. This program allows you to create personalized form letters for each person listed in data.form.

EXAMPLE 6.171

```
(The Awk Script)
% cat form.awk
# form.awk is an awk script that requires access to 2 files: The
# first file is called "form.letter." This file contains the
# format for a form letter. The awk script uses another file,
# "data.form," as its input file. This file contains the
# information that will be substituted into the form letters in
# the place of the numbers preceded by pound signs. Today's date
# is substituted in the place of "@date" in "form.letter."
1   BEGIN{ FS=":"; n=1
2   while(getline < "form.letter" > 0)
3       form[n++] = $0    # Store lines from form.letter in an array
4   "date" | getline d; split(d, today, " ")
         # Output of date is Fri Mar 2 14:35:50   PST 2004
5   thisday=today[2]". "today[3]", "today[6]
6   }
7   { for( i = 1; i < n; i++ ){
8       temp=form[i]
9       for ( j = 1; j <=NF; j++ ){
             gsub("@date", thisday, temp)
10           gsub("#" j, $j , temp )
         }
11  print temp
     }
     }
```

---

4. Alfred V. Aho, Brian W. Kernighan, and Peter J. Weinberger, *The AWK Programming Language* (Boston: Addison-Wesley, 1988). © 1988 Bell Telephone Laboratories, Inc. Reprinted by permission of Pearson Education, Inc.

EXAMPLE 6.171 (CONTINUED)

```
% cat form.letter
    The form letter, form.letter, looks like this:
************************************************************
    Subject: Status Report for Project "#1"
    To: #2
    From: #3
    Date: @date
    This letter is to tell you, #2, that project "#1" is up to
    date.
    We expect that everything will be completed and ready for
    shipment as scheduled on #4.

    Sincerely,

    #3

*************************************************************
```

The file, *data.form*, is awk's **input file** containing the data that will replace the #1-4 and the @date in *form.letter*.

```
% cat data.form
    Dynamo:John Stevens:Dana Smith, Mgr:4/12/2004
    Gallactius:Guy Sterling:Dana Smith, Mgr:5/18/2004
```

(The Command Line)

```
    % nawk  -f form.awk  data.form
    *************************************************************
    Subject: Status Report for Project "Dynamo"
    To: John Stevens
    From: Dana Smith, Mgr
    Date: Mar. 2, 2004
    This letter is to tell you, John Stevens, that project
    "Dynamo" is up to date.
    We expect that everything will be completed and ready for
    shipment as scheduled on 4/12/2001.
    Sincerely,

    Dana Smith, Mgr
    Subject: Status Report for Project "Gallactius"
    To: Guy Sterling
    From: Dana Smith, Mgr
    Date: Mar. 2, 2004
    This letter is to tell you, Guy Sterling, that project "Gallactius"
    is up to date.
```

EXAMPLE   6.171 (CONTINUED)

We expect that everything will be completed and ready for
shipment as scheduled on 5/18/2004.

Sincerely,

Dana Smith, Mgr

EXPLANATION

1   In the BEGIN block, the field separator (FS) is assigned a colon, and a user-defined variable n is assigned 1.

2   In the while loop, the getline function reads a line at a time from the file called form.letter. If getline fails to find the file, it returns a −1. When it reaches the end of file, it returns 0. Therefore, by testing for a return value of greater than 1, we know that the function has read in a line from the input file.

3   Each line from form.letter is assigned to an array called form.

4   The output from the UNIX/Linux date command is piped to the getline function and assigned to the user-defined variable d. The split function then splits up the variable d with whitespace, creating an array called today.

5   The user-defined variable thisday is assigned the month, day, and year.

6   The BEGIN block ends.

7   The for loop will loop n times.

8   The user-defined variable temp is assigned a line from the form array.

9   The nested for loop is looping through a line from the input file, data.form, NF number of times. Each line stored in the temp variable is checked for the string @date. If @date is matched, the gsub function replaces it with today's date (the value stored in thisday).

10 If a # and a number are found in the line stored in temp, the gsub function will replace the # and number with the value of the corresponding field in the input file, data.form. For example, if the first line stored is being tested, #1 would be replaced with Dynamo, #2 with John Stevens, #3 with Dana Smith, #4 with 4/12/2004, and so forth.

11 The line stored in temp is printed after the substitutions.

6.25.4   Interaction with the Shell

Now that you have seen how awk works, you will find that awk is a very powerful utility when writing shell scripts. You can embed one-line awk commands or awk scripts within your shell scripts. The following is a sample of a Korn shell program embedded with awk commands.

EXAMPLE 6.172

```
    !#/bin/ksh
    # This korn shell script will collect data for awk to use in
    # generating form letter(s). See above.
    print "Hello $LOGNAME. "
    print "This report is for the month and year:"
1   cal | nawk 'NR==1{print $0}'

    if [[ -f data.form  || -f formletter? ]]
    then
         rm data.form formletter?  2> /dev/null
    fi
    integer num=1
    while true
    do
         print "Form letter #$num:"
         read project?"What is the name of the project? "
         read sender?"Who is the status report from? "
         read recipient?"Who is the status report to? "
         read due_date?"What is the completion date scheduled? "
         echo $project:$recipient:$sender:$due_date > data.form
         print -n "Do you wish to generate another form letter? "
         read answer
         if [[ "$answer" != [Yy]* ]]
         then
              break
         else
2             nawk -f form.awk  data.form  > formletter$num
         fi
         (( num+=1 ))
    done
    nawk -f form.awk data.form > formletter$num
```

EXPLANATION

1. The UNIX cal command is piped to nawk. The first line that contains the current month and year is printed.
2. The nawk script form.awk generates form letters, which are redirected to a UNIX file.

(Refer to the database called lab7.data on the CD.)

Mike Harrington:(510) 548-1278:250:100:175
Christian Dobbins:(408) 538-2358:155:90:201
Susan Dalsass:(206) 654-6279:250:60:50
Archie McNichol:(206) 548-1348:250:100:175
Jody Savage:(206) 548-1278:15:188:150
Guy Quigley:(916) 343-6410:250:100:175
Dan Savage:(406) 298-7744:450:300:275
Nancy McNeil:(206) 548-1278:250:80:75
John Goldenrod:(916) 348-4278:250:100:175
Chet Main:(510) 548-5258:50:95:135
Tom Savage:(408) 926-3456:250:168:200
Elizabeth Stachelin:(916) 440-1763:175:75:300

The database contains the names, phone numbers, and money contributions to the party campaign for the past three months.Write a user-defined function to return the average of all the contributions for a given month. The month will be passed in at the command line.

6.26 awk **Built-In Functions**

Unless otherwise noted, the examples in this section use the following datafile, repeated periodically for your convenience.

% **cat datafile**						
northwest	NW	Joel Craig	3.0	.98	3	4
western	WE	Sharon Kelly	5.3	.97	5	23
southwest	SW	Chris Foster	2.7	.8	2	18
southern	SO	May Chin	5.1	.95	4	15
southeast	SE	Derek Johnson	4.0	.7	4	17
eastern	EA	Susan Beal	4.4	.84	5	20
northeast	NE	TJ Nichols	5.1	.94	3	13
north	NO	Val Shultz	4.5	.89	5	9
central	CT	Sheri Watson	5.7	.94	5	13

6.26.1 String Functions

EXAMPLE 6.173

```
% nawk 'NR==1{gsub(/northwest/,"southeast", $1) ;print}' datafile
southeast          NW      Joel Craig        3.0   .98   3   4
```

EXPLANATION

If this is the first record (NR == 1), *globally substitute* the regular expression northwest with southeast, if northwest is found in the first field.

EXAMPLE 6.174

```
% nawk 'NR==1{print substr($3, 1, 3)}' datafile
Joe
```

EXPLANATION

If this is the first record, display the *substring* of the third field, starting at the first character, and extracting a length of 3 characters. The substring Joe is printed.

EXAMPLE 6.175

```
% nawk 'NR==1{print length($1)}' datafile
9
```

EXPLANATION

If this is the first record, the *length* (number of characters) in the first field is printed.

EXAMPLE 6.176

```
% nawk 'NR==1{print index($1,"west")}' datafile
6
```

EXPLANATION

If this is the first record, print the first position where the substring west is found in the first field. The string west starts at the sixth position (*index*) in the string northwest.

% **cat datafile**						
northwest	NW	Joel Craig	3.0	.98	3	4
western	WE	Sharon Kelly	5.3	.97	5	23
southwest	SW	Chris Foster	2.7	.8	2	18
southern	SO	May Chin	5.1	.95	4	15
southeast	SE	Derek Johnson	4.0	.7	4	17
eastern	EA	Susan Beal	4.4	.84	5	20
northeast	NE	TJ Nichols	5.1	.94	3	13
north	NO	Val Shultz	4.5	.89	5	9
central	CT	Sheri Watson	5.7	.94	5	13

EXAMPLE 6.177

```
% nawk '{if(match($1,/^no/)){print substr($1,RSTART,RLENGTH)}}' datafile
no
no
no
```

EXPLANATION

If the match function finds the regular expression /^no/ in the first field, the index position of the leftmost character is returned. The built-in variable RSTART is set to the index position and the RLENGTH variable is set to the length of the matched substring. The substr function returns the string in the first field starting at position RSTART, RLENGTH number of characters.

EXAMPLE 6.178

```
% nawk 'BEGIN{split("10/14/04",now,"/");print now[1],now[2],now[3]}'
10 14 04
```

EXPLANATION

The string 10/14/04 is *split* into an array called now. The delimiter is the forward slash. The elements of the array are printed, starting at the first element of the array.

The following datafile2 is used for Example 6.179.

% cat datafile2
Joel Craig:northwest:NW:3.0:.98:3:4
Sharon Kelly:western:WE:5.3:.97:5:23
Chris Foster:southwest:SW:2.7:.8:2:18
May Chin:southern:SO:5.1:.95:4:15
Derek Johnson:southeast:SE:4.0:.7:4:17
Susan Beal:eastern:EA:4.4:.84:5:20
TJ Nichols:northeast:NE:5.1:.94:3:13
Val Shultz:north:NO:4.5:.89:5:9
Sheri Watson:central:CT:5.7:.94:5:13

EXAMPLE 6.179

```
% nawk -F: '/north/{split($1, name, " ");\
   print "First name: "name[1];\
   print "Last name: " name[2];\
   print "\n-------------------"}' datafile2


First name: Joel
Last name: Craig
-------------------

First name: TJ
Last name: Nichols
-------------------

First name: Val
last name: Shultz
-------------------
```

EXPLANATION

The input field separator is set to a colon (-F:). If the record contains the regular expression north, the first field is *split* into an array called name, where a space is the delimiter. The elements of the array are printed.

```
% cat datafile
northwest     NW     Joel Craig          3.0    .98    3     4
western       WE     Sharon Kelly        5.3    .97    5     23
southwest     SW     Chris Foster        2.7    .8     2     18
southern      SO     May Chin            5.1    .95    4     15
southeast     SE     Derek Johnson       4.0    .7     4     17
eastern       EA     Susan Beal          4.4    .84    5     20
northeast     NE     TJ Nichols          5.1    .94    3     13
north         NO     Val Shultz          4.5    .89    5     9
central       CT     Sheri Watson        5.7    .94    5     13
```

EXAMPLE 6.180

```
% nawk '{line=sprintf("%10.2f%5s\n",$7,$2); print line}' datafile
3.00    NW
5.00    WE
2.00    SW
4.00    SO
4.00    SE
5.00    EA
3.00    NE
5.00    NO
5.00    CT
```

EXPLANATION

The sprintf function formats the seventh and the second fields ($7, $2) using the formatting conventions of the printf function. The formatted string is returned and assigned to the user-defined variable line and printed.

The toupper and tolower Functions (gawk only).   The toupper function returns a string with all the lowercase characters translated to uppercase, and leaves nonalphabetic characters unchanged. Likewise, the tolower function translates all uppercase letters to lowercase. Strings must be quoted.

FORMAT

```
toupper (string)
tolower (string)
```

EXAMPLE 6.181

```
% awk 'BEGIN{print toupper("linux"), tolower("BASH 2.0")}'
LINUX bash 2.0
```

6.26.2   Time Functions with gawk

Gawk provides two functions for getting the time and formatting timestamps: systime and strftime.

The systime Function.   The systime function returns the time of day in non-leap-year seconds since January 1, 1970 (called the Epoch).

FORMAT

systime()

EXAMPLE 6.182

```
% awk 'BEGIN{now=systime(); print now}'
939515282
```

EXPLANATION

The return value of the systime function is returned to a user-defined variable, now. The value is the time of day in non-leap-year seconds since January 1, 1970.

The strftime Function.   The strftime function formats the time using the C library strftime function. The format specifications are in the form %T %D, and so on (see Table 6.14). The timestamp is in the same form as the return value from systime. If the timestamp is omitted, then the current time of day is used as the default.

Table 6.14   Date and Time Format Specifications

Date Format	Definition
For the following definitions, assume the current date and time as *Date: Sunday, October 17, 2004* *Time: 15:26:26 PDT*	
%a	Abbreviated weekday name (Sun)
%A	Full weekday name (Sunday)
%b	Abbreviated month name (Oct)
%B	Full month name (October)
%c	Date and time for locale (Sun Oct 17 15:26:46 2004)
%d	Day of month in decimal (17)
%D	Date as 10/17/04[a]
%e	Day of the month, padded with space if only one digit

Table 6.14 Date and Time Format Specifications (continued)

Date Format	Definition
%H	Hour for a 24-hour clock in decimal (15)
%I	Hour for a 12-hour clock in decimal (03)
%j	Day of the year since January 1 in decimal (290)
%m	Month in decimal (10)
%M	Minute in decimal (26)
%p	AM/PM notation assuming a 12-hour clock (PM)
%S	Second as a decimal number (26)
%U	Week number of the year (with the first Sunday as the first day of week one) as a decimal number (42)
%w	Weekday (Sunday is 0) as a decimal number (0)
%W	The week number of the year (the first Monday as the first day of week one) as a decimal number (41)
%x	Date representation for locale (10/17/04)
%X	Time representation for locale (15:26:26)
%y	Year as two digits in decimal (04)
%Y	Year with century (2004)
%Z	Time zone (PDT)
%%	A literal percent sign (%)

a. %D and %e are available only on some versions of gawk.

FORMAT

```
systime([format specification][,timestamp])
```

EXAMPLE 6.183

```
% awk 'BEGIN{now=strftime("%D", systime()); print now}'
10/09/04

% awk 'BEGIN{now=strftime("%T"); print now}'
17:58:03

% awk 'BEGIN{now=strftime("%m/%d/%y"); print now}'
10/09/04
```

The strftime function formats the time and date according to the format instruction provided as an argument. (See Table 6.14.) If systime is given as a second argument or no argument is given at all, the current time for this locale is assumed. If a second argument is given, it must be in the same format as the return value from the systime function.

The examples in the next sections use the following datafile database, repeated periodically for your convenience.

% **cat datafile**						
northwest	NW	Joel Craig	3.0	.98	3	4
western	WE	Sharon Kelly	5.3	.97	5	23
southwest	SW	Chris Foster	2.7	.8	2	18
southern	SO	May Chin	5.1	.95	4	15
southeast	SE	Derek Johnson	4.0	.7	4	17
eastern	EA	Susan Beal	4.4	.84	5	20
northeast	NE	TJ Nichols	5.1	.94	3	13
north	NO	Val Shultz	4.5	.89	5	9
central	CT	Sheri Watson	5.7	.94	5	13

6.26.3 Command-Line Arguments

EXAMPLE 6.184

```
% cat argvs.sc
# Testing command-line arguments with ARGV and ARGC using a for loop.

BEGIN{
    for(i=0;i < ARGC;i++)
        printf("argv[%d] is %s\n", i, ARGV[i])
        printf("The number of arguments, ARGC=%d\n", ARGC)
}

% nawk -f argvs.sc datafile
argv[0] is nawk
argv[1] is datafile
The number of arguments, ARGC=2
```

The BEGIN block contains a for loop to process the *command-line arguments*. ARGC is the number of arguments and ARGV is an array that contains the actual arguments. Nawk does not count options as arguments. The only valid arguments in this example are the nawk command and the input file, datafile.

```
% cat datafile
northwest     NW     Joel Craig         3.0     .98     3     4
western       WE     Sharon Kelly       5.3     .97     5     23
southwest     SW     Chris Foster       2.7     .8      2     18
southern      SO     May Chin           5.1     .95     4     15
southeast     SE     Derek Johnson      4.0     .7      4     17
eastern       EA     Susan Beal         4.4     .84     5     20
northeast     NE     TJ Nichols         5.1     .94     3     13
north         NO     Val Shultz         4.5     .89     5     9
central       CT     Sheri Watson       5.7     .94     5     13
```

EXAMPLE 6.185

1   % nawk 'BEGIN{name=ARGV[1]};\
    $0 ~ name {print $3 , $4}' "Derek" datafile
    nawk: can't open Derek
    source line number 1

2   % nawk 'BEGIN{name=ARGV[1]; delete ARGV[1]};\
    $0 ~ name {print $3, $4}' "Derek" datafile
    Derek Johnson

EXPLANATION

1   The name "Derek" was assigned to the variable name in the BEGIN block. In the pattern-action block, nawk attempted to open "Derek" as an input file and failed.

2   After assigning "Derek" to the variable name, ARGV[1] is deleted. When starting the pattern-action block, nawk does not try to open "Derek" as the input file, but opens datafile instead.

6.26.4 Reading Input (getline)

EXAMPLE 6.186

    % nawk 'BEGIN{ "date" | getline d; print d}' datafile
    Mon Jan 15 11:24:24 PST 2004

EXPLANATION

The UNIX/Linux date command is piped to the getline function. The results are stored in the variable d and printed.

EXAMPLE 6.187

```
% nawk 'BEGIN{ "date " | getline d; split( d, mon) ;print mon[2]}' datafile
Jan
```

EXPLANATION

The UNIX/Linux date command is piped to the getline function and the results are stored in d. The split function splits the string d into an array called mon. The second element of the array is printed.

EXAMPLE 6.188

```
% nawk 'BEGIN{ printf "Who are you looking for?" ; \
    getline name < "/dev/tty"};\
```

EXPLANATION

Input is read from the terminal, /dev/tty, and stored in the array called name.

EXAMPLE 6.189

```
% nawk 'BEGIN{while(getline < "/etc/passwd"  > 0 ){lc++}; print lc}' datafile
16
```

EXPLANATION

The while loop is used to loop through the /etc/passwd file one line at a time. Each time the loop is entered, a line is read by getline and the value of the variable lc is incremented. When the loop exits, the value of lc is printed (i.e., the number of lines in the /etc/passwd file). As long as the return value from getline is not 0 (i.e., a line has been read), the looping continues.

6.26.5 Control Functions

EXAMPLE 6.190

```
% nawk '{if ( $5 >= 4.5) next; print $1}' datafile
northwest
southwest
southeast
eastern
north
```

EXPLANATION

If the fifth field is greater than 4.5, the next line is read from the input file (datafile) and processing starts at the beginning of the awk script (after the BEGIN block). Otherwise, the first field is printed.

```
% cat datafile
northwest       NW      Joel Craig          3.0     .98     3       4
western         WE      Sharon Kelly        5.3     .97     5       23
southwest       SW      Chris Foster        2.7     .8      2       18
southern        SO      May Chin            5.1     .95     4       15
southeast       SE      Derek Johnson       4.0     .7      4       17
eastern         EA      Susan Beal          4.4     .84     5       20
northeast       NE      TJ Nichols          5.1     .94     3       13
north           NO      Val Shultz          4.5     .89     5       9
central         CT      Sheri Watson        5.7     .94     5       13
```

EXAMPLE 6.191

```
% nawk '{if ($2 ~ /S/){print ; exit 0}}' datafile
southwest       SW      Chris   Foster 2.7      .8      2       18

% echo $status (csh) or echo $? (sh or ksh)
0
```

EXPLANATION

If the second field contains an S, the record is printed and the awk program exits. The C shell status variable contains the exit value. If using the Bourne or Korn shells, the $? variable contains the exit status.

6.26.6   User-Defined Functions

EXAMPLE 6.192

```
(The Command Line)
% cat nawk.sc7
1    BEGIN{largest=0}
2    {maximum=max($5)}

3    function max ( num ) {
4        if ( num > largest){ largest=num }
         return largest
5    }
6    END{ print "The maximum is " maximum "."}

% nawk -f nawk.sc7 datafile
The maximum is 5.7.
```

EXPLANATION

1 In the BEGIN block, the user-defined variable largest is initialized to 0.

2 For each line in the file, the variable maximum is assigned the value returned from the function max. The function max is given $5 as its argument.

3 The user-defined function max is defined. The function statements are enclosed in curly braces. Each time a new record is read from the input file, datafile, the function max will be called.

4 It will compare the values in num and largest and return the larger of the two numbers.

5 The function definition block ends.

6 The END block prints the final value in maximum.

6.26.7 awk/gawk Command-Line Options

Awk has a number of comand-line options. Gawk has two formats for command-line options: the GNU long format starting with a double dash (--) and a word; and the traditional short POSIX format, consisting of a dash and one letter. Gawk-specific options are used with the -W option or its corresponding long option. Any arguments provided to long options are either joined by an = sign (with no intervening spaces), or may be provided in the next command-line argument. The --help option (see Example 6.193) to gawk lists all the gawk options. See Table 6.15.

EXAMPLE 6.193

```
% awk --help
Usage: awk [POSIX or GNU style options] -f progfile [--] file ...
       awk [POSIX or GNU style options] [--] 'program' file ...
POSIX options:          GNU long options:
        -f progfile             --file=progfile
        -F fs                   --field-separator=fs
        -v var=val              --assign=var=val
        -m[fr] val
        -W compat               --compat
        -W copyleft             --copyleft
        -W copyright            --copyright
        -W help                 --help
        -W lint                 --lint
        -W lint-old             --lint-old
        -W posix                --posix
        -W re-interval          --re-interval
        -W source=program-text  --source=program-text
        -W traditional          --traditional
        -W usage                --usage
        -W version              --version
```

EXAMPLE 6.193 (CONTINUED)

Report bugs to bug-gnu-utils@prep.ai.mit.edu,
with a Cc: to arnold@gnu.ai.mit.edu

Table 6.15 gawk Command-Line Options

Options	*Meaning*
-F fs, --field-separator fs	Specifies the input field separator,where fs is either a string or regular expression; for example, FS=":" or FS="[\t:]".
-v var=value, --assign var=value	Assigns a value to a user-defined variable, var before the awk script starts execution. Available to the BEGIN block.
-f scriptfile, --file scriptfile	Reads awk commands from the scriptfile.
-mf nnn, -mr nnn	Sets memory limits to the value of nnn. With -mf as the option, limits the maximum number of fields to nnn; with -mr as the option, sets the maximum number of records. Not applicable for gawk.
-W traditional, -W compat, --traditional --compat	Runs in compatibility mode so that gawk behaves exactly as UNIX versions of awk. All gawk extensions are ignored. Both modes do the same thing; --traditional is preferred.
-W copyleft -W copyright --copyleft	Prints abbreviated version of copyright information.
-W help -W usage --help --usage	Prints the available awk options and a short summary of what they do.
-W lint --lint	Prints warnings about the use of constructs that may not be portable to traditional versions of UNIX awk.
-W lint-old, --lint-old	Provides warnings about constructs that are not portable to the original version of UNIX implementations.
-W posix --posix	Turns on the compatibility mode. Does not recognize \x escape sequences, newlines as a field separator character if FS is assigned a single space, the function keyword (func), operators ** and **= to replace ^ and ^=, and fflush.
-W re-interval, --re-interval	Allows the use of interval regular expressions (see "The POSIX Character Class" on page 176); that is, the bracketed expressions such as [[:alpha:]].

Table 6.15   gawk Command-Line Options (continued)

Options	*Meaning*
-W source program-text --source program-text	Uses program-text as awk's source code allowing awk commands at the command line to be intermixed with -f files; for example, awk -W source '{print $1} -f cmdfile inputfile.
-W version --version	Prints version and bug reporting information.
--	Signals the end of option processing.

7

The Interactive Bourne Shell

7.1 Introduction

When you are at the command line you are using the shell interactively. The shell has a special built-in variable that contains a string of options. If one of the options is the letter i, the shell is running interactively. To test this, type in the following small script at the prompt:

```
case "$-" in
*i*) echo This shell is interactive ;;
*) echo This shell is not interactive ;;
esac
```

The Bourne shell offers you many features to make life easier when you are working at the command line. Although the Bourne shell isn't as robust in this area as the other shells discussed in this book, it provides filename expansion, I/O redirection, command substitution, functions, and a host of other features. Once you have become familiar with the interactive shell, you will be ready to start using these features in shell scripts.

If the Bourne shell is your login shell, it follows a chain of processes before you see a shell prompt (see Figure 7.1).

Here's a very rough sketch of what goes on: The first process to run is called init, PID 1. It gets instructions from a file called inittab (System V), or it spawns a getty process (BSD). These processes open up the terminal ports, providing a place where standard input comes from and a place where standard output and error go, and they put a login prompt on your screen. The /bin/login program is then executed. The login program prompts for a password, encrypts and verifies the password, sets up an initial environment, and starts up the login shell, /bin/sh, the last entry in the passwd file. The sh process looks for the system file, /etc/profile, and executes its commands. It then looks in the user's home directory for an initialization file called .profile. After executing commands from .profile, the default dollar sign ($) prompt appears on your screen and the Bourne shell awaits commands. Of course, most systems today start up with a graphical user

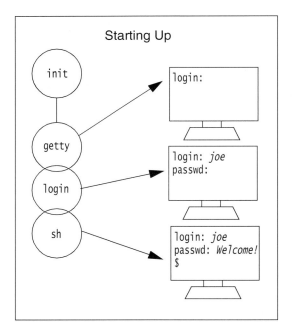

Figure 7.1   Starting the Bourne shell.

interface that provides a login window, a virtual desktop, and submenus to start up shell terminals and other applications. This is more a more complex setup than shown in Figure 7.1, but once the user selects a terminal window, a prompt will appear, and the shell will wait for commands.

7.2   The Environment

The environment of a process consists of variables, open files, the current working directory, functions, resource limits, signals, and so forth. It defines those features that are inherited from one shell to the next and the configuration for the working environment. The configuration for the user's shell is defined in the shell initialization files.

7.2.1   The Initialization Files

After the Bourne shell program starts up, it first checks for the system file /etc/profile. After executing the commands in that initialization file, .profile in the user's home directory is executed. Skeleton files for initial setup can be found in /etc/skel (SVR4).

The /etc/profile File.   The /etc/profile file is a systemwide initialization file set up by the system administrator to perform tasks when the user logs on. It is executed when the Bourne shell starts up. It is available to all Bourne and Korn shell users on the system and normally performs such tasks as checking the mail spooler for new mail and displaying the message of the day from the /etc/motd file. (The following examples will make more sense after you have completed this chapter.)

EXAMPLE 7.1

```
(Sample /etc/profile)
# The profile that all logins get before using their own .profile
1    trap " " 2 3
2    export LOGNAME PATH
3    if [ "$TERM" = " " ]
     then
             if /bin/i386
             then
                    TERM=AT386     # Sets the terminal
             else
                    TERM=sun
             fi
             export TERM
     fi
     # Login and -su shells get /etc/profile services.
     # -rsh is given its environment in its own .profile.
4        case "$0" in
         -sh | -ksh | -jsh )
5            if [ ! -f .hushlogin ]
             then
                    /usr/sbin/quota
                    # Allow the user to break the Message-Of-The-Day only.
6                   trap "trap ' ' 2" 2
7                   /bin/cat -s /etc/motd
                    # Message of the day displayed
                    trap " " 2
8                   /bin/mail -E     # Checks for new mail
9                   case $? in
                    0)
                        echo "You have new mail. "
                    ;;
                    2)
                        echo "You have mail. "
                    ;;
                    esac
             fi
         esac
10       umask 022
11       trap 2 3
```

EXPLANATION

1   The trap command controls signals coming into this program while it is running. If signals 2 (Ctrl-C) or 3 (Ctrl-\) are sent while the program is in execution, those signals will be ignored.

2   The variables LOGNAME and PATH are exported so that their values will be known in subshells started from this process.

3   The command /bin/i386 is executed. If the exit status of the command is 0, the terminal variable, TERM, is assigned the value AT386; if not, the TERM variable is assigned sun.

4   If the value of $0, the name of the program running the /etc/profile file, is either a login Bourne, Korn, or job shell, the following commands will be executed.

5   If the .hushlogin file does not exist, quota will be run to display the disk usage warnings if usage is over the quota.

6   The trap is reset so that the user can terminate the message of the day (motd) with Ctrl-C.

7   After the message of the day has been displayed, the trap is reset to ignore Ctrl-C.

8   The mail program checks for new incoming mail.

9   If the exit status ($?) of the mail program is 0 or 2, the message You have new mail. or You have mail., respectively, is displayed.

10 The umask command is set to determine the initial permissions of files and directories when they are created.

11 The trap command sets signals 2 and 3 back to their defaults; that is, to kill the program if either Ctrl-C or Ctrl-\ arrive.

The .profile File.   The .profile file is a user-defined initialization file executed once at login and found in your home directory. It gives you the ability to customize and modify the shell environment. Environment and terminal settings are normally put here, and if a window application or database application is to be initiated, it is started here. The settings in this file will be discussed in detail as the chapter progresses, but a brief synopsis of each line in the file is explained here.

EXAMPLE   7.2

```
(Sample .profile)
1    TERM=vt102
2    HOSTNAME=`uname -n`
3    EDITOR=/usr/ucb/vi
4    PATH=/bin:/usr/ucb:/usr/bin:/usr/local:/etc:/bin:/usr/bin:.
5    PS1="$HOSTNAME $ > "
6    export TERM HOSTNAME EDITOR PATH PS1
7    stty erase ^h
8    go () { cd $1; PS1=`pwd`; PS1=`basename $PS1`; }
9    trap '$HOME/.logout' EXIT
10   clear
```

EXPLANATION

1   The TERM variable is assigned the value of the terminal type, vt102.

2   Because the uname -n command is enclosed in backquotes, the shell will perform command substitution; that is, the output of the command (the name of the host machine) will be assigned to the variable HOSTNAME.

3   The EDITOR variable is assigned /usr/ucb/vi. Programs such as mail will now have this variable available when defining an editor.

4   The PATH variable is assigned the directory entries that the shell searches to find a UNIX/Linux program. If, for example, you type ls, the shell will search the PATH until it finds that program in one of the listed directories. If it never finds the program, the shell will tell you so.

5   The primary prompt is assigned the value of HOSTNAME, the machine name, and the $ and > symbols.

6   All of the variables listed are exported. They will be known by child processes started from this shell.

7   The stty command sets terminal options. The erase key is set to ^h, so that when you press the Backspace key, the letter typed preceding the cursor is erased.

8   A function called go is defined. The purpose of this function is to take one argument, a directory name, cd to that directory, and set the primary prompt to the present working directory. The basename command removes all but the last entry of the path. The prompt will show you the current directory.

9   The trap command is a signal handling command. When you exit the shell, that is, log out, the .logout file will be executed.

10   The clear command clears the screen.

7.2.2   The Prompts

When used interactively, the shell prompts you for input. When you see the prompt, you know that you can start typing commands. The Bourne shell provides two prompts: the primary prompt, a dollar sign ($), and the secondary prompt, a right angle bracket symbol (>). The prompts are displayed when the shell is running interactively. You can change these prompts. The variable PS1 is the primary prompt set initially to a dollar sign. The primary prompt appears when you log on and the shell waits for you to type commands. The variable PS2 is the secondary prompt, initially set to the right angle bracket character. It appears if you have partially typed a command and then pressed the carriage return. You can change the primary and secondary prompts.

The Primary Prompt.   The dollar sign is the default primary prompt. You can change your prompt. Normally prompts are defined in .profile, the user initialization file.

EXAMPLE 7.3

```
1   $ PS1="`uname -n > `"
2   chargers >
```

EXPLANATION

1   The default primary prompt is a dollar sign ($). The PS1 prompt is being reset to the name of the machine (uname -n) and a > symbol. (Don't confuse backquotes and single quotes.)

2   The new prompt is displayed.

The Secondary Prompt.   The PS2 prompt is the secondary prompt. Its value is displayed to standard error, which is the screen by default. This prompt appears when you have not completed a command and have pressed the carriage return.

EXAMPLE 7.4

```
1   $ echo "Hello
2   > there"
3   Hello
    there
4   $

5   $ PS2="----> "
6   $ echo 'Hi
7   ---->
    ---->
    ----> there'
    Hi


    there
    $
```

EXPLANATION

1   The double quotes must be matched after the string "Hello.

2   When a newline is entered, the secondary prompt appears. Until the closing double quotes are entered, the secondary prompt will be displayed.

3   The output of the echo command is displayed.

4   The primary prompt is displayed.

5   The secondary prompt is reset.

6   The single quote must be matched after the string 'Hi.

7   When a newline is entered, the new secondary prompt appears. Until the closing single quote is entered, the secondary prompt will be displayed.

7.2.3 The Search Path

The PATH variable is used by the Bourne shell to locate commands typed at the command line. The path is a colon-separated list of directories used by the shell when searching for commands. The search is from left to right. The dot at the end of the path represents the current working directory. If the command is not found in any of the directories listed in the path, the Bourne shell sends to standard error the message filename: not found. It is recommended that the path be set in the .profile file.

   If the dot is not included in the path and you are executing a command or script from the current working directory, the name of the script must be preceded with a ./, such as ./program_name, so that shell can find the program.

EXAMPLE 7.5

```
(Printing the PATH)
1    $ echo $PATH
     /home/gsa12/bin:/usr/ucb:/usr/bin:/usr/local/bin:/usr/bin:/usr/local/bin:.

(Setting the PATH)
2    $ PATH=$HOME:/usr/ucb:/usr:/usr/bin:/usr/local/bin:.
3    $ export PATH
```

EXPLANATION

1   By echoing $PATH, the value of the PATH variable is displayed. The path consists of a list of colon-separated elements and is searched from left to right. The dot at the end of the path represents the user's current working directory.

2   To set the path, a list of colon-separated directories are assigned to the PATH variable.

3   By exporting the path, child processes will have access to it.

7.2.4 The hash Command

The hash command controls the internal hash table used by the shell to improve efficiency in searching for commands. Instead of searching the path each time a command is entered, the first time you type a command, the shell uses the search path to find the command, and then stores it in a table in the shell's memory. The next time you use the same command, the shell uses the hash table to find it. This makes it much faster to access a command than having to search the complete path. If you know that you will be using a command often, you can add the command to the hash table. You can also remove commands from the table. The output of the hash command displays both the number of times the shell has used the table to find a command (hits) and the relative cost of looking up the command (cost), that is, how far down the search path it had to go before it found the command. The hash command with the -r option clears the hash table.

EXAMPLE 7.6

```
1   $ hash
    hits  cost    command
    3     8       /usr/bin/date
    1     8       /usr/bin/who
    1     8       /usr/bin/ls
2   $ hash vi
    3     8       /usr/bin/date
    1     8       /usr/bin/who
    1     8       /usr/bin/ls
    0     6       /usr/ucb/vi
3   $ hash -r
```

EXPLANATION

1   The hash command displays the commands currently stored in the internal hash table. The shell will not have to search the search path to find the commands listed when they are entered at the command line. This saves time. Otherwise, the shell has to go out to the disk to search the path. When you type a new command, the shell will search the path first, and then place it on the hash table. The next time you use that command, the shell finds it in memory.

2   The hash command can take arguments; the names of commands you want to guarantee get stored on the hash table ahead of time.

3   The hash command with the -r option clears the hash table.

7.2.5 The dot Command

The dot command is a built-in Bourne shell command. It takes a script name as an argument. The script will be executed in the environment of the current shell; that is, a child process will not be started. All variables set in the script will become part of the current shell's environment. Likewise, all variables set in the current shell will become part of the script's environment. The dot command is normally used to re-execute the .profile file if it has been modified. For example, if one of the settings, such as the EDITOR or TERM variable, has been changed since you logged on, you can use the dot command to re-execute the .profile without logging out and then logging back in.

EXAMPLE 7.7

```
$ . .profile
```

EXPLANATION

The dot command executes the initialization file, .profile, within this shell. Local and global variables are redefined within this shell. The dot command makes it unnecessary to log out and then log back in again.[a]

---

a. If the .profile were executed directly as a script, a subshell would be started. Then the variables would be set in the subshell, but not in the login shell (parent shell).

7.3 The Command Line

After logging on, the shell displays its primary prompt, a dollar sign by default. The shell is your command interpreter. When the shell is running interactively, it reads commands from the terminal and breaks the command line into words. A command line consists of one or more words (tokens), separated by whitespace (blanks and/or tabs), and terminated with a newline, which is generated by pressing Enter. The first word is the command and subsequent words are the command's arguments. The command may be a UNIX executable program such as ls or pwd, a built-in command such as cd or test, or a shell script. The command may contain special characters, called *metacharacters,* that the shell must interpret while parsing the command line. If a command line is long and you want to continue typing on the next line, the backslash character, followed by a newline, will allow you to continue typing on the next line. The secondary prompt will appear until the command line is terminated.

7.3.1 The Exit Status

After a command or program terminates, it returns an exit status to the parent process. The exit status is a number between 0 and 255. By convention, when a program exits, if the status returned is 0, the command was successful in its execution. When the exit status is nonzero, the command failed in some way. The shell status variable, ?, is set to the value of the exit status of the last command that was executed. Success or failure of a program is determined by the programmer who wrote the program.

EXAMPLE 7.8

```
1   $ grep "john" /etc/passwd
    john:MgVyBsZJavd16s:9496:40:John Doe:/home/falcon/john:/bin/sh
2   $ echo $?
    0
3   $ grep "nicky" /etc/passwd
4   $ echo $?
    1
5   $ grep "scott" /etc/passssswd
    grep: /etc/passssswd: No such file or directory
6   $ echo $?
    2
```

EXPLANATION

1   The grep program searches for the pattern john in the /etc/passwd file and is successful. The line from /etc/passwd is displayed.

2   The ? variable is set to the exit value of the grep command. Zero indicates success.

3   The grep program cannot find user nicky in the /etc/passwd file.

EXPLANATION (CONTINUED)

    4   If the grep program cannot find the pattern, it returns an exit status of 1.

    5   The grep program fails because the /etc/passsswd file cannot be opened.

    6   If grep cannot find the file, it returns an exit status of 2.

7.3.2   Multiple Commands at the Command Line

A command line can consist of multiple commands. Each command is separated by a semicolon, and the command line is terminated with a newline.

EXAMPLE 7.9

```
$ ls; pwd; date
```

EXPLANATION

The commands are executed from left to right, one after the other, until the newline is reached.

Grouping Commands.   Commands may also be grouped so that all of the output is either piped to another command or redirected to a file.

EXAMPLE 7.10

```
$ ( ls ; pwd; date ) > outputfile
```

EXPLANATION

The output of each of the commands is sent to the file called outputfile. The spaces inside the parentheses are necessary.

7.3.3   Conditional Execution of Commands

With conditional execution, two command strings are separated by the special meta-characters, double ampersands (&&) and double vertical bars (||). The command on the right of either of these metacharacters will or will not be executed based on the exit condition of the command on the left.

EXAMPLE 7.11

```
$ cc prgm1.c -o prgm1 && prgm1
```

EXPLANATION

If the first command is successful (has a 0 exit status), the command after the && is executed; that is, if the cc program can successfully compile prgm1.c, the resulting executable program, prgm1, will be executed.

EXAMPLE 7.12

$ cc prog.c 2> err || mail bob < err

EXPLANATION

If the first command fails (has a nonzero exit status), the command after the || is executed; that is, if the cc program cannot compile prog.c, the errors are sent to a file called err, and user bob will be mailed the err file.

7.3.4 Commands in the Background

Normally, when you execute a command, it runs in the foreground, and the prompt does not reappear until the command has completed execution. It is not always convenient to wait for the command to complete. By placing an ampersand (&) at the end of the command line, the shell will return the shell prompt immediately and execute the command in the background concurrently. You do not have to wait to start up another command. The output from a background job will be sent to the screen as it processes. Therefore, if you intend to run a command in the background, the output of that command might be redirected to a file or piped to another device, such as a printer, so that the output does not interfere with what you are doing.

The $! variable contains the PID number of the last job put in the background.

EXAMPLE 7.13

```
1   $ man sh | lp&
2   [1] 1557
3   $ kill -9 $!
```

EXPLANATION

1   The output of the man command (the manual pages for the sh command) is piped to the printer. The ampersand at the end of the command line puts the job in the background.

2   There are two numbers that appear on the screen: the number in square brackets indicates that this is the first job to be placed in the background; the second number is the PID, or the process identification number of this job.

3   The shell prompt appears immediately. While your program is running in the background, the shell is waiting for another command in the foreground. The ! variable evaluates to the PID of the job most recently put in the background. If you get it in time, you will kill this job before it goes to the print queue.

7.4   Shell Metacharacters (Wildcards)

Like grep, sed, and awk, the shell has metacharacters. At first glance, they may look the same, but they don't always represent the same characters when the shell evaluates them. Metacharacters, as we discussed in "Metacharacters" on page 83 of Chapter 4, are special characters used to represent something other than themselves. Shell metacharacters are often called *wildcards*. Table 7.1 lists the Bourne shell metacharacters and what they do.

Table 7.1   Bourne Shell Metacharacters

Metacharacter	Meaning
\	Literally interprets the following character
&	Processes in the background
;	Separates commands
$	Substitutes variables
?	Matches for a single character
[abc]	Matches for one character from a set of characters
[!abc]	Matches for one character *not* from the set of characters
*	Matches for zero or more characters
(cmds)	Executes commands in a subshell
{cmds}	Executes commands in current shell

7.5   Filename Substitution

When evaluating the command line, the shell uses metacharacters to abbreviate filenames or pathnames that match a certain set of characters. The filename substitution metacharacters listed in Table 7.2 are expanded into an alphabetically listed set of filenames. The process of expanding the metacharacter into filenames is also called *filename substitution*, or *globbing*. If a metacharacter is used and there is no filename that matches it, the shell treats the metacharacter as a literal character.

Table 7.2   Bourne Shell Metacharacters and Filename Substitution

Metacharacter	Meaning
*	Matches zero or more characters
?	Matches exactly one character
[abc]	Matches one character in the set a, b, or c

Table 7.2 Bourne Shell Metacharacters and Filename Substitution (continued)

Metacharacter	Meaning
[a–z]	Matches one character in the range from a to z
[!a–z]	Matches one character *not* in the range from a to z
\	Escapes or disables the metacharacter

7.5.1 The Asterisk

The asterisk is a wildcard that matches for zero or more of any characters in a filename.

EXAMPLE 7.14

```
1   $ ls *
    abc abc1 abc122 abc123 abc2 file1 file1.bak file2 file2.bak none
    nonsense nobody nothing nowhere one
2   $ ls *.bak
    file1.bak file2.bak
3   $ echo a*
    ab abc1 abc122 abc123 abc2
```

EXPLANATION

1. The asterisk expands to all of the files in the present working directory. All of the files are passed as arguments to ls and displayed.
2. All files starting with zero or more characters and ending with .bak are matched and listed.
3. All files starting with a, followed by zero or more characters, are matched and passed as arguments to the echo command.

7.5.2 The Question Mark

The question mark represents a single character in a filename. When a filename contains one or more question marks, the shell performs filename substitution by replacing the question mark with the character it matches in the filename.

EXAMPLE 7.15

```
1   $ ls
    abc abc122 abc2 file1.bak file2.bak nonsense nothing one
    abc1 abc123 file1 file2 none noone nowhere
2   $ ls a?c?
    abc1 abc2
```

EXAMPLE 7.15 (CONTINUED)

```
3   $ ls ??
    ?? not found
4   $ echo  abc???
    abc122 abc123
5   $ echo ??
    ??
```

EXPLANATION

1   The files in the current directory are listed.

2   Filenames starting with a, followed by a single character, followed by c and a single character, are matched and listed.

3   Filenames containing exactly two characters are listed if found. Because there are no two-character filenames, the question marks are treated as a literal filename.

4   Filenames starting with abc and followed by exactly three characters are expanded and displayed by the echo command.

5   There are no files in the directory that contain exactly two characters. The shell treats the question mark as a literal question mark if it cannot find a match.

7.5.3   The Square Brackets

The brackets are used to match filenames containing one character in a set or range of characters.

EXAMPLE 7.16

```
1   $ ls
    abc  abc122 abc2 file1.bak file2.bak nonsense nothing
    one  abc1 abc123 file1 file2 none noone nowhere
2   $ ls abc[123]
    abc1   abc2
3   $ ls abc[1-3]
    abc1   abc2
4   $ ls [a-z][a-z][a-z]
    abc one
5   $ ls [!f-z]???
    abc1   abc2
6   $ ls abc12[23]
    abc122 abc123
```

EXPLANATION

1   All of the files in the present working directory are listed.

2   All filenames containing four characters are matched and listed if the filename starts with abc, followed by 1, 2, or 3. Only one character from the set in the brackets is matched.

3 All filenames containing four characters are matched and listed if the filename starts with abc and is followed by a number in the range from 1 to 3.

4 All filenames containing three characters are matched and listed if the filename contains exactly three lowercase alphabetic characters.

5 All filenames containing four characters are listed if the first character is *not* a lowercase letter between f and z ([!f-z]), followed by three of any character (e.g., ???).

6 Files are listed if the filenames contain abc12 followed by 2 or 3.

7.5.4 Escaping Metacharacters

To use a metacharacter as a literal character, the backslash may be used to prevent the metacharacter from being interpreted.

EXAMPLE 7.17

```
1   $ ls
    abc file1 youx
2   $ echo How are you?
    How are youx
3   $ echo How are you\?
    How are you?
4   $ echo  When does this line \
    > ever end\?
    When does this line ever end?
```

EXPLANATION

1 The files in the present working directory are listed. (Note the file youx.)

2 The shell will perform filename expansion on the ?. Any files in the current directory starting with y-o-u and followed by exactly one character are matched and substituted in the string. The filename youx will be substituted in the string to read How are youx (probably not what you wanted to happen).

3 By preceding the question mark with a backslash, it is escaped, meaning that the shell will not try to interpret it as a wildcard.

4 The newline is escaped by preceding it with a backslash. The secondary prompt is displayed until the string is terminated with a newline. The question mark (?) is escaped to protect it from filename expansion.

7.6 Variables

There are two types of variables: local and environment. Some variables are created by the user and others are special shell variables.

7.6.1 Local Variables

Local variables are given values that are known only to the shell in which they are created. Variable names must begin with an alphabetic or underscore character. The remaining characters can be alphabetic, decimal digits 0 to 9, or an underscore character. Any other characters mark the termination of the variable name. When assigning a value, there can be no whitespace surrounding the equal sign. To set the variable to null, the equal sign is followed by a newline.[1]

A dollar sign is used in front of a variable to extract the value stored there.

Setting Local Variables.   See Example 7.18 for a demonstration on setting a local variable.

EXAMPLE 7.18

```
1   $ round=world
    $ echo $round
    world
2   $ name="Peter Piper"
    $ echo $name
    Peter Piper
3   $ x=
    $ echo $x

4   $ file.bak="$HOME/junk"
    file.bak=/home/jody/ellie/junk: not found
```

EXPLANATION

1   The variable round is assigned the value world. When the shell encounters the dollar sign preceding a variable name, it performs variable substitution. The value of the variable is displayed.

2   The variable name is assigned the value "Peter Piper". The quotes are needed to hide the whitespace so that the shell will not split the string into separate words when it parses the command line. The value of the variable is displayed.

---

1. A variable set to some value or to null will be displayed by using the set command, whereas an unset variable will not.

3 The variable x is not assigned a value. The shell will assign the null value. The null value, an empty string, is displayed.

4 The period in the variable name is illegal. The only characters allowed in a variable name are numbers, letters, and the underscore. The shell tries to execute the string as a command.

The Scope of Local Variables. A local variable is known only to the shell in which it was created. It is not passed on to subshells. The double dollar sign variable is a special variable containing the PID of the current shell.

EXAMPLE 7.19

```
1   $ echo $$
    1313
2   $ round=world
    $ echo $round
    world
3   $ sh            # Start a subshell
4   $ echo $$
    1326
5   $ echo $round

6   $ exit          # Exits this shell, returns to parent shell
7   $ echo $$
    1313
8   $ echo $round
    world
```

EXPLANATION

1 The value of the double dollar sign variable evaluates to the PID of the current shell. The PID of this shell is 1313.

2 The local variable round is assigned the string value world, and the value of the variable is displayed.

3 A new Bourne shell is started. This is called a *subshell*, or *child shell*.

4 The PID of this shell is 1326. The parent shell's PID is 1313.

5 The variable round is not defined in this shell. A blank line is printed.

6 The exit command terminates this shell and returns to the parent shell. (Ctrl-D will also exit this shell.)

7 The parent shell returns. Its PID is displayed.

8 The value of the variable round is displayed.

Setting Read-Only Variables.   A read-only variable cannot be redefined or unset.

EXAMPLE 7.20

```
1   $ name=Tom
2   $ readonly name
    $ echo $name
    Tom
3   $ unset name
    name: readonly
4   $ name=Joe
    name: readonly
```

EXPLANATION

1   The local variable name is assigned the value Tom.
2   The variable is made readonly.
3   A read-only variable cannot be unset.
4   A read-only variable cannot be redefined.

7.6.2   Environment Variables

Environment variables are available to the shell in which they are created and any sub-shells or processes spawned from that shell. By convention, environment variables are capitalized. Environment variables are variables that have been exported.

The shell in which a variable is created is called the *parent shell*. If a new shell is started from the parent shell, it is called the *child shell*. Some of the environment variables, such as HOME, LOGNAME, PATH, and SHELL, are set before you log on by the /bin/login program. Normally, environment variables are defined and stored in the .profile file in the user's home directory. See Table 7.3 for a list of environment variables.

Table 7.3   Bourne Shell Environment Variables

Variable	*Value*
PATH	The search path for commands.
HOME	Home directory; used by cd when no directory is specified.
IFS	Internal field separators, normally space, tab, and newline.
LOGNAME	The user's login name.
MAIL	If this parameter is set to the name of a mail file and the MAILPATH parameter is not set, the shell informs the user of the arrival of mail in the specified file.
MAILCHECK	This parameter specifies how often (in seconds) the shell will check for the arrival of mail in the files specified by the MAILPATH or MAIL parameters. The default value is 600 seconds (10 minutes). If set to zero, the shell will check before issuing each primary prompt.

Table 7.3   Bourne Shell Environment Variables (continued)

Variable	Value
MAILPATH	A colon-separated list of filenames. If this parameter is set, the shell informs the user of the arrival of mail in any of the specified files. Each filename can be followed by a percent sign and a message that will be printed when the modification time changes. The default message is You have mail.
PWD	Present working directory.
PS1	Primary prompt string, which is a dollar sign by default.
PS2	Secondary prompt string, which is a right angle bracket by default.
SHELL	When the shell is invoked, it scans the environment for this name. The shell gives default values to PATH, PS1, PS2, MAILCHECK, and IFS. HOME and MAIL are set by login.

Setting Environment Variables.   To set environment variables, the export command is used either after assigning a value or when the variable is set. (Do not use the dollar sign on a variable when exporting it.)

EXAMPLE 7.21

```
1    $ TERM=wyse
     $ export TERM
2    $ NAME="John Smith"
     $ export NAME
     $ echo $NAME
     John Smith
3    $ echo $$
     319              # pid number for parent shell
4    $ sh             # Start a subshell
5    $ echo $$
     340              # pid number for new shell
6    $ echo $NAME
     John Smith
7    $ NAME="April Jenner"
     $ export NAME
     $ echo $NAME
     April Jenner
8    $ exit           # Exit the subshell and go back to parent shell
9    $ echo $$
     319              # pid number for parent shell
10   $ echo $NAME
     John Smith
```

EXPLANATION

1   The TERM variable is assigned wyse. The variable is exported. Now, processes started from this shell will inherit the variable.

2   The variable is defined and exported to make it available to subshells started from the shell.

3   The value of this shell's PID is printed.

4   A new Bourne shell is started. The new shell is called the *child*. The original shell is its *parent*.

5   The PID of the new Bourne shell is stored in the $$ variable and its value is echoed.

6   The variable, set in the parent shell, was exported to this new shell and is displayed.

7   The variable is reset to April Jenner. It is exported to all subshells, but will not affect the parent shell. Exported values are not propagated upward to the parent shell.

8   This Bourne child shell is exited.

9   The PID of the parent is displayed again.

10   The variable NAME contains its original value. Variables retain their values when exported from parent to child shell. The child cannot change the value of a variable for its parent.

7.6.3   Listing Set Variables

There are two built-in commands that print the value of a variable: set and env. The set command prints all variables, local and global. The env command prints just the global variables.

EXAMPLE 7.22

```
1   $ env      (Partial list)
    LOGNAME=ellie
    TERMCAP=sun-cmd
    USER=ellie
    DISPLAY=:0.0
    SHELL=/bin/sh
    HOME=/home/jody/ellie
    TERM=sun-cmd
    LD_LIBRARY_PATH=/usr/local/OW3/lib
    PWD=/home/jody/ellie/perl

2   $ set
    DISPLAY=:0.0
    FMHOME=/usr/local/Frame-2.1X
    FONTPATH=/usr/local/OW3/lib/fonts
    HELPPATH=/usr/local/OW3/lib/locale:/usr/local/OW3/lib/help
```

EXAMPLE 7.22 (CONTINUED)

```
HOME=/home/jody/ellie
HZ=100
IFS=
LANG=C
LD_LIBRARY_PATH=/usr/local/OW3/lib
LOGNAME=ellie
MAILCHECK=600
MANPATH=/usr/local/OW3/share/man:/usr/local/OW3/man:/
usr/local/man:/usr/local/doctools/man:/usr/man
OPTIND=1
PATH=/home/jody/ellie:/usr/local/OW3/bin:/usr/ucb:/usr/local/
doctools/bin:/usr/bin:/usr/local:/usr/etc:/etc:/usr/spool/
news/bin:/home/jody/ellie/bin:/usr/lo
PS1=$
PS2=>
PWD=/home/jody/ellie/kshprog/joke
SHELL=/bin/sh
TERM=sun-cmd
TERMCAP=sun-cmd:te=\E[>4h:ti=\E[>4l:tc=sun:
USER=ellie
name=Tom
place="San Francisco"
```

EXPLANATION

1 The env command lists all environment (exported) variables. These variables are, by convention, named with all uppercase letters. They are passed from the process in which they are created to any of its child processes.

2 The set command, without options, prints all set variables, local and exported (including variables set to null).

7.6.4 Unsetting Variables

Both local and environment variables can be unset by using the unset command, unless the variables are set as read-only.

EXAMPLE 7.23

```
unset name; unset TERM
```

EXPLANATION

The unset command removes the variable from the shell's memory.

7.6.5   Printing the Values of Variables: The echo Command

The echo command prints its arguments to standard output and is used primarily in Bourne and C shells. The Korn shell has a built-in print command. There are different versions of the echo command; for example, the Berkeley (BSD) echo is different from the System V echo. Unless you specify a full pathname, you will use the built-in version of the echo command. The built-in version will reflect the version of UNIX you are using. The System V echo allows the use of numerous escape sequences, whereas the BSD version does not. Table 7.4 lists the BSD echo option and escape sequences.

Table 7.4   BSD echo Option and System V Escape Sequences

Option	Meaning
BSD	
-n	Suppress newline at the end of a line of output
System V	
\b	Backspace
\c	Print the line without a newline
\f	Form feed
\n	Newline
\r	Return
\t	Tab
\v	Vertical tab
\\	Backslash

EXAMPLE 7.24

```
1    $ echo The username is $LOGNAME.
     The username is ellie.
2    $ echo "\t\tHello there\c"    # System V
         Hello there$
3    $ echo -n "Hello there"       # BSD
     Hello there$
```

EXPLANATION

1   The echo command prints its arguments to the screen. Variable substitution is performed by the shell before the echo command is executed.

2   The System V version of the echo command supports escape sequences similar to those of the C programming language. The $ is the shell prompt.

3   The -n option to the echo command indicates the BSD version of the echo command is being used. The line is printed without the newline. The escape sequences are not supported by this version of echo.

7.6.6 Variable Expansion Modifiers

Variables can be tested and modified by using special modifiers. The modifier provides a shortcut conditional test to check if a variable has been set, and then assigns a value to the variable based on the outcome of the test. See Table 7.5 for a list of Bourne shell variable modifiers.

Table 7.5 Bourne Shell Variable Modifiers

Modifier	Value
${variable:-word}	If variable is set and is non-null, substitute its value; otherwise, substitute word.
${variable:=word}	If variable is set or is non-null, substitute its value; otherwise, set it to word. The value of variable is substituted permanently. Positional parameters may not be assigned in this way.
${variable:+word}	If parameter is set and is non-null, substitute word; otherwise, substitute nothing.
${variable:?word}	If variable is set and is non-null, substitute its value; otherwise, print word and exit from the shell. If word is omitted, the message parameter null or not set is printed.

Using the colon with any of the modifiers (-, =, +, ?) checks whether the variable is not set or is null; without the colon, a variable set to null is considered to be set.

EXAMPLE 7.25

```
(Assigning temporary default values)
1   $ fruit=peach
2   $ echo ${fruit:-plum}
    peach
3   $ echo ${newfruit:-apple}
    apple
4   $ echo $newfruit

5   $ echo $EDITOR        # More realistic example

6   $ echo ${EDITOR:-/bin/vi}
    /bin/vi
7   $ echo $EDITOR

8   $ name=
    $ echo ${name-Joe}

9   $ echo ${name:-Joe}
    Joe
```

EXPLANATION

1   The variable fruit is assigned the value peach.

2   The special modifier will check to see if the variable fruit has been set. If it has, the value is printed; if not, plum is substituted for fruit and its value is printed.

3   The variable newfruit has not been set. The value apple will be temporarily substituted for newfruit.

4   The setting was only temporary. The variable newfruit is not set.

5   The environment variable EDITOR has not been set.

6   The :- modifier substitutes EDITOR with /bin/vi.

7   The EDITOR was never set. Nothing prints.

8   The variable name is set to null. By not prefixing the modifier with a colon, the variable is considered to be set, even if to null, and the new value Joe is not assigned to name.

9   The colon causes the modifier to check that a variable is either *not* set or is set to null. In either case, the value Joe will be substituted for name.

EXAMPLE 7.26

```
(Assigning permanent default values)
1   $ name=
2   $ echo  ${name:=Patty}
    Patty
3   $ echo $name
    Patty
4   $ echo ${EDITOR:=/bin/vi}
    /bin/vi
5   $ echo $EDITOR
    /bin/vi
```

EXPLANATION

1   The variable name is assigned the value null.

2   The special modifier := will check to see if the variable name has been set. If it has been set, it will not be changed; if it is either null or not set, it will be assigned the value to the right of the equal sign. Patty is assigned to name because the variable is set to null. The setting is permanent.

3   The variable name still contains the value Patty.

4   The value of the variable EDITOR is set to /bin/vi.

5   The value of the variable EDITOR is displayed.

EXAMPLE 7.27

```
(Assigning temporary alternate values)
1   $ foo=grapes
2   $ echo ${foo:+pears}
    pears
3   $ echo $foo
    grapes
    $
```

EXPLANATION

1   The variable foo has been assigned the value grapes.

2   The special modifier :+ will check to see if the variable has been set. If it has been set, pears will temporarily be substituted for foo; if not, null is returned.

3   The variable foo now has its original value.

EXAMPLE 7.28

```
(Creating error messages based on default values)
1   $ echo ${namex:?"namex is undefined"}
    namex: namex is undefined
2   $ echo ${y?}
    y: parameter null or not set
```

EXPLANATION

1   The :? modifier will check to see if the variable has been set. If not, the string to the right of the ? is printed to standard error, after the name of the variable. If in a script, the script exits.

2   If a message is not provided after the ?, the shell sends a default message to standard error.

7.6.7 Positional Parameters

Normally, the special built-in variables, often called *positional parameters*, are used in shell scripts when passing arguments from the command line, or used in functions to hold the value of arguments passed to the function. See Table 7.6. The variables are called positional parameters because they are denoted by their position on the command line. The Bourne shell allows up to nine positional parameters. The name of the shell script is stored in the $0 variable. The positional parameters can be set and reset with the set command.

Table 7.6 Bourne Shell Positional Parameters

Positional Parameter	Meaning
$0	References the name of the current shell script
$1–$9	Denotes positional parameters 1 through 9
$#	Evaluates to the number of positional parameters
$*	Evaluates to all the positional parameters
$@	Means the same as $*, except when double quoted
"$*"	Evaluates to "$1 $2 $3"
"$@"	Evaluates to "$1" "$2" "$3"

EXAMPLE 7.29

```
1   $ set tim bill ann fred
    $ echo $*      # Prints all the positional parameters.
    tim bill ann fred
2   $ echo $1      # Prints the first positional parameter.
    tim
3   $ echo $2 $3   # Prints the second and third positional parameters.
    bill ann
4   $ echo $#      # Prints the total number of positional parameters.
    4
5   $ set a b c d e f g h i j k l m
    $ echo  $10    # Prints the first positional parameter followed by a zero.
    a0
6   $ echo  $*
    a b c d e f g h i j k l m
7   $ set file1 file2 file3
    $ echo  \$$#
    $3
8   $ eval echo  \$$#
    file3
```

EXPLANATION

1   The set command assigns values to positional parameters. The $* special variable contains all of the parameters set.

2   The value of the first positional parameter, tim, is displayed.

3   The value of the second and third parameters, bill and ann, are displayed.

4   The $# special variable contains the number of positional parameters currently set.

EXPLANATION (CONTINUED)

5   The set command resets all of the positional parameters. The original set is destroyed. Positional parameters cannot be numbered beyond nine. The value of the first positional parameter is printed, followed by the number 0.

6   The $* allows you to print all of the parameters, even past nine.

7   The positional parameters are reset to file1, file2, and file3. The dollar sign is escaped; $# is the number of arguments. The echo command displays $3.

8   The eval command parses the command line a second time before executing the command. The first time parsed, the shell substitutes \$$# with $3, and the second time, the shell substitutes the value of $3 with file3.

7.6.8   Other Special Variables

The shell has special variables consisting of a single character. The dollar sign preceding the character allows you to access the value stored in the variable. See Table 7.7.

Table 7.7   Bourne Shell Special Variables

Variable	Meaning
$	The PID of the shell
-	The sh options currently set
?	The exit value of last executed command
!	The PID of the last job put in the background

EXAMPLE 7.30

```
1    $ echo The pid of this shell is $$
     The pid of this shell is 4725
2    $ echo The options for this shell are $-
     The options for this shell are s
3    $ grep dodo /etc/passwd
     $ echo $?
     1
4    $ sleep 25&
     4736
     $ echo $!
     4736
```

EXPLANATION

1   The $ variable holds the value of the PID for this process.

2   The - variable lists all options for this interactive Bourne shell.

EXPLANATION (CONTINUED)

3   The grep command searches for the string dodo in the /etc/passwd file. The ? variable holds the exit status of the last command executed. Because the value returned from grep is 1, grep is assumed to have failed in its search. An exit status of 0 indicates a successful exit.

4   The ! variable holds the PID number of the last command placed in the background. The & appended to the sleep command sends the command to the background.

7.7 Quoting

Quoting is used to protect special metacharacters from interpretation. There are three methods of quoting: the backslash, single quotes, and double quotes. The characters listed in Table 7.8 are special to the shell and must be quoted.

Table 7.8   Special Metacharacters Requiring Quotes

Metacharacter	Meaning
;	Command separator
&	Background processing
( )	Command grouping; creates a subshell
{ }	Command grouping; does not create a subshell
|	Pipe
<	Input redirection
>	Output redirection
newline	Command termination
space/tab	Word delimiter
$	Variable substitution character
* [ ] ?	Shell metacharacters for filename expansion

Single and double quotes must be matched. Single quotes protect special metacharacters, such as $, *, ?, |, >, and <, from interpretation. Double quotes also protect special metacharacters from being interpreted, but allow variable and command substitution characters (the dollar sign and backquotes) to be processed. Single quotes will protect double quotes and double quotes will protect single quotes.

The Bourne shell does not let you know if you have mismatched quotes. If running interactively, a secondary prompt appears when quotes are not matched. If in a shell script, the file is scanned and if the quote is not matched, the shell will attempt to match it with the next available quote; if the shell cannot match it with the next available quote, the program aborts and the message 'end of file' unexpected appears on the terminal. Quoting can be a real hassle for even the best of shell programmers! See "What You Should Know About Quotes" on page 985 for shell quoting rules.

7.7.1 The Backslash

The backslash is used to quote (or escape) a single character from interpretation. The backslash is not interpreted if placed in single quotes. The backslash will protect the dollar sign ($), backquotes (` `), and the backslash from interpretation if enclosed in double quotes.

EXAMPLE 7.31

```
1   $ echo Where are you going\?
    Where are you going?
2   $ echo Start on this line and \
    >  go to the next line.
    Start on this line and go to the next line.
3   $ echo \\
    \
4   $ echo '\\'
    \\
5   $ echo '\$5.00'
    \$5.00
6   $ echo "\$5.00"
    $5.00
```

EXPLANATION

1   The backslash prevents the shell from performing filename substitution on the question mark.
2   The backslash escapes the newline, allowing the next line to become part of this line.
3   Because the backslash itself is a special character, it prevents the backslash following it from interpretation.
4   The backslash is not interpreted when enclosed in single quotes.
5   All characters in single quotes are treated literally. The backslash does not serve any purpose here.
6   When enclosed in double quotes, the backslash prevents the dollar sign from being interpreted for variable substitution.

7.7.2   Single Quotes

Single quotes must be matched. They protect all metacharacters from interpretation. To print a single quote, it must be enclosed in double quotes or escaped with a backslash.

EXAMPLE 7.32

```
1   $ echo 'hi there
    > how are you?
    > When will this end?
    > When the quote is matched
    > oh'
    hi there
    how are you?
    When will this end?
    When the quote is matched
    oh
2   $ echo 'Don\'t  you need $5.00?'
    Don't you need $5.00?
3   $ echo 'Mother yelled, "Time to eat!"'
    Mother yelled, "Time to eat!"
```

EXPLANATION

1   The single quote is not matched on the line. The Bourne shell produces a secondary prompt. It is waiting for the quote to be matched.

2   The single quotes protect all metacharacters from interpretation. The apostrophe in Don't is escaped with a backslash. Otherwise, it would match the first quote, and the single quote at the end of the string would not have a mate. In this example, the $ and the ? are protected from the shell and will be treated as literals.

3   The single quotes protect the double quotes in this string.

7.7.3   Double Quotes

Double quotes must be matched, will allow variable and command substitution, and protect any other special metacharacters from being interpreted by the shell.

EXAMPLE 7.33

```
1   $ name=Jody
2   $ echo "Hi $name, I'm glad to meet you!"
    Hi Jody, I'm glad to meet you!
3   $ echo "Hey $name, the time is `date`"
    Hey Jody, the time is Wed Oct 13 14:04:11 PST 2004
```

EXPLANATION

1   The variable name is assigned the string Jody.

2   The double quotes surrounding the string will protect all special metacharacters from interpretation, with the exception of $ in $name. Variable substitution is performed within double quotes.

3   Variable substitution and command substitution are both performed when enclosed within double quotes. The variable name is expanded, and the command in backquotes, date, is executed.

7.8   Command Substitution

When a command is enclosed in backquotes, it will be executed and its output returned. This process is called *command substitution*. It is used when assigning the output of a command to a variable or when substituting the output of a command within a string. All three shells use backquotes to perform command substitution.[2]

EXAMPLE 7.34

```
1    $ name=`nawk -F: '{print $1}' database`
     $ echo $name
     Ebenezer Scrooge
2    $ set `date`
3    $ echo $*
     Fri Oct 22 09:35:21 PDT 2004
4    $ echo  $2 $6
     Oct 2004
```

EXPLANATION

1   The nawk command is enclosed in backquotes. Command substitution is performed. The output is assigned to the variable name, as a string, and displayed.

2   The set command assigns the output of the date command to positional parameters. Whitespace separates the list of words into its respective parameters.

3   The $* variable holds all of the positional parameters. The output of the date command was stored in the $* variable. Each parameter is separated by whitespace.

4   The second and sixth parameters are printed.

---

2.   The Korn shell allows backquotes for command substitution for upward compatibility, but provides an alternate method as well.

7.9 An Introduction to Functions

Although the Bourne shell does not have an *alias* mechanism for abbreviating commands, it does support functions (introduced to the shell in SVR2). Functions are used to execute a group of commands with a name. They are like scripts, only more efficient. Once defined, they become part of the shell's memory so that when the function is called, the shell does not have to read it in from the disk as it does with a file. Often functions are used to improve the modularity of a script (discussed in the programming section of this chapter). Once defined, they can be used again and again. Functions are often defined in the user's initialization file, .profile. They must be defined before they are invoked, and cannot be exported.

7.9.1 Defining Functions

The function name is followed by a set of empty parentheses. The definition of the function consists of a set of commands separated by semicolons and enclosed in curly braces. The last command is terminated with a semicolon. Spaces around the curly braces are required.

FORMAT

```
function_name () { commands ; commands; }
```

EXAMPLE 7.35

```
1   $ greet () { echo "Hello $LOGNAME, today is `date`; }
2   $ greet
    Hello ellie, today is Thu Oct 21 19:56:31 PDT 2004
```

EXPLANATION

1   The function is called greet.

2   When the greet function is invoked, the command(s) enclosed within the curly braces are executed.

EXAMPLE 7.36

```
1   $ fun () { pwd; ls; date; }
2   $ fun
    /home/jody/ellie/prac
    abc      abc123   file1.bak   none       nothing   tmp
    abc1     abc2     file2       nonsense   nowhere   touch
    abc122   file1    file2.bak   noone      one
    Sat Feb 21 11:15:48 PST 2004
```

EXAMPLE   7.36 (CONTINUED)

```
3   $ welcome () { echo "Hi $1 and $2"; }
4   $ welcome tom joe
    Hi tom and joe
5   $ set jane nina lizzy
6   $ echo $*
    jane nina lizzy
7   $ welcome tom joe
    hi tom and joe
8   $ echo  $1 $2
    jane nina
```

EXPLANATION

1   The function fun is named and defined. The name is followed by a list of commands enclosed in curly braces. Each command is separated by a semicolon. A space is required after the first curly brace or you will get a syntax error. A function must be defined before it can be used.

2   The function behaves just like a script when invoked. Each of the commands in the function definition are executed in turn.

3   There are two positional parameters used in the function welcome. When arguments are given to the function, the positional parameters are assigned those values.

4   The arguments to the function, tom and joe, are assigned to $1 and $2, respectively. The positional parameters in a function are private to the function and will not interfere with any used outside the function.

5   The positional parameters are set at the command line. These variables have nothing to do with the ones set in the function.

6   $* displays the values of the currently set positional parameters.

7   The function welcome is called. The values assigned to the positional parameters are tom and joe.

8   The positional variables assigned at the command line are unaffected by those set in the function.

7.9.2   Listing and Unsetting Functions

To list functions and their definitions, use the set command. The function and its definition will appear in the output, along with the exported and local variables. Functions and their definitions are unset with the unset command.

7.10 Standard I/O and Redirection

When the shell starts up, it inherits three files: stdin, stdout, and stderr. Standard input normally comes from the keyboard. Standard output and standard error normally go to the screen. There are times when you want to read input from a file or send output or error to a file. This can be accomplished by using I/O redirection. See Table 7.9 for a list of redirection operators.

Table 7.9 Redirection Operators

Operator	What It Does
<	Redirect input
>	Redirect output
>>	Append output
2>	Redirect error
1>&2	Redirect output to where error is going
2>&1	Redirect error to where output is going

EXAMPLE 7.37

```
1   $ tr '[A-Z]' '[a-z]' < myfile    # Redirect  input
2   $ ls > lsfile                    # Redirect output
    $ cat lsfile
    dir1
    dir2
    file1
    file2
    file3
3   $ date >> lsfile                 # Redirect and append otuput
    $ cat lsfile
    dir1
    dir2
    file1
    file2
    file3
    Mon Sept 20 12:57:22 PDT 2004
4   $ cc prog.c 2> errfile           # Redirect error
5   $ find . -name \*.c -print > foundit 2> /dev/null    # Redirect output to foundit,
                                                         # and error to /dev/null
6   $ find . -name \*.c -print > foundit 2>&1    # Redirect output and send standard
                                                 # error to where output is going
7   $ echo "File needs an argument" 1>&2    # Send standard output to error
```

EXPLANATION

1   Instead of getting input from the keyboard, standard input is redirected from the file myfile to the UNIX tr command. All uppercase letters are converted to lowercase letters.

2   Instead of sending output to the screen, the ls command redirects its output to the file lsfile.

3   The output of the date command is redirected and appended to lsfile.

4   The file prog.c is compiled. If the compile fails, the standard error is redirected to the file errfile. Now you can take your error file to the local guru for an explanation (of sorts)!

5   The find command starts searching in the current working directory for filenames ending in .c, and prints the filenames to a file named foundit. Errors from the find command are sent to /dev/null.

6   The find command starts searching in the current working directory for filenames ending in .c, and prints the filenames to a file named foundit. The errors are also sent to foundit.

7   The echo command sends its message to standard error. Its standard output is merged with standard error.

7.10.1 The exec Command and Redirection

The exec command can be used to replace the current program with a new one without starting a new process. Standard output or input can be changed with the exec command without creating a subshell (see Table 7.10). If a file is opened with exec, subsequent read commands will move the file pointer down the file a line at a time until the end of the file. The file must be closed to start reading from the beginning again. However, if using UNIX utilities such as cat and sort, the operating system closes the file after each command has completed. For examples on how to use exec commands in scripts, see "Looping Control Commands" on page 358.

Table 7.10   The exec Command

Command	*What It Does*
exec ls	Execute ls in place of the shell. When ls is finished, the shell in which it was started does not return.
exec < filea	Open filea for reading standard input.
exec > filex	Open filex for writing standard output.
exec 3< datfile	Open datfile as file descriptor 3 for reading input.
sort <&3	Sort datfile.
exec 4>newfile	Open newfile as file descriptor (fd) 4 for writing.

Table 7.10   The exec Command (continued)

Command	What It Does
ls >&4	Output of ls is redirected to newfile.
exec 5<&4	Make fd 5 a copy of fd 4.
exec 3<&–	Close fd 3.

EXAMPLE 7.38

```
1   $ exec date
    Sun Oct 17 10:07:34  PDT 2004
     <Login prompt appears if you are in your login shell >
2   $ exec > temp
    $ ls
    $ pwd
    $ echo Hello
3   $ exec > /dev/tty
4   $ echo Hello
    Hello
```

EXPLANATION

1   The exec command executes the date command in the current shell (it does not fork a child shell). Because the date command is executed in place of the current shell, when the date command exits, the shell terminates. If a Bourne shell had been started from the C shell, the Bourne shell would exit and the C shell prompt would appear. If you are in your login shell when you try this, you will be logged out. If you are working interactively in a shell window, the window exits.

2   The exec command opens standard output for the current shell to the temp file. Output from ls, pwd, and echo will no longer go to the screen, but to temp.

3   The exec command reopens standard output to the terminal. Now, output will go to the screen as shown in line 4.

4   Standard output has been directed back to the terminal (/dev/tty).

EXAMPLE 7.39

```
1   $ cat doit
    pwd
    echo hello
    date
2   $ exec < doit
    /home/jody/ellie/shell
    hello
    Sun Oct 17 10:07:34  PDT 2004
3   %
```

EXPLANATION

1   The contents of a file called doit are displayed.

2   The exec command opens standard input to the file called doit. Input is read from the file instead of from the keyboard. The commands from the file doit are executed in place of the current shell. When the last command exits, so does the shell. See Figure 7.2.

3   The Bourne shell exited when the exec command completed. The C shell prompt appeared. It was the parent shell. If you had been in your login shell when the exec finished, you would be logged out; if in a window, the window would have disappeared.

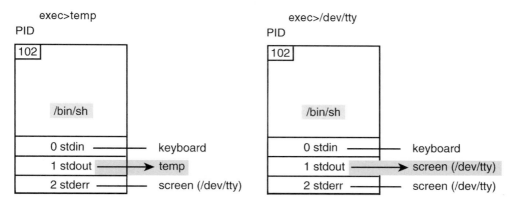

Figure 7.2   The exec command.

EXAMPLE 7.40

```
1    $ exec 3> filex
2    $ who >& 3
3    $ date >& 3
4    $ exec 3>&-
5    $ exec 3< filex
6    $ cat <&3
     ellie   console   Oct 7    09:53
     ellie   ttyp0     Oct 7    09:54
     ellie   ttyp1     Oct 7    09:54
     ellie   ttyp2     Oct 11   15:42
     Sun Oct 17 13:31:31  PDT 2004
7    $ exec 3<&-
8    $ date >& 3
     Sun Oct 17 13:41:14  PDT 2004
```

1   File descriptor 3 (fd 3) is assigned to filex and opened for redirection of output. See Figure 7.3.

2   The output of the who command is sent to fd 3, filex.

3   The output of the date command is sent to fd 3; filex is already opened, so the output is appended to filex.

4   Fd 3 is closed.

5   The exec command opens fd 3 for reading input. Input will be redirected from filex.

6   The cat program reads from fd 3, assigned to filex.

7   The exec command closes fd 3. (Actually, the operating system will close the file once end of file is reached.)

8   When attempting to send the output of the date command to fd 3, the output goes to the screen, because the file descriptor was closed.

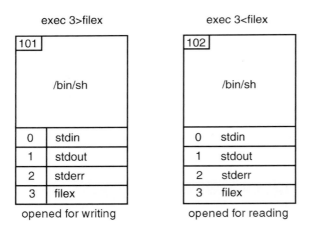

Figure 7.3 exec and file descriptors.

7.11 Pipes

A *pipe* takes the output from the command on the left-hand side of the pipe symbol and sends it to the input of the command on the right-hand side of the pipe symbol. A pipeline can consist of more than one pipe.

The purpose of the next three commands is to count the number of people logged on (who), save the output of the command in a file (tmp), use the wc -l to count the number of lines in the tmp file (wc -l), and then remove the tmp file (i.e., find the number of people logged on). See Figures 7.4 and 7.5.

EXAMPLE 7.41

```
1   $ who > tmp
2   $ wc -l tmp
    4 tmp
3   $ rm tmp

# Using a pipe saves disk space and time.
4   $ who | wc -l
    4
5   $ du . | sort -n | sed -n '$p'
    72388   /home/jody/ellie
```

EXPLANATION

1   The output of the who command is redirected to the tmp file.

2   The wc -l command displays the number of lines in tmp.

3   The tmp file is removed.

4   With the pipe facility, you can perform all three of the preceding steps in one step. The output of the who command is sent to an anonymous kernel buffer; the wc -l command reads from the buffer and sends its output to the screen.

5   The output of the du command, the number of disk blocks used per directory, is piped to the sort command and sorted numerically. It is then piped to the sed command, which prints the last line of the output it receives.

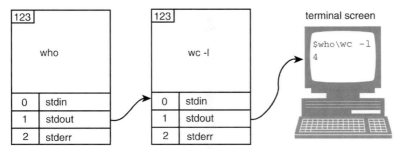

Figure 7.4   The pipe.

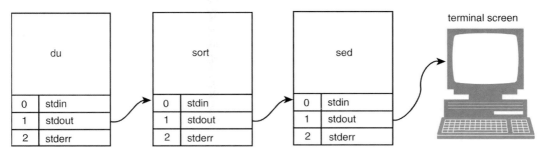

Figure 7.5   Multiple pipes (filter).

7.12 The here document **and Input**

The here document accepts inline text for a program expecting input, such as mail, sort, or cat, until a user-defined terminator is reached. It is often used in shell scripts for creating menus. The command receiving the input is appended with a << symbol, followed by a user-defined word or symbol, and a newline. The next lines of text will be the lines of input to be sent to the command. The input is terminated when the user-defined word or symbol is then placed on a line by itself in the leftmost column (it cannot have spaces surrounding it). The word is used in place of Ctrl-D to stop the program from reading input.

EXAMPLE 7.42

```
1    $ sort            # Sort waits for user input if it does get a file
     pears
     apples
     bananas
     ^D (Ctrl-D)       # User presses Ctrl-D to stop input to sort

     (Output)
     apples
     bananas
     pears
     $
2    $ sort <<DONE      # DONE is a user-defined terminator
     >  pears
     >  apples          # The user input is called the "document"
     >  bananas
3    DONE               # Marks end of here document
                        # Here is where input stops

     (Output)
4    apples
     bananas
     pears
5    $
```

EXPLANATION

1 The UNIX/Linux sort command waits for user input because it was not provided with a filename as its argument. The user types three lines of input, and then must press Ctrl-D, the key sequence that stops input to the program. (Don't mistake Ctrl-D with Ctrl-C. Ctrl-C kills the program so that you won't get any output at all!) After the user presses Ctrl-D, the sort command will send the sorted output to the screen.

2 A here document will provide input to the sort command. The << is followed by what is called a user-defined terminator, a word or symbol. A secondary prompt appears. The following text is input for the sort command.

3   The DONE terminator marks the end of the here document. The DONE cannot have space on either side of it. The terminator replaces typing Ctrl-D. The sort command will not receive further input. When finished, sort will send its output to the screen.

4   The output from the sort program is displayed.

5   The shell prompt reappears.

If the terminator is preceded by the <<- operator, leading tabs, and only tabs, may precede the final terminator. The user-defined terminating word or symbol must match exactly from "here" to "here." The following examples illustrate the use of the here document at the command line to demonstrate the syntax. It is much more practical to use them in scripts.

EXAMPLE 7.43

```
1   $ cat << FINISH              ◄──┐   # FINISH is a user-defined terminator
2   > Hello there $LOGNAME          │
3   > The time is `date`            │
    > I can't wait to see you!!!    │
4   > FINISH                     ◄──┘   # terminator matches first FINISH on line 1.

5   Hello there ellie
    The time is Wed April 22 19:42:16 PST 2004
    I can't wait to see you!!!
6   $
```

EXPLANATION

1   The UNIX cat program will accept input until the word FINISH appears on a line by itself.

2   A secondary prompt appears. The following text is input for the cat command. Variable substitution is performed within the here document.

3   Command substitution, `date`, is performed within the here document.

4   The user-defined terminator FINISH marks the end of input for the cat program. It cannot have any spaces before or after it and is on a line by itself.

5   The output from the cat program is displayed.

6   The shell prompt reappears.

EXAMPLE 7.44

```
1   $ cat <<- DONE
    >    Hello there
    >    What's up?
    >    Bye now The time is `date`.
2   >    DONE
    Hello there
    What's up?
    Bye now The time is Thu Oct 28 19:48:23 PST 2004.
    $
```

EXPLANATION

1   The cat program accepts input until DONE appears on a line by itself. The <<- operator allows the input and final terminator to be preceded by one or more tabs.

2   The final matching terminator, DONE, is preceded by a tab. The output of the cat program is displayed on the screen.

7.12.1   Now What?

Now that we have completed our discussion on the interactive shell, it is time to combine many of these features in scripts, to produce programs that will automate repetitive tasks, produce information, monitor processes, and so on. If you are not a programmer, writing shell scripts may be a good place for you to start. It's fun and you get results quickly.

chapter

8

Programming the Bourne Shell

8.1 Introduction

Shell programs are usually called shell *scripts*. Now that you have learned how to use the shell interactively, you are ready to start scripting using what you have learned in addition to the programming constructs provided in this chapter. It doesn't matter whether you are a system administrator, a programmer, or a user. Shell scripts can automate a number of routine tasks to make life a lot easier—and they are fun to write and use!

8.1.1 The Steps in Creating a Shell Script

A shell script is normally written in an editor and consists of commands interspersed with comments. Comments are preceded by a pound sign (#) and consist of text used to document what is going on.

The First Line.   The first line at the top left corner of the script will indicate the program that will be executing the lines in the script. This line, known as the *shbang* line, is commonly written as

```
#!/bin/sh
```

  The #! is called a magic number and is used by the kernel to identify the program that should be interpreting the lines in the script. This line must be the top line of your script.

Comments.   *Comments* are lines preceded by a pound sign and can be on a line by themselves or on a line following a script command. They are used to document your script. It is sometimes difficult to understand what the script is supposed to do if it is not commented. Although comments are important, they are often too sparse or not used at all. Try to get used to commenting what you are doing not only for someone else, but also for yourself. Two days from now you may not recall exactly what you were trying to do.

Executable Statements and Bourne Shell Constructs.   A Bourne shell program consists of a combination of UNIX commands, Bourne shell commands, programming constructs, and comments.

Making the Script Executable.   When you create a file, it is not given the execute permission. You need this permission to run your script. Use the chmod command to turn on the execute permission.

EXAMPLE 8.1

```
1   $ chmod +x myscript
2   $ ls -1F  myscript
    -rwxr-xr-x     1   ellie   0 Jul   13:00 myscript*
```

EXPLANATION

1   The chmod command is used to turn on the execute permission for the user, group, and others.

2   The output of the ls command indicates that all users have execute permission on the myscript file. The asterisk at the end of the filename also indicates that this is an executable program.

A Scripting Session.   In the following example, the user creates a script in the editor. After saving the file, the execute permissions are turned on, and the script is executed. If there are errors in the program, the shell will respond immediately.

EXAMPLE 8.2

```
(The Script)
1   #!/bin/sh
2   # Scriptname: greetings
    # Written by:  Barbara Born
    # This is the first Bourne shell program of the day.
3   echo "Hello $LOGNAME, it's nice talking to you."
4   echo "Your present working directory is `pwd`."
    echo "You are working on a machine called `uname -n`."
    echo "Here is a list of your files."
5   ls     # List files in the present working directory
6   echo  "Bye for now $LOGNAME. The time is `date +%T`!"

(The Command Line)
7   $ chmod +x greetings
    $ greetings
3   Hello barbara, it's nice talking to you.
```

EXAMPLE 8.2 (CONTINUED)

```
4    Your present working directory is /home/lion/barbara/prog
     You are working on a machine called lion.
     Here is a list of your files.
5    Afile        cplus    letter    prac
     Answerbook   cprog    library   prac1
     bourne       joke     notes     perl5
6    Bye for now barbara. The time is 18:05:07!
```

EXPLANATION

1. The first line of the script, #!/bin/sh, lets the kernel know what interpreter will execute the lines in this program, in this case the sh (Bourne shell) interpreter.

2. The comments are nonexecutable lines preceded by a pound sign. They can be on a line by themselves or appended to a line after a command.

3. After variable substitution is performed by the shell, the echo command displays the line on the screen.

4. After command substitution is performed by the shell, the echo command displays the line on the screen.

5. The ls command is executed. The comment will be ignored by the shell.

6. The echo command displays the string enclosed within double quotes. Variables and command substitution (backquotes) are expanded when placed within double quotes. In this case, the quotes were really not necessary.

7. The greetings script is given permission to execute by the user, group, and others, and is run from the command line.

8.2 Reading User Input

The read command is a built-in command used to read input from the terminal or from a file (see Table 8.1). The read command takes a line of input until a newline is reached. The newline at the end of a line will be translated into a null byte when read. You can also use the read command to cause a program to stop until the user enters a carriage return. To see how the read command is most effectively used for reading lines of input from a file, see "Looping Commands" on page 349.

Table 8.1 The read Command

Format	Meaning
read answer	Reads a line from standard input and assigns it to the variable answer.
read first last	Reads a line from standard input to the first whitespace or newline, putting the first word typed into the variable first and the rest of the line into the variable last.

EXAMPLE 8.3

```
(The Script)
    #!/bin/sh
    # Scriptname: nosy
    echo "Are you happy? \c"
1   read answer
    echo "$answer is the right response."
    echo "What is your full name? \c"
2   read first middle last
    echo "Hello  $first"
    --------------------------------------------------------------
(The Output)
    Are you happy? Yes
1   Yes is the right response.
2   What is your full name? Jon Jake Jones
    Hello Jon
```

EXPLANATION

1   The read command accepts a line of user input and assigns the input to the variable answer.

2   The read command accepts input from the user and assigns the first word of input to the variable first, the second word of input to the variable middle, and all the rest of the words up to the end of the line to the variable last.

EXAMPLE 8.4

```
(The Script)
    #!/bin/sh
    # Scriptname: printer_check
    # Script to clear a hung up printer for SVR4
1   if [ $LOGNAME != root ]
    then
        echo "Must have root privileges to run this program"
        exit 1
    fi
2   cat << EOF
    Warning: All jobs in the printer queue will be removed.
    Please turn off the printer now. Press Enter when you
    are ready to continue. Otherwise press Ctrl-C.
    EOF
3   read ANYTHING      # Wait until the user turns off the printer
    echo
4   /etc/init.d/lp stop      # Stop the printer
```

EXAMPLE 8.4 (CONTINUED)

```
5   rm -f /var/spool/lp/SCHEDLOCK /var/spool/lp/temp*
    echo
    echo "Please turn the printer on now."
6   echo "Press Enter to continue"
7   read ANYTHING            # Stall until the user turns the printer back on
    echo                     # A blank line is printed
8   /etc/init.d/lp start     # Start the printer
```

EXPLANATION

1   Checks to see if user is root. If not, sends an error and exits.

2   Creates a here document. Warning message is displayed on the screen.

3   The read command waits for user input. When the user presses Enter, the variable ANYTHING accepts whatever is typed. The variable is not used for anything. The read in this case is used to wait until the user turns off the printer, comes back, and presses Enter.

4   The lp program stops the printer daemon.

5   The SCHEDLOCK file must be removed before the scheduler can start again, as well as temporary files in /var/spool/lp.

6   The user is asked to press Enter when ready.

7   Whatever the user types is read into the variable ANYTHING, and when Enter is pressed, the program will resume execution.

8   The lp program starts the print daemons.

8.3 Arithmetic

Arithmetic is not built into the Bourne shell. If you need to perform simple integer arithmetic calculations, the UNIX expr command is most commonly used in Bourne shell scripts. For floating-point arithmetic, the awk or bc programs can be used. Because arithmetic was not built in, the performance of the shell is degraded when iterating through loops a number of times. Each time a counter is incremented or decremented in a looping mechanism, it is necessary to fork another process to handle the arithmetic.

8.3.1   Integer Arithmetic and the expr Command

The expr command is an expression-handling program. When used to evaluate arithmetic expressions, it can perform simple integer operations (see Table 8.2). Each of its arguments must be separated by a space. The +, -, *, /, and % operators are supported, and the normal programming rules of associativity and precedence apply.

Table 8.2 The expr Command Arithmetic Operators

Operator	Function
*	Multiplication
/	Division
%	Modulus
+	Addition
–	Subtraction

EXAMPLE 8.5

```
1   $ expr 1 + 4
    5
2   $ expr 1+4
    1+4
3   $ expr 5 + 9 / 3
    8
4   $ expr 5 * 4
    expr: syntax error
5   $ expr 5 \* 4 - 2
    18
6   $ expr 11 % 3
    2
7   $ num=1
    $ num=`expr $num + 1`
    $ echo $num
    2
```

EXPLANATION

1   The expr command evaluates the expression. The two numbers are added.
2   Because there are no spaces between the operator, the expression is evaluated as a string.
3   Addition and division are combined. The division is performed first and then the addition.
4   The asterisk (*) is evaluated by the shell as one of its wildcards, causing the expr command to fail.
5   The asterisk (*) is escaped with a backslash to prevent shell interpretation. The expr command performs arithmetic.
6   The modulus operator (%) returns the remainder after division is performed.
7   The variable num is assigned 1. The expr command adds 1 to the value of the variable and assigns the result to num. The value of num is echoed to the screen.

8.3.2 Floating-Point Arithmetic

The bc, awk, and nawk utilities are useful if you need to perform more complex calculations.

EXAMPLE 8.6

```
(The Command Line)
1    $ n=`echo "scale=3; 13 / 2" | bc`
     $ echo $n
     6.500
2    $ n=`bc << EOF
     scale=3
     13/2
     EOF`
     $ echo $n
     6.500
3    $ product=`nawk -v x=2.45 -v y=3.123 'BEGIN{printf "%.2f\n",x*y}'`
     $ echo $product
     7.65
```

EXPLANATION

1   The output of the echo command is piped to the bc program. The scale is set to 3, which is the number of significant digits to the right of the decimal point that will be printed. The calculation is to divide 13 by 2. The entire pipeline is enclosed in backquotes. Command substitution will be performed and the output assigned to the variable n.

2   This example uses the here document within backquotes to perform the same function as the first example. The output of the command will be asssigned to the variable n and then displayed with the echo command.

3   The nawk program gets its values from the argument list passed in at the command line, x=2.45 y=3.123. (The -v switch works with nawk, not awk.) After the numbers are multiplied, the printf function formats and prints the result with a precision of two places to the right of the decimal point. The output is assigned to the variable product.

8.4 Positional Parameters and Command-Line Arguments

Information can be passed into a script via the command line. Each word (separated by whitespace) following the script name is called an *argument*.

Command-line arguments can be referenced in scripts with positional parameters; for example, $1 for the first argument, $2 for the second argument, $3 for the third argument, and so on. The $# variable is used to test for the number of parameters, and $* is used to display all of them. Positional parameters can be set or reset with the set command. When the set command is used, any positional parameters previously set are cleared out. See Table 8.3.

Table 8.3   Bourne Shell Positional Parameters

Positional Parameter	What It References
$0	References the name of the script
$#	Holds the value of the number of positional parameters
$*	Lists all of the positional parameters
$@	Means the same as $*, except when enclosed in double quotes
"$*"	Expands to a single argument (e.g., "$1 $2 $3")
"$@"	Expands to separate arguments (e.g., "$1" "$2" "$3")
$1 .. $9	References up to nine positional parameters

EXAMPLE 8.7

```
(The Script)
    #!/bin/sh
    # Scriptname: greetings
    echo "This script is called $0."
1   echo "$0  $1 and $2"
    echo "The number of positional parameters is $#"
    ----------------------------------------------------------
(The Command Line)
    $ chmod +x greetings
2   $ greetings
    This script is called  greetings.
    greetings  and
    The number of positional parameters is

3   $ greetings Tommy
    This script is called greetings.
    greetings Tommy and
    The number of positional parameters is 1

4   $ greetings Tommy  Kimberly
    This script is called greetings.
    greetings Tommy and Kimberly
    The number of positional parameters is 2
```

EXPLANATION

1   In the script greetings, positional parameter $0 references the script name, $1 the first command-line argument, and $2 the second command-line argument.

2   The greetings script is executed without any arguments passed. The output illustrates that the script is called greetings ($0 in the script) and that $1 and $2 were never assigned anything; therefore, their values are null and nothing is printed.

3   This time, one argument is passed, Tommy. Tommy is assigned to positional parameter 1.

4   Two arguments are entered, Tommy and Kimberly. Tommy is assigned to $1 and Kimberly is assigned to $2.

8.4.1   The set Command and Positional Parameters

The set command with arguments resets the positional parameters.[1] Once reset, the old parameter list is lost. To unset all of the positional parameters, use set --. $0 is always the name of the script.

EXAMPLE   8.8

```
(The Script)
    #!/bin/sh
    # Scriptname: args
    # Script to test command-line arguments

1   echo The name of this script is $0.
2   echo The arguments are $*.
3   echo The first argument is $1.
4   echo The second argument is $2.
5   echo The number of arguments is $#.
6   oldargs=$*             # Save parameters passed in from the command line
7   set Jake Nicky Scott   # Reset the positional parameters
8   echo All the positional parameters are $*.
9   echo The number of postional parameters is $#.
10  echo "Good-bye for now, $1 "
11  set `date`             # Reset the positional parameters
12  echo The date is $2 $3, $6.
13  echo "The value of \$oldargs is $oldargs."
14  set $oldargs
15  echo $1 $2 $3
```

---

1.   Remember, without arguments, the set command displays all the variables that have been set for this shell, local and exported. With options, the set command turns on and off shell control options such as -x and -v.

EXAMPLE   8.8 (CONTINUED)

(The Command Line and Output)
```
$ args a b c d
```
1   *The name of this script is args.*
2   *The arguments are a b c d.*
3   *The first argument is a.*
4   *The second argument is b.*
5   *The number of arguments is 4.*
8   *All the positional parameters are Jake Nicky Scott.*
9   *The number of positional parameters is 3.*
10 *Good-bye for now, Jake*
12 *The date is Mar 25, 2004.*
13 *The value of $oldargs is a b c d.*
15 *a b c*

EXPLANATION

1   The name of the script is stored in the $0 variable.

2   $* represents all of the positional parameters.

3   $1 represents the first positional parameter (command-line argument).

4   $2 represents the second positional parameter.

5   $# is the total number of positional parameters (command-line arguments).

6   All positional parameters are saved in a variable called oldargs.

7   The set command allows you to reset the positional parameters, clearing out the old list. Now, $1 is Jake, $2 is Nicky, and $3 is Scott.

8   $* represents all of the parameters, Jake, Nicky, and Scott.

9   $# represents the number of parameters, 3.

10 $1 is Jake.

11 After command substitution is performed—that is, date is executed—the positional parameters are reset to the output of the date command.

12 The new values of $2, $3, and $6 are displayed.

13 The values saved in oldargs are printed.

14 The set command creates positional parameters from the value stored in oldargs.

15 The first three positional parameters are displayed.

EXAMPLE 8.9

(The Script)
```
#!/bin/sh
# Scriptname: checker
# Script to demonstrate the use of special variable modifiers and arguments
1   name=${1:?"requires an argument" }
    echo Hello $name
```

(The Command Line)
```
2   $ checker
    ./checker: 1: requires an argument
3   $ checker Sue
    Hello Sue
```

EXPLANATION

1. The special variable modifier :? will check whether $1 has a value. If not, the script exits and the message is printed.

2. The program is executed without an argument. $1 is not assigned a value; an error is displayed.

3. The checker program is given a command-line argument, Sue. In the script, $1 is assigned Sue. The program continues.

8.4.2 How $* and $@ Differ

The $* and $@ differ only when enclosed in double quotes. When $* is enclosed within double quotes, the parameter list becomes a single string. When $@ is enclosed within double quotes, each of the parameters is quoted; that is, each word is treated as a separate string.

EXAMPLE 8.10

```
1   $ set 'apple pie' pears peaches
2   $ for i in $*
    > do
    > echo $i
    > done
    apple
    pie
    pears
    peaches
```

EXAMPLE   8.10 (CONTINUED)

```
3   $ set 'apple pie' pears peaches
4   $ for i in "$*"
    > do
    > echo $i
    > done
apple pie pears peaches

5   $ set 'apple pie' pears peaches
6   $ for i in $@
    > do
    > echo $i
    > done
apple
pie
pears
peaches

7   $ set 'apple pie' pears peaches
8   $ for i in "$@"          # At last!!
    > do
    > echo $i
    > done
apple pie
pears
peaches
```

EXPLANATION

1   The positional parameters are set.

2   When $* is expanded, the quotes surrounding apple pie are stripped; apple and pie become two separate words. The for loop assigns each of the words, in turn, to the variable i, and then prints the value of i. Each time through the loop, the word on the left is shifted off, and the next word is assigned to the variable i.

3   The positional parameters are set.

4   By enclosing $* in double quotes, the entire parameter list becomes one string, "apple pie pears peaches". The entire list is assigned to i as a single word. The loop makes one iteration.

5   The positional parameters are set.

6   Unquoted, $@ and $* behave the same way (see line 2 of this explanation).

7   The positional parameters are set.

8   By surrounding $@ with double quotes, each of the positional parameters is treated as a quoted string. The list would be "apple pie", "pears", "peaches". The desired result is finally achieved.

8.5 Conditional Constructs and Flow Control

Conditional commands allow you to perform some task(s) based on whether a condition succeeds or fails. The if command is the simplest form of decision making; the if/else command allows a two-way decision; and the if/elif/else command allows a multiway decision.

The Bourne shell expects a command to follow an if. The command can be a system command or a built-in command. The exit status of the command is used to evaluate the condition.

To evaluate an expression, the built-in test command is used. This command is also linked to the bracket symbol. Either the test command is used, or the expression can be enclosed in set of single brackets. Shell metacharacters (wildcards) are not expanded by the test command. The result of a command is tested, with zero status indicating success and nonzero status indicating failure. See Table 8.4.

Table 8.4 String, Integer, and File Testing

Test Operator	Test For
String Test	
string1 = string2	String1 is equal to String2 (space surrounding = required)
string1 != string2	String1 is not equal to String2 (space surrounding != required)
string	String is not null
-z string	Length of string is zero
-n string	Length of string is nonzero
	EXAMPLE test -n $word or [-n $word] test tom = sue or [tom = sue]
Integer Test	
int1 -eq int2	Int1 is equal to int2
int1 -ne int2	Int1 is not equal to int2
int1 -gt int2	Int1 is greater than int2
int1 -ge int2	Int1 is greater than or equal to int2
int1 -lt int2	Int1 is less than int2
int1 -le int2	Int1 is less than or equal to int2

Table 8.4   String, Integer, and File Testing (continued)

Test Operator	Test For
Logical Test	
expr1 -a expr2	Logical AND
expr1 -o expr2	Logical OR
! expr	Logical NOT
File Test	
-b filename	Block special file
-c filename	Character special file
-d filename	Directory existence
-f filename	Regular file existence and not a directory
-g filename	Set-group-ID is set
-k filename	Sticky bit is set
-p filename	File is a named pipe
-r filename	File is readable
-s filename	File is nonzero size
-u filename	Set-user-ID bit is set
-w filename	File is writable
-x filename	File is executable

8.5.1   Testing Exit Status: The test Command

The following examples illustrate how the exit status is tested.

The test command is used to evaluate conditional expressions, returning true or false. It will return a zero exit status for true and a nonzero exit status for false. The test command or brackets can be used. (Refer back to Table 8.4.)

EXAMPLE   8.11

```
(At the Command Line)
1   $ name=Tom
2   $ grep "$name"  /etc/passwd
    Tom:8ZKX2F:5102:40:Tom Savage:/home/tom:/bin/ksh
3   $ echo $?
    0              Success!
4   $ test $name != Tom
5   $ echo $?
    1              Failure
6   $ [ $name = Tom ]          # Brackets replace the test command
7   $ echo $?
    0              Success
8   $ [ $name = [Tt]?m ]       # Wildcards are not evaluated by the test command
9   $ echo  $?
    1              Failure
```

EXPLANATION

1   The variable name is assigned the string Tom.

2   The grep command will search for string Tom in the passwd file.

3   The ? variable contains the exit status of the last command executed, in this case, the exit status of grep. If grep is successful in finding the string Tom, it will return an exit status of 0. The grep command was successful.

4   The test command is used to evaluate strings, numbers, and perform file testing. Like all commands, it returns an exit status. If the exit status is 0, the expression is true; if the exit status is 1, the expression evaluates to false. There *must* be spaces surrounding the equal sign. The value of name is tested to see if it is not equal to Tom.

5   The test fails and returns an exit status of 1.

6   The brackets are an alternate notation for the test command. There must be spaces after the first bracket. The expression is tested to see if $name evaluates to the string Tom.

7   The exit status of the test is 0. The test was successful because $name is equal to Tom.

8   The test command does not allow wildcard expansion. Because the question mark is treated as a literal character, the test fails. Tom and [Tt]?m are not equal.

9   The exit status is 1, indicating that the text in line 8 failed.

8.5.2   The if Command

The simplest form of conditional is the if command. The command or UNIX utility following the if construct is executed and its exit status is returned. The exit status is usually determined by the programmer who wrote the utility. Typically, if the exit status is zero, the command succeeded and the statement(s) after the then keyword are executed. In the C shell, the expression following the if command is a Boolean-type expression as in C. But in the Bourne and Korn shells, the statement following the if is a command or group of commands. If the exit status of the command being evaluated is zero, the block of statements after the then is executed until fi is reached. The fi terminates the if block. If the exit status is nonzero, meaning that the command failed in some way, the statement(s) after the then keyword are ignored and control goes to the line directly after the fi statement. It is important that you know the exit status of the commands being tested. For example, the exit status of grep is reliable in letting you know whether grep found the pattern it was searching for in a file. If grep is successful in its search, it returns a 0 exit status; if not, it returns 1. The sed and awk programs also search for patterns, but they will report a successful exit status regardless of whether they find the pattern. The criteria for success with sed and awk is correct syntax, not functionality.[2]

FORMAT

```
if command
then
        command
        command
fi
-----------------------------------
if test expression
then
        command
fi


            or


if [ expression ]
then
        command
fi
------------------------------
```

EXAMPLE 8.12

```
1    if ypmatch "$name" passwd > /dev/null 2>&1
2    then
            echo Found $name!
3    fi
```

2. Unlike the C shell, the Bourne shell does not support an if statement without a then, even for a simple statement.

EXPLANATION

1 The ypmatch command is an NIS (Sun's Network Information Services) command that searches for its argument, name, in the NIS passwd database on the server machine. Standard output and standard error are redirected to /dev/null, the UNIX bit bucket. If ypmatch is not supported on your system, try

   `if grep "$name" /etc/passwd > /dev/null 2>&1`

2 If the exit status of the ypmatch command is 0, the program goes to the then statement and executes commands until fi is reached.

3 The fi terminates the list of commands following the then statement.

EXAMPLE 8.13

```
1   echo  "Are you okay (y/n) ?"
    read answer
2   if [ "$answer" = Y -o "$answer" = y  ]
    then
          echo  "Glad to hear it."
3   fi
```

EXPLANATION

1 The user is asked the question and told to respond. The read command waits for a response.

2 The test command, represented by square brackets, is used to test expressions. It returns an exit status of zero if the expression is true and nonzero if the expression is false. If the variable answer evaluates to Y or y, the commands after the then statement are executed. (The test command does not allow the use of wildcards when testing expressions, and spaces must surround the square brackets (as well as the = operators). Refer to Table 8.4 on page 333.

   The variable $answer is double quoted to hold it together as a single string. The test command fails if more than one word appears before the = operator. For example, if the user entered yes, you betcha, the answer variable would evaluate to three words, causing the test to fail, *unless* $answer is enclosed in double quotes.

3 The fi terminates the list of commands following the then statement.

8.5.3   The exit Command and the ? Variable

The exit command is used to terminate the script and return to the command line. You may want the script to exit if some condition occurs. The argument given to the exit command is a number ranging from 0 to 255. If the program exits with 0 as an argument, the program exited with success. A nonzero argument indicates some kind of failure. The argument given to the exit command is stored in the shell's ? variable.

EXAMPLE 8.14

```
(The Script)
    # Name: bigfiles
    # Purpose: Use the find command to find any files in the root
    # partition that have not been modified within the past n (any
    # number within 30 days) days and are larger than 20 blocks
    # (512-byte blocks)

1   if  [ $# -ne 2 ]
    then
        echo  "Usage: $0 mdays size " 1>&2
        exit 1
2   fi
3   if  [ $1 -lt 0 -o $1 -gt 30 ]
    then
        echo "mdays is out of range"
        exit 2
4   fi
5   if [ $2 -le 20 ]
    then
        echo "size is out of range"
        exit 3
6   fi
7   find / -xdev -mtime $1 -size +$2 -print

(The Command Line)
$ bigfiles
Usage: bigfiles mdays size
$ echo $?
1
$ bigfiles 400 80
mdays is out of range
$ echo $?
2
$ bigfiles 25 2
size is out of range
$ echo $?
3
$ bigfiles 2 25
(Output of find prints here)
```

EXPLANATION

1 The statement reads: If the number of arguments is not equal to 2, print the error message and send it to standard error, then exit the script with an exit status of 1.

2 The fi marks the end of the block of statements after then.

3 The statement reads: If the value of the first positional parameter passed in from the command line is less than 0 or greater than 30, then print the message and exit with a status of 2. See Table 8.4 on page 333 for numeric operators.

4 The fi ends the if block.

5 The statement reads: If the value of the second positional parameter passed in at the command line is less than or equal to 20 (512-byte blocks), then print the message and exit with a status of 3.

6 The fi ends the if block.

7 The find command starts its search in the root directory. The -xdev option prevents find from searching other partitions. The -mtime option takes a number argument, which is the number of days since the file was modified, and the -size option takes a number argument, which is the size of the file in 512-byte blocks.

8.5.4 Checking for Null Values

When checking for null values in a variable, use double quotes to hold the null value or the test command will fail.

EXAMPLE 8.15

```
(The Script)
1   if [ "$name" = "" ]    # Alternative to  [ ! "$name" ]  or  [ -z "$name" ]
    then
        echo The name variable is null
    fi

(From System showmount program, which displays all remotely mounted systems)
    remotes=`/usr/sbin/showmount`
2   if [ "X${remotes}" != "X" ]
    then
        /usr/sbin/wall ${remotes}
                    ...
3   fi
```

EXPLANATION

1 If the `name` variable evaluates to null, the test is true. The double quotes are used to represent null.

2 The `showmount` command lists all clients remotely mounted from a host machine. The command will list either one or more clients, or nothing. The variable `remotes` will either have a value assigned or will be null. The letter `X` precedes the variable `remotes` when being tested. If `remotes` evaluates to null, no clients are remotely logged on and X will be equal to X, causing the program to start execution again on line 3. If the variable has a value, for example, the hostname `pluto`, the expression would read `if Xpluto != X`, and the `wall` command would be executed. (All users on remote machines will be sent a message.) The purpose of using X in the expression is to guarantee that even if the value of `remotes` is null, there will always be a placeholder on either side of the `!=` operator in the expression.

3 The `fi` terminates the `if`.

8.5.5 The `if/else` Command

The `if/else` command allows a two-way decision-making process. If the command after the `if` fails, the commands after the `else` are executed.

FORMAT

```
if  command
then
     command(s)
else
     command(s)
fi
```

EXAMPLE 8.16

```
(The Script)
    #!/bin/sh
1   if ypmatch "$name" passwd > /dev/null 2>&1ᵃ
2   then
         echo Found $name!
3   else
         echo "Can't find $name."
         exit 1
5   fi
```

---

a. If using NIS+, the command would read: If `nismatch "$name" passwd.org_dir`.

EXPLANATION

1   The ypmatch command searches for its argument, name, in the NIS passwd database. Because the user does not need to see the output, standard output and standard error are redirected to /dev/null, the UNIX bit bucket.

2   If the exit status of the ypmatch command is 0, program control goes to the then statement and executes commands until else is reached.

3   The commands under the else statement are executed if the ypmatch command fails to find $name in the passwd database; that is, the exit status of ypmatch must be non-zero for the commands in the else block to be executed.

4   If the value in $name is not found in the passwd database, this echo statement is executed and the program exits with a value of 1, indicating failure.

5   The fi terminates the if.

EXAMPLE 8.17

```
(The Script)
#!/bin/sh
# Scriptname: idcheck
# purpose: check user ID to see if user is root.
# Only root has a uid of 0.
# Format for id output:uid=9496(ellie) gid=40 groups=40
# root's uid=0

1   id=`id | nawk -F'[=()]' '{print $2}'`      # Get user ID
    echo your user id is: $id
2   if [ $id -eq 0 ]
    then
3       echo "you are superuser."
4   else
        echo "you are not superuser."
5   fi

    (The Command Line)
6   $ idcheck
    your user id is: 9496
    you are not superuser.
7   $ su
    Password:
8   # idcheck
    your user id is: 0
    you are superuser
```

EXPLANATION

1   The id command is piped to the nawk command. Nawk uses either an equal sign or
     an open parenthesis as field separator, extracts the user ID from the output, and
     assigns the output to the variable id.

2   If the value of id is equal to 0, then line 3 is executed.

4   If id is not equal to 0, the else statement is executed.

5   The fi marks the end of the if command.

6   The idcheck script is executed by the current user, whose UID is 9496.

7   The su command switches the user to root.

8   The # prompt indicates that the superuser (root) is the new user. The UID for root
     is 0.

8.5.6 The if/elif/else Command

The if/elif/else command allows a multiway decision-making process. If the command
following the if fails, the command following the elif is tested. If that command succeeds, the commands under its then statement are executed. If the command after the
elif fails, the next elif command is checked. If none of the commands succeeds, the else
commands are executed. The else block is called the default.

FORMAT

```
if  command
then
     command(s)
elif command
then
     commands(s)
elif command
then
     command(s)
else
     command(s)
fi
```

EXAMPLE 8.18

```
(The Script)
    #!/bin/sh
    # Scriptname: tellme
1   echo -n "How old are you? "
    read age
```

EXAMPLE 8.18 (CONTINUED)

```
2    if [ $age -lt 0 -o $age -gt 120 ]
     then
         echo  "Welcome to our planet! "
         exit 1
     fi
3    if [ $age -ge 0 -a  $age -lt 13 ]
     then
         echo "A child is a garden of verses"
     elif [ $age -ge 13 -a $age -lt  20 ]
     then
         echo "Rebel without a cause"
     elif [ $age  -ge 20 -a $age -lt  30 ]
     then
         echo "You got the world by the tail!!"
     elif [ $age -ge  30 -a  $age -lt 40 ]
     then
         echo "Thirty something..."
4    else
         echo "Sorry I asked"
5    fi
```

```
(The Output)
$ tellme
How old are you? 200
Welcome to our planet!
$ tellme
How old are you? 13
Rebel without a cause
$ tellme
How old are you? 55
Sorry I asked
```

EXPLANATION

1   The user is asked for input. The input is assigned to the variable age.

2   A numeric test is performed within the square brackets. If age is less than 0 or greater than 120, the echo command is executed and the program terminates with an exit status of 1. The interactive shell prompt will appear.

3   A numeric test is performed within the square brackets. If age is greater than or equal to 0 and less than 13, the test command returns exit status 0, true, and the statement after the then is executed. Otherwise, program control goes to the elif. If that test is false, the next elif is tested.

4   The else construct is the default. If none of the above statements are true, the else commands will be executed.

5   The fi terminates the initial if statement.

8.5.7   File Testing

Often when writing scripts, your script will require that there are certain files available and that those files have specific permissions, are of a certain type, or have other attributes. (See Table 8.4 on page 333.) You will find file testing a necessary part of writing dependable scripts.

When if statements are nested, the fi statement always goes with the nearest if statement. Indenting the nested ifs makes it easier to see which if statement goes with which fi statement.

EXAMPLE 8.19

```
(The Script)
    #!/bin/sh
    file=./testing

1 ┌─if [ -d $file ]
  │  then
  │         echo "$file is a directory"
2 │  elif [ -f $file ]
  │  then
3 │      ┌─ if [ -r $file -a -w $file -a -x $file ]
  │      │   then    # nested if command
  │      │       echo "You have read, write, and execute permission on $file."
4 │      └─ fi
5 │  else
  │         echo "$file is neither a file nor a directory."
6 └─fi
```

EXPLANATION

1   If the file testing is a directory, print testing is a directory.
2   If the file testing is not a directory, else if the file is a plain file, then . . .
3   If the file testing is readable, writable, and executable, then . . .
4   The fi terminates the innermost if command.
5   The else commands are executed if lines 1 and 2 are not true.
6   This fi goes with the first if.

8.5.8   The null Command

The null command, represented by a colon, is a built-in, do-nothing command that returns an exit status of 0. It is used as a placeholder after an if command when you have nothing to say, but need a command or the program will produce an error message because it requires something after the then statement. Often the null command is used as an argument to a looping command to make the loop a forever loop.

EXAMPLE 8.20

```
(The Script)
1    name=Tom
2    if grep "$name" databasefile > /dev/null 2>&1
     then
3        :
4    else
         echo  "$1 not found in databasefile"
         exit 1
     fi
```

EXPLANATION

1   The variable name is assigned the string Tom.

2   The if command tests the exit status of the grep command. If Tom is found in the database file, the null command, a colon, is executed and does nothing.

3   The colon is the null command. It does nothing other than returning a 0 exit status.

4   What we really want to do is print an error message and exit if Tom is *not* found. The commands after the else will be executed if the grep command fails.

EXAMPLE 8.21

```
(The Command Line)
1    $ DATAFILE=
2    $ : ${DATAFILE:=$HOME/db/datafile}
     $ echo $DATAFILE
     /home/jody/ellie/db/datafile
3    $ : ${DATAFILE:=$HOME/junk}
     $ echo $DATAFILE
     /home/jody/ellie/db/datafile
```

EXPLANATION

1   The variable DATAFILE is assigned null.

2   The colon command is a "do-nothing" command. The modifier (:=) returns a value that can be assigned to a variable or used in a test. In this example, the expression is passed as an argument to the do-nothing command. The shell will perform variable substitution; that is, assign the pathname to DATAFILE if DATAFILE does not already have a value. The variable DATAFILE is permanently set.

3   Because the variable has already been set, it will not be reset with the default value provided on the right of the modifier.

EXAMPLE 8.22

```
(The Script)
     #!/bin/sh
1    # Name:wholenum
     # Purpose:The expr command tests that the user enters an integer
     echo "Enter a number."
     read number
2    if expr "$number" + 0 > /dev/null 2>&1
     then
3         :
     else
4         echo "You did not enter an integer value." 1782
          exit 1
5    fi
```

EXPLANATION

1   The user is asked to enter an integer. The number is assigned to the variable number.

2   The expr command evaluates the expression. If addition can be performed, the number is a whole number and expr returns a successful exit status. All output is redirected to the bit bucket /dev/null.

3   If expr is successful, it returns a 0 exit status, and the colon command does nothing.

4   If the expr command fails, it returns a nonzero exit status, the echo command displays the message to standard error (1782), and the program exits.

5   The fi ends the if block.

8.5.9 The case Command

The case command is a multiway branching command used as an alternative to the if/elif command. The value of the case variable is matched against value1, value2, and so forth, until a match is found. When a value matches the case variable, the commands following the value are executed until the double semicolons are reached. Then execution starts after the word esac (case spelled backwards).

If the case variable is not matched, the program executes the commands after the *), the default value, until ;; or esac is reached. The *) value functions the same as the else statement in if/else conditionals. The case values allow the use of shell wildcards and the vertical bar (pipe symbol) for ORing two values.

FORMAT

```
case variable in
value1)
    command(s)
    ;;
value2)
    command(s)
    ;;
*)
command(s)
    ;;
esac
```

EXAMPLE 8.23

```
(The Script)
    #!/bin/sh
    # Scriptname: colors

1   echo -n "Which color do you like?"
    read color
2   case "$color" in
3   [Bb]l??)
4       echo I feel $color
        echo The sky is $color
5       ;;
6   [Gg]ree*)
        echo  $color is for trees
        echo  $color is for seasick;;
7   red | orange)          # The vertical bar means "OR"
        echo  $color is very warm!;;
8   *)
        echo  No such color as $color;;
9   esac
10  echo  "Out of case"
```

EXPLANATION

1   The user is asked for input. The input is assigned to the variable color.

2   The case command evaluates the expression $color.

3   If the color begins with a B or b, followed by the letter l and any two characters, the case expression matches the first value. The value is terminated with a single closed parenthesis. The wildcards are shell metacharacters used for filename expansion.

4   The statements are executed if the value in line 3 matches the case expression.

5   The double semicolons are required after the last command in this block of commands. Control branches to line 10 when the semicolons are reached. The script is easier to debug if the semicolons are on their own line.

6   If the case expression matches a G or g, followed by the letters ree and ending in zero or more of any other characters, the echo commands are executed. The double semicolons terminate the block of statements and control branches to line 10.

7   The vertical bar is used as an OR conditional operator. If the case expression matches either red or orange, the echo command is executed.

8   This is the default value. If none of the above values match the case expression, the commands after the *) are executed.

9   The esac statement terminates the case command.

10 After one of the case values is matched, execution continues here.

8.5.10 Creating Menus with the here document and case Command

The here document and case command are often used together. The here document is used to create a menu of choices that will be displayed to the screen. The user will be asked to select one of the menu items, and the case command will test against the set of choices to execute the appropriate command.

EXAMPLE 8.24

```
    (The .profile file)
        echo "Select a terminal type: "
1   cat << ENDIT
            1) vt 120
            2) wyse50
            3) sun
2   ENDIT
3   read choice
4   case "$choice" in
5   1)   TERM=vt120
        export TERM
        ;;
    2)   TERM=wyse50
        export TERM
        ;;
6   3)   TERM=sun
        export TERM
        ;;
```

> EXAMPLE 8.24 (CONTINUED)
>
> ```
> 7    esac
> 8    echo "TERM is $TERM."
> ```
>
> (The Output)
> ```
> $ . .profile
> Select a terminal type:
> 1) vt120
> 2) wyse50
> 3) sun
> 3                      <-- User input
> TERM is sun.
> ```

> EXPLANATION
>
> 1 If this segment of script is put in the .profile, when you log on, you will be given a chance to select the proper terminal type. The here document is used to display a menu of choices.
>
> 2 The user-defined ENDIT terminator marks the end of the here document.
>
> 3 The read command stores the user input in the variable TERM.
>
> 4 The case command evaluates the variable choice and compares that value with one of the values preceding the closing parenthesis: 1, 2, or *.
>
> 5 The first value tested is 1. If there is a match, the terminal is set to a vt120. The TERM variable is exported so that subshells will inherit it.
>
> 6 A default value is not required. The TERM variable is normally assigned in /etc/profile at login time. If the choice is 3, the terminal is set to a sun.
>
> 7 The esac terminates the case command.
>
> 8 After the case command has finished, this line is executed.

8.6 Looping Commands

Looping commands are used to execute a command or group of commands a set number of times or until a certain condition is met. The Bourne shell has three types of loops: for, while, and until.

8.6.1 The for Command

The for looping command is used to execute commands a finite number of times on a list of items. For example, you might use this loop to execute the same commands on a list of files or usernames. The for command is followed by a user-defined variable, the keyword in, and a list of words. The first time in the loop, the first word from the wordlist is assigned to the variable, and then shifted off the list. Once the word is assigned to the variable, the body of the loop is entered, and commands between the do and done keywords are executed. The next time around the loop, the second word is assigned to the variable, and so on. The body of the loop starts at the do keyword and ends at the done keyword. When all of the words in the list have been shifted off, the loop ends and program control continues after the done keyword.

FORMAT

```
for variable in word_list
do
     command(s)
done
```

EXAMPLE 8.25

```
(The Script)
    #!/bin/sh
    # Scriptname: forloop
1   for pal in Tom Dick Harry Joe
2   do
3       echo "Hi $pal"
4   done
5   echo "Out of loop"

(The Output)
$ forloop
Hi Tom
Hi Dick
Hi Harry
Hi Joe
Out of loop
```

EXPLANATION

1   This for loop will iterate through the list of names, Tom, Dick, Harry, and Joe, shifting each one off (to the left and assigning its value to the user-defined variable, pal) after it is used. As soon as all of the words are shifted and the wordlist is empty, the loop ends and execution starts after the done keyword. The first time in the loop, the variable pal will be assigned the word Tom. The second time through the loop, pal will be assigned Dick, the next time pal will be assigned Harry, and the last time pal will be assigned Joe.

2   The do keyword is required after the wordlist. If it is used on the same line, the list must be terminated with a semicolon. Example:

    for pal in Tom Dick Harry Joe; do

3   This is the body of the loop. After Tom is assigned to the variable pal, the commands in the body of the loop (i.e., all commands between the do and done keywords) are executed.

4 The done keyword ends the loop. Once the last word in the list (Joe) has been assigned and shifted off, the loop exits.

5 Control resumes here when the loop exits.

EXAMPLE 8.26

```
(The Command Line)
1   $ cat mylist
    tom
    patty
    ann
    jake

(The Script)
    #!/bin/sh
    # Scriptname: mailer
2   for person in `cat mylist`
    do
3       mail $person < letter
        echo  $person was sent a letter.
4   done
5   echo "The letter has been sent."
```

EXPLANATION

1 The contents of a file, called mylist, are displayed.

2 Command substitution is performed and the contents of mylist becomes the wordlist. The first time in the loop, tom is assigned to the variable person, then it is shifted off to be replaced with patty, and so forth.

3 In the body of the loop, each user is mailed a copy of a file called letter.

4 The done keyword marks the end of this loop iteration.

5 When all of the users in the list have been sent mail and the loop has exited, this line is executed.

EXAMPLE 8.27

```
(The Script)
    #!/bin/sh
    # Scriptname: backup
    # Purpose:
    # Create backup files and store them in a backup directory
1   dir=/home/jody/ellie/backupscripts
```

EXAMPLE 8.27 (CONTINUED)

```
2    for file in memo[1-5]
     do
3        if [ -f $file ]
         then
             cp $file $dir/$file.bak
             echo "$file is backed up in $dir"
         fi
     done

(The Output)
memo1 is backed up in /home/jody/ellie/backupscripts
memo2 is backed up in /home/jody/ellie/backupscripts
memo3 is backed up in /home/jody/ellie/backupscripts
memo4 is backed up in /home/jody/ellie/backupscripts
memo5 is backed up in /home/jody/ellie/backupscripts
```

EXPLANATION

1   The variable `dir` is assigned.
2   The wordlist will consist of all files in the current working directory with names starting with `memo` and ending with a number between 1 and 5. Each filename will be assigned, one at time, to the variable `file` for each iteration of the loop.
3   When the body of the loop is entered, the file will be tested to make sure it exists and is a real file. If so, it will be copied into the directory /home/jody/ellie/backup-scripts with the .bak extension appended to its name.

8.6.2 The $* and $@ Variables in Wordlists

When expanded, the $* and $@ are the same unless enclosed in double quotes. $* evaluates to one string, whereas $@ evaluates to a list of separate words.

EXAMPLE 8.28

```
(The Script)
    #!/bin/sh
    # Scriptname: greet
1   for name in $*          # Same as for name in $@
2   do
        echo Hi $name
3   done
```

EXAMPLE 8.28

(The Command Line)
$ **greet Dee Bert Lizzy Tommy**
Hi Dee
Hi Bert
Hi Lizzy
Hi Tommy

EXPLANATION

1   $* and $@ expand to a list of all the positional parameters, in this case, the arguments passed in from the command line: Dee, Bert, Lizzy, and Tommy. Each name in the list will be assigned, in turn, to the variable name in the for loop.

2   The commands in the body of the loop are executed until the list is empty.

3   The done keyword marks the end of the loop body.

EXAMPLE 8.29

(The Script)
```
#!/bin/sh
# Scriptname:permx
1   for file          # Empty wordlist
    do
2       if [ -f $file -a ! -x $file ]
        then
3           chmod +x $file
            echo $file now has execute permission
        fi
    done
```

(The Command Line)
4   $ **permx** *
addon now has execute permission
checkon now has execute permission
doit now has execute permission

EXPLANATION

1   If the for loop is not provided with a wordlist, it iterates through the positional parameters. This is the same as for file in $*.

2   The filenames are coming in from the command line. The shell expands the asterisk (*) to all filenames in the current working directory. If the file is a plain file and does not have execute permission, line 3 is executed.

3   Execute permission is added for each file being processed.

4   At the command line, the asterisk will be evaluated by the shell as a wildcard and all files in the current directory will be replaced for the *. The files will be passed as arguments to the permx script.

8.6.3   The while Command

The while command evaluates the command immediately following it and, if its exit status is 0, the commands in the body of the loop (commands between do and done) are executed. When the done keyword is reached, control is returned to the top of the loop and the while command checks the exit status of the command again. Until the exit status of the command being evaluated by the while becomes nonzero, the loop continues. When the exit status reaches nonzero, program execution starts after the done keyword.

FORMAT

```
while command
do
      command(s)
done
```

EXAMPLE 8.30

```
(The Script)
      #!/bin/sh
      # Scriptname: num
1     num=0                    # Initialize num
2     while [ $num -lt 10 ]    # Test num with test command
      do
            echo  -n $num
3            num=`expr  $num + 1`  # Increment num
      done
      echo "\nAfter loop exits, continue running here"

(The Output)
0123456789
After loop exits, continue running here
```

EXPLANATION

1   This is the initialization step. The variable num is assigned 0.

2   The while command is followed by the test (square brackets) command. If the value of num is less than 10, the body of the loop is entered.

3   In the body of the loop, the value of num is incremented by 1. If the value of num never changes, the loop would iterate infinitely or until the process is killed.

EXAMPLE 8.31

```
(The Script)
    #!/bin/sh
    # Scriptname: quiz
1   echo "Who was the chief defense lawyer in the OJ case?"
    read answer
2   while [ "$answer" != "Johnny" ]
3   do
4       echo  "Wrong try again!"
        read answer
5   done
6   echo You got it!

(The Output)
$ quiz
Who was the chief defense lawyer in the OJ case? Marcia
Wrong try again!
Who was the chief defense lawyer in the OJ case?  I give up
Wrong try again!
Who was the chief defense lawyer in the OJ case?  Johnny
You got it!
```

EXPLANATION

1   The echo command prompts the user, Who was the chief defense lawyer in the OJ case? The read command waits for input from the user. The input will be stored in the variable answer.

2   The while loop is entered and the test command, the bracket, tests the expression. If the variable answer does not equal the string Johnny, the body of the loop is entered and commands between the do and done are executed.

3   The do keyword is the start of the loop body.

4   The user is asked to re-enter input.

5   The done keyword marks the end of the loop body. Control is returned to the top of the while loop, and the expression is tested again. As long as $answer does not evaluate to Johnny, the loop will continue to iterate. When the user enters Johnny, the loop ends. Program control goes to line 6.

6   When the body of the loop ends, control starts here.

EXAMPLE 8.32

```
(The Script)
    #!/bin/sh
    # Scriptname: sayit
    echo Type q to quit.
    go=start
1   while [ -n "$go" ]        # Make sure to double quote the variable
    do
2       echo -n I love you.
3       read word
4       if [ "$word" = q -o "$word" = Q ]
        then
            echo "I'll always love you!"
            go=
        fi
    done

(The Output)
$ sayit
Type q to quit.
I love you.      <- When user presses the Enter key, the program continues
I love you.
I love you.
I love you.
I love you.q
I'll always love you!
$
```

EXPLANATION

1   The command after the while is executed and its exit status tested. The -n option
    to the test command tests for a non-null string. Because go initially has a value,
    the test is successful, producing a zero exit status. If the variable go is not enclosed
    in double quotes and the variable is null, the test command would complain:

    `go: test: argument expected`

2   The loop is entered. The string I love you. is echoed to the screen.

3   The read command waits for user input.

4   The expression is tested. If the user enters a q or Q, the string I'll always love you!
    is displayed, and the variable go is set to null. When the while loop is re-entered,
    the test is unsuccessful because the variable is null. The loop terminates. Control
    goes to the line after the done statement. In this example, the script will terminate
    because there are no more lines to execute.

8.6.4 The until Command

The until command is used like the while command, but executes the loop statements only if the command after until fails; that is, if the command returns an exit status of nonzero. When the done keyword is reached, control is returned to the top of the loop and the until command checks the exit status of the command again. Until the exit status of the command being evaluated by until becomes 0, the loop continues. When the exit status reaches 0, the loop exits, and program execution starts after the done keyword.

FORMAT

```
until command
do
      command(s)
done
```

EXAMPLE 8.33

```
(The Script)
      #!/bin/sh
1     until who | grep linda
2     do
            sleep 5
3     done
      talk linda@dragonwings
```

EXPLANATION

1 The until loop tests the exit status of the last command in the pipeline, grep. The who command lists who is logged on this machine and pipes its output to grep. The grep command will return a 0 exit status (success) only when it finds user linda.

2 If user linda has not logged on, the body of the loop is entered and the program sleeps for five seconds.

3 When linda logs on, the exit status of the grep command will be 0 and control will go to the statements following the done keyword.

EXAMPLE 8.34

```
(The Script)
      #!/bin/sh
      # Scriptname: hour
1     hour=1
2     until [ $hour  -gt 24 ]
      do
```

EXAMPLE 8.34 (CONTINUED)

```
3       case "$hour" in
        [0-9] |1[0-1])echo  "Good morning!"
            ;;
        12) echo  "Lunch time."


            ;;
        1[3-7])echo  "Siesta time."
            ;;
        *)  echo  "Good night."
            ;;
        esac
4       hour=`expr $hour + 1`
5   done
```

```
(The Output)
$ hour
Good morning!
Good morning!
   ...
Lunch time.
Siesta time.
   ...
Good night.
   ...
```

EXPLANATION

1   The variable hour is initialized to 1.

2   The test command tests if the hour is greater than 24. If the hour is not greater than 24, the body of the loop is entered. The until loop is entered if the command following it returns a nonzero exit status. Until the condition is true, the loop continues to iterate.

3   The case command evaluates the hour variable and tests each of the case statements for a match.

4   The hour variable is incremented before control returns to the top of the loop.

5   The done command marks the end of the loop body.

8.6.5 Looping Control Commands

If some condition occurs, you may want to break out of a loop, return to the top of the loop, or provide a way to stop an infinite loop. The Bourne shell provides loop control commands to handle these kinds of situations.

The shift Command. The shift command shifts the parameter list to the left a specified number of times. The shift command without an argument shifts the parameter list once to the left. Once the list is shifted, the parameter is removed permanently. Often, the shift command is used in a while loop when iterating through a list of positional parameters.

FORMAT

```
shift [n]
```

EXAMPLE 8.35

```
(Without a loop)
(The Script)
      #!/bin/sh
1     set joe mary tom sam
2     shift
3     echo $*
4     set `date`
5     echo  $*
6     shift 5
7     echo  $*
8     shift 2

(The Output)
3     mary tom sam
5     Fri Sep 9 10:00:12 PDT 2004
7     2004
8     cannot shift
```

EXPLANATION

1 The set command sets the positional parameters. $1 is assigned joe, $2 is assigned mary, $3 is assigned tom, and $4 is assigned sam. $* represents all of the parameters.

2 The shift command shifts the positional parameters to the left; joe is shifted off.

3 The parameter list is printed after the shift.

4 The set command resets the positional parameters to the output of the UNIX date command.

5 The new parameter list is printed.

6 This time the list is shifted 5 times to the left.

7 The new parameter list is printed.

8 By attempting to shift more times than there are parameters, the shell sends a message to standard error.

EXAMPLE 8.36

```
(With a loop)
(The Script)
    #!/bin/sh
    # Name: doit
    # Purpose: shift through command-line arguments
    # Usage: doit [args]
1   while [  $# -gt  0 ]
    do
2       echo  $*
3       shift
4   done

(The Command Line)
$ doit a b c d e
a b c d e
b c d e
c d e
d e
e
```

EXPLANATION

1   The while command tests the numeric expression. If the number of positional parameters ($#) is greater than 0, the body of the loop is entered. The positional parameters are coming from the command line as arguments. There are five.

2   All positional parameters are printed.

3   The parameter list is shifted once to the left.

4   The body of the loop ends here; control returns to the top of the loop. Each time the loop is entered, the shift command causes the parameter list to be decreased by 1. After the first shift, $# (number of positional parameters) is four. When $# has been decreased to zero, the loop ends.

EXAMPLE 8.37

```
(The Script)
    #!/bin/sh
    # Scriptname: dater
    # Purpose: set positional parameters with the set command
    # and shift through the parameters.
```

EXAMPLE 8.37 (CONTINUED)

```
1    set `date`
2    while [ $# -gt 0 ]
     do
3        echo $1
4        shift
     done

(The Output)
$ dater
Sat
Oct
16
12:12:13
PDT
2004
```

EXPLANATION

1 The set command takes the output of the date command and assigns the output to positional parameters $1 through $6.

2 The while command tests whether the number of positional parameters ($#) is greater than 0. If true, the body of the loop is entered.

3 The echo command displays the value of $1, the first positional parameter.

4 The shift command shifts the parameter list once to the left. Each time through the loop, the list is shifted until the list is empty. At that time, $# will be zero and the loop terminates.

The break Command.   The built-in break command is used to force immediate exit from a loop, but not from a program. (To leave a program, the exit command is used.) After the break command is executed, control starts after the done keyword. The break command causes an exit from the innermost loop, so if you have nested loops, the break command takes a number as an argument, allowing you to break out of a specific outer loop. If you are nested in three loops, the outermost loop is loop number 3, the next nested loop is loop number 2, and the innermost nested loop is loop number 1. The break is useful for exiting from an infinite loop.

FORMAT

```
break [n]
```

EXAMPLE 8.38

```
     #!/bin/sh
1    while true; do
2         echo Are you ready to move on\?
          read answer
3         if [  "$answer"  =  Y -o "$answer" = y  ]
          then
4              break
5         else
               ....commands...
          fi
6    done
7    print "Here we are"
```

EXPLANATION

1   The true command is a UNIX command that always exits with 0 status. It is often used to start an infinite loop. It is okay to put the do statement on the same line as the while command, as long as a semicolon separates them. The body of the loop is entered.

2   The user is asked for input. The user's input is assigned to the variable answer.

3   If $answer evaluates to Y or y, control goes to line 4.

4   The break command is executed, the loop is exited, and control goes to line 7. The line Here we are is printed. Until the user answers with a Y or y, the program will continue to ask for input. This could go on forever!

5   If the test fails in line 3, the else commands are executed. When the body of the loop ends at the done keyword, control starts again at the top of the while at line 1.

6   This is the end of the loop body.

7   Control starts here after the break command is executed.

The continue Command.   The continue command returns control to the top of the loop if some condition becomes true. All commands below the continue will be ignored. If nested within a number of loops, the continue command returns control to the inner-most loop. If a number is given as its argument, control can then be started at the top of any loop. If you are nested in three loops, the outermost loop is loop number 3, the next nested loop is loop number 2, and the innermost nested loop is loop number 1.[3]

FORMAT

```
continue [n]
```

---

3. If the continue command is given a number higher than the number of loops, the loop exits.

EXAMPLE 8.39

```
(The mailing List)
$ cat mail_list
ernie
john
richard
melanie
greg
robin


(The Script)
    #!/bin/sh
    # Scriptname: mailem
    # Purpose: To send a list
1   for name in `cat  mail_list`
    do
2       if [ "$name" = "richard" ] ; then
3           continue
        else
4           mail $name < memo
        fi
5   done
```

EXPLANATION

1   After command substitution, cat mail_list, the for loop will iterate through the list of names from the file called mail_list (i.e., ernie john richard melanie greg robin).

2   If the name matches richard, the continue command is executed and control goes back to top of the loop where the loop expression is evalutated. Because richard has already been shifted off the list, the next user, melanie, will be assigned to the variable name. The string richard does not need to be quoted here because it is only one word. But, it is good practice to quote the string after the test's = operator because if the string consisted of more than one word, for example, richard jones, the test command would produce an error message:

test: unknown operator richard

3   The continue command returns control to the top of the loop, skipping any commands in the rest of the loop body.

4   All users in the list, except richard, will be mailed a copy of the file memo.

5   This is the end of the loop body.

8.6.6 Nested Loops and Loop Control

When using nested loops, the break and continue commands can be given a numeric, integer argument so that control can go from the inner loop to an outer loop.

EXAMPLE 8.40

```
(The Script)
      #!/bin/sh
      # Scriptname: months
1     for month in Jan Feb Mar Apr May Jun Jul Aug Sep Oct Nov Dec
   ┌─ do
2  │      for week in  1 2 3 4
   │   ┌─ do
   │   │      echo -n "Processing the month of $month. Okay? "
   │   │      read ans
3  │   │      if [ "$ans" = n  -o -z "$ans" ]
   │   │      then
4  │   │          continue 2
   │   │      else
   │   │          echo -n "Process week $week of $month? "
   │   │          read ans
   │   │          if [ "$ans" = n -o -z "$ans" ]
   │   │          then
5  │   │              continue
   │   │          else
   │   │              echo "Now processing week $week of $month."
   │   │              sleep 1
   │   │                  # Commands go here
   │   │              echo "Done processing..."
   │   │          fi
   │   │      fi
6  │   └─ done
7  └─ done
```

```
(The Output)
$ months
Processing the month of Jan. Okay?
Processing the month of Feb. Okay? y
Process week 1 of Feb? y
Now processing week 1 of Feb.
Done processing...
Processing the month of Feb. Okay? y
Process week 2 of Feb? y
Now processing week 2 of Feb.
Done processing...
Processing the month of Feb. Okay? n
Processing the month of Mar. Okay? n
Processing the month of Apr. Okay? n
Processing the month of May. Okay? n
```

EXPLANATION

1   The outer for loop is started. The first time in the loop, Jan is assigned to month.

2   The inner for loop starts. The first time in this loop, 1 is assigned to week. The inner loop iterates completely before going back to the outer loop.

3   If the user enters either an n or presses Enter, line 4 is executed.

4   The continue command with an argument of 2 starts control at the top of the second outermost loop. The continue without an argument returns control to the top of the innermost loop.

5   Control is returned to the innermost for loop.

6   This done terminates the innermost loop.

7   This done terminates the outermost loop.

8.6.7   I/O Redirection and Subshells

Input can be piped or redirected to a loop from a file. Output can also be piped or redirected to a file from a loop. The shell starts a subshell to handle I/O redirection and pipes. Any variables defined within the loop will not be known to the rest of the script when the loop terminates.

Redirecting the Output of a Loop to a File.   See Example 8.41 for a demonstration of how to redirect the output of a loop to a file.

EXAMPLE 8.41

```
(The Command Line)
1   $ cat memo
    abc
    def
    ghi

(The Script)
    #!/bin/sh
    # Program name: numberit
    # Put line numbers on all lines of memo
2   if [ $# -lt 1 ]
    then
3       echo  "Usage: $0 filename " >&2
        exit 1
    fi
4   count=1                     # Initialize count
5   cat $1 | while read line    # Input is coming from file on command line
    do
```

EXAMPLE 8.41 (CONTINUED)

```
6        [ $count -eq 1 ] && echo "Processing file $1..." > /dev/tty
7        echo $count $line
8        count=`expr $count + 1`
9   done > tmp$$                    # Output is going to a temporary file
10  mv tmp$$ $1
```

```
(The Command Line)
11  $ numberit memo
    Processing file memo...

12  $ cat memo
    1 abc
    2 def
    3 ghi
```

EXPLANATION

1   The contents of file memo are displayed.

2   If the user did not provide a command-line argument when running this script, the number of arguments ($#) will be less than 1 and the error message appears.

3   The usage message is sent to stderr (>&2) if the number of arguments is less than 1.

4   The count variable is assigned the value 1.

5   The UNIX cat command displays the contents of the filename stored in $1, and the output is piped to the while loop. The read command is assigned the first line of the file the first time in the loop, the second line of the file the next time through the loop, and so forth. The read command returns a 0 exit status if it is successful in reading input and 1 if it fails.

6   If the value of count is 1, the echo command is executed and its output is sent to /dev/tty, the screen.

7   The echo command prints the value of count, followed by the line in the file.

8   The count is incremented by 1.

9   The output of this entire loop, each line of the file in $1, is redirected to the file tmp$$, with the exception of the first line of the file, which is redirected to the terminal, /dev/tty.[a]

10 The tmp file is renamed to the filename assigned to $1.

11 The program is executed. The file to be processed is called memo.

12 The file memo is displayed after the script has finished, demonstrating that line numbers have been prepended to each line.

---

a. $$ expands to the PID number of the current shell. By appending this number to the filename, the filename is made unique.

EXAMPLE 8.42

```
(The Input File)
$ cat testing
apples
pears
peaches

(The Script)
    #!/bin/sh
    # This program demonstrates the scope of variables when
    # assigned within loops where the looping command uses
    # redirection. A subshell is started when the loop uses
    # redirection, making all variables created within the loop
    # local to the shell where the loop is being executed.
1   while read line
    do
2        echo $line     # This line will be redirected to outfile
3        name=JOE
4   done < testing > outfile   # Redirection of input and output
5   echo Hi there $name

(The Output)
5   Hi there
```

EXPLANATION

1   If the exit status of the read command is successful, the body of the while loop is entered. The read command is getting input from the file testing, named after the done on line 4. Each time through the loop, the read command reads another line from the file testing.

2   The value of line will be redirected to outfile in line 4.

3   The variable name is assigned JOE. Because redirection is utilized in this loop, the variable is local to the loop.

4   The done keyword consists of the redirection of input from the file testing, and the redirection of output to the file outfile. All output from this loop will go to outfile.

5   When out of the loop, name is undefined. It was local to the while loop and known only within the body of that loop. Because the variable name has no value, only the string Hi there is displayed.

Piping the Output of a Loop to a UNIX Command.   Output can be either piped to another command(s) or redirected to a file.

EXAMPLE   8.43

```
(The Script)
    #!/bin/sh
1   for i in 7 9 2 3 4  5
2   do
        echo  $i
3   done | sort -n

(The Output)
2
3
4
5
7
9
```

EXPLANATION

1   The for loop iterates through a list of unsorted numbers.

2   In the body of the loop, the numbers are printed. This output will be piped into the UNIX sort command, a numerical sort.

3   The pipe is created after the done keyword. The loop is run in a subshell.

8.6.8   Running Loops in the Background

Loops can be executed to run in the background. The program can continue without waiting for the loop to finish processing.

EXAMPLE   8.44

```
(The Script)
    #!/bin/sh
1   for person in bob jim joe sam
    do
2       mail $person < memo
3   done &
```

EXPLANATION

1   The for loop shifts through each of the names in the wordlist: bob, jim, joe, and sam. Each of the names is assigned to the variable person, in turn.

2   In the body of the loop, each person is sent the contents of the memo file.

3   The ampersand at the end of the done keyword causes the loop to be executed in the background. The program will continue to run while the loop is executing.

8.6.9 The exec Command and Loops

The exec command can be used to open or close standard input or output without creating a subshell. Therefore, when starting a loop, any variables created within the body of the loop will remain when the loop completes. When using redirection in loops, any variables created within the loop are lost.

The exec command is often used to open files for reading and writing, either by name or by file descriptor number. Recall that file descriptors 0, 1, and 2 are reserved for standard input, output, and error. If a file is opened, it will receive the next available file descriptor. For example, if file descriptor 3 is the next free descriptor, the new file will be assigned file descriptor 3.

EXAMPLE 8.45

```
(The File)
1    $ cat tmp
     apples
     pears
     bananas
     pleaches
     plums

(The Script)
     #!/bin/sh
     # Scriptname: speller
     # Purpose: Check and fix spelling errors in a file
2    exec < tmp                    # Opens the tmp file
3    while read line               # Read from the tmp file
     do
4        echo $line
5        echo -n "Is this word correct? [Y/N] "
6        read answer < /dev/tty   # Read from the terminal
7        case "$answer" in
8        [Yy]*)
9            continue;;
         *)
             echo "What is the correct spelling? "
10           read word < /dev/tty
11           sed "s/$line/$word/g" tmp > error
12           mv error tmp
13           echo $line has been changed to $word.
         esac
14   done
```

EXPLANATION

1.   The contents of the tmp file are displayed.
2.   The exec command changes standard input (file descriptor 0) so that instead of input coming from the keyboard, it is coming from the tmp file.
3.   The while loop starts. The read command gets a line of input from the tmp file.
4.   The value stored in the line variable is printed.
5.   The user is asked if the word is correct.
6.   The read gets the user's response from the terminal, /dev/tty. If the input is not redirected directly from the terminal, it will continue to be read from the file tmp, still opened for reading.
7.   The case command evalutates the user's answer.
8.   If the variable answer evaluates to a string starting with a Y or y, the continue statement on the next line will be executed.
9.   The continue statement causes the program to go to the beginning of the while loop on line 3.
10.   The user is again asked for input (the correct spelling of the word). The input is redirected from the terminal, /dev/tty.
11.   The sed command will replace the value of line with the value of word wherever it occurs in the tmp file, and send the output to the error file.
12.   The error file will be renamed tmp, thus overwriting the old contents of tmp with the contents of the error file.
13.   This line is displayed to indicate that the change has been made.
14.   The done keyword marks the end of the loop body.

8.6.10   IFS and Loops

The shell's internal field separator (IFS) evaluates to spaces, tabs, and the newline character. It is used as a word (token) separator for commands that parse lists of words, such as read, set, and for. It can be reset by the user if a different separator will be used in a list. Before changing its value, it is a good idea to save the original value of the IFS in another variable. Then it is easy to return to its default value, if needed.

EXAMPLE   8.46

```
(The Script )
    #/bin/sh
    # Scriptname: runit
    # IFS is the internal field separator and defaults to
    # spaces, tabs, and newlines.
    # In this script it is changed to a colon.
```

EXAMPLE 8.46 (CONTINUED)

```
1    names=Tom:Dick:Harry:John
2    OLDIFS="$IFS"        # Save the original value of IFS
3    IFS=":"
4    for persons in $names
     do
5          echo  Hi $persons
     done
6    IFS="$OLDIFS"                # Reset the IFS to old value
7    set Jill Jane Jolene        # Set positional parameters
8    for girl in $*
     do
9          echo Howdy $girl
     done


(The Output)
5    Hi Tom
     Hi Dick
     Hi Harry
     Hi John
9    Howdy Jill
     Howdy Jane
     Howdy Jolene
```

EXPLANATION

1   The names variable is assigned the string Tom:Dick:Harry:John. Each of the words is separated by a colon.

2   The value of IFS, whitespace, is assigned to another variable, OLDIFS. Because the value of the IFS is whitespace, it must be quoted to preserve it.

3   The IFS is assigned a colon. Now the colon is used to separate words.

4   After variable substitution, the for loop will iterate through each of the names, using the colon as the internal field separator between the words.

5   Each of the names in the wordlist are displayed.

6   The IFS is reassigned its original value stored in OLDIFS.

7   The positional parameters are set. $1 is assigned Jill, $2 is assigned Jane, and $3 is assigned Jolene.

8    $* evaluates to all the positional parameters, Jill, Jane, and Jolene. The for loop assigns each of the names to the girl variable, in turn, through each iteration of the loop.

9   Each of the names in the parameter list is displayed.

8.7 Functions

Functions were introduced to the Bourne shell in AT&T's UNIX System VR2. A function is a name for a command or group of commands. Functions are used to modularize your program and make it more efficient. You may even store functions in another file and load them into your script when you are ready to use them.

Here is a review of some of the important rules about using functions.

1. The Bourne shell determines whether you are using a built-in command, a function, or an executable program found on the disk. It looks for built-in commands first, then functions, and last, executables.
2. A function must be defined before it is used.
3. The function runs in the current environment; it shares variables with the script that invoked it, and lets you pass arguments by assigning them as positional parameters. If you use the exit command in a function, you exit the entire script. If, however, either the input or output of the function is redirected or the function is enclosed within backquotes (command substitution), a subshell is created and the function and its variables and present working directory are known only within the subshell. When the function exits, any variables set there will be lost, and if you have changed directories, you will revert to the directory you were in before invoking the function. If you exit the function, you return to where the script left off when the function was invoked.
4. The return statement returns the exit status of the last command executed within the function or the value of the argument given, and cannot exceed a value of 255.
5. Functions exist only in the shell where they are defined; they cannot be exported to subshells. The dot command can be used to execute functions stored in files.
6. To list functions and definitions, use the set command.
7. Traps, like variables, are global within functions. They are shared by both the script and the functions invoked in the script. If a trap is defined in a function, it is also shared by the script. This could have unwanted side effects.
8. If functions are stored in another file, they can be loaded into the current script with the dot command.

FORMAT

```
function_name () { commands ; commands; }
```

EXAMPLE 8.47

```
dir () { echo "Directories: " ; ls -l | nawk '/^d/ {print $NF}' ; }
```

The name of the function is dir. The empty parentheses are necessary syntax for naming the function but have no other purpose. The commands within the curly braces will be executed when dir is typed. The purpose of the function is to list only the subdirectories below the present working directory. *The spaces surrounding the curly braces are required.*

8.7.1 Unsetting Functions

To remove a function from memory, the unset command is used.

```
unset function_name
```

8.7.2 Function Arguments and the Return Value

Because the function is executed within the current shell, the variables will be known to both the function and the shell. Any changes made to your environment in the function will also be made to the shell. Arguments can be passed to functions by using positional parameters. The positional parameters are private to the function; that is, arguments to the function will not affect any positional parameters used outside the function.

The return command can be used to exit the function and return control to the program at the place where the function was invoked. (Remember, if you use exit anywhere in your script, including within a function, the script terminates.) The return value of a function is really just the value of the exit status of the last command in the script, unless you give a specific argument to the return command. If a value is assigned to the return command, that value is stored in the ? variable and can hold an integer value between 0 and 255. Because the return command is limited to returning only an integer between 0 and 255, you can use command substitution to capture the output of a function. Place the entire function in backquotes and assign the output to a variable just as you would if getting the output of a UNIX command.

```
(Using the return command)
(The Script)
    #!/bin/sh
    # Scriptname: do_increment
1   increment () {
2       sum=`expr $1 + 1`
3       return $sum      # Return the value of sum to the script.
    }
```

EXAMPLE   8.48 (CONTINUED)

```
4    echo  -n "The sum is "
5    increment 5     # Call function increment; pass 5 as a parameter.
                     # 5 becomes $1 for the increment function.
6    echo $?         # The return value is stored in $?
7    echo  $sum      # The variable "sum" is known to the function,
                     # and is also known to the main script.


(The Output)
4,6    The sum is 6
7      6
```

EXPLANATION

1   The function called increment is defined.

2   When the function is called, the value of the first argument, $1, will be incremented by 1 and the result assigned to sum.

3   The built-in return command, when given an argument, returns to the main script after the line where the function was invoked. It stores its argument in the ? variable.

4   The string is echoed to the screen.

5   The increment function is called with an argument of 5.

6   When the function returns, its exit status is stored in the ? variable. The exit status is the exit value of the last command executed in the function unless an explicit argument is used in the return statement. The argument for return must be an integer between 0 and 255.

7   Although sum was defined in the function increment, it is global in scope, and therefore also known within the script that invoked the function. Its value is printed.

EXAMPLE   8.49

```
(Using command substitution)
(The Script)
     #!/bin/sh
     # Scriptname: do_square
1    function square {
         sq=`expr $1 \* $1`
         echo  "Number to be squared is $1."
2        echo  "The result is $sq "
     }
3    echo "Give me a number to square. "
     read number
```

EXAMPLE 8.49 (CONTINUED)

```
4   value_returned=`square $number`     # Command substitution
5   echo    $value_returned
```

(The Output)
```
3   Give me a number to square.
    10
5   Number to be squared is 10. The result is 100
```

EXPLANATION

1 The function called square is defined. Its function, when called, is to multiply its argument, $1, by itself.

2 The result of squaring the number is printed.

3 The user is asked for input. This is the line where the program starts executing.

4 The function square is called with a number (input from the user) as its argument. Command substitution is performed because the function is enclosed in back-quotes. The output of the function, both of its echo statements, is assigned to the variable value_returned.

5 The command substitution removes the newline between the strings Number to be squared is 10. and The result is 100.

8.7.3 Functions and the dot Command

Storing Functions.   Functions are often defined in the .profile file, so that when you log in, they will be defined. Functions cannot be exported, but they can be stored in a file. Then, when you need the function, the dot command is used with the name of the file to activate the definitions of the functions within it.

EXAMPLE 8.50

```
1   $ cat myfunctions
2   go() {   # This file contains two functions
        cd $HOME/bin/prog
        PS1='`pwd` > '
          ls
    }
3   greetings() { echo "Hi $1! Welcome to my world." ; }

4   $ . myfunctions
5   $ greetings george
    Hi george! Welcome to my world.
```

EXPLANATION

1   The file myfunctions is displayed. It contains two function definitions.

2   The first function defined is called go. It sets the primary prompt to the present working directory.

3   The second function defined is called greetings. It will greet the name of the user passed in as an argument.

4   The dot command loads the contents of the file myfunctions into the shell's memory. Now both functions are defined for this shell.

5   The greetings function is invoked and executed.

EXAMPLE 8.51

(The .dbfunctions file shown below contains functions to be used by the main program.)

```
1   $ cat .dbfunctions
2   addon () {    # Function is named and defined in file .dbfunctions
3       while true
        do
            echo "Adding information "
            echo "Type the full name of employee "
            read name
            echo "Type address for employee "
            read address
            echo "Type start date for employee (4/10/88 ) :"
            read startdate
            echo $name:$address:$startdate
            echo -n "Is this correct? "
            read ans
            case "$ans"  in
            [Yy]*)
                    echo "Adding info..."
                    echo $name:$address:$startdate>>datafile
                sort -u datafile -o datafile
                echo -n "Do you want to go back to the main menu? "
                read ans
                if [ $ans = Y -o $ans = y ]
                then
4                   return        # Return to calling program
                else
5                   continue      # Go to the top of the loop
                fi
                ;;
            *)
                echo "Do you want to try again? "
                read answer
```

EXAMPLE 8.51 (CONTINUED)

```
                case "$answer" in
                [Yy]*) continue;;
                *) exit;;
                esac
                     ;;
            esac
        done
6   }   # End of function definition
    -----------------------------------------------------------------
(The Script)
7   #!/bin/sh
    # Scriptname: mainprog
    # This is the main script that will call the function, addon

    datafile=$HOME/bourne/datafile
8   . .dbfunctions      # The dot command reads the dbfunctions file into memory
    if [ ! -f $datafile ]
    then
        echo "`basename $datafile` does not exist" 1>&2
        exit 1
    fi
9   echo "Select one: "
    cat <<EOF
        [1] Add info
        [2] Delete info
        [3] Exit
    EOF
    read choice
    case "$choice" in
10      1)   addon           # Calling the addon function
              ;;
        2)   delete          # Calling the delete function
              ;;
        3)   update
              ;;
        4)
             echo Bye
             exit 0
              ;;
        *)   echo Bad choice
             exit 2
              ;;
    esac
    echo Returned from function call
    echo The name is $name
    # Variables set in the function are known in this shell.
```

EXPLANATION

1   The .dbfunctions file is displayed. It is not a script. It contains only functions.

2   The addon function is defined. Its function is to add new information to the file datafile.

3   A while loop is entered. It will loop forever unless a loop control statement such as break or continue is included in the body of the loop.

4   The return command sends control back to the calling program where the function was called.

5   Control is returned to the top of the while loop.

6   The closing curly brace ends the function definition.

7   This is the main script. The function addon will be used in this script.

8   The dot command loads the file .dbfunctions into the program's memory. Now the function addon is defined for this script and available for use. It is as though you had just defined the function right here in the script.

9   A menu is displayed with the here document. The user is asked to select a menu item.

10   The addon function is invoked.

8.8   Trapping Signals

While your program is running, if you press Ctrl-C or Ctrl-\, your program terminates as soon as the signal arrives. There are times when you would rather not have the program terminate immediately after the signal arrives. You could arrange to ignore the signal and keep running or perform some sort of cleanup operation before actually exiting the script. The trap command allows you to control the way a program behaves when it receives a signal.

A signal is defined as an asynchronous message that consists of a number that can be sent from one process to another, or by the operating system to a process if certain keys are pressed or if something exceptional happens.[4] The trap command tells the shell to terminate the command currently in execution upon the receipt of a signal. If the trap command is followed by commands within quotes, the command string will be executed upon receipt of a specified signal. The shell reads the command string twice, once when the trap is set, and again when the signal arrives. If the command string is surrounded by double quotes, all variable and command substitution will be performed when the trap is set the first time. If single quotes enclose the command string, variable and command substitution do not take place until the signal is detected and the trap is executed.

Use the command kill -l to get a list of all signals. Table 8.5 provides a list of signal numbers and their corresponding names.

---

4. Morris I. Bolsky and David G. Korn, *The New KornShell Command and Programming Language* (Englewood Cliffs, NJ: Prentice Hall PTR, 1995), p. 327.

Table 8.5   Signal Numbers and Signals[a, b]

1) HUP	12) SYS	23) POLL
2) INT	13) PIPE	24) XCPU
3) QUIT	14) ALRM	25) XFSZ
4) ILL	15) TERM	26) VTALRM
5) TRAP	16) URG	27) PROF
6) IOT	17) STOP	28) WINCH
7) EMT	18) TSTP	29) LOST
8) FPE	19) CONT	30) USR1
9) KILL	20) CHLD	31) USR2
10) BUS	21) TTIN	
11) SEGV	22) TTOU	

a.   The output of the kill command may differ depending on the OS and/or the shell.
b.   For a complete list of UNIX signals and their meanings, go to www.cybermagician.co.uk/technet/unixsignals.htm. For Linux signals, go to www.comptechdoc.org/os/linux/programming/linux_pgsignals.html.

FORMAT

```
trap 'command; command' signal-number
```

EXAMPLE 8.52

```
trap 'rm tmp*; exit 1' 1 2 15
```

EXPLANATION

When any of the signals 1 (hangup), 2 (interrupt), or 15 (software termination) arrive, remove all the tmp files and exit.

If an interrupt signal comes in while the script is running, the trap command lets you handle the signal in several ways. You can let the signal behave normally (default), ignore the signal, or create a handler function to be called when the signal arrives.

8.8.1   Resetting Signals

To reset a signal to its default behavior, the trap command is followed by the signal name or number.

EXAMPLE 8.53

```
trap 2
```

EXPLANATION

Resets the default action for signal 2, SIGINT, which is used to kill a process (i.e., Ctrl-C).

EXAMPLE 8.54

```
trap 'trap 2' 2
```

EXPLANATION

Sets the default action for signal 2 (SIGINT) to execute the command string within quotes when the signal arrives. The user must press Ctrl-C twice to terminate the program. The first trap catches the signal, the second trap resets the trap back to its default action, which is to kill the process.

8.8.2 Ignoring Signals

If the trap command is followed by a pair of empty quotes, the signals listed will be ignored by the process.

EXAMPLE 8.55

```
trap " "  1  2
```

EXPLANATION

Signals 1 and 2 will be ignored by the shell.

8.8.3 Listing Traps

To list all traps and the commands assigned to them, type trap.

EXAMPLE 8.56

```
(The Script)
    #/bin/sh
    # Scriptname: trapping
    # Script to illustrate the trap command and signals
1   trap 'echo "Ctrl-C will not terminate $0."' 2
2   trap 'echo "Ctrl-\ will not terminate $0."' 3
```

EXAMPLE 8.56 (CONTINUED)

```
3    echo "Enter any string after the prompt."
     echo "When you are ready to exit, type \"stop\"."
4    while true
     do
         echo  -n "Go ahead...> "
         read reply
5        if [ "$reply" = stop ]
         then
6            break
         fi
7    done
```

```
(The Output)
Enter any string after the prompt.
When you are ready to exit, type "stop".
Go ahead...> this is it^C
Ctrl-C will not terminate trapping.
Go ahead...> this is never it ^\
Ctrl-\ will not terminate trapping.
Go ahead...> stop
$
```

EXPLANATION

1   The first trap catches the INT signal, Ctrl-C. If Ctrl-C is pressed while the program is running, the command enclosed in quotes will be executed. Instead of aborting, the program will print Ctrl-C will not terminate trapping., and continue to prompt the user for input.

2   The second trap command will be executed when the user presses Ctrl-\, the QUIT signal. The string Ctrl-\ will not terminate trapping. will be displayed, and the program will continue to run. This signal, by default, kills the process and produces a core file.

3   The user is prompted for input.

4   The while loop is entered and a prompt, Go ahead...>, is displayed.

5   The user input is assigned to the reply variable and, if its value matches stop, the loop exits and the program terminates. This is the way we will get out of this program unless it is killed with the kill command.

6   The break command causes the body of the loop to be exited with control starting after line 7. In this case, the program is at its end.

7   This is the end of the while loop.

8.8.4 Traps in Functions

If you use a trap to handle a signal in a function, it will affect the entire script, once the function is called. The trap is global to the script. In the following example, the trap is set to ignore the interrupt key, Ctrl-C. This script had to be killed with the kill command to stop the looping. It demonstrates potential undesirable side effects when using traps in functions.

EXAMPLE 8.57

```
(The Script)
    #!/bin/sh
1   trapper () {
        echo "In trapper"
2       trap 'echo "Caught in a trap!"' 2
        # Once set, this trap affects the entire script. Anytime
        # ^C is entered, the script will ignore it.
    }
3   while :
    do
        echo "In the main script"
4       trapper
5       echo "Still in main"
        sleep 5
    done

(The Output)
In the main script
In trapper
Still in main
^CCaught in a trap!
In the main script
In trapper
Still in main
^CCaught in a trap!
In the main script
```

EXPLANATION

1   The trapper function is defined. All variables and traps set in the function are global to the script.

2   The trap command will ignore signal 2, the interrupt key (^C). If ^C is pressed, the message Caught in a trap! is printed, and the script continues forever.

3   The main script starts a forever loop.

4   The function trapper is called.

5   When the function returns, execution starts here.

8.8.5 Debugging

By using the -n option to the sh command, you can check the sytnax of your scripts without really executing any of the commands. If there is a syntax error in the script, the shell will report the error. If there are no errors, nothing is displayed.

The most commonly used method for debugging scripts is to use the set command with the -x option, or to use the -x option as an argument to the sh command, followed by the script name. See Table 8.6 for a list of debugging options. These options allow an execution trace of your script. Each command from your script is displayed after substitution has been performed, and then the command is executed. When a line from your script is displayed, it is preceded with a plus (+) sign.

With the verbose option turned on, or by invoking the Bourne shell with the -v option (sh -v scriptname), each line of the script will be displayed just as it was typed in the script, and then executed.

Table 8.6 Debugging Options

Command	*Option*	*What It Does*
sh -x scriptname	Echo option	Displays each line of script after variable substitutions and before execution
sh -v scriptname	Verbose option	Displays each line of script before execution, just as you typed it
sh -n scriptname	Noexec option	Interprets but does not execute commands
set -x	Turns on echo	Traces execution in a script
set +x	Turns off echo	Turns off tracing

EXAMPLE 8.58

```
(The Script)
    #!/bin/sh
1   # Scriptname: todebug
    name="Joe Blow"
    if [ "$name" = "Joe Blow" ]
    then
        echo "Hi $name"
    fi
    num=1
    while [ $num -lt 5 ]
    do
        num=`expr $num + 1`
    done
    echo The grand total is $num
```

EXAMPLE 8.58 (CONTINUED)

```
   (The Command Line and Output)
2  $ sh -x todebug
   + name=Joe Blow
   + [ Joe Blow = Joe Blow ]
   + echo Hi Joe Blow

   Hi Joe Blow
   num=1
   + [ 1 -lt 5 ]
   + expr 1 + 1
   num=2
   + [ 2 -lt 5 ]
   + expr 2 + 1
   num=3
   + [ 3 -lt 5 ]
   + expr 3 + 1
    num=4
   + [ 4 -lt 5 ]
   + expr 4 + 1
    num=5
   + [ 5 -lt 5 ]
   + echo The grand total is 5
   The grand total is 5
```

EXPLANATION

1 The script is called todebug. You can watch the script run with the -x switch turned on. Each iteration of the loop is displayed and the values of variables are printed as they are set and when they change.

2 The sh command starts the Bourne shell with the -x option. Echoing is turned on. Each line of the script will be displayed to the screen prepended with a plus sign (+). Variable substitution is performed before the line is displayed. The result of the execution of the command appears after the line has been displayed.

8.9 The Command Line

8.9.1 Processing Command-Line Options with getopts

If you are writing scripts that require a number of command-line options, positional parameters are not always the most efficient. For example, the UNIX ls command takes a number of command-line options and arguments. (An option requires a leading dash; an argument does not.) Options can be passed to the program in several ways: ls -laFi, ls -i -a -l -F, ls -ia -F, and so forth. If you have a script that requires arguments, positional parameters might be used to process the arguments individually, such as ls -l -i -F. Each dash option would be stored in $1, $2, and $3, respectively. But what if the user listed all of the options as one dash option, as in `ls -liF`? Now the `-liF` would all be assigned to $1 in the script. The getopts function makes it possible to process command-line options and arguments in the same way they are processed by the `ls` program.[5] The getopts function will allow the runit program to process its arguments using any variety of combinations.

EXAMPLE 8.59

```
(The Command Line )
1   $ runit -x -n  200 filex

2   $ runit -xn200 filex

3   $ runit -xy

4   $ runit -yx -n 30

5   $ runit -n250 -xy filey

( any other combination of these arguments )
```

EXPLANATION

1   The program runit takes four arguments: x is an option, n is an option requiring a number argument after it, and filex is an argument that stands alone.
2   The program runit combines the options x and n and the number argument 200; filex is also an argument.
3   The program runit is invoked with the x and y options combined.
4   The program runit is invoked with the y and x options combined; the n option is passed separately, as is the number argument, 30.
5   The program runit is invoked with the n option combined with the number argument, the x and y options are combined, and the filey is separate.

Before getting into all the details of the runit program, we examine the line from the program where getopts is used to see how it processes the arguments.

EXAMPLE 8.60

```
(A line from the script called "runit")
while getopts :xyn: name
```

---

5.   See the UNIX manual pages (Section 3) for the C library function getopt.

EXPLANATION

- x, y, and n are the options. Options are the allowable arguments that can be passed to this script from the command line; for example, runit -x -y -n.

- Options typed at the command line begin with a leading dash: -x -y -z, -xyz, -x -yz, and so forth. If there is a colon after option, it means that the option requires a named argument, such as -x filename, where -x is the option and filename is the named argument.

- Any options that do not contain a dash tell getopts that the option list is at an end.

- Each time getopts is called, it places the next option it finds in the variable name. (You can use any variable name here.) If an illegal argument is given, name is assigned a question mark.

- OPTIND is a special variable that is initialized to 1, and is incremented each time getopts completes processing a command-line argument to the number of the *next* argument getopts will process.

- If an option requires an argument, getopts puts it in the OPTARG variable. If the first character in the option list is a colon, the shell variable, name, will be set to the colon character, and the OPTARG variable will be set to the to the value of the illegal option.

getopts Scripts.   The following examples illustrate how getopts processes arguments.

EXAMPLE 8.61

```
(The Script)
    #!/bin/sh
    # Program opts1
    # Using getopts -- First try --
1   while getopts xy options
    do
2       case $options in
3       x) echo "you entered -x as an option";;
        y) echo "you entered -y as an option";;
        esac
    done

(The Command Line)
4   $ opts1 -x
    you entered -x as an option
5   $ opts1 -xy
    you entered -x as an option
    you entered -y as an option
6   $ opts1 -y
    you entered -y as an option
7   $ opts1 -b
    opts1:  illegal option -- b
8   $ opts1 b
```

EXPLANATION

1 The getopts command is used as a condition for the while command. The valid options for this program are listed after the getopts command; they are x and y. Each option is tested in the body of the loop, one after the other. Each option will be assigned to the variable options, without the leading dash. When there are no longer any arguments to process, getopts will exit with a nonzero status, causing the while loop to terminate.

2 The case command is used to test each of the possible options found in the options variable, either x or y.

3 If x was an option, the string You entered -x as an option is displayed.

4 At the command line, the opts1 script is given an x option, a legal option to be processed by getopts.

5 At the command line, the opts1 script is given an xy option; x and y are legal options to be processed by getopts.

6 At the command line, the opts1 script is given a y option, a legal option to be processed by getopts.

7 The opts1 script is given a b option, an illegal option. Getopts sends an error message to stderr.

8 An option without a dash prepended to it is not an option and causes getopts to stop processing arguments.

EXAMPLE 8.62

```
(The Script)
    #!/bin/sh
    # Program opts2
    # Using getopts -- Second try --
1   while getopts xy options 2> /dev/null
    do
2       case $options in
        x) echo "you entered -x as an option";;
        y) echo "you entered -y as an option";;
3       \?) echo "Only -x and -y are valid options"  1>&2;;
        esac
    done

(The Command Line)
    $ opts2 -x
    you entered -x as an option

    $ opts2 -y
    you entered -y as an option
```

EXAMPLE 8.62 (CONTINUED)

```
        $ opts2 xy

        $ opts2 -xy
        you entered -x as an option
        you entered -y as an option
```

4
```
        $ opts2 -g
        Only -x and -y are valid options
```

5
```
        $ opts2 -c
        Only -x and -y are valid options
```

EXPLANATION

1   If there is an error message from getopts, it is redirected to /dev/null.

2   If the option is a bad option, a question mark will be assigned to the options variable. The case command can be used to test for the question mark, allowing you to print your own error message to standard error.

3   If the options variable is assigned the question mark, the case statement is executed. The question mark is protected with the backslash so that the shell does not see it as a wildcard and try to perform filename substitution.

4   g is not a legal option. A question mark is assigned to the variable options, and the error message is displayed.

5   c is not a legal option. A question mark is assigned to the variable options, and the error message is displayed.

EXAMPLE 8.63

```
(The Script)
    #!/bin/sh
    # Program opts3
    # Using getopts -- Third try --
1   while getopts dq: options
    do
        case $options in
2           d) echo "-d is a valid switch ";;
3           q) echo "The argument for -q is $OPTARG";;
            \?) echo "Usage:opts3 -dq filename ... " 1>&2;;
        esac
    done
```

EXAMPLE 8.63 (CONTINUED)

(The Command Line)
```
4   $ opts3 -d
    -d is a valid switch

5   $ opts3 -q  foo
    The argument for -q is foo

6   $ opts3 -q
    Usage:opts3 -dq filename ...

7   $ opts3 -e
    Usage:opts3 -dq filename ...

8   $ opts3 e
```

EXPLANATION

1   The while command tests the exit status of getopts. If getopts can successfully process an argument, it returns 0 exit status, and the body of the while loop is entered. The colon appended to the argument list means that the q option requires an argument. The argument will be stored in the special variable, OPTARG.

2   One of the legal options is d. If d is entered as an option, the d (without the dash) is stored in the options variable.

3   One of the legal options is q. The q option requires an argument. There must be a space between the q option and its argument. If q is entered as an option followed by an argument, the q, without the dash, is stored in the options variable and the argument is stored in the OPTARG variable. If an argument does not follow the q option, the question mark is stored in the variable options.

4   The d option is a legal option to opts3.

5   The q option with an argument is also a legal option to opts3.

6   The q option without an argument is an error.

7   The e option is invalid. A question mark is stored in the options variable if the option is illegal.

8   The option is prepended with neither a dash nor a plus sign. The getopts command will not process it as an option and returns a nonzero exit status. The while loop is terminated.

EXAMPLE 8.64

```
(The Script)
    #!/bin/sh
    # Program opts4
    # Using getopts -- Fourth try --
1   while getopts xyz: arguments 2>/dev/null
    do
          case $arguments  in
2         x) echo "you entered -x as an option.";;
          y) echo "you entered -y as an option.";;
3         z) echo "you entered -z as an option."
                echo "\$OPTARG is $OPTARG.";;
4         \?) echo "Usage opts4 [-xy] [-z  argument]"
                exit 1;;
          esac
    done
5   echo "The initial value of \$OPTIND is 1.
          The final value of \$OPTIND is $OPTIND.
          Since this reflects the number of the next command-line argument,
          the number of arguments passed was `expr $OPTIND - 1`. "
```

```
(The Command Line)
$ opts4 -xyz foo
you entered -x as an option.
you entered -y as an option.
you entered -z as an option.
$OPTARG is foo.
The initial value of $OPTIND is 1.
The final value of $OPTIND is 3.
Since this reflects the number of the next command-line argument, the number of
arguments passed was 2.

$ opts4 -x -y -z  boo
you entered -x as an option.
you entered -y as an option.
you entered -z as an option.
$OPTARG is boo.
The initial value of $OPTIND is 1.
The final value of $OPTIND is 5.
Since this reflects the number of the next command-line argument, the number of
arguments passed was 4.

$ opts4 -d
Usage: opts4  [-xy] [-z argument]
```

1. The while command tests the exit status of getopts. If getopts can successfully process an argument, it returns 0 exit status, and the body of the while loop is entered. The colon appended to the z option tells getopts that an argument must follow the -z option. If the option takes an argument, the argument is stored in the getopts built-in variable OPTARG.

2. If x is given as an option, it is stored in the variable arguments.

3. If z is given as an option with an argument, the argument is stored in the built-in variable OPTARG.

4. If an invalid option is entered, the question mark is stored in the variable arguments, and an error message is displayed.

5. The special getopts variable, OPTIND, holds the number of the next option to be processed. Its value is always one more than the actual number of command-line arguments.

8.9.2 The eval Command and Parsing the Command Line

The eval command evaluates a command line, performs all shell substitutions, and then executes the command line. Essentially, it parses the command line twice. It is used when normal parsing of the command line is not enough.

EXAMPLE 8.65

```
1   $ set a b c d
2   $ echo The last argument is \$$#
3   The last argument is $4
4   $ eval echo The last argument is \$$#
    The last argument is d
5   $ set -x
    $ eval echo The last argument is \$$#
    + eval echo the last argument is $4
    + echo the last argument is d
    The last argument is d
```

1. Four positional parameters are set.

2. The desired result is to print the value of the last positional parameter. The \$ will print a literal dollar sign. The $# evaluates to 4, the number of positional parameters. After the shell evaluates the $#, it does not parse the line again to get the value of $4.

3. $4 is printed instead of the last argument.

4. After the shell performs variable substitution, the eval command performs the variable substitution and then executes the echo command.

5. Turn on the echoing to watch the order of parsing.

EXAMPLE 8.66

```
(From SVR4 Shutdown Program)
1   eval `/usr/bin/id | /usr/bin/sed 's/[^a-z0-9=].*//'`
2   if [ "${uid:=0}" -ne 0 ]
    then
3       echo $0: Only root can run $0
        exit 2
    fi
```

EXPLANATION

1   This is a tricky one. The id program's output is sent to sed to extract the uid part of the string. The output for id is

    ```
    uid=9496(ellie) gid=40 groups=40
    uid=0(root) gid=1(daemon) groups=1(daemon)
    ```

    The sed regular expression reads: Find any character that is not a letter, number, or an equal sign and remove that character and all characters following it. The result is to substitute everything from the first opening parenthesis to the end of the line with nothing. What is left is either uid=9496 or uid=0.

    After eval evaluates the command line, it then executes the resulting command:

    ```
    uid=9496
    or
    uid=0
    ```

    For example, if the user's ID is root, the command executed would be uid=0. This creates a local variable in the shell called uid and assigns 0 to it.

2   The value of the uid variable is tested for 0, using command modifiers.

3   If the uid is not 0, the echo command displays the script name ($0) and the message.

8.10 Shell Invocation Options

When the shell is started using the sh command, it can take options to modify its behavior. See Table 8.7.

Table 8.7   Shell Invocation Options

Option	Meaning
-i	Shell is in the interactive mode. QUIT and INTERRUPT are ignored.
-s	Commands are read from standard input and output is sent to standard error.
-c string	Commands are read from string.

8.10.1 The set Command and Options

The set command can be used to turn shell options on and off, as well as for handling command-line arguments. To turn an option on, the dash (-) is prepended to the option; to turn an option off, the plus sign (+) is prepended to the option. See Table 8.8 for a list of set options.

EXAMPLE 8.67

```
1   $ set -f
2   $ echo *
    *
3   $ echo ??
    ??
4   $ set +f
```

EXPLANATION

1   The f option is turned on; filename expansion is disabled.
2   The asterisk is not expanded.
3   The question marks are not expanded.
4   The f is turned off; filename expansion is enabled.

Table 8.8 The set Command Options

Option	Meaning
-a	Marks variables that have been modified or exported
-e	Exits the program if a command returns a nonzero status
-f	Disables globbing (filename expansion)
-h	Locates and remembers function commands as functions when they are defined, not just when they are executed
-k	Places all keyword arguments in the environment for a command, not just those that precede the command name
-n	Reads commands but does not execute them; used for debugging
-t	Exits after reading and executing one command
-u	Treats unset variables as an error when performing substitution
-v	Prints shell input lines as they are read; used for debugging
-x	Prints commands and their arguments as they are being executed; used for debugging
--	Does not change any of the flags

8.10.2 Shell Built-In Commands

The shell has a number of commands that are built into its source code. Because the commands are built-in, the shell doesn't have to locate them on disk, making execution much faster. The built-in commands are listed in Table 8.9.

Table 8.9   Built-In Commands

Command	What It Does
:	Do-nothing command; returns exit status 0
. file	The dot command reads and executes command from file
break [n]	See "The break Command" on page 361
cd	Change directory
continue [n]	See "The continue Command" on page 362
echo [args]	Echo arguments
eval command	Shell scans the command line twice before execution
exec command	Runs command in place of this shell
exit [n]	Exit the shell with status n
export [var]	Make var known to subshells
hash	Controls the internal hash table for quicker searches for commands
kill [-signal process]	Sends the signal to the PID number or job number of the process; see /usr/include/sys/signal.h for a list of signals
getopts	Used in shell scripts to parse command line and check for legal options
login [username]	Sign onto the system
newgrp [arg]	Logs a user into a new group by changing the real group and effective group ID
pwd	Print present working directory
read [var]	Read line from standard input into variable var
readonly [var]	Make variable var read-only; cannot be reset
return [n]	Return from a function where n is the exit value given to the return
set	See Table 8.8
shift [n]	Shift positional parameters to the left n times

Table 8.9   Built-In Commands (continued)

Command	What It Does
stop pid	Halt execution of the process number PID
suspend	Stops execution of the current shell (but not if a login shell)
times	Print accumulated user and system times for processes run from this shell
trap [arg] [n]	When shell receives signal n (0, 1, 2, or 15), execute arg
type [command]	Prints the type of command; for example, pwd has a built-in shell, in ksh, an alias for the command whence -v
umask [octal digits]	User file creation mode mask for owner, group, and others
unset [name]	Unset value of variable or function
wait [pid#n]	Wait for background process with PID number n and report termination status
ulimit [options size]	Set maximum limits on processes
umask [mask]	Without argument, print out file creation mask for permissions
wait [pid#n]	Wait for background process with PID number n and report termination status

LAB 8: BOURNE SHELL—GETTING STARTED

1. What process puts the login prompt on your screen?

2. What process assigns values to HOME, LOGNAME, and PATH?

3. How do you know what shell you are using?

4. Where is your login shell assigned? (What file?)

5. Explain the difference between the /etc/profile and .profile file. Which one is executed first?

6. Edit your .profile file as follows:

   a. Welcome the user.

   b. Add your home directory to the path if it is not there.

   c. Set the erase function to the Backspace key using stty.

   d. Type: . .profile
      What is the function of the dot command?

LAB 9: METACHARACTERS

1. Make a directory called `wildcards`. `cd` to that directory and type at the prompt:

   `touch ab abc a1 a2 a3 a11 a12 ba ba.1 ba.2 filex filey AbC ABC ABc2 abc`

2. Write and test the command that will do the following:

   a. List all files starting with a.

   b. List all files ending in at least one digit.

   c. List all files starting with an a or A.

   d. List all files ending in a period, followed by a digit.

   e. List all files containing the letter a anywhere in the filename.

   f. List three-character files where all letters are uppercase.

   g. List files ending in 10, 11, or 12.

   h. List files ending in x or y.

   i. List all files ending in a digit, an uppercase letter, or a lowercase letter.

   j. List all files *not* starting with a letter b or B.

   k. Remove two-character files starting with a or A.

LAB 10: REDIRECTION

1. What are the names of the three file streams associated with your terminal?

2. What is a file descriptor?

3. What command would you use to do the following:

   a. Redirect the output of the `ls` command to a file called `lsfile`?

   b. Redirect and append the output of the `date` command to `lsfile`?

   c. Redirect the output of the `who` command to `lsfile`? What happened?

4. Perform the following:

   a. Type `cp` all by itself. What happens?

   b. Save the error message from the above example to a file.

   c. Use the `find` command to find all files, starting from the parent directory, of type directory. Save the standard output in a file called `found` and any errors in a file called `found.errs`.

   d. Take the output of three commands and redirect the output to a file called `gottem_all`.

   e. Use a pipe(s) with the `ps` and `wc` commands to find out how many processes you are currently running.

LAB 11: FIRST SCRIPT

1. Write a script called greetme that will do the following:

   a. Contain a comment section with your name, the name of this script, and the purpose of this script.

   b. Greet the user.

   c. Print the date and the time.

   d. Print a calendar for this month.

   e. Print the name of your machine.

   f. Print the name and release of this operating system, (cat /etc/motd).

   g. Print a list of all files in your parent directory.

   h. Print all the processes root is running.

   i. Print the value of the TERM, PATH, and HOME variables.

   j. Print your disk usage (du).

   k. Use the id command to print your group ID.

   l. Print Please, could you loan me $50.00?

   m. Tell the user Good-bye and the current hour (see *man* pages for the date command).

2. Make sure your script is executable.

   chmod +x greetme

3. What was the first line of your script? Why do you need this line?

LAB 12: COMMAND-LINE ARGUMENTS

1. Write a script called rename that will take two arguments: the first argument is the name of the original file and the second argument is the new name for the file. If the user does not provide two arguments, a usage message will appear on the screen and the script will exit. Here is an example of how the script works:

   ```
   $ rename
   Usage: rename oldfilename newfilename
   $

   $ rename file1 file2
   file1 has been renamed file2
   Here is a listing of the directory:
   a file2
   b file.bak
   ```

2. The following find command (SunOS) will list all files in the root partition that are larger than 100K and that have been modified in the last week. (Check your *man* pages for the correct find syntax on your system.)

   ```
   find / -xdev -mtime -7 -size +200 -print
   ```

3. Write a script called bigfiles that will take two arguments: One will be the mtime and one the size value. An appropriate error message will be sent to stderr if the user does not provide two arguments.

4. If you have time, write a script called vib that creates backup files for vi. The backup files will have the extension .bak appended to the original name.

LAB 13: GETTING USER INPUT

1. Write a script called nosy that will do the following:

   a. Ask the user's full name—first, last, and middle name.

   b. Greet the user by his or her first name.

   c. Ask the user's year of birth and calculate his or her age (use expr).

   d. Ask the user's login name and print his or her user ID (from /etc/passwd).

   e. Tell the user his or her home directory.

   f. Show the user the processes he or she is running.

   g. Tell the user the day of the week, and the current time in nonmilitary time. The output should resemble

      ```
      The day of the week is Tuesday and the current time is 04:07:38 PM.
      ```

2. Create a text file called datafile (unless this file has already been provided for you). Each entry consists of fields separated by colons. The fields are as follows:

   a. First and last name

   b. Phone number

   c. Address

   d. Birth date

   e. Salary

3. Create a script called lookup that will do the following:

   a. Contain a comment section with the script name, your name, the date, and the reason for writing this script. The reason for writing this script is to display the datafile in sorted order.

   b. Sort datafile by last names.

   c. Show the user the contents of datafile.

   d. Tell the user the number of entries in the file.

4. Try the -x and -v options for debugging your script. How did you use these commands? How do they differ?

LAB 14: CONDITIONAL STATEMENTS

1. Write a script called checking that will do the following:

    a. Take a command-line argument: a user's login name.

    b. Test to see if a command-line argument was provided.

    c. Check to see if the user is in the /etc/passwd file. If so, it will print

       Found <user> in the /etc/passwd file.

    d. Otherwise, it will print

       No such user on our system.

2. In the lookup script, ask the user if he or she would like to add an entry to datafile. If the answer is yes or y:

    a. Prompt the user for a new name, phone, address, birth date, and salary. Each item will be stored in a separate variable. You will provide the colons between the fields and append the information to datafile.

    b. Sort the file by last names. Tell the user you added the entry, and show him or her the line preceded by the line number.

LAB 15: CONDITIONALS AND FILE TESTING

1. Rewrite checking. After checking whether the named user is in the /etc/passwd file, the program will check to see if the user is logged on. If so, the program will print all the processes that are running; otherwise, it will tell the user

    <user> is not logged on.

2. The lookup script depends on datafile to run. In the lookup script, check to see if the datafile exists and if it is readable and writable. Add a menu to the lookup script to resemble the following:

       [1] Add entry.
       [2] Delete entry.
       [3] View entry.
       [4] Exit.

    a. You already have the Add entry part of the script written. The Add entry routine should now include code that will check to see if the name is already in datafile and if it is, tell the user so. If the name is not there, add the new entry.

    b. Now write the code for the Delete entry, View entry, and Exit functions.

    c. The Delete part of the script should first check to see if the entry exists before trying to remove it. If it does not exist, notify the user; otherwise, remove the entry and tell the user you removed it. On exit, make sure that you use a digit to represent the appropriate exit status.

    d. How do you check the exit status from the command line?

LAB 16: THE case STATEMENT

1. The ps command is different on BSD and AT&T UNIX. On AT&T UNIX, the command to list all processes is:

   ps -ef

   On BSD UNIX and Linux, the command is

   ps -aux

   Write a program called systype that will check for a number of different system types. The cases to test for will be

   AIX
   Darwin (Mac OS X)
   Free BSD
   HP-UX
   IRIX
   Linux
   OS
   OSF1
   SCO
   SunOS (Solaris / SunOS)
   ULTRIX

   Solaris, HP-UX (10.x+) , SCO, and IRIX are AT&T-type systems. The rest are BSD-ish.

   The version of UNIX/Linux you are using will be printed to stdout. The system name can be found with the uname -s command or from the /etc/motd file.

LAB 17: LOOPS

Select one of the following:

1. Write a program called mchecker to check for new mail and write a message to the screen if new mail has arrived.

   The program will get the size of the mail spool file for the user. (The spool files are found in /usr/mail/$LOGNAME on AT&T systems and /usr/spool/mail/$USER on UCB systems. Use the find command if you cannot locate the file.) The script will execute in a continuous loop, once every 30 seconds. Each time the loop executes, it will compare the size of the mail spool file with its size from the previous loop. If the new size is greater than the old size, a message will be printed on your screen, saying Username, You have new mail.

   The size of a file can be found by looking at the output from ls -l, wc -c, or from the find command.

2. Write a program called dusage that will mail a list of users, one at a time, a listing of the number of blocks they are currently using. The list of users will be in a file called potential_hogs. One of the users listed in the potential_hogs file will be admin.

   a. Use file testing to check that potential_hogs file exists and is readable.

b. A loop will be used to iterate through the list of users. Only those users who are using over 500 blocks will be sent mail. The user admin will be skipped over (i.e., he or she does not get a mail message). The mail message will be stored in a here document in your dusage script.

c. Keep a list of the names of each person who received mail. Do this by creating a log file. After everyone on the list has been sent mail, print the number of people who received mail and a list of their names.

LAB 18: FUNCTIONS

1. Rewrite the systype program from Lab 16 as a function that returns the name of the system. Use this function to determine what options you will use with the ps command in the checking program.

   The ps command to list all processes on AT&T UNIX is

   ps -ef

   On BSD UNIX, the command is

   ps -aux

2. Write a function called cleanup that will remove all temporary files and exit the script. If the interrupt or hangup signal is sent while the program is running, the trap command will call the cleanup function.

3. Use a here document to add a new menu item to the lookup script to resemble the following:

   [1] Add entry
   [2] Delete entry
   [3] Change entry
   [4] View entry
   [5] Exit

   Write a function to handle each of the items in the menu. After the user has selected a valid entry and the function has completed, ask if the user would like to see the menu again. If an invalid entry is entered, the program should print

   Invalid entry, try again.

   and the menu will be redisplayed.

4. Create a submenu under View entry in the lookup script. The user will be asked if he or she would like to view specific information for a selected individual:

   a) Phone
   b) Address
   c) Birthday
   d) Salary

5. Use the trap command in a script to perform a cleanup operation if the interrupt signal is sent while the program is running.

9

The Interactive C and TC Shells

9.1 Introduction

An interactive shell is one in which the standard input, output, and errors are connected to a terminal. The C shell (csh) and TC shell (tcsh) provide a number of convenient features for interactive use that are not available with the Bourne shell, including filename completion, command aliasing, history substitution, job control, and more. These shells are almost identical when used as a programming language, but the TC shell has many more interactive features than its predecessor, the C shell. This section covers the common features of the C shell and TC shell for interactive use. If you are looking for some nice shortcuts at the command line, the new TC shell enhancements are covered in the second half of this chapter, beginning with "New Features of the Interactive TC Shell" on page 460.

9.1.1 C/TC Shell Startup

Before the shell displays a prompt, it is preceded by a number of processes. (See Figure 9.1.) After the system boots, the first process to run is called init; it is assigned process identification number (PID) 1. It gets instructions from a file called inittab (System V) or spawns a getty process (BSD). These processes are responsible for opening up the terminal ports, for providing a place where input comes from (stdin), where standard output (stdout) and error (stderr) go, and for putting a login prompt on your screen. The /bin/login program is then executed. The login program prompts for a password, encrypts and verifies your password, sets up an initial working environment, and then initiates the shell, /bin/csh or bin/tcsh for the C or TC shell, respectively.

When the shell is a login shell, this is the sequence of invocations: The C/TC shell looks in the /etc directory for system startup files, which are executed if they exist. For the C shell, for example, these files are /etc/csh.cshrc and /etc/csh.login. (See Chapter 16, "The System Administrator and the Shell," on page 1023 for details.) Then the C/TC shell looks in the user's home directory for a file called .cshrc or .tcshrc, respectively,

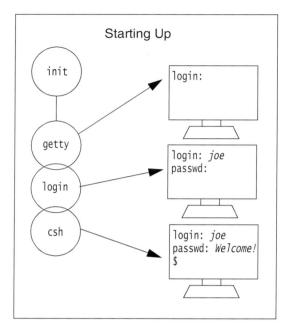

Figure 9.1   Starting the C shell.

which is an initialization file that allows you to customize the C/TC shell environment in which you will be working. After executing commands in the .cshrc or .tcshrc file, commands in the .login file are executed. The .cshrc or .tcshrc file will be executed every time a new C/TC shell is started. The .login file is executed only once when the user logs on, and also contains commands and variables to initialize the user's environment. After executing commands from those files, the prompt appears on your screen and the C/TC shell awaits commands. Most systems today start up with a graphical user interface, adding to the steps just mentioned. When you are in the desktop, such as CDE, you will see icons and menus. Once you select a terminal from the menu, the shell prompt will appear and you can start typing commands.

9.2   The Environment

9.2.1   Initialization Files

After the csh/tcsh program starts, it is programmed to execute two files in the user's home directory: the .cshrc or .tcshrc file, respectively, and the .login file. These files allow users to initialize their own environments.

The .cshrc and .tcshrc Files.   The .cshrc file contains C shell variable settings and is executed when you log in and every time a csh subshell is started. Likewise, the .tcshrc file contains TC shell variable settings and is executed when you log in and every time a tcsh subshell is started. These files share similar settings. For example, aliases and history are normally set here.

EXAMPLE · 9.1

```
    (The .cshrc File)
1   if ( $?prompt ) then
2       set prompt = "\! stardust > "
3       set history = 32
4       set savehist = 5
5       set noclobber
6       set filec fignore = ( .o )
7       set cdpath = ( /home/jody/ellie/bin /usr/local/bin /usr/bin )
8       set ignoreeof
9       alias m more
        alias status 'date;du -s'
        alias cd 'cd \!*;set prompt = "\! <$cwd> "'
    endif
```

EXPLANATION

1   If the prompt has been set ($?prompt), the shell is running interactively; that is, it is not running in a script.

2   The primary prompt is set to the number of the current history event, the name stardust, and a > character. This will change the % prompt, the default.

3   The history variable is set to 32. This controls the number of history events that will appear on the screen. The last 32 commands you entered will be displayed when you type history (see "Command-Line History" on page 413).

4   Normally, when you log out, the history list is cleared. The savehist variable allows you to save a specified number of commands from the end of the history list. In this example, the last 5 commands will be saved in a file in your home directory, the .history file, so that when you log in again, the shell can check to see if that file exists and put the history lines saved at the top of the new history list.

5   The noclobber variable is set to protect the user from inadvertently removing files when using redirection. For example, sort myfile > myfile will destroy myfile. With noclobber set, the message file exists will appear on the screen.

6   The filec variable is used for filename completion so that you only need to type the first number of significant characters in a filename, press the Esc key, and the shell will complete the rest of the filename. By pressing ^D (Ctrl-D) when typing in the filename, the C shell will display a list of files that match that string. The fignore variable allows you to exclude files that you do not want affected by filename completion. In this case, all the .o filenames (object files) will not be affected by filec, even though filec is set (see "Filename Completion: The filec Variable" on page 431).

EXPLANATION (CONTINUED)

7   The cdpath variable is assigned a list of path elements. When changing directories, if you specify just the directory name, and that directory is not a subdirectory directly below the current working directory, the shell will search the cdpath directory entries to see if it can find the directory in any of those locations and then will change the directory.

8   The ignoreeof variable prevents you from logging out with ^D. UNIX utilities that accept input from the keyboard, such as the mail program, are terminated by pressing ^D. Often, on a slow system, the user will be tempted to press ^D more than once. The first time, the mail program would be terminated, the second time, the user is logged out. By setting ignoreeof, you are required to type logout to log out.

9   The aliases are set to give a shorthand notation for a single command or group of commands. Now when you type the alias, the command(s) assigned to it will be executed. The alias for the more command is m. Every time you type m, the more command is executed. The status alias prints the date and a summary of the user's disk usage. The cd alias creates a new prompt every time the user changes directory. The new prompt will contain the number of the current history event (\!*) and the current working directory, $cwd surrounded by < > (see "Aliases" on page 418).

The .login File.   The .login file is executed one time when you first log in. It normally contains environment variables and terminal settings. It is the file where window applications are usually started. Because environment variables are inherited by processes spawned from this shell and only need to be set once, and terminal settings do not have to be reset for every process, those settings belong in the .login file.

EXAMPLE 9.2

```
(The .login File)
1    stty -istrip
2    stty erase ^h
3    stty kill ^u
     #
     # If possible start the windows system.
     # Give a user a chance to bail out
     #
4    if ( $TERM == "linux" ) then
5            echo "Starting X windows.  Press Ctrl-C \
                 to exit within the next 5 seconds "
             sleep 5
6            startx
7    endif
8    set autologout=60
```

1   The stty command sets options for the terminal. Input characters will not be stripped to seven bits if -istrip is used.

2   The stty command sets Ctrl-H, the Backspace key, to erase.

3   Any line beginning with # is a comment. It is not an executable statement.

4   If the current terminal window (tty) is the console (linux), the next line is executed; otherwise, program control goes to the last endif.

5   This line is echoed to the screen, and if the user does not press Ctrl-C to kill the process, the program will sleep (pause) for five seconds, and then the X Windows program will start.

6   The startx program launches X Windows if this system is Linux.

7   The endif marks the end of the innermost if construct.

8   The autologout variable is set to 60 so that after 60 minutes of inactivity, the user will automatically be logged out (from the login shell).

9.2.2 The Search Path

The path variable is used by the shell to locate commands typed at the command line. The search is from left to right. The dot represents the current working directory. If the command is not found in any of the directories listed in the path, or in the present working directory, the shell sends the message Command not found to standard error. It is recommended that the path be set in the .login file.[1] The search path is set differently in the C/TC shell than it is in the Bourne and Korn shells. Each of the elements is separated by whitespace.

```
set path = (/usr/bin /usr/ucb /bin /usr .)
echo $path
/usr/bin /usr/ucb /bin /usr .
```

The environment variable PATH will display as

```
echo $PATH
/usr/bin:/usr/ucb:/bin:.
```

The C/TC shell internally updates the environment variable for PATH to maintain compatibility with other programs (such as the Bourne or Korn shells) that may be started from this shell and will need to use the path variable.

---

1. Do not confuse the search path variable with the cdpath variable set in the .cshrc file.

9.2.3 The rehash Command

The shell builds an internal hash table consisting of the contents of the directories listed in the search path. (If the dot is in the search path, the files in the dot directory, the current working directory, are not put in the hash table.) For efficiency, the shell uses the hash table to find commands that are typed at the command line, rather than searching the path each time. If a new command is added to one of the directories already listed in the search path, the internal hash table must be recomputed. This is done by typing

```
% rehash
```

(The % is the C shell prompt.) The hash table is also automatically recomputed when you change your path at the prompt or start another shell.

9.2.4 The hashstat Command

The hashstat command displays performance statistics to show the effectiveness of its search for commands from the hash table. The statistics are in terms of "hits" and "misses." If the shell finds most of its commands you use at the end of your path, it has to work harder than if they were at the front of the path, resulting in a higher number of misses than hits. In such cases, you can put the most heavily hit directory toward the front of the path to improve performance.

```
% hashstat
2 hits, 13 misses, 13%[2]
```

9.2.5 The source Command

The source command is a shell built-in command, that is, part of the shell's internal code. It is used to execute a command or set of commands from a file. Normally, when a command is executed, the shell forks a child process to execute the command, so that any changes made will not affect the original shell, called the parent shell. The source command causes the program to be executed in the current shell, so that any variables set within the file will become part of the environment of the current shell. The source command is normally used to re-execute the .cshrc or .login if either has been modified. For example, if the path is changed after logging in, type

```
% source .login or .cshrc
```

---

2. On systems without vfork, prints the number and size of hash buckets; for example, 1024 hash buckets of 16 bits each.

9.2.6 The Shell Prompts

The C shell has two prompts: the *primary* prompt, a percent sign (%), and the *secondary* prompt, a question mark (?). The TC shell uses a > as its primary default prompt. (See "The Shell Prompts" on page 461 for coverage of the tcsh enhanced prompt settings.) The primary prompt is the one displayed on the terminal after you have logged in; it waits for you to type commands. The primary prompt can be reset. If you are writing scripts at the prompt that require C/TC shell programming constructs, for example, decision making or looping, the secondary prompt will appear so that you can continue onto the next line. It will continue to appear after each newline, until the construct has been properly terminated. The secondary prompt cannot be reset.

The Primary Prompt.   When running interactively, the prompt waits for you to type a command and press the Enter key. If you do not want to use the default prompt, reset it in the .cshrc file and it will be set for this and all other C subshells. If you only want it set for this login session, set it at the shell prompt.

EXAMPLE 9.3

```
1   % set prompt = "$LOGNAME > "
2   ellie >
```

EXPLANATION

1   The primary prompt is assigned the user's login name, followed by a > symbol and a space.
2   The new prompt is displayed.

The Secondary Prompt.   The secondary prompt appears when you are writing online scripts at the prompt. Whenever shell programming constructs are entered, followed by a newline, the secondary prompt appears and continues to appear until the construct is properly terminated. Writing scripts correctly at the prompt takes practice. Once the command is entered and you press Enter, you cannot back up, and the C shell history mechanism does not save commands typed at the secondary prompt.

EXAMPLE 9.4

```
1   % foreach pal (joe tom ann)
2   ? mail $pal < memo
3   ? end
4   %
```

EXPLANATION

1   This is an example of online scripting. Because the C shell is expecting further in-put after the foreach loop is entered, the secondary prompt appears. The foreach loop processes each word in the parenthesized list.

2   The first time in the loop, joe is assigned to the variable pal. The user joe is sent the contents of memo in the mail. Then next time through the loop, tom is assigned to the variable pal, and so on.

3   The end statement marks the end of the loop. When all of the items in the paren-thesized list have been processed, the loop ends and the primary prompt is dis-played.

4   The primary prompt is displayed.

9.3   The C/TC Shell Command Line

After logging in, the C/TC shell displays its primary prompt, a % or >, respectively. The shell is your command interpreter. When the shell is running interactively, it reads com-mands from the terminal and breaks the command line into words. A command line consists of one or more words (or tokens) separated by whitespace (blanks and/or tabs) and terminated with a newline, generated by pressing the Enter key. The first word is the command, and subsequent words are the command's options and/or arguments. The command may be a UNIX/Linux executable program such as ls or pwd, an alias, a built-in command such as cd or jobs, or a shell script. The command may contain special char-acters, called *metacharacters*, that the shell must interpret while parsing the command line. If the last character in the command line is a backslash, followed by a newline, the line can be continued to the next line.[3]

9.3.1   The Exit Status

After a command or program terminates, it returns an exit status to the parent process. The exit status is a number between 0 and 255. By convention, when a program exits, if the status returned is 0, the command was successful in its execution. When the exit sta-tus is nonzero, the command failed in some way. The C/TC shell status variable is set to the value of the exit status of the last command that was executed. Success or failure of a program is determined by the programmer who wrote the program.

---

3. The length of the command line can be 256 characters or more; it can be even higher on different versions of UNIX.

EXAMPLE 9.5

```
1  % grep "ellie" /etc/passwd
   ellie:GgMyBsSJavd16s:9496:40:Ellie Quigley:/home/jody/ellie
2  % echo $status
   0
3  % grep "nicky" /etc/passwd
4  % echo $status
   1
5  % grep "scott" /etc/passsswd
   grep: /etc/passsswd: No such file or directory
6  % echo $status
   2
```

EXPLANATION

1 The grep program searches for the pattern ellie in the /etc/passwd file and is successful. The line from /etc/passwd is displayed.

2 The status variable is set to the exit value of the grep command; 0 indicates success.

3 The grep program cannot find user nicky in the /etc/passwd file.

4 The grep program cannot find the pattern, so it returns an exit status of 1.

5 The grep program fails because the file /etc/passsswd cannot be opened.

6 Grep cannot find the file, so it returns an exit status of 2.

9.3.2 Command Grouping

A command line can consist of multiple commands. Each command is separated by a semicolon and the command line is terminated with a newline.

EXAMPLE 9.6

```
% ls; pwd; cal 2004
```

EXPLANATION

The commands are executed from left to right until the newline is reached.

Commands may also be grouped so that all of the output is either piped to another command or redirected to a file. The shell executes commands in a subshell.

EXAMPLE 9.7

```
1  % ( ls ; pwd; cal 2004 ) > outputfile
2  % pwd; ( cd / ; pwd ) ; pwd
   /home/jody/ellie
   /
   /home/jody/ellie
```

EXPLANATION

1   The output of each of the commands is sent to the file called outputfile. Without
     the parentheses, the output of the first two commands would go to the screen, and
     only the output of the cal command would be redirected to the output file.

2   The pwd command displays the present working directory. The parentheses cause
     the commands enclosed within them to be processed by a subshell. The cd com-
     mand is built into the shell. While in the subshell, the directory is changed to root
     and the present working directory is displayed. When out of the subshell, the
     present working directory of the original shell is displayed.

9.3.3   Conditional Execution of Commands

With conditional execution, two command strings are separated by two special meta-
characters, double ampersand and double vertical (&& and ||). The command on the
right of either of these metacharacters will or will not be executed based on the exit condition of the command on the left.

EXAMPLE 9.8

```
% grep '^tom:' /etc/passwd && mail tom < letter
```

EXPLANATION

If the first command is successful (has a 0 exit status), the second command, after the
&&, is executed. If the grep command successfully finds tom in the passwd file, the command on the right will be executed: The mail program will send tom the contents of the
letter file.

EXAMPLE 9.9

```
% grep '^tom:' /etc/passwd || echo "tom is not a user here."
```

EXPLANATION

If the first command fails (has a nonzero exit status), the second command, after the ||,
is executed. If the grep command does not find tom in the passwd file, the command on the
right will be executed: The echo program will print tom is not a user here. to the screen.

9.3.4   Commands in the Background

Normally, when you execute a command, it runs in the foreground, and the prompt does
not reappear until the command has completed execution. It is not always convenient
to wait for the command to complete. By placing an ampersand at the end of the command line, the shell will return the shell prompt immediately so that you do not have to
wait for the last command to complete before starting another one. The command run-

ning in the background is called a *background job* and its output will be sent to the screen as it processes. It can be confusing if two commands are sending output to the screen concurrently. To avoid confusion, you can send the output of the job running in the background to a file, or pipe it to another device such as a printer. It is often handy to start a new shell window in the background, so you will have access to both the window from which you started and the new shell window.

EXAMPLE 9.10

```
1   % man xview | lp&
2   [1] 1557
3   %
```

EXPLANATION

1   The output from the man pages for the xview program is piped to the printer. The ampersand at the end of the command line puts the job in the background.

2   There are two numbers that appear on the screen: The number in square brackets indicates that this is the first job to be placed in the background, and the second number is the PID of this job.

3   The shell prompt appears immediately. While your program is running in the background, the shell is prompting you for another command in the foreground.

9.3.5 Command-Line History

The history mechanism is built into the C/TC shell. (For tcsh enhancements to history see "TC Shell Command-Line History" on page 466.) It keeps a numbered list of the commands (called *history events*) that you have typed at the command line. You can recall a command from the history list and re-execute it without retyping the command. The history substitution character, the exclamation point, is often called the *bang* character. The history built-in command displays the history list.

EXAMPLE 9.11

```
(The Command Line)
% history
1 cd
2 ls
3 more /etc/fstab
4 /etc/mount
5 sort index
6 vi index
```

EXPLANATION

The history list displays the last commands that were typed at the command line. Each event in the list is preceded with a number.

Setting History. The C shell history variable is set to the number of events you want to save from the history list and display on the screen. Normally, this is set in the .cshrc file, the user's initialization file.

EXAMPLE 9.12

```
set history=50
```

EXPLANATION

The last 50 commands typed at the terminal are saved and may be displayed on the screen by typing the history command.

Saving History. To save history events across logins, set the savehist variable. This variable is normally set in the .cshrc file, the user's initialization file.

EXAMPLE 9.13

```
set savehist=25
```

EXPLANATION

The last 25 commands from the history list are saved and will be at the top of the history list the next time you log in.

Displaying History. The history command displays the events in the history list. The history command also has options that control the number of events and the format of the events that will be displayed. The numbering of events does not necessarily start at 1. If you have 100 commands on the history list, and you have set the history variable to 25, you will only see the last 25 commands saved. (The TC shell supports the use of the arrow keys. See "Accessing Commands from the History File" on page 470.)

EXAMPLE 9.14

```
% history
1 ls
2 vi file1
3 df
4 ps -eaf
5 history
6 more /etc/passwd
7 cd
8 echo $USER
9 set
```

EXPLANATION

The history list is displayed. Each command is numbered.

EXAMPLE 9.15

```
% history -h        # Print without line numbers
ls
vi file1
df
ps -eaf
history
more /etc/passwd
cd
echo $USER
set
history -n
```

EXPLANATION

The history list is displayed without line numbers.

EXAMPLE 9.16

```
% history -r        # Print the history list in reverse
11 history -r
10 history -h
 9 set
 8 echo $USER
 7 cd
 6 more /etc/passwd
 5 history
 4 ps -eaf
 3 df
 2 vi file1
 1 ls
```

EXPLANATION

The history list is displayed in reverse order.

EXAMPLE 9.17

```
% history 5         # Prints the last 5 events on the history list
 7   echo $USER
 8   cd
 9   set
10   history -n
11   history 5
```

EXPLANATION

The last five commands on the history list are displayed.

Re-executing Commands.   To re-execute a command from the history list, the exclamation point (bang) is used. If you type two exclamation points (!!), the last command is re-executed. If you type the exclamation point followed by a number, the number is associated with the command from the history list and the command is executed. If you type an exclamation point and a letter, the last command that started with that letter is executed. The caret (∧) is also used as a shortcut method for editing the previous command.

EXAMPLE 9.18

```
1   % date
    Mon Apr 26  8 12:27:35 PST 2004
2   % !!
    date
    Mon Apr 26 12:28:25 PST 2004
3   % !3
    date
    Mon Apr 26 12:29:26 PST 2004
4   % !d
    date
    Mon Apr 26 12:30:09 PST 2004
5   % dare
    dare: Command not found.
6   % ^r^t
    date
    Mon Apr 26 12:33:25 PST 2004
```

EXPLANATION

1   The date command is executed at the command line. The history list is updated. This is the last command on the list.

2   The !! (bang bang) gets the last command from the history list; the command is re-executed.

3   The third command on the history list is re-executed.

4   The last command on the history list that started with the letter d is re-executed.

5   The command is mistyped.

6   The carets are used to substitute letters from the last command on the history list. The first occurrence of an r is replaced with a t.

EXAMPLE 9.19

```
1   % cat file1 file2 file3
        <Contents of file1, file2, and file3 are displayed here>
    % vi !:1
    vi file1
```

EXAMPLE 9.19 (CONTINUED)

```
2   % cat file1 file2 file3
        <Contents of file1, file2, and file3 are displayed here>

    % ls !:2
    ls file2
    file2

3   % cat file1 file2 file3
    % ls  !:3
    ls file3
    file3

4   % echo a b c
    a b c
    % echo !$
    echo c
    c

5   % echo a b c
    a b c
    % echo !^
    echo a
    a

6   % echo a b c
    a b c
    % echo !*
    echo a b c
    a b c

7   % !!:p
    echo a b c
```

EXPLANATION

1   The cat command displays the contents of file1, file2, and file3 to the screen. The history list is updated. The command line is broken into words, starting with word number 0. If the word number is preceded by a colon, that word can be extracted from the history list. The !:1 notation means: get the first argument from the last command on the history list and replace it in the command string. The first argument from the last command is file1. (Word 0 is the command itself.)

2   The !:2 is replaced with the second argument of the last command, file2, and given as an argument to ls. file2 is printed. (file2 is the third word.)

3   ls !:3 reads: go to the last command on the history list and get the fourth word (words start at 0) and pass it to the ls command as an argument (file3 is the fourth word).

4   The bang (!) with the dollar sign ($) refers to the last argument of the last command on the history list. The last argument is c.

5   The caret (^) represents the first argument after the command. The bang (!) with the ^ refers to the first argument of the last command on the history list. The first argument of the last command is a.

6   The asterisk (*) represents all arguments after the command. The bang (!) with the * refers to all of the arguments of the last command on the history list.

7   The last command from the history list is printed but not executed. The history list is updated. You could now perform caret substitutions on that line.

9.4 Aliases

An *alias* is a C/TC shell user-defined abbreviation for a command. (For tcsh enhancements to the alias mechanism, see "TC Shell Aliases" on page 491.) Aliases are useful when a command has a number of options and arguments or the syntax is difficult to remember. Aliases set at the command line are not inherited by subshells. Aliases are normally set in the .cshrc or .tcshrc file. Because the .cshrc or .tcshrc is executed when a new shell is started, any aliases set there will get reset for the new shell. Aliases may also be passed into shell scripts, but will cause potential portability problems unless they are directly set within the script.

9.4.1 Listing Aliases

The alias built-in command lists all set aliases. The alias is printed first, followed by the real command or commands it represents.

EXAMPLE 9.20

```
% alias
co       compress
cp       cp -i
ls1      enscript -B -r -Porange -f Courier8 !* &
mailq    /usr/lib/sendmail -bp
mroe     more
mv       mv -i
rn       /usr/spool/news/bin/rn3
uc       uncompress
uu       uudecode
vg       vgrind -t -s11 !:1 | lpr -t
weekly   (cd /home/jody/ellie/activity; ./weekly_report; echo Done)
```

EXPLANATION

The alias command lists the alias (nickname) for the command in the first column and the real command the alias represents in the second column.

9.4.2 Creating Aliases

The alias command is used to create an alias. The first argument is the name of the alias, the nickname for the command. The rest of the line consists of the command or commands that will be executed when the alias is executed. Multiple commands are separated by a semicolon, and commands containing spaces and metacharacters are surrounded by single quotes.

EXAMPLE 9.21

```
1   % alias m more
2   % alias mroe more
3   % alias lF 'ls -alF'
4   % alias cd  'cd \!*; set prompt = "$cwd   >"'
    % cd ..
    /home/jody > cd /          # New prompt displayed
    / >
```

EXPLANATION

1   The nickname for the more command is set to m.
2   The alias for the more command is set to mroe. This is handy if you can't spell.
3   The alias definition is enclosed in quotes because of the whitespace. The alias lF is a nickname for the command ls -alF.
4   When cd is executed, the alias for cd will cause cd to go to the directory named as an argument and will then reset the prompt to the current working directory followed by the string >. The !* is used by the alias in the same way it is used by the history mechanism. The backslash prevents the history mechanism from evaluating the !* first before the alias has a chance to use it. The \!* represents the arguments from the most recent command on the history list.

9.4.3 Deleting Aliases

The unalias command is used to delete an alias. To temporarily turn off an alias, the alias name is preceded by a backslash.

EXAMPLE 9.22

```
1   % unalias mroe
2   % \cd ..
```

EXPLANATION

1   The unalias command deletes the alias mroe from the list of defined aliases.
2   The alias cd is temporarily turned off for this execution of the command only.

9.4.4   Alias Loop

An alias loop occurs when an alias definition references another alias that references back to the original alias.

EXAMPLE 9.23

```
1    % alias m more
2    % alias mroe m
3    % alias m mroe        # Causes a loop
4    % m datafile
     Alias loop.
```

EXPLANATION

1   The alias is m. The alias definition is more. Every time m is used, the more command is executed.

2   The alias is mroe. The alias definition is m. If mroe is typed, the alias m is invoked and the more command is executed.

3   This is the culprit. If alias m is used, it invokes alias mroe, and alias mroe references back to m, causing an alias loop. Nothing bad happens. You just get an error message.

4   Alias m is used. It is circular. m calls mroe and mroe calls m, then m calls mroe, and so on. Rather than looping forever, the C shell catches the problem and displays an error message.

9.5   Manipulating the Directory Stack

If you find that as you work, you cd up and down the directory tree into many of the same directories, you can make it easy to access those directories by pushing them onto a directory stack and manipulating the stack. The directory stack is often compared to stacking trays in a cafeteria where the trays are stacked on top of each other, the first one being at the bottom of the stack. The pushd built-in command pushes directories onto a stack and the popd command removes them. (See following examples.) The stack is a numbered list of directories with the top directory being the most recent directory pushed onto the stack. The directories are numbered starting with the top directory at 0, the next one numbered 1, and so on. The built-in command, dirs, with a -v option, displays the numbered directory stack.

9.5.1   The pushd and popd Commands

The pushd command with a directory as an argument causes the new directory to be added to the directory stack and, at the same time, changes to that directory. If the argument is a dash (-), the dash refers to the previous working directory. If the argument is a + and a number (n), pushd extracts the nth directory from the stack and pushes it onto the top, then changes to that directory. Without arguments, pushd exchanges the top two elements of the directory stack, making it easy to switch back and forth between directories. There are a number of shell variables that control the way pushd works. (See "Setting Local Variables" on page 441.)

To save a directory stack across login sessions, you must set the savedirs variable in one of the tcsh initialization files (e.g., ~/.tcshrc). The directory stack will be stored in a file called ~/.cshdirs and will be automatically sourced when the shell starts up.

The popd command removes a directory from the top of the stack, and changes to that directory.

See Table 9.1 for a list of directory stack variables.

Table 9.1 Directory Stack Variables

Variable	What It Does
deextract	If set, pushd +n extracts the nth directory from the directory stack before pushing it onto the stack.
dirsfile	Can be assigned a filename where the directory stack can be saved across logins.
dirstack	Used to display the stack or assign directories to it.
dunique	Before pushing a directory onto the stack, removes any directories with the same name.
pushdsilent	Doesn't print the directory stack when pushd is executed.
pushdtohome	If set, pushd without arguments, is same as pushd ~ or cd.
pushtohome	Without arguments, pushes to ~, the user's home directory.
savedirs	Saves the directory stack across logins.

EXAMPLE 9.24

```
1   % pwd
    /home/ellie

    % pushd ..
    /home ~

    % pwd
    /home

2   % pushd          # swap the two top directories on the stack
    ~ /home

    % pwd
    /home/ellie
```

EXAMPLE 9.24 (CONTINUED)

```
3   % pushd perlclass
    ~/perlclass  ~  /home

4   % dirs -v
    0       ~/perlclass
    1       ~
    2       /home

5   % popd
    ~       /home
    % pwd
    /home/ellie

6   % popd
    /home

    % pwd
    /home

7   % popd
    popd: Directory stack empty.
```

EXPLANATION

1   First the pwd command displays the present working directory, /home/ellie. Next the pushd command with .. as its argument pushes the parent directory (..) onto the directory stack. The output of pushd indicates that /home is at the top of the directory stack and the user's home directory (~), /home/ellie, is at the bottom of the stack. pushd also changes the directory to the one that was pushed onto the stack; that is, .. , which translates to /home. The new directory is displayed with the second pwd command.

2   pushd, without arguments, exchanges the two top directory entries on the stack and changes to the swapped directory; in this example, the directory is switched back to the user's home directory, /home/ellie.

3   The pushd command will push its argument, ~/perlclass, onto the stack, and change to that directory.

4   The built-in dirs command displays the numbered directory stack, with 0 being the top level.

5   The popd command removes a directory from the top of the stack, and changes to that directory.

6   The popd command removes another directory from the top of the stack, and changes to that directory.

7   The popd command cannot remove any more directory entries because the stack is empty, and issues an error message saying so.

9.6 Job Control

Job control is a powerful feature of the C/TC shell that allows you to run programs, called jobs, in the background or foreground. Normally, a command typed at the command line runs in the foreground, and will continue until it has finished. If you have windows, job control may not be necessary, because you can simply open another window to start a new task. On the other hand, with a single terminal, job control is a very useful feature. For a list of job commands, see Table 9.2. (See "TC Shell Job Control" on page 495 for TC shell enhancements for job control.)

Table 9.2 Job Control Commands

Command	Meaning
jobs	Lists all the jobs running
^Z (Ctrl-Z)	Stops (suspends) the job; the prompt appears on the screen
bg	Starts running the stopped job in the background
fg	Brings a background job to the foreground
kill	Sends the kill signal to a specified job

9.6.1 The Ampersand and Background Jobs

If you expect a command to take a long time to complete, you can append the command with an ampersand and the job will execute in the background. The C/TC shell prompt returns immediately and now you can type another command. Now the two commands are running concurrently, one in the background and one in the foreground. They both send their standard output to the screen. If you place a job in the background, it is a good idea to redirect its output either to a file or pipe it to a device such as a printer.

EXAMPLE 9.25

```
1   % find . -name core -exec rm {} \; &
2   [1]  543
3   %
```

EXPLANATION

1   The find command runs in the background. (Without the -print option, the find command does not send any output to the screen).[a]

2   The number in square brackets indicates this is the first job to be run in the background and the PID for this process is 543.

3   The prompt returns immediately. The shell waits for user input.

a. The find syntax requires a semicolon at the end of an exec statement. The semicolon is preceded by a backslash to prevent the shell from interpreting it.

9.6.2   The Suspend Key Sequence and Background Jobs

To suspend a program, the suspend key sequence, Ctrl-Z, is issued. The job is now suspended (stopped), the shell prompt is displayed, and the program will not resume until the fg or bg commands are issued. (When using the vi editor, the ZZ command writes and saves a file. Do not confuse this with Ctrl-Z, which would suspend the vi session.) If you try to log out when a job is suspended, the message There are stopped jobs appears on the screen.

9.6.3   The jobs Command

The C/TC shell jobs built-in command displays the programs that are currently active and either running or suspended in the background. Running means the job is executing in the background. When a job is stopped, it is suspended; it is not in execution. In both cases, the terminal is free to accept other commands.

EXAMPLE 9.26

```
(The Command Line)
1    % jobs
2    [1] + Stopped    vi filex
     [2] - Running    sleep 25

3    % jobs -1
     [1] + 355  Stopped    vi filex
     [2] - 356  Running    sleep 25

4    [2] Done sleep 25
```

EXPLANATION

1   The jobs command lists the currently active jobs.

2   The notation [1] is the number of the first job; the plus sign indicates that the job is not the most recent job to be placed in the background; the dash indicates that this is the most recent job put in the background; Stopped means that this job was suspended with ^Z and is not currently active.

3   The -1 option (long listing) displays the number of the job as well as the PID of the job. The notation [2] is the number of the second job, in this case, the last job placed in the background. The dash indicates that this is the most recent job. The sleep command is running in the background.

4   After sleep has been running for 25 seconds, the job will complete and a message saying that it has finished appears on the screen.

9.6.4   The Foreground and Background Commands

The fg command brings a background job into the foreground. The bg command starts a suspended job running in the background. A percent sign and the number of a job can be used as arguments to the fg and bg commands if you want to select a particular job for job control.

EXAMPLE 9.27

```
1    % jobs
2    [1] + Stopped     vi filex
     [2] - Running     cc prog.c -o prog

3    % fg %1
     vi filex
     (vi session starts)

4    % kill %2
     [2] Terminated    cc prog.c -o prog

5    % sleep 15
     (Press ^z)
     Stopped

6    % bg
     [1] sleep 15 &
     [1] Done      sleep 15
```

EXPLANATION

1   The jobs command lists currently running processes, called jobs.

2   The first job stopped is the vi session, the second job is the cc command.

3   The job numbered [1] is brought to the foreground. The number is preceded with a percent sign.

4   The kill command is built-in. It sends the TERM (terminate) signal, by default, to a process. The argument is either the number or the PID of the process.

5   The sleep command is stopped by pressing ^Z. The sleep command is not using the CPU and is suspended in the background.

6   The bg command causes the last background job to start executing in the background. The sleep program will start the countdown in seconds before execution resumes.

9.7　Shell Metacharacters

Metacharacters are special characters that are used to represent something other than themselves. As a rule of thumb, characters that are neither letters nor numbers may be metacharacters. Like grep, sed, and awk, the shell has its own set of metacharacters, often called *shell wildcards*.[4] Shell metacharacters can be used to group commands together, to abbreviate filenames and pathnames, to redirect and pipe input/output, to place commands in the background, and so forth. Table 9.3 presents a partial list of shell metacharacters.

Table 9.3　Shell Metacharacters

Metacharacter	Purpose	Example	Meaning
$	Variable substitution	set name=Tom echo $name *Tom*	Sets the variable name to Tom; displays the value stored there.
!	History substitution	!3	Re-executes the third event from the history list.
*	Filename substitution	rm *	Removes all files.
?	Filename substitution	ls ??	Lists all two-character files.
[ ]	Filename substitution	cat f[123]	Displays contents of f1, f2, f3.
;	Command separator	ls;date;pwd	Each command is executed in turn.
&	Background processing	lp mbox&	Printing is done in the background. Prompt returns immediately.
>	Redirection of output	ls > file	Redirects standard output to file.
<	Redirection of input	ls < file	Redirects standard input from file.
>&	Redirection of output and error	ls >& file	Redirects both output and errors to file.
>!	If noclobber is set, override it	ls >! file	If file exists, truncate and overwrite it, even if noclobber is set.
>>!	If noclobber is set, override it	ls >>! file	If file does not exist, create it; even if noclobber is set.

---

4. Programs such as grep, sed, and awk have a set of metacharacters, called *regular expression metacharacters*, for pattern matching. These should not be confused with shell metacharacters.

Table 9.3   Shell Metacharacters (continued)

Metacharacter	Purpose	Example	Meaning
( )	Groups commands to be executed in a subshell	`(ls ; pwd) >tmp`	Executes commands and sends output to `tmp` file.
{ }	Groups commands to be executed in this shell	`{ cd /; echo $cwd }`	Changes to root directory and displays current working directory.

9.8   Filename Substitution

When evaluating the command line, the shell uses metacharacters to abbreviate filenames or pathnames that match a certain set of characters. The filename substitution metacharacters listed in Table 9.4 are expanded into an alphabetically listed set of filenames. The process of expanding a metacharacter into filenames is also called *globbing*. Unlike the other shells, when the C shell cannot substitute a filename for the metacharacter it is supposed to represent, the shell reports `No match`.

Table 9.4   Shell Metacharacters and Filename Substitution

Metacharacter	Meaning
`*`	Matches zero or more characters
`?`	Matches exactly one character
`[abc]`	Matches one character in the set: a, b, or c
`[a-z]`	Matches one character in the range a to z
`{a, ile,ax}`	Matches for a character or set of characters
`~`	Substitutes the user's home directory for tilde
`\`	Escapes or disables the metacharacter

The shell performs filename substitution by evaluating its metacharacters and replacing them with the appropriate letters or digits in a filename.

9.8.1   The Asterisk

The asterisk matches zero or more characters in a filename.

EXAMPLE 9.28

```
1   % ls
    a.c b.c abc ab3 file1 file2 file3 file4 file5
2   % echo *
    a.c b.c abc ab3 file1 file2 file3 file4 file5
3   % ls *.c
    a.c b.c
4   % rm z*p
    No match.
```

EXPLANATION

1   All the files in the current directory are listed.

2   The echo program prints all its arguments to the screen. The asterisk (also called a splat) is a wildcard that means: match for zero or more of any characters found in a filename. All the files in the directory are matched and echoed to the screen.

3   Filenames ending in .c are listed.

4   Because none of the files in the directory start with z, the shell reports No match.

9.8.2 The Question Mark

The question mark matches exactly one character in a filename.

EXAMPLE 9.29

```
1   % ls
    a.c b.c abc ab3 file1 file2 file3 file4 file5
2   % ls ???
    abc ab3
3   % echo How are you?
    No match.
4   % echo How are you\?
    How are you?
```

EXPLANATION

1   All the files in the current directory are listed.

2   The question mark matches for a single-character filename. Any filenames consisting of three characters are listed.

3   The shell looks for a filename spelled y-o-u followed by one character. There is not a file in the directory that matches these characters. The shell prints No match.

4   The backslash preceding the question mark is used to turn off the special meaning of the question mark. Now the shell treats the question mark as a literal character.

9.8.3   The Square Brackets

The square brackets match a filename for one character from a set or range of characters.

EXAMPLE   9.30

```
1   % ls
    a.c b.c abc ab3 file1 file2 file3 file4 file5 file10 file11 file12
2   % ls file[123]
    file1 file2 file3
3   % ls [A-Za-z][a-z][1-5]
    ab3
4   % ls file1[0-2]
    file10 file11 file12
```

EXPLANATION

1   All the files in the current directory are listed.

2   Filenames starting with file and followed by a 1, 2, or 3 are matched and listed.

3   Filenames starting with a letter (either uppercase or lowercase) followed by a lowercase letter, and followed by a number between 1 and 5 are matched and listed.

4   Filenames starting with file1 and followed by a 0, 1, or 2 are listed.

9.8.4   The Curly Braces

The curly braces ({}) match for a character or string of characters in a filename.

EXAMPLE   9.31

```
1   % ls
    a.c b.c abc ab3 ab4 ab5 file1 file2 file3 file4 file5 foo faa fumble
2   % ls f{oo,aa,umble}
    foo faa fumble
3   % ls a{.c,c,b[3-5]}
    a.c ab3 ab4 ab5
```

EXPLANATION

1   All the files in the current directory are listed.

2   Files starting with f and followed by the strings oo, aa, or umble are listed. Spaces inside the curly braces will cause the error message Missing }.

3   Files starting with a followed by .c, c, or b3, b4, or b5 are listed. (The square brackets can be used inside the curly braces.)

9.8.5   Escaping Metacharacters

The backslash is used to escape the special meaning of a single character. The escaped character will represent itself.

EXAMPLE 9.32

```
1   % gotta light?
    No match.
2   % gotta light\?
    gotta: Command not found.
```

EXPLANATION

1   This is a little UNIX joke. The question mark is a file substitution metacharacter and evaluates to a single character. The shell looks for a file in the present working directory that contains the characters l-i-g-h-t, followed by a single character. If the shell cannot find the file, it reports No match. This shows you something about the order in which the shell parses the command line. The metacharacters are evaluated before the shell tries to locate the gotta command.

2   The backslash protects the metacharacter from interpretation, often called escaping the metacharacter. Now the shell does not complain about a No match, but searches the path for the gotta command, which is not found.

9.8.6   Tilde Expansion

The tilde character by itself expands to the full pathname of the user's home directory. When the tilde is prepended to a username, it expands to the full pathname of that user's home directory. When prepended to a path, it expands to the home directory and the rest of the pathname.

EXAMPLE 9.33

```
1   % echo ~
    /home/jody/ellie
2   % cd ~/desktop/perlstuff
    % pwd
    /home/jody/ellie/desktop/perlstuff
3   % cd ~joe
    % pwd
    /home/bambi/joe
```

EXPLANATION

1   The tilde expands to the user's home directory.

2   The tilde followed by a pathname expands to the user's home directory, followed by /desktop/perlstuff.

3   The tilde followed by a username expands to the home directory of the user. In this example, the directory is changed to that user's home directory.

9.8.7   Filename Completion: The `filec` Variable

When running interactively, the C/TC shell provides a shortcut method for typing a file-name or username. The built-in `filec` variable, when set, is used for what is called file-name completion. If you type the first few significant characters of a file in the current working directory and press the Esc key, the shell fills in the rest of the filename, pro-vided that there are not a number of other files beginning with the same characters. If you type Ctrl-D after the partial spelling of the file, the shell will print out a list of files that match those characters. The terminal beeps if there are multiple matches. If the list begins with a tilde, the shell attempts to expand that list to a username.

EXAMPLE   9.34

```
1   % set filec
2   % ls
    rum rumple rumplestilsken run2
3   % ls ru[ESC]ᵃ     # terminal beeps
4   % ls rum^D
    rum rumple rumplestilsken
5   % ls rump[ESC]
    rumple
6   % echo ~ell[ESC]
    /home/jody/ellie
```

a.   [ESC] stands for Esc key.

EXPLANATION

1   The special C shell variable `filec` is set. Filename completion can be used.
2   The files in the present working directory are listed.
3   Filename completion is attempted. The letters r and u are not unique; that is, the shell does not know which one to pick, so it causes the terminal to beep.
4   After the letters r-u-m are typed, ^D is pressed. A list of all filenames beginning with rum are displayed.
5   The first filename starting with rump is completed and displayed.
6   If a tilde precedes a partially spelled username, the shell will attempt to complete the spelling of the user's name and display the user's home directory.

9.8.8   Turning Off Metacharacters with `noglob`

If the `noglob` variable is set, filename substitution is turned off, meaning that all meta-characters represent themselves; they are not used as wildcards. This can be useful when searching for patterns in programs like grep, sed, or awk, which may contain metacharac-ters that the shell may try to expand.

EXAMPLE 9.35

```
1   % set noglob
2   % echo * ?? [] ~
    * ?? [] ~
```

EXPLANATION

1   The variable noglob is set. It turns off the special meaning of the wildcards.

2   The metacharacters are displayed as themselves without any interpretation.

9.9 Redirection and Pipes

Normally, standard output (stdout) from a command goes to the screen, standard input (stdin) comes from the keyboard, and error messages (stderr) go to the screen. The shell allows you to use the special redirection metacharacters to redirect the input/output to or from a file. The redirection operators (<, >, >>, >&) are followed by a filename. This file is opened by the shell before the command on the left-hand side is executed.

Pipes, represented by a vertical bar (|) symbol, allow the output of one command to be sent to the input of another command. The command on the left-hand side of the pipe is called the *writer* because it writes to the pipe. The command on the right-hand side of the pipe is the *reader* because it reads from the pipe. See Table 9.5 for a list of redirection and pipe metacharacters.

Table 9.5   Redirection Metacharacters

Metacharacter	Meaning
command < file	Redirects input from file to command.
command > file	Redirects output from command to file.
command >& file	Redirects output and errors to file.
command >> file	Redirects output of command and appends it to file.
command >>& file	Redirects and appends output and errors of command to file.
command << WORD <input> WORD	Redirects input from first WORD to terminating WORD to command; start of here document. User input goes here. It will be treated as a doubly quoted string of text. WORD marks the termination of input to command; end of here document.
command | command	Pipes output of first command to input of second command.
command |& command	Pipes output and errors of first command to input of second command.
command >! file	If the noclobber variable is set, override its effects for this command and either open or overwrite file.

Table 9.5 Redirection Metacharacters (continued)

Metacharacter	Meaning
command >>! file	Override noclobber variable; if file does not exist, it is created and output from command is appended to it.
command >>&! file	Override noclobber variable; if file does not exist, it is created and both output and errors are appended to it.

9.9.1 Redirecting Input

Instead of the input coming from the terminal keyboard, it can be redirected from a file. The shell will open the file on the right-hand side of the < symbol and the program on the left will read from the file. If the file does not exist, the error No such file or directory will be reported by the C shell.

FORMAT

    command < file

EXAMPLE 9.36

    mail bob < memo

EXPLANATION

The file memo is opened by the shell, and the input is redirected to the mail program. Simply, the user bob is sent a file called memo by the mail program.

9.9.2 The here document

The here document is another way to redirect input to a command. It is used in shell scripts for creating menus and processing input from other programs. Normally, programs that accept input from the keyboard are terminated with Ctrl-D (^D). The here document provides an alternate way of sending input to a program and terminating the input without typing ^D. The << symbol is followed by a user-defined word, often called a *terminator*. Input will be directed to the command on the left-hand side of the << symbol until the user-defined terminator is reached. The final terminator is on a line by itself, and cannot be surrounded by any spaces. Variable and command substitution are performed within the here document. (Normally, a here document is used in shell scripts to create menus and provide input to commands such as mail, bc, ex, ftp, etc.)

FORMAT

```
command << MARK
        ... input ...
MARK
```

EXAMPLE 9.37

```
(Without the here document)
(The Command Line)
1    % cat
2    Hello There.
     How are you?
     I'm tired of this.
3    ^D

(The Output)
4    Hello There.
     How are you?
     I'm tired of this.
```

EXPLANATION

1 The cat program, without arguments, waits for keyboard input.

2 The user types input at the keyboard.

3 The user types ^D to terminate input to the cat program.

4 The cat program sends its output to the screen.

EXAMPLE 9.38

```
(With the here document)
(The Command Line)
1    % cat << DONE
2    Hello There.
     How are you?
     I'm tired of this.
3    DONE

(The Output)
4    Hello There.
     How are you?
     I'm tired of this.
```

EXPLANATION

1 The cat program will receive input from the first DONE to the terminating DONE. The words are user-defined terminators.

2 These lines are input. When the word DONE is reached, no more input is accepted.

EXPLANATION (CONTINUED)

3   The final terminator marks the end of input. There cannot be any spaces on either side of this word.

4   The text between the first word DONE and the final word DONE is the output of the cat command (from "here" to "here") and is sent to the screen. The final DONE must be against the left margin with no space or other text to the right of it.

EXAMPLE 9.39

```
(The Command Line)
1    % set name = steve
2    % mail $name << EOF
3    Hello there, $name
4    The hour is now `date +%H`
5    EOF
```

EXPLANATION

1   The shell variable name is assigned the username steve. (Normally, this example would be included in a shell script.)

2   The variable name is expanded within the here document.

3   The mail program will receive input until the terminator EOF is reached.

4   Command substitution is performed within the here document; that is, the command within the backquotes is executed and the output of the command is replaced within the string.

5   The terminator EOF is reached, and input to the mail program is stopped.

9.9.3   Redirecting Output

By default, the standard output of a command or commands goes to the terminal screen. To redirect standard output from the screen to a file, the > symbol is used. The command is on the left-hand side of the > symbol, and a filename is on the right-hand side. The shell will open the file on the right-hand side of the > symbol. If the file does not exist, the shell will create it; if it does exist, the shell will open the file and truncate it. Often files are inadvertently removed when using redirection. (A special C/TC shell variable, called noclobber, can be set to prevent redirection from clobbering an existing file. See Table 9.6 on page 439.)

FORMAT

```
command > file
```

EXAMPLE 9.40

```
cat file1 file2 > file3
```

EXPLANATION

The contents of file1 and file2 are concatenated and the output is sent to file3. Remember that the shell opens file3 before it attempts to execute the cat command. If file3 already exists and contains data, the data will be lost. If file3 does not exist, it will be created.

9.9.4   Appending Output to an Existing File

To append output to an existing file, the >> symbol is used. If the file on the right-hand side of the >> symbol does not exist, it is created; if it does exist, the file is opened and output is appended to the end of the file.

FORMAT

```
command >> file
```

EXAMPLE 9.41

```
date >> outfile
```

EXPLANATION

The standard output of the date command is redirected and appended to outfile.

9.9.5   Redirecting Output and Error

The >& symbol is used to redirect both standard output and standard error to a file. Normally, a command is either successful and sends its output to stdout, or fails and sends its error messages to stderr. Some recursive programs, such as find and du, send both standard output and errors to the screen as they move through the directory tree. By using the >& symbol, both standard output and standard error can be saved in a file and examined. The C/TC shell does not provide a symbol for redirection of only standard error, but it is possible to get just the standard error by executing the command in a subshell. See Example 9.42 and Figure 9.2.

EXAMPLE 9.42

```
1   % date
    Tue Aug 9 10:31:56  PDT  2004
2   % date >& outfile
3   % cat outfile
    Tue Aug 9 10:31:56  PDT  2004
```

EXPLANATION

1   The output of the date command is sent to standard output, the screen.

2   The output and errors are sent to outfile.

3   Because there were no errors, the standard output is sent to outfile and the contents of the file are displayed.

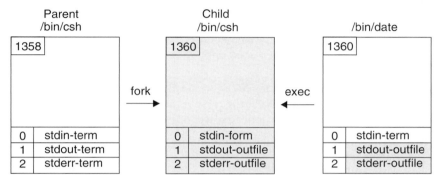

Figure 9.2   Redirecting stdout and stderr. See Example 9.42.

EXAMPLE 9.43

```
1    % cp file1 file2
2    % cp file1
     Usage: cp [-ip] f1 f2; or: cp [-ipr] f1 ... fn d2
3    % cp file1 >& errorfile
4    % cat errorfile
     Usage: cp [-ip] f1 f2; or: cp [-ipr] f1 ... fn d2
```

EXPLANATION

1   To copy a file, the cp command requires both a source file and a destination file. The cp command makes a copy of file1 and puts the copy in file2. Because the cp command is given the correct syntax, nothing is displayed to the screen. The copy was successful.

2   This time the destination file is missing and the cp command fails, sending an error to stderr, the terminal.

3   The >& symbol is used to send both stdout and stderr to errorfile. Because the only output from the command is the error message, that is what is saved in errorfile.

4   The contents of errorfile are displayed, showing that it contains the error message produced by the cp command.

9.9.6   Separating Output and Errors

Standard output and standard error can be separated by enclosing the command in parentheses. When a command is enclosed in parentheses, the C/TC shell starts up a subshell, handles redirection from within the subshell, and then executes the command. By using the technique shown in Example 9.44, the standard output can be separated from the errors.

EXAMPLE 9.44

(The Command Line)
```
1   % find . -name '*.c' -print >& outputfile
2   % (find . -name '*.c' -print > goodstuff) >& badstuff
```

EXPLANATION

1   The find command will start at the current directory, searching for all files ending in .c, and will print the output to outputfile. If an error occurs, that will also go into outputfile.

2   The find command is enclosed within parentheses. The shell will create a subshell to handle the command. Before creating the subshell, the words outside the parentheses will be processed; that is, the badstuff file will be opened for both standard output and error. When the subshell is started, it inherits the standard input, output, and errors from its parent. The subshell then has standard input coming from the keyboard, and both standard output and standard error going to the badstuff file. Now the subshell will handle the > operator. The stdout will be assigned the file goodstuff. The output is going to goodstuff, and the errors are going to badstuff. See Figure 9.3.

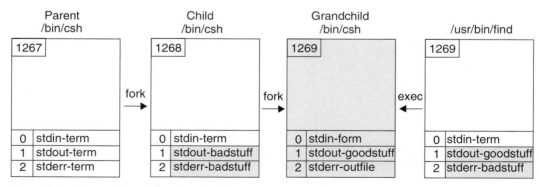

Figure 9.3   Separating stdout and stderr.

9.9.7 The noclobber Variable

The special shell built-in variable noclobber, when set, protects you from clobbering files with redirection. See Table 9.6.

Table 9.6 The noclobber Variable and Redirection

noclobber **Is Not Set**	**If File Exists**	**If File Does Not Exist**
command > file	file is overwritten	file is created
command >> file	file is appended to	file is created
noclobber **Is Set**		
command > file	Error message	file is created
command >> file	file is appended to	Error message
Overwriting noclobber		
command >! file	If the noclobber variable is set, override its effects for this command and either open or truncate file, redirecting output of command to file.	
command >>! file	Override noclobber variable; if file does not exist, it is created and output from command is appended to it. (See Example 9.45.)	

EXAMPLE 9.45

```
1   % cat filex
    abc
    123
2   % date > filex
3   % cat filex
    Wed Aug 5 11:51:04  PDT 2004
4   % set noclobber
5   % date > filex
    filex: File exists.
6   % ls >! filex      # Override noclobber for this command only
    % cat filex
    abc
    ab1
    dir
    filex
    plan.c
7   % ls > filex
    filex:  File exists.
8   % unset noclobber    # Turn off noclobber permanently
```

EXPLANATION

1   The contents of `filex` are displayed on the screen.

2   The output of the `date` command is redirected to `filex`. The file is truncated and its original contents overwritten.

3   The contents of `filex` are displayed.

4   The `noclobber` variable is set.

5   Since `filex` already exists and `noclobber` is set, the shell reports that the file exists and will not allow it to be overwritten.

6   The output of `ls` is redirected to `filex` because the `>!` operator overrides the effects of `noclobber`.

7   The effects of the `>!` symbol were temporary. It does not turn off `noclobber`. It simply overrides `noclobber` for the command where it is implemented.

8   The `noclobber` variable is unset.

9.10 Variables

C/TC shell variables hold only strings or a set of strings. Some variables are built into the shell and can be set by turning them on or off, such as the `noclobber` or `filec` variable. Others are assigned a string value, such as the `path` variable. You can create your own variables and assign them to strings or the output of commands. Variable names are case sensitive and may contain up to 20 characters consisting of numbers, letters, and the underscore.

There are two types of variables: *local* and *environment*. Local variables are created with the `set` command. Global variables are created with the `setenv` command. The scope of a variable is its visibility. A local variable is visible to the shell where it is defined. The scope of environment variables is often called *global*. Their scope is for this shell and all processes spawned (started) from this shell.

The dollar sign ($) is a special metacharacter that, when preceding a variable name, tells the shell to extract the value of that variable. The `echo` command, when given the variable as an argument, will display the value of the variable after the shell has processed the command line and performed variable substitution.

The special notation $?, when prepended to the variable name, lets you know whether the variable has been set. If a one is returned, it means true, the variable has been set. If a zero is returned, it means false, the variable has not been set.

EXAMPLE   9.46

```
1   % set filec
2   % set history = 50
3   % set name = George
4   % set machine = `uname -n`
5   % echo  $?machine
    1
6   % echo  $?blah
    0
```

1 Sets the built-in variable filec for filename completion. It is either on or off.
2 Sets the built-in variable history to 50 to control the number of events displayed.
3 Sets the user-defined variable name to George.
4 Sets the user-defined variable machine to the output of the UNIX command. The command is in backquotes, telling the shell to perform command substitution.
5 Because $? is prepended to the variable name to test whether the variable has been set. Since the test yields a 1 (true), the variable has been set.
6 The $? yields 0 (false). The variable has not been set.

9.10.1 Curly Braces

Curly braces insulate a variable from any characters that may follow it.

EXAMPLE 9.47

```
1    % set var = net
     % echo $var
     net
2    % echo $varwork
     varwork: Undefined variable.
3    % echo ${var}work
     network
```

EXPLANATION

1 The curly braces surrounding the variable name insulate the variable from characters that follow it.
2 A variable called varwork has not been defined. The shell prints an error message.
3 The curly braces shield the variable from characters appended to it. $var is expanded and the string work is appended.

9.10.2 Local Variables

Local variables are known only in the shell where they were created. If a local variable is set in the .cshrc file, the variable will be reset every time a new C shell is started. By convention, local variables are named with lowercase letters.

Setting Local Variables. If the string being assigned contains more than one word, it must be quoted; otherwise, only the first word will be assigned to the variable. It does not matter if there are spaces around the equal sign, but if there is a space on one side of the equal sign, there must be one on the other side.

EXAMPLE 9.48

```
1   % set round = world
2   % set name = "Santa Claus"
3   % echo $round
     world
4   % echo $name
    Santa Claus
5   % csh             # Start a subshell
6   % echo $name
    name: Undefined variable.
```

EXPLANATION

1   The local variable round is assigned the value world.

2   The local variable name is assigned the value Santa Claus. The double quotes keep the shell from evaluating the whitespace between Santa and Claus.

3   The dollar sign prepended to the variable allows the shell to perform variable substitution, that is, to extract the value stored in the variable.

4   Variable substitution is performed.

5   A new C shell (called a subshell) process is started.

6   In the subshell, the variable name has not been defined. It was defined in the parent shell as a local variable.

The set Command.   The set command prints all local variables set for this shell.

EXAMPLE 9.49

```
(The Command Line--Linux/tcsh)
> set
addsuffix
argv          ()
cwd           /home/jody/meta
dirstack      /home/ellie/meta
echo_style both
edit
gid       501
group     ellie
history   500
home    /home/ellie
i         /etc/profile.d/mc.csh
owd     /home/ellie
noclobber
path    (/usr/sbin /sbin /usr/local/bin /bin  /usr/bin /usr/X11R6/bin )
```

EXAMPLE 9.49 (CONTINUED)

```
prompt     [%n@%m  %c]#
prompt2    %R?
prompt3    CORRECT>%R  (y|n|e|a)?
savedirs
shell      /bin/tcsh
shlvl      2
status     0
tcsh       6.07.09
term       xterm
user       ellie
version tcsh 6.07.09 (Astron) 2004-07-07 (i386-intel-linux)
options 8b,nls,dl,al,rh,color
```

EXPLANATION

All of the local variables set for this shell are printed. Many of these variables, such as history, dirstack, and noclobber, are set in the .tcshrc file. Others, such as argv, cwd, shell, term, user, version, and status variables are preset, built-in variables.

EXAMPLE 9.50

```
(The Command Line--UNIX/csh)
% set
argv       ()
cwd        /home/jody/ellie
fignore    .o
filec
history    500
home       /home/jody/ellie
hostname   jody
ignoreeof
noclobber
notify
path       (/home/jody/ellie /bin /usr/local /usr/usr/bin/usr/etc .)
prompt     jody%
shell      /bin/csh
status     0
term       sun-cmd
user       ellie
```

EXPLANATION

All of the local variables set for this shell are printed. Most of these variables are set in the .cshrc file. The argv, cwd, shell, term, user, and status variables are preset, built-in variables.

Read-Only Variables (tcsh).   Read-only variables are local variables that, once set, cannot be changed or unset or an error message will result. Environment variables cannot be made read-only. If using the C shell, the following example will cause the error: set: Syntax error.

EXAMPLE 9.51

```
1   > set -r name = Tommy
2   > unset name
    unset: $name is read-only.
3   > set name = Danny
    set: $name is read-only
```

Built-In Local Variables.   The shell has a number of predefined variables with their own definitions. Some of the variables are either on or off. For example, if you set noclobber, the variable is on and effective, and when you unset noclobber, it is turned off. Some variables require a definition when set. Built-in variables are usually set in the .cshrc file for the C shell and the .tschrc file for the TC shell if they are to be effective for different C/TC shells. Some of the built-in variables already discussed include noclobber, cdpath, history, filec, and noglob. For a complete list, see Table 9.26 on page 514.

9.10.3 Environment Variables

Environment variables are often called *global* variables. They are defined in the shell where they were created and inherited by all shells spawned from that shell. Although environment variables are inherited by subshells, those defined in subshells are not passed back to parent shells. Inheritance is from parent to child, not the other way around (like real life). By convention, environment variables are named with uppercase letters.

EXAMPLE 9.52

```
(The Command Line)
1   % setenv TERM wyse
2   % setenv PERSON "Joe Jr."
3   % echo $TERM
    wyse
4   % echo $PERSON
    Joe Jr.
5   % echo $$         # $$ evaluates to the PID of the current shell
    206
6   % csh             # Start a subshell
7   % echo $$
    211
```

EXAMPLE   9.52 (CONTINUED)

```
8    % echo $PERSON
     Joe Jr.
9    % setenv PERSON "Nelly Nerd"
10   % echo $PERSON
     % Nelly Nerd
11   % exit              # Exit the subshell
12   % echo $$
     206
13   % echo $PERSON      # Back in parent shell
     Joe Jr.
```

EXPLANATION

1   The shell environment variable TERM is set to a wyse terminal.

2   The user-defined variable PERSON is set to Joe Jr.. The quotes are used to protect the space.

3   The dollar sign ($) prepended to the variable name allows the shell to evaluate the contents of the variable, called variable substitution.

4   The value of the environment variable PERSON is printed.

5   The $$ variable contains the PID of the current shell. The PID is 206.

6   The csh command starts a new C shell, called a subshell.

7   The PID of the current shell is printed. Because this is a new C shell, it has a different PID number. The PID is 211.

8   The environment variable PERSON was inherited by the new shell.

9   The PERSON variable is reset to Nelly Nerd. This variable will be inherited by any shells spawned from this shell.

10   The new value of the PERSON variable is printed.

11   This C shell is exited.

12   The original C shell is running; to attest to that, the PID 206 is printed. It is the same as it was before the subshell was started.

13   The PERSON variable contains its original value.

Printing Environment Variables.   The printenv (BSD) and env (SVR4) commands (both work in Linux) print all the environment variables set for this shell and its subshells. The setenv command prints variables and their values on both the BSD and SVR4 versions of the C shell.

EXAMPLE 9.53

(Linux/tcsh Example)

```
> env  or  printenv  or  setenv
USERNAME=root
COLORTERM=rxvt-xpm
HISTSIZE=1000
HOSTNAME=homebound
LOGNAME=ellie
HISTFILESIZE=1000
MAIL=/var/spool/mail/ellie
MACHTYPE=i386
COLORFGBG=0;default;15
TERM=xterm
HOSTTYPE=i386-linux
PATH=/usr/sbin:/sbin:/usr/local/bin:/bin:/usr/bin:/usr/
X11R6/bin:/home/ellie/bin;/root/bash-2.03/:/usr/X11R6/bin:/home/
ellie/bin;/root/bash-2.03/:/usr/X11R6/bin
HOME=/root
SHELL=/bin/bash
PS1=[\u@\h \W]\$
USER=ellie
VENDOR=intel
GROUP=ellie
HOSTDISPLAY=homebound:0.0
DISPLAY=:0.0
HOST=homebound
OSTYPE=linux
WINDOWID=37748738
PWD=/home/ellie
SHLVL=6
_=/usr/bin/env
```

EXPLANATION

The environment variables are set for this session and all processes that are started from this shell are displayed by using either one of the built-in commands: env or print-env. Many applications require the setting of environment variables. For example, the mail command has a MAIL variable set to the location of the user's mail spooler and the xterm program has a DISPLAY variable that determines which bit map display terminal to use. When any of these programs are executed, the values in their respective variables are passed on to them.

EXAMPLE 9.54

(UNIX/Solaris/csh Example)

```
% env
FONTPATH=/usr/local/OW3/lib/fonts
HELPPATH=/usr/local/OW3/lib/locale:/usr/local/OW3/lib/help
HOME=/home/jody/ellie
LD_LIBRARY_PATH=/usr/local/OW3/lib
LOGNAME=ellie
MANPATH=/ur/local/man:/usr/local/man:/usr/local/doctools/man:/usr/man
NOSUNVIEW=0
OPENWINHOME=/usr/local/OW3
PATH=/bin:/usr/local:/usr:/usr/bin:/usr/etc:/home/5bin:/usr/
    doctools:/usr:.
PWD=/home/jody/ellie
SHELL=/bin/csh
TERM=sun-cmd
USER=ellie
WINDOW_PARENT=/dev/win0
WINDOW_TTYPARMS=
WMGR_ENV_PLACEHOLDER=/dev/win3
```

9.10.4 Arrays

In the C shell, an array is simply a list of words, separated by spaces or tabs, and enclosed in parentheses. The elements of the array are numbered by subscripts starting at 1. If there is not an array element for a subscript, the message Subscript out of range is displayed. Command substitution will also create an array. If the $# notation precedes an array name, the number of elements in the array is displayed.

EXAMPLE 9.55

```
1   % set fruit = ( apples pears peaches plums )
2   % echo $fruit
    apples pears peaches plums
3   % echo $fruit[1]        # Subscripts start at 1
    apples
4   % echo $fruit[2-4]      # Prints the 2nd, 3rd, and 4th elements
    pears peaches plums
5   $ echo $fruit[6]
    Subscript out of range.
6   % echo $fruit[*]        # Prints all elements of the array
    apples pears peaches plums
7   % echo $#fruit          # Prints the number of elements
    4
```

EXAMPLE 9.55 (CONTINUED)

```
8   % echo $fruit[$#fruit]       # Prints the last element
    plums
9   % set fruit[2] = bananas     # Reassigns the second element
    % echo $fruit
    apples bananas peaches plums
10  % set path = ( ~ /usr/bin /usr /usr/local/bin . )
    % echo $path
    /home/jody/ellie /usr/bin /usr /usr/local/bin .
11  % echo $path[1]
    /home/jody/ellie
```

EXPLANATION

1   The wordlist is enclosed within parentheses. Each word is separated by whitespace. The array is called fruit.

2   The words in the fruit array are printed.

3   The first element of the fruit array is printed. The subscripts start at 1.

4   The second, third, and fourth elements of the wordlist are printed. The dash allows you to specify a range.

5   The array does not have six elements. The subscript is out of range.

6   All elements of the fruit array are printed.

7   The $# preceding the array is used to obtain the number of elements in the array. There are four elements in the fruit array.

8   Because the subscript $#fruit evaluates to the total number of elements in the array, if that value is used as an index value of the array, that is, [$#fruit], the last element of the fruit array is printed.

9   The second element of the array is assigned a new value. The array is printed with its replaced value, bananas.

10 The path variable is a special C shell array of directories used to search for commands. By creating an array, the individual elements of the path can be accessed or changed.

11 The first element of path is printed.

The shift Command and Arrays.   If the built-in shift command takes an array name as its argument, it shifts off (to the left) the first element of the array. The length of the array is decreased by one. (Without an argument, the shift command shifts off the first element of the built-in argv array. See "Command-Line Arguments" on page 534.)

EXAMPLE 9.56

```
1   % set names = ( Mark Tom Liz Dan Jody )
2   % echo $names
    Mark Tom Liz Dan Jody
3   % echo $names[1]
    Mark
4   % shift  names
5   % echo $names
    Tom Liz Dan Jody
6   % echo $names[1]
    Tom
7   % set days = ( Monday Tuesday )
8   % shift days
9   % echo $days
    Tuesday
10  % shift days
11  % echo $days
12  % shift days
    shift: no more words.
```

EXPLANATION

1   The array is called names. It is assigned the list of words in parentheses. Each word is separated by whitespace.

2   The array is printed.

3   The first element of the array is printed.

4   The array is shifted to the left by one element. The word Mark is shifted off.

5   The array was decreased by one element after the shift.

6   The first element of the array, after the shift, is Tom.

7   An array called days is created. It has two elements, Monday and Tuesday.

8   The array days is shifted one to the left.

9   The array is printed. Tuesday is the only element left.

10 The array days is shifted again. The array is empty.

11 The days array is empty.

12 This time, attempting to shift causes the shell to send an error message indicating that it cannot shift elements from an empty array.

Creating an Array from a String.   You may want to create a wordlist out of a quoted string. This is accomplished by placing the string variable within a set of parentheses.

EXAMPLE 9.57

```
1   % set name = "Thomas Ben Savage"
    % echo $name[1]
    Thomas Ben Savage
2   % echo $name[2]
    Subscript out of range.
3   % set name = ( $name )
4   % echo $name[1] $name[2] $name[3]
    Thomas Ben Savage
```

EXPLANATION

1   The variable name is assigned the string Thomas Ben Savage.
2   When treated as an array, there is only one element, the entire string.
3   The variable is enclosed in parentheses, creating an array of words, called name.
4   The three elements of the new array are displayed.

9.10.5 Special Variables

Built into the C shell are several variables consisting of one character. The $ preceding the character allows variable interpretation. See Table 9.7.

Table 9.7 Variables and Their Meanings

Variable	Example	Meaning
$?var	echo $?name	Returns 1 if variable has been set, 0 if not.
$#var	echo $#fruit	Prints the number of elements in an array.
$$	echo $$	Prints the PID of the current shell.
$<	set name = $<	Accepts a line of input from user up to newline.

EXAMPLE 9.58

```
1   % set num
    % echo $?num
    1
2   % echo $path
    /home/jody/ellie   /usr/bin/   usr/local/bin
    % echo $#path
    3
```

EXAMPLE 9.58 (CONTINUED)

```
3   % echo $$
    245
    % csh              # Start a subshell
    % echo $$
    248
4   % set name = $<
    Christy Campbell
    % echo $name
    Christy Campbell
```

EXPLANATION

1   The variable num is set to null. The $? preceding the variable evaluates to one if the variable has been set (either to null or some value), and to zero if the variable has not been set.

2   The path variable is printed. It is an array of three elements. The $# preceding the variable extracts and prints the number of elements in the array.

3   The $$ is the PID of the current process, in this case, the C shell.

4   The $< variable accepts a line of input from the user up to, but not including, the newline, and stores the line in the name variable. The value of the name variable is displayed.

Pathname Variable Modifiers.   If a pathname is assigned to a variable, it is possible to manipulate the pathname variable by appending special C shell extensions to it. The pathname is divided into four parts: *head*, *tail*, *root*, and *extension*. See Table 9.8 for examples of pathname modifiers and what they do.

Table 9.8   Pathname Modifiers
set pn = /home/ellie/prog/check.c

Modifier	*Meaning*	*Example*	*Result*
:r	Root	echo $pn:r	/home/ellie/prog/check
:h	Head	echo $pn:h	/home/ellie/prog
:t	Tail	echo $pn:t	check.c
:e	Extension	echo $pn:e	c
:g	Global	echo $p:gt	(See Example 9.59)

EXAMPLE 9.59

```
1   % set pathvar = /home/danny/program.c
2   % echo $pathvar:r
    /home/danny/program
3   % echo $pathvar:h
    /home/danny
4   % echo $pathvar:t
    program.c
5   % echo $pathvar:e
    c
6   % set pathvar = ( /home/* )
    echo $pathvar
    /home/jody /home/local /home/lost+found /home/perl /home/tmp
7   % echo $pathvar:gt
    jody  local  lost+found  perl  tmp
```

EXPLANATION

1   The variable pathvar is set to /home/danny/program.c.

2   When :r is appended to the variable, the extension is removed when displayed.

3   When :h is appended to the variable, the head of the path is displayed; that is, the last element of the path is removed.

4   When :t is appended to the variable, the tail end of the path (the last element) is displayed.

5   When :e is appended to the variable, the extension is displayed.

6   The variable is set to /home/*. The asterisk expands to all the pathnames in the current directory starting in /home/.

7   When :gt is appended to the variable, the tail end of each (global) of the path elements is displayed.

9.11 Command Substitution

A string or variable can be assigned the output of a UNIX command by placing the command in backquotes. This is called *command substitution*. (On the keyboard, the backquote is normally below the tilde character.) If the output of a command is assigned to a variable, it is stored as a wordlist (see "Arrays" on page 447), not a string, so that each of the words in the list can be accessed separately. To access a word from the list, a subscript is appended to the variable name. Subscripts start at 1.

```
1  % echo The name of my machine is `uname -n`.
   The name of my machine is stardust.
2  % echo The present working directory is `pwd`.
   The present working directory is /home/stardust/john.
3  % set d = `date`
   % echo $d
   Sat Jun 20 14:24:21 PDT 2004
4  % echo $d[2] $d[6]
   Jun 2004
5  % set d = "`date`"
   % echo $d[1]
   Sat Jun 20 14:24:21 PDT 2004
```

EXPLANATION

1   The UNIX command uname -n is enclosed in backquotes. When the shell encounters the backquotes, it will execute the enclosed command, uname -n, and substitute the output of the command, stardust, into the string. When the echo command prints its arguments to standard output, the name of the machine will be one of its arguments.

2   The UNIX command pwd is executed by the shell and the output is substituted in place within the string.

3   The local variable d is assigned the output of the date command. The output is stored as a list of words (an array).

4   Elements 2 and 6 of the d array are printed. The subscripts start at 1.

5   Because the output is enclosed in double quotes, it is a single string rather than a wordlist.

9.11.1 Wordlists and Command Substitution

When a command is enclosed in backquotes and assigned to a variable, the resulting value is an array (wordlist). Each element of the array can be accessed by appending a subscript to the array name. The subscripts start at 1. If a subscript that is greater than the number of words in the array is used, the C shell prints Subscript out of range. If the output of a command consists of more than one line, the newlines are stripped from each line and replaced with a single space.

```
1  % set d = `date`
   % echo $d
   Fri Aug 27 14:04:49 PDT 2004
```

EXAMPLE 9.61 (CONTINUED)

```
2    % echo $d[1-3]
     Fri Aug 27
3    % echo $d[6]
     2004
4    % echo $d[7]
     Subscript out of range.
5    % echo "The calendar for the month of November is `cal 11 2004`"
     The calendar for month of November is November 2004 S M Tu W
     Th F S 1 2 3 4 5 6 7 8 9 10 11 12 13 14 15 16 17 18 19 20 21
     22 23 24 25 26 27 28 29 30
```

EXPLANATION

1   The variable d is assigned the output of the UNIX date command. The output is stored as an array. The value of the variable is displayed.

2   The first three elements of the array are displayed.

3   The sixth element of the array is displayed.

4   There are not seven elements in the array. The shell reports that the subscript is out of range.

5   The output spans more than one line. Each newline is replaced with a space. This may not be the output you expected.

EXAMPLE 9.62

```
1    % set machine = `rusers | awk '/tom/{print $1}'`
2    % echo $machine
     dumbo bambi dolphin
3    % echo $#machine
     3
4    % echo $machine[$#machine]
     dolphin
5    % echo $machine
     dumbo bambi dolphin
6    % shift $machine
     % echo $machine
     bambi dolphin
7    % echo $machine[1]
     bambi
8    % echo $#machine
     2
```

EXPLANATION

1   The output of the rusers command is piped to awk. If the regular expression tom is found, awk prints the first field. The first field, in this case, is the name of the machine(s) where user tom is logged on.

2   User tom is logged on three machines. The names of the machines are displayed.

3   The number of elements in the array is accessed by preceding the array name with $#. There are three elements in the array.

4   The last element of the array is displayed. The number of elements in the array ($#machine) is used as a subscript.

5   The array is displayed.

6   The shift command shifts the array to the left. The first element of the array is dropped and the subscripts are renumbered, starting at 1.

7   The first element of the array after the shift is displayed.

8   After the shift, the length of the array has decreased by one.

9.12 Quoting

The C/TC shell has a whole set of metacharacters that have some special meaning. In fact, almost any character on your keyboard that is not a letter or a number has some special meaning for the shell. Here is a partial list:

∗ ? [ ] $ ~ ! ∧ & { } ( ) > < | ; : %

The backslash and quotes are used to escape the interpretation of metacharacters by the shell. Whereas the backslash is used to escape a single character, the quotes can be used to protect a string of characters. There are some general rules for using quotes:

1. Quotes are paired and must be matched on a line. The backslash character can be used to escape a newline so that a quote can be matched on the next line.
2. Single quotes will protect double quotes, and double quotes will protect single quotes.
3. Single quotes protect all metacharacters from interpretation, with the exception of the history character (!).
4. Double quotes protect all metacharacters from interpretation, with the exception of the history character (!), the variable substitution character ($), and the backquotes (used for command substitution).

9.12.1   The Backslash

The backslash is used to escape the interpretation of a single character and, in the C shell, is the only character that can be used to escape the history character, the exclamation point (also called the bang). Often the backslash is used to escape the newline character. Backslash interpretation does not take place within quotes.

EXAMPLE 9.63

```
1   % echo Who are you?
    echo: No match.
2   % echo Who are you\?
    Who are you?
3   % echo This is a very,very long line and this is where \
    break the line.
    This is a very, very long line and this is where
    I break the line.
4   % echo "\\abc"
    \\abc
    % echo '\\abc'
    \\abc
    % echo \\abc
    \abc
5   % echo Wow\!
    Wow!
```

EXPLANATION

1   The question mark is used for filename expansion. It matches for a single character. The shell is looking for a file in the current directory that is spelled y-o-u, followed by a single character. Because there is not a file by that name in the directory, the shell complains that it could not find a match with No match.

2   The shell will not try to interpret the question mark, because it is escaped with the backslash.

3   The string is continued to the next line by escaping the newline with a backslash.

4   If the backslash is enclosed in either single or double quotes, it is printed. When not enclosed in quotes, the backslash escapes itself.

5   The exclamation point must be escaped with a backslash. Otherwise the C shell will perform history substitution.

9.12.2 Single Quotes

Single quotes must be matched on the same line and will escape all metacharacters with the exception of the history (bang) character (!). The history character is not protected because the C shell evaluates history before it does quotes, but not before backslashes.

EXAMPLE 9.64

```
1   % echo 'I need $5.00'
    I need $5.00
2   % echo 'I need $500.00 now\!\!'
    I need $500.00 now!!
```

EXAMPLE 9.64 (CONTINUED)

```
3  % echo 'This is going to be a long line so
   Unmatched '.
4  % echo 'This is going to be a long line so \
   I used the backslash to suppress the newline'
   This is going to be a long line so
   I used the backslash to suppress the newline
```

EXPLANATION

1 The string is enclosed in single quotes. All characters, except the history (bang) character (!), are protected from shell interpretation.

2 The !! must be protected from shell interpretation by using the backslash character.

3 The quotes must be matched on the same line, or the shell reports Unmatched '.

4 If the line is to be continued, the backslash character is used to escape the newline character. The quote is matched at the end of the next line. Even though the shell ignored the newline, the echo command did not.

9.12.3 Double Quotes

Double quotes must be matched, will allow variable and command substitution, and hide everything else except the history (bang) character (!). The backslash will not escape the dollar sign when enclosed in double quotes.

EXAMPLE 9.65

```
1  % set name = Bob
   % echo "Hi $name"
   Hi Bob
2  % echo "I don't have time."
   I don't have time.
3  % echo "WOW!"        # Watch the history metacharacter!
   ": Event not found.
4  % echo "Whoopie\!"
   Whoopie!
5  % echo "I need \$5.00"
   I need \.00
```

EXPLANATION

1 The local variable name is assigned the value Bob. The double quotes allow the dollar sign to be used for variable substitution.

2 The single quote is protected within double quotes.

EXPLANATION (CONTINUED)

3   Double or single quotes will not protect the exclamation point from shell inter-
    pretation. The built-in history command is looking for the last command that be-
    gan with a double quote and that event was not found.

4   The backslash is used to protect the exclamation point.

5   The backslash does not escape the dollar sign when used within double quotes.

9.12.4   The Quoting Game

As long as the quoting rules are adhered to, double quotes and single quotes can be used
in a variety of combinations in a single command. (See Chapter 15, "Debugging Shell
Scripts," on page 967 for a complete discussion on quoting.)

EXAMPLE   9.66

```
1   % set name = Tom
2   % echo "I can't give $name" ' $5.00\!'
    I can't give Tom $5.00!
3   % echo She cried, \"Oh help me\!' "', $name.
    She cried, "Oh help me!", Tom.
```

EXPLANATION

1   The local variable name is assigned Tom.

2   The single quote in the word can't is protected when enclosed within double
    quotes. The shell would try to perform variable substitution if the dollar sign in
    $5.00 were within double quotes. Therefore, the string $5.00 is enclosed in single
    quotes so that the dollar sign will be a literal. The exclamation point is protected
    with a backslash because neither double nor single quotes can protect it from shell
    interpretation.

3   The first conversational quotes are protected by the backslash. The exclamation
    point is also protected with a backslash. The last conversational quotes are en-
    closed in a set of single quotes. Single quotes will protect double quotes.

Quoting with the :q Modifier.   The :q modifier is used to replace double quotes.

EXAMPLE   9.67

```
1   % set name = "Daniel Savage"
2   % grep $name:q database
        same as
3   % grep "$name" database
4   % set food = "apple pie"
```

EXAMPLE 9.67 (CONTINUED)

```
5   % set dessert = ( $food "ice cream")
6   % echo $#dessert
    3
7   % echo $dessert[1]
    apple
8   % echo $dessert[2]
    pie
9   % echo $dessert[3]
    ice cream
10  % set dessert = ($food:q "ice cream")
11  % echo $#dessert
    2
12  % echo $dessert[1]
    apple pie
13  % echo $dessert[2]
    ice cream
```

EXPLANATION

1   The variable is assigned the string Daniel Savage.

2   When :q is appended to the variable, the variable is quoted. This is the same as enclosing the variable in double quotes.

3   The double quotes surrounding the variable $name allow variable substitution to take place, but protect any whitespace characters. Without the double quotes, the grep program will search for Daniel in a file called Savage and a file called database.

4   The variable food is assigned the string apple pie.

5   The variable dessert is assigned an array (wordlist) consisting of apple pie and ice cream.

6   The number of elements in the dessert array is three. When the food variable was expanded, the quotes were removed. There are three elements, apple, pie, and ice cream.

7   The first element of the array is printed. The variable expands to separated words if not quoted.

8   The second element of the array is printed.

9   Because "ice cream" is quoted, it is treated as one word.

10 The dessert array is assigned apple pie and ice cream. The :q can be used to quote the variable in the same way double quotes quote the variable; that is, $food:q is the same as "$food".

11 The array consists of two strings, apple pie and ice cream.

12 The first element of the array, apple pie, is printed.

13 The second element of the array, ice cream, is printed.

Quoting with the :x Modifier.   If you are creating an array and any of the words in the list contain metacharacters, :x prevents the shell from interpreting the metacharacters when performing variable substitution.

EXAMPLE 9.68

```
1   % set  things = "*.c  a??  file[1-5]"
    % echo $#things
    1
2   % set newthings = ( $things )
    set: No match.
3   % set newthings = ( $things:x )
4   % echo $#newthings
    3
5   % echo "$newthings[1] $newthings[2] $newthings[3] "
    *.c  a??   file[1-5]
6   % grep $newthings[2]:q filex
    The question marks in a?? would be used for filename expansion
    it is not quoted
```

EXPLANATION

1   The variable things is assigned a string. Each string contains a wildcard. The number of elements in the variable is one, one string.

2   When attempting to create an array out of the string things, the C shell tries to expand the wildcard characters to perform filename substitution within things and produces a No match.

3   The :x extension prevents the shell from expanding the wildcards in the things variable.

4   The array newthings consists of three elements.

5   To print the elements of the array, they must be quoted or, again, the shell will try to expand the wildcards.

6   The :q quotes the variable just as though the variable were surrounded by double quotes. The grep program will print any lines containing the pattern a?? in file filex.

9.13 New Features of the Interactive TC Shell

The TC shell is a public domain enhanced version of its predecessor, the Berkeley UNIX C shell. If you are using Linux, you will have this available to you rather than the traditional C shell. Although tcsh is included in most Linux distributions, it can also be ported to a number of other operating systems, including Solaris, Windows NT, HP-UX, QNX, and more. There are an assortment of new features in the TC shell. The remainder of this chapter covers these additional features, most of them shortcuts, including command-line editing, fancy prompts, programmable completions (filenames, commands, and variables), spelling correction, and so forth.

This section focuses only on the new features added to the TC shell. The topics covered in the last section apply to **both** the C shell and TC shell.

9.13.1 Versions of tcsh

To find out what version of tcsh you are using, type at the shell prompt:

```
which tcsh
```

To tell you in what directory tcsh is installed (normally /bin), and to print the version information, type:

```
/directory_path/tcsh -c 'echo $version'
```

EXAMPLE 9.69

```
1   which tcsh
    /bin/tcsh
2   /bin/tcsh -c 'echo $version'
    tcsh 6.07.09 (Astron) 1998-07-07 (i386-intel-linux) options
    8b,nls,dl,al,rh,color
```

9.13.2 The Shell Prompts

The TC shell has three prompts: the *primary* prompt, a > symbol; the *secondary* prompt, a question mark (?) followed by a tcsh command such as while, foreach, or if; and a third prompt used for the spelling correction feature. The primary prompt is the prompt that is displayed on the terminal after you have logged in. It can be reset. If you are writing scripts at the prompt that require tcsh programming constructs, for example, decision making or looping, the secondary prompt will appear so that you can continue on to the next line. It will continue to appear after each newline, until the construct has been properly terminated. The third prompt appears to confirm automatic spelling correction if spelling correction is turned on. (See "TC Shell Spelling Correction" on page 490.) It contains the string CORRECT > corrected command (y|n|e|a)?. The prompts can be customized by adding special formatting sequences to the prompt string. See Table 9.9.

Table 9.9 Prompt Strings

String	Description
%/	The current working directory
%~	The current working directory, where ~ represents the user's home directory and other users' home directories are represented by ~user
%c[[0]n], %.[[0]n]	The trailing component of the current working directory, or if n (a digit) is given, n trailing components

Table 9.9　Prompt Strings　(continued)

String	Description
%C	Like %c, but without ~ substitution
%h, %!, !	The current history event number
%M	The full hostname
%m	The hostname up to the first "."
%S (%s)	Start (stop) standout mode
%B (%b)	Start (stop) boldfacing mode
%U (%u)	Start (stop) underline mode
%t, %@	The time of day in 12-hour AM/PM format
%T	Like %t, but in 24-hour format
%p	The "precise" time of day in 12-hour AM/PM format, with seconds
%P	Like %p, but in 24-hour format
^c	c is parsed as in bindkey
\c	c is parsed as in bindkey
%%	A single %
%n	The user name
%d	The weekday in "Day" format
%D	The day in "dd" format
%w	The month in "Mon" format
%W	The month in "mm" format
%y	The year in "yy" format
%Y	The year in "yyyy" format
%l	The shell's tty
%L	Clears from the end of the prompt to the end of the display or the end of the line
%$	Expands the shell or environment variable name immediately after the $
%#	> (or the first character of the promptchars shell variable) for normal users, # (or the second character of promptchars) for the superuser
%{string%}	Includes string as a literal escape sequence; should be used only to change terminal attributes and should not move the cursor location; cannot be the last sequence in prompt
%?	The return code of the command executed just before the prompt
%R	In prompt2, the status of the parser; in prompt3, the corrected string; in history, the history string

The Primary Prompt. When running interactively, the prompt waits for you to type a command and press the Enter key. If you do not want to use the default prompt, reset it in the .tcshrc file and it will be set for this and all TC shells subsequently started. If you only want it set for this login session, set it at the shell prompt.

EXAMPLE 9.70

```
1   > set prompt = '[ %n@%m %c]# '
2   [ ellie@homebound ~]#  cd ..
3   [ ellie@homebound /home]#  cd ..
```

EXPLANATION

1   The primary prompt is assigned the user's login name (%n), followed by the host-name (%m), a space, and the current working directory. The string is enclosed in square brackets, followed by a #.

2   The new prompt is displayed. The ~ appearing in the prompt represents the user's home directory. The cd command changes directory to the parent directory.

3   The new prompt indicates the current working directory, /home. In this way the user always know what directory he or she is in.

The Secondary Prompt. The secondary prompt appears when you are writing online scripts at the prompt. The secondary prompt can be changed. Whenever shell programming constructs are entered, followed by a newline, the secondary prompt appears and continues to appear until the construct is properly terminated. Writing scripts correctly at the prompt takes practice. Once the command is entered and you press Enter, you cannot back up, and the tcsh history mechanism does not save commands typed at the secondary prompt.

EXAMPLE 9.71

```
1        > foreach pal (joe tom ann)
2        foreach? echo Hi $pal
3        foreach? end
         Hi joe
         Hi tom
         Hi ann
4        >
```

EXPLANATION

1   This is an example of online scripting. Because the TC shell is expecting further input after the foreach loop is entered, the secondary prompt appears. The foreach loop processes each word in the parenthesized list.

EXPLANATION (CONTINUED)

2   The first time in the loop, joe is assigned to the variable pal. The user joe is sent the contents of memo in the mail. Then next time through the loop, tom is assigned to the variable pal, and so on.

3   The end statement marks the end of the loop. When all of the items in the parenthe-sized list have been processed, the loop ends and the primary prompt is displayed.

4   The primary prompt is displayed.

EXAMPLE 9.72

```
1        > set prompt2='%R %% '
2        > foreach name ( joe tom ann )
3        foreach % echo Hi $name
4        foreach % end
         Hi joe
         Hi tom
         Hi ann
5        >
```

EXPLANATION

1   The secondary prompt, prompt2, is reset to the formatted string where %R is the name of the conditional or looping construct entered in line 2 at the primary prompt. The two percent signs will evaluate to one percent sign.

2   The foreach command has been started. This is a looping construct that must end with the keyword end. The secondary prompt will continue to appear until the loop is properly terminated.

3   The secondary prompt is foreach %.

4   After the end keyword is typed, the loop executes.

5   The primary prompt reappears awaiting user input.

9.14 The TC Shell Command Line

9.14.1   The Command Line and Exit Status

After logging in, the TC shell displays its primary prompt, by default a > symbol. The shell is your command interpreter. When the shell is running interactively, it reads com-mands from the terminal and breaks the command line into words. A command line consists of one or more words (or tokens) separated by whitespace (blanks and/or tabs) and terminated by a newline, generated by pressing the Enter key. The first word is the command, and subsequent words are the command's options and/or arguments. The command may be a Linux executable program such as ls or pwd, an alias, a built-in com-mand such as cd or jobs, or a shell script. The command may contain special characters, called *metacharacters,* that the shell must interpret while parsing the command line. If the last character in the command line is a backslash, followed by a newline, the line can be continued to the next line.[5]

Exit Status and the `printexitvalue` Variable. After a command or program terminates, it returns an *exit status* to the parent process. The exit status is a number between 0 and 255. By convention, when a program exits, if the status returned is 0, the program was successful in its execution. When the exit status is nonzero, then it failed in some way. If the program terminated abnormally, then 0200 is added to the status. Built-in commands that fail return an exit status of 1; otherwise, they return a status of 0.

The `tcsh` *status* variable or ? variable is set to the value of the exit status of the last command that was executed. Success or failure of a program is determined by the programmer who wrote the program. By setting the `tcsh` variable, `printexitvalue`, any time a program exits with a value other than 0, its status will automatically be printed.

EXAMPLE 9.73

```
1   > grep "ellie" /etc/passwd
    ellie:GgMyBsSJavd16s:501:40:E Quigley:/home/jody/ellie:/bin/tcsh
2   > echo $status   or echo $?
    0
3   > grep "nicky" /etc/passwd
4   > echo $status
    1
5   > grep "scott" /etc/passssswd
    grep: /etc/passssswd: No such file or directory
6   > echo $status
    2
7   > set printexitvalue
    > grep "XXX" /etc/passwd
    Exit 1
    >
```

EXPLANATION

1   The `grep` program searches for the pattern "`ellie`" in the /etc/passwd file and is successful. The line from /etc/passwd is displayed.

2   The status variable is set to the exit value of the `grep` command; 0 indicates success. The ? variable also holds the exit status. This is the variable used by the `bash` and `ksh` shells for checking exit status. (It is not used by `csh`.)

3   The `grep` program cannot find user `nicky` in the /etc/passwd file.

4   The `grep` program cannot find the pattern, so it returns an exit status of 1.

---

5. The length of the command line can be at least 256 characters.

5   The grep fails because the file /etc/passsswd cannot be opened.

6   Grep cannot find the file, so it returns an exit status of 2.

7   The special tcsh variable printexitvalue is set. It will automatically print the exit
    value of any command that exits with a nonzero value.

9.14.2   TC Shell Command-Line History

The history mechanism is built into the TC shell. It keeps in memory a sequentially
numbered list of the commands, called *events*, that you have typed at the command line.
As well as the number of the history event, it also keeps track of the time the event was
entered at the terminal. When the shell reads a command from the terminal, it breaks
the command line into words (using whitespace to designate a word break), saves the
line to the history list, parses it, and then executes it. The previous command typed is
always saved. You can recall a command at any time from the history list and re-execute
it without retyping the command. During a login session, the commands you type are
appended to the history list until you exit, at which time they can be saved in a file in
your home directory, called .history.[6] The terms *history list* and *history file* can be some-
what confusing. The history list consists of the command lines currently held in the
shell's memory. The history file, normally called .history, is the text file where those commands are saved for future use. The built-in variable, savehist, saves the history list to
the .history file when you log out, and loads its contents into memory when you start
up. (See –S and –L options to the history command in Table 9.10.) The history built-in
command displays the history list. It supports a number of arguments to control how
the history is displayed.

Table 9.10   The history Command and Options

Option	Meaning
-c	Clears the history list in memory, not the history file
-h	Prints history list without numbers
-L [filename]	Appends history file (.history or filename) to the history list
-M [filename]	Like -L, except merges contents of history file with current history list
n	n is a number, for example, history 5, controlling the number of lines displayed
-r	Prints history list in reverse
-S [filename]	Saves history list to .history or filename if given
-T	Prints timestamps in comment form

---

6. The name of the .history file can be changed by assigning the new name to the histfile shell variable.

Although the default name for the history file is .history, its name can be changed by assigning an alternative name to the built-in shell variable, histfile. The history shell variable is set to a number specifying how many commands to display and the histdup variable can be set so that duplicate entries are not added to the history file.

EXAMPLE 9.74

```
(The Command Line)
> history
1 17:12   cd
2 17:13   ls
3 17:13   more /etc/fstab
4 17:24   /etc/mount
5 17:54   sort index
6 17:56   vi index
```

EXPLANATION

The history list displays the last commands that were typed at the command line. Each event in the list is preceded with a number (called an event number) and the time that it was entered at the command line.

The history Variable.   The TC shell history variable can be set to the number of events from the history list that will be displayed on the terminal. Normally, this is set in the /etc/.cshrc or ~/.tcshrc file, the user's initialization file. It is set to 100 by default. You can also provide an optional second value for the history variable to control the way the history is formatted. This value uses the same formatting sequences as the prompt variable. (See Table 9.10.) The default format string for history is %h\t%T\t%R\n.

EXAMPLE 9.75

```
1  set history=1000
2  set history= ( 1000 '%B%h %R\n' )
3  history
   136 history
   137 set history = ( 1000 '%B%h %R\n' )
   138 history
   139 ls
   140 pwd
   141 cal
   141 pwd
   142 cd
```

EXPLANATION

1   The last 1,000 commands typed at the terminal can be displayed on the screen by typing the history command.

EXPLANATION (CONTINUED)

2   The last 1,000 commands typed at the terminal are displayed. The format string causes the history list to be displayed in bold text (%B) first with the event number (%h), then a space, and finally the command that was typed (%R) at the command line followed by a newline (\n).

3   When you type history, the new format is shown. This is only a selected section of the real history list.

Saving History and the savehist Variable.   To save history events across logins, set the savehist variable. This variable is normally set in the .tcshrc file, the user's initialization file. If the first value assigned to savehist is a number, it cannot exceed the number set in the history variable, if the history variable is set. If the second value is set to merge, the history list is merged with the existing history file instead of replacing it. It is sorted by timestamp, and the most recent events saved.

EXAMPLE   9.76

```
1  set savehist
2  set savehist = 1000
3  set savehist = 1000 merge
```

EXPLANATION

1   The commands from the history list are saved in the history file and will be at the top of the history list the next time you log in.

2   The history file is replaced with the last 1,000 commands from the history list, and saved. It will be displayed when you next log in.

3   Rather than replacing the existing history file, the current history list will be merged with the existing history file when you log out, and loaded into memory after you log in.

Displaying History.   The history command displays the events in the history list. The history command also has options that control the number of events and the format of the events that will be displayed. The numbering of events does not necessarily start at one. If you have 100 commands on the history list, and you have set the history variable to 25, you will only see the last 25 commands saved.

EXAMPLE   9.77

```
1  > set history = 10
2  > history
   1 ls
   2 vi file1
   3 df
```

EXAMPLE 9.77 (CONTINUED)

```
4 ps -eaf
5 history
6 more /etc/passwd
7 cd
8 echo $USER
9 set
10 ls
```

EXPLANATION

1   The history variable is set to 10. Only the last 10 lines of the history list will be displayed, even if there are many more.

2   The last 10 events from the history are displayed. Each command is numbered.

EXAMPLE 9.78

```
1   > history -h        # print without line numbers
    ls
    vi file1
    df
    ps -eaf
    history
    more /etc/passwd
    cd
    echo $USER
    set
    history -n
2   > history -c
```

EXPLANATION

1   With the h option, the history list is displayed without line numbers.

2   With the c option, the history list is cleared.

EXAMPLE 9.79

```
> history -r       # print the history list in reverse
11 history -r
10 history -h
 9 set
 8 echo $USER
 7 cd
 6 more /etc/passwd
 5 history
 4 ps -eaf
 3 df
 2 vi file1
 1 ls
```

EXPLANATION

The history list is displayed in reverse order.

EXAMPLE 9.80

```
> history 5        # prints the last 5 events on the history list
7    echo $USER
8    cd
9    set
10   history -n
11   history 5
```

EXPLANATION

The last five commands on the history list are displayed.

Accessing Commands from the History File.   There are several ways to access and repeat commands from the history list. A nice new feature is included with tcsh: You can use the arrow keys with history. They allow you to scroll up and down the history list, and to move left and right across lines, editing as you go; you can use a mechanism called history substitution to re-execute and fix spelling mistakes; or you can use the built-in emacs or vi editors to retrieve, edit, and execute previous commands. We'll step through each of these procedures and then you can choose whatever way works best for you.

1. **The Arrow Keys**

    To access commands from the history list, you can use the arrow keys on the keyboard to move up and down through the history list, and from left to right. You can edit any of the lines in the history list by using the standard keys for deleting, backspacing, and so on. As soon as you have edited the line, pressing the carriage return (Enter key) will cause the command line to re-execute. You can also use standard emacs or vi commands to edit the history list. (See Table 9.13 on page 475 and Table 9.14 on page 476.) The arrow keys behave the same way for both the vi and emacs keybindings. (See Table 9.11.)

Table 9.11   The Arrow Keys

Key	What It Does
↑	Up arrow moves up the history list
↓	Down arrow moves down the history list
→	Right arrow moves cursor to the right of history command
←	Left arrow moves cursor to the left of history command

2. **Re-executing and Bang! Bang!**

   To re-execute a command from the history list, use the exclamation point (bang) to start history substitution. The exclamation point can begin anywhere on the line and can be escaped with a backslash. If the ! is followed by a space, tab, or newline, it will not be interpreted. There are a number of ways to use history substitution to designate what part of the history list you want to redo. (See Table 9.12 on page 474.) If you type two exclamation points (!!), the last command is re-executed. If you type the exclamation point followed by a number, the number is associated with the command from the history list and the command is executed. If you type an exclamation point and a letter, the last command that started with that letter is executed. The caret (∧) is also used as a shortcut method for editing the previous command.

   After history substitution is performed, the history list is updated with the results of the substitution shown in the command. For example, if you type !! the last command will be re-executed and saved in the history list in its expanded form. If you want the last command to be added to the history list in its literal form; that is, !!, then set the histlit shell variable.

EXAMPLE 9.81

```
1   > date
    Mon Feb  8 12:27:35 PST 2004
2   > !!
    date
    Mon Aug  10 12:28:25 PST 2004
3   > !3
    date
    Mon Aug  10 12:29:26 PST 2004
4   > !d
    date
    Mon Aug  10 12:30:09 PST 2004
5   > dare
    dare: Command not found.
6   > ^r^t
    date
    Mon Apr  10 16:15:25 PDT 2004
7   > history
    1 16:16  ls
    2 16:16  date
    3 16:17  date
    4 16:18  date
    5 16:18  dare
    6 16:18  date
```

EXAMPLE   9.81 (CONTINUED)

```
8  > set histlit
9  > history
   1 16:18  ls
   2 16:19  date
   3 16:19  !!
   4 16:20  !3
   5 16:21  dare
   6 16:21  ^r^t
```

EXPLANATION

1   The date command is executed at the command line. The history list is updated. This is the last command on the list.

2   The !! (bang bang) gets the last command from the history list; the command is re-executed.

3   The third command on the history list is re-executed.

4   The last command on the history list that started with the letter d is re-executed.

5   The command is mistyped.

6   The carets are used to substitute letters from the last command on the history list. The first occurrence of an r is replaced with a t.

7   The history command displays the history list, after history substitution has been performed.

8   By setting histlit, the shell will perform history substitution, but will put the literal command typed on the history list; that is, just as it was typed.

9   When histlit is set, the output of the history command shows what commands were literally typed before history substitution took place. (This is just a demo; the history numbers are not accurate.)

EXAMPLE   9.82

```
1  % cat file1 file2 file3
      <Contents of files displayed here>
   > vi !:1
   vi file1
2  > cat file1 file2 file3
   <Contents of file, file2, and file3 are displayed here>
   > ls !:2
   ls file2
   file2
3  > cat file1 file2 file3
   > ls  !:3
   ls file3
   file3
```

EXAMPLE 9.82 (CONTINUED)

```
4   > echo a b c
    a b c
    > echo !$
    echo c
    c
5   > echo a b c
    a b c
    > echo !^
    echo a
    a
6   > echo a b c
    a b c
    > echo !*
    echo a b c
    a b c
7   > !!:p
    echo a b c
```

EXPLANATION

1 The cat command displays the contents of file1 to the screen. The history list is updated. The command line is broken into words, starting with word number zero. If the word number is preceded by a colon, that word can be extracted from the history list. The !:1 notation means: get the first argument from the last command on the history list and replace it in the command string. The first argument from the last command is file1. (Word 0 is the command itself.)

2 The !:2 is replaced with the second argument of the last command, file2, and given as an argument to ls. File2 is printed. (File2 is the third word.)

3 ls !:3 reads: go to the last command on the history list and get the fourth word (words start at zero) and pass it to the ls command as an argument. (File3 is the fourth word.)

4 The bang (!) with the dollar sign ($) refers to the last argument of the last command on the history list. The last argument is c.

5 The caret (^) represents the first argument after the command. The bang (!) with the ^ refers to the first argument of the last command on the history list. The first argument of the last command is a.

6 The asterisk (*) represents all arguments after the command. The bang (!) with the * refers to all of the arguments of the last command on the history list.

7 The last command from the history list is printed but not executed. The history list is updated. You could now perform caret substitutions on that line.

Table 9.12 Substitution and History

Event Designators	Meaning
!	Indicates the start of history substitution
!!	Re-executes the previous command
!N	Re-executes the Nth command from the history list
!-N	Re-executes the Nth command back from present command
!string	Re-executes the last command starting with string
!?string?	Re-executes the last command containing string
!?string?%	Re-executes the most recent command-line argument from the history list containing string
!^	Uses the first argument of the last history command in the current command line
!*	Uses all of the arguments from the last history command in the current command line
!$	Uses the last argument from the last history command in the current command line
!! string	Appends string to the previous command and executes
!N string	Appends string to Nth command in history list and executes
!N:s/old/new/	In previous Nth command, substitutes the first occurrence of old string with new string
!N:gs/old/new/	In previous Nth command, globally substitutes old string with new string
^old^new^	In last history command, substitutes old string with new string
command !N:wn	Executes current command appending an argument (wn) from the Nth previous command; wn is a number starting at 0, 1, 2, . . . designating the number of the word from the previous command; word 0 is the command itself, and 1 is its first argument, and so on
!N:p	Puts the command at the bottom of the history list and prints it, but doesn't execute it

9.14.3 The Built-In Command-Line Editors

The command line can be edited by using the same type of key sequences that you use in either the emacs or vi editors. You can use editor commands to scroll up and down the history list. Once the command is found, it can be edited, and by pressing the Enter key, re-executed. When the shell was compiled, it was given a default set of keybindings for the emacs editor.

The bindkey Built-In Command. The built-in bindkey command is used to select either vi or emacs for command-line editing and to list and set keybindings for the respective editors. To use vi as your command-line editor, use bindkey with the -v option:

bindkey -v

and to go back to emacs, type

bindkey -e

To see a list of editor commands and a short description of what each does, type

bindkey -1

To see the actual keys and how they are bound, type

bindkey

To actually bind keys to commands, see "Binding Keys" on page 477.

The vi Built-In Editor. To edit the history list, go to the command line and press the Esc key. Then press the K key if you want to scroll upward in the history list, and the J key to move downward, just like standard vi motion keys. When you find the command that you want to edit, use the standard keys that you would use in vi for moving left and right, deleting, inserting, and changing text. (See Table 9.13.) After making the edit, press the Enter key. The command will be executed and added to the bottom of the history list. If you want to add or insert text, then use any of the insertion commands (i, e, o, 0, etc.). Remember, vi has two modes: the command mode and the insert mode. You are always in the insert mode when you are actually typing text. To get back to the command mode, press the Esc key.

Table 9.13 vi Commands

Command	Function
Moving Through the History File	
Esc K *or* +	Move up the history list
Esc J *or* -	Move down the history list
G	Move to first line in history file
5G	Move to fifth command in history file
/string	Search upward through history file
?	String search downward through history file

Table 9.13 vi Commands (continued)

Command	Function
Moving Around on a Line	
h	Move left on a line
l	Move right on a line
b	Move backward a word
e or w	Move forward a word
^ or 0	Move to beginning of first character on the line
$	Move to end of line
Editing with vi	
a A	Append text
i I	Insert text
dd dw x	Delete text into a buffer (line, word, or character)
cc C	Change text
u U	Undo
yy Y	Yank (copy a line into buffer)
p P	Put yanked or deleted line down below or above the line
r R	Replace a letter or any amount of text on a line

The emacs Built-In Editor.   If you are using the emacs built-in editor, like vi, start at the command line. To start moving upward through the history file, press ^P. To move down, press ^N. Use emacs editing commands to change or correct text, then press Enter, and the command will be re-executed. See Table 9.14.

Table 9.14 emacs Commands

Command	Function
Ctrl-P	Move up history file
Ctrl-N	Move down history file
Esc <	Move to first line of history file
Esc >	Move to last line of history file
Ctrl-B	Move backward one character

Table 9.14 emacs Commands (continued)

Command	Function
Ctrl-R	Search backward for string
Esc B	Move back one word
Ctrl-F	Move forward one character
Esc F	Move forward one word
Ctrl-A	Move to the beginning of the line
Ctrl-E	Move to the end of the line
Esc <	Move to the first line of the history file
Esc >	Move to the last line of the history file

Editing with emacs

Ctrl-U	Delete the line
Ctrl-Y	Put the line back
Ctrl-K	Delete from cursor to the end line
Ctrl-D	Delete a letter
Esc D	Delete one word forward
Esc H	Delete one word backward
Esc (space)	Set a mark at cursor position
Ctrl-X Ctrl-X	Exchange cursor and mark
Ctrl-P Ctrl-Y	Push region from cursor to mark into a buffer (Ctrl-P) and put it down (Ctrl-Y)

Binding Keys.   The bindkey built-in command lists all the standard keybindings including keybindings for emacs and vi. The keybindings are divided up into four groups: the standard key bindings, alternative key bindings, multicharacter key bindings, and the arrow key bindings. The bindkey command also allows you to change the current bindings of keys.

EXAMPLE 9.83

```
1   > bindkey
    Standard key bindings
    "^@"          ->  is undefined
    "^A"          ->  beginning-of-line
    "^B"          ->  backward-char
    "^C"          ->  tty-sigintr
    "^D"          ->  list-or-eof
    "^E"          ->  end-of-line
    "^F"          ->  forward-char
    "^L"          ->  clear-screen
    "^M"          ->  newline
          ...      ....
    Alternative key bindings
    "^@"          ->  is undefined
    "^A"          ->  beginning-of-line
    "^B"          ->  is undefined
    "^C"          ->  tty-sigintr
    "^D"          ->  list-choices
    "^E"          ->  end-of-line
    "^F"          ->  is undefined
          ......   .....
    Multi-character bindings
    "^[[A"        -> up-history
    "^[[B"        -> down-history
    "^[[C"        -> forward-char
    "^[[D"        -> backward-char
    "^[OA"        -> up-history
    "^[OB"        -> down-history
          ...      ....
    Arrow key bindings
    down          -> down-history
    up            -> up-history
    left          -> backward-char
    right         -> forward-char
```

The -l option to bindkey lists the editor commands and what they do. See Example 9.84.

EXAMPLE 9.84

```
> bindkey -l

backward-char
        Move back a character
backward-delete-char
        Delete the character behind cursor
```

EXAMPLE 9.84 (CONTINUED)

```
backward-delete-word
        Cut from beginning of current word to cursor - saved in cut buffer
backward-kill-line
        Cut from beginning of line to cursor - save in cut buffer
backward-word
        Move to beginning of current word
beginning-of-line
        Move to beginning of line
capitalize-word
        Capitalize the characters from cursor to end of current word
change-case
        Vi change case of character under cursor and advance one character
change-till-end-of-line
        Vi change to end of line
clear-screen
Standard key bindings
        .....   ...
```

The bindkey command can also display the values for individual key bindings as shown in Example 9.85. The emacs mappings are shown by default, but with the -a option to bindkey, the alternate mappings for vi keys are displayed. The arguments to bindkey are specified as a sequence of special characters to represent the key sequences followed by the editing command key to which the key will be bound. See Table 9.15 for a list of these keybinding characters. You can bind keys not only to emacs or vi editor commands, but also to Linux commands and strings.

Table 9.15   Keybinding Characters

Characters	Meaning
^C	Ctrl-C
^[	Escape
^?	Delete
\a	Ctrl-G (bell)
\b	Ctrl-H (backspace)
\e	Esc (escape)
\f	Formfeed
\n	Newline
\r	Return

Table 9.15   Keybinding Characters (continued)

Characters	Meaning
\t	Tab
\v	Ctrl-K (vertical tab)
\nnn	ASCII octal number

Table 9.16   bindkey Options

bindkey	Lists All Key Bindings
bindkey -a	Allow alternate key mapping
bindkey -d	Restore default bindings
bindkey -e	Use emacs bindings
bindkey -l	Display all editing commands and what they mean
bindkey -u	Display usage message
bindkey -v	Use vi key bindings
bindkey key	Display binding for key
bindkey key command	Bind key to emacs or vi command
bindkey -c key command	Bind key to UNIX/Linux command
bindkey -s key string	Bind key to string
bindkey -r key	Remove key binding

EXAMPLE 9.85

```
1   > bindkey ^L
    "^L"       ->     clear-screen
2   > bindkey ^C
    "^C"       ->     tty-sigintr
3   > bindkey "j"
    "j"        ->     self-insert-command
4   > bindkey -v
5   > bindkey -a "j"
    "j"        ->     down-history
```

EXPLANATION

1   The bindkey command with a Ctrl key (^L) displays to what command the Ctrl key is bound. ^L causes the screen to be cleared.

2   Ctrl-C (^C) is bound to the interrupt signal, which normally terminates a process.

3   Lowercase "j" is an emacs self-insert command, which does nothing but insert that letter into the buffer.

4   In order to see the alternate vi key bindings, be sure you have set the vi command-line editor with bindkey -v as shown here.

5   With the -a option, bindkey displays the alternate key mapping for "j"; that is, the vi key for moving down the history list.

EXAMPLE 9.86

```
1   > bindkey "^T" clear-screen          # Create a new keybinding
2   > bindkey "^T"
    "^T"      ->      clear-screen
3   > bindkey -a "^T"                     # Alternate keybinding undefined
    "^T"      ->      undefined-key
4   > bindkey -a [Ctrl-v Control t] clear-screen    # Create an alternate keybinding
       Press keys one after the other
5   > bindkey -a [Ctrl-v Control t]
    "^T"      ->      clear-screen
6   > bindkey -s '\ehi'  'Hello to you!\n'        # Bind a key to a string
    > echo [Esc]hi    Press escape followed by 'h' and 'i'
    Hello to you!
    >
7   > bindkey '^[hi'
    "^[hi"    ->     "Hello to you!"
8   > bindkey -r '\[hi'               # Remove keybinding
9   > bindkey '\ehi'
    Unbound extended key "^[hi"
10  > bindkey -c '\ex' 'ls | more'    # Bind a key to a command
```

EXPLANATION

1   Ctrl-T is bound to the command to clear the screen, a default emacs key mapping. This key sequence was not originally bound to anything. Now when the Ctrl and T keys are pressed together, the screen will be cleared.

2   The bindkey command, with the key sequence as an argument, will display the mapping for that sequence, if there is one.

3   With the -a option and a key sequence, bindkey displays the value of the alternate key map, vi. In this example, bindkey with the -a option and the key sequence shows that the alternate mapping (vi) does not have this sequence bound to anything.

EXPLANATION (CONTINUED)

4   With the -a option, bindkey can bind keys to the alternate key map, vi. By pressing
     Ctrl-V followed by Ctrl-T, the key sequence is created and assigned the value
     clear-screen. Ctrl-V/Ctrl-T can also be represented as "^T" as shown in the previ-
     ous example.

5   The bindkey function displays the alternate mapping for ^T and its command.

6   With the -s command, bindkey will bind a literal string to a key sequence. Here the
     string "Hello to you!\n" is bound to the escape sequence hi. By pressing the Esc key
     and then an h and an i, the string will be sent to standard output.

7   The bindkey command displays the binding for the escape sequence hi. The ^[is
     another way to represent Esc (escape).

8   With the -r option, bindkey removes a key binding.

9   Because the keybinding was removed, the output says that this extended key se-
     quence is not bound.

10   With the -c option, bindkey can bind a key sequence to a Linux command. In this
     example, pressing the Esc key, followed by the "x" key, will cause the command
     ls to be piped to more.

9.15 TC Shell Command, Filename, and Variable Completion

To save typing, tcsh has a mechanism called *completion* that allows you to type part of a
command, filename, or variable, and then by pressing the Tab key, have the rest of the
word completed for you.

   If you type the first few letters of a command, and press the Tab key, tcsh will attempt
to complete the command name. If tcsh cannot complete the command, because it
doesn't exist, the terminal will beep and the cursor will stay at the end of the command.
If there is more than one command starting with those characters, by pressing Ctrl-D,
all commands that start with those characters will be listed.

   Filename and variable completion work the same as command completion. With filename completion, if there are several files starting with the same letters, tcsh will complete the shortest name that matches, expand out the filename until the characters differ,
and then flash the cursor for you to complete the rest. See Example 9.87.

9.15.1 The autolist Variable

If the autolist variable is set, and there are a number of possible completions, all of the
possible commands, variables, or filenames will be listed depending on what type of
completion is being performed when the Tab key is entered.

EXAMPLE 9.87

```
1    > ls
     file1 file2 foo foobarckle fumble
2    > ls fu[tab]           # expands to filename to fumble
3    > ls fx[tab]           # terminal beeps, nothing happens
4    > ls fi[tab]           # expands to file_  (_ is a cursor)
5    > set autolist
6    > ls f[tab]            # lists all possibilities
     file1 file2 foo foobarckle fumble
7    > ls foob[tab]         # expands to foobarckle
8    > da[tab]              # completes the date command
     date
     Fri Aug 9 21:15:38 PDT 2004
9    > ca[tab]              # lists all commands starting with ca
     cal    captoinfo  case   cat
10   > echo $ho[tab]me      # expands shell variables
     /home/ellie/
11   > echo $h[tab]
     history home
```

EXPLANATION

1   All files are listed for the current working directory.

2   After fu is typed, the Tab key is pressed, causing the filename to be completed to fumble, and listed.

3   Because none of the files start with fx, the terminal beeps and the cursor remains but does nothing.

4   There are a number of files starting with fi; the filenames are completed until the letters are no longer the same. When you press Ctrl-D, all files with that spelling are listed.

5   The autolist variable is set. If there are a number of choices, when you press the Tab key, autolist displays all the possibilities.

6   After you press the Tab key, a list of all files beginning with f are printed.

7   When the Tab key is pressed, the filename is expanded to foobarckle.

8   When the Tab key is pressed after da, the only command that begins with da is the date command. The command name is expanded and executed.

9   Because autolist is set, when the Tab key is pressed after ca, all commands starting with ca are listed. If autolist is not set, type Ctrl-D to get a list.

10 The leading $ on a word indicates that the shell should perform variable expansion when the Tab key is pressed to complete the word. The variable home is completed.

11 Variable completion is ambiguous in this example. When completion is attempted by pressing the Tab key, all possible shell variables are listed.

9.15.2   The fignore Variable

The shell variable, fignore, can be set to ignore certain filename extensions when file-name completion is in use. For example, you may not want to expand files that end in .o because they are unreadable object files. Or maybe you don't want the .gif files to be accidently removed when filenames are expanded. For whatever reason, the fignore vari-able can be assigned a list of extensions for files that will be excluded from filename expansion.

EXAMPLE   9.88

```
1   > ls
    baby       box.gif    file2     prog.c
    baby.gif   file1      file3     prog.o
2   > set fignore = (.o .gif )
3   > echo ba[tab]     # Completes baby but ignores baby.gif
    baby
4   > echo box[tab].gif    # fignore is ignored if only one completion is possible
    box.gif
5   > vi prog[tab]           # expands to prog.c
    Starts vi with prog.c as its argument
```

EXPLANATION

1   The files in the current working directory are listed. Note that some of the files have extensions on their names.

2   The fignore variable allows you to list those filename extensions that should be ig-nored when filename completion is performed. All filenames ending in either .o or .gif will be ignored.

3   By pressing the Tab key, only the file baby is listed, not baby.gif. The .gif files are ignored.

4   Even though .gif is listed as a suffix to be ignored, fignore will not take effect when there are no other possible completions, such as the same filename without the .gif extension as in line 3.

5   When the vi editor is invoked, prog is expanded to prog.c.

9.15.3   The complete Shell Variable

This is a variable that does a lot! It is a little tricky trying to decipher all it can do from the tcsh *man* page, but you may find some of these examples helpful for a start. You can control what kind of completion you are doing. For example, maybe you only want completion to expand directory names, or a filename depending on its position in the command line, or maybe you would like certain commands to be expanded and others excluded, or even create a list of possible words that can be expanded. Whatever it is you want to do with completion the complete shell variable will no doubt accommodate you.

Filename completion can be even more sophisticated if the complete shell variable is set to enhance. This causes Tab completion to ignore case; to treat hyphens, periods, and underscores as word separators; and to consider hyphens and underscores as equivalent.

EXAMPLE 9.89

```
1   > set complete=enhance
2   > ls g..[tab]    # expands to gawk-3.0.3
    gawk-3.0.3
3   > ls GAW[tab]    # expands to gawk-3.0.3
    gawk-3.0.3
```

EXPLANATION

1   By setting the complete shell variable to enhance, Tab completion will ignore case; will treat hyphens, periods, and underscores as word separators; and will consider hyphens and underscores as equivalent.

2   With enhance set, filename completion expands g.. to any files starting with a g, followed by any two characters (..), and any characters to complete the filename, including hyphens, periods, and so forth.

3   With enhance set, filename completion expands GAW to any files starting with GAW, where GAW can be any combination of uppercase and lowercase letters, and the remaining characters can be any characters even if they contain hyphens, periods, and underscores.

9.15.4   Programming Completions

To customize completions to a more specific functionality, you can program the completions, and then store them in the ~/.tcshrc file, making them part of your tcsh environment each time you start a new TC shell. The purpose of programming completions is to improve efficiency and select types of commands and arguments that will be affected. (The Tab key for word completion and Ctrl-D to list possible completions still work the same way as they did for simple completions.)

Types of Completions.   There three types of completions: p, n, and c. A p-type completion is position-dependent. It rules the way a completion is performed based on the *position* of a word in the command line, where position 0 is the command, position 1 is the first argument, position 2 is the second argument, and so on. Suppose, for example, you wanted to guarantee that any time a completion is performed for the built-in cd command, the first (and only) argument to cd is completed only if it is a directory name, nothing else; then you can program the completion as shown in the following example:

```
complete cd   'p/1/d/'
```

The complete command is followed by the cd command and what is called the completion *rule*. The p stands for the word *position* in the command line. The command, cd, is position 0 and its first argument is position 1. The pattern part of the rule is enclosed in slashes (p/1/ means position 1, the first argument to cd), and will be affected by the completion rule. The d part of the pattern is called a *word type*. See Table 9.17 on page 487 for a complete list of word types. The d word type means that only directories are to be affected by the completion. A filename or alias, for example, would not be completed if given as the first argument to cd. The rule states that whenever Tab completion is performed on the cd command, it will only take place if the first argument is a directory, and Ctrl-D will only list directories if the match is ambiguous; that is, there is more than one possible completion. See Example 9.90 for p-type completions.

EXAMPLE 9.90

```
# p-type completions (positional completion)

1   > complete
    alias    'p/1/a/'
    cd       'p/1/d/'
    ftp      'p/1/( owl ftp.funet.fi prep.ai.mit.edu )'
    man      'p/*/c/'
2   > complete vi 'p/*/t/'
3   > complete vi
    vi 'p/*/t/'
4   > set autolist
5   > man fin[tab]    # Completes command names
    find      find2perl   findaffix  findsmb   finger
6   > vi b[tab]        # Completes only  filenames, not directories
    bashtest binded bindings bindit
7   > vi na[tab]mes
8   > cd sh[tab]ellsolutions/
9   > set hosts = ( netcom.com 192.100.1.10 192.0.0.200 )
10  > complete telnet 'p/1/$hosts/'
11  > telnet net[tab]com.com
    telnet netcom.com
12  > alias m[tab]    # Completes alias names
    mc mroe mv
13  > ftp prep[tab]
```

EXPLANATION

1   The complete built-in command, without arguments, lists all programmed completions. The following examples (lines 2 through 11) use these completion rules.

2   This rule states that if Tab completion is used when typing arguments to the vi command, that all arguments (*), must be of type "t" (i.e., plain text files) for completion to performed.

EXPLANATION (CONTINUED)

3   The complete command, with the name of a command as its argument, displays the completion rule for that command. The completion rule for vi is displayed.

4   By setting the built-in command, autolist, all possible Tab completions will automatically be printed. (You don't have to press Ctrl-D.)

5   The man command has a programmed completion: complete man 'p/1/c/'. This rule states that the first argument given to the man command must be a command, because c is defined as a command word type. In this example, completion is attempted with the letters fin as the argument to man. All manual commands starting with fin will be displayed.

6   Only filenames will be completed, because the vi editor completion was programmed to complete only text files, not directories.

7   According to the vi completion rule, only text filenames will be completed, no matter how many arguments are passed.

8   When filename completion is performed on the first argument to the built-in cd command, the only word that will be completed must be the name of a directory as stated in the completion rule. The argument in this example will expand to a directory called shellsolutions.

9   The variable hosts is set to a list of IP addresses or hostnames.

10 The completion rule for telnet states that completion will be performed if position 1 contains one of the hostnames set in the hosts variable. This is a list word type completion.

11 The telnet command is executed and the word beginning with net, followed by pressing the Tab key, is completed to netcom.com, which is one of the hostnames in the hosts variable, previously set.

12 The alias completion is performed if the user types the word alias followed by a word that will be expanded to all aliases that contain that word. Word type a means only aliases are expanded for p, position 1.

Table 9.17   Completion Word Types

Word	Type
a	Alias
b	Editor keybinding commands
c	Commands (built-in or external commands)
C	External commands that begin with the supplied path prefix
d	Directory
D	Directories that begin with the supplied path prefix
e	Environment variables

Table 9.17   Completion Word Types (continued)

Word	Type
f	Filenames (not directory)
F	Filenames that begin with the supplied path prefix
g	Groupnames
j	Jobs
l	Limits
n	Nothing
s	Shell variables
S	Signals
t	Plain ("text") files
T	Plain ("text") files beginning with the supplied path prefix
v	Any variables
u	Usernames
X	Command names for which completions have been defined
x	Like n, but prints a message if ^D is typed
C, D, F, T	Like c, d, f, t, but selects completions from a given directory
(list)	Selects completions from words in a list

A c-type completion is used to complete a pattern in the current word. The current word refers to the pattern enclosed in forward slashes. It rules that if the pattern is matched, any completion performed will finish the pattern.

EXAMPLE 9.91

```
# c-type completions

1    > complete
     stty    'c/-/(raw xcase noflsh)/'
     bash    'c/-no/(profile rc braceexpansion)/'
     find    'c/-/(user name type exec)/'
     man     'c/perl/(delta faq toc data modlib locale)/'
2    > stty -r[tab]aw
     stty -raw
3    > bash -nop[tab]rofile
     bash -noprofile
4    > find / -n[tab]ame .tcshrc -p[tab]rint
     find / -name .tcshrc -print
```

EXAMPLE 9.91 (CONTINUED)

```
5  > man perlde[tab]lta
   man perldelta
6  > uncomplete stty
   > complete
   bash   'c/-no/(profile rc braceexpansion)/'
   find   'c/-/(user name type exec)/'
   man    'c/perl/(delta faq toc data modlib locale)/'
7  > uncomplete *
```

EXPLANATION

1 These examples demonstrate a c-type completion. If the pattern in the first set of forward slashes is typed, that pattern will be completed by one of the words listed in the parentheses when a character(s) from that list is typed, followed by the Tab key.

2 When the stty command is typed, followed by a dash (-) character, the word will be completed to -raw if a dash, an r, and the Tab key are entered. One of the words from the rule list in parentheses (raw xcase noflsh) can be completed.

3 When the bash command is typed, followed by the pattern, -no, that pattern will be completed to -noprofile if the pattern -no is followed by a p and the Tab key. Completion is performed from one of the words in the rule list (profile rc braceexpansion); in this example, resulting in -noprofile.

4 Arguments to the find command are completed if the dash (-) character is completed by typing significant characters from any of the words in the find rule list (user name type exec).

5 When the man command is typed, the pattern perl is completed to perldelta because the pattern is followed by one of the words from the list (delta faq toc data modlib locale).

6 The uncomplete built-in command removes the completion rule for stty. The other completion rules remain.

7 The uncomplete built-in command, with the asterisk as its argument, removes all completion rules.

N-type completions match the first word and complete the second one.

EXAMPLE 9.92

```
# n-type completions (next word completion)

1  > complete
   rm   'n/-r/d/'
   find 'n/-exec/c/'
2  > ls -ld testing
   drwxr-sr-x  2  ellie  root   1024 Aug 29 11:02 testing
3  > rm -r te[tab]sting
```

EXPLANATION

1   These examples demonstrate an n-type completion. If the word in the first set of forward slashes is typed (the current word) and matched, the next word (in the second set of forward slashes) will be completed according to the word type. The `complete` command lists two n-type completions, one for the `rm` command and one for the `find` command. When the `rm` command is executed with the -r switch, the word following -r must be of type directory if completion is to be performed. The rule for the `find` command is: if the -exec option is given, any words following it must be commands if completion is to be performed.

2   The output of the `ls` command shows that `testing` is a directory.

3   Filename completion is successful for the `rm` command because word completion is attempted for a directory named `testing`. If `testing` were a plain file, the completion would not have been performed.

9.16 TC Shell Spelling Correction

Spelling correction, a feature added to the TC shell, is the ability to correct spelling errors in filenames, commands, and variables. If using the emacs built-in editor, the spelling error can be corrected by using the spelling correction keys, bound to the Meta-s or Meta-S keys (use the Alt or Esc key if you don't have Meta) and Meta-$ to correct an entire line. The value of the prompt, `prompt3`, displays the spelling correction prompt.[7]

If you are using the vi built-in editor, set the built-in variable `correct`, and the shell will prompt you to fix the spelling.

Table 9.18   The `correct` Variable Arguments

Argument	What It Does
`all`	Spell-corrects entire command line
`cmd`	Spell-corrects commands
`complete`	Completes commands

EXAMPLE 9.93

```
1   > fimger[Alt-s]    # Replaces fimger with finger
2   > set correct=all
3   > dite
    CORRECT>date (y|n|e|a)? yes
    Wed Aug 8 19:26:27 PDT 2004
```

---

7. From the tcsh *man* page: "Beware: Spelling correction is not guaranteed to work the way one intends, and is provided as an experimental feature. Suggestions and improvements are welcome."

EXAMPLE 9.93 (CONTINUED)

```
4   > dite
    CORRECT>date (y|n|e|a)? no
    dite: Command not found.
    >
5   > dite
    CORRECT>date (y|n|e|a)? edit
    > dite        # Waits for user to edit and then executes command
6   > dite
    CORRECT>date (y|n|e|a)? abort
    >
```

EXPLANATION

1 By pressing the Meta (or Alt or Esc) key together with an s, the spelling of a command, filename, or variable can be corrected. This does not work if you are using the built-in vi editor.

2 By setting correct to all, tcsh will attempt to correct all spelling errors in the command line. This feature is available for both emacs and vi keybindings.

3 Because the command was incorrectly spelled, the third prompt, prompt3, "CORRECT>date (y|n|e|a)?" appears on the screen, and the user is supposed to type the letter y if he or she wants the spelling corrected, an n if not, an e if he or she wants to edit the line, or an a if he or she wants to abort the whole operation.

4 If the user wants the command to be unchanged, he types an n for no.

5 If the user wants to edit the correction, he or she types an e, and will be prompted to fix or enhance the command.

6 If the correction is incorrect or not wanted, the user types an a, and the spelling correction is aborted.

9.17 TC Shell Aliases

An *alias* is a TC shell user-defined abbreviation for a command. Aliases are useful if a command has a number of options and arguments or the syntax is difficult to remember. Aliases set at the command line are not inherited by subshells. Aliases are normally set in the .tcshrc file. Because the .tcshrc is executed when a new shell is started, any aliases set there will get reset for the new shell. Aliases may also be passed into shell scripts but will cause potential portability problems, unless they are directly set within the script.

The TC shell has some additional preset aliases, which remain undefined until you define them. They are: beepcmd, cwdcmd, periodic, and precomd. These aliases are listed and defined in "Special tcsh Aliases" on page 494.

9.17.1 Listing Aliases

The alias built-in command lists all set aliases. The alias is printed first, followed by the real command or commands it represents.

EXAMPLE 9.94

```
> alias
apache    $HOME/apache/httpd -f $HOME/apache/conf/httpd.conf
co        compress
cp        cp -i
ls1       enscript -B -r -Porange -f Courier8 !* &
mailq     /usr/lib/sendmail -bp
mc        setenv MC '/usr/bin/mc -P !*'; cd $MC; unsetenv MC
mroe      more
mv        mv -i
uc        uncompress
uu        uudecode
vg        vgrind -t -s11 !:1 | lpr -t
weekly    (cd /home/jody/ellie/activity; ./weekly_report; echo
Done)
```

EXPLANATION

The alias command lists the alias (nickname) for the command in the first column and the real command the alias represents in the second column.

9.17.2 Creating Aliases

The alias command is used to create an alias. The first argument is the name of the alias, the nickname for the command. The rest of the line consists of the command or commands that will be executed when the alias is executed. Multiple commands are separated by a semicolon, and commands containing spaces and metacharacters are surrounded by single quotes.

FORMAT

```
alias
alias aliasname command
alias aliasname 'command command(s)'
unalias aliasname
```

EXAMPLE 9.95

```
1  > alias m more
2  > alias mroe more
3  > alias lf ls-F
4  > alias cd 'cd \!*; set prompt = "%/ > "'
5  > cd ..
6  /home/jody > cd /          # new prompt displayed
   / >
```

EXAMPLE 9.95 (CONTINUED)

```
7   > set tperiod = 60
    > alias periodic 'echo You have worked an hour, nonstop'
8   > alias Usage 'echo "Error: \!* " ; exit 1'
```

EXPLANATION

1. The nickname for the more command is set to m.
2. The alias for the more command is set to mroe. This is handy if you can't spell.
3. The alias lf is a nickname for the tcsh built-in command ls-F. It lists files like ls -F, but is faster.
4. When cd is executed, the alias for cd will cause cd to go to the directory named as an argument and will then reset the prompt to the current working directory (%/) followed by the string "%/ > ". The !* is used by the alias in the same way it is used by the history mechanism. The backslash prevents the history mechanism from evaluating the !* first before the alias has a chance to use it. The \!* represents the arguments from the most recent command on the history list. The alias definition is enclosed in quotes because of the whitespace.
5. After the cd command changes to the parent directory, the prompt is expanded to the current working directory (%/) and a > symbol.[a]
6. The new directory is /home/jody, which is reflected in the prompt; after changing directory to root (/), the prompt again reflects the change.
7. The tperiod variable is set to 60 minutes. The alias, periodic, is a preset alias. Every 60 minutes, the echo statement will be displayed.
8. This alias is useful in scripts to produce a diagnostic message and to then exit the script. For an example of this alias in use, see Example 10.20 on page 545.

a. If using /bin/csh as your shell, replace %/ with $cwd when setting the prompt.

9.17.3 Deleting Aliases

The unalias command is used to delete an alias. To temporarily turn off an alias, precede the alias name by a backslash.

EXAMPLE 9.96

```
1   > unalias mroe
2   > \cd ..
```

EXPLANATION

1. The unalias command deletes the alias mroe from the list of defined aliases.
2. The alias cd is temporarily turned off for this execution of the command only.

9.17.4   Alias Loop

An alias loop occurs when an alias definition references another alias that references back to the original alias.

EXAMPLE 9.97

```
1   > alias m more
2   > alias mroe m
3   > alias m mroe        # Causes a loop
4   > m datafile
    Alias loop.
```

EXPLANATION

1   The alias is m. The alias definition is more. Every time m is used, the more command is executed.

2   The alias is mroe. The alias definition is m. If mroe is typed, the alias m is invoked and the more command is executed.

3   This is the culprit. If alias m is used, it invokes alias mroe, and alias mroe references back to m, causing an alias loop. Nothing bad happens. You just get an error message.

4   Alias m is used. It is circular. M calls mroe and mroe calls m, then m calls mroe, and so on. Rather than looping forever, the TC shell catches the problem and displays an error message.

9.17.5   Special tcsh Aliases

If set, each of the TC shell aliases executes automatically at the indicated time. They are all initially undefined.

Table 9.19   tcsh Aliases

Alias	*What It Does*
beepcmd	Runs when the shell wants to ring the terminal bell
cwdcmd	Runs after every change of working directory
periodic	Runs every tperiod minutes; e.g., > set tperiod = 30 > alias periodic date
precmd	Runs just before each prompt is printed; e.g., alias precmd date

9.18 TC Shell Job Control

Job control is a powerful feature of the TC shell that allows you to run programs, called *jobs*, in the background or foreground. Normally, a command typed at the command line is running in the foreground and will continue until it has finished. If you have a windowing program, job control may not be necessary, because you can simply open another window to start a new task. On the other hand, with a single terminal, job control is a very useful feature. For a list of job commands, see Table 9.20.

Table 9.20   Job Control Commands

Command	Meaning
jobs	Lists all the jobs running
^Z (Ctrl-Z)	Stops (suspends) the job; the prompt appears on the screen
bg	Starts running the stopped job in the background
fg	Brings a background job to the foreground
kill	Sends the kill signal to a specified job
Argument to jobs Command	
%n	Job number n
%string	Job name starting with string
%?string	Job name containing string
%%	Current job
%+	Current job
%-	Previous job, before current job

9.18.1   The jobs Command and the listjobs Variable

The tcsh built-in jobs command displays the programs that are currently active and either running or suspended in the background. Running means the job is executing in the background. When a job is suspended, it is stopped; it is not in execution. In both cases, the terminal is free to accept other commands. If you attempt to exit the shell while jobs are stopped, the warning, "There are suspended jobs" will appear on the screen. When you attempt to exit immediately a second time, the shell will go ahead and terminate the suspended jobs. You set the tcsh built-in listjobs variable if you want to automatically print a message when you suspend a job.

EXAMPLE 9.98

(The Command Line)

```
1   > jobs
2   [1]  +              Suspended     vi filex
    [2]  -              Running       sleep 25
3   > jobs -1
    [1]  +    355       Suspended     vi filex
    [2]  -    356       Running       sleep 25
4   [2] Done                          sleep 25
5   > set listjobs = long
    > sleep 1000
    Press Ctrl-Z to suspend job
    [1]  +    3337      Suspended        sleep 1000
    >
6   > set notify
```

EXPLANATION

1   The jobs command lists the currently active jobs.

2   The notation [1] is the number of the first job; the plus sign indicates that the job is not the most recent job to be placed in the background; the dash indicates that this is the most recent job put in the background; Suspended means that this job was stopped with ^Z and is not currently active.

3   The –1 option (long listing) displays the number of the job as well as the PID of the job. The notation [2] is the number of the second job, in this case, the last job placed in the background. The dash indicates that this is the most recent job. The sleep command is running in the background.

4   After sleep has been running for 25 seconds, the job will complete and a message saying that it has finished appears on the screen.

5   The tcsh listjobs variable, when set to long, will print the number of a job as well as its process id number when it is suspended. (See Table 9.26 on page 514 for a list of built-in tcsh variables.).

6   Normally the shell notifies you if a job is stopped just before it prints a prompt, but if the shell variable notify is set, the shell will notify you immediately if there is any change in the status of a background job. For example, if you are working in the vi editor, and a background job is terminated, a message will appear immediately in your vi window like this:

```
[1]      Terminated                   sleep 20
```

9.18.2 Foreground and Background Commands

The fg command brings a background job into the foreground. The bg command starts a suspended job running in the background. A percent sign and the number of a job can be used as arguments to fg and bg if you want to select a particular job for job control.

EXAMPLE 9.99

```
1   > jobs
2   [1] + Suspended          vi filex
    [2] - Running            cc prog.c -o prog
3   > fg %1
    vi filex
    (vi session starts)
4   > kill %2
    [2] Terminated           c prog.c -o prog
5   > sleep 15
    (Press ^z)
    Suspended
6   > bg
    [1] sleep 15 &
    [1] Done    sleep 15
```

EXPLANATION

1   The jobs command lists currently running processes, called jobs.

2   The first job stopped is the vi session, the second job is the cc command.

3   The job numbered [1] is brought to the foreground. The number is preceded with a percent sign.

4   The kill command is built-in. It sends the TERM (terminate) signal, by default, to a process. The argument is either the number or the PID of the process.

5   The sleep command is stopped by pressing ^Z. The sleep command is not using the CPU and is suspended in the background.

6   The bg command causes the last background job to start executing in the background. The sleep program will start the countdown in seconds before execution resumes.[a]

---

a. Programs such as grep, sed, and awk have a set of metacharacters, called regular expression metacharacters, for pattern matching. These should not be confused with shell metacharacters.

9.18.3 Scheduling Jobs

The sched built-in command allows you to create a list of jobs that will be scheduled to run at some specific time. The sched command, without arguments, displays a numbered list of all the scheduled events. It sets times in the form hh:mm (hour:minute) where hour can be in military or 12-hour AM/PM format. Time can also be specified as a relative to the current time with a + sign. With a – sign, the event is removed from the list.[8]

FORMAT

```
sched
sched [+]hh:mm   command
sched -n
```

EXAMPLE 9.100

```
1   > sched 14:30  echo '^G Time to start your lecture!'
2   > sched 5PM  echo Time to go home.
3   > sched +1:30 /home/ellie/scripts/logfile.sc
4   > sched
    1    17:47 /home/scripts/logfile.sc
    2    5PM  echo Time to go home.
    3    14:30  echo '^G Time to start your lecture!'
5   > sched -2
    > sched
    1    17:47 /home/scripts/logfile.sc
    2    14:30  echo '^G Time to start your lecture!'
```

EXPLANATION

1   The sched command schedules the echo command to be executed at 14:30. At that time a beep will sound (Ctrl-G)[a] and the message will be displayed.

2   The sched command will schedule the echo command to be executed at 5 PM.

3   The script, logfile.sc, is scheduled to be executed 1 hour and 30 minutes from now.

4   The sched command displays the scheduled events, in numeric order, the last one first.

5   With a numeric argument, sched will remove the numbered job from the scheduled list. Job number 2 was removed, as shown in the output of sched.

a.   To get the ^G into the echo statement, type Ctrl-M, followed by Ctrl-V, followed by Ctrl-G.

---

8.   From the tcsh *man* page: "A command in the scheduled-event list is executed just before the first prompt is printed after the time when the command is scheduled. It is possible to miss the exact time when the command is to be run, but an overdue command will execute at the next prompt."

9.19 Printing the Values of Variables in the TC Shell

9.19.1   The echo Command

The built-in echo command prints its arguments to standard output. The echo allows the use of numerous escape sequences that are interpreted and displayed as tabs, newlines, form feed, and so on. Table 9.21 lists the echo options and escape sequences.

The TC shell uses the style of both BSD and SVR4, but allows you to modify the behavior of the echo command by using the built-in echo_style variable; for example, set echo_style=bsd. See Table 9.22, and the manual page for echo.

Table 9.21   echo Options and Escape Sequences

Option	Meaning
-n	Suppresses newline at the end of a line of output

Escape Sequences	
\a	Alert (bell)
\b	Backspace
\c	Print the line without a newline
\f	Form feed
\n	Newline
\r	Return
\t	Tab
\v	Vertical tab
\\	Backslash
\nnn	The character whose ASCII code is nnn (octal)

Table 9.22   The echo_style Variable (SVR4 and BSD)

System	Behavior
bsd	If the first argument is -n, the newline is suppressed
both	Both -n and escape sequences are in effect (the default)
none	Recognizes neither sysv or bsd
sysv	Expands escape sequences in echo strings

EXAMPLE 9.101

```
1   > echo The username is $LOGNAME.
    The username is ellie.
2   > echo "\t\tHello there\c"
              Hello there>
3   > echo -n "Hello there"
    Hello there$
4   > set echo_style=none
5   > echo  "\t\tHello there\c"
    -n \t\tHello there\c
```

EXPLANATION

1   The echo command prints its arguments to the screen. Variable substitution is performed by the shell before the echo command is executed.

2   The echo command by default, supports escape sequences similar to those of the C programming language and used in the SVR4 version of echo. The > is the shell prompt.

3   With the -n option, echo displays the string without the newline.

4   The echo_style variable is assigned the value none. Neither the BSD -n switch nor the SVR4 escape sequences are in effect.

5   With the new echo style, the string is displayed.

9.19.2 The printf Command

The GNU version of printf can be used to format printed output. It prints the formatted string, in the same way as the C printf function. The format consists of a string that may contain formatting instructions to describe how the printed output will look. The formatting instructions are designated with a % followed by specifiers (diouxXfeEgGcs), where %f would represent a floating-point number and %d would represent a whole (decimal) number.

To see a complete listing of printf specifiers and how to use them, type at the command-line prompt printf --help. (See Table 9.23.) To see what version of printf you are using, type printf --version.

FORMAT

```
printf format [argument...]
```

EXAMPLE 9.102

```
printf "%10.2f%5d\n" 10.5  25
```

Table 9.23   Format Specifiers for the `printf` Command

Format Specifier	Value
\"	Double quote
\0NNN	An octal character in which NNN represents 0 to 3 digits
\\	Backslash
\a	Alert or beep
\b	Backspace
\c	Produce no further output
\f	Form feed
\n	Newline
\r	Carriage return
\t	Horizontal tab
\v	Vertical tab
\xNNN	Hexadecimal character in which NNN is 1 to 3 digits
%%	Single %
%b	ARGUMENT as a string with \ escapes interpreted

EXAMPLE   9.103

```
1   > printf --version
    printf (GNU sh-utils) 1.16
2   > printf "The number is %.2f\n" 100
    The number is 100.00
3   > printf "%-20s%-15s%10.2f\n" "Jody" "Savage" 28
    Jody                Savage              28.00
4   > printf "|%-20s|%-15s|%10.2f|\n" "Jody" "Savage" 28
    |Jody                |Savage         |     28.00|
```

EXPLANATION

1   The GNU version of the `printf` command is printed. It is found in /usr/bin.

2   The argument 100 is printed as a floating-point number with only two places to the right of the decimal point printing, designated by the format specification %.2f in the format string. Note that unlike C, there are no commas separating the arguments.

3   This time the format string specifies that three conversions will take place: the first one is %-20s (a left-justified, 20-character string), next is %-15s (a left-justified, 15-character string), and last is %10.2f (a right-justified 10-character floating-point number; one of those characters is the period and the last two characters are the two numbers to the right of the decimal point). Each argument is formatted in the order of the corresponding % signs, so that string "Jody" corresponds to first %, string "Savage" corresponds to the second %, and the number 28 to the last % sign. The vertical bars are used to demonstrate the width of the fields.

9.19.3 Curly Braces and Variables

Curly braces insulate a variable from any characters that may follow it. They can be used to concatenate a string to the end of the variable.

EXAMPLE 9.104

```
1   > set var = net
    > echo $var
    net
2   > echo $varwork
    varwork: Undefined variable.
3   > echo ${var}work
    network
```

EXPLANATION

1   The curly braces surrounding the variable name insulate the variable from characters that follow it.

2   A variable called varwork has not been defined. The shell prints an error message.

3   The curly braces shield the variable from characters appended to it. $var is expanded and the string work is appended.

9.19.4 Uppercase and Lowercase Modifiers

A special history modifier can be used to change the case of letters in a variable.

Table 9.24 TC Shell Case Modifiers

Modifier	What It Does
:a	Apply a modifier as many times as possible to a single word.
:g	Apply a modifier once to each word.
:l	Lowercase the first uppercase letter in a word.
:u	Uppercase the first lowercase letter in a word.

EXAMPLE 9.105

```
1   > set name = nicky
    > echo $name:u
    Nicky
2   > set name = ( nicky jake )
    > echo $name:gu
    Nicky Jake
3   > echo $name:agu
    NICKY JAKE
4   > set name = ( TOMMY DANNY )
    > echo $name:agl
    tommy danny
5   > set name = "$name:agu"
    > echo $name
    TOMMY DANNY
```

EXPLANATION

1   When :u is appended to the variable, the first letter in its value is uppercased.

2   When :gu is appended to the variable, the first letter in each word in the list of values is uppercased.

3   When :agu is appended to the variable, all letters in its value are uppercased.

4   When :agl is appended to the variable, all letters in its value are lowercased.

5   The variable is reset with all letters in its list uppercased.

9.20 TC Shell Built-In Commands

Rather than residing on disk like UNIX/Linux executable commands, built-in commands are part of the C/TC shell's internal code and are executed from within the shell. If a built-in command occurs as any component of a pipeline except the last, it is executed in a subshell. The tcsh built-in command aptly called builtins lists all the built-in commands.

EXAMPLE 9.106

```
1  > builtins
:            @          alias       alloc      bg         bindkey     break
breaksw      builtins   case        cd         chdir      complete    continue
default      dirs       echo        echotc     else       end         endif
endsw        eval       exec        exit       fg         filetest    foreach
glob         goto       hashstat    history    hup        if          jobs
kill         limit      log         login      logout     ls-F        nice
nohup        notify     onintr      popd       printenv   pushd       rehash
repeat       sched      set         setenv     settc      setty       shift
source       stop       suspend     switch     telltc     time        umask
unalias      uncomplete unhash      unlimit    unset      unsetenv    wait
where        which      while
```

See Table 9.25 for a list of built-in commands.

Table 9.25   tcsh Built-In Commands and Their Meanings

Command	*Meaning*
:	Interprets null command, but performs no action.
alias [name [wordlist]]	A nickname for a command. Without arguments, prints all aliases; with a name, prints the name for the alias; and with a name and wordlist, sets the alias.
alloc	Displays amount of dynamic memory acquired, broken down into used and free memory. Varies across systems.
bg [%job] %job &	Runs the current or specified jobs in the background. A synonym for the bg built-in command.
bindkey [-l|-d|-e|-v|-u] (+) bindkey [-a] [-b] [-k] [-r] [--] key bindkey [-a] [-b] [-k] [-c|-s] [--] key command	Without options, the first form lists all bound keys and the editor command to which each is bound; the second form lists the editor command to which key is bound; and the third form binds the editor command command to key. Options include: -a Lists or changes keybindings in the alternative key map. This is the key map used in vi command mode. -b This key is interpreted as a control character written as ^character (e.g., ^A) or C-character (e.g., C-A), a meta-character written M-character (e.g., M-A), a function key written F-string (e.g., F-string), or an extended prefix key written X-character (e.g., X-A). -c This command is interpreted as a built-in or external command, instead of an editor command. -d Binds all keys to the standard bindings for the default editor. -e Binds all keys to the standard GNU emacs-like bindings. -k This key is interpreted as a symbolic arrow key name, which may be one of "down," "up," "left," or "right." -l Lists all editor commands and a short description of each. -r Removes key's binding. Be careful: bindkey-r does not bind key to self-insert command (q.v.), it unbinds key completely. -s This command is taken as a literal string and treated as terminal input when key is typed. Bound keys in commands are themselves reinterpreted, and this continues for 10 levels of interpretation. -u (or any invalid option) Prints a usage message. This key may be a single character or a string. If a command is bound to a string, the first character of the string is bound to sequence-lead-in and the entire string is bound to the command. -v Binds all keys to the standard vi(1)-like bindings. -- Forces a break from option processing, so the next word is taken as a key even if it begins with a hyphen (-).

Table 9.25   tcsh Built-In Commands and Their Meanings (continued)

Command	*Meaning*
bindkey *(continued)*	Control characters in key can be literal (they can be typed by preceding them with the editor command quoted-insert, normally bound to ^V), or written caret-character style (e.g., ^A). Delete is written ^? (caret-question mark). Key and command can contain backslashed escape sequences (in the style of System V echo(1)) as follows: \a Bell \b Backspace \e Escape \f Form feed \n Newline \r Carriage return \t Horizontal tab \v Vertical tab \nnn The ASCII character corresponding to the octal number nnn \ nullifies the special meaning of the following character, if it has any, notably backslash (\) and caret (^).
break	Breaks out of the innermost foreach or while loop.
breaksw	Breaks from a switch, resuming after the endsw.
builtins	Prints the names of all built-in commands.
bye	A synonym for the logout built-in command. Available only if the shell was so compiled; see the version shell variable.
case label:	A label in a switch statement.
cd [dir]	Changes the shell's working directory to dir. If no argument is given, changes to the home directory of the user.
cd [-p] [-l] [-n|-v] [name]	If a directory name is given, changes the shell's working directory to name. If not, changes to home. If name is "-" it is interpreted as the previous working directory. -p prints the final directory stack, just like dirs. -l, -n, and -v flags have the same effect on cd as on dirs, and they imply -p.
chdir	A synonym for the cd built-in command.
complete [command [word/pattern/ list[:select]/[[suffix]/] ...]]	Without arguments, lists all completions. With command, lists completions for command. With command and word etc., defines completions. (See "Programming Completions" on page 485.)
continue	Continues execution of the nearest enclosing while or foreach.

Table 9.25   tcsh Built-In Commands and Their Meanings (continued)

Command	*Meaning*
default:	Labels the default case in a switch statement. The default should come after all case labels.

dirs [-l] [-n|-v]
 	
dirs -S|-L [filename]
 	
dirs -c
	The first form prints the directory stack. The top of the stack is at the left and the first directory in the stack is the current directory. -l, ~, or ~name in the output is expanded explicitly to home or the pathname of the home directory for username.
	    (+) -n, entries are wrapped before they reach the edge of the screen.
	    (+) -v, entries are printed one per line preceded by their stack postions.
	    -S, the second form saves the directory stack to filename as a series of cd and pushd commands.
	    -L, the shell source's filename, which is presumably a directory stack file saved.
	In either case dirsfile is used if filename is not given and ~/.cshdirs is used if dirsfile is unset.
	    With -c, form clears the directory stack.

echo [-n] list	Writes the words in list to the shell's standard output, separated by space characters. The output is terminated with a newline unless the -n option is used.
echo [-n] word ...	Writes each word to the shell's standard output, separated by spaces and terminated with a newline. The echo_style shell variable may be set to emulate (or not) the flags and escape sequences of the BSD and/or System V versions of echo.
echotc [-sv] arg ...	Exercises the terminal capabilities (see term-cap(5)) in args. For example, echotc home sends the cursor to the home position. If arg is baud, cols, lines, meta, or tabs, prints the value of that capability. With -s, nonexistent capabilities return the empty string rather than causing an error. With -v, messages are verbose.
else if (expr2) then	See "Conditional Constructs and Flow Control" on page 535.

else
end
endif
endsw
	See the description of the foreach, if, switch, and while statements below.

end	Executes the commands between the while and the matching end while expr evaluates nonzero. while and end must appear alone on their input lines. break and continue may be used to terminate or continue the loop prematurely. If the input is a terminal, the user is prompted the first time through the loop as with foreach.

Table 9.25   tcsh Built-In Commands and Their Meanings (continued)

Command	Meaning
eval arg ...	Treats the arguments as input to the shell and executes the resulting command(s) in the context of the current shell. This is usually used to execute commands generated as the result of command or variable substitution, as parsing occurs before these substitutions.
eval command	Runs command as standard input to the shell and executes the resulting commands. This is usually used to execute commands generated as the result of command or variable substitution, as parsing occurs before these substitutions (e.g., eval 'tset -s options').
exec command	Executes command in place of the current shell, which terminates.
exit [(expr)]	Exits the shell, either with the value of the status variable or with the value specified by expr.
fg [% job] %job	Brings the current or specified job into the foreground. A synonym for the fg built-in command.
filetest -op file ...	Applies op (which is a file inquiry operator) to each file and returns the results as a space-separated list.
foreach name (wordlist) ... end	See "Looping Control Commands" on page 566.
foreach var (wordlist)	See "The foreach Loop" on page 561.
getspath	Prints the system execution path.
getxvers	Prints the experimental version prefix.
glob wordlist	Performs filename expansion on wordlist. Like echo, but no escapes (\) are recognized. Words are delimited by null characters in the output.
goto label	See "The goto" on page 547.
goto word	word is filename and command-substituted to yield a string of the form "label." The shell rewinds its input as much as possible, searches for a line of the form "label:", possibly preceded by blanks or tabs, and continues execution after that line.
hashstat	Prints a statistics line indicating how effective the internal hash table has been at locating commands (and avoiding execs). An exec is attempted for each component of the path where the hash function indicates a possible hit, and in each component that does not begin with a backslash.

Table 9.25　tcsh Built-In Commands and Their Meanings (continued)

Command	Meaning
history [-hTr] [n] history -S|-L|-M [filename] history -c	The first form prints the history event list. If n is given, only the n most recent events are printed or saved. With -h, the history list is printed without leading numbers. If -T is specified, timestamps are printed also in comment form. (This can be used to produce files suitable for loading with history -L or source -h.) With -r, the order of printing is most recent first rather than oldest first. (See "TC Shell Command-Line History" on page 466.) With -c, clears the history list.
hup [command]	With command, runs command such that it will exit on a hangup signal and arranges for the shell to send it a hangup signal when the shell exits. Note that commands may set their own response to hangups, overriding hup. Without an argument (allowed only in a shell script), causes the shell to exit on a hangup for the remainder of the script.
if (expr) command	If expr evaluates true, then command is executed. Variable substitution on command happens early, at the same time it does for the rest of the if command. Command must be a simple command, not an alias, a pipeline, a command list, or a parenthesized command list, but it may have arguments. Input/output redirection occurs even if expr is false and command is thus not executed; this is a bug.

if (expr) then
...
else if (expr2) then
...
else
...
endif
	If the specified expr is true then the commands to the first else are executed; otherwise if expr2 is true then the commands to the second else are executed, and so on. Any number of else if pairs are possible; only one endif is needed. The else part is likewise optional. (The words else and endif must appear at the beginning of input lines; the if must appear alone on its input line or after an else.)

inlib shared-library ...	Adds each shared library to the current environment. There is no way to remove a shared library. (Domain/OS only)
jobs [-l]	Lists the active jobs under job control. With -l, lists IDs in addition to the normal information.
kill [-sig] [pid] [%job] ... kill -l	Sends the TERM (terminate) signal, by default or by the signal specified, to the specified ID, the job indicated, or the current job. Signals are given either by number or name. There is no default. Typing kill does not send a signal to the current job. If the signal being sent is TERM (terminate) or HUP (hangup), then the job or process is sent a CONT (continue) signal as well. With -l lists the signal names that can be sent.

Table 9.25 tcsh Built-In Commands and Their Meanings (continued)

Command	*Meaning*
limit [-h] [resource [max-use]]	Limits the consumption by the current process or any process it spawns, each not to exceed max-use on the specified resource. If max-use is omitted, print the current limit; if resource is omitted, display all limits. With -h, uses hard limits instead of the current limits. Hard limits impose a ceiling on the values of the current limits. Only the superuser may raise the hard limits. Resource is one of: cputime, maximum CPU seconds per process; filesize, largest single file allowed; datasize, maximum data size (including stack) for the process; stacksize, maximum stack size for the process; coredump, maximum size of a core dump; and descriptors, maximum value for a file descriptor.
log	Prints the watch shell variable and reports on each user indicated in watch who is logged in, regardless of when they last logged in. See also watchlog.
login	Terminates a login shell, replacing it with an instance of /bin/login.
login [username|-p]	Terminates a login shell and invokes login(1). The .logout file is not processed. If username is omitted, login prompts for the name of a user. With -p, preserves the current environment (variables).
logout	Terminates a login shell.
ls-F [-switch ...] [file ...]	Lists files like ls -F, but much faster. It identifies each type of special file in the listing with a special character: / Directory * Executable # Block device % Character device | Named pipe (systems with named pipes only) = Socket (systems with sockets only) @ Symbolic link (systems with symbolic links only) + Hidden directory (AIX only) or context-dependent (HP-UX only) : Network special (HP-UX only) If the listlinks shell variable is set, symbolic links are identified in more detail (only, of course, on systems that have them): @ Symbolic link to a nondirectory > Symbolic link to a directory & Symbolic link to nowhere The ls-F built-in can list files using different colors depending on the filetype or extension.

Table 9.25 tcsh Built-In Commands and Their Meanings (continued)

Command	Meaning
migrate [-site] pid|%jobid ... migrate -site	The first form migrates the process or job to the site specified or the default site determined by the system path. The second form is equivalent to migrate -site $$. It migrates the current process to the specified site. Migrating the shell itself can cause unexpected behavior, because the shell does not like to lose its tty.
@ @ name = expr @ name[index] = expr @ name++|-- @ name[index]++|--	The first form prints the values of all shell variables. The second form assigns the value of expr to name. The third form assigns the value of expr to the index'th component of name; both name and its index'th component must already exist. The fourth and fifth forms increment (++) or decrement (--) name or its index'th component.
newgrp [-] group	Equivalent to exec newgrp; see newgrp(1). Available only if the shell was so compiled; see the version shell variable.
nice [+number] [command]	Sets the scheduling priority for the shell to number, or, without number, to 4. With command, runs command at the appropriate priority. The greater the number, the less CPU the process gets. The superuser may specify negative priority by using nice -number. Command is always executed in a subshell, and the restrictions placed on commands in simple if statements apply.
nohup [command]	Runs command with HUPs (hangups) ignored. With no arguments, ignores HUPs throughout the remainder of a script.
notify [%job]	Notifies the user asynchronously when the status of the current or of a specified job changes.
onintr [- | label]	Controls the action of the shell on interrupts. With no arguments, onintr restores the default action of the shell on interrupts. (The shell terminates shell scripts and returns to the terminal command input level.) With the minus sign argument, the shell ignores all interrupts. With a label argument, the shell executes a goto label when an interrupt is received or a child process terminates because it was interrupted.
popd [+n]	Pops the directory stack and cd to the new top directory. The elements of the directory stack are numbered from zero, starting at the top. With +n, discard the nth entry in the stack.
printenv [name]	Prints the names and values of all environment variables or, with name, the value of the environment variable name.

Table 9.25 tcsh Built-In Commands and Their Meanings (continued)

Command	Meaning
pushd [+n | dir]	Pushes a directory onto the directory stack. With no arguments, exchanges the top two elements. With +n, rotates the nth entry to the top of the stack and cd to it. With dir, pushes the current working directory onto the stack and changes to dir.
rehash	Recomputes the internal hash table of the contents of directories listed in the path variable to account for new commands added.
repeat count command	Repeats command count times.
rootnode //nodename	Changes the rootnode to //nodename, so that / will be interpreted as //nodename. (Domain/OS only)
sched sched [+]hh:mm command sched -n	The first form prints the scheduled-event list. The sched shell variable may be set to define the format in which the scheduled-event list is printed. The second form adds a command to the scheduled-event list.
set set name ... set name=word ... set [-r] [-f|-l] name=(wordlist) ... (+) set name[index]=word ... set -r set -r name ... set -r name=word ...	The first form of the command prints the value of all shell variables. Variables that contain more than a single word print as a parenthesized word list. The second form sets name to the null string. The third form sets name to the single word. The fourth form sets name to the list of words in wordlist. In all cases the value is command and filename expanded. If -r is specified, the value is set read-only. If -f or -l are specified, set only unique words keeping their order. -f prefers the first occurrence of a word, and -l the last occurrence of the word. The fifth form sets the index'th component of name to word; this component must already exist. The sixth form lists the names (only) of all shell variables that are read-only. The seventh form makes name read-only, whether or not it has a value. The eighth form is the same as the third form, but makes name read-only at the same time .
set [var [= value]]	See "Variables" on page 440.
setenv [VAR [word]]	See "Variables" on page 440. The most commonly used environment variables, USER, TERM, and PATH, are automatically imported to and exported from the csh variables, user, term, and path; there is no need to use setenv for these. In addition, the shell sets the PWD environment variable from the csh variable cwd whenever the latter changes.
setenv [name [value]]	Without arguments, prints the names and values of all environment variables. Given name, sets the environment variable name to value or, without value, to the null string.
setpath path	Equivalent to setpath(1). (Mach only)

Table 9.25 tcsh Built-In Commands and Their Meanings (continued)

Command	Meaning
setspath LOCAL|site|cpu ...	Sets the system execution path.
settc cap value	Tells the shell to believe that the terminal capability cap (as defined in termcap(5)) has the value value. No sanity checking is done. Concept terminal users may have to settc xn no to get proper wrapping at the rightmost column.
setty [-d|-q|-x] [-a] [[+|-]mode]	Controls which tty modes the shell does not allow to change. -d, -q, or -x tells setty to act on the edit, quote, or execute set of tty modes, respectively; without -d, -q, or -x, execute is used. Without other arguments, setty lists the modes in the chosen set that are fixed on (+mode) or off (-mode). The available modes, and thus the display, vary from system to system. With -a, lists all tty modes in the chosen set whether or not they are fixed. With +mode, -mode, or mode, fixes mode on or off or removes control from mode in the chosen set. For example, setty +echok echoe fixes echok mode on and allows commands to turn echoe mode on or off, both when the shell is executing commands.
setxvers [string]	Sets the experimental version prefix to string, or removes it if string is omitted.
shift [variable]	The components of argv, or variable, if supplied, are shifted to the left, discarding the first component. It is an error for variable not to be set, or to have a null value.
source [-h] name	Reads commands from name. Source commands may be nested, but if they are nested too deeply, the shell may run out of file descriptors. An error in a sourced file at any level terminates all nested source commands. Commonly used to re-execute the .login or .cshrc files to ensure variable settings are handled within the current shell, i.e., shell does not create a child shell (fork). With -h, places commands from the filename on the history list without executing them.
stop [%job] ...	Stops the current or specified background job.
suspend	Stops the shell in its tracks, much as if it had been sent a stop signal with ^Z. This is most often used to stop shells started by su.
switch (string)	See "The switch Command" on page 557.
telltc	Lists the values of all terminal capabilities (see termcap(5)).
time [command]	With no argument, prints a summary of time used by this shell and its children. With an optional command, executes command and prints a summary of the time it uses.

Table 9.25 tcsh Built-In Commands and Their Meanings (continued)

Command	*Meaning*
umask [value]	Displays the file creation mask. With value, sets the file creation mask. Value, given in octal, is XORed with the permissions of 666 for files and 777 for directories to arrive at the permissions for new files. Permissions cannot be added via umask.
unalias pattern	Removes all aliases whose names match pattern. unalias * thus removes all aliases. It is not an error for nothing to be unaliased.
uncomplete pattern	Removes all completions whose names match pattern. uncomplete * thus removes all completions.
unhash	Disables the internal hash table.
universe universe	Sets the universe to universe. (Masscomp/RTU only)
unlimit [-h] [resource]	Removes the limitation on resource or, if no resource is specified, all resource limitations. With -h, the corresponding hard limits are removed. Only the superuser may do this.
unsetenv pattern	Removes all environment variables whose names match pattern. unsetenv * thus removes all environment variables; this is a bad idea. If there is no pattern to be unsetenved, no error will result from this built-in.
unsetenv variable	Removes variable from the environment. Pattern matching, as with unset, is not performed.
@ [var =expr] @ [var[n] =expr]	With no arguments, displays the values for all shell variables. With arguments, the variable var, or the nth word in the value of var, is set to the value that expr evaluates to.
ver [systype [command]]	Without arguments, prints SYSTYPE. With systype, sets SYSTYPE to systype. With systype and command, executes command under systype. systype may be bsd4.3 or sys5.3. (Domain/OS only)
wait	Waits for background jobs to finish (or for an interrupt) before prompting.
warp universe	Sets the universe to universe. (Convex/OS only)
watchlog	An alternate name for the log built-in command (q.v.). Available only if the shell was so compiled; see the version shell variable.
where command	Reports all known instances of command, including aliases, built-ins, and executables in path.

Table 9.25 tcsh Built-In Commands and Their Meanings (continued)

Command	Meaning
which command	Displays the command that will be executed by the shell after substitutions, path searching, etc. The built-in command is just like which(1), but it correctly reports tcsh aliases and built-ins and is 10 to 100 times faster.
while (expr)	See "Looping Control Commands" on page 566.

9.20.1 Special Built-In T/TC Shell Variables

The built-in shell variables have special meaning to the shell and are used to modify and control the way many of the shell commmands behave. They are local variables and therefore most of them are set in the .tcshrc file for the TC shell, and the .cshrc file for the C shell if they are to be passed on to and affect child C/TC shells.

When the shell starts up, it automatically sets the following variables: addsuffix, argv, autologout, command, echo_style, edit, gid, group, home, loginsh, oid, path, prompt, prompt2, prompt3, shell, shlvl, tcsh, term, tty, uid, user, and version. Unless the user decides to change them, these variables will remain fixed. The shell also keeps track of and changes special variables that may need period updates, such as cwd, dirstack, owd, and status, and when the user logs out, the shell sets the logout variable.

Some of the local variables have a corresponding environment variable of the same name. If one of the environment or local variables is affected by a change in the user's environment, the shell will synchronize the local and environment variables[9] so that their values always match. Examples of cross-matched variables are afuser, group, home, path, shlvl, term, and user. (Although cwd and PWD have the same meaning, they are not cross-matched. Even though the syntax is different for the path and PATH variables, they are automatically cross-matched if either one is changed.)

Table 9.26 Special C/TC Shell Variables[a] [b]

Variable	Meaning
addsufix (+)	For filename completion, adds slashes at the end of directories and space to the end of normal files if they are matched. Set by default.
afsuser (+)	If set, autologout's autolock feature uses its value instead of the local username for Kerberos authentication.
ampm (+)	If set, all times are shown in 12-hour AM/PM format.
argv	An array of command-line arguments to the shell; also represented as $1, $2, and so on.

---

9. This is true unless the variable is a read-only variable, and then there will be no synchronization.

Table 9.26 Special C/TC Shell Variables[a] [b] (continued)

Variable	Meaning
autocorrect (+)	Invokes the spell checker before each attempt at filename, command, or variable completion.
autoexpand (+)	If set, the expand-history editor command is invoked automatically before each completion attempt.
autolist (+)	If set, possibilities are listed after an ambiguous completion. If set to ambiguous, possibilities are listed only when no new characters are added by completion.
autologout (+)	Its argument is the number of minutes of inactivity before automatic logout; the second optional argument is the number of minutes before automatic locking causes the screen to lock.
backslash_quote (+)	If set, a backslash will always quote itself, a single quote or a double quote.
cdpath	A list of directories in which cd should search for subdirectories if they aren't found in the current directory.
color (+)	Enables color display for the built-in command ls-F and passes --color=auto to ls.
complete (+)	If set to enhance, completion ignores case, considers periods, hyphens, and underscores to be word separators, and hyphens and underscores to be equivalent.
correct (+)	If set to cmd, commands are automatically spelling-corrected. If set to complete, commands are automatically completed. If set to all, the entire command line is corrected.
cwd	The full pathname of the current working directory.
dextract (+)	If set, pushd +n extracts the nth directory from the directory stack rather than rotating it to the top.
dirsfile (+)	The default location in which dirs -S and dirs -L look for a history file. If unset, ~/.cshdirs is used.
dirstack (+)	A list of all directories on the directory stack.
dunique (+)	Will not allow pushd to keep duplicate directory entries on the stack.
echo	If set, each command with its arguments is echoed just before it is executed. Set by the -x command-line option.
echo-style (+)	Sets the style for echo. If set to bsd will not echo a newline if the first argument is -n; if set to sysv, recognizes backslashed escape sequences in echo strings; if set to both, recognizes both the -n flag and backslashed escape sequences; the default, and if set to none, recognizes neither.
edit (+)	Sets the command-line editor for interactive shells; set by default.

Table 9.26   Special C/TC Shell Variables[a] [b] (continued)

Variable	Meaning
ellipsis (+)	If set, the %c, %., and %C prompt sequences (see the "The Shell Prompts" on page 461) indicate skipped directories with an ellipsis (…) instead of /<skipped>.
fignore	Lists filename suffixes to be ignored by completion.
filec (+)	In tcsh, completion is always used and this variable is ignored. If set in csh, filename completion is used.
gid (+)	The user's read group ID number.
group (+)	The user's group name.
hardpaths	If set, pathnames in the directory stack are resolved to contain no symbolic-link components.
histchars	A string value determining the characters used in history substitution. The first character of its value is used as the history substitution character to replace the default character, !. The second character of its value replaces the character ^ in quick substitutions.
histdup (+)	Controls handling of duplicate entries in the history list. Can be set to all (removes all duplicates), prev (removes the current command if it duplicates the previous command), or erase (inserts the current event for an older duplicate event).
histfile (+)	The default location in which history -S and history -L look for a history file. If unset, ~/.history is used.
histlit (+)	Enters events on the history list literally; that is, unexpanded by history substitution.
history	The first word indicates the number of history events to save. The optional second word (+) indicates the format in which history is printed.
home	The home directory of the user; same as ~.
ignoreeof	If logging out by pressing Ctrl-D, prints Use "exit" to leave tcsh. Prevents inadvertently logging out.
implicitcd (+)	If set, the shell treats a directory name typed as a command as though it were a request to change to that directory and changes to it.
inputmode (+)	If set to insert or overwrite, puts the editor into that input mode at the beginning of each line.
listflags (+)	If set to x, a, or A, or any combination (e.g., xA), values are used as flags to ls-F, making it act like ls -xF, ls -Fa, ls -FA, or any combination of those flags.
listjobs (+)	If set, all jobs are listed when a job is suspended. If set to long, the listing is in long format.

Table 9.26 Special C/TC Shell Variables[a] [b] (continued)

Variable	Meaning
listlinks (+)	If set, the ls -F built-in command shows the type of file to which each symbolic link points.
listmax (+)	The maximum number of items the list-choices editor command will list without asking first.
listmaxrows (+)	The maximum number of rows of items the list-choices editor command will list without asking first.
loginsh (+)	Set by the shell if it is a login shell. Setting or unsetting it within a shell has no effect. See also shlvl.
logout (+)	Set by the shell to normal before a normal logout, automatic before an automatic logout, and hangup if the shell was killed by a hangup signal.
mail	The names of the files or directories to check for incoming mail. After 10 minutes if new mail has come in, will print You have new mail.
matchbeep (+)	If set to never, completion never beeps; if set to nomatch, completion beeps only when there is no match; and when set to ambiguous, beeps when there are multiple matches.
nobeep	Disables all beeping.
noclobber	Safeguards against the accidental removal of existing files when redirection is used; for example, ls > file.
noglob	If set, inhibits filename and directory stack substitutions when using wildcards.
nokanji (+)	If set and the shell supports Kanji (see the version shell variable), it is disabled so that the Meta key can be used.
nonomatch	If set, a filename substitution or directory stack substitution that does not match any existing files is left untouched rather than causing an error.
nostat (+)	A list of directories (or glob patterns that match directories) that should not be stat(2)ed during a completion operation. This is usually used to exclude directories that take too much time to stat(2).
notify	If set, the shell announces job completions asynchronously instead of waiting until just before the prompt appears.
oid (+)	The user's real organization ID. (Domain/OS only)
owd (+)	The old or previous working directory.
path	A list of directories in which to look for executable commands. path is set by the shell at startup from the PATH environment variable or, if PATH does not exist, to a system-dependent default, something like /usr/local/bin /usr/bsd /bin /usr/bin.

Table 9.26   Special C/TC Shell Variables[a, b] (continued)

Variable	Meaning
printexitvalue (+)	If set and an interactive program exits with a nonzero status, the shell prints Exit status.
prompt	The string that is printed before reading each command from the terminal; may include special formatting sequences (see "The Shell Prompts" on page 461).
prompt2 (+)	The string with which to prompt in while and foreach loops and after lines ending in \. The same format sequences may be used as in prompt; note the variable meaning of %R. Set by default to %R? in interactive shells.
prompt3 (+)	The string with which to prompt when confirming automatic spelling correction. The same format sequences may be used as in prompt; note the variable meaning of %R. Set by default to CORRECT>%R (y|n|e|a)? in interactive shells.
promptchars (+)	If set (to a two-character string), the %# formatting sequence in the prompt shell variable is replaced with the first character for normal users and the second character for the superuser.
pushtohome (+)	If set, pushd without arguments does pushd ~, like cd.
pushdsilent (+)	If set, pushd and popd to not print the directory stack.
recexact (+)	If set, completion completes on an exact match even if a longer match is possible.
recognize_only_ executables (+)	If set, command listing displays only files in the path that are executable.
rmstar (+)	If set, the user is prompted before rm * is executed.
rprompt (+)	The string to print on the right-hand side of the screen (after the command input) when the prompt is being displayed on the left. It recognizes the same formatting characters as prompt. It will automatically disappear and reappear as necessary, to ensure that command input isn't obscured, and will only appear if the prompt, command input, and itself will fit together on the first line. If edit isn't set, then rprompt will be printed after the prompt and before the command input.
savedirs (+)	If set, the shell does dirs -S before exiting.
savehist	If set, the shell does history -S before exiting. If the first word is set to a number, at most that many lines are saved. (The number must be less than or equal to history.) If the second word is set to merge, the history list is merged with the existing history file instead of replacing it (if there is one) and sorted by timestamp and the most recent events are retained.
sched (+)	The format in which the sched built-in command prints scheduled events; if not given, %h\t%T\t%R\n is used. The format sequences are described above under prompt; note the variable meaning of %R.

Table 9.26 Special C/TC Shell Variables[a, b] (continued)

Variable	Meaning
shell	The file in which the shell resides. This is used in forking shells to interpret files that have execute bits set, but are not executable by the system. (See the description of built-in and non-built-in command execution.) Initialized to the (system-dependent) home of the shell.
shlvl (+)	The number of nested shells. Reset to 1 in login shells. See also loginsh.
status	The status returned by the last command. If it terminated abnormally, then 0200 is added to the status. Built-in commands that fail return exit status 1, all other built-in commands return status 0.
symlinks (+)	Can be set to several different values to control symbolic link (symlink) resolution. (See tcsh *man* page for examples.)
tcsh (+)	The version number of the shell in the format R.W.PP, where R is the major release number, W the current version, and PP the patch level.
term (+)	The terminal type. Usually set in ~/.login as described under "C/TC Shell Startup" on page 403.
time	If set to a number, then the time built-in executes automatically after each command that takes more than that many CPU seconds. If there is a second word, it is used as a format string for the output of the time built-in. The following sequences may be used in the format string: %c The number of involuntary context switches. %D The average amount in (unshared) data/stack space used in KB. %E The elapsed (wall clock) time in seconds. %F The number of major page faults (page needed to be brought from disk). %I The number of input operations. %K The total space used (%X + %D) in KB. %k The number of signals received. %M The maximum memory the process had in use at any time in KB. %O The number of output operations. %P The CPU percentage computed as (%U + %S) / %E. %R (+) The number of minor page faults. %r The number of socket messages received. %S The time the process spent in kernel mode in CPU seconds. %s The number of socket messages sent. %U The time the process spent in user mode in CPU seconds. %W Number of times the process was swapped. %w The number of voluntary context switches (waits). %X The average amount in (shared) text space used in KB. Only the %U, %S, %F, and %P sequences are supported on systems without BSD resource limit functions. The default time format is %Uu %Ss %E %P %X+%Dk %I+%Oio %Fpf+%Ww for systems that support resource usage reporting and %Uu %Ss %E %P for systems that do not.

Table 9.26 Special C/TC Shell Variables[a, b] (continued)

Variable	Meaning
time (*continued*)	Under Sequent's DYNIX/ptx, %X, %D, %K, %r, and %s are not available, but the following additional sequences are:

	%Y	The number of system calls performed.
	%Z	The number of pages that are zero-filled on demand.
	%i	The number of times a process's resident set size was increased by the kernel.
	%d	The number of times a process's resident set size was decreased by the kernel.
	%l	The number of read system calls performed.
	%m	The number of write system calls performed.
	%p	The number of reads from raw disk devices.
	%q	The number of writes to raw disk devices.

	The default time format is %Uu %Ss $E %P %I+%Oio %Fpf+%Ww. Note that the CPU percentage can be higher than 100 percent on multiprocessors.
tperiod (+)	The period, in minutes, between executions of the periodic special alias.
tty (+)	The name of the tty, or empty if not attached to one.
uid (+)	The user's real user ID.
user (+)	The user's login name.
verbose	If set, causes the words of each command to be printed, after history substitution (if any). Set by the -v command-line option.
version (+)	The version ID stamp. It contains the shell's version number (see tcsh), origin, release date, vendor, operating system, and so forth.

a. Variables with a (+) are TC shell only. All others are built in for both TC and C shells.
b. Descriptions taken from tcsh manual pages.

9.20.2 TC Shell Command-Line Switches

The TC shell can take a number of command-line switches (also called flag arguments) to control or modify its behavior. The command-line switches are listed in Table 9.27.

Table 9.27 TC Shell Command-Line Switches

Switch	Meaning
-	Specifies the shell is a login shell.
-b	Forces a "break" from option processing. Any shell arguments thereafter will not be treated as options. The remaining arguments will not be interpreted as shell options. Must include this option if shell is set-user id.
-c	If a single argument follows the -c; commands are read from the argument (a filename). Remaining arguments are placed in the argv shell variable.

Table 9.27 TC Shell Command-Line Switches (continued)

Switch	Meaning
-d	The shell loads the directory stack from ~/.cshdirs.
-Dname[=value]	Sets the environment variable name to value.
-e	The shell exits if any invoked command terminates abnormally or yields a nonzero exit status.
-f	Called the fast startup because the shell ignores ~/.tcshrc, when starting a new TC shell.
-F	The shell uses fork(2) instead of vfork(2) to spawn processes. (Convex/OS only)
-i	The shell is interactive and prompts input, even if it appears to not be a terminal. This option isn't necessary if input and output are connected to a terminal.
-l	The shell is a login shell if -l is the only flag specified.
-m	The shell loads ~/.tcshrc even if it does not belong to the effective user.
-n	Used for debugging scripts. The shell parses commands but does not execute them.
-q	The shell accepts the SIGQUIT signal and behaves when it is used under a debugger. Job control is disabled.
-s	Command input is taken from the standard input.
-t	The shell reads and executes a single line of input. A backslash (\) may be used to escape the newline at the end of this line and continue on to another line.
-v	Sets the verbose shell variable, so that command input is echoed after history substitution. Used to debug shell scripts.
-x	Sets the echo shell variable, so that commands are echoed before execution and after history and variable substitution. Used to debug shell scripts.
-V	Sets the verbose shell variable before executing the ~/.tcshrc file.
-X	Sets the echo shell variable before executing the ~/.tcshrc file.

LAB 19: THE TC SHELL—GETTING STARTED

1. What does the `init` process do?

2. What is the function of the `login` process?

3. How do you know what shell you are using?

4. How can you change your login shell?

5. Explain the difference between the `.tcshrc`, `.cshrc`, and `.login` files. Which one is executed first?

6. Edit your `.tcshrc` or `.cshrc` file as follows:

    a. Create three of your own aliases.

    b. Reset your prompt with the host machine name, time, username.

    c. Set the following variables and put a comment after each variable explaining what it does: `noclobber`, `history`, `ignoreof`, `savehist`, `prompt`.

7. Type the following:

   ```
   source .tcshrc   or   source .cshrc
   ```

   What does the source command do?

8. Edit your `.login` file as follows:

    a. Welcome the user.

    b. Add your home directory to the path if it is not there.

    c. Source the `.login` file.

9. What is the difference between `path` and `PATH`?

LAB 20: HISTORY

1. In what file are history events stored when you log out? What variable controls the number of history events to be displayed? What is the purpose of the `savehist` variable?

2. Print your history list in reverse.

3. Print your history list without line numbers.

4. Type the following commands:

    a. `ls -a`

    b. `date '+%T'`

    c. `cal 2004`

    d. `cat /etc/passwd`

    e. `cd`

5. Type history. What is the output?

    a. How do you re-execute the last command?

    b. Now type: echo a b c

    Use the history command to re-execute the echo command with only its last argument, c.

6. Use history to print and execute the last command in your history list that started with the letter d.

7. Execute the last command that started with the letter c.

8. Execute the echo command and the last argument from the previous command.

9. Use the history substitution command to replace the T in the date command with an H.

10. How do you use the bindkey command to start the vi editor for command-line editing?

11. How do you list the editor commands and what they do?

12. How do you see how the editing keys are actually bound?

13. Describe what the fignore variable does.

LAB 21: SHELL METACHARACTERS

1. Type at the prompt:

   touch ab abc a1 a2 a3 a11 a12 ba ba.1 ba.2 filex filey AbC ABC ABc2 abc

   Write and test the command that will:

    a. List all files starting with a.

    b. List all files ending in at least one digit.

    c. List all files not starting with an a or A.

    d. List all files ending in a period, followed by a digit.

    e. List all files containing just two alphas.

    f. List three character files where all letters are uppercase.

    g. List files ending in 11 or 12.

    h. List files ending in x or y.

    i. List all files ending in a digit, an uppercase letter, or a lowercase letter.

    j. List all files containing a b.

    k. Remove two-character files starting with a.

LAB 22: REDIRECTION

1. What are the names of the three file streams associated with your terminal?

2. What is a file descriptor?

3. What command would you use to:

    a. Redirect the output of the ls command to a file called lsfile?

    b. Redirect and append the output of the date command to lsfile?

    c. Redirect the output of the who command to lsfile? What happened?

    d. What happens when you type cp all by itself?

    e. How do you save the error message from the above example to a file?

    f. Use the find command to find all files, starting from the parent directory, and of type "directory." Save the standard output in a file called found and any errors in a file called found.errs.

    g. What is noclobber? How do you override it?

    h. Take the output of three commands and redirect the output to a file called gottemall.

    i. Use a pipe(s) with the ps and wc commands to find out how many processes you are currently running.

LAB 23: VARIABLES AND ARRAYS

1. What is the difference between a local variable and an environment variable?

2. How do you list all local variables? Environmental variables?

3. In what initialization file would you store local variables? Why?

4. Create an array called fruit. Put five kinds of fruit in the array.

    a. Print the array.

    b. Print the last element of the array.

    c. Print the number of elements in the array.

    d. Remove the first element from the array.

    e. If you store an item that isn't fruit in the array, is it okay?

5. Describe the difference between a wordlist and a string.

chapter

10

Programming the C and TC Shells

10.1 Introduction

10.1.1 The Steps in Creating a Shell Script

A shell script is normally written in an editor and consists of commands interspersed with comments. Comments are preceded by a pound sign (#) and consist of text used to document what is going on.

The First Line. At the top left corner, the line preceded by #! (often called *shbang*) indicates the program that will be executing the lines in the script.

```
#!/bin/csh   or   #!/bin/tcsh
```

The #!, also called a *magic number*, is used by the kernel to identify the program that should be interpreting the lines in the script. When a program is loaded into memory, the kernel will examine the first line. If the first line is binary data, the program will be executed as a compiled program; if the first line contains the #!, the kernel will look at the path following the #! and start that program as the interpreter. If the path is /bin/csh, the C shell will interpret the lines in the program. If the path is /bin/tcsh, the TC shell will interpret the lines in the program. This line must be the top line of your script or the line will be treated as a comment line.

When the script starts, the .cshrc file (for csh) or .tcshrc file (for tcsh) is read first and executed, so that anything set within that file will become part of your script. You can prevent the .cshrc or .tcshrc file from being read into your script by using the -f (fast) option to the C shell program. This option is written as

```
#!/bin/csh -f   or   #!/bin/tcsh -f
```

Note: In all the following examples, if you are using tcsh, change the shbang line to

```
#!/bin/tcsh -f
```

Comments.   Comments are lines preceded by a pound sign. They are used to document your script. It is sometimes difficult to understand what the script is supposed to do if it is not commented. Although comments are important, they are often too sparse or not even used at all. Try to get used to commenting what you are doing not only for someone else, but also for yourself. Two days from now you may not remember exactly what you were trying to do.

Making the Script Executable.   When you create a file, it is not given execute permission. You need this permission to run your script. Use the chmod command to turn on execute permission.

EXAMPLE 10.1

```
1    % chmod +x myscript
2    % ls -lF  myscript
     -rwxr--xr--x    1 ellie  0 Jul  13:00 myscript*
```

EXPLANATION

1   The chmod command is used to turn on execute permission for the user, the group, and others.

2   The output of the ls command indicates that all users have execute permission on the myscript file. The asterisk at the end of the filename (resulting from the -F option) also indicates that this is an executable program.

An Example Scripting Session.   In the following example, the user will create the script in the editor. After saving the file, the execute permissions are turned on with the chmod command, and the script is executed. If there are errors in the program, the C shell will respond immediately.

EXAMPLE 10.2

```
(The Script - info)
    #!/bin/csh -f
    # Scriptname: info
1   echo Hello ${LOGNAME}!
2   echo The hour is `date +%H`
3   echo "This machine is `uname -n`"
4   echo The calendar for this month is
5   cal
6   echo The processes you are running are:
7   ps -ef | grep  "^ *$LOGNAME"
8   echo "Thanks for coming. See you soon\!\!"

    (The Command Line)
    % chmod +x info
    % info
```

EXAMPLE 10.2 (CONTINUED)

```
1    Hello ellie!
2    The hour is 09
3    This machine is jody
4    The calendar for this month is
5        July 2004
      S   M   Tu   W   Th   F   S
                         1   2   3
      4   5   6    7    8    9   10
     11  12  13   14   15   16   17
     18  19  20   21   22   23   24
     25  26  27   28   29   30   31
7    The processes you are running are:
     < output of ps prints here >
8    Thanks for coming. See you soon!!
```

EXPLANATION

1   The user is greeted. The variable LOGNAME holds the user's name. On BSD systems, USER is used. The curly braces shield the variable from the exclamation point. The exclamation point does not need to be escaped because it will not be interpreted as a history character unless there is a character appended to it.

2   The date command is enclosed in backquotes. The shell will perform command substitution and the date's output, the current hour, will be substituted into the echo string.

3   The uname -n command displays the machine name.

4, 5   The cal command is not enclosed in backquotes because when the shell performs command substitution, the newlines are all stripped from the output. This produces a strange-looking calendar. By putting the cal command on a line by itself, the formatting is preserved. The calendar for this month is printed.

6, 7   The user's processes are printed. Use ps -aux for BSD or ps au with Linux.[a]

8   The string is printed. Note that the two exclamation points are prepended with backslashes. This is necessary to prevent history substitution.

a. Linux supports a variety of different style options, including UNIX98, BSD and GNU. See your *man* page for ps.

10.2 Reading User Input

10.2.1 The $< Variable

To make a script interactive, a special C shell variable is used to read standard input into a variable. The $< symbol reads a line from standard input up to but not including the newline, and assigns the line to a variable.[1]

---

1. Another way to read one line of input is setvariable = 'head -1'.

EXAMPLE 10.3

```
(The Script - greeting)
    #/bin/csh -f
    # The greeting script
1   echo -n  "What is your name? "
2   set name = $<
3   echo Greetings to you, $name.

(The Command Line)
    % chmod +x greeting
    % greeting
1   What is your name? Dan Savage
3   Greetings to you, Dan Savage.
```

EXPLANATION

1   The string is echoed to the screen. The -n option causes the echo command to suppress the newline at the end of the string. On some versions of echo, use a \c at the end of the string to suppress the newline; for example, echo hello\c.

2   Whatever is typed at the terminal, up to a newline, is stored as a string in the name variable.

3   The string is printed after variable substitution is performed.

10.2.2   Creating a Wordlist from the Input String

Because the input from the $< variable is stored as a string, you may want to break the string into a wordlist.

EXAMPLE 10.4

```
1   % echo What is your full name\?
2   % set name = $<
    Lola Justin Lue
3   % echo Hi $name[1]
    Hi Lola Justin Lue
4   % echo $name[2]
    Subscript out of range.
5   % set name = ( $name )
6   % echo Hi $name[1]
    Hi Lola
7   % echo $name[2] $name[3]
    Justin Lue
```

1   The user is asked for input.

2   The special variable $< accepts input from the user in a string format.

3   Because the value Lola Justin Lue is stored as a single string, the subscript [1] displays the whole string. Subscripts start at 1.

4   The string consists of one word. There are not two words, so by using a subscript of [2], the shell complains Subscript out of range.

5   To create a wordlist, the string is enclosed in parentheses. An array is created. The string is broken up into a list of words and assigned to the variable name.

6   The first element of the array is printed.

7   The second and third elements of the array are printed.

10.3 Arithmetic

There is not really a need to do math problems in a shell script, but sometimes arithmetic is necessary, for instance, to increment or decrement a loop counter. The C shell supports integer arithmetic only. The @ symbol is used to assign the results of calculations to numeric variables.

10.3.1 Arithmetic Operators

The following operators shown in Table 10.1 are used to perform integer arithmetic operations. They are the same operators as found in the C programming language. See Table 10.6 on page 538 for operator precedence. Also borrowed from the C language are shortcut assignment operators, shown in Table 10.2.

Table 10.1   Integer Arithmetic Operators

Operator	Function
+	Addition
-	Subtraction
/	Division
*	Multiplication
%	Modulus
<<	Left shift
>>	Right shift

Table 10.2 Shortcut Operators

Operator	Example	Equivalent To
+=	@ num += 2	@ num = $num + 2
-=	@ num -= 4	@ num = $num - 4
*=	@ num *= 3	@ num = $num * 3
/=	@ num /= 2	@ num = $num / 2
++	@ num++	@ num = $num + 1
--	@ num--	@ num = $num - 1

EXAMPLE 10.5

```
1   % @ sum = 4 + 6
    echo $sum
    10
2   % @ sum++
    echo $sum
    11
3   % @ sum += 3
    echo $sum
    14
4   % @ sum--
    echo $sum
    13
5   % @ n = 3+4
    @: Badly formed number
```

EXPLANATION

1   The variable sum is assigned the result of adding 4 and 6. (The space after the @ is required.)
2   The variable sum is incremented by 1.
3   The variable sum is incremented by 3.
4   The variable sum is decremented by 1.
5   Spaces are required after the @ symbol and surrounding the operator.

10.3.2 Floating-Point Arithmetic

Because floating-point arithmetic is not supported by this shell, if you should need more complex mathematical operations, you can use UNIX utilities.

The bc and nawk utilities are useful if you need to perform complex calculations.

EXAMPLE 10.6

```
(The Command Line)
1    set n=`echo "scale=3; 13 / 2" | bc`
     echo $n
     6.500

2    set product=`nawk -v x=2.45 -v y=3.124 'BEGIN{\
     printf "%.2f\n", x * y }'`
     % echo $product
     7.65
```

EXPLANATION

1   The output of the echo command is piped to the bc program. The scale is set to 3; that is, the number of significant digits to the right of the decimal point that will be printed. The calculation is to divide 13 by 2. The entire pipeline is enclosed in backquotes. Command substitution will be performed and the output assigned to the variable n.

2   The nawk program gets its values from the argument list passed in at the command line. Each argument passed to nawk is preceded by the -v switch; for example, -v x=2.45 and -v y=3.124. After the numbers are multiplied, the printf function formats and prints the result with a precision of 2 places to the right of the decimal point. The output is assigned to the variable product.

10.4 Debugging Scripts

C/TC shell scripts often fail because of some simple syntax error or logic error. Options to the csh command to help you debug your programs are provided in Table 10.3.

Table 10.3   echo (-x) and verbose (-v)

Option	What It Does
As Options to csh and tcsh	
csh -x scriptname tcsh -x scriptname	Display each line of script after variable substitution and before execution.
csh -v scriptname tcsh -v scriptname	Display each line of script before execution, just as you typed it.
csh -n scriptname tcsh -n scriptname	Interpret but do not execute commands.
As Arguments to the set Command	
set echo	Display each line of script after variable substitution and before execution.
set verbose	Display each line of script before execution, just as you typed it.

Table 10.3 echo (-x) and verbose (-v) (continued)

Option	What It Does
As the First Line in a Script	
#!/bin/csh -xv #!/bin/tcsh -xv	Turns on both echo and verbose. These options can be invoked separately or combined with other csh invocation arguments.

EXAMPLE 10.7

```
(The -v and -x Options)
1   % cat practice
    #!/bin/csh
    echo Hello $LOGNAME
    echo The date is `date`
    echo Your home shell is $SHELL
    echo Good-bye $LOGNAME

2   % csh -v practice
    echo Hello $LOGNAME
    Hello ellie
    echo The date is `date`
    The date is Sun May 23 12:24:07 PDT  2004
    echo Your login shell is $SHELL
    Your login shell is /bin/csh
    echo Good-bye $LOGNAME
    Good-bye ellie

3   % csh -x practice
    echo Hello ellie
    Hello ellie
    echo The date is `date`
    date
    The date is Sun May 23 12:24:15 PDT  2004
    echo Your login shell is /bin/csh
    Your login shell is /bin/csh
    echo Good-bye ellie
    Good-bye ellie
```

EXPLANATION

1. The contents of the C shell script are displayed. Variable and command substitution lines are included so that you can see how echo and verbose differ.

2. The -v option to the csh command causes the verbose feature to be enabled. Each line of the script is displayed as it was typed in the script, and then the line is executed.

3. The -x option to the csh command enables echoing. Each line of the script is displayed after variable and command substitution are performed, and then the line is executed. Because this feature lets you examine what is being replaced as a result of command and variable substitution, it is used more often than the verbose option.

EXAMPLE 10.8

(Echo and Verbose)

1   % **cat practice**
     #!/bin/csh
     echo Hello $LOGNAME
     echo The date is `date`
     set echo
     echo Your home shell is $SHELL
     unset echo
     echo Good-bye $LOGNAME

     % chmod +x practice

2   % **practice**
     Hello ellie
     The date is Sun May 26 12:25:16 PDT 2004
     --> *echo Your login shell is /bin/csh*
     --> *Your login shell is /bin/csh*
     --> *unset echo*
     Good-bye ellie

EXPLANATION

1   The echo option is set and unset within the script. This enables you to debug certain sections of your script where you have run into a bottleneck, rather than echoing each line of the entire script.

2   The --> marks where the echoing was turned on. Each line is printed after variable and command substitution and then executed.

EXAMPLE 10.9

1   % **cat practice**
     #!/bin/csh
     echo Hello $LOGNAME
     echo The date is `date`
     set verbose
     echo Your home shell is $SHELL
     unset verbose
     echo Good-bye $LOGNAME

2   % **practice**
     Hello ellie
     The date is Sun May 23 12:30:09 PDT 2004
     --> *echo Your login shell is $SHELL*
     --> *Your login shell is /bin/csh*
     --> *unset verbose*
     Good-bye ellie

10.5 Command-Line Arguments

Shell scripts can take command-line arguments. Arguments are used to modify the behavior of the program in some way. The C shell assigns command-line arguments to positional parameters and enforces no specific limit on the number of arguments that can be assigned (the Bourne shell sets a limit of nine positional parameters). Positional parameters are number variables. The script name is assigned to $0, and any words following the scriptname are assigned to $1, $2, $3 . . . ${10}, ${11}, and so on. $1 is the first command-line argument. In addition to using positional parameters, the C shell provides the `argv` built-in array.

10.5.1   Positional Parameters and argv

If using the `argv` array notation, a valid subscript must be provided to correspond to the argument being passed in from the command line or the error message `Subscript out of range` is sent by the C shell. The `argv` array does not include the script name. The first argument is $argv[1], and the number of arguments is represented by $#argv. (There is no other way to represent the number of arguments.) See Table 10.4.

Table 10.4   Command-Line Arguments

Argument	Meaning
$0	The name of the script.
$1, $2, . . . ${10} . . .	The first and second positional parameters are referenced by the number preceded by a dollar sign. The curly braces shield the number 10 so that it does not print the first positional parameter followed by a 0.
$*	All the positional parameters.
$argv[0]	Not valid; nothing is printed. C shell array subscripts start at 1.
$argv[1] $argv[2]...	The first argument, second argument, and so on.
$argv[*]	All arguments.
$argv	All arguments.
$#argv	The number of arguments.
$argv[$#argv]	The last argument.

EXAMPLE 10.10

```
(The Script)
#!/bin/csh -f
# The greetings script
# This script greets a user whose name is typed in at the command line.
1   echo $0 to you $1 $2 $3
2   echo Welcome to this day `date | awk '{print $1, $2, $3}'`
3   echo Hope you have a nice day, $argv[1]\!
4   echo Good-bye $argv[1] $argv[2] $argv[3]


(The Command Line)
    % chmod +x greetings
    % greetings Guy Quigley
1   greetings to you Guy Quigley
2   Welcome to this day Fri Aug 28
3   Hope you have a nice day, Guy!
4   Subscript out of range
```

EXPLANATION

1   The name of the script and the first three positional parameters are to be displayed. Because there are only two positional parameters coming in from the command line, Guy and Quigley, $1 becomes Guy, $2 becomes Quigley, and $3 is not defined.

2   The awk command is quoted with single quotes so that the shell does not confuse awk's field numbers $1, $2, and $3 with positional parameters. (Do not confuse awk's field designators $1, $2, and $3 with the shell's positional parameters.)

3   The argv array is assigned values coming in from the command line. Guy is assigned to argv[1] and its value is displayed. You can use the argv array to represent the command-line arguments within your script, or you can use positional parameters. The difference is that positional parameters do not produce an error if you reference one that has no value, whereas an unassigned argv value causes the script to exit with the Subscript out of range error message.

4   The shell prints the error Subscript out of range because there is no value for argv[3].

10.6 Conditional Constructs and Flow Control

When making decisions, the if, if/else, if/else if, and switch commands are used. These commands control the flow of the program by allowing decision making based on whether an expression is true or false.

10.6.1 Testing Expressions

An expression consists of a set of operands separated by operators. Operators and precedence are listed in Tables 10.5 and 10.6, respectively. To test an expression, the expression is surrounded by parentheses. The C shell evaluates the expression, resulting in either a zero or nonzero numeric value. If the result is *nonzero*, the expression is *true*; if the result is *zero*, the expression is *false*.

Table 10.5 Comparison and Logical Operators

Operator	Meaning	Example
==	Equal to	$x == $y
!=	Not equal to	$x != $y
>	Greater than	$x > $y
>=	Greater than or equal to	$x >= $y
<	Less than	$x < $y
<=	Less than or equal to	$x <= $y
=~	String matches	$ans =~ [Yy]*
!~	String does not match	$ans !~ [Yy]*
!	Logical NOT	! $x
||	Logical OR	$x || $y
&&	Logical AND	$x && $y

When evaluating an expression with the logical AND (&&), the shell evaluates from left to right. If the first expression (before the &&) is false, the shell assigns *false* as the result of the entire expression, never checking the remaining expressions. Both expressions surrounding a logical && operator must be true for the entire expression to evaluate to true.

```
( 5 && 6 )   Expression is true
( 5 && 0 )   Expression is false
( 0 && 3 && 2 )   Expression is false
```

When evaluating an expression with the logical OR (||), if the first expression to the left of the || is true, the shell assigns *true* to the entire expression and never checks further. In a logical || expression, only one of the expressions must be true.

```
( 5 || 6 )    Expression is true
( 5 || 0 )    Expression is true
( 0 || 0 )    Expression is false
( 0 || 4 || 2 )   Expression is true
```

The logical NOT is a unary operator; that is, it evaluates one expression. If the expression to the right of the NOT operator is *true*, the expression becomes false. If it is false, the expression becomes true.

```
! 5   Expression is false
! 0   Expression is true
```

10.6.2   Precedence and Associativity

Like C, the C shell uses precedence and associativity rules when testing expressions. If you have an expression with a mix of different operators, such as the following, the shell reads the operators in a certain order:

```
@  x = 5 + 3 * 2
echo $x
11
```

Precedence refers to the order of importance of the operator. *Associativity* refers to whether the shell reads the expression from left to right or right to left when the precedence is equal.[2] Other than in arithmetic expressions (which you will not readily need in shell scripts anyway), the order of associativity is from left to right if the precedence is equal. You can change the order by using parentheses. (See Table 10.6.)

```
@ x = ( 5 + 3 ) * 2
echo $x
16
```

Expressions can be numeric, relational, or logical. Numeric expressions use the following arithmetic operators:

```
+ - * /   ++ -- %
```

Relational expressions use the operators that yield either a true (nonzero) or false (zero) result:

```
>  <   >=   <=   ==   !=
```

Logical expressions use these operators that also yield true or false:

```
!   && ||
```

---

2. Associativity in arithmetic expressions is right to left in cases of equal precedence.

Table 10.6 Operator Precedence

Operator	Precedence	Meaning
( )	High	Change precedence; group
~		Complement
!		Logical NOT, negation
* / %		Multiply, divide, modulo
+ -		Add, subtract
<< >>		Bitwise left and right shift
> >= < <=		Relational operators: greater than, less than
== !=		Equality: equal to, not equal to
=~ !~		Pattern matching: matches, does not match
&		Bitwise AND
^		Bitwise exclusive OR
|		Bitwise inclusive OR
&&		Logical AND
||	Low	Logical OR

10.6.3 The if Statement

The simplest form of conditional is the if statement. After the if expression is tested, and if the expression evaluates to true, the commands after the then keyword are executed until the endif is reached. The endif keyword terminates the block. The if statement may be nested as long as every single if statement is terminated with a matching endif. The endif goes with the nearest enclosing if.

FORMAT

```
if ( expression ) then
      command
      command
endif
```

EXAMPLE 10.11

```
(In the Script: Checking for Arguments)
1   if ( $#argv != 1 ) then
2       echo "$0 requires an argument"
3       exit 1
4   endif
```

EXPLANATION

1 This line reads: If the number of arguments ($#argv) passed in from the command line is not equal to one, then . . .

2 If the first line is true, this line and line 3 are executed.

3 The program exits with a value of 1, meaning it failed.

4 Every if block is closed with an endif statement.

10.6.4 Testing and Unset or Null Variables

The $? special variable is used to test if a variable has been set. It will return true if the variable is set to some value, including null.

EXAMPLE 10.12

```
(From .cshrc/.tcshrc File)
if ( $?prompt ) then
    set history = 32
endif
```

EXPLANATION

The .cshrc file is executed every time you start a new csh program. $? is used to check to see if a variable has been set. In this example, the shell checks to see if the prompt has been set. If the prompt is set, you are running an interactive shell, not a script. The prompt is only set for interactive use. Because the history mechanism is only useful when running interactively, the shell will not set history if you are running a script.

EXAMPLE 10.13

```
(The Script)
    echo -n "What is your name? "
1   set name = $<
2   if ( "$name" != "" ) then
        grep "$name" datafile
    endif
```

EXPLANATION

1   The user is asked for input. If the user just presses Enter, the variable name is set, but it is set to null.

2   The variable is double quoted so that if the user enters more than one word in name, the expression will still be evaluated. If the quotes were removed and the user entered first and last name, the shell would exit the script with the error message if: Expression syntax. The empty double quotes represent a null string.

10.6.5   The if/else Statement

The if/else construct is a two-way branching control structure. If the expression following the if is true, the statements following it are executed; otherwise, the statements after the else are executed. The endif matches the innermost if statement and terminates the statement.

FORMAT

```
if ( expression ) then
    command
else
    command
endif
```

EXAMPLE 10.14

```
1   if ( $answer =~ [Yy]* ) then
2       mail bob < message
3   else
4       mail john < datafile
5   endif
```

EXPLANATION

1   This line reads: If the value of $answer matches a Y or a y, followed by zero or more characters, then go to line 2; otherwise, go to line 3. (The * is a shell metacharacter.)

2   The user bob is mailed the contents of the file message.

3   The commands under the else are executed if line 1 is not true.

4   The user john is mailed the contents of the file datafile.

5   The endif block ends the if block.

10.6.6   Logical Expressions

The logical operators are &&, ||, and !. The AND operator, &&, evaluates the expression on the left-hand side of &&; if true, the expression on the right side of && is tested and must also be true. If one expression is false, the expression is false. The OR operator, ||, evaluates the expression on the left-hand side of ||; if true, the expression is true; if false, the expression on the right side of the || operator is tested. If it is true, the expression is true. If both expressions are false, the expression is false. The NOT operator, !, is a unary operator. It evaluates the expression on the right and if that expression is true, it becomes false, and if it is false, it becomes true. If one expression is false, the expression is false.

The -x option (called echoing) to the C/TC shell allows you to trace what is going on in your script as it executes. (See Chapter 15, "Debugging Shell Scripts," on page 967.)

EXAMPLE 10.15

```
(The Script: Using Logical Expressions and Checking Values)
    #!/bin/csh -f
    # Scriptname: logical
    set x = 1
    set y = 2
    set z = 3
1   if ( ( "$x" && "$y" ) || ! "$z" ) then
        # Note: grouping and parentheses
2       echo TRUE
    else
        echo FALSE
    endif

(The Output)
3   % csh -x logical
    set x = 1
    set y = 2
    set z = 3
    if ( ( 1 && 2 ) || ! 3 ) then
    echo TRUE
    TRUE
    else
    %
```

EXPLANATION

1   The logical expression is being evaluated. The first expression is enclosed in parentheses (not necessary because && is of higher precedence than ||). The parentheses do not require spaces when nested, but the negation operator (!) must have a space after it.

2   If the expression evaluates true, this line is executed.

3   The csh program is executed with the -x switch. This turns on echoing. Every line in your script is echoed back to you after variable substitution has been performed.

10.6.7 The if Statement and a Single Command

If an expression is followed by a single command, the then and endif keywords are not
necessary.

FORMAT

```
if ( expression ) single command
```

EXAMPLE 10.16

```
if ($#argv == 0) exit 1
```

EXPLANATION

The expression is tested. If the number of command-line arguments, $#argv, is equal to
0, the program is exited with a status of 1.

10.6.8 The if/else if Statement

The if/else if construct offers a multiway decision-making mechanism. A number of
expressions can be tested, and when one of the expressions evaluated is true, the block
of statements that follow is executed. If none of the expressions is true, the else block is
executed.

FORMAT

```
if ( expression ) then
    command
    command
else if ( expression ) then
    command
    command
else
    command
endif
```

EXAMPLE 10.17

```
(The Script: grade)
    #!/bin/csh -f
    # Scriptname: grade
    echo -n "What was your grade? "
    set grade = $<
1   if ( $grade >= 90 && $grade <= 100 ) then
        echo "You got an A\!"
```

EXAMPLE 10.17 (CONTINUED)

```
2   else if ( $grade > 79 ) then
        echo "You got a B"
3   else if ( $grade > 69 ) then
        echo "You're average"
    else
4       echo "Better study"
5   endif
```

EXPLANATION

1   If grade is greater than or equal to 90 and grade is less than or equal to 100, then You got an A! is printed. *Both* expressions surrounding the && must be true or program control will go to the else if on line 2.

2   If line 1 is false, test the expression (line 2), and if it is true, You got a B is printed.

3   If line 1 and 2 are both false, try this one. If this expression is true, then You're average is printed.

4   If all of the above expressions test false, the statements in the else block are executed.

5   The endif ends the entire if construct.

10.6.9 Exit Status and the Status Variable

Every UNIX/Linux command returns an exit status. If the command was successful, it returns an exit status of zero. If the command failed, it returns a nonzero exit status. You can test to see whether the command succeeded or failed by looking at the value of the C shell status variable. The status variable contains the exit status of the last command executed.

EXAMPLE 10.18

```
1   % grep ellie /etc/passwd
    ellie:pHAZk66gA:9496:41:Ellie:/home/jody/ellie:/bin/csh
2   % echo $status
    0                   # Zero shows that grep was a success

3   % grep joe /etc/passwd
4   % echo $status
    1                   # Nonzero shows that grep failed
```

EXPLANATION

1   The grep program found ellie in the /etc/passwd file.

2   The grep program, if it finds the pattern ellie, returns a zero status when it exits.

3   The grep program did not find joe in the /etc/passwd file.

4   The grep program returns a nonzero status if the pattern is not found.

10.6.10   Exiting from a Shell Script

In your shell script, the exit command will take you back to the shell prompt. The exit command takes an integer value to indicate the type of exit. A nonzero argument indicates failure; zero indicates success. The number must be between 0 and 255.

EXAMPLE 10.19

```
(The checkon Shell Script)
    #!/bin/csh -f
1   if ( $#argv != 1 ) then
2           echo "$0 requires an argument"
3           exit 2
4   endif


(At the command line)
5   % checkon
    checkon requires an argument
6   % echo $status
    2
```

EXPLANATION

1   If the number of arguments passed in from the command line ($#argv) is not equal to 1, then go to line 2.

2   The echo prints the script name ($0) and the string requires an argument.

3   The program exits back to the prompt with a value of 2. This value will be stored in the status variable of the parent shell.

4   The end of the conditional if.

5   At the command line, the program checkon is executed without an argument.

6   The program exits with a value of 2, which is stored in the status variable.

10.6.11   Using an Alias to Create an Error Message

You may want to create a customized diagnostic message when exiting from a script due to some error condition. This can be accomplished with an alias, as shown in Example 10.20.

EXAMPLE   10.20

```
(The Script)
    #!/bin/tcsh -f
    # Scriptname: filecheck
    # Usage: filecheck filename
1   alias Usage 'echo "    Usage: $0 filename\!*" ; exit 1'
2   alias Error 'echo "    Error: \!* "; exit 2'
3   set file=$1
4   if ( $#argv == 0 ) then
        Usage
    endif
5   if ( ! -e $file ) then
        Error "$file does not exist"
    endif

(The Command Line)
% filecheck
Usage: filecheck filename
% echo status
1


% filecheck xyzfile
Error: xyzfile does not exist
% echo $status
2
```

10.6.12   Using the Status Variable in a Script

The status variable can be used in a script to test the status of a command. The status variable is assigned the value of the last command that was executed.

EXAMPLE   10.21

```
(The Script)
    #!/bin/csh -f
1   ypmatch  $1  passwd >& /dev/null
2   if ( $status == 0 ) then
3       echo Found $1 in the NIS database
    endif
```

EXPLANATION

1   The ypmatch program checks the NIS database to see if the name of the user, passed in as the first argument, is in the database.

2   If the status returned from the last command is 0, the then block is executed.

3   This line is executed if the if test expression evaluated to be true.

10.6.13   Evaluating Commands Within Conditionals

The C shell evaluates *expressions* in conditionals. To evaluate *commands* in conditionals, curly braces must enclose the command. If the command is successful, that is, returns an exit status of zero, the curly braces tell the shell to evaluate the expression as true (1).[3] If the command fails, the exit status is nonzero, and the expression is evaluated as false (0).

It is important, when using a command in a conditional, to know the exit status of that command. For example, the grep program returns an exit status of 0 when it finds the pattern it is searching for, 1 when it cannot find the pattern, and 2 when it cannot find the file. When awk or sed are searching for patterns, those programs return 0 whether or not they are successful in the pattern search. The criterion for success with awk and sed is based on whether the syntax is correct; that is, if you typed the command correctly, the exit status of awk and sed is 0.

If the exclamation mark is placed before the expression, it NOTs the entire expression so that if true, it is now false, and vice versa. Make sure a space follows the exclamation mark, or the C shell will invoke the history mechanism.

FORMAT

```
if  { ( command ) }  then
    command
    command
endif
```

EXAMPLE 10.22

```
#!/bin/csh -f
1   if  { ( who | grep $1 >& /dev/null ) } then
2       echo $1 is logged on and running:
3       ps -ef | grep "^ *$1"        # ps -aux for BSD
4   endif
```

EXPLANATION

1   The who command is piped to the grep command. All of the output is sent to /dev/null, the UNIX/Linux "bit bucket." The output of the who command is sent to grep; grep searches for the name of the user stored in the $1 variable (the first command-line argument). If grep is successful and finds the user, an exit status of 0 is returned. The shell will then invert the exit status of the grep command to yield 1, or true. If the shell evaluates the expression to be true, it executes the commands between the then and endif.

2   If the C/TC shell evaluates the expression in line 1 to be true, lines 2 and 3 are executed.

3   All the processes running and owned by $1 are displayed.

4   The endif ends the if statements.

---

3. The command's exit status is inverted by the shell so that the expression yields a true or false result.

FORMAT

```
if ! { (command) } then
```

EXAMPLE 10.23

```
1   if  !  { ( ypmatch $user passwd >& /dev/null ) } then
2       echo $user is not a user here.
        exit 1
3   endif
```

EXPLANATION

1   The ypmatch command is used to search the NIS passwd file, if you are using a network. If the command succeeds in finding the user ($user) in the passwd file, the expression evaluates to be true. The exclamation point (!) preceding the expression NOTs or complements the expression; that is, makes it false if it is true, and vice versa.

2   If the expression is not true, the user is not found and this line is executed.

3   The endif ends this if block.

10.6.14   The goto

A goto allows you to jump to some label in the program and start execution at that point. Although gotos are frowned on by many programmers, they are sometimes useful for breaking out of nested loops.

EXAMPLE 10.24

```
(The Script)
    #!/bin/csh -f
1   startover:
2   echo "What was your grade? "
    set grade = $<
3   if ( "$grade" < 0 || "$grade" > 100 ) then
4       echo "Illegal grade"
5       goto startover
    endif
    if ( $grade >= 89 ) then
        echo "A for the genius\!"
    else if ( $grade >= 79 ) then
        .. < Program continues >
```

EXPLANATION

1   The label is a user-defined word with a colon appended. The label is called start-over. During execution of the program, the label is ignored by the shell, unless the shell is explicitly directed to go to the label.

EXPLANATION (CONTINUED)

2   The user is asked for input.

3   If the expression is true (the user entered a grade less than 0 or greater than 100), the string Illegal grade is printed, and the goto starts execution at the named label, startover. The program continues to execute from that point.

4   The if expression tested false, so this line is printed.

5   The goto sends control to line 1 and execution starts after the label, startover.

10.6.15   File Testing with the C Shell

Both the C and TC shells have a built-in set of options for testing attributes of files, such as whether it is a directory, a plain file (not a directory), a readable file, and so forth. The TC shell adds a few more features in this area, which will be discussed in "File Testing with the TC Shell" on page 551. For other types of file tests, the UNIX/Linux test command is used. The built-in options for file inquiry are listed in Table 10.7.

Table 10.7   File Testing with the C Shell

Test Flag	(What It Tests) True If
-d	File is a directory
-e	File exists
-f	File is a plain file
-o	Current user owns the file
-r	Current user can read the file
-w	Current user can write to the file
-x	Current user can execute the file
-z	File is zero length

EXAMPLE 10.25

```
    #!/bin/csh -f
1   if ( -e file ) then
        echo file exists
    endif
2   if ( -d file ) then
        echo file is a directory
    endif
```

EXAMPLE 10.25 (CONTINUED)

```
3   if ( ! -z file ) then
         echo file is not of zero length
    endif
4   if ( -r file && -w file ) then
         echo file is readable and writable
    endif
```

EXPLANATION

1   The statement reads: if the file exists, then . . .
2   The statement reads: if the file is a directory, then . . .
3   The statement reads: if the file is not of zero length, then . . .
4   The statement reads: if the file is readable and writable, then . . . . The file-testing flags cannot be stacked, as in -rwx file. A single option precedes the filename (e.g., -r file && -w file && -x file).

10.6.16   The test Command and File Testing

The UNIX/Linux test command includes options that were built into the C shell, as well as a number of options that were not. See Table 10.8 for a list of test options. You may need these additional options when testing less common attributes of files such as block and special character files, or setuid files. The test command evaluates an expression and returns an exit status of either 0 for success or 1 for failure. When using the test command in an if conditional statement, curly braces must surround the command so that the shell can evaluate the exit status properly.[4]

Table 10.8   File Testing with the test Command

Option	Meaning—Tests True If
-b	File is a block special device file
-c	File is a character special device file
-d	File exists and is a directory file
-f	File exists and is a plain file
-g	File has the set-group-ID bit set
-k	File has the sticky bit set

4. A common error is to name your script test. If your search path contains the UNIX test command first, it will execute it instead of your script. The test command either displays an error or nothing at all if the syntax is correct.

Table 10.8   File Testing with the `test` Command (continued)

Option	Meaning—Tests True If
-p	File is a named pipe
-r	Current user can read the file
-s	File exists and is not empty
-t n	n is file descriptor for terminal
-u	File has the set-user-ID bit set
-w	Current user can write to the file
-x	Current user can execute the file

EXAMPLE 10.26

```
1    if { test -b file } echo file is a block special device file

2    if { test -u file }  echo file has the set-user-id bit set
```

EXPLANATION

1   The statement reads: if the file is a block special device file (found in /dev), then . . .
2   The statement reads: if the file is a setuid program (set user ID), then . . .

10.6.17   Nesting Conditionals

Conditional statements can be nested. Every if must have a corresponding endif (else if does not have an endif). It is a good idea to indent nested statements and line up the ifs and endifs so that you can read and test the program more effectively.

EXAMPLE 10.27

```
(The Script)
    #!/bin/csh -f
    # Scriptname: filecheck

    # Usage: filecheck filename

    set file=$1
1  ┌─if ( ! -e $file ) then
   │      echo "$file does not exist"
   │      exit 1
   └─endif
```

EXAMPLE 10.27 (CONTINUED)

```
2  ┌─ if ( -d $file ) then
   │       echo "$file is a directory"
3  │  else if (-f $file) then
4  │     ┌─ if ( -r $file && -x $file ) then     # Nested if construct
   │     │      echo "You have read and execute permission on $file"
5  │     └─ endif
   │  else
   │       print "$file is neither a plain file nor a directory."
6  └─ endif
```

(The Command Line)
$ **filecheck testing**
You have read and execute permission of file testing.

EXPLANATION

1 If file (after variable substitution) is a file that does not exist (note the NOT operator, !), the commands under the then keyword are executed. An exit value of 1 means that the program failed.

2 If the file is a directory, print testing is a directory.

3 If the file is not a directory, else if the file is a plain file, then . . . the next statement is executed, another if.

4 This if is nested in the previous if. If file is readable, writable, and executable, then . . . . This if has its own endif and is lined up to indicate where it belongs.

5 The endif terminates the innermost if construct.

6 The endif terminates the outermost if construct.

10.6.18 File Testing with the TC Shell

The TC shell, like the C shell, has a built-in set of options for testing attributes of files, such as whether the file is a directory, a plain file (not a directory), a readable file, and so forth. But the TC shell provides additional techniques for file testing as listed below.

The operators listed in Table 10.9 return 1 for true and 0 for false after testing an attribute of a file or directory in terms of the real user. The built-in options for file inquiry are listed in Table 10.10 on page 554. The TC shell allows these operators to be bound together (the C shell does not). The form -rwx is the same as -r && -w && -x.

Table 10.9 File Testing with the TC Shell

Test Flag	(What It Tests) True If
-b	File is a block special file
-c	File is a character special file

Table 10.9   File Testing with the TC Shell (continued)

Test Flag	(What It Tests) True If
-d	File is a directory
-e	File exists
-f	File is a plain file
-g	Set-group-ID bit is set
-k	Sticky bit is set
-l	File is a symbolic link
-L	Applies subsequent operators in a multiple-operator list to a symbolic link rather than to the file to which it is linked
-o	Current user owns the file
-p	File is named pipe (fifo)
-r	Current user can read the file
-R	Has been migrated (convex only)
-s	File is nonzero size
-S	File is a socket special file
-t file	file (must be a digit) is an open file descriptor for a terminal device
-w	Current user can write to the file
-x	Current user can execute the file
-z	File is zero length

EXAMPLE 10.28

```
(The Script)
    #!/bin/tcsh -f
    # Scriptname: filetest1
1   if ( -e file ) then
        echo file exists
    endif
2   if ( -d file ) then
        echo file is a directory
    endif
3   if ( ! -z file ) then
        echo file is not of zero length
    endif
```

EXAMPLE 10.28 (CONTINUED)

```
4   if ( -r file && -w file && -x file) then
        echo  file is readable and writable and executable.
    endif
5   if ( -rwx file ) then
        echo file is readable and writable and executable.
    endif
```

EXPLANATION

1   The statement reads: if the file exists, then . . .

2   The statement reads: if the file is a directory, then . . .

3   The statement reads: if the file is not of zero length, then . . .

4   The statement reads: if the file is readable and writable, then . . . A single option precedes the filename (e.g., -r file && -w file && -x file).

5   The file-testing flags can be stacked (only with tcsh), as in -rwx file.

EXAMPLE 10.29

```
(The Script)
    #!/bin/tcsh -f
    # Scriptname: filetest2
1   foreach file (`ls`)
2      if ( -rwf $file ) then
3          echo "${file}: readable/writable/plain file"
       endif
    end

(Output)
3 complete: readable/writable/plain file
  dirstack: readable/writable/plain file
  file.sc: readable/writable/plain file
  filetest: readable/writable/plain file
  glob: readable/writable/plain file
  modifiers: readable/writable/plain file
  env: readable/writable/plain file
```

EXPLANATION

1   The foreach loop iterates through the list of files produced by the UNIX/Linux ls program, one file at a file, assigning each filename to the variable file.

2   If the file is readable, writable, and a plain file (-rwf), line number 3 is executed. The stacking of these file-testing options is legal in tcsh, but not in csh.

3   This line is executed if the filename being tested is readable, writable, and executable.

10.6.19 The filetest Built-In (tcsh)

The tcsh built-in filetest command applies one of the file inquiry operators to a file or list of files and returns a space-separated list of numbers; 1 for true and 0 for false.

EXAMPLE 10.30

```
1   > filetest -rwf dirstack file.sc xxx
    1 1 0
2   > filetest -b hdd
    1
3   > filetest -lrx /dev/fd
    1
```

EXPLANATION

1   Each of the files, dirstack, file.sc, and xxx, are tested to see if they are readable, writable, plain files. For the first two files the test returns true (1 1), and for the last the test returns false (0).

2   The filetest command returns 1 if the file, hdd, is a block special device file. It is. Otherwise, 0 is returned.

3   The filetest command returns 1 if the file, fd, is a symbolic link and is readable and executable. It is. Otherwise, 0 is returned.

10.6.20 Additional TC Shell File-Testing Operators

There is an additional set of file-testing operators (tcsh only), shown in Table 10.10, that return information about files. Because the returned values are not true/false values, a −1 indicates failure (except F, which returns a :).

Table 10.10 Additional tcsh File Tests

Operator	What It Does
-A	Last file access time, as the number of seconds since the epoch (Jan. 1, 1970)
-A:	Like A, but in timestamp format, e.g., Fri. Aug. 27 16:36:10 2004
-M	Last file modification time
-M:	Like M, but in timestamp format
-C	Last inode modification time
-C:	Like C, but in timestamp format
-F	Composite file identifier, in the form device:inode
-G	Numeric group ID

Table 10.10   Additional tcsh File Tests (continued)

Operator	What It Does
-G:	Group name or numeric group ID if the group name is unknown
-L	The name of the file pointed to by a symbolic link
-N	Number of (hard) links
-P	Permissions, in octal, without a leading zero
-P:	Like P, with leading a zero
-Pmode	Equivalent to -P file & mode; e.g., -P22 file returns 22 if file is writable by group and other, 20 if by group only, and 0 if by neither
-Mode:	Like PMode:, with leading zero
-U	Numeric user ID
-U:	Username, or the numeric user ID if the username is unknown
-Z	Size, in bytes

EXAMPLE 10.31

```
1  > date
   Wed Apr 22 13:36:11 PST 2004
2  > filetest -A myfile
   934407771
3  > filetest -A: myfile
   Wed Apr 22 14:42:51 2004
4  > filetest -U myfile
   501
5  > filetest -P: myfile
   0600
   > filetest -P myfile
   600
```

EXPLANATION

1 Today's date is printed.
2 With the -A option, the filetest built-in prints the date (in epoch form) when myfile was last accessed.
3 With the -A: option, the filetest built-in prints the date in timestamp format.
4 With the -U option, the filetest built-in prints the numeric user ID for the owner of myfile.
5 With the -P: option, the filetest built-in prints the octal permission mode with a leading 0. Without the colon, the leading 0 is removed.

EXAMPLE 10.32

```
(The Script)
    #!/bin/tcsh -f
    # Scriptname: filecheck
    # Usage: filecheck filename
1   alias Usage 'echo "    Usage: $0 filename\!*" ; exit 1'
2   alias Error 'echo "    Error: \!* "; exit 2'
3   set file=$1                          # The first argument, $1, is assigned
4   if ( $#argv == 0 ) then              # to a variable called
file
        Usage
    endif
5   if ( ! -e $file ) then
        Error "$file does not exist"
    endif
6   if ( -d $file ) then
        echo "$file is a directory"
7   else if (-f $file) then
8       if ( -rx $file ) then    # nested if construct
            echo "You have read and execute permission on $file"
9       endif
    else
        print "$file is neither a plain file nor a directory."
10  endif

(The Command Line)
    % filecheck testing1
    You have read and execute permission on file testing1.
```

EXPLANATION

1   This alias, Usage, can be used to produce an error message and exit the program.

2   This is an alias called Error that will produce an error message followed by any arguments passed when called.

3   The variable file is set to the first argument passed in from the command line, $1 (i.e., testing1).

4   If the number of arguments passed is 0, that is, no arguments were provided, the alias Usage will print its message to the screen.

5   If file (after variable substitution) is a file that does not exist (note the NOT operator, !), the alias, Error, under the then keyword displays its message.

6   If the file is a directory, print "testing1 is a directory."

7   If the file is not a directory, else if the file is a plain file, then . . . the next statement is executed, another if.

8   This if is nested in the previous if. If file is readable and executable, then . . . This if has its own endif and is lined up to indicate where it belongs.

9   The endif terminates the innermost if construct.

10 The endif terminates the outermost if construct.

10.6.21   The switch Command

The switch command is an alternative to using the if-then-else if construct. Sometimes the switch command makes a program clearer to read when handling multiple options. The value in the switch expression is matched against the expressions, called labels, following the case keyword. The case labels will accept constant expressions and wildcards. The label is terminated with a colon. The default label is optional, but its action is taken if none of the other cases match the switch expression. The breaksw is used to transfer execution to the endsw. If a breaksw is omitted and a label is matched, any statements below the matched label are executed until either a breaksw or endsw is reached.

FORMAT

```
switch (variable)
case constant:
     commands
     breaksw
case constant:
     commands
     breaksw
endsw
```

EXAMPLE 10.33

```
(The Script)
#!/bin/csh -f
# Scriptname: colors
1    echo -n "Which color do you like? "
2    set color = $<
3    switch ("$color")
4    case bl*:
         echo I feel $color
         echo The sky is $color
5        breaksw
6    case red:           # Is is red or is it yellow?
7    case yellow:
8        echo The sun is sometimes $color.
9        breaksw
10   default:
11       echo $color is not one of the categories.
12       breaksw
13   endsw
```

EXAMPLE 10.33 (CONTINUED)

```
(The Command Line)
% colors

(The Output)
1   Which color do you like? red
8   The sun is sometimes red.
1   Which color do you like? Doesn't matter
11  Doesn't matter is not one of the categories.
```

EXPLANATION

1   The user is asked for input.

2   The input is assigned to the color variable.

3   The switch statement evaluates the variable. The switch statement evaluates a single word or string of words if the string of words is held together with double quotes.

4   The case label is bl*, meaning that the switch expression will be matched against any set of characters starting with b, followed by an l. If the user entered blue, black, blah, blast, and so forth, the commands under this case label would be executed.

5   The breaksw transfers program control to the endsw statement.

6   If the switch statement matches this label, red, the program starts executing statements until the breaksw on line 9 is reached. Line 8 will be executed. The sun is sometimes red. is displayed.

7   If line 6 is not matched (i.e., the color is not red), case yellow is tested.

8   If either label, red or yellow, is matched, this line is executed.

9   The breaksw transfers program control to the endsw statement.

10 The default label is reached if none of the case labels matches the switch expression. This is like the if/else if/else construct.

11 This line is printed if the user enters something not matched in any of the above cases.

12 This breaksw is optional because the switch will end here. It is recommended to leave the breaksw here so that if more cases are added later, they will not be overlooked.

13 The endsw terminates the switch statement.

Nesting Switches.   Switches can be nested; that is, a switch statement and its cases can be contained within another switch statement as one of its cases. There must be an endsw to terminate each switch statement. A default case is not required.

EXAMPLE 10.34

```
(The Script)
    #!/bin/csh -f
    # Scriptname: systype
    # Program to determine the type of system you are on.
    echo "Your system type is: "
1   set release = (`uname -r`)
2   switch (`uname -s`)
3   case SunOS:
4       switch ("$release")
5       case 4.*:
                echo "SunOS $release"
                breaksw
6       case [5-9].*:
                echo "Solaris $release"
                breaksw
7       endsw
        breaksw
    case HP*:
        echo HP-UX
        breaksw
    case Linux:
        echo Linux
        breaksw
8   endsw
```

```
(The Output)
Your system type:
SunOS 4.1.2
```

EXPLANATION

1   The variable release is assigned the output of uname -r, the release number for the version of the operating system.

2   The switch command evaluates the output of uname -s, the name of the operating system.

3   If the system type is SunOS, the case command on line 3 is executed.

4   The value of the variable release is evaluated in each of the cases for a match.

5   The case for all release versions 4 are tested.

6   The case for all release versions 5–9 are tested.

7   The inner switch statement is terminated.

8   The outer switch statement is terminated.

10.6.22   The here document and Menus

The here document (discussed in "The here document" on page 433) is used in shell scripts to produce a menu. It is often used in conjunction with the switch statement. Once the user has seen the menu, he or she selects an item, and then the choice is matched in the switch statement to the case that corresponds to the choice. The here document reduces the number of echo statements that would otherwise be needed and makes the program easier to read.

EXAMPLE   10.35

```
(The Script)
    #! /bin/tcsh
1   echo "Select from the following menu:"
2   cat << EOF
        1) Red
        2) Green
        3) Blue
        4) Exit
3   EOF
4   set choice = $<
5   switch ("$choice")
6   case 1:
            echo Red is stop.
7           breaksw
    case 2:
            echo Green is go\!
            breaksw
    case 3:
            echo Blue is a feeling...
            breaksw
    case 4:
            exit
            breaksw
    default:
            echo Not a choice\!\!
    endsw
8   echo Good-bye

(The Output)
Select from the following menu:
    1) Red
    2) Green
    3) Blue
    4) Exit
2
Green is go!
Good-bye
```

1   The user is asked to select from the menu produced by the here document on line 2.

2   The here document is used to display a list of color choices.

3   EOF marks the end of the here document.

4   The user input is assigned to the variable choice.

5   The switch statement evaluates the variable choice and proceeds to match the user's choice to one of the cases.

6   If the user selected 1, Red is stop is displayed and the breaksw command on line 7 causes the program to exit the switch and go to line 8. If the user didn't select 1, then the program starts at case 2, and so on.

10.7 Looping Commands

Looping constructs allow you to execute the same statements a number of times. The C shell supports two types of loops: foreach and while. The foreach loop is used when you need to execute commands on a list of items, one item at a time, such as a list of files or a list of usernames. The while loop is used when you want to keep executing a command until a certain condition is met.

10.7.1 The foreach Loop

The foreach command is followed by a variable and a wordlist enclosed in parentheses. The first time the loop is entered, the first word in the list is assigned to the variable. The list is shifted to the left by one and the body of the loop is entered. Each command in the loop body is executed until the end statement is reached. Control returns to the top of the loop. The next word on the list is assigned to the variable, the commands after the foreach line are executed, the end is reached, control returns to the top of the foreach loop, the next word in the wordlist is processed, and so on. When the wordlist is empty, the loop ends.

```
foreach variable (wordlist)
    commands
end
```

EXAMPLE 10.36

```
1   foreach person (bob sam sue fred)
2       mail $person < letter
3   end
```

EXPLANATION

1   The foreach command is followed by a variable, person, and a wordlist enclosed in parentheses. The variable person will be assigned the value bob the first time the foreach loop is entered. Once bob has been assigned to person, bob is shifted off (to the left) and sam is at the beginning of the list. When the end statement is reached, control starts at the top of the loop, and sam is assigned to the variable person. This procedure continues until fred is shifted off, at which time the list is empty and the loop is over.

2   The user bob will be mailed the contents of the file letter the first time through the loop.

3   When the end statement is reached, loop control is returned to the foreach, and the next element in the list is assigned to the variable person.

EXAMPLE 10.37

```
(The Command Line)
% cat maillist
tom
dick
harry
dan

(The Script)
    #!/bin/csh -f
    # Scriptname: mailtomaillist
1   foreach person (`cat maillist`)
2       mail $person <<EOF
        Hi $person,
        How are you?  I've missed you. Come on over
        to my place.
        Your pal,
                $LOGNAME@`uname -n`
    EOF
3   end
```

EXPLANATION

1   Command substitution is performed within the parentheses. The contents of the file maillist become the wordlist. Each name in the wordlist (tom, dick, harry, dan) is assigned, in turn, to the variable person. After the looping statements are executed and the end is reached, control returns to the foreach, a name is shifted off from the list, and assigned to the variable person. The next name in the list replaces the one that was just shifted off. The list therefore decreases in size by one. This process continues until all the names have been shifted off and the list is empty.

2   The here document is used. Input is sent to the mail program from the first EOF to the terminating EOF. (It is important that the last EOF is against the left-hand margin and has no surrounding whitespace.) Each person in the list will be sent the mail message.

3   The end statement for the foreach loop marks the end of the block of lines that is executed within this loop. Control returns to the top of the loop.

EXAMPLE 10.38

```
1   foreach file (*.c)
2       cc $file -o $file:r
    end
```

EXPLANATION

1   The wordlist for the foreach command is a list of files in the current directory ending in .c (i.e., all the C source files).

2   Each file in the list will be compiled. If, for example, the first file to be processed is program.c, the shell will expand the cc command line to

```
cc program.c -o program
```

The :r causes the .c extension to be removed.

EXAMPLE 10.39

```
(The Command Line)
1   % runit f1 f2 f3 dir2 dir3

(The Script)
    #!/bin/csh -f
    # Scriptname: runit
    # It loops through a list of files passed as arguments.

2   foreach arg ($*)
3       if ( -e $arg ) then
        ...             Program code continues here

        else
        ...             Program code continues here
        endif
4   end
5   echo "Program continues here"
```

1   The script name is runit; the command-line arguments are f1, f2, f3, dir2, and dir3.

2   The $* variable evaluates to a list of all the arguments (positional parameters) passed in at the command line. The foreach command processes, in turn, each of the words in the wordlist, f1, f2, f3, dir2, and dir3. Each time through the loop, the first word in the list is assigned to the variable arg. After a word is assigned, it is shifted off (to the left) and the next word is assigned to arg, until the list is empty.

3   The commands in this block are executed for each item in the list until the end statement is reached.

4   The end statement terminates the loop after the wordlist is empty.

5   After the loop ends, the program continues to run.

10.7.2   The while Loop

The while loop evaluates an expression, and as long as the expression is true (nonzero), the commands below the while command will be executed until the end statement is reached. Control will then return to the while expression, the expression will be evaluated, and if still true, the commands will be executed again, and so on. When the while expression is false, the loop ends and control starts after the end statement.

EXAMPLE 10.40

```
(The Script)
    #!/bin/csh -f
1   set num = 0
2   while ($num < 10)
3       echo $num
4       @ num++        # See arithmetic.
5   end
6   echo "Program continues here"
```

EXPLANATION

1   The variable num is set to an initial value of 0.

2   The while loop is entered and the expression is tested. If the value of num is less than 10, the expression is true, and lines 3 and 4 are executed.

3   The value of num is displayed each time through the loop.

4   The value of the variable num is incremented. If this statement were omitted, the loop would continue forever.

5   The end statement terminates the block of executable statements. When this line is reached, control is returned to the top of the while loop and the expression is evaluated again. This continues until the while expression is false (i.e., when $num is 10).

6   Program execution continues here after the loop terminates.

EXAMPLE 10.41

```
(The Script)
   #!/bin/csh -f
1  echo -n  "Who wrote \"War and Peace\"?"
2  set answer = $<
3  while ("$answer" != "Tolstoy")
       echo "Wrong, try again\!"
4      set answer = $<
5  end
6  echo Yeah!
```

EXPLANATION

1   The user is asked for input.

2   The variable answer is assigned whatever the user inputs.

3   The while command evaluates the expression. If the value of $answer is not equal
    to the string Tolstoy exactly, the message Wrong, try again! is printed and the pro-
    gram waits for user input.

4   The variable answer is assigned the new input. This line is important. If the value
    of the variable answer never changes, the loop expression will never become false,
    thus causing the loop to spin infinitely.

5   The end statement terminates the block of code inside the while loop.

6   If the user enters Tolstoy, the loop expression tests false, and control goes to this
    line. Yeah! is printed.

10.7.3 The repeat Command

The repeat command takes two arguments, a number and a command. The *command* is
executed *that* number of times.

EXAMPLE 10.42

```
% repeat 3 echo hello
hello
hello
hello
```

EXPLANATION

The echo command is executed three times.

10.7.4 Looping Control Commands

The shift Command.   The shift command, without an array name as its argument, shifts the argv array by one word from the left, thereby decreasing the size of the argv array by one. Once shifted off, the array element is lost.

EXAMPLE 10.43

```
(The Script)
    #!/bin/csh -f
    # Scriptname: loop.args
1   while ($#argv)
2       echo $argv
3       shift
4   end

(The Command Line)
5   % loop.args a b c d e
    a b c d e
    b c d e
    c d e
    d e
    e
```

EXPLANATION

1   $#argv evaluates to the number of command-line arguments. If there are five command-line arguments, a, b, c, d, and e, the value of $#argv is 5 the first time in the loop. The expression is tested and yields 5, true.

2   The command-line arguments are printed.

3   The argv array is shifted one to the left. There are only four arguments left, starting with b.

4   The end of the loop is reached, and control goes back to the top of the loop. The expression is re-evaluated. This time, $#argv is 4. The arguments are printed, and the array is shifted again. This goes on until all of the arguments are shifted off. At that time, when the expression is evaluated, it will be 0, which is false, and the loop exits.

5   The arguments a, b, c, d, and e are passed to the script via the argv array.

The break Command.   The break command is used to break out of a loop so that control starts after the end statement. It breaks out of the innermost loop. Execution continues after the end statement of the loop.

EXAMPLE 10.44

```
#!/bin/csh -f
# Scriptname: baseball
1   echo -n "What baseball hero died in August 1995? "
2   set answer = $<
3   while ("$answer" !~ [Mm]*)
4           echo "Wrong\! Try again."
            set answer = $<
5           if ( "$answer" =~ [Mm]* ) break
6   end
7   echo "You are a scholar."
```

EXPLANATION

1   The user is asked for input.

2   The input from the user is assigned to the variable answer (answer: Mickey Mantle).

3   The while expression reads: While the value of answer does not begin with a big M or little m, followed by zero or more of any character, enter the loop.

4   The user gets to try again. The variable is reset.

5   If the variable answer matches M or m, break out of the loop. Go to the end statement and start executing statements at line 7.

6   The end statement terminates this block of statements after the loop.

7   After the loop exits, control starts here and this line is executed.

EXAMPLE 10.45

```
#!/bin/csh -f
# Scriptname: database
1   while (1)
        echo "Select a menu item"
2       cat << EOF
        1) Append
        2) Delete
        3) Update
        4) Exit
EOF
3       set choice = $<
4       switch ($choice)
        case 1:
                echo "Appending"
5               break           # Break out of loop; not a breaksw
        case 2:
                echo "Deleting"
                break
```

EXAMPLE 10.45 (CONTINUED)

```
        case 3:
                echo "Updating"
                break
        case 4:
                exit 0
        default:
6               echo "Invalid choice. Try again.
        endsw
7   end
8   echo "Program continues here"
```

EXPLANATION

1   This is called an *infinite* loop. The expression always evaluates to 1, which is true.
2   This is a here document. A menu is printed to the screen.
3   The user selects a menu item.
4   The switch command evaluates the variable.
5   If the user selects a valid choice, between 1 and 4, the command after the appropriate matching case label is executed. The break statement causes the program to break out of the loop and start execution on line 8. Don't confuse this with the breaksw statement, which merely exits the switch at endsw.
6   The default is selected when none of the cases above it are matched. After the echo message is displayed, control goes to the end of the loop and then starts again at the top of the while. Because the expression after the while always evaluates true, the body of the loop is entered and the menu is displayed again.
7   End of the while loop statements.
8   After the loop is exited, this line is executed.

Nested Loops and the repeat Command.   Rather than a goto, the repeat command can be used to break out of nested loops. The repeat command will not do this with the continue command.

EXAMPLE 10.46

```
(Simple Script)
    #!/bin/csh -f
1 ┌─while (1)
  │     echo "Hello, in 1st loop"
2 │   ┌─while (1)
  │   │     echo "In 2nd loop"
3 │   │   ┌─while (1)
  │   │   │     echo "In 3rd loop"
4 │   │   │     repeat 3 break
  │   │   └─end
  │   └─end
  └─end
5   echo "Out of all loops"
```

EXAMPLE 10.46 (CONTINUED)

```
(The Output)
Hello, in 1st loop
In 2nd loop
In 3rd loop
Out of all loops
```

EXPLANATION

1   Start the first while loop.

2   Enter the second nested while loop.

3   Enter the third nested while loop.

4   The repeat command will cause break to be executed three times; it will break first out of this innermost loop, then the second loop, and last, the first loop. Control continues at line 5.

5   Program control starts here after loop terminates.

The continue Command. The continue statement starts execution at the top of the innermost loop.

EXAMPLE 10.47

```
1   set done = 0
2   while ( ! $done )
        echo "Are you finished yet?"
        set answer = $<
3       if ("$answer" =~ [Nn]*) continue
4       set done = 1
5   end
```

EXPLANATION

1   The variable done is assigned 0.

2   The expression is tested. It reads: while (! 0). Not 0 is evaluated as true (logical NOT).

3   If the user entered No, no, or nope (anything starting with N or n), the expression is true and the continue statement returns control to the top of the loop where the expression is re-evaluated.

4   If answer does not start with N or n, the variable done is reset to one. When the end of the loop is reached, control starts at the top of the loop and the expression is tested. It reads: while (! 1). Not 1 is false. The loop exits.

5   This marks the end of the while loop.

EXAMPLE 10.48

```
(The Script)
    #!/bin/csh -f
1   if ( ! -e memo ) then
        echo  "memo file non existent"
        exit 1
    endif
2   foreach person (anish bob don karl jaye)
3       if ("$person" =~ [Kk]arl) continue
4       mail -s "Party time" $person < memo
    end
```

EXPLANATION

1   A file check is done. If the file memo does not exist, the user is sent an error message and the program exits with a status of 1.

2   The loop will assign each person in the list to the variable person, in turn, and then shift off the name in the list to process the next one.

3   If the person's name is Karl or karl, the continue statement starts execution at the top of the foreach loop (Karl is not sent the memo because his name was shifted off after being assigned to person.) The next name in the list is assigned to person.

4   Everyone on the mailing list is sent the memo, except karl.

10.8 Interrupt Handling

If a script is interrupted with the Interrupt key, it terminates and control is returned to the C shell; that is, you get your prompt back. The onintr command is used to process interrupts within a script. It allows you to either ignore the interrupt (^C) or transfer control to another part of the program before exiting. Normally, the interrupt command is used with a label to "clean up" before exiting. The onintr command without arguments restores the default action.

EXAMPLE 10.49

```
(The Script)
1   onintr  finish
2       < Script continues here >
3   finish:
4   onintr -        # Disable further interrupts
5   echo Cleaning temp files
6   rm $$tmp* ; exit 1
```

EXPLANATION

1 The onintr command is followed by a label name. The label finish is a user-defined label; control will be transferred to the finish label if an interrupt occurs. Usually this line is at the beginning of the script. It is not in effect until it is executed in the script.

2 The rest of the script lines are executed unless ^C (Interrupt key) is pressed while the program is in execution, at which time, control is transferred to the label.

3 This is the label; when the interrupt comes in, the program will continue to run, executing the statements below the label.

4 To shield this part of the script from further interrupts, the onintr - is used. If ^C is entered now, it will be ignored.

5 This line is echoed to the screen.

6 All tmp files are removed. The tmp files are prefixed with the shell's PID ($$) number and suffixed with any number of characters. The program exits with a status of 1.

10.9 setuid **Scripts**

Whoever runs a setuid program temporarily (as long as he or she is running the setuid program) becomes the owner of that program and has the same permissions as the owner. The passwd program is a good example of a setuid program. When you change your password, you temporarily become root, but only during the execution of the passwd program. That is why you are able to change your password in the /etc/passwd (or /etc/shadow) file, which normally is off-limits to regular users.

Shell programs can be written as setuid programs. You might want to do this if you have a script that is accessing a file containing information that should not be accessible to regular users, such as salary or other personal information. If the script is a setuid script, the person running the script can have access to the data, but it is still restricted from others. A setuid program requires the following steps:

1. In the script, the first line is

    ```
    #!/bin/csh -feb
    ```

    where the -feb options are

    ```
    -f  fast start up; don't execute .cshrc
    -e  abort immediately if interrupted
    -b  this is a setuid script
    ```

2. Next, change the permissions on the script so that it can run as a setuid program:

    ```
    % chmod 4755 script_name
              or
    % chmod +srx script_name
    % ls -l
    -rwsr-xr-x   2 ellie        512 Oct 10 17:18 script_name
    ```

10.10 Storing Scripts

After creating successful scripts, it is customary to collect them in a common script directory and change your path so that the scripts can be executed from any location.

EXAMPLE 10.50

```
1   % mkdir ~/bin
2   % mv myscript ~/bin
3   % vi .login

    (In .login reset the path to add ~/bin.)
4       set path = ( /usr/ucb /usr /usr/etc ~/bin . )

5   (At command line)
    % source .login
```

EXPLANATION

1   Make a directory under your home directory called bin, or any other name you choose.

2   Move any error-free scripts into the bin directory. Putting buggy scripts here will just cause problems.

3   Go into your .login file and reset the path.

4   The new path contains the directory ~/bin, which is where the shell will look for executable programs. Because it is near the end of the path, a system program that may have the same name as one of your scripts will be executed first.

5   By sourcing the .login, the path changes are affected; it is not necessary to log out and back in again.

10.11 Built-In Commands

Rather than residing on disk like UNIX/Linux commands, built-in commands are part of the C/TC shell's internal code and are executed from within the shell. If a built-in command occurs as any component of a pipeline except the last, it is executed in a sub-shell. See Table 10.11 for a list of built-in commands that apply to both the C and TC shells. For an extended list of TC shell only built-in commands, see Table 9.25 on page 504.

Table 10.11   C and TC Shell Built-In Commands and Their Meanings

Command	Meaning
:	Interprets null command, but performs no action.
alias	A nickname for a command.
bg [%job]	Runs the current or specified jobs in the background.
break	Breaks out of the innermost foreach or while loop.
breaksw	Breaks from a switch, resuming after the endsw.
case label:	A label in a switch statement.
cd [dir] chdir [dir]	Changes the shell's working directory to dir. If no argument is given, change to the home directory of the user.
continue	Continues execution of the nearest enclosing while or foreach.
default:	Labels the default case in a switch statement. The default should come after all case labels.
dirs [-l]	Prints the directory stack, most recent to the left; the first directory shown is the current directory. With the -l argument, produces an unabbreviated printout; use of the ~ notation is suppressed.
echo [-n] list	Writes the words in list to the shell's standard output, separated by space characters. The output is terminated with a newline unless the -n option is used.
eval command	Runs command as standard input to the shell and executes the resulting commands. This is usually used to execute commands generated as the result of command or variable substitution, as parsing occurs before these substitutions (e.g., eval 'tset -s options').
exec command	Executes command in place of the current shell, which terminates.
exit [(expr)]	Exits the shell, either with the value of the status variable or with the value specified by expr.
fg [% job]	Brings the current or specified job into the foreground.
foreach var (wordlist)	See "The foreach Loop" on page 561.
glob wordlist	Performs filename expansion on wordlist. Like echo, but no escapes (\) are recognized. Words are delimited by null characters in the output.
goto label	See "The goto" on page 547.

Table 10.11   C and TC Shell Built-In Commands and Their Meanings (continued)

Command	Meaning
hashstat	Prints a statistics line indicating how effective the internal hash table has been at locating commands (and avoiding execs). An exec is attempted for each component of the path where the hash function indicates a possible hit, and in each component that does not begin with a backslash.
history [-hr] [n]	Displays the history list; if n is given, display only the n most recent events. -r Reverses the order of the printout to be most recent first rather than oldest first. -h Displays the history list without leading numbers. This is used to produce files suitable for sourcing using the -h option to source.
if (expr)	See "Conditional Constructs and Flow Control" on page 535.
else if (expr2) then	See "Conditional Constructs and Flow Control" on page 535.
jobs [-1]	Lists the active jobs under job control. -1 Lists IDs in addition to the normal information.
kill [-sig] [pid][%job] ... kill -1	Sends the TERM (terminate) signal, by default or by the signal specified, to the specified ID, the job indicated, or the current job. Signals are given either by number or name. There is no default. Typing kill does not send a signal to the current job. If the signal being sent is TERM (terminate) or HUP (hangup), then the job or process is sent a CONT (continue) signal as well. -1 List the signal names that can be sent.
limit [-h] [resource [max-use]]	Limit the consumption by the current process or any process it spawns, each not to exceed max-use on the specified resource. If max-use is omitted, print the current limit; if resource is omitted, display all limits. -h Uses hard limits instead of the current limits. Hard limits impose a ceiling on the values of the current limits. Only the superuser may raise the hard limits. Resource is one of: cputime, maximum CPU seconds per process; filesize, largest single file allowed; datasize, maximum data size (including stack) for the process; stacksize, maximum stack size for the process; coredump, maximum size of a core dump; and descriptors, maximum value for a file descriptor.
login [username|-p]	Terminates a login shell and invokes login(1). The .logout file is not processed. If username is omitted, login prompts for the name of a user. -p Preserves the current environment (variables).
logout	Terminates a login shell.

Table 10.11   C and TC Shell Built-In Commands and Their Meanings (continued)

Command	*Meaning*
nice [+n|-n] [command]	Increments the process priority value for the shell or command by n. The higher the priority value, the lower the priority of a process and the slower it runs. If command is omitted, nice increments the value for the current shell. If no increment is specified, nice sets the nice value to 4. The range of nice values is from −20 through 19. Values of n outside this range set the value to the lower or higher boundary, respectively. +n Increments the process priority value by n. -n Decrements by n. This argument can be used only by the superuser.
nohup [command]	Runs command with HUPs (hangups) ignored. With no arguments, ignores HUPs throughout the remainder of a script.
notify [%job]	Notifies the user asynchronously when the status of the current or of a specified job changes.
onintr [- | label]	Controls the action of the shell on interrupts. With no arguments, onintr restores the default action of the shell on interrupts. (The shell terminates shell scripts and returns to the terminal command input level.) With the minus sign argument, the shell ignores all interrupts. With a label argument, the shell executes a goto label when an interrupt is received or a child process terminates because it was interrupted.
popd [+n]	Pops the directory stack and cd to the new top directory. The elements of the directory stack are numbered from zero, starting at the top. +n Discard the nth entry in the stack.
pushd [+n | dir]	Pushes a directory onto the directory stack. With no arguments, exchange the top two elements. +n Rotates the nth entry to the top of the stack and cd to it. dir Pushes the current working directory onto the stack and change to dir.
rehash	Recomputes the internal hash table of the contents of directories listed in the path variable to account for new commands added.
repeat count command	Repeat command count times.
set [var [= value]]	See "Variables" on page 440.
setenv [VAR [word]]	See "Variables" on page 440. The most commonly used environment variables, USER, TERM, and PATH, are automatically imported to and exported from the csh variables, user, term, and path; there is no need to use setenv for these. In addition, the shell sets the PWD environment variable from the csh variable cwd whenever the latter changes.
shift [variable]	The components of argv, or variable, if supplied, are shifted to the left, discarding the first component. It is an error for variable not to be set, or to have a null value.

Table 10.11   C and TC Shell Built-In Commands and Their Meanings (continued)

Command	Meaning
source [-h] name	Reads commands from name. Source commands may be nested, but if they are nested too deeply, the shell may run out of file descriptors. An error in a sourced file at any level terminates all nested source commands. Used commonly to re-execute the .login or .cshrc files to ensure variable settings are handled within the current shell, that is, to make sure the shell does not create (fork) a child shell. -h Places commands from the filename on the history list without executing them.
stop [%job] ...	Stops the current or specified background job.
suspend	Stops the shell in its tracks, much as if it had been sent a stop signal with ^Z. This is most often used to stop shells started by su.
switch (string)	See "The switch Command" on page 557.
time [command]	With no argument, print a summary of time used by this shell and its children. With an optional command, execute command and print a summary of the time it uses.
umask [value]	Displays the file creation mask. With value, sets the file creation mask. Value, given in octal, is XORed with the permissions of 666 for files and 777 for directories to arrive at the permissions for new files. Permissions cannot be added via umask.
unalias pattern	Discards aliases that match (filename substitution) pattern. All aliases are removed by unalias *.
unhash	Disables the internal hash table.
unlimit [-h] [resource]	Removes a limitation on resource. If no resource is specified, all resource limitations are removed. See the description of the limit command for the list of resource names. -h Removes corresponding hard limits. Only the superuser may do this.
unset pattern	Removes variables whose names match (filename substitution) pattern. All variables are removed by unset *; this has noticeably distasteful side effects.
unsetenv variable	Removes variable from the environment. Pattern matching, as with unset, is not performed.
wait	Waits for background jobs to finish (or for an interrupt) before prompting.
while (expr)	See "The while Loop" on page 564.

LAB 24: C/TC SHELLS—GETTING STARTED

1. What does the init process do?

2. What is the function of the login process?

3. How do you know what shell you are using?

4. How can you change your login shell?

5. Explain the difference between the .cshrc/.tcshrc and .login files. Which one is executed first?

6. Edit your .cshrc/.tcshrc file as follows:

    a. Create three of your own aliases.

    b. Reset your prompt.

7. Set the following variables and put a comment after each variable explaining what it does:

    noclobber   # Protects clobbering files from redirection overwriting
    history
    ignoreeof
    savehist
    filec

8. Type the following: source .cshrc source .tcshrc. What does the source command do?

9. Edit your .login file as follows:

    a. Welcome the user.

    b. Add your home directory to the path if it is not there.

    c. Source the .login file.

10. Type history. What is the output?

    a. How do you re-execute the last command?

    b. Now type echo a b c. Use the history command to re-execute the echo command with only its last argument, c.

LAB 25: SHELL METACHARACTERS

1. Type the following at the prompt:

    touch ab abc a1 a2 a3 a11 a12 ba ba.1 ba.2 filex filey AbC ABC ABc2 abc

    Write and test the command that will do the following:

    a. List all files starting with a.

    b. List all files ending in at least one digit.

    c. List all files starting with an a or A.

d. List all files ending in a period, followed by a digit.

e. List all files containing just two of the letter a.

f. List three-character files where all letters are uppercase.

g. List files ending in 11 or 12.

h. List files ending in x or y.

i. List all files ending in a digit, an uppercase letter, or a lowercase letter.

j. List all files containing the letter b.

k. Remove two-character files starting with an a.

LAB 26: REDIRECTION

1. What are the names of the three file streams associated with your terminal?

2. What is a file descriptor?

3. What command would you use to do the following:

    a. Redirect the output of the ls command to a file called lsfile.

    b. Redirect and append the output of the date command to lsfile.

    c. Redirect the output of the who command to lsfile. What happened?

4. What happens when you type cp all by itself?

    a. How do you save the error message from the above example to a file?

5. Use the find command to find all files, starting from the parent directory, of type directory. Save the standard output in a file called found and any errors in a file called found.errs.

6. What is noclobber? How do you override it?

7. Take the output of three commands and redirect the output to a file called gotemail.

8. Use a pipe(s) with the ps and wc commands to find out how many processes you are currently running.

LAB 27: FIRST SCRIPT

1. Write a script called greetme that will do the following:

    a. Greet the user.

    b. Print the date and time.

    c. Print a calendar for this month.

    d. Print the name of your machine.

    e. Print a list of all files in your parent directory.

    f. Print all the processes you are running.

    g. Print the value of the TERM, PATH, and HOME variables.

    h. Print Please, could you loan me $50.00?

    i. Tell the user Good-bye and the current hour. (See *man* pages for the date command.)

2. Make sure your script is executable.

    chmod +x greetme

3. What was the first line of your script?

LAB 28: GETTING USER INPUT

1. Write a script called nosy that will do the following:

    a. Ask the user's full name—first, last, and middle name.

    b. Greet the user by his or her first name.

    c. Ask the user's year of birth and calculate the user's age.

    d. Ask the user's login name and print the user's ID (from /etc/passwd).

    e. Tell the user his or her home directory.

    f. Show the user the processes he or she is running.

    g. Tell the user the day of the week, and the current time in nonmilitary time.

    The output should resemble the following:

    The day of the week is Tuesday and the current time is 04:07:38 PM.

2. Create a text file called datafile (unless this file has already been provided for you). Each entry consists of fields separated by colons. The fields are as follows:

    a. First and last name

    b. Phone number

    c. Address

    d. Birth date

    e. Salary

3. Create a script called lookup that will do the following:

    a. Contain a comment section with the script name, your name, the date, and the reason for writing this script. The reason for writing this script is to display datafile in sorted order.

    b. Sort datafile by last names.

    c. Show the user the contents of datafile.

    d. Tell the user the number of entries in the file.

4. Try the echo and verbose commands for debugging your script. How did you use these commands?

LAB 29: COMMAND-LINE ARGUMENTS

1. Write a script called rename that will do the following:

   a. Take two filenames as command-line arguments; the first file is the old file and the second file is the new one.

   b. Rename the old filename with the new filename.

   c. List the files in the directory to show the change.

2. Write a script called checking that will do the following:

   a. Take a command-line argument, a user's login name.

   b. Test to see if a command-line argument was provided.

   c. Check to see if the user is in the /etc/passwd file. If so, print the following:

      Found <user> in the /etc/passwd file.

      Otherwise, print the following:

      No such user on our system.

LAB 30: CONDITIONALS AND FILE TESTING

1. In the lookup script, ask the user if he or she would like to add an entry to the datafile. If yes or y:

   a. Prompt the user for a new name, phone, address, birth date, and salary. Each item will be stored in a separate variable. You will provide the colons between the fields and append the information to datafile.

   b. Sort the file by last names. Tell the user you added the entry, and show the added line preceded by the line number.

2. Rewrite checking from Lab 29. After checking whether the named user is in the /etc/passwd file, the program will check to see if he or she is logged on. If so, the program will print all the processes that are running; otherwise it will tell the user the following:

      <user> is not logged on.

3. The lookup script depends on datafile in order to run. In the lookup script, check to see if datafile exists and if it is readable and writable.

4. Add a menu to the lookup script to resemble the following:

   [1] Add entry
   [2] Delete entry
   [3] View entry
   [4] Exit

5. You already have the Add entry part of the script written. The Add entry routine should now include code that will check to see if the name is already in datafile and if it is, tell the user so. If the name is not there, add the new entry.

6. Now write the code for the Delete entry, View entry, and Exit functions.

7. The Delete entry part of the script should first check to see if the entry exists before trying to remove it. If the entry does not exist, notify the user; otherwise, remove the entry and tell the user you removed it. On Exit, make sure that you use a digit to represent the appropriate exit status.

8. How do you check the exit status from the command line?

LAB 31: THE switch STATEMENT

1. Rewrite the following script using a switch statement:

```
#!/bin/csh -f
# Grades program
echo -n "What was your grade on the test? "
set score = $<
if ( $grade >= 90 && $grade <= 100 ) then
    echo You got an A\!
else if ( $grade >= 80 && $grade <= 89 ) then
    echo You got a B.
else if ( $grade >= 70 && $grade <= 79 ) then
    echo "You're average."
else if ( $grade >= 60 && $grade <= 69 ) then
    echo Better study harder
else
    echo Better luck next time.
endif
```

2. Rewrite the lookup script using switch statements for each of the menu items.

LAB 32: LOOPS

1. Write a program called picnic that will mail a list of users, one at a time, an invitation to a picnic. The list of users will be in a file called friends. One of the users listed in the friends file will be Popeye.

   a. The invitation will be in another file, called invite.

   b. Use file testing to check that both files exist and are readable.

   c. A loop will be used to iterate through the list of users. When Popeye is reached, he will be skipped over (i.e., he does not get an invitation), and the next user on the list sent an invitation, and so forth.

   d. Keep a list with the names of each person who received an invitation. Do this by building an array. After everyone on the list has been sent mail, print the number of people who received mail and a list of their names.

Bonus: If you have time, you may want to customize your invite file so that each user receives a letter containing his or her name. For example, the message might start:

```
Dear John,
I hope you can make it to our picnic....
```

To do this your invite file may be written:

```
Dear XXX,
I hope you can make it to our picnic....
```

With sed or awk, you could then substitute XXX with the user name. (It might be tricky putting the capital letter in the user name, as user names are always lowercase.)

2. Add a new menu item to the lookup script to resemble the following:

```
[1] Add entry
[2] Delete entry
[3] Change entry
[4] View entry
[5] Exit
```

After the user has selected a valid entry, when the function has completed, ask the user if he or she would like to see the menu again. If an invalid entry is entered, the program should print the following:

```
Invalid entry, try again.
```

The menu will be redisplayed.

3. Create a submenu under View entry in the lookup script. The user will be asked if he or she would like to view specific information for a selected individual:

```
a) Phone
b) Address
c) Birth date
d) Salary
```

4. Add the onintr command to your script using a label. When the program starts execution at the label, any temporary files will be removed, the user will be told Good-bye, and the program will exit.

chapter

11

The Interactive Korn Shell

11.1 Introduction

With an interactive shell, the standard input, output, and error are tied to a terminal. When using the Korn (ksh) shell interactively, you type UNIX/Linux commands at the ksh prompt and wait for a response. The interactive Korn shell combined the best of the UNIX Bourne and C shells to provide you with a large assortment of built-in commands and command-line shortcuts, such as history, aliases, file and command completion, and so forth. David Korn expanded his shell to include a lot more, such as command-line editing with vi and emacs, new metacharacters, coprocessing, and error handling. The Korn shell is very popular and, although it started at AT&T, has been adapted to run on most operating systems.

This chapter focuses on how you interact with ksh at the command line and how to customize your working environment. You will learn how to take advantage of all short-cuts and built-in features in order to create an efficient and fun working environment. Chapter 12 takes you a step further. At that point, you will be ready to write ksh shell scripts to further tailor the working environment for yourself by automating everyday tasks and developing sophisticated scripts, and if you are an administrator, doing the same not only for yourself but also for whole groups of users.

11.1.1 Startup

Before the Korn shell displays a prompt, it is preceded by a number of processes. (See Figure 11.1.) The first process to run is called init, PID 1. It gets instructions from a file called inittab (System V) or spawns a getty (BSD) process. These processes open up the terminal ports, provide a place where input comes from (stdin) and the place where standard output (stdout) and standard error (stderr) go, and put a login prompt on your screen. The /bin/login program is then executed. The login program prompts you for a password, encrypts and verifies the password, sets up an initial environment, and starts up the login shell, /bin/ksh, the last entry in the passwd file. The ksh program looks for the system file, /etc/profile, and executes its commands. It then looks in the user's home directory for an initialization file called .profile, and an environment file, conventionally called .kshrc. After executing commands from those files, the dollar sign prompt appears on your screen and the Korn shell awaits commands.

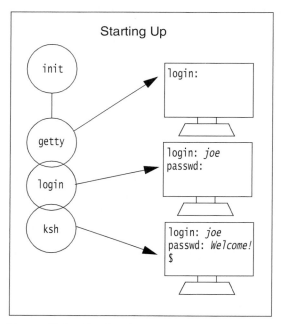

Figure 11.1   Starting the Korn shell.

11.2 The Environment

11.2.1   The Initialization Files

After executing the commands in /etc/profile, the initialization files in the user's home directory are executed. The .profile is executed, followed by the ENV file, commonly called the .kshrc file.

The /etc/profile File.   The /etc/profile is a systemwide readable file set up by the system administrator to perform tasks when the user logs on and the Korn shell starts up. It is available to all Bourne and Korn shell users on the system, and normally performs such tasks as checking the mail spooler for new mail and displaying the message of the day from the /etc/motd file. The following text is an example of the /etc/profile. See Chapter 8, "Programming the Bourne Shell," on page 321 for a complete explanation of each line of /etc/profile.

EXAMPLE 11.1

```
# The profile that all logins get before using their own .profile
    trap " " 2 3
    export LOGNAME PATH  # Initially set by /bin/login
    if [ "$TERM" = " " ]
    then
        if /bin/i386
        then    # Set the terminal type
            TERM=AT386
        else
            TERM=sun
        fi
        export TERM
    fi
    # Login and -su shells get /etc/profile services.
    # -rsh is given its environment in the .profile.
    case "$0" in
    -sh | -ksh | -jsh )
        if [ ! -f .hushlogin ]
        then
            /usr/sbin/quota
    # Allow the user to break the Message-Of-The-Day only.
            trap "trap ' ' 2" 2
            /bin/cat -s /etc/motd
            # Display the message of the day
            trap " " 2
            /bin/mail -E
            case $? in
            0)   # Check for new mail
                echo "You have new mail. "
                ;;
            2)   echo "You have mail. "
                ;;
            esac
        fi
    esac
    umask 022
    trap 2 3
```

The .profile File.   The .profile file is a user-defined initialization file that is executed once at login (by the Bourne and Korn shells) and is found in your home directory. It gives you the ability to customize and modify your working environment. Environment variables and terminal settings are normally set here, and if a window application or dbm is to be initiated, it is started here. If the .profile file contains a special variable called ENV, the filename that is assigned to that variable will be executed next. The ENV file is often named .kshrc; it contains aliases and set -o commands. The ENV file is executed every time a ksh subshell is spawned. The lines from the following files may not be meaningful to you now, but all of the concepts, such as exporting variables, history, the search path, and so on, will be discussed in detail throughout the text of this book.

EXAMPLE 11.2

```
1    set -o allexport
2    TERM=vt102
3    HOSTNAME=$(uname -n)
4    HISTSIZE=50
5    EDITOR=/usr/ucb/vi
6    ENV=$HOME/.kshrc
7    PATH=$HOME/bin:/usr/ucb:/usr/bin:\
     /usr/local:/etc:/bin:/usr/bin:/usr/local\
     /bin:/usr/hosts:/usr/5bin:/usr/etc:/usr/bin:.
8    PS1="$HOSTNAME ! $ "
9    set +o allexport
10   alias openwin=/usr/openwin/bin/openwin
11   trap '$HOME/.logout' EXIT
12   clear
```

EXPLANATION

1 By setting the allexport option, all variables created will automatically be exported (made available to subshells).

2 The terminal is set to vt102.

3 The variable HOSTNAME is assigned the name of this machine, $(uname -n).

4 The HISTSIZE variable is assigned 50; 50 lines from the history file will be displayed on the terminal when the user types history.

5 The EDITOR variable is assigned the pathname for the vi editor. Programs such as mail allow you to select an editor in which to work.

6 The ENV variable is assigned the path to the home directory ($HOME) and the name of the file that contains further Korn shell customization settings. After the .profile is executed, the ENV file is executed. The name of the ENV file is your choice; it is commonly called .kshrc.

7 The search path is defined. It is a colon-separated list of directories used by the shell in its search for commands typed at the prompt or in a script file. The shell searches each element of the path from left to right for the command. The dot at the end represents the current working directory. If the command cannot be found in any of the listed directories, the shell will look in the current directory.

8 The primary prompt, by default a dollar sign ($), is set to the name of the host machine, the number of the current command in the history file, and a dollar sign ($).

9 The allexport option is turned off.

10 An alias is a nickname for a command. The alias for openwin is assigned the full pathname of the openwin command, which starts Sun's window application.

11 The trap command will execute the .logout file when you exit this shell, that is, when you log out. The .logout file is a user-defined file containing commands that are executed at the time of logging out. For example, you may want to record the time you log out, clean up a temporary file, or simply say So long.

12 The clear command clears the screen.

The ENV File.   The ENV variable is assigned the name of a file that will be executed every time an interactive ksh or a ksh program (script) is started. The ENV variable is set in the .profile and is assigned the name of the file that will contain special ksh variables and aliases. The name is conventionally .kshrc, but you can call it anything you want. (The ENV file is not processed when the privileged option is on. See Table 11.1.)

EXAMPLE 11.3

```
1   $ export ENV=.kshrc
2   $ cat .kshrc
    # The .kshrc file
3   set -o trackall
4   set -o vi
5   alias l='ls -laF'
    alias ls='ls -aF'
    alias hi='fc -l'
    alias c=clear
6   function pushd { pwd > $HOME/.lastdir.$$ ; }
    function popd { cd $(< $HOME/.lastdir.$$) ;
            rm $HOME/.lastdir.$$; pwd; }
    function psg { ps -ef | egrep $1 | egrep -v egrep; }
    function vg { vgrind -s11 -t $* | lpr -t ; }
```

EXPLANATION

1 The ENV variable is assigned the name of the file that will be exectued every time the Korn shell is invoked. Exporting ENV makes it available to all subshells.

2 The contents of the .kshrc file are displayed.

3 The set option for tracked aliases is turned on. (For a complete description, see "Aliases" on page 604.)

4 The set option for the vi editor is turned on for in-line editing of the history file. (See "Command-Line History" on page 595.)

5 The aliases (nicknames) for the commands are defined.

6 The functions are named and defined. (See "Functions" on page 639.)

The set -o Options. The set command, used by itself, sets positional parameters (see "Positional Parameters" on page 633), but with the -o switch, it can be used to turn on and turn off ksh options that allow you to customize the shell environment. The options are either on or off, and are normally set in the ENV file. (See Table 11.1 for a list of shell set options.)

FORMAT

```
set -o option      Turns on the option.
set +o option      Turns off the option
set -[a-z]         Abbreviation for an option; the minus turns it on
set +[a-z]         Abbreviation for an option; the plus turns it off
```

EXAMPLE 11.4

```
1 set -o allexport
2 set +o allexport
3 set -a
4 set +a
```

EXPLANATION

1   Sets the allexport option. This option causes all variables to be automatically exported to subshells.
2   Unsets the allexport option. All variables will now be local to the current shell.
3   Sets the allexport option. Same as 1. Not every option has an abbreviation (see Table 11.1).
4   Unsets the allexport option. Same as 2.

Table 11.1 Korn Shell set Options

Name of Option	Abbreviation	What It Does
allexport	-a	Causes set variables to be automatically exported.
bgnice		Runs background jobs with a lower priority.
emacs		For command-line editing, uses the emacs built-in editor.
errexit	-e	If a command returns a nonzero exit status (fails), executes the ERR trap, if set, and exits. Not set when reading initialization files.
gmacs		For command-line editing, uses the gmacs built-in editor.
ignoreeof		Prevents logout with ^D; must type exit to exit the shell.
markdirs		Puts a trailing backslash (/) on directory names when filename expansion is used.

Table 11.1 Korn Shell set Options (continued)

Name of Option	Abbreviation	What It Does
monitor	−m	Allows job control.
noclobber		Protects files from being overwritten when redirection is used.
noexec	−n	Reads commands, but does not execute them. Used to check the syntax of scripts. Not on when running interactively.
noglob	−f	Disables pathname expansion; that is, turns off wildcards.
nolog		Does not store function definitions in the history file.
notify		Notifies user when background job finishes.
nounset		Displays an error when expanding a variable that has not been set.
privileged	−p	When set, the shell does not read the .profile or ENV file; used with setuid scripts.
trackall		Enables alias tracking.
verbose	−v	Turns on the verbose mode for debugging.
vi		For command-line editing, uses the vi built-in editor.
xtrace	−x	Turns on the echo mode for debugging.

11.2.2 The Prompts

The Korn shell provides four prompts. The primary and secondary prompts are used when the Korn shell is running interactively. You can change these prompts. The variable PS1 is the primary prompt, set initially to a dollar sign ($). It appears when you log on and waits for you to type commands. The variable PS2 is the secondary prompt, initially set to the > character. It appears if you have partially typed a command and then pressed Enter. You can change the primary and secondary prompts.

The Primary Prompt. $ is the default primary prompt. You can change your prompt. Normally, prompts are defined in .profile.

EXAMPLE 11.5

```
1   $ PS1="$(uname -n) ! $ "
2   jody 1141 $
```

EXPLANATION

1   The default primary prompt is a $. The PS1 prompt is being reset to the name of
    the machine $(uname -n), the number of the current history number, and the $. The
    exclamation point evaluates to the current history number. (To print an exclama-
    tion point, type two exclamation points (!!) in the PS1 definition.)

2   The new prompt is displayed.

The Secondary Prompt.   The PS2 prompt is the secondary prompt. Its value is displayed to standard error (the screen). This prompt appears when you have not completed a command and have pressed the carriage return.

EXAMPLE 11.6

```
1   $ print "Hello
2   > there"
3   Hello
    there
4   $

5   $ PS2="----> "
6   $ print "Hi
7   ------>
    ------>
    ------> there"
    Hi


    there
    $
```

EXPLANATION

1   The double quotes must be matched after the string "Hello.

2   When a newline is entered, the secondary prompt appears. Until the closing dou-
    ble quotes are entered, the secondary prompt will be displayed.

3   The output of the print command is displayed.

4   The primary prompt is displayed.

5   The secondary prompt is reset.

6   The double quotes must be matched after the string "Hi.

7   When a newline is entered, the new secondary prompt appears. Until the closing
    double quotes are entered, the secondary prompt will be displayed.

11.2.3 The Search Path

To execute a command typed at the command line or within a shell script, the Korn shell searches the directories listed in the PATH variable. The PATH is a colon-separated list of directories, searched by the shell from left to right. The dot in the PATH represents the current working directory. If the command is not found in any of the directories listed in the path, the shell sends the message ksh: filename: not found to standard error. It is recommended that the path be set in the .profile file. To speed up the searching process, the Korn shell has implemented tracked aliases. See "Tracked Aliases" on page 606.

EXAMPLE 11.7

```
$ echo $PATH
/home/gsa12/bin:/usr/ucb:/usr/bin:/usr/local/bin:.
```

EXPLANATION

The Korn shell will search for commands starting in /home/gsa12/bin. If the command is not found there, /usr/ucb is searched, then /usr/bin, /usr/local/bin, and finally the user's current working directory represented by the period.

11.2.4 The dot Command

The dot command (.) is a built-in Korn shell command. It takes a script name as an argument. The script will be executed in the environment of the current shell. A child process will not be started. The dot command is normally used to re-execute the .profile file or the ENV file, if either of those files has been modified. For example, if one of the settings in either file has been changed after you have logged on, you can use the dot command to re-execute the initialization files without logging out and then logging back in.

EXAMPLE 11.8

```
$ . .profile
$ . .kshrc
$ . $ENV
```

EXPLANATION

Normally a child process is started when commands are executed. The dot command executes each of the initialization files, .profile and the ENV file (.kshrc), in the current shell. Local and global variables in these files are defined within this shell. Otherwise, the user would have to log out and log back in to cause these files to be executed for the login shell. The dot command makes that unnecessary.

11.3 The Command Line

After logging in, the Korn shell displays its primary prompt. The shell is your command interpreter. When the shell is running interactively, it reads commands from the terminal and breaks the command line into words. A command line consists of one or more words (or tokens), separated by whitespace (blanks and/or tabs), and terminated with a newline, generated by pressing Enter. The first word is the command, and subsequent words are the command's arguments. The command may be a UNIX executable program such as `ls` or `pwd`, a built-in command such as `cd` or `jobs`, or a shell script. The command may contain special characters, called metacharacters, which the shell must interpret while parsing the command line. If a command line is too long, the backslash character, followed by a newline, will allow you to continue typing on the next line. The secondary prompt will appear until the command line is terminated.

11.3.1   The Order of Processing Commands

The first word on the command line is the command to be executed. The command may be a keyword, a special built-in command or utility, a function, a script, or an executable program. The command is executed according to its type in the following order:[1]

1. Keywords (such as `if`, `while`, `until`)
2. Aliases (see `typeset -f`)
3. Built-in commands
4. Functions
5. Scripts and executables

The special built-in commands and functions are defined within the shell, and therefore are executed from within the current shell, making them much faster in execution. Scripts and executable programs such as `ls` and `pwd` are stored on disk, and the shell must locate them within the directory hierarchy by searching the `PATH` environment variable; the shell then forks a new shell that executes the script. To find out the type of command you are using, use the built-in command, `whence -v`, or its alias, `type`. (See Example 11.9.)

EXAMPLE 11.9

```
$ type print
print is a shell builtin
$ type test
test is a shell builtin
$ type ls
ls is a tracked alias for /usr/bin/ls
```

---

1. A built-in command will override a function; therefore, an alias must be defined to the name of the function. (See "Aliases" on page 604.) In the 1994 version of the Korn shell, the order of processing functions and built-ins was reversed, thus alleviating this problem.

EXAMPLE 11.9 (CONTINUED)

```
$ type type
type is an exported alias for whence -v
$ type bc
bc is /usr/bin/bc
$ type if
if is a keyword
```

11.3.2 The Exit Status

After a command or program terminates, it returns an exit status to the parent process. The exit status is a number between 0 and 255. By convention, when a program exits, if the status returned is 0, the command was successful in its execution. When the exit status is nonzero, the command failed in some way. The Korn shell status variable ? is set to the value of the exit status of the last command that was executed. Success or failure of a program is determined by the programmer who wrote the program. In shell scripts, you can explicitly control the exit status by using the exit command.

EXAMPLE 11.10

```
1   $ grep "ellie" /etc/passwd
    ellie:GgMyBsSJavd16s:9496:40:Ellie Quigley:/home/jody/ellie
2   $ echo $?
    0

3   $ grep "nicky" /etc/passwd
4   $ echo $?
    1

5   $ grep "scott" /etc/passsswd
    grep: /etc/passsswd: No such file or directory
6   $ echo $?
    2
```

EXPLANATION

1   The grep program searches for the pattern ellie in the /etc/passwd file and is successful. The line from /etc/passwd is displayed.

2   The ? variable is set to the exit value of the grep command. Zero indicates success.

3   The grep program cannot find user nicky in the /etc/passwd file.

4   If the grep program cannot find the pattern, it returns an exit status of 1.

5   The grep fails because the file /etc/passsswd cannot be opened.

6   If grep cannot find the file, it returns an exit status of 2.

11.3.3   Multiple Commands and Command Grouping

A command line can consist of multiple commands. Each command is separated by a semicolon, and the command line is terminated with a newline.

EXAMPLE 11.11

```
$ ls; pwd; date
```

EXPLANATION

The commands are executed from left to right until the newline is reached. Commands may also be grouped so that all of the output is either piped to another command or redirected to a file.

EXAMPLE 11.12

```
$ ( ls ; pwd; date ) > outputfile
```

EXPLANATION

The output of each of the commands is sent to the file called outputfile.

11.3.4   Conditional Execution of Commands

With conditional execution, two command strings are separated by two special metacharacters, && and ||. The command on the right of either of these metacharacters will or will not be executed, based on the exit condition of the command on the left.

EXAMPLE 11.13

```
$ cc prgm1.c -o prgm1 && prgm1
```

EXPLANATION

If the first command is *successful* (has a 0 exit status), the command after the && is executed.

EXAMPLE 11.14

```
$ cc prog.c >& err || mail bob < err
```

EXPLANATION

If the first command *fails* (has a nonzero exit status), the command after the || is executed.

11.3.5 Commands in the Background

Normally, when you execute a command, it runs in the foreground and the prompt does not reappear until the command has completed execution. It is not always convenient to wait for the command to complete. By placing an ampersand (&) at the end of the command line, the shell will return the shell prompt immediately and execute the command in the background concurrently. You do not have to wait to start up another command. The output from a background job will be sent to the screen as it processes. Therefore, if you intend to run a command in the background, the output of that command should be redirected to a file or piped to another device such as a printer so that the output does not interfere with what you are doing.

EXAMPLE 11.15

```
1    $ man ksh | lp&
2    [1] 1557
3    $
```

EXPLANATION

1   The output of the manual pages for the Korn shell is piped to the printer. The ampersand at the end of the command line puts the job in the background.

2   Two numbers appear on the screen: The number in square brackets indicates that this is the first job to be placed in the background; the second number is the PID, the process identification number, of this job.

3   The Korn shell prompt appears immediately. While your program is running in the background, the shell is waiting for another command in the foreground.

11.3.6 Command-Line History

The history mechanism keeps a numbered record of the commands that you have typed at the command line in a history file. You can recall a command from the history file and re-execute it without retyping the command. The history built-in command displays the history list. The default name for the history file is .sh_history, and it is located in your home directory.

The HISTSIZE variable, accessed when ksh first accesses the history file, specifies how many commands can be accessed from the history file. The default size is 128. The HIST-FILE variable specifies the name of the command history file (~/.sh_history is the default) where commands are stored. The history file grows from one login session to the next; it becomes very large unless you clean it out. The history command is a preset alias for the fc -l command.

EXAMPLE   11.16

(The ~/sh_history File)
(This file contains a list of the commands the user has typed at the command line)

```
netscape&
ls
mkdir javascript
cd javascript
&cp ../javapdf.zip .
gunzip javapdf.zip
unzip javapdf.zip
ls
more chapter10*
ls -l
rm chapter9.pdf
ls
ls -l
```

... continues ...

```
1   $ history -1 -5        # List last 5 commands, preceding this one in reversed order.
    13   history -3
    12   history 8
    11   history -n
    10   history
    9    set
2   $ history -5 -1        # Print last 5 commands, preceding this one in order.
    10   history
    11   history -n
    12   history 8
    13   history -3
    14   history -1 -5
3   $ history              # (Different history list)
    78   date
    79   ls
    80   who
    81   echo hi
    82   history
4   $ history ls echo      # Display from most recent ls command to
    79   ls                # most recent echo command.
    80   who
    81   echo hi
5   $ history -r ls echo    # -r reverses the list
    81   echo hi
    80   who
    79   ls
```

The history Command/Redisplay Commands. The built-in history command lists previously typed commands preceded by a number. The command can take arguments to control the display.

EXAMPLE 11.17

```
1  $ history           # Same as fc -l
   1 ls
   2 vi file1
   3 df
   4 ps -eaf
   5 history
   6 more /etc/passwd
   7 cd
   8 echo $USER
   9 set
   10 history
2  $ history -n        # Print without line numbers
   ls
   vi file1
   df
   ps -eaf
   history
   more /etc/passwd
   cd
   echo $USER
   set
   history
   history -n
3  $ history 8         # List from 8th command to present
   8    echo $USER
   9    set
   10   history
   11   history -n
   12   history 8
4  $ history -3        # List this command and the 3 preceding it
   10   history
   11   history -n
   12   history 8
   13   history -3
5  $ history -1 -5     # List last 5 commands, preceding this one in reversed order.
   13   history -3
   12   history 8
   11   history -n
   10   history
   9    set
```

EXAMPLE 11.17 (CONTINUED)

```
6    $ history -5 -1        # Print last 5 commands, preceding this one in order.
     10   history
     11   history -n
     12   history 8
     13   history -3
     14   history -1 -5
7    $ history              # (Different history list)
     78   date
     79   ls
     80   who
     81   echo hi
     82   history
```

Re-executing Commands with the r Command.   The r command redoes the last command typed at the command line. If the r command is followed by a space and a number, the command at that number is re-executed. If the r command is followed by a space and a letter, the last command that began with that letter is executed. Without any arguments, the r command re-executes the most previous command on the history list.

EXAMPLE 11.18

```
1    $ r date
     date
     Mon May 15 12:27:35 PST 2004
2    $ r 3      redo command number 3
     df
     Filesystem   kbytes    used      avail     capacity   Mounted on
     /dev/sd0a    7735      6282      680       90%        /
     /dev/sd0g    144613    131183    0         101%       /usr
     /dev/sd2c    388998    211395    138704    60%        /home.
3    $ r vi         # Redo the last command that began with pattern vi.
4    $ r vi file1=file2    # Redo last command that began with vi and substitute the
                           # first occurrence of file1 with file2.
```

EXPLANATION

1   The last command, date, is re-executed.
2   The third command in the history file is executed.
3   The last command, starting with the string vi, is executed.
4   The string file1 is replaced with the string file2. The last command, vi file1, is replaced with vi file2.

11.3.7   Command-Line Editing

The Korn shell provides two built-in editors, emacs and vi, that allow you to interactively edit your history list. To enable the vi editor, add the set command listed below and put this line in your .profile file. The emacs built-in editor works on lines in the history file one line at a time, whereas the vi built-in editor works on commands consisting of more than one line. To set vi, type

set -o vi   or   **VISUAL=vi**   or   **EDITOR=/usr/bin/vi**

   If using emacs, type

set -o emacs   or   **VISUAL=emacs**   or   **EDITOR=/usr/bin/emacs**

Note that set -o vi overrides VISUAL, and VISUAL overrides EDITOR.

The vi Built-In Editor.   To edit the history list, press the Esc key and use the standard keys that you would use in vi for moving up and down, left and right, deleting, inserting, and changing text. See Table 11.2. After making the edit, press the Enter key. The command will be executed and added to the bottom of the history list. To scroll upward in the history file, press the Esc key and then the K key.

Table 11.2   vi Commands

Command	Function
Moving Through the History File	
Esc k *or* +	Move up the history list
Esc j *or* –	Move down the history list
Esc *G*	Move to first line in history file
Esc *5G*	Move to fifth command in history file for string
/string	Search upward through history file
?	String search downward through history file
Moving Around on a Line (Press the Esc Key First)	
h	Move left on a line
l	Move right on a line
b	Move backward a word
e or w	Move forward a word

Table 11.2 vi Commands (continued)

Command	Function
∧ or 0	Move to beginning of first character on the line
$	Move to end of line
Editing with vi	
a A	Append text
i I	Insert text
dd dw x	Delete text into a buffer (line, word, or character)
cc C	Change text
u U	Undo
yy Y	Yank (copy a line into buffer)
p P	Put yanked or deleted line down below or above the line
r R	Replace a letter or any amount of text on a line

The emacs Built-In Editor.   To start moving backward through the history file, press ∧P. To move forward, press ∧N. Use emacs editing commands to change or correct text, then press Enter and the command will be re-executed. See Table 11.3.

Table 11.3   emacs Commands

Command	Function
Moving Through the History File	
Ctrl-P	Move up history file
Ctrl-N	Move down history file
Ctrl-B	Move backward one character
Ctrl-R	Search backward for string
Esc B	Move back one word
Ctrl-F	Move forward one character
Esc F	Move forward one word
Ctrl-A	Move to the beginning of the line
Ctrl-E	Move to the end of the line

Table 11.3 emacs Commands (continued)

Command	Function
Esc <	Move to the first line of the history file
Esc >	Move to the last line of the history file
Editing with emacs	
Ctrl-U	Delete the line
Ctrl-Y	Put the line back
Ctrl-K	Delete from cursor to the end line
Ctrl-D	Delete a letter
Esc D	Delete one word forward
Esc H	Delete one word backward
Esc space	Set a mark at cursor position
Ctrl-X Ctrl-X	Exchange cursor and mark
Ctrl-P Ctrl-Y	Push region from cursor to mark into a buffer (Ctrl-P) and put it down (Ctrl-Y)

FCEDIT and Editing Commands. The fc command is a built-in command that can be used with the FCEDIT[2] variable (typically set in the .profile file) to invoke the editor of your choice for editing the history file. This can be any editor on your system. The FCEDIT variable is set to the full pathname of your favorite editor. If FCEDIT is not set, the default editor, /bin/ed, is invoked when you type the fc command.

The FCEDIT variable should be set to the chosen editor. You can specify a number of items from the history list that you want to edit. After you edit the commands, the Korn shell will execute the whole file. Any commands that are preceded by a pound sign (#) will be treated as comments and will not be executed. See Table 11.4 on page 603 for more on commenting and filename expansion.

---

2. On versions of the Korn shell newer than 1988, the FCEDIT variable has been renamed HISTEDIT, and the fc command has been renamed hist.

EXAMPLE   11.19

```
1   $ FCEDIT=/usr/bin/vi
2   $ pwd
3   $ fc
```
<Starts up the full-screen vi editor with the pwd command on line 1>

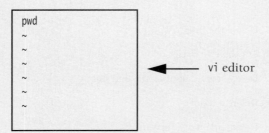

vi editor

```
4   $ history
    1 date
    2 ls -l
    3 echo "hello"
    4 pwd

5   $ fc -3 -1        # Start vi, edit, write/quit, and execute last 3 commands.
```

EXPLANATION

1   The FCEDIT variable can be assigned the pathname for any of the UNIX text editors you have on your system, such as vi, emacs, textedit, and so on. If not set, the ed editor is the default.

2   The pwd command is typed at the command line. It will be placed in the history file.

3   The fc command caused the editor (set in FCEDIT) to be invoked with the last command typed in the editor window. If the user writes and quits the editor, any commands typed there will be executed.

4   The history command lists recently typed commands.

5   The fc command is used to start up the editor with the last three commands from the history file in the editor's buffer.

11.4 Commenting and Filename Expansion

Filename expansion is a mechanism that allows the user to type part of a filename and press the Esc key to see the rest of the filename(s). In the following examples, [Esc] represents the Esc key.

Table 11.4 Using the Esc Key and Filename Expansion

Combination	Result
command [Esc]#	# precedes command with a #; puts it on the history list commented; command will not be executed.
command [Esc]_	Underscore inserts the last word of the last command at the cursor.
command [Esc] 2_	Inserts the second word of the last command at the cursor position.
word[Esc] *	* replaces the current word with all files matched.
word[Esc] \	\ replaces the current word with the first filename that starts with the same characters; filename expansion.
word[Esc]=	Displays all filenames beginning with the same character as the current word and displays them in a numbered list.

EXAMPLE 11.20

(Press the Esc Key for [Esc].

```
1   $ ls a[Esc]=
    1) abc
    2) abc1
    3) abc122
    4) abc123
    5) abc2
2   $ ls a[Esc]*
    ls abc abc1 abc122 abc123 abc2
    abc   abc1  abc122 abc123 abc2
3   $ print apples pears peaches
    apples pears peaches
4   $ print [Esc]_
    print peaches
    peaches
5   $ print apples pears peaches plums
    apples pears peaches
6   $ print [Esc]2_
    print pears
    pears
```

EXPLANATION

1   By typing an a, followed by the Esc key and an equal sign (=), all files starting with an a are numbered and listed. (The numbers do not serve any special purpose.)

2   By typing an a, then the Esc key and an asterisk (*), the filenames starting with an a are displayed.

EXPLANATION (CONTINUED)

3   The print command displays its arguments: apples, pears, and peaches.

4   The Esc key, followed by an underscore (_), is replaced with the last argument.

5   The print command displays its arguments: apples, pears, and peaches.

6   The Esc key, followed by the number 2 and an underscore, is replaced by the second argument. The command (print) is the first argument, starting at word zero.

11.5 Aliases

An alias is a Korn shell or user-defined abbreviation for a command. The alias name contains alphanumeric characters. Default aliases are provided by the shell and can be redefined or unset. Unlike the C shell aliases, the Korn shell does not support passing arguments. (If you need to use arguments, see "Functions" on page 639.)

Aliases can be exported to subshells by storing them in the ENV file. (The commands in the ENV file are executed every time a new shell is spawned.) Starting with the 1988 version of the Korn shell, the -x option allows aliases to be exported to subshells as long as the new shell is not a separate invocation of ksh. Tracked aliases are provided by the Korn shell to speed up the time it takes the shell to search the path. Aliases can alias themselves; that is, they are recursive.

11.5.1   Listing Aliases

The alias built-in command lists all set aliases.

EXAMPLE 11.21

```
1    $ alias
2    autoload=typeset -fu
3    false=let 0
4    functions=typeset -f
5    hash=alias -t
6    history=fc -l
7    integer=typeset -i
8    r=fc -e -
9    stop=kill -STOP
10   suspend=kill -STOP $$
11   true=:
12   type=whence -v
```

EXPLANATION

1   The alias command, without arguments, lists all aliases. This is a list of preset aliases, including those you have set.

2   The autoload alias is used for invoking functions dynamically.

3   The false alias is used in expressions testing for a false condition.

EXPLANATION (CONTINUED)

4   The functions alias lists all functions and their definitions.

5   The hash alias lists all tracked aliases.

6   The history alias lists and numbers all commands in the history file, .sh_history.

7   The integer alias allows you to create integer-type variables.

8   The r alias lets you redo a previous command from the history list.

9   The stop alias causes a process to be suspended if a job number or PID is provided to the kill command. The job can be resumed in the foreground by typing fg.

10 The suspend alias suspends the current job by sending the STOP signal and the PID ($$) of this process to the kill command.

11 The true alias is set to the do-nothing command, often used to start an infinite loop.

12 The type alias indicates the type of command you are executing: an alias, a binary executable, and so forth.

11.5.2 Creating Aliases

The user can create aliases in the Korn shell. An alias is a nickname for an existing command or commands. The real command(s) is substituted for the alias when the shell evaluates the command line.

EXAMPLE 11.22

```
1   $ alias cl='clear'
2   $ alias l='ls -laF'
3   $ alias ls='ls -aF'
4   $ \ls ..
```

EXPLANATION

1   The alias cl is an alias for clear.

2   The alias is l. The letter l is a nickname for the command ls -laF.

3   The alias ls is assigned the command ls -aF.

4   The backslash turns off the meaning of the alias for the execution of this line. The real ls command, not the alias, is executed.

11.5.3 Deleting Aliases

The unalias command deletes an alias.

EXAMPLE 11.23

```
unalias cl
```

EXPLANATION

The alias cl is removed from the list of set aliases.

11.5.4 Tracked Aliases

To reduce the amount of time needed to do a search of the path, the Korn shell creates an alias when a command is first encountered and sets the alias equal to the full pathname of the command. This is called a *tracked alias*.[3]

The Korn shell has some preset tracked aliases that are defined when it is installed. To use tracked aliases, the `set -o trackall` command is issued; it is normally set in the ENV file. To see all tracked aliases, type `alias -t`.

EXAMPLE 11.24

```
$ alias -t
chmod=/bin/chmod
ls=/bin/ls
vi=/usr/ucb/vi
who=/bin/who
```

EXPLANATION

The `-t` option to the built-in `alias` command displays those commands that have been aliased via the tracking mechanism. When the user types any of these commands, the shell will not search the path, but use the alias definition to invoke the command.

11.6 Job Control

Job control is used to control the execution of background and foreground jobs.

To use Korn shell job control, the monitor option (`set -o monitor`) must be set on systems that do not support job control. See Table 11.5 for job control commands.

Table 11.5 Job Control Commands

Command	Function
jobs	Lists all unfinished processes in a numerically ordered list where the number of the job is enclosed in brackets
jobs -l	Same as jobs, but includes the PID number of the job
^Z	Stops the current job
fg %n	Runs background job in foreground
bg %n	Runs job in background
wait %n	Waits for job number n to finish
kill %n	Kills job number n

---

3. Tracked aliases will be undefined if the PATH variable is reset.

EXAMPLE 11.25

```
1   $ vi
    [1]  + Stopped          # vi
2   $ sleep 25&
    [2] 4538
3   $ jobs
    [2] +  Running          # sleep 25&
    [1] -  Stopped          # vi
4   $ jobs -1
    [2] + 4538   Running    # sleep 25&
    [1] - 4537   Stopped    # vi
5   $ fg %1
```

EXPLANATION

1   After the vi editor is invoked, you can press ^Z (Ctrl-Z) to suspend the vi session. The editor will be suspended in the background, and after the message Stopped appears, the shell prompt will appear immediately.

2   The ampersand at the end of the command causes the sleep command, with an argument of 25, to execute in the background. The notation [2] means that this is the second job to be run in the background and the PID of this job is 4538.

3   The jobs command displays the jobs currently in the background.

4   The jobs command with the -1 option displays the processes (jobs) running in the background and the PID numbers of those jobs.

5   The fg command followed by a percent sign and the job number will bring that numbererd job into the foreground. Without a number, fg brings the most recently backgrounded job back into the foreground.

11.7 Metacharacters

Metacharacters are special characters used to represent something other than themselves. Table 11.6 lists some common Korn shell metacharacters and their functions.

Table 11.6 Korn Shell Metacharacters

Command	Function
\	Literal interpretation of the following character
&	Background processing
;	Command separator
$	Variable substitution
?	Match for a single character

Table 11.6   Korn Shell Metacharacters (continued)

Command	Function
[abc]	Match for one from a set of characters
[!abc]	Match for one *not* from the set of characters
*	Match for zero or more characters
(cmds)	Execute commands in a subshell
{cmds}	Execute commands in current shell

EXAMPLE 11.26

```
1   $ ls -d *     all files are displayed
    abc   abc122   abc2   file1.bak file2.bak nonsense  nothing one
    abc1 abc123   file1    file2    none     noone

2   $ print hello \        # The carriage return is escaped
    > there
    hello there

3   $ rusers&              # Process the rusers command in the background
    [1]   4334
    $

4   $ who; date; uptime    # Commands are executed one at a time
    ellie   console Feb 10 10:46
    ellie   ttyp0   Feb 15 12:41
    ellie   ttyp1   Feb 10 10:47
    ellie   ttyp2   Feb 5  10:53
    Mon Feb 15 17:16:43 PST 2004
    5:16pm up 5 days, 6:32, 1 user, load average: 0.28, 0.23, 0.01

5   $ print $HOME          # The value of the HOME variable is printed
    /home/jody/ellie

6   $ print $LOGNAME       # The value of the LOGNAME variable is printed
    ellie

7   $ ( pwd; cd / ; pwd )
    /home/jody/ellie
    /
```

EXAMPLE 11.26 (CONTINUED)

```
    $ pwd
    /home/jody/ellie

8   $ { pwd; cd /; pwd; }
    /home/jody/ellie
    /
    $ pwd
    /

9   $ ( date; pwd; ls ) > outfile
    $ cat outfile
    Mon Feb 15 15:56:34 PDT 2004
    /home/jody/ellie
    foo1
    foo2
    foo3
```

EXPLANATION

1   The asterisk matches all the files in the current directory. (The -d option to the ls command prevents the contents of subdirectories from being displayed.)

2   The backslash escapes the newline so that the command line can be continued on the next line.

3   The ampersand (&) causes the rusers program to be executed in the background; the shell prompt returns immediately. Both processes will run concurrently.

4   Each command is separated by a semicolon. Each command will be executed one at a time.

5   If a dollar sign precedes the variable, the shell will perform variable substitution. The value of the env variable, HOME, is displayed. The HOME variable contains the full pathname of the user's home directory.

6   Again, the dollar sign precedes the variable name. The value of the LOGNAME variable is the user's login name.

7   The parentheses indicate that the enclosed commands will be executed in a subshell. The cd command is built into the shell, so that each shell that is invoked has its own copy of cd. The pwd command prints the present working directory, /home/jody/ellie. After cding to the root directory, the pwd command displays that the new directory is root. After the subshell exits, the output of the pwd command in the parent shell indicates that the directory is still set to /home/jody/ellie as it was before entering the subshell.

8   The curly braces indicate that the enclosed commands will be executed in the current shell. The `pwd` command prints the present working directory, `/home/jody/ellie`. After `cd`ing to the `root` directory, the `pwd` command displays that the new directory is `root`. After the commands within the curly braces exit, the output of the `pwd` command indicates that the directory is still set to the root directory.

9   The parentheses are used to group the commands so that the output of all three commands is sent to `outfile`.

11.8 Filename Substitution (Wildcards)

When evaluating the command line, the shell uses metacharacters to abbreviate filenames or pathnames that match a certain set of characters, often called *wildcards*. The filename substitution metacharacters listed in Table 11.7 are expanded into an alphabetically listed set of filenames. The process of expanding a metacharacter into filenames is also called filename substitution, or *globbing*. If a metacharacter is used and there is no filename that matches it, the Korn shell treats the metacharacter as a literal character.

Table 11.7   Shell Metacharacters and Filename Substitution

Metacharacter	Meaning
*	Matches zero or more characters
?	Matches exactly one character
[abc]	Matches one character in the set, a, b, or c
[!abc]	Matches one character *not* in the set a, b, or c
[a-z]	Matches one character in the range: any character in the set between a and z
~	Substitutes the user's home directory for ~
\	Escapes or disables the metacharacter

11.8.1   The Asterisk

The asterisk is a wildcard that matches for zero or more of any character in a filename.

EXAMPLE 11.27

```
1    $ ls *
     abc abc1 abc122 abc123 abc2 file1 file1.bak file2 file2.bak none
     nonsense noone nothing nowhere one
```

EXAMPLE 11.27 (CONTINUED)

```
2   $ ls *.bak
    file1.bak file2.bak
3   $ print a*c
    abc
```

EXPLANATION

1   The asterisk expands to all of the files in the present working directory. All of the files are passed to ls and displayed.

2   All files starting with zero or more characters and ending with .bak are matched and listed.

3   All files starting with a, followed by zero or more characters, and ending in c are matched and passed as arguments to the print command.

11.8.2 The Question Mark

The question mark represents a single character in a filename. When a filename contains one or more question marks, the shell performs filename substitution by replacing the question mark with the character it matches in the filename.

EXAMPLE 11.28

```
1   $ ls
    abc abc1 abc122 abc123 abc2 file1 file1.bak file2 file2.bak
    none nonsense noone nothing nowhere one
2   $ ls a?c?
    abc1 abc2
3   $ ls ??
    ?? not found
4   $ print abc???
    abc122 abc123
5   $ print ??
    ??
```

EXPLANATION

1   The files in the current directory are listed.

2   Filenames containing four characters are matched and listed if the filename starts with an a, followed by a single character, followed by a c and a single character.

3   Filenames containing exactly two characters are listed. There are none, so the two question marks are treated as literal characters. Because there is no file in the directory called ??, the shell sends the message ?? not found.

4   Filenames containing six characters are matched and printed, starting with abc and followed by exactly three of any character.

EXPLANATION (CONTINUED)

5   The ksh print function gets the two question marks as an argument. The shell tries
    to match for any filenames with exactly two characters. There are no files in the
    directory that contain exactly two characters. The shell treats the question mark
    as a literal question mark if it cannot find a match. The two literal question marks
    are passed as arguments to the print command.

11.8.3 The Square Brackets

Brackets are used to match filenames containing *one* character from a set or range of
characters.

EXAMPLE 11.29

```
1   $ ls
    abc abc1 abc122 abc123 abc2 file1 file1.bak file2 file2.bak
    none nonsense noone nothing nowhere one
2   $ ls abc[123]
    abc1 abc2
3   $ ls abc[1-3]
    abc1 abc2
4   $ ls [a-z][a-z][a-z]
    abc one
5   $ ls [!f-z]???
    abc1 abc2
6   $ ls abc12[2-3]
    abc122 abc123
```

EXPLANATION

1   All of the files in the present working directory are listed.

2   All four-character names are matched and listed if the filename starts with abc, fol-
    lowed by 1, 2, or 3. Only one character from the set in the brackets is matched for
    a filename.

3   All four-character filenames are matched and listed if the filename starts with abc,
    and is followed by a number in the range from 1 to 3.

4   All three-character filenames are matched and listed, if the filename contains ex-
    actly three lowercase alphabetic characters.

5   All four-character files are listed if the first character is *not* a letter between f and
    z, followed by three of any character (???).

6   Files are listed if the filenames contain abc12, followed by 2 or 3.

11.8.4   Escaping Metacharacters

To use a metacharacter as a literal character, use the backslash to prevent the metacharacter from being interpreted.

EXAMPLE 11.30

```
1   $ ls
    abc file1 youx
2   $ print How are you?
    How are youx
3   $ print How are you\?
    How are you?
4   $ print When does this line \
    > ever end\?
    When does this line ever end?
```

EXPLANATION

1   The files in the present working directory are listed. Note the file youx.

2   The shell will perform filename expansion on the question mark. Any files in the current directory starting with y-o-u and followed by exactly one character are matched and substituted in the string. The filename youx will be substituted in the string to read, How are youx (probably not what you wanted to happen).

3   By preceding the question mark (?) with a backslash, it is escaped, meaning that the shell will not try to interpret it as a wildcard.

4   The newline is escaped by preceding it with a backslash. The secondary prompt is displayed until the string is terminated with a newline. The question mark (?) is escaped to protect it from filename expansion.

11.8.5   Tilde and Hyphen Expansion

The tilde character was adopted by the Korn shell (from the C shell) for pathname expansion. The tilde by itself evaluates to the full pathname of the user's home directory. When the tilde is appended with a username, it expands to the full pathname of that user.

The hyphen character refers to the previous working directory; OLDPWD also refers to the previous working directory.

EXAMPLE 11.31

```
1   $ echo ~
    /home/jody/ellie
2   $ echo ~joe
    /home/joe
```

EXAMPLE 11.31 (CONTINUED)

```
3   $ echo ~+
    /home/jody/ellie/perl
4   $ echo ~-
    /home/jody/ellie/prac
5   $ echo $OLDPWD
    /home/jody/ellie/prac
6   $ cd -
    /home/jody/ellie/prac
```

EXPLANATION

1   The tilde evaluates to the full pathname of the user's home directory.

2   The tilde preceding the username evaluates to the full pathname of joe's home directory.

3   The ~+ notation evaluates to the full pathname of the working directory.

4   The ~- notation evaluates to the previous working directory.

5   The OLDPWD variable contains the previous working directory.

6   The hyphen refers to the previous working directory; cd to go to the previous working directory and display the directory.

11.8.6 New ksh Metacharacters

The new Korn shell metacharacters are used for filename expansion in a way that is similar to the regular expression metacharacters of egrep and awk. The metacharacter preceding the characters enclosed in parentheses controls what the pattern matches. See Table 11.8.

Table 11.8 Regular Expression Wildcards

Regular Expression	Meaning
abc?(2|9)1	? matches zero or one occurrences of any pattern in the parentheses. The vertical bar represents an OR condition; for example, either 2 or 9. Matches abc21, abc91, or abc1.
abc*([0-9])	* matches zero or more occurrences of any pattern in the parentheses. Matches abc followed by zero or more digits; for example, abc, abc1234, abc3, or abc2.
abc+([0-9])	+ matches one or more occurrences of any pattern in the parentheses. Matches abc followed by one or more digits; for example, abc3 or abc123.
no@(one|ne)	@ matches exactly one occurrence of any pattern in the parentheses. Matches noone or none.

Table 11.8   Regular Expression Wildcards (continued)

Regular Expression	Meaning
no!(thing|where)	! matches all strings *except* those matched by any of the patterns in the parentheses. Matches no, nobody, or noone, but not nothing or nowhere.

EXAMPLE 11.32

```
1   $ ls
    abc abc1 abc122 abc123 abc2 file1 file1.bak file2 file2.bak none
    nonsense noone nothing nowhere one
2   $ ls abc?(1|2)
    abc  abc1 abc2
3   $ ls abc*([1-5])
    abc   abc1  abc122 abc123 abc2
4   $ ls abc+([1-5])
    abc1  abc122 abc123 abc2
5   $ ls no@(thing|ne)
    none   nothing
6   $ ls no!(one|nsense)
    none  nothing nowhere
```

EXPLANATION

1   All the files in the present working directory are listed.

2   Matches filenames starting with abc and followed by *zero characters or one* of either of the patterns in parentheses. Matches abc, abc1, or abc2.

3   Matches filenames starting with abc and followed by *zero or more* numbers between 1 and 5. Matches abc, abc1, abc122, abc123, and abc2.

4   Matches filenames starting with abc and followed by *one or more* numbers between 1 and 5. Matches abc1, abc122, abc123, and abc2.

5   Matches filenames starting with *no* and followed by exactly thing or ne. Matches nothing or none.

6   Matches filenames starting with no and followed by anything except one or nsense. Matches none, nothing, and nowhere.

11.8.7   The noglob Variable

If the noglob variable is set, filename substitution is turned off, meaning that all metacharacters represent themselves; they are not used as wildcards. This can be useful when searching for patterns containing metacharacters in programs like grep, sed, or awk. If noglob is not set, all metacharacters must be escaped with a backslash if they are not to be interpreted.

EXAMPLE 11.33

```
1   % set -o noglob        # or set -f
2   % print * ?? [] ~ $LOGNAME
    * ?? [] /home/jody/ellie ellie
3   % set +o noglob        # or set +f
```

EXPLANATION

1   The noglob variable is set. It turns off the special meaning of the wildcards for file-name expansion. You can use the -f option to set the command to achieve the same results.

2   The filename expansion metacharacters are displayed as themselves without any interpretation. Note that the tilde and the dollar sign are still expanded.

3   The noglob option is reset. Filename metacharacters will be expanded.

11.9 Variables

11.9.1   Local Variables

Local variables are given values that are known only to the shell in which they are created. Variable names must begin with an alphabetic or underscore character. The remaining characters can be alphabetic, decimal digits zero to nine, or an underscore character. Any other characters mark the termination of the variable name.

Setting and Referencing Local Variables.   When assigning a value to a variable, there can be no whitespace surrounding the equal sign. To set the variable to null, the equal sign is followed by nothing. If more than one word is assigned to a variable, it must be quoted to protect the whitespace; otherwise, the shell prints an error message and the variable is undefined.

If a dollar sign is prepended to the variable name, the value assigned to that variable can be referenced. If other characters are attached to a variable name, curly braces are used to shield the name of the variable from the extra characters.

EXAMPLE 11.34

```
1   $ state=Cal
    $ echo $state
    Cal
2   $ name="Peter Piper"
    $ echo $name
    Peter Piper
```

EXAMPLE 11.34 (CONTINUED)

```
3    $ x=
     $ echo $x
                    # Blank line appears when a variable is either unset or set to null
     $
4    $ state=Cal
     $ print ${state}ifornia
     California
```

EXPLANATION

1   The variable state is assigned the value Cal. When the shell encounters the dollar sign preceding a variable name, it performs variable substitution. The value of the variable is displayed.

2   The variable name is assigned the value "Peter Piper". The quotes are needed to hide the whitespace so that the shell will not split the string into separate words when it parses the command line. The value of the variable is displayed.

3   The variable x is not assigned a value. It will be assigned a null string. The null value, an empty string, is displayed. The same output would be displayed if the variable had not been set at all.

4   The variable state is assigned the value Cal. The variable is enclosed in curly braces to shield it from the characters that are appended. The value of the variable Cal is displayed with ifornia appended.

The Scope of Local Variables.   A local variable is known only to the shell in which it was created. It is not passed on to subshells. The $$ variable is a special variable containing the PID of the current shell.

EXAMPLE 11.35

```
1    $ echo $$
     1313
2    $ round=world
     $ echo $round
     world
3    $ ksh      # Start a subshell
4    $ echo $$
     1326
5    $ echo $round
6    $ exit       # Exits this shell, returns to parent shell
7    $ echo $$
     1313
8    $ echo $round
     world
```

EXPLANATION

1   The value of the $$ variable evaluates to the PID of the current shell. The PID of this shell is 1313.

2   The local variable round is assigned the string value world and the value of the variable is displayed.

3   A new Korn shell is invoked. This is called a *subshell*, or *child shell*.

4   The PID of this shell is 1326. The parent shell's PID is 1313.

5   The variable round is not defined in this shell.

6   The exit command terminates this shell and returns to the parent shell. If the ignoreeof option is not set, Ctrl-D will also exit this shell.

7   The parent shell returns. Its PID is displayed.

8   The value of the variable is displayed.

Setting Read-Only Variables.   A read-only variable cannot be redefined or unset. It can be set with the readonly or typeset -r built-in commands. You may want to set variables to readonly for security reasons when running in privileged mode.

EXAMPLE   11.36

```
1   $ readonly name=Tom
    $ print $name
    Tom
2   $ unset name
    ksh: name: is read only
3   $ name=Joe
    ksh name: is read only
4   $ typeset -r PATH
    $ PATH=${PATH}:/usr/local/bin
    ksh: PATH: is read only
```

EXPLANATION

1   The readonly local variable name is assigned the value Tom.

2   A readonly variable cannot be unset.

3   A readonly variable cannot be redefined.

4   The PATH variable is set to be readonly. Any effort to unset or change the variable will produce an error message.

11.9.2   Environment Variables

Environment variables are available to the shell in which they are created and any subshells or processes spawned from that shell. By convention, environment variables are capitalized.

The shell in which a variable is created is called the *parent shell*. If a new shell is started from the parent shell, it is called the *child shell*. Some of the environment variables, such as HOME, LOGNAME, PATH, and SHELL, are set before you log in by the /bin/login program. Normally, environment variables are set in the .profile file in the user's home directory.

Setting Environment Variables.   To set environment variables, the export command is used either after assigning a value or when the variable is set. All variables in a script can be exported by turning on the allexport option to the set command (e.g., set -o allexport).

EXAMPLE 11.37

```
1   $ TERM=wyse ; export TERM
2   $ export NAME ="John Smith"
    $ print $NAME
    John Smith
3   $ print $$
    319
4   $ ksh
5   $ print $$
    340
6   $ print $NAME
    John Smith
7   $ NAME="April Jenner"
    $ print $NAME
    April Jenner
8   $ exit
9   $ print $$
    319
10  $ print $NAME
    John Smith
```

EXPLANATION

1   The TERM variable is assigned wyse. The variable is exported. Now processes started from this shell will inherit the variable.

2   The variable is exported and defined in the same step. (New with the Korn shell.)

3   The value of this shell's PID is printed.

4   A new Korn shell is started. The new shell is the *child*; the original shell is its *parent*.

5   The PID of the new Korn shell, stored in the $$ (340) variable, is printed.

6   The variable was exported to the new shell and is displayed.

7   The variable is reset to April Jenner and displayed.

8   This Korn child shell is exited. The parent shell will return.

9   The PID of the parent, 319, is displayed again.

10   The variable NAME contains its original value. Variables retain their values when exported from parent to child. The child cannot change the value of a variable for its parent.

Special Environment Variables.   The Korn shell assigns default values to the environment variables, PATH, PS1, PS2, PS3, PS4, MAILCHECK, FCEDIT, TMOUT, and IFS. The SHELL, LOGNAME, USER, and HOME are set by the /bin/login program. You can change the values of the defaults and set the others listed in Table 11.9.

Table 11.9   Korn Shell Environment Variables

Variable Name	*Meaning*
_ (underscore)	The last argument of the previous command.
CDPATH	The search path for the cd command. A colon-separated list of directories used to find a directory if the /, ./, or ../ is not at the beginning of the pathname.
COLUMNS	If set, defines the width of the edit window for shell edit modes and the select command.
EDITOR	Pathname for a built-in editor: emacs, gmacs, or vi.
ENV	A variable set to the name of a file, containing functions and aliases, that the Korn shell will invoke when the ksh program is invoked. On versions newer than 1988, this file is only executed when ksh is invoked interactively, not for noninteractive shells. The variable is not expanded if the privileged option is turned on.
ERRNO	System error number. Its value is the error number of the most recently failed system call.
FCEDIT	Default editor name for the fc command. On versions newer than 1988, this variable is called HISTEDIT, and the fc command is hist.
FPATH	A colon-separated list of directories that defines the search path for directories containing auto-loaded functions.
HISTEDIT	For versions of the Korn shell newer than 1988, the new name for FCEDIT.
HISTFILE	Specifies file in which to store command history.
HISTSIZE	Maximum number of commands from the history that can be accessed; default is 128.
HOME	Home directory; used by cd when no directory is specified.
IFS	Internal field separators, normally space, tab, and newline, used for field splitting of words resulting from command substitution, lists in loop constructs, and reading input.
LINENO	Current line number in script.
LINES	Used in select loops for vertically displaying menu items; default is 24.

Table 11.9 Korn Shell Environment Variables (continued)

Variable Name	Meaning
MAIL	If this parameter is set to the name of a mail file and the MAILPATH parameter is not set, the shell informs the user of the arrival of mail in the specified file.
MAILCHECK	This parameter specifies how often (in seconds) the shell will check for the arrival of mail in the files specified by the MAILPATH or MAIL parameters. The default value is 600 seconds (10 minutes). If set to zero, the shell will check before issuing each primary prompt.
MAILPATH	A colon-separated list of filenames. If this parameter is set, the shell informs the user of the arrival of mail in any of the specified files. Each filename can be followed by a % and a message that will be printed when the modification time changes. The default message is You have mail.
OLDPWD	Last working directory.
PATH	The search path for commands; a colon-separated list of directories the shell uses to search for the command you want to execute.
PWD	Present working directory; set by cd.
PPID	Process ID of the parent process.
PS1	Primary prompt string, by default $.
PS2	Secondary prompt string, by default >.
PS3	Selection prompt string used with the select command, by default #?.
PS4	Debug prompt string used when tracing is turned on, by default +.
RANDOM	Random number generated each time the variable is referenced.
REPLY	Set when read is not supplied arguments.
SHELL	When the shell is invoked, it scans the environment for this name. The shell gives default values to PATH, PS1, PS2, MAILCHECK, and IFS. HOME and MAIL are set by login.
TMOUT	Specifies number of seconds to wait for input before exiting.
VISUAL	Specifies editor for in-line command editing: emacs, gmacs, or vi.

11.9.3 Listing Set Variables

There are three built-in commands that print the value of variables: set, env, and typeset. The set command prints all variables, local and global. The env command prints only global variables. The typeset command prints all variables, integers, functions, and exported variables. The set -o command prints all options set for the Korn shell.

EXAMPLE 11.38

```
1   $ env       # Partial list
    LOGNAME=ellie
    TERMCAP=sun-cmd:te=\E[>4h:ti=\E[>4l:tc=sun:
    USER=ellie
    DISPLAY=:0.0
    SHELL=/bin/ksh
    HOME=/home/jody/ellie
    TERM=sun-cmd
    LD_LIBRARY_PATH=/usr/local/OW3/lib
    PWD=/home/jody/ellie/perl

2   $ typeset
    export MANPATH
    export PATH
    integer ERRNO
    export FONTPATH
    integer OPTIND
    function LINENO
    export OPENWINHOME
    export LOGNAME
    function SECONDS
    integer PPID
    PS3
    PS2
    export TERMCAP
    OPTARG
    export USER
    export DISPLAY
    function RANDOM
    export SHELL
    integer TMOUT
    integer MAILCHECK

3   $ set
    DISPLAY=:0.0
    ERRNO=10
    FCEDIT=/bin/ed
    FMHOME=/usr/local/Frame-2.1X
    FONTPATH=/usr/local/OW3/lib/fonts
    HELPPATH=/usr/local/OW3/lib/locale:/usr/local/OW3/lib/help
    HOME=/home/jody/ellie
    IFS=
    LD_LIBRARY_PATH=/usr/local/OW3/lib
    LINENO=1
    LOGNAME=ellie
    MAILCHECK=600
```

EXAMPLE 11.38 (CONTINUED)

```
MANPATH=/usr/local/OW3/share/man:/usr/local/OW3/man:/
usr/local/man:/usr/local/doctools/man:/usr/man
OPTIND=1
PATH=/home/jody/ellie:/usr/local/OW3/bin:/usr/ucb:/
usr/local/doctools/bin:/usr/bin:/usr/local:/usr/etc:/etc:/
usr/spool/news/bin:/home/jody/ellie/bin:/usr/lo
PID=1332
PS1=$
PS2=>
PS3=#?
PS4=+
PWD=/home/jody/ellie/kshprog/joke
RANDOM=4251
SECONDS=36
SHELL=/bin/ksh
TERM=sun-cmd
TERMCAP=sun-cmd:te=\E[>4h:ti=\E[>4l:tc=sun:
      TMOUT=0
USER=ellie
_=pwd
name=Joe
place=San Francisco
x=
```

4   **set -o**
```
    allexport      off
    bgnice         on
    emacs          off
    errexit        off
    gmacs          off
    ignoreeof      off
    interactive    on
    keyword        off
    markdirs       off
    monitor        on
    noexec         off
    noclobber      off
    noglob         off
    nolog          off
    nounset        off
    privileged     off
    restricted     off
    trackall       off
    verbose        off
    viraw          off
    xtrace         off
```

EXPLANATION

1   The env command lists all environment (exported) variables. These variables are, by convention, named with uppercase letters. They are passed from the process in which they are created to any of the child processes.

2   The typeset command displays all variables and their attributes, functions, and integers. The typeset command with the + option displays only the names of the variables.

3   The set command, without options, prints all set variables, local and exported, including variables set to null.

4   The set command with the -o option lists all built-in variables that are set to on or off. To turn options off, use the plus sign (+), and to turn options on, use the minus sign (-); for example, set -o allexport turns on the allexport option, causing all variables to be set as global.

11.9.4   Unsetting Variables

Both local and environment variables can be unset by using the unset command (unless the variables are set to readonly).

EXAMPLE 11.39

```
unset name; unset TERM
```

EXPLANATION

The variables name and TERM are no longer defined for this shell.

11.9.5   Printing the Values of Variables

The echo command (used in Bourne and C shells) is still effective in this shell, but the print command has more options and is more efficient. Both the echo command and print command are built into the shell. The print command has a number of options to control its output. They are listed in Table 11.10.

Table 11.10   print Options

Option	Meaning
-	Any arguments that follow are not print options. The dash allows arguments that contain a hyphen, for example, -2.
-f	For versions newer than 1988, used to emulate printf.
-n	No newline in output; like echo -n.

Table 11.10 print Options (continued)

Option	Meaning
-p	Sends output to a coprocess or pipe (&|) rather than to standard output.
-r	Prevents the print command from interpreting escape sequences.
-R	Prevents ksh from treating a -2 or -x as a print argument; turns off the dash if preceding an argument (except -n); \t, \c, \c are not recognized as special and appear unchanged when printed without the \.
-s	Output is appended to the history file as a command rather than to standard output.
-un	Redirects output to file descriptor n.

EXAMPLE 11.40

```
1  $ print Hello my friend and neighbor!
   Hello my friend and neighbor!
2  $ print "Hello          friends"
   Hello          friends

3  $ print -r "\n"
   \n
4  $ print -s "date +%H"
   $ history -2
   132 print -s "date +%H"
   133 date +%H
   134 history -2
   $ r 133
   09
5  $ print -n $HOME
   /home/jody/ellie
6  $ var=world
   $ print ${var}wide
   worldwide
7  $ print -x is an option
   ksh: print: bad option(s)
8  $ print - -x is an option
   -x is an option
```

EXPLANATION

1   The shell parses the command line, breaks the command line into words (tokens) separated by space, and passes the words as arguments to the print command. The shell removes all the extra whitespace between words.

EXPLANATION (CONTINUED)

2   The quotes create a single string. The shell evaluates the string as a single word and the whitespace is preserved.

3   This is the `raw` option. Any escape sequences, such as \r, are not interpreted.

4   The `-s` option appends the `print` command's arguments to the history file as a command. The string `"date +%H"` is the argument to the `print` command. The `date` string is appended to the history list as a command and then executed with the `r` command (history's `redo` command).

5   The `-n` option suppresses the newline. The Korn shell prompt is on the same line as the output from the `print` command.

6   The local variable is assigned the value `world`. The braces insulate the variable from characters appended to it.

7   When the first argument to the `print` function begins with a dash, the `print` command interprets the argument as one of its options, unless an additional preceding dash is provided.

8   The dash as an option allows you to use a dash as the first character in the string to be printed.

11.9.6   Escape Sequences

Escape sequences consist of a character preceded by a backslash and have a special meaning when enclosed within quotes. (See Table 11.11.)

The `print` command, without the `-r` and `-R` options, formats output when any of the following escape sequences are placed within a string. The string must be enclosed in double or single quotes.

EXAMPLE 11.41

```
1   $ print '\t\t\tHello\n'
                Hello

    $

2   $ print "\aTea \tTime!\n\n"
    Ding ( bell rings ) Tea     Time!
```

EXPLANATION

1   The backslash characters must be quoted with either single or double quotes. The \t escape sequence represents a tab, and \n represents a newline. The output is three tabs, followed by the string `Hello`, and a newline.

2   The \a escape sequence causes a bell to ring (\07) and the \t creates a tab. The two \n sequences will print two newline characters.

Table 11.11 Escape Sequences

Backslash Character	Meaning
\a	Bell character
\b	Backspace
\c	Suppress newline and ignore any arguments that follow \c
\f	Formfeed
\n	Newline
\r	Return
\t	Tab
\v	Vertical tab
\\	Backslash
\0x	Eight-bit character with a 1-, 2-, or 3-digit ASCII value, as in print \0124
\E	Only on versions newer than 1988; used for an escape sequence

11.9.7 Variable Expressions and Expansion Modifiers

Variable expressions can be tested and modified by using special modifiers. The modifier provides a shortcut conditional test to check whether a variable has been set, and then, depending on the modifier, may assign a default value to the variable. These expressions can be used with conditional constructs such as if and elif. See Table 11.12.

The colon does not have to be used with the modifier. Using the colon with the modifier checks whether the variable is not set or is null; without the colon, a variable set to null is considered a set variable.

Table 11.12 Variable Expressions and Modifiers

Expression	Function
${variable:-word}	If variable is set and is nonnull, substitute its value; otherwise, substitute word.
${variable:=word}	If variable is not set or is null, set it to word; the value of variable is substituted permanently. Positional parameters may not be assigned in this way.
${variable:+word}	If variable is set and is nonnull, substitute word; otherwise substitute nothing.
${variable:?word}	If variable is set and is nonnull, substitute its value; otherwise, print word and exit from the shell. If word is omitted, the message parameter null or not set is printed.

EXAMPLE 11.42

```
(Using Temporary Default Values)
1   $ fruit=peach
2   $ print ${fruit:-plum}
    peach
3   $ print ${newfruit:-apple}
    apple
4   $ print $newfruit

5   $ print ${TERM:-vt120}
    sun-cmd
```

EXPLANATION

1   The variable fruit is assigned the value peach.

2   The special modifier will check to see if the variable fruit has been set. If it has, the value peach is printed; if not, plum is printed.

3   The variable newfruit has not been set. The value apple will be printed.

4   The variable newfruit was not set, so nothing prints. In step 3, the expression was simply replaced with the word apple and printed.

5   If the TERM variable has not been set, a default value vt120 will be displayed. In this example, the terminal has already been set to sun-cmd, a Sun workstation.

EXAMPLE 11.43

```
(Assigning Permanent Default Values)
1   $ name=
2   $ print ${name:=Patty}
    Patty
3   $ print $name
    Patty
4   $ print ${TERM:=vt120}
    vt120
    $ print $TERM
    vt120
```

EXPLANATION

1   The variable name is assigned the value null.

2   The special modifier := will check to see if the variable name has been set to some value other than null. If it has been set, it will not be changed; if it is either null or not set, it will be assigned the value to the right of the equal sign. Patty is assigned to name because the variable is set to null. The setting is permanent.

3   The variable name still contains the value Patty.

4   If the variable TERM is not set, it will be assigned the default value vt120 permanently.

EXAMPLE 11.44

```
(Assigning Temporary Alternate Value)
1   $ foo=grapes
2   $ print ${foo:+pears}
    pears
    $ print $foo
    grapes
```

EXPLANATION

1   The variable foo has been assigned the value grapes.
2   The special modifier :+ will check to see if the variable has been set. If it has been set, it will temporarily be reset to grapes. If it has not been set, null is returned.

EXAMPLE 11.45

```
(Creating Error Messages Based on Default Values)
1   $ print ${namex:?"namex is undefined"}
    ksh: namex: namex is undefined
2   $ print ${y?}
    ksh: y: parameter null or not set
```

EXPLANATION

1   The :? modifier will check to see if the variable has been set. If not, the string to the right of the ? is printed to standard error, after the name of the variable. If in a script, the script exits.
2   If a message is not provided after the ?, the Korn shell sends a default message to standard error. Without the colon, the ? modifier would consider a variable set to null a set variable, and the message would not be printed.

EXAMPLE 11.46

```
(Line from a System Script)
if [ "${uid:=0}" -ne 0 ]
```

EXPLANATION

If the UID (user ID) has a value, it will not be changed; if it does not have a value, it will be assigned the value zero (superuser). The value of the variable will be tested for nonzero. This line was taken from the /etc/shutdown program (SVR4/Solaris 2.5). It is here to give you an example of how variable modifiers are used.

11.9.8 Variable Expansion of Substrings

Pattern-matching arguments are used to strip off certain portions of a string from either the front or end of the string. The most common use for these operators is stripping off pathname elements from the head or tail of the path. See Table 11.13.

Table 11.13 Variable Expansion Substrings

Expression	Function
${variable%pattern}	Matches the *smallest trailing portion* of the value of variable to pattern and removes it.
${variable%%pattern}	Matches the *largest trailing portion* of the value of variable to pattern and removes it.
${variable#pattern}	Matches the *smallest leading portion* of the value of variable to pattern and removes it.
${variable##pattern}	Matches the *largest leading portion* of the value of variable to pattern and removes it.

EXAMPLE 11.47

```
1   $ pathname="/usr/bin/local/bin"
2   $ print ${pathname%/bin*}
    /usr/bin/local
```

EXPLANATION

1   The local variable pathname is assigned /usr/bin/local/bin.

2   The % removes the *smallest trailing portion* of pathname containing the pattern /bin, followed by zero or more characters; that is, it strips off /bin.

EXAMPLE 11.48

```
1   $ pathname="usr/bin/local/bin"
2   $ print ${pathname%%/bin*}
    /usr
```

EXPLANATION

1   The local variable pathname is assigned /usr/bin/local/bin.

2   The %% removes the *largest trailing portion* of pathname containing the pattern /bin, followed by zero or more characters; that is, it strips off /bin/local/bin.

EXAMPLE 11.49

```
1   $ pathname=/home/lilliput/jake/.cshrc
2   $ print ${pathname#/home}
    /lilliput/jake/.cshrc
```

EXPLANATION

1   The local variable pathname is assigned /home/liliput/jake/.cshrc.

2   The # removes the *smallest leading portion* of pathname containing the pattern /home; that is, /home is stripped from the beginning of the path variable.

EXAMPLE 11.50

```
1   $ pathname=/home/liliput/jake/.cshrc
2   $ print ${pathname##*/}
    .cshrc
```

EXPLANATION

1   The local variable pathname is assigned /home/liliput/jake/.cshrc.

2   The ## removes the *largest leading portion* of pathname containing zero or more characters up to and including the last slash; that is, it strips off /home/lilliput/jake/ from the path variable.

11.9.9   Variable Attributes: The typeset Command

The attributes of a variable, such as its case, width, and left or right justification, can be controlled by the typeset command. When the typeset command changes the attributes of a variable, the change is permanent. The typeset function has a number of other functions. See Table 11.14.

EXAMPLE 11.51

```
1   $ typeset -u name="john doe"
    $ print "$name"
    JOHN DOE            # Changes all characters to uppercase.

2   $ typeset -l name
    $ print $name
    john doe            # Changes all characters to lowercase.

3   $ typeset -L4 name
    $ print $name
    john               # Left-justified fixed-width 4-character field.
```

EXAMPLE   11.51 (CONTINUED)

```
4   $ typeset -R2 name
    $ print $name                 # Right-justified fixed-width 2-character field.
    hn

5   $ name="John Doe"
    $ typeset -Z15 name           # Null-padded sting, 15-space field width
    $ print "$name"
     John Doe

6   $ typeset -LZ15 name          # Left-justified, 15-space field width.
    $ print "$name$name"
    John Doe        John Doe

7   $ integer n=25
    $ typeset -Z15 n              # Left-justified, zero-padded integer.
    $ print "$n"
    000000000000025

8   $ typeset -lL1 answer=Yes     # Left justify one lowercase letter.
    $ print $answer
    y
```

EXPLANATION

1   The -u option to the typeset command converts all characters in a variable to uppercase.

2   The -l option to the typeset command converts all characters in a variable to lowercase.

3   The -L option to the typeset command converts the variable name to a left-justified, four-character string, john.

4   The -R option to the typeset command converts the variable name to a right-justified, two-character string, hn.

5   The variable name is set to John Doe. The -Z option to the typeset command will convert the string to a null-padded, 15-space string. The variable is quoted to preserve whitespace.

6   The variable name is converted to a left-justified, 15-space, null-padded string.

7   The variable n is an integer (see typeset -i, Table 11.14) assigned the value 25. The typeset command will convert the integer n to a zero-filled, 15-space, left-justified number.

8   The variable answer is assigned the value Yes and converted to a lowercase, left-justified, one-character string. (This can be very useful when handling user input in a script.)

Table 11.14 Other Uses of the typeset Command

Command	What It Does
typeset	Displays all variables
typeset -i num	Will only accept integer values for num
typeset -x	Displays exported variables
typeset a b c	If defined in a function, creates a, b, and c to be local variables
typeset -r x=foo	Sets x to foo and then makes it read-only

11.9.10 Positional Parameters

Normally, the special built-in variables, often called *positional parameters*, are used in shell scripts when passing arguments from the command line, or used in functions to hold the value of arguments passed to the function. The variables are called positional parameters because they are referenced by numbers 1, 2, 3, and so on, representing their respective positions in the parameter list. See Table 11.15.

The name of the shell script is stored in the $0 variable. The positional parameters can be set and reset with the set command.

Table 11.15 Positional Parameters

Expression	Function
$0	References the name of the current shell script
$1–$9	Positional parameters 1-9
${10}	Positional parameter 10
$#	Evaluates to the number of positional parameters
$*	Evaluates to all the positional parameters
$@	Same as $*, except when double quoted
"$*"	Evaluates to "$1 $2 $3", and so on
"$@"	Evaluates to "$1" "$2" "$3", and so on

EXAMPLE 11.52

```
1   $ set tim bill ann fred
    $ print $*          # Prints all the positional parameters.
    tim bill ann fred
```

EXAMPLE   11.52 (CONTINUED)

```
2   $ print $1          # Prints the first position.
    tim

3   $ print $2 $3        # Prints the second and third position.
    bill ann

4   $ print $#           # Prints the total number of positional parameters.
    4

5   $ set a b c d e f g h i j k l m
    $ print $10          # Prints the first positional parameter followed by a 0.
    a0

    $ print ${10} ${11}  # Prints the 10th and 11th positions.
    j k

6   $ print $#
    13

7   $ print $*
    a b c d e f g h i j k l m

8   $ set file1 file2 file3
    $ print \$$#
    $3

9   $ eval print \$$#
    file3
```

EXPLANATION

1   The set command assigns values to positional parameters. The $* special variable contains all of the parameters set.

2   The value of the first positional parameter, tim, is displayed.

3   The value of the second and third parameters, bill and ann, are displayed.

4   The $# special variable contains the number of positional parameters currently set.

5   The set command resets all of the positional parameters. The original parameter list is cleared. To print any positional parameters beyond 9, the curly braces are used to keep the two digits together. Otherwise, the value of the first positional parameter is printed, followed by the number appended to it.

6   The number of positional parameters is now 13.

7   The values of all the positional parameters are printed.

8   The dollar sign is escaped; $# is the number of arguments. The print command displays $3, a literal dollar sign followed by the number of positional parameters.

9   The eval command parses the command line a second time before executing the command. The first time parsed by the shell, the print would display $3; the second time, after eval, the print displays the value of $3, file3.

11.9.11   Other Special Variables

The Korn shell has some special built-in variables, as shown in Table 11.16.

Table 11.16   Special Variables

Variable	Meaning
$$	PID of the shell
$-	ksh options currently set
$?	Exit value of last executed command
$!	PID of last job put in background

EXAMPLE   11.53

```
1   $ print The pid of this shell is $$
    The pid of this shell is 4725
2   $ print The options for this korn shell are $-
    The options for this korn shell are ismh
3   $ grep dodo /etc/passwd
    $ print $?
    1
4   $ sleep 25&
    [1]    400
    $ print $!
    400
```

EXPLANATION

1   The $$ variable holds the value of the PID for this process.

2   The $- variable lists all options for this interactive Korn shell.

3   The grep command searches for the string dodo in the /etc/passwd file. The ? variable holds the exit status of the last command executed. Because the value returned from grep is 1, grep is assumed to have failed in its search. An exit status of 0 indicates a successful exit.

4   The & appended to the sleep command causes the command to be executed in the background. The $! variable holds the PID of the last command placed in the background.

11.10 Quoting

Quotes are used to protect special metacharacters from interpretation. They can cause major debugging hassles in all shell scripts. Single quotes must be matched. They protect special metacharacters from being interpreted by the shell. Double quotes also must be matched. They protect most characters from interpretation by the shell, but allow variable and command substitution characters to be processed. Single quotes will protect double quotes, and double quotes will protect single quotes. The Korn shell, unlike the Bourne shell, will inform you if you have mismatched quotes by sending an error message to standard error with the line where it detects that the quotes were mismatched.

11.10.1   The Backslash

The backslash is used to protect (or escape) a single character from interpretation.

EXAMPLE 11.54

```
1   $ print Where are you going\?
    Where are you going?
2   $ print Start on this line and \
    > go to the next line.
    Start on this line and go to the next line.
```

EXPLANATION

1   The special metacharacter ? is escaped with the backslash. It will not be interpreted for filename expansion by the shell.

2   The newline is escaped. The next line will become part of the first line. The > is the Korn shell's secondary prompt.

11.10.2   Single Quotes

Single quotes must be matched. They protect all metacharacters from interpretation. To print a single quote, it must be enclosed in double quotes or escaped with a backslash.

EXAMPLE 11.55

```
1   $ print 'hi there
    > how are you?
    > When will this end?
    > When the quote is matched
    > oh'
    hi there
    how are you?
    When will this end?
    When the quote is matched
    oh
```

EXAMPLE 11.55 (CONTINUED)

```
2   $ print 'Do you need $5.00?'
    Do you need $5.00?
```

```
3   $ print 'Mother yelled, "Time to eat!"'
    Mother yelled, "Time to eat!"
```

EXPLANATION

1   The single quote is not matched on the line. The Korn shell produces a secondary prompt. It is waiting for the quote to be matched.

2   The single quotes protect all metacharacters from interpretation. In this example, the $ and the ? are protected from the shell and will be treated as literals.

3   The single quotes protect the double quotes in this string. The double quotes here are conversational quotes.

11.10.3   Double Quotes

Double quotes must be matched. They allow variable and command substitution, and protect any other special metacharacters from being interpreted by the shell.

EXAMPLE 11.56

```
1   $ name=Jody
2   $ print "Hi $name, I'm glad to meet you!"
    Hi Jody, I'm glad to meet you!
```

```
3   $ print "Hey $name, the time is `date`"
    Hey Jody, the time is Fri Dec 18 14:04:11 PST 2004
```

EXPLANATION

1   The variable name is assigned the string Jody.

2   The double quotes surrounding the string will protect all special metacharacters from interpretation, with the exception of $ in $name. Variable substitution is performed within double quotes.

3   Variable substitution and command substitution are both performed when enclosed within double quotes. The variable name is expanded and the command in backquotes, date, is executed.

11.11 Command Substitution

Command substitution is used when assigning the output of a command to a variable, or when substituting the output of a command into a string. The Bourne and C shells use backquotes to perform command substitution. The Korn shell does allow the back-quote format (calling it "obsolescent"),[4] but placing the command in parentheses is the preferred method because it has simpler quoting rules and makes nesting commands easier.

FORMAT

```
`Unix/Linux command`      # Old method with backquotes
$(Unix/Linux command)     # New method
```

EXAMPLE 11.57

```
(Old Way)
1   $ print "The hour is `date +%H`"
    The hour is 09
2   $ name=`nawk -F: '{print $1}' database`
    $ print $name
    Ebenezer Scrooge
3   $ ls `ls /etc`
    shutdown
4   $ set `date`
5   $ print $*
    Sat Oct 13 09:35:21 PDT 2004
6   $ print $2 $6
    Oct 2004
```

EXPLANATION

1   The output of the date command is substituted into the string.

2   The output of the nawk command is assigned to the variable name, and displayed.

3   The output of the ls command, enclosed in backquotes, is a list of files from the /etc directory. The filenames will be arguments to the first ls command. All files with the same name in /etc as are in the current directory are listed.

4   The set command assigns the output of the date command to positional parameters. Whitespace separates the list of words into its respective parameters.

5   The $* variable holds all of the parameters. The output of the date command was stored in the $* variable. Each parameter is separated by whitespace.

6   The second and sixth parameters are printed.

---

4. Using backquotes for command substitution is an old form still used in the Bourne and C shells. Although still legal syntax, the Korn shell introduces a new method shown in this section.

The ksh alternate for using backquotes in command substitution is presented in Example 11.58.

EXAMPLE 11.58

```
(The New ksh Way)
1    $ d=$(date)
     $ print $d
     Sat Oct 20 09:35:21 PDT 2004
2    $ line = $(< filex)
3    $ print The time is $(date +%H)
     The time is 09
4    $ machine=$(uname -n)
     $ print $machine
     jody
5    $ dirname="$(basename $(pwd))"          # Nesting commands
     $ print $dirname
     bin
```

EXPLANATION

1   The date command is enclosed within parentheses. The output of the command is returned to the expression, assigned to the variable d, and displayed.

2   The input from the file is assigned to the variable line. The < filex notation has the same effect as `cat filex`. Command substitution is performed within the parentheses when the parentheses are preceded with a dollar sign.

3   The UNIX date command and its hour argument, +%H, are enclosed within parentheses. Command substitution is performed, and the results are placed within the print string.

4   Command substitution has been performed. The output of the UNIX uname command is assigned to the variable machine.

5   To set the variable dirname to the name (only) of the present working directory, command substitution is nested. The pwd command is executed first, passing the full pathname of the present working directory as an argument to the UNIX command basename. The basename command strips off all but the last element of a pathname. Nesting commands within backquotes is not allowed.

11.12 Functions

This section introduces functions so that you can use them interactively or store them in your initialization files. Later, when discussing scripts, functions will be covered in more depth. Functions can be used when an alias is not enough, that is, for passing arguments. Functions are often defined in the user's initialization file, .profile. They are like mini-scripts, but unlike scripts, functions run in the current environment; that is, the shell does not fork a child process to execute a function. All variables are shared with the shell that invoked the function. Often functions are used to improve the modularity of a script. Once defined, they can be used repeatedly and even stored in another directory.

Functions must be defined before they are invoked; there are two formats used to define them. One format came from the Bourne shell and the other is new with the Korn shell. Functions can be exported from one invocation of the shell to the next. The `typeset` function and `unset` command can be used to list and unset functions. See Table 11.17.

Table 11.17 Commands to List and Set Functions

Command	Function
`typeset -f`	Lists functions and their definitions; `functions` is an alias for `typeset -f`
`typeset +f`	Lists only function names
`unset -f name`	Unsets a function

11.12.1   Defining Functions

There are two acceptable formats for defining functions: the Bourne shell format (still allowed for upward compatibility) and the new Korn shell format. A function must be defined before it can be used.[5]

FORMAT

```
(Bourne Shell)
functionname() { commands ; commands; }

(Korn Shell)
function functionname { commands; commands; }
```

EXAMPLE 11.59

```
1   $ function fun { pwd; ls; date; }

2   $ fun
    /home/jody/ellie/prac
    abc      abc123   file1.bak  none      nothing  tmp
    abc1     abc2     file2      nonsense  nowhere  touch
    abc122   file1    file2.bak  noone     one
    Mon Feb 9 11:15:48 PST 2004
```

---

5. The POSIX standard defines functions with the Bourne shell syntax, but variables and traps cannot be local in scope, as with the new Korn shell definition.

EXAMPLE 11.59 (CONTINUED)

```
3    $ function greet { print "Hi $1 and $2"; }

4    $ greet tom joe          # Here $1 is tom and $2 is joe
     Hi tom and joe

5    $ set jane nina lizzy
6    $ print $*
     jane nina lizzy

7    $ greet tom joe
     Hi tom and joe

8    $ print $1 $2
     jane nina
```

EXPLANATION

1   The function fun is named and defined. The name is followed by a list of commands enclosed in curly braces. Each command is separated by a semicolon. There must be a space after the first curly brace or you will get a syntax error such as ksh: syntax error: `}' unexpected. A function must be defined before it can be used.

2   The function behaves like a script or an alias when invoked. Each of the commands in the function definition is executed in turn.

3   There are two positional parameters used in the function greet. When arguments are given to the function, the positional parameters are assigned those values.

4   The arguments to the function tom and joe are assigned to $1 and $2, respectively. The positional parameters in a function are private to the function and will not interfere with any used outside the function.

5   The positional parameters are set at the command line. These variables have nothing to do with the ones set in the function.

6   $* displays the values of the currently set positional parameters.

7   The function greet is called. The values assigned to the positional parameters $1 and $2 are tom and joe, respectively.

8   The positional variables assigned at the command line are unaffected by those set in the function.

11.12.2 Functions and Aliases

When processing the command line, the shell looks for aliases before special built-in commands and for special built-ins before functions. If a function has the same name as a built-in, the built-in will take priority over the function. An alias for a special built-in can be defined, and then the function name can be given the name of the alias to override the order of processing.

EXAMPLE 11.60

```
(The ENV File)
1   alias cd=_cd
2   function _cd {
3   \cd $1
4   print $(basename $PWD)
5   }

(The Command Line)
$ cd /
/
$ cd $HOME/bin
bin
$ cd ..
ellie
```

EXPLANATION

1   The alias for cd is assigned _cd.

2   The function _cd is defined. The opening curly brace marks the start of the function definition.

3   If an alias is preceded by a backslash, alias substitution is not performed. The backslash precedes cd to execute the built-in cd command, not the alias. Without the backslash, the function would be recursive and the shell would display an error message: cd_: recursion too deep. $1 is the argument (name of a directory) passed to cd.

4   The name of the directory (not the full pathname) is printed.

5   The closing curly brace marks the end of the function definition.

11.12.3   Listing Functions

To list functions and their definitions, use the typeset command.

EXAMPLE 11.61

```
(The Command Line)
1   $ typeset -f
    function fun
    {
    pwd; ls; date; }
    function greet
    {
    print "hi $1 and $2"; }
2   $ typeset +f
    fun
    greet
```

1   The typeset command, with the –f option, lists the function and its definition.

2   The typeset command, with the +f option, lists only the names of defined functions.

11.12.4   Unsetting Functions

When a function is unset, it will be removed from the shell's memory.

EXAMPLE   11.62

```
(The Command Line)
1    $ typeset -f
     function fun
     {
         pwd; ls; date; }
     function greet
     {
     print "hi $1 and $2"; }

2    $ unset -f fun
3    $ typeset -f
     function greet
     {
     print "hi $1 and $2"; }
```

EXPLANATION

1   The typeset –f command displays the function and its definition. Two functions, fun and greet, are displayed.

2   The built-in command unset, with the –f option, undefines the fun function, removing it from the shell's memory.

3   The fun function is no longer shown as one of the functions defined when the typeset –f command is executed.

11.13 Standard I/O and Redirection

The Korn shell opens three files (called *streams*) whenever a program is started: stdin, stdout, and stderr. Standard input normally comes from the keyboard and is associated with file descriptor 0. Standard output normally goes to the screen, file descriptor 1. Standard error normally goes to the screen, file descriptor 2. Standard input, output, and error can be redirected to or from a file. See Table 11.18 for a list of redirection operators.

Table 11.18   Redirection

Operator	Function
< file	Redirect input from file
> file	Redirect output to file
>> file	Redirect and append output to file
2> file	Redirect errors to file
2>> file	Redirect and append errors to file
1>&2	Redirect output to where error is going
2>&1	Redirect error to where output is going

EXAMPLE 11.63

```
(The Command Line)
1    $ tr '[A-Z]' '[a-z]' < myfile    # Redirect input
2    $ ls > lsfile              # Redirect output
     $ cat lsfile
     dir1
     dir2
     file1
     file2
     file3
3    $ date >> lsfile           # Redirect and append output
     $ cat lsfile
     dir1
     dir2
     file1
     file2
     file3
     Mon Sept 20 12:57:22 PDT 2004
4    $ cc prog.c 2> errfile              # Redirect error
5    $ find . -name \*.c -print > founditfile 2> /dev/null
6    $ find . -name \*.c -print > foundit 2>&1
7    $ print "File needs an argument" 1>&2
8    $ function usage { print "Usage: $0 [-y] [-g] filename" 1>&2 ; exit 1; }
```

EXPLANATION

1   The standard input is redirected from the file myfile to the UNIX tr command. All uppercase letters are converted to lowercase letters.

2   The ls command redirects its output to the file lsfile.

3   The output of the date command is redirected and appended to lsfile.

EXPLANATION (CONTINUED)

4   The file prog.c is compiled. If the compile fails, standard error is redirected to errfile.

5   The find command starts searching in the current working directory for filenames ending in .c and prints the files to a file named founditfile. Errors from the find command are sent to /dev/null.

6   The find command starts searching in the current working directory for filenames ending in .c and prints the files to a filenamed foundit. The standard error (file descriptor 2) is being sent to the same place that the standard output (file descriptor 1) is being sent, to the file called foundit.

7   The print command sends its message to standard error. Standard output is merged with standard error; that is, standard output is being redirected to the place where standard error goes, the terminal. This makes it possible to separate error messages from "good" output.

8   The function usage is defined. This function, when called, will print a usage message, send the output to standard error, and exit. This type of function is often used in scripts.

11.13.1   The exec Command and Redirection

The exec command can be used to replace the current program with the one being execed. Another use for the exec command is to change standard output or input without creating a subshell. If a file is opened with exec, subsequent read commands will move the file pointer down the file a line at a time until end of file. The file must be closed to start reading from the beginning again. However, if using UNIX utilities such as cat and sort, the operating system closes the file after each command has completed. See Table 11.19 for exec functionality.

Table 11.19   exec Commands

Command	Function
exec ls	ls will execute in place of the shell. When ls is finished, the shell in which it was started does not return.
exec < filea	Open filea for reading standard input.
exec > filex	Open filex for writing standard output.
exec 2> errors	Open errors for writing standard error.
exec 2>> errors	Open errors for writing and appending standard error.
exec 2> /dev/console	Sends all error messages to the console.
exec 3< datfile	Open datfile as file descriptor 3 for reading input.

Table 11.19   exec Commands (continued)

Command	Function
sort <&3	datfile is sorted.
exec 4>newfile	Open newfile as file descriptor 4 for writing.
ls >&4	Output of ls is redirected to newfile.
exec 5<&4	Make fd 5 a copy of fd 4. Both descriptors refer to newfile.
exec 3<&–	Close file descriptor 3, datfile.

11.13.2   Redirection and the Child Shell

When the output of a command is redirected from the screen to a file, the Korn shell creates (forks) a child shell to rearrange the file descriptors, as shown in Figure 11.2.

11.14 Pipes

A pipe takes the output from the command on the left-hand side of the pipe symbol and sends it to the input of a command on the right-hand side of the pipe symbol. A pipeline can consist of more than one pipe.

EXAMPLE   11.64

```
1    $ who > tmp
2    $ wc -l tmp
     4 tmp
3    $ rm tmp
4    $ who | wc -l          # Using the pipe
```

EXPLANATION

The purpose of lines 1 through 3 is to count the number of people logged on (who), save the output of the command in a file (tmp), use the wc -l to count the number of lines in the tmp file (wc -l), and then remove the tmp file; that is, find the number of people logged on. The pipe performs the same task in one command.

1   The output of the who command is redirected to the tmp file.

2   The wc -l command displays the number of lines in tmp.

3   The tmp file is removed.

4   With the pipe facility, you can perform steps 1, 2, and 3 in one step. The output of the who command is sent to an anonymous kernel buffer (instead of to a temporary file that requires disk space); the wc -l command reads from the buffer and sends its output to the screen.

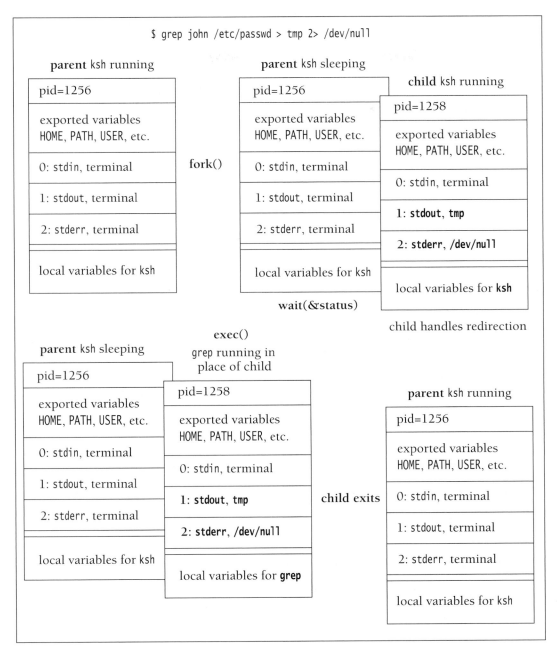

Figure 11.2   Redirection of standard output and errors.

EXAMPLE 11.65

```
1    $ ls | more
     < lists (ls) all files one page at a time (more) >
2    $ du ~ | sort -n | sed -n '$p'
     72388   /home/jody/ellie
3    $ cat | lp  or  cat | lpr
```

EXPLANATION

1   The ls output is piped to the more command, which accepts input. Output is displayed one page at a time.
2   The output of the du command (disk usage) is sorted numerically and piped to the sed command (stream editor), which displays only the last line ($p).
3   The cat command reads from standard input; its output is piped to the line printer (lp in SVR4 and lpr in BSD).

11.14.1   The here document and Redirecting Input

A here document captures in-line input for programs such as mail, sort, and cat. Input is placed between two words or symbols. The first word is preceded by a UNIX command and the << symbol. The next lines consist of the input to be received by the command. The last line consists of a second word that exactly matches the first word. This word is called the final terminator and marks the end of input. It is used in the same way Ctrl-D is used to terminate input. There can be no spaces surrounding the final terminator. If the first word is preceded by the <<-, leading tabs (and only tabs) may precede the final terminator. Normally, a here document is used in shell scripts, rather than interactively. A good use for a here document is to create a menu in a script.

FORMAT

```
UNIX command << TERMINATOR
     lines of input
     input
TERMINATOR
```

EXAMPLE 11.66

```
(The Command Line)
1    $ cat << FINISH
2    > Hello there $LOGNAME
3    > The time is $(date)
     > I can't wait to see you!!!
4    > FINISH
```

EXAMPLE 11.66 (CONTINUED)

5 *Hello there ellie*
The time is Sun May 30 19:42:16 PDT 2004
I can't wait to see you!!
6 *$*

EXPLANATION

1 The UNIX/Linux cat program will accept input until the word FINISH appears on a line by itself. FINISH is called a user-defined terminator.

2 Variable substitution is performed within the here document. The > is the Korn shell's secondary prompt.

3 Command substitution is performed within the here document.

4 The user-defined terminator, FINISH, marks the end of input for the cat program. It cannot have any spaces before or after it and is on a line by itself.

5 The output from the cat program is displayed.

6 The shell prompt reappears.

EXAMPLE 11.67

```
(From the .profile File)
1   print "Select a terminal type"
2   cat << EOF
        [1] sun
        [2] ansi
        [3] wyse50
3   EOF
4   read TERM
    ...
```

EXPLANATION

1 The user is asked to select a terminal type.

2 The menu will appear on the screen. This is a here document, meaning from here until the matching EOF on line 3 is reached, input will be given to the cat command. You could use a series of echo commands to get the same results, but visually, the here document is nicer.

3 EOF is a user-defined terminator, marking the end of the here document. It must be at the left margin with no spaces surrounding it.

4 The user input will be read in from the keyboard and assigned to TERM.

EXAMPLE 11.68

(The Command Line)
```
1   $ cat <<- DONE
    >Hello there
    >What's up?
    >Bye now The time is $(date).

2   >       DONE

3   Hello there
    What's up?
    Bye now The time is Sun May 30 19:48:23 PDT 2004.
```

EXPLANATION

1   The cat program accepts input until DONE appears on a line by itself. The <<– operator allows the final terminator to be preceded by one or more tabs. (The > is the shell's secondary prompt.)

2   The final matching DONE terminator is preceded by a tab. From the first DONE on line 1 to the last DONE on this line, the text in between is sent as input to the cat command.

3   The output of the cat program is displayed on the screen.

11.15 Timing Commands

11.15.1   The time Command

The time command is a ksh built-in command. The time command prints the following to standard error: elapsed time, the user time, and the system time used to execute a command.

EXAMPLE 11.69

```
1   $ time sleep 3
    real  0m3.15s    took 3.15 seconds to run
    user  0m0.01s    sleep used its own code for .01 seconds
    sys   0m0.08s    and kernel code for .08 seconds

2   $ time ps -ef | wc -l    # time is measured for all commands in the pipeline
    38
    real  0m1.03s
    user  0m0.01s
    sys   0m0.10s
```

1 The time command will display the total amount of time elapsed to run the command, the time the user part of the program took to run, and the time the kernel spent running the program. The sleep command took 3.15 seconds to run.

2 The time is measured for the ps command and wc command.

11.15.2 The TMOUT Variable

The TMOUT variable is an integer type. It can be set to force users to type commands within a certain period of time. TMOUT, by default, is set to zero, allowing the user an infinite amount of time to type commands after the PS1 prompt. If TMOUT is set to a value greater than zero, the shell will terminate after the time has expired. Sixty additional seconds will be allotted as the grace period before actually exiting the shell.

```
$ TMOUT=600
time out in 60 seconds due to inactivity
ksh: timed out waiting for input
```

The TMOUT variable is set to 600 seconds. If the user does nothing for 600 seconds, a message will appear on the screen and then an additional 60 seconds grace period will be allotted before the shell exits. If you do this at the prompt, your current shell exits.

chapter
12

Programming the Korn Shell

12.1 Introduction

When commands are executed from within a file, instead of from the command line, the file is called a shell script and the shell is running noninteractively. Writing Korn shell scripts requires a few steps, as outlined in the following section.

12.1.1   The Steps in Creating a Shell Script

A shell script is normally written in an editor and consists of commands interspersed with comments. Comments are preceded by a pound sign (#).

The First Line.   At the top left corner, the line preceded by #! (often called *shbang*) indicates the program that will be executing the lines in the script. In Korn shell scripts, this appears as

```
#!/bin/ksh
```

The #!, also called the *magic number*, is used by the kernel to identify the program that should be interpreting the lines in the script. This line must be the top line of your script. The Korn shell also provides a number of invocation options that control how the shell behaves. These options are listed at the end of this chapter in "Korn Shell Invocation Arguments" on page 740.

Comments.   Comments are lines preceded by a pound sign. They are used to document your script. It is sometimes difficult to understand what the script is supposed to do if it is not commented. Although comments are important, they are often too sparse or not even used at all. Try to get used to commenting what you are doing, not only for someone else, but also for yourself.

Executable Statements and Korn Shell Constructs.   A Korn shell program consists of a combination of UNIX/Linux commands, Korn shell commands, programming constructs, and comments.

Naming and Storing Scripts.   When naming scripts, it is a good idea to give the script a meaningful name that does not conflict with other UNIX/Linux commands or aliases. For example, you may want to call the script test because it is merely performing some simple test procedure, but test is a built-in command and you may find you are executing the wrong test. Additionally, if you name the file foo, goo, boobar, and so forth, in a few days or even hours you may not have any idea what is in that script!

After you have tested your script and found it bug-free, make a directory where you can store the scripts, then set the path so that your scripts can be executed from anywhere in the directory hierarchy.

EXAMPLE 12.1

```
1    $ mkdir ~/bin
2    $ mv myscript ~/bin

(In .profile)
3    export PATH=${PATH}:~/bin
4    $ . .profile
```

EXPLANATION

1   A common place to store scripts is in a directory under your home directory called bin.

2   The script, called myscript, is moved into the new bin directory.

3   The new directory is added to the PATH variable in the .profile initialization file.

4   The dot command causes the .profile file to be executed in the current environment so that you do not have to log out and then back in to enable the new setting.

Making a Script Executable.   When you create a file, it is not automatically given execute permission (regardless of how umask is set). You need this permission to run your script. Use the chmod command to turn on execute permission.

EXAMPLE 12.2

```
1    $ chmod +x myscript
2    $ ls -lF myscript
     -rwxr--xr--x  1 ellie       0 Jul 12 13:00 myscript*
```

EXPLANATION

1   The chmod command is used to turn on execute permission for the user, group, and others.

2   The output of the ls command indicates that all users have execute permission on the myscript file. The asterisk at the end of the filename also indicates that this is an executable program.

Using a Script As an Argument to ksh.   If you don't make a script executable, you can execute it by passing it as an argument to the ksh command.

EXAMPLE 12.3

```
(The Command Line)
$ ksh myscript
```

EXPLANATION

If the ksh program is given a script name as its argument, it will execute the script and the #! line is not necessary or even used.

A Scripting Session.   In Example 12.4, the user will create a script in the editor. After saving the file, the execute permissions are turned on, and the script is executed. If there are errors in the program, the Korn shell will respond immediately.

EXAMPLE 12.4

```
(The Script)
1   #!/bin/ksh
2   # This is the first Korn shell program of the day.
    # Scriptname: greetings
    # Written by: Karen Korny
3   print "Hello $LOGNAME, it's nice talking to you."
4   print "Your present working directory is $(pwd)."
    print "You are working on a machine called $(uname -n)."
    print "Here is a list of your files."
5   ls      # List files in the present working directory
    print "Bye for now $LOGNAME. The time is $(date +%T)!"

(The Command Line)
    $ chmod +x greetings
    $ greetings
3   Hello karen, it's nice talking to you.
4   Your present working directory is /home/lion/karen/junk
    You are working on a machine called lion.
    Here is a list of your files.
5   Afile       cplus  letter   prac
    Answerbook cprog  library  prac1
    bourne      joke   notes    perl5
    Bye for now karen. The time is 18:05:07!
```

EXPLANATION

1   The first line of the script, #!/bin/ksh, lets the kernel know what interpreter will execute the lines in this program.

2   The comments are nonexecutable lines preceded by a #. They can be on a line by themselves or inserted in a line after a command.

EXPLANATION (CONTINUED)

3   The print command displays the line on the screen, after variable substitution is performed by the shell.

4   The print command displays the line on the screen, after command substitution is performed by the shell.

5   The ls command is executed. The comment, any text on the line after the pound sign (#), will be ignored by the shell.

12.2 Reading User Input

The read command is used to take input from the terminal or from a file until the newline is reached. The Korn shell provides some additional options for the read command. See Table 12.1 for different read formats. See Table 12.2 for read options.

Table 12.1   read Formats

Format	Meaning
read answer	Reads a line from standard input and assigns it to the variable answer.
read first last	Reads a line from standard input to the first whitespace or newline, putting the first word typed into the variable first and the rest of the line into the variable last.
read response?"Do you feel okay?"	Displays the string Do you feel okay? to standard error and waits for the user to type a reply, then puts the reply in the variable response. This form of read requires and accepts only one variable. Whatever the user types, until the newline, will be stored in response.
read -u3 line	Reads a line from file descriptor 3 into variable line.
read	Reads input into a built-in variable, REPLY.

Table 12.2   read Options

Options	Meaning
-p	Reads a line of input from a coprocess.
-r	Treats newline character, the \n, as a literal.
-s	Copies a line into the history file.
-un	Reads from file descriptor n; the default is fd 0, or standard input.

Table 12.2   read Options (continued)

Options	Meaning
On Versions of ksh Newer Than 1988	
-A	Stores the fields as an array, index starting at zero.
-d char	Used as an alternate delimiter for terminating input; newline is the default.
-t sec	Puts a limit of seconds on the user's response time.

EXAMPLE 12.5

```
(The Script)
    #!/bin/ksh
    # Scriptname: nosy
    print -n "Are you happy? "
1   read answer
    print "$answer is the right response."
    print -n "What is your full name? "
2   read first middle last
    print "Hello $first"
    print -n "Where do you work? "
3   read
4   print I guess $REPLY keeps you busy!
5   read place?"Where do you live? "
    # New ksh read and print combined
    print Welcome to $place, $first $last


(The Output)
    $ nosy
    Are you happy? Yes
1   Yes is the right response.
2   What is your full name? Jon Jake Jones
    Hello Jon
3   Where do you work? Tandem
4   I guess Tandem keeps you busy!
5   Where do you live? Timbuktu
    Welcome to Timbuktu, Jon Jones
```

EXPLANATION

1   The read command accepts a line of user input and assigns the input to the variable answer.

2   The read command accepts input from the user and assigns the first word of input to the variable first, assigns the second word of input to the variable middle, and all the rest of the words to the end of the line to the variable last.

EXPLANATION (CONTINUED)

3   The read command, without an argument, accepts a line of input from the user and assigns the input to the built-in variable REPLY.

4   After the shell has performed variable substitution, the print function prints the string, showing the value of the built-in REPLY variable.

5   If the variable following the read command is appended with a question mark (?), the string after the question mark is displayed as a prompt. The user input is stored in the variable place.

12.2.1   read and File Descriptors

When the system boots up, three files called *streams* (stdin, stdout, and stderr) are opened and assigned to an array of file descriptors. The first three file descriptors, 0, 1, and 2, are for standard input, standard output, and standard error, respectively. The next file descriptor available is file descriptor 3. The -u option allows the read command to read directly from the file descriptor.

EXAMPLE 12.6

```
(The Command Line)
1   $ cat filex
    Captain Kidd
    Scarlett O'Hara
2   $ exec 3< filex        # filex is assigned to file descriptor 3 for reading
3   $ read -u3 name1       # read from filex and store input in variable, name1
4   $ print $name1
    Captain Kidd
5   $ read -u3 name2
    $ print $name2
    Scarlett O'Hara
6   $ exec 3<&-            # close file descriptor 3
7   $ read -u3 line
    ksh: read: bad file unit number
```

EXPLANATION

1   The contents of filex are displayed.

2   The exec command is used to open file descriptor 3 for reading from filex.

3   The read command reads one line directly from unit 3 (file descriptor 3, filex) and assigns that line to the variable name1.

4   The line stored in name1 is printed.

5   The file filex is still open, and this read command reads the next line from the file and stores that line in the variable name2.

6   File descriptor 3 (unit 3) is closed. filex is no longer open.

7   Because file descriptor 3 (filex) has been closed, the read command fails when attempting to read input from that descriptor into variable line.

12.2.2   Reading Through Files

Example 12.7 uses the read command with a while loop. The loop will iterate through the file one line at a time. When end of file is reached, the loop terminates. The files are opened with descriptors (units) for reading.

EXAMPLE 12.7

```
(The Files)
1   $ cat names
    Merry Melody
    Nancy Drew
    Rex Allen
    $ cat addresses
    150 Piano Place
    5 Mystery Lane
    130 Cowboy Terrace
```

```
(The Script)
    #!/bin/ksh
    # Scriptname: readit
2   while read -u3 line1 && read -u4 line2
    do
3        print "$line1:$line2"
4   done 3<$1 4<$2
```

```
(The Command Line)
5   $ readit names addresses
    Merry Melody:150 Piano Place
    Nancy Drew:5 Mystery Lane
    Rex Allen:130 Cowboy Terrace
```

EXPLANATION

1   The contents of two files, names and addresses, are displayed.

2   The while loop is started. The read command reads a line of input from file descriptor 3 (unit 3) and, if successful, reads another line from file descriptor 4. The file descriptors (units) are assigned filenames on line 4. The filenames are being passed as arguments, or positional parameters 1 and 2.

3   The value of the first variable, a colon, and the value of the second variable are displayed.

4   The input assigned to file descriptor 3 is the first command-line argument, names. The input assigned to file descriptor 4 is the second command-line argument, addresses.

5   The script is executed with command-line arguments (the names of two files).

12.3 Arithmetic

The Korn shell supports both integer and floating-point arithmetic, but floating-point arithmetic is available only on versions of the Korn shell newer than 1988. The typeset command is used for assigning types. See Table 12.3 for the typeset command.

Table 12.3   typeset and Arithmetic

Command	Alias	Meaning
typeset –i variable	integer variable	variable is only allowed integer assignment
typeset –i#		# is the base number for the integer
On Versions of ksh Newer Than 1988		
typeset –F variable		Floating-point number assignment
typeset –E variable	float variable	Floating-point number assignment

12.3.1   The Integer Type

Variables can be declared as integers with the typeset –i command or its alias, integer. If you attempt to assign any string value, ksh returns an error. If you assign a floating-point number, the decimal point and the fractional value will be truncated. The integer alias can be used instead of typeset –i. Numbers can also be represented in different bases such as *binary*, *octal*, and *hex*.

EXAMPLE 12.8

```
1   $ typeset -i num or integer num      # integer is an alias for typeset -i
2   $ num=hello
    /bin/ksh: hello: bad number
3   $ num=5 + 5
    /bin/ksh: +: not found
4   $ num=5+5
    $ echo $num
    10
5   $ num=4*6
    $ echo $num
    24
6   $ num="4 * 6"
    $ echo $num
    24
7   $ num=6.789
    $ echo $num
    6
```

EXPLANATION

1 The typeset command with the –i option creates an integer variable, num.

2 Trying to assign the string hello to the integer variable num causes an error.

3 The whitespace must be quoted or removed unless the (( )) operators are used (see "Arithmetic Operators and the let Command" on page 662).

4 The whitespace is removed and arithmetic is performed.

5 Multiplication is performed and the result assigned to num.

6 The whitespace is quoted so that the multiplication can be performed and to keep the shell from expanding the wildcard (*).

7 Since the variable is set to integer, the fractional part of the number is truncated.

12.3.2 Using Different Bases

Numbers can be represented in decimal (base 10), octal (base 8), and so forth, by using the typeset command and with the –i option and the base number.[1]

EXAMPLE 12.9

```
1   $ num=15
2   $ typeset -i2 num     # binary
    $ print $num
    2#1111
3   $ typeset -i8 num     # octal
    $ print $num
    8#17
4   $ typeset -i16 num    # hex
    $ print $num
    16#f
5   $ read number
    2#1101
    $ print $number
    2#1101
6   $ typeset -i number
    $ print $number
    2#1101
7   $ typeset -i10 number   # decimal
    $ print $number
    13
8   $ typeset -i8 number    # octal
    $ print $number
    8#15
```

---

1. Bases greater than 36 are available on versions of the Korn shell that are newer than 1988.

EXPLANATION

1   The variable num is assigned the value 15.

2   The typeset command converts the number to a binary format. The display is the base of the number (2), followed by a pound sign (#), and the value of the number in binary.

3   The typeset command converts the number to an octal format and displays the value of the number in base 8.

4   The typeset command converts the number to hexadecimal format and displays the value of the number in base 16.

5   The read command accepts input from the user. The input is entered in binary format, stored in the variable number, and displayed in binary format.

6   The typeset command converts number to an integer. It still displays in binary format.

7   The typeset command converts number to a decimal integer and displays it.

8   The typeset command converts number to octal and displays its value in base 8.

12.3.3   Listing Integers

The typeset command with only the –i argument will list all preset integers and their values, as shown in the following display.

```
$ typeset -i
ERRNO=2
LINENO=1
MAILCHECK=600
OPTIND=1
PPID=4881
RANDOM=25022
SECONDS=47366
TMOUT=0
n=5
number=#15
```

12.3.4   Arithmetic Operators and the let Command

The let command is a Korn shell built-in command that is used to perform integer arithmetic. (See Table 12.4.) This replaces the Bourne shell method of integer testing. The alternative and preferred way to use the let command is with the (( )) operator.

Table 12.4   let Operators[a]

Operator	Meaning
–	Unary minus
!	Logical NOT

Table 12.4 let Operators[a] (continued)

Operator	Meaning
~	Bitwise NOT
*	Multiply
/	Divide
%	Remainder
+	Add
–	Subtract
<<	Bitwise left shift
>>	Bitwise right shift
<= >= < > == !=	Comparison operators
&	Bitwise AND
^|	Exclusive OR
&&	Logical AND
||	Logical OR
!	Unary NOT
=	Assignment
*= /= %= += -= <<= >>= &= ^= |=	Shortcut assignments

a.   The ++ and -- operators are supported on versions of ksh that are newer than 1988

EXAMPLE   12.10

```
1   $ i=5
2   $ let i=i+1
    $ print $i
    6
3   $ let "i = i + 2"
    $ print $i
    8
4   $ let "i+=1"
    $ print $i
    9
```

EXPLANATION

1   The variable i is assigned the value 5.

2   The let command will add 1 to the value of i. The $ (dollar sign) is not required for variable substitution when performing arithmetic.

3   The quotes are needed if the arguments contain whitespace.

4   The shortcut operator += is used to add 1 to the value of i.

EXAMPLE 12.11

```
(The Command Line)
1   $ (( i = 9 ))
2   $ (( i = i * 6 ))
    $ print $i
    54
3   $ (( i > 0 && i <= 10 ))
4   $ print $?
    1
    $ j=100
5   $ (( i < j || i == 5 ))
6   $ print $?
    0
7   $ if (( i < j && i == 54 ))
    > then
    > print True
    >fi
    True
    $
```

EXPLANATION

1   The variable i is assigned the value 9. The (( )) operators are an alternate form of the let command. Because the expression is enclosed in double parentheses, spaces are allowed between the operators.

2   The variable i is assigned the product of i*6.

3   The numeric expressions are tested. If both expressions are true, 0 exit status is returned.

4   The special ? variable holds the exit status of the last command (the let command) executed. Because the value is 1, the command failed (evaluated as false).

5   The numeric expressions are tested. If one of the expressions is true, 0 exit status is returned.

6   The special ? variable holds the exit status of the last command (the let command) executed. Because the value is 0, the command succeeded (evaluated as true).

7   The if conditional command precedes the let command. The secondary prompt appears while waiting for the command to be completed. If the exit status is 0, the commands after the then statement are executed; otherwise, the primary prompt returns.

12.4 Positional Parameters and Command-Line Arguments

Command-line arguments can be referenced in scripts with positional parameters; for example, $1 is set to the first argument, $2 to the second argument, and $3 to the third argument. Positional parameters can be reset with the set command. See Table 12.5.

Table 12.5 Positional Parameters

Variable	Function
$0	References the name of the script
$#	Holds the value of the number of positional parameters
$*	Contains a list of all the positional parameters
$@	Means the same as $*, except when enclosed in double quotes
"$*"	Expands to a single argument, for example, "$1 $2 $3"
"$@"	Expands to separate arguments, for example, "$1" "$2" "$3"

12.4.1 The set Command and Positional Parameters

The set command sets the positional parameters. If the positional parameters have already been set, the set command will reset them, removing any values in the old list. To unset all of the positional parameters, use set --.

EXAMPLE 12.12

```
     (The Script)
     $ cat args
     #!/bin/ksh
     # Script to test command-line arguments
1    print The name of this script is $0.
2    print The arguments are $*.
3    print The first argument is $1.
4    print The second argument is $2.
5    print The number of arguments is $#.
6    oldparameters=$*
7    set Jake Nicky Scott
8    print All the positional parameters are $*.
9    print The number of positional parameters is $#.
10   print $oldparameters
```

EXAMPLE 12.12 (CONTINUED)

```
11  set --
12  print Good-bye for now, $1.
13  set $oldparameters
14  print $*
```

(The Output)
```
$ args a b c d
```
1   *The name of this script is* ***args.***
2   *The arguments are* ***a b c d.***
3   *The first argument is* ***a.***
4   *The second argument is* ***b.***
5   *The number of arguments is* ***4.***
8   *All the positional parameters are* ***Jake Nicky Scott.***
9   *The number of positional parameters is* ***3.***
10 *a b c d*
12 *Good-bye for now ,.*
14 *a b c d*
    $

EXPLANATION

1   The name of the script is stored in the $0 variable.

2   $* (and $@) both represent all of the positional parameters.

3   $1 represents the first positional parameter (command-line argument).

4   $2 represents the second positional parameter.

5   $# is the total number of positional parameters (command-line arguments).

6   The variable oldparameters is assigned all of the positional parameters ($*). Later on, if you want to get back your original parameters, you can do so by typing set $oldparameters.

7   Reset positional parameters with the set command. The set command completely clears all previously set parameters. Jake is assigned to $1, Nicky is assigned to $2, and Scott is assigned to $3.

8   The new positional parameters are printed.

9   The number of positional parameters is printed.

10 The original parameters were stored in the variable oldparameters. They are printed.

11 All parameters are unassigned.

12 $1 has no value. The parameters list was cleared with the set -- command.

13 A new parameter list is assigned by substituting the values in oldparameters to the parameter list with the set command.

14 All the positional parameters are printed.

EXAMPLE 12.13

```
(How $* and $@ Differ)
1   $ set 'apple pie' pears peaches
2   $ for i in $*
    > do
    > echo $i
    > done
    apple
    pie
    pears
    peaches

3   $ set 'apple pie' pears peaches
4   $ for i in "$*"
    > do
    > echo $i
    > done
    apple pie pears peaches

5   $ set 'apple pie' pears peaches
6   $ for i in $@
    > do
    > echo $i
    > done
    apple
    pie
    pears
    peaches

7   $ set 'apple pie' pears peaches
8   $ for i in "$@"              # At last!!
    > do
    > echo $i
    > done
    apple pie
    pears
    peaches
```

EXPLANATION

1   The positional parameters are set. When the $* is expanded, the quotes are stripped and apple pie becomes two separate words. The for loop assigns each of the words, in turn, to the variable i and then prints the value of i. Each time through the loop, the word on the left is shifted off, and the next word is assigned to i.

2   If $* is surrounded by double quotes, all of the words in the list become one single string, and the whole string is assigned to the variable i.

3   The positional parameters are set.

EXPLANATION (CONTINUED)

4   By enclosing $* in double quotes, the entire parameter list becomes one string.

5   The positional parameters are set.

6   Unquoted, the $@ behaves the same way as the $*.

7   The positional parameters are set.

8   By surrounding $@ with double quotes, each of the positional parameters is treated as a quoted string. The list would consist of "apple pie", "pears", and "peaches". Each of the quoted words is assigned to i, in turn, as the loop goes through each iteration.

12.5 Conditional Constructs and Flow Control

Conditional commands allow you to perform some task(s) based on whether a condition succeeds or fails. The if command is the simplest form of decision making. The if/else commands allow a two-way decision construct, and the if/elif/else commands allow a multiway decision construct.

The Korn shell expects a command to follow an if. The command can be a system command or a built-in command. The exit status of the command is used to evaluate the condition. To evaluate an expression, the built-in test command is used. This command is also linked to the [and the [[symbols. The Bourne shell encloses an expression in a set of single brackets: [and]. The Korn shell has a more sophisticated method for testing expressions. The expression is enclosed in double brackets: [[and]]. In the single brackets, the expansion of wildcards is not allowed; with the double brackets, wildcard expansion is supported and a new set of operators has been added. The result of a command is tested, with zero status indicating success, and nonzero status indicating failure.

12.5.1   Testing Exit Status and the $? Variable

The ? variable contains a number value (between 0 and 255) representing the exit status of the last command that exited. If the exit status is zero, the command exited with success; if nonzero, the command failed in some way. You can test the exit status of commands and use the test command to test the exit status of expressions.

The following examples illustrate how the exit status is tested. The single brackets are used in the Bourne shell, and although perfectly acceptable in the Korn shell, Dr. Korn provides you with the new double-bracket notation for testing expressions.

EXAMPLE 12.14

```
    (The Command Line)
1   $ name=Tom
2   $ grep "$name" datafile
    Tom Savage:408-124-2345
```

EXAMPLE 12.14 (CONTINUED)

```
3   $ print $?
    0                           # Success
4   $ test $name = Tom
5   $ print $?
    0                           # Success
6   $ test $name != Tom
    $ print $?
    1                           # Failure
7   $ [ $name = Tom ]           # Brackets instead of the test command
8   $ print $?
    0
9   $ [[ $name = [Tt]?m ]]      # New ksh test command
10  $ print $?
    0
```

EXPLANATION

1   The string Tom is assigned to the variable name.

2   The grep command will search for string Tom in datafile, and if successful in its search, will display the line found.

3   The ? variable, accessed by $?, contains the exit status of the last command executed, in this case, the exit status of grep. If grep is successful in finding the string Tom, it will return an exit status of 0. The grep command was successful.

4   The test command is used to evaluate strings and numbers, and to perform file testing. It returns an exit status of 0 if the expression is true, and an exit status of 1 if the expression fails. There must be spaces surrounding the equal sign.

5   The value of name is tested to see if it is equal to Tom. The test command returns an exit status of 0, meaning that $name does evaluate to Tom.

6   The value of name is tested to see if it is equal to Tom. The test command returns an exit status of 1, meaning that name is not equal to Tom.

7   The brackets are an alternate notation for the test command. There must be spaces after the first bracket. The expression is tested to see if $name evaluates to the string Tom.

8   The exit status of the test is 0. The test was successful because $name is equal to Tom.

9   The new Korn shell test command, [[, is used. The new test allows shell metacharacter expansion. If the variable matches Tom, tom, Tim, tim, and so on, the test will return a successful status, 0.

10 The variable name did match a string beginning with T or t and ending in m, resulting in a successful exit status ($?) of 0.

12.5.2   The Old test Command

The test command is used to evaluate conditional expressions, returning true or false. It returns zero exit status for true, and nonzero exit status for false. Either the test command or the brackets can be used. The Korn shell introduced a new way of testing expressions with double brackets. For backward compatibility with the Bourne shell, the older form of test can be used with either the test command or the single brackets. However, the preferred method for Korn shell programmers is the new test with double brackets. A complete list of test operators (both old and new style) appear in Table 12.6.

Table 12.6   Testing and Logical Operators

Test/Operator	Tests For
String Testing	
string1 = string2	string1 is equal to string2
string1 != string2	string1 is not equal to string2
string	string is not null
-z string	length of string is zero
-n string	length of string is nonzero
	EXAMPLE test -n $word or [-n $word] test tom = sue or [tom = sue]
Integer Testing (Old-Style test Used with Bourne Shell)	
int1 -eq int2	int1 is equal to int2
int1 -ge int2	int1 is greater than or equal to int2
int1 -gt int2	int1 is greater than int2
int1 -le int2	int1 is less than or equal to int2
int1 -lt int2	int1 is less than int2
int1 -ne int2	int1 is not equal to int2
Logical Operators (Old-Style test)	
!	NOT operator
-a	AND operator
-o	OR operator

Table 12.6   Testing and Logical Operators (continued)

Test/Operator	*Tests For*
File Testing (Old-Style test)	
-b filename	Block special file
-c filename	Character special file
-d filename	Directory existence
-f filename	File existence and not a directory
-g filename	Set-group-ID is set
-h filename	Symbolic link
-k filename	Sticky bit is set
-p filename	File is a named pipe
-r filename	File is readable
-s filename	File is nonzero size
-u filename	Set-user-ID bit is set
-w filename	File is writable
-x filename	File is executable

12.5.3   The New test Command

With the [[. . .]] compound test command, additional operators are available. Wildcards can be used in string-matching tests, and many of the errors from the old test have been eliminated. New string test operators are listed in Table 12.7.

Table 12.7   String Testing (New-Style Test)

String Testing Operator	*Tests For*
string = pattern	string matches pattern[a]
string != pattern	string does not match pattern
string1 < string2	ASCII value of string1 is less than string2
string1 > string2	ASCII value of string1 is greater than string2
-n string	string is nonzero in length, nonnull parameter
-z string	string is zero in length, null parameter

a.   On versions newer than 1988, the == operator is permitted.

EXAMPLE 12.15

```
(The Script)
    read answer
1   if [[ $answer = [Yy]* ]]        # Test for Yes or yes or Y or y, etc.
    then...


    Example:
    (The Script)
    guess=Noone
2   if [[ $guess != [Nn]o@(one|body) ]]     # Test for Noone, noone, or Nobody, nobody...
    then. . .


    Example:
    (The Command Line)
3   [[ apples < oranges ]]
    print $?
    0
4   [[ apples > oranges ]]
    print $?
    1
5   $ name="Joe Shmoe"
    $ [ $name = "Abe Lincoln" ]                # old style
    ksh: Shmoe: unknown test operator
6   $ [[ $name = "Abe Lincoln" ]]              # new style
    $ echo $?
    1
```

EXPLANATION

1   The answer read in from the user is tested to see if it matches anything starting with
    Y or y.

2   The variable guess is tested. If it is not equal to a string starting with N or n, fol-
    lowed by an o, and exactly one or body (for example, noone or nobody) the then com-
    mand would be executed.

3   The string apples is tested to see if it comes before oranges in the ASCII collating
    sequence. It does.

4   The string apples is tested to see if it comes after oranges in the ASCII collating se-
    quences. It does not.

5   In the old-style test, the variable name is split into separate words. Because the =
    operator expects a single string as its left operand, the test command fails. To fix
    the problem, the variable should be enclosed in double quotes.

6   In the new-style test, the variable is not split up into separate words; therefore,
    double quotes are not required around $name.

12.5.4 File Testing with Binary Operators

The binary operators for testing files require two operands (i.e., a file on either side of the operator). See Table 12.8 for a list of binary file-testing operators.

Table 12.8 Binary File Testing and Logical Operators

Operator	Tests For
file1 -nt file2	True if file1 is newer than file2
file1 -ot file2	True if file1 is older than file2
file1 -ef file2	True if file1 is another name for file2

12.5.5 Expression Testing with Logical Operators

The Korn shell, like C, provides logical testing of the truth or falsity of expressions. They are listed in Table 12.9.

Table 12.9 Logical Operators

Operator	Tests For
&&	The AND operator evaluates the expression on the left-hand side of &&; if true, the expression on the right side of && is tested and must also be true. If one expression is false, the expression is false. The && operator replaces -a; for example, ((($x && $y) > 5)).
||	The OR operator evaluates the expression on the left-hand side of the || operator; if true, the expression is true; if false, the expression on the right-hand side of the || is evaluated; if true, the expression is true. Only if both expressions are false will the expression evaluate to false. The || operator replaces -o; for example, ((($x || $y).

12.5.6 File Testing with Flags

The Korn shell provides a number of built-in test commands for checking the attributes of files, such as existence, type, permissions, and so forth. The file-testing options (also called *flags*) are listed in Table 12.10.

Table 12.10 File Testing (New test Flags)

Flag	Tests For
Korn Shell Only	
-a file	file exists
-e file	file exists (versions newer than 1988)

Table 12.10 File Testing (New test Flags) (continued)

Flag	Tests For
-L file	file exists and is a symbolic link
-O file	You are the owner of file
-G file	Your group ID is the same as file's
-S file	file exists and is a socket
Bourne and Korn Shells	
-b file	file exists and is a block special file
-c file	file exists and is a character special file
-d file	file exists and is a directory
-f file	file exists and is not a directory
-g file	file exists and is setgid
-k file	file exists and sticky bit is set
-p file	file exists and is a named pipe
-r file	file exists and is readable
-s file	file has a nonzero size
-u file	file exists and is setuid
-w fle	file exists and is writable
-x file	file exists and is executable

EXAMPLE 12.16

```
    (The Script)
1   file=/etc/passwd
2   if [[ -f $file && (-r $file || -w $file) ]]
    then
3      print $file is a plain file and is either readable or writable
    fi
```

EXPLANATION

1   The variable file is assigned /etc/passwd.

2   The file test operators test if the file is a plain file and is either readable or writable. The parentheses are used for grouping. In the old test, the parentheses had to be escaped with a backslash.

3   If both of the tests are true, the file is a plain file, and it is either readable or writable, this line is executed.

12.5.7 The if Command

The simplest form of conditional is the if command. The command following the if keyword is executed and its exit status is returned. If the exit status is 0, the command succeeded and the statement(s) after the then keyword are executed.

In the C shell and C language, the expression following the if command is a Boolean-type expression. But in the Bourne and Korn shells, the statement following the if is a command or group of commands. The exit status of the last command of the if line is used to determine whether to continue and execute commands under the then statement. If the exit status of the last command on the if line is 0, the commands under the then statement are executed. The fi terminates the command list to be executed after the then. If the exit status is nonzero, meaning that the command failed in some way, the statement(s) after the then statement are ignored and control goes to the line directly after the fi statement.

Conditional commands can be nested. Every if must have a corresponding fi. The fi is paired with the closest if. Using indentation to format your if blocks helps when debugging your programs.

FORMAT

```
if command
then      # Testing command exit status
    command
    command
fi
---------------------------------------
if test expression
then      # Using the test command to test expressions
    command
fi


            or


if [ expression ]
then                  # Using the old-style test command--
    command           # brackets replace the word test
fi
-----------------------------------
if [[ expression ]]
then                  # New-style brackets for testing expressions
    command
fi
---------------------------------------------
```

FORMAT (CONTINUED)

```
if command
then
...
    if command
    then
    ...
        if command          # Nested conditionals
        then
        ...
        fi
    fi
fi
```

EXAMPLE 12.17

```
1   if ypmatch $name passwd > /dev/null 2>&1
2   then
            echo Found $name!
3   fi
```

EXPLANATION

1   The ypmatch command is an NIS command that searches for its argument, name, in the NIS passwd database on the server machine. Standard output and standard error are redirected to /dev/null, the UNIX bit bucket.

2   If the exit status of the ypmatch command is 0, the program goes to the then statement and executes commands until fi is reached.

3   The fi terminates the list of commands following the then statement.

12.5.8   Using the Old-Style Bourne test

If you have been programming in the Bourne shell, the Korn shell is backward-compatible, allowing your Bourne shell scripts to be executed properly by the Korn shell. Many Bourne shell programmers, when converting to Korn shell, still use the old-style test command when evaluating expressions. If you are reading or maintaining scripts, you may find the old syntax alive and well. Therefore, a brief discussion of the old syntax may help you, even if you are writing your own scripts with the new Korn shell test command.

EXAMPLE 12.18

```
    #!/bin/ksh
    # Scriptname: are_you_ok
1   print "Are you ok (y/n) ?"
    read answer
```

EXAMPLE 12.18 (CONTINUED)

```
2   if [ "$answer" = Y -o "$answer" = y ]      # Old-style test
    then
          print "Glad to hear it."
3   fi
```

EXPLANATION

1   The user is asked the question, Are you ok (y/n) ?. The read command causes the program to wait for user input.

2   The test command, represented by a [, is used to test expressions and returns an exit status of 0 if the expression is true and nonzero if the expression is false. If the variable answer evaluates to Y or y, the commands after the then statement are executed. (The test command does not allow the use of wildcards when testing expressions.)

3   The fi terminates the list of commands following the then statement.

12.5.9   Using the New-Style Korn test

The new-style Korn shell testing allows expressions to contain shell metacharacters and Korn shell operators such as && and ||.

EXAMPLE 12.19

```
    #!/bin/ksh
    # Scriptname: are_you_ok2
1   print "Are you ok (y/n) ?"
    read answer
2   if [[ "$answer" = [Yy]* ]]          # New-style test
    then
          print "Glad to hear it."
3   fi
```

EXPLANATION

1   The user is asked the question, Are you ok (y/n) ?. The read command causes the program to wait for user input.

2   The [[ ]] is a special Korn shell construct used to test expressions. If the answer evaluates to Y or y followed by any number of characters, the commands after the then statement are executed.

3   The fi statement terminates the if.

12.5.10   Using the Old-Style Bourne test with Numbers

To test numeric expressions, the old-style Bourne shell test command and its operators are still acceptable in the Korn shell, but the new-style let command is preferred.

EXAMPLE 12.20

```
1   if [ $# -lt 1 ]
    then
        print "$0: Insufficient arguments " 1>&2
        exit 1
2   fi
```

EXPLANATION

1   The statement reads: If the number of arguments is less than 1, print the error message and send it to standard error. Then exit the script. The old style of testing integers is used with the test command.

2   The fi marks the end of the block of statements after then.

12.5.11   The let Command and Testing Numbers

Although it is still acceptable to use single square brackets and old-style Bourne shell numeric operators for testing numeric expressions, the preferred Korn shell method is to use the double parentheses and the new C language–style numeric operators when testing *numeric* expressions. Note that the double brackets are only used for testing *string* expressions and for file tests (see Table 12.10).

EXAMPLE 12.21

```
1   if (( $# < 1 ))
    then
        print "$0: Insufficient arguments " 1>&2
        exit 1
2   fi
```

EXPLANATION

1   The statement reads: If the number of arguments is less than 1, print the error message and send it to standard error. Then exit the script. This is the preferred way to perform numeric tests in the Korn shell.

2   The fi marks the end of the block of statements after then.

12.5.12 The `if/else` Command

The `if/else` command allows a two-way decision-making process. If the command after the `if` fails, the commands after the `else` are executed.

FORMAT

```
if command
then
    command(s)
else
    command(s)
fi
```

EXAMPLE 12.22

```
1    if ypmatch "$name" passwd > /dev/null 2>&1
2    then
         print Found $name!
3    else
4        print "Can't find $name."
         exit 1
5    fi
```

EXPLANATION

1   The ypmatch command searches for its argument, $name, in the NIS passwd database. Standard output and standard error are redirected to /dev/null, the UNIX bit bucket.

2   If the exit status of the ypmatch command is 0, program control goes to the then statement and executes commands until else is reached.

3   The commands under the else statement are executed if the ypmatch command fails to find name in the passwd database; that is, the exit status of ypmatch must be nonzero for the commands in the else block to be executed.

4   The print function sends output to the screen and the program exits.

5   This marks the end of the if construct.

12.5.13 The `if/elif/else` Command

The `if/elif/else` command allows a multiway decision-making process. If the command following the `if` fails, the command following the `elif` is tested. If that command succeeds, the commands under its then statement are executed. If the command after the `elif` fails, the next `elif` command is checked. If none of the commands succeeds, the `else` commands are executed. The `else` block is called the default.

FORMAT

```
if command
then
     command(s)
elif command
then
     commands(s)
elif command
then
     command(s)
else
     command(s)
fi
```

```
if [[ string expression ]]      or       if (( numeric expression ))
then
     command(s)
elif [[ string expression  ]]   or       elif (( numeric expression ))
then
     commands(s)
elif [[ string expression ]]    or       elif(( numeric expression ))
then
     command(s)
else
     command(s)
fi
```

EXAMPLE 12.23

```
(The Script)
     #!/bin/ksh
     # Scriptname: tellme
1    read age?"How old are you? "
2    if (( age < 0 || age > 120 ))
     then
          print "Welcome to our planet! "
          exit 1
     fi
3    if (( age >= 0 && age < 13 ))
     then
          print "A child is a garden of verses"
     elif (( age > 12 && age < 20 ))
     then
          print "Rebel without a cause"
```

EXAMPLE 12.23 (CONTINUED)

```
    elif (( age >= 20 && age < 30 ))
    then
         print "You got the world by the tail!!"
    elif (( age >= 30 && age < 40 ))
    then
         print "Thirty something..."
4   else
         print "Sorry I asked"
5   fi
```

```
(The Output)
    $ tellme
1   How old are you? 200
2   Welcome to our planet!

    $ tellme
1   How old are you? 13
3   Rebel without a cause

    $ tellme
1   How old are you? 55
4   Sorry I asked
```

EXPLANATION

1   The user is asked for input. The input is assigned to the variable age.

2   A numeric test is performed within the double parentheses. If age is less than 0 or greater than 120, the print command is executed and the program terminates with an exit status of 1. The interactive shell prompt will appear. Note that the dollar sign ($) is not required to perform variable substitution when using the (( )) operators.

3   A numeric test is performed within the double parentheses. If age is greater than 0 and less than 13, the let command returns exit status 0, true.

4   The else construct is the default. If none of the above statements are true, the else commands will be executed.

5   The fi terminates the initial if statement.

12.5.14   The exit Command

The exit command is used to terminate the script and get back to the command line. You may want the script to exit if some condition does not test true. The argument to the exit command is an integer, ranging from 0 to 255. When the program exits, the exit number is stored in the shell's ? variable.

EXAMPLE 12.24

```
(The Script)
    #!/bin/ksh
    # Scriptname: filecheck
    # Purpose: Check to see if a file exists, what type it is, and its permissions.

1   file=$1      # Variable is set to first command-line argument
2   if [[ ! -a $file ]]
    then
        print "$file does not exist"
        exit 1
    fi
3   if [[ -d $file ]]
    then
        print "$file is a directory"
4   elif [[ -f $file ]]
    then
5       if [[ -r $file && -w $file && -x $file ]]
        then
            print "You have read, write, and execute permission on
            file $file"
        else
6           print "You don't have the correct permissions"
            exit 2
        fi
    else
7       print "$file is neither a file nor a directory. "
        exit 3
8   fi

(The Command Line)
9   $ filecheck testing
    testing does not exist
10  $ echo $?
    1
```

EXPLANATION

1   The first command-line argument passed to this program ($1) is assigned to the variable file.

2   The test command follows the if. If $file (after variable substitution) is a file that does not exist (note the NOT operator, !), the commands under the then keyword are executed. An exit value of 1 means that the program failed in some way. (In this case, the test failed.)

3   If the file is a directory, print that it is a directory.

4   If the file is not a directory, else if the file is a plain file, then . . .

EXPLANATION (CONTINUED)

5 If the file is readable, writable, and executable, then . . .

6 The fi terminates the innermost if command. The program exits with an argument of 2 if the file does not have read, write, and execute permission.

7 The else commands are executed if lines 2 and 3 fail. The program exits with a value of 3.

8 This fi goes with the if on line 3 in the example.

9 The file called testing does not exist.

10 The $? variable holds the exit status, 1.

12.5.15 The null Command

The null command is a colon. It is a built-in, do-nothing command that returns an exit status of 0. It is used as a placeholder after an if command when you have nothing to say, but need a command or the program will produce an error message because it requires something after the then statement. Often the null command is used as an argument to the loop command to make the loop a forever loop or for testing variable expression modifiers such as {EDITOR:-/bin/vi}.

EXAMPLE 12.25

```
(The Script)
1    name=Tom
2    if grep "$name" databasefile > /dev/null 2>&1
     then
3        :
4    else
         print "$1 not found in databasefile"
         exit 1
     fi
```

EXPLANATION

1 The string Tom is assigned to the variable name.

2 The if command tests the exit status of the grep command. If Tom is found in databasefile, the null command is executed and does nothing.

3 The colon is the null command. It always exits with a 0 exit status.

4 What we really want to do is print an error message and exit if Tom is not found. The commands after the else will be executed if the grep command fails.

EXAMPLE 12.26

```
(The Script)
1    : ${EDITOR:=/bin/vi}
2    echo $EDITOR
```

EXPLANATION

1. The colon command takes an argument that is evaluated by the shell. The expression `${EDITOR:=/bin/vi}` is used as an argument to the colon command. If the variable EDITOR has been previously set, its value will not be changed; if it has not been set, the value /bin/vi will be assigned to it. The Korn shell would have responded with an error such as ksh: /bin/vi: not found if the colon command had not preceded the expression.
2. The value of the EDITOR variable is displayed.

12.5.16 The case Command

The case command is a multiway branching command used as an alternative to the if/elif commands. The value of the case variable is matched against value1, value2, and so forth until a match is found. When a value matches the case variable, the commands following the value are executed until the double semicolons are reached. Then, instruction starts after the word esac (case spelled backwards).

If a case variable is not matched, the program executes commands after the *), the default value, until the double semicolons or esac is reached. The *) value serves the same purpose as the else statement in if/else conditionals. The case values can use shell wildcards and the vertical bar (pipe symbol) for ORing two values.

FORMAT

```
case variable in
value1)
    command(s);;
value2)
    command(s);;
*)
    command(s);;
esac
```

EXAMPLE 12.27

```
(The Script)
    #!/bin/ksh
    # Scriptname: xtermcolor
    # Sets the xterm foreground color (the color of the prompt and
    # input typed for interactive windows.
1   read color?"Choose a foreground color for your terminal?"
2   case "$color" in
3   *[Bb]1??)
4       xterm -fg blue -fn terminal &
5           ;;
```

EXAMPLE 12.27 (CONTINUED)

```
6    *[Gg]reen)
         xterm -fg darkgreen -fn terminal &
             ;;
7    red | orange)                  # The vertical bar means "OR"
         xterm -fg "$color" -fn terminal &
             ;;
8    *)  xterm -fn terminal &        # default
             ;;
9    esac
10   print "Out of case..."
```

EXPLANATION

1 The user is asked for input. The input is assigned to the variable color.

2 The case command evaluates the expression $color.

3 If color begins with a B or b, followed by the letter l and any two characters, the case expression matches the first value. The value is terminated with a single closed parenthesis. The wildcards are shell metacharacters.

4 The statement is executed if the value in line 3 matches the case expression. The xterm command sets the foreground color to blue.

5 The double semicolons are required after the last command in this block of commands. Control branches to line 10, after the semicolons are reached.

6 If the case expression matches a G or g, followed by the letters r-e-e-n, the xterm window foreground color is set to dark green. The double semicolons terminate the block of statements and control branches to line 10.

7 The vertical bar is used as an OR conditional operator. If the case expression matches either red or orange, the xterm command is executed.

8 This is the default value. If none of the above values match the case expression, the command(s) after the * value are executed. The default color for the terminal foreground is black.

9 The esac statement (case spelled backwards) terminates the case command.

10 After one of the values is matched, execution continues here.

The case Command and the here document.   Often, the here document is used to create a menu. After the user has selected a choice from the menu, the case command is used to match against one of the choices. The Korn shell also provides a select loop for creating menus.

EXAMPLE 12.28

```
   (The .profile File)
       print "Select a terminal type "
1   cat << EOF
           1) vt120
           2) wyse50
           3) ansi
           4) sun
2   EOF
3   read TERM
4   case "$TERM" in
    1)   export TERM=vt120
         ;;
    2)   export TERM=wyse50
         ;;
    3)   export TERM=ansi
         ;;
    *)   export TERM=sun
         ;;
5   esac
    print "TERM is $TERM"
```

EXPLANATION

1   A here document is used to display a menu of choices.

2   EOF is the user-defined terminator. Input for the here document stops here.

3   The read command waits for user input and assigns it to the TERM variable.

4   The case command evaluates the variable TERM and matches it against one of the numbers in the list. If a match is found, the terminal is set.

5   The case command terminates with esac.

12.6 Looping Commands

The looping commands are used to execute a command or group of commands a set number of times, or until a certain condition is met. The Korn shell has four types of loops: for, while, until, and select.

12.6.1 The for Command

The for looping command is used to execute commands for each member of a set of arguments. You might use this loop to execute the same commands on a list of files or usernames. The for command is followed by a user-defined variable, the keyword in, and a list of words. The first time in the loop, the first word from the wordlist is assigned to the variable, and then shifted off. The next time around the loop, the second word is assigned to the variable, and so on. The body of the loop starts at the do keyword and ends at the done keyword. When all of the words in the list have been shifted off, the loop ends and program control continues after the done keyword.

FORMAT

```
for variable in wordlist
do
    command(s)
done
```

EXAMPLE 12.29

```
(The Script)
1    for pal in Tom Dick Harry Joe
2    do
3        print "Hi $pal"
4    done
5    print "Out of loop"

(The Output)
     Hi Tom
     Hi Dick
     Hi Harry
     Hi Joe
     Out of loop
```

EXPLANATION

1   This for loop will iterate through the list of names, Tom, Dick, Harry, and Joe, shifting each one off (to the left) after it is assigned to the variable pal. As soon as all of the words are shifted and the wordlist is empty, the loop ends and execution starts after the done keyword. The word following the for command, pal, is a variable that will be assigned the value after the in keyword, one at a time, for each iteration of the loop. The first time in the loop, the variable pal will be assigned the word Tom. The second time through the loop, pal will be assigned Dick, the next time pal will be assigned Harry, and the last time, pal will be assigned Joe.

2   The do keyword is required after the wordlist. If it is used on the same line, the list must be terminated with a semicolon. For example:

     for pal in Tom Dick Harry Joe; do

3   This is the body of the loop. After Tom is assigned to the variable pal, the commands in the body of the loop, that is, all commands between the do and the done keywords, are executed.

4   The done keyword ends the loop. If there are no words left to be processed in the wordlist on line 1, the loop exits, and execution starts at line 5.

5   This line is executed when the loop terminates.

EXAMPLE 12.30

```
(The Command Line)
1    $ cat mylist
     tom
     patty
     ann
     jake

(The Script)
2    for person in $(< mylist)     #same as for person in `cat mylist`
     do
3        mail $person < letter
         print $person was sent a letter.
4    done
5    print "The letter has been sent."
```

EXPLANATION

1   The contents of a file, mylist, are displayed.

2   Command substitution is performed and the contents of mylist become the wordlist. The first time in the loop, tom is assigned to the variable person, and then shifted off, to be replaced with patty, and so on.

3   In the body of the loop, each user is mailed a copy of a file called letter.

4   The done keyword marks the end of this loop iteration.

5   When all of the users in the list have been sent mail, the loop will exit, and this line will be executed.

EXAMPLE 12.31

```
1    for file in *.c
2    do
         if [[ -f $file ]] ; then
             cc $file -o ${file%.c}
         fi
     done
```

EXPLANATION

1   The wordlist will consist of all files in the current working directory ending with the extension .c (C source files). Each filename will be assigned to variable file, in turn, for each iteration of the loop.

2   When the body of the loop is entered, the file will be tested to make sure it exists and is a real file. If so, it will be compiled. ${file%.c} expands to the filename without its extension.

12.6.2 The $* and $@ Variables in Wordlists

When expanded, the $* and $@ are the same unless enclosed in double quotes. "$*" eval-uates to one string, whereas "$@" evaluates to a list of separate words.

EXAMPLE 12.32

```
(The Script)
    #!/bin/ksh
1   for name in $*      # or for name in $@
2   do
          echo Hi $name
3   done

(The Command Line)
$ greet Dee Bert Lizzy Tommy
Hi Dee
Hi Bert
Hi Lizzy
Hi Tommy
```

EXPLANATION

1   $* and $@ expand to a list of all the positional parameters; in this case, the argu-ments passed in from the command line: Dee, Bert, Lizzy, and Tommy. Each name in the list will be assigned, in turn, to the name variable in the for loop.

2   The commands in the body of the loop are executed until the list is empty.

3   The done keyword marks the end of the loop body.

12.6.3 The while Command

The while evaluates the command immediately following it, and if its exit status is 0, the commands in the body of the loop (commands between do and done) are executed. When the done keyword is reached, control is returned to the top of the loop and the while com-mand checks the exit status of the command again. Until the exit status of the command being evaluated by the while becomes nonzero, the loop continues. When the exit status reaches nonzero, program execution starts after the done keyword. If the exit status never becomes nonzero, the loop goes around and around infinitely. (Of course, pressing Ctrl-C or Ctrl-\ will stop the looping.)

FORMAT

```
while command
do
      command(s)
done
```

EXAMPLE 12.33

```
(The Script)
1    num=0                    # Initialize num
2    while (( num < 10 ))     # Test num with the let
     do
         print -n $num
3        (( num=num + 1 ))    # Increment num
     done
     print "\nAfter loop exits, continue running here"

(The Output)
0123456789
After loop exits, continue running here
```

EXPLANATION

1   This is the initialization step. The variable num is assigned 0.

2   The while command is followed by the let command. If the value of num is less than 10, the body of the loop is entered.

3   In the body of the loop, the value of num is incremented by one. If the value of num was never changed, the loop would iterate infinitely or until the process was killed.

EXAMPLE 12.34

```
(The Script)
    #!/bin/ksh
    # Scriptname: quiz
1   read answer?"Who was the U.S. President in 1992? "
2   while [[ $answer != "Bush" ]]
3   do
        print "Wrong try again!"
4       read answer
5   done
6   print Good guess!

(The Output)
$ quiz
Who was the U.S. President in 1992? George
Wrong try again!
Who was the U.S. President in 1992? I give up
Wrong try again!
Who was the U.S. President in 1992? Bush
Good guess!
```

EXPLANATION

1 The read command prints the string after the question mark (?), Who was the U.S. President in 1992?, and waits for input from the user. The input will be stored in the variable answer.

2 The while loop is entered and the test command, [[, evaluates the expression. If the variable answer does not equal the string Bush, the body of the loop is entered and commands between the do and done are executed.

3 The do keyword is the start of the loop body.

4 The user is asked to re-enter input.

5 The done keyword marks the end of the loop body. Control is returned to the top of the while loop, and the expression is tested again. As long as $answer does not evaluate to Bush, the loop will continue to iterate. When the user's input is Bush, the loop ends. Program control goes to line 6.

EXAMPLE 12.35

```
(The Script)
1   go=1
    print Type q to quit.
2   while let go or (( go ))
    do
        print I love you.
        read word
3       if [[ $word = [qQ]* ]]
        then
            print "I'll always love you"
4           go=0
        fi
5   done

(The Output)
$ sayit
Type q to quit.
I love you.
I love you.
I love you.
I love you.
I love you.
q
I'll always love you
$
```

EXPLANATION

1   The variable go is assigned 1.

2   The loop is entered. The let command tests the expression. The expression evaluates to one. The program goes into the body of the while loop and executes commands from the do keyword to the done keyword.

3   If the user enters a q or Q as input to the variable word, the commands between then and fi are executed. Anything else will cause I love you. to be displayed.

4   The variable go is assigned 0. When program control starts at the top of the while loop, the expression will be tested. Because the expression evaluates to false, the loop exits and the script starts execution after the done keyword on line 5.

5   The done marks the end of the body of the loop.

12.6.4   The until Command

The until command is used like the while command, but evaluates the exit status in the opposite way. The until evaluates the command immediately following it, and if its exit status is not 0, the commands in the body of the loop (commands between do and done) are executed. When the done keyword is reached, control is returned to the top of the loop and the until command checks the exit status of the command again. Until the exit status of the command being evaluated by until becomes 0, the loop continues. When the exit status reaches 0, program execution starts after the done keyword.

FORMAT

```
until command
do
      command(s)
done
```

EXAMPLE 12.36

```
      #!/bin/ksh
1     until who | grep linda
2     do
          sleep 5
3     done
      talk linda@dragonwings
```

EXPLANATION

1   The until loop tests the exit status of the last command in the pipeline, grep. The who command lists who is logged on this machine and pipes its output to grep. The grep command will return 0 exit status (success) only when it finds user linda.

2   If user linda has not logged in, the body of the loop is entered and the program sleeps for 5 seconds.

3   When linda logs on, the exit status of the grep command will be 0 and control will go to the statements following the done keyword.

EXAMPLE 12.37

```
    #!/bin/ksh
1   hour=0
2   until (( hour > 23 ))
    do
3       case "$hour" in
        [0-9]|1[0-1]) print "Good morning!"
            ;;
        12) print "Lunch time"
            ;;
        1[3-7]) print "Siesta time"
            ;;
        *) print "Good night"
            ;;
        esac
4       (( hour+=1 ))
5   done
```

EXPLANATION

1   The hour variable is assigned 0. The variable must be initialized before being used in the until loop.

2   The until command is followed by the let command. If the hour is not greater than 23, that is, the exit status is nonzero, the loop body is entered.

3   The case command matches the value of the hour variable against one of the hour values, or matches the default, executing the command that applies.

4   The hour is incremented by 1; otherwise, the hour will never become greater than 23 and the loop will never exit. Control is returned to the until command and the hour is evaluated again.

5   The done keyword marks the end of the loop. When the hour is greater than 23, control will go to the line under the done, if there is one; otherwise, the program is exited.

12.6.5 The select Command and Menus

The here document is an easy method for creating menus, but the Korn shell introduces a new loop, called the select loop, which is used primarily for creating menus. A menu of numerically listed items is displayed to standard error. The PS3 prompt is used to prompt the user for input; by default, PS3 is #?. After the PS3 prompt is displayed, the shell waits for user input. The input should be one of the numbers in the menu list. The input is stored in the special Korn shell REPLY variable. The number in the REPLY variable is associated with the string to the right of the parentheses in the list of selections.[2]

---

2. If you want the menu to reappear when the loop starts again, set the REPLY variable to null just before the done keyword.

The case command is used with the select command to allow the user to make a selection from the menu and, based on that selection, execute commands. The LINES and COL-UMNS variables can be used to determine the layout of the menu items displayed on the terminal. The output is displayed to standard error, each item preceded by a number and closing parenthesis, and the PS3 prompt is displayed at the bottom of the menu. Because the select command is a looping command, it is important to remember to use either the break command to get out of the loop, or the exit command to exit the script.

FORMAT

```
select var in wordlist
do
     command(s)
done
```

EXAMPLE 12.38

```
(The Script)
     #!/bin/ksh
     # Program name: goodboys
1    PS3="Please choose one of the three boys : "
2    select choice in tom dan guy
3    do
4         case $choice in
          tom)
               print Tom is a cool dude!
5              break;;          # break out of the select loop
6         dan | guy )
               print Dan and Guy are both sweethearts.
               break;;
          *)
7              print " $REPLY is not one of your choices" 1>&2
               print "Try again."
               ;;
8         esac
9    done

(The Command Line)
$ goodboys
1) tom
2) dan
3) guy
Please choose one of the three boys : 2
Dan and Guy are both sweethearts.
```

EXAMPLE 12.38 (CONTINUED)

```
$ goodboys
1) tom
2) dan
3) guy
Please choose one of the three boys : 4
4 is not one of your choices
Try again.
Please choose one of the three boys : 1
Tom is a cool dude!
$
```

EXPLANATION

1 The PS3 variable is assigned the prompt that will appear below the list of menu selections. After the prompt is displayed, the program waits for user input. The input is stored in the built-in variable called REPLY.

2 The select command is followed by the variable choice. This syntax is similar to that of the for loop. The variable choice is assigned, in turn, each of the items in the list that follows it; in this case, tom, dan, and guy. It is this wordlist that will be displayed in the menu, preceded by a number and a right parenthesis.

3 The do keyword indicates the start of the body of the loop.

4 The first command in the body of the select loop is the case command. The case command is normally used with the select loop. The value in the REPLY variable is associated with one of the choices: 1 is associated with tom, 2 is associated with dan, and 3 is associated with guy.

5 If tom is the choice, after printing the string Tom is a cool dude!, the break command causes the select loop to be exited. Program control starts after the done keyword.

6 If either menu item, 2 (dan) or 3 (tom), is selected, the REPLY variable contains the user's selection.

7 If the selection is not 1, 2, or 3, an error message is sent to standard error. The user is asked to try again and control starts at the beginning of the select loop.

8 The end of the case command.

9 The end of the select loop.

EXAMPLE 12.39

```
(The Script)
    #!/bin/ksh
    # Program name: ttype
    # Purpose: set the terminal type
    # Author: Andy Admin
```

EXAMPLE 12.39 (CONTINUED)

```
1    COLUMNS=60
2    LINES=1
3    PS3="Please enter the terminal type: "
4    select choice in wyse50 vt200 vt100 sun
     do
5        case $REPLY in
         1)
6            export TERM=$choice
             print "TERM=$choice"
             break;;                    # break out of the select loop
         2 | 3 )
             export TERM=$choice
             print "TERM=$choice"
             break;;
         4)
             export TERM=$choice
             print "TERM=$choice"
             break;;
         *)
7            print "$REPLY is not a valid choice. Try again" 1>&2
                 ;;
         esac
8    done
```

```
(The Command Line)
$ ttype
1) wyse50    2) vt200   3) vt100    4) sun
Please enter the terminal type : 4
TERM=sun


$ ttype
1) wyse50    2) vt200   3) vt100    4) sun
Please enter the terminal type : 3
TERM=vt100


$ ttype
1) wyse50    2) vt200   3) vt100    4) sun
Please enter the terminal type : 7
7 is not a valid choice. Try again.
Please enter the terminal type: 2
TERM=vt200
```

1   The COLUMNS variable is set to the width of the terminal display in columns for menus created with the select loop. The default is 80.

2   The LINES variable controls the vertical display of the select menu on the terminal. The default is 24 lines. By changing the LINES value to 1, the menu items will be printed on one line, instead of vertically as in the last example.

3   The PS3 prompt is set and will appear under the menu choices.

4   The select loop will print a menu with four selections: wyse50, vt200, vt100, and sun. The variable choice will be assigned one of these values based on the user's response held in the REPLY variable. If REPLY is 1, wyse50 is assigned to choice; if REPLY is 2, vt200 is assigned to choice; if REPLY is 3, vt100 is assigned to choice; and if REPLY is 4, sun is assigned to choice.

5   The REPLY variable evaluates to the user's input selection.

6   The terminal type is assigned, exported, and printed.

7   If the user does not enter a number between 1 and 4, he or she will be prompted again. Note that the menu does not appear, just the PS3 prompt. To make the menu reappear, set the REPLY variable to null. Type above line 8: REPLY =

8   The end of the select loop.

12.6.6 Looping Control Commands

If some condition occurs, you may want to break out of a loop, return to the top of the loop, or provide a way to stop an infinite loop. The Korn shell provides loop control commands to control loops.

The shift Command.   The shift command shifts the parameter list to the left a specified number of times. The shift command without an argument shifts the parameter list once to the left. Once the list is shifted, the parameter is removed permanently. Often the shift command is used in while loops when iterating through a list of positional parameters.

shift [n]

EXAMPLE 12.40

```
(Without a Loop)
(The Script)
    #!/bin/ksh
    # Scriptname: doit0
1   set joe mary tom sam
2   shift
```

EXAMPLE 12.40 (CONTINUED)

```
3    print $*
4    set $(date)
5    print $*
6    shift 5
7    print $*
8    shift 2
```

(The Output)
```
    $ doit0
3    mary tom sam
5    Sun Sep 9 10:00:12 PDT 2004
7    2004
8    ksh: shift: bad number
```

EXPLANATION

1   The set command sets the positional parameters. $1 is assigned joe, $2 is assigned mary, $3 is assigned tom, and $4 is assigned sam.

2   The shift command shifts the positional parameters to the left; joe is shifted off.

3   The parameter list is printed after the shift. $* represents all of the parameters.

4   The set command resets the positional parameters to the output of the UNIX date command.

5   The new parameter list is printed.

6   This time the list is shifted five times to the left.

7   The new parameter list is printed.

8   By attempting to shift more times than there are parameters, the shell sends a message to standard error.

EXAMPLE 12.41

```
(With a Loop)
(The Script)
    #!/bin/ksh
    # Usage: doit [args]
1    while (( $# > 0 ))
    do
2        print $*
3        shift
4    done
```

EXAMPLE 12.41 (CONTINUED)

(The Command Line)
$ **doit a b c d e**
a b c d e
b c d e
c d e
d e
e

EXPLANATION

1   The while command tests the numeric expression. If the number of positional parameters ($#) is greater than 0, the body of the loop is entered. The positional parameters are coming from the command line as arguments. There are five.

2   All the positional parameters are printed.

3   The parameter list is shifted once to the left.

4   The body of the loop ends here; control returns to the top of the loop. The parameter list has decreased by one. After the first shift, $# is four. When $# has been decreased to 0, the loop ends.

The break Command.   The built-in break command is used to force immediate exit from a loop, but not from a program. (To leave a program, the exit command is used.) After the break command is executed, control starts after the done keyword. The break command causes an exit from the innermost loop, so if you have nested loops, the break command takes a number as an argument, allowing you to exit out of any number of outer loops. The break is useful for exiting from an infinite loop.

FORMAT

break [n]

EXAMPLE 12.42

```
1    while true; do
2        read answer? Are you ready to move on\?
3        if [[ $answer = [Yy]* ]]; then
             break
4        else
             ....commands...
         fi
5    done
6    print "Here we are"
```

EXPLANATION

1   The true command is a UNIX command, and an alias for the colon command in the Korn shell. It always exits with 0 status and is often used to start an infinite loop. (The null command (:) can be used to do the same thing.) The body of the loop is entered.

2   The user is asked for input. The user's input is assigned to the variable answer.

3   If answer evaluates to Y, y, Yes, Yup, or Ya (anything beginning with Y or y), the break command is executed and control goes to line 6. The line Here we are is printed. Until the user answers something that starts with a Y or y, the program will continue to ask for input. This could go on forever!

4   If the test fails in line 3, the else commands are executed. When the body of the loop ends at the done keyword, control starts again at the top of the while at line 1.

5   The end of the loop body.

6   Control starts here after the break command is executed.

The continue Command.   The continue command starts back at the top of the loop if some condition becomes true. All commands below the continue will be ignored. The continue command returns control to the top of the innermost loop; if nested within a number of loops, the continue command may take a number as its argument. Control can be started at the top of any number of outer loops.

FORMAT

```
continue [n]
```

EXAMPLE 12.43

```
(The Mailing List)
$ cat mail_list
ernie
john
richard
melanie
greg
robin

(The Script)
      # Scriptname: mailtomaillist
      #!/bin/ksh
1     for name in $(< mail_list)
      do
2       if [[ "$name" = "richard" ]] then
3             continue
        else
4             mail $name < memo
        fi
5     done
```

1   The for loop will iterate through a list of names stored in a file called mail_list. Each time a name from the list is assigned to the variable name, it is shifted off the list and replaced by the next name on the list.

2   The name matches richard; the continue command is executed. Because richard has already been shifted off, the next user, melanie, is assigned to the variable name.

3   The continue command returns control to the top of the loop, skipping any commands in the rest of the loop body.

4   All users in the list, except richard, will be mailed a copy of the file memo.

5   The end of the loop body.

12.6.7 Nested Loops and Loop Control

If using nested loops, the break and continue commands let you control which loop to terminate.

```
(The Script)
    #!/bin/ksh
1   while true ; do  ◄
            < Commands here>
2       for user in tom dick harry joe
        do
            if [[ $user = [Dd]* ]]
            then
3               continue 2
                < Commands here >
4               while true
                do
                    < Commands here>
5                   break 3
6                done
7           fi
        done
8   done  ◄
9   print Out of loop
```

1   The true command always returns an exit status of zero. The loop is designed to go forever unless you use loop control commands.

2   The for loop is entered.

EXPLANATION (CONTINUED)

3   The for loop will loop through each of the names in the list. If the user variable
     begins with a D or d, the continue command causes control to go to the top of the
     while loop. Without an argument, the continue command would start control at the
     top of the for loop. The argument 2 tells the shell to go to the top of the second
     enclosing loop and restart execution there.

4   The while loop is nested. The true command always exits with zero status. The
     loop will go forever.

5   The break command terminates the outermost while loop. Execution starts at line 9.

6   The done keyword marks the end of the innermost while loop.

7   This done keyword marks the end of the for loop.

8   This done keyword marks the end of outermost while loop.

9   Out of the loop.

12.6.8   I/O Redirection and Loops

The Korn shell allows you to use redirection and pipes in loops. Unlike the Bourne shell,
the loop runs in this shell, not a subshell. Variables set within the loop will still be set
when the loop exits.

Redirecting the Output of a Loop to a File.   Instead of sending the output of a
loop to the screen, it can be redirected to a file or a pipe. See Example 12.45.

EXAMPLE   12.45

```
(The Command Line)
1    $ cat memo
     abc
     def
     ghi
--------------------------------------------------------------------
(The Script)
     #!/bin/ksh
     # Program name: numberit
     # Put line numbers on all lines of memo
2    if (( $# < 1 ))
     then
           print "Usage: $0 filename " >&2
           exit 1
     fi
3    integer count=1              # Initialize count
4    cat $1 | while read line     # Input is coming from memo
     do
```

EXAMPLE 12.45 (CONTINUED)

```
5          (( count == 1 )) && print "Processing file $1..." > /dev/tty
6          print $count $line
7          (( count+=1 ))
8      done > tmp$$                   # Output is going to a temporary file
9      mv tmp$$ $1
```

```
(The Command Line)
10   $ numberit memo
     Processing file memo...

11   $ cat memo
     1 abc
     2 def
     3 ghi
```

EXPLANATION

1   The contents of file memo are displayed.

2   If the number of arguments is less than one, a usage message is sent to standard error, the screen.

3   The count variable is declared an integer and is assigned the value 1.

4   The UNIX cat command displays the contents of the filename stored in $1, and the output is piped to the while loop. The read command is assigned the first line of the file the first time in the loop, the second line of the file the next time through the loop, and so forth.

5   The output of this print statement is sent to /dev/tty, the screen. If not explicitly redirected to /dev/tty, the output will be redirected to tmp$$ on line 8.

6   The print function prints the value of count, followed by the line in the file.

7   The count variable is incremented by 1.

8   The output of this entire loop, with the exception of line 3, is redirected to the file tmp$$ (where $$ evaluates to the PID of this process). The tmp file is given a unique name by appending the PID of this process to its name.

9   The tmp file is renamed to the name of the file that was assigned to $1.

10 The program is executed. The file to be processed is called memo.

11 The file is displayed with line numbers.

Piping the Output of a Loop to a UNIX Command.   The output of a loop can be redirected from the screen to a pipe. See Example 12.46.

EXAMPLE 12.46

```
(The Script)
1    for i in 7 9 2 3 4 5
2    do
          print $i
3    done | sort -n

(The Output)
2
3
4
5
7
9
```

EXPLANATION

1　　The for loop iterates through a list of unsorted numbers.

2　　In the body of the loop, the numbers are printed. This output will be piped into the UNIX sort command.

3　　The pipe is created after the done keyword.

12.6.9　Running Loops in the Background

If the loop is going to take a while to process, it can be run as a background job so that the rest of the program can continue.

EXAMPLE 12.47

```
1    for person in bob jim joe sam
     do
2         mail $person < memo
3    done &
```

EXPLANATION

1　　The for loop shifts through each of the names in the wordlist: bob, jim, joe, and sam. Each of the names is assigned to the variable person, in turn.

2　　In the body of the loop, each person is sent the contents of the file memo.

3　　The ampersand at the end of the done keyword causes the loop to be executed in the background. The program will continue to run while the loop is executing.

12.6.10 The exec Command and Loops

The exec command can be used to close standard input or output without creating a sub-shell.

```
(The File)
1   cat tmp
    apples
    pears
    bananas
    peaches
    plums
--------------------------------------------------------------

(The Script)
    #!/bin/ksh
    # Scriptname: speller
    # Purpose: Check and fix spelling errors in a file

2   exec < tmp          # Opens the tmp file
3   while read line     # Read from the tmp file
    do
4       print $line
5       print -n "Is this word correct? [Y/N] "
6       read answer < /dev/tty     # Read from the terminal
        case $answer in
        [Yy]*)
            continue
               ;;
        *)
            print "New word? "
7           read word < /dev/tty
            sed "s/$line/$word/" tmp > error
            mv error tmp

8           print $word has been changed.
               ;;
        esac
    done
```

1   The contents of the tmp file are displayed.

2   The exec command changes standard input (file descriptor 0), so that instead of input coming from the keyboard, it is coming from the tmp file.

3   The while loop starts. The read command gets a line of input from the tmp file.

4   The value stored in the line variable is printed to the screen.

5   The user is asked if the word is correct.

6   The read command gets the user's response from the terminal, /dev/tty. If the input is not redirected directly from the terminal, it will continue to be read from the file tmp, still opened for input.

7   The user is again asked for input, and the input is redirected from the terminal, /dev/tty.

8   The new word is displayed.

12.6.11   The IFS and Loops

The IFS, the shell's internal field separator, evaluates to spaces, tabs, and the newline character. It is used as a word (token) separator for commands that parse lists of words such as read, set, for, and select. It can be reset by the user if a different separator will be used in a list. It is a good idea to save the original value of the IFS in another variable before changing it. Then it is easy to return to its default value.

EXAMPLE   12.49

```
(The Script)
    #!/bin/ksh
    # Scriptname: runit
    # IFS is the internal field separator and defaults to
    # spaces, tabs, and newlines.
    # In this script it is changed to a colon.

1   names=Tom:Dick:Harry:John
2   OLDIFS="$IFS"              # Save the original value of IFS
3   IFS=":"
4   for persons in $names
    do
5        print Hi $persons
    done
6   IFS="$OLDIFS"             # Reset the IFS to old value

7   set Jill Jane Jolene      # Set positional parameters
8   for girl in $*
    do
         print Howdy $girl
    done
```

EXAMPLE 12.49 (CONTINUED)

```
(The Output)
$ runit
Hi Tom
Hi Dick
Hi Harry
Hi John
Howdy Jill
Howdy Jane
Howdy Jolene
```

EXPLANATION

1   The names variable is set to the string Tom:Dick:Harry:John. Each of the words is separated by a colon.

2   The value of IFS is assigned to another variable, OLDIFS. Because the value of the IFS is whitespace, it must be quoted to preserve the whitespace.

3   The IFS is assigned a colon. Now the colon is used to separate words.

4   After variable substitution, the for loop will iterate through each of the names using the colon as the internal field separator between the words.

5   Each of the names in the wordlist is displayed.

6   IFS is reassigned its original values, stored in OLDIFS.

7   The positional parameters are set. $1 is assigned Jill, $2 is assigned Jane, and $3 is assigned Jolene.

8   $* evaluates to all the positional parameters, Jill, Jane, and Jolene. The for loop assigns each of the names to the girl variable, in turn, through each iteration of the loop.

12.7 Arrays

Korn shell arrays are one-dimensional arrays that may contain up to 1,024 (size varies) elements consisting of words or integers. The index starts at 0. Each element of an array can be set or unset individually. Values do not have to be set in any particular order. For example, you can assign a value to the tenth element before you assign a value to the first element. An array can be set using the set command with the -A option.

Associative arrays are supported under versions of the Korn shell that are more recent than 1988.

EXAMPLE 12.50

```
(The Command Line)
1    $ array[0]=tom
     $ array[1]=dan
     $ array[2]=bill
2    $ print ${array[0]}        # Curly braces are required.
     tom
3    $ print ${array[1]}
     dan
4    $ print ${array[2]}
     bill
5    $ print ${array[*]}        # Display all elements.
     tom dan bill
6    $ print ${#array[*]}       # Display the number of elements.
     3
```

EXPLANATION

1   The first three elements of the array are assigned values. The index starts at 0.

2   The value of the first array element, tom, is printed. Make sure you remember to surround the variable with curly braces. $array[0] would print tom[0].

3   The value of the second element of the array, dan, is printed.

4   The value of the third element of the array, bill, is printed.

5   All elements in the array are printed.

6   The number of elements in the array is printed. An array can be declared with typeset if you know the size and type.

EXAMPLE 12.51

```
(At The Command Line)
1    $ typeset -i ints[4]       # Declare an array of four integers.
2    $ ints[0]=50
     $ ints[1]=75
     $ ints[2]=100
3    $ ints[3]=happy
     ksh: happy: bad number
```

EXPLANATION

1   The typeset command creates an array of 4 integers.

2   Integer values are assigned to the array.

3   A string value is assigned to the fourth element of the array, and the Korn shell sends a message to standard error.

12.7.1 Creating Arrays with the set Command

You can assign the values of an array using the set command. The first word after the –A option is the name of the array; the rest of the words are the elements of the array.

EXAMPLE 12.52

```
(The Command Line)
1   $ set -A fruit apples pears peaches
2   $ print ${fruit[0]}
    apples
3   $ print ${fruit[*]}
    apples pears peaches
4   $ fruit[1]=plums
5   $ print ${fruit[*]}
    apples plums peaches
```

EXPLANATION
---

1   The set command with the –A option creates an array. The name of the array, fruit, follows the –A option. Each of the elements of the fruit array follow its name.
2   Subscripts start at 0. Curly braces are required around the variable for it to be evaluated properly. The first element of the array is printed.
3   When the asterisk is used as a subscript, all elements of the array are displayed.
4   The second element of the array is reassigned the value plums.
5   All elements of the array are displayed.

12.8 Functions

Korn shell functions are similar to those used in the Bourne shell, and are used to modularize your program. A function is a collection of one or more commands that can be executed simply by entering the function's name, similar to a built-in command. Here is a review of some of the important rules about using functions.

1. The Korn shell executes built-in commands first, then functions, and then executables. Functions are read into memory once when they are defined, not every time they are referenced.
2. A function must be defined before it is used; therefore, it is best to place function definitions at the beginning of the script.
3. The function runs in the current environment; it shares variables with the script that invoked it, and lets you pass arguments by setting them as positional parameters. The present working directory is that of the calling script. If you change the directory in the function, it will be changed in the calling script.
4. In the Korn shell, you can declare local variables in the function using the typeset command. Ksh functions can be exported to subshells.

5. The `return` statement returns the exit status of the last command executed within the function or the value of the argument given, and cannot exceed a value of 255.
6. To list functions and definitions, use the preset alias, `functions`.
7. Traps are local to functions and will be reset to their previous value when the function exits (not so with the Bourne shell).
8. Functions can be recursive, that is, call themselves. Recursion should be handled carefully. The Korn shell will warn you otherwise with the message, `recursion too deep`.
9. Functions can be autoloaded; they are defined only if referenced. If never referenced, they are not loaded into memory.
10. Versions of the Korn shell that are more recent than 1988 also support discipline functions, passing variables by reference, and compound variables. A built-in command is no longer found before a function of the same name. In older versions it was necessary to use a combination of aliases and functions to write a function that would override a built-in command.[3]

12.8.1   Defining Functions

A function must be defined before it can be invoked. Korn shell functions are defined with the keyword `function` preceding the function name. The curly braces must have a space on the inside of each brace. (Please see "Functions" on page 372 for the older-style Bourne shell function definition; these are still compatible in Korn shell scripts.)

FORMAT

```
function function_name { commands; commands; }
```

EXAMPLE   12.53

```
function usage { print "Usage $0 [-y] [-g] " ; exit 1; }
```

EXPLANATION

The function name is `usage`. It is used to print a diagnostic message and exit the script if the script does not receive the proper arguments, either -y or -g.

12.8.2   Listing and Unsetting Functions

To list local function definitions, type `typeset -f`. To list exported function definitions, type `typeset -fx`. To unset a function, type `unset -f function_name`. See the `typeset` command, Table 12.11 on page 714.

---

3. David G. Korn and Morris I. Bolsky, *The Korn Shell Command and Programming Language* (Englewood Cliffs, NJ: Prentice-Hall, Inc., 1988), p. 77.

12.8.3 Local Variables and the Return Value

The typeset command can be used to create local variables. These variables will be known only in the function where they are created. Once out of the function, the local variables are undefined.

The return value of a function is really just the value of the exit status of the last command in the script unless a specific return command is used. If a value is assigned to the return command, that value is stored in the ? variable. It can hold an integer value between 0 and 255. Because the return command is limited to returning only integer values, you can use command substitution to return the output of a function and assign the output to a variable, just as you would if getting the output of a UNIX command.

EXAMPLE 12.54

```
(The Script)
    #!/bin/ksh
    # Scriptname: do_increment
    # Using the return Command)
1   function increment {
2       typeset sum        # sum is a local variable.
        (( sum = $1 + 1 ))
3       return $sum        # Return the value of sum to the script.
    }

    print -n "The sum is "
4   increment 5            # Call the function increment and pass 5 as a
                           # parameter. 5 becomes $1 for the increment function.
5   print $?              # The return value is stored in the ? variable
6   print $sum            # The variable "sum" was local to the function, and
                           # is undefined in the main script. Nothing is printed.

(The Output)
    $ do_increment
5   The sum is 6
    6
```

EXPLANATION

1   The function called increment is defined.

2   The typeset command defines the variable sum to be local to this function.

3   The return built-in command, when given an argument, returns to the main script after the line where the function was invoked and stores its argument in the ? variable. In the script, the increment function is called with an argument.

4   The increment function is called with an argument of 5.

EXPLANATION (CONTINUED)

5   The exit status of the function is stored in ? unless an explicit argument is given
     to the return command. The return command argument specifies a return status
     for the function, its value is stored in the ? variable, and it must be an integer be-
     tween 0 and 255.

6   Because sum was defined as a local variable in the function increment, it is not de-
     fined in the script that invoked the function. Nothing is printed.

EXAMPLE 12.55

```
(Using Command Substitution)
(The Script)
    # Scriptname: do_square
    #!/bin/ksh
1   function square {
    (( sq = $1 * $1 ))
        print "Number to be squared is $1."
2       print "The result is $sq "
    }
3   read number?"Give me a number to square. "
4   value_returned=$(square $number)
5   print $value_returned

(The Output)
    $ do_square
5   Number to be squared is 10. The result is 100
```

EXPLANATION

1   The function called square is defined. It will multiply its argument times itself.

2   The result of squaring the number is printed.

3   The user is asked for input.

4   The function square is called with a number (input from the user) as its argument.
     Command substitution is performed because the function is enclosed in paren-
     theses preceded by a $. The output of the function (both of its print statements) is
     assigned to the variable value_returned.

5   The command substitution removes the newline between the strings Number to be
     squared is and The result is 100.

12.8.4   Exported Functions

Function definitions are not inherited by subshells unless you define them in the ENV file
with the typeset command, for example, typeset -fx function_names.

     You can export functions with typeset -fx from the current Korn shell to a script, or
from one script to another, but not from one invocation of ksh to the next (e.g., a separate

invocation means that if you type ksh at the prompt, a brand new shell is started up). Exported function definitions will not be inherited by the new shell.

EXAMPLE 12.56

```
(The First Script)
    $ cat calling_script
    #!/bin/ksh
1   function sayit { print "How are ya $1?" ; }
2   typeset -fx sayit    # Export sayit to other scripts
3   sayit Tommy
4   print "Going to other script"
5   other_script         # Call other_script
    print "Back in calling script"
******************************************************************
(The Second Script)
    $ cat other_script   # NOTE: This script cannot be invoked with #!/bin/ksh
6   print "In other script "
7   sayit Dan
8   print "Returning to calling script"

(The Output)
    $ calling_script
3   How are ya Tommy?
4   Going to other script
6   In other script
7   How are ya Dan?
8   Returning to calling script
    Back in calling script
```

EXPLANATION

1   The function sayit is defined. It will accept one argument to be stored in $1.

2   The typeset command with the -fx option allows the function to be exported to any script called from this script.

3   The function sayit is invoked with Tommy as an argument. Tommy will be stored in $1 in the function.

4   After the sayit function terminates, the program resumes here.

5   The script, called other_script, is executed.

6   We are now in the other script. This script is called from the first script, sayit. It cannot start with the line #!/bin/ksh because this line causes a ksh subshell to be started, and exporting functions does not work if a separate Korn shell is invoked.

7   The function sayit is invoked. Dan is passed as an argument, which will be stored in $1 in the function.

8   After this line is printed, other_script terminates and control goes back to the calling script at the line where it left off after the function was invoked.

12.8.5　Function Options and the typeset Command

The typeset command is used to display function attributes. See Table 12.11.

Table 12.11　typeset and Function Options

Option	What It Does
typeset -f	Displays all functions and their values. Must have a history file, as all function definitions are stored there.
typeset +f	Displays just function names.
typeset -fx	Displays all function definitions that will be exported across shell scripts, but not as a separate invocation of ksh.
typeset -fu func	func is the name of a function that has not yet been defined.

Autoloaded Functions.　An autoloaded function is not loaded into your program until you reference it. The autoloaded function can be defined in a file somewhere else and the definition will not appear in your script, allowing you to keep the script small and compact. To use autoload, you need to set the FPATH variable in your ENV file. The FPATH variable contains a search path for directories containing function files. The files in this directory have the same names as the functions defined within them.

The autoload alias for typeset -fu specifies that the function names that have not yet been defined are to be autoloaded functions. After the autoload command is executed with the function as its argument, you must invoke the function to execute the commands contained in it. The primary advantage of autoloading functions is better performance, because the Korn shell does not have to read the function definition if it has never been referenced.[4]

EXAMPLE　12.57

```
(The Command Line)
1   $ mkdir functionlibrary
2   $ cd functionlibrary
3   $ vi foobar

(In Editor)
4   function foobar { pwd; ls; whoami; }   # function has the same name as the file.

(In .profile File)
5   export FPATH=$HOME/functionlibrary    # This path is searched for functions.
```

---

4. Morris I. Bolsky and David G. Korn, *The New Kornshell* (Upper Saddle River, NJ: Prentice Hall, 1995), p. 78.

EXAMPLE 12.57 (CONTINUED)

```
(In Your Script)
6   autoload foobar
7   foobar
```

EXPLANATION

1   Make a directory in which to store functions.

2   Go to the directory.

3   foobar is a file in functionlibrary. The file foobar contains the definition of function foobar. The filename and function name must match.

4   The function foobar is defined in the file called foobar.

5   In the user's .profile initialization file, the FPATH variable is assigned the path where the functions are stored. This is the path the Korn shell will search when auto-loading a function. FPATH is exported.

6   In your script, the function foobar is brought into the program's memory.

7   The function foobar is invoked.

A number of functions can be stored in one file; for example, calculation functions may be contained in a file called math. Because the function must have the same name as the file in which it is stored, you may create hard links to the function file. Each function name will be a link to the file in which the function is defined. For example, if a function in the math file is called square, use the UNIX/Linux ln command to give the math file another name, square. Now the math file and square file can be referenced, and in either case you are referencing the file by the corresponding function name. Now the square function can be autoloaded by its own name.

EXAMPLE 12.58

```
(The Command Line)
1   $ ln math square add divide
2   $ ls -i
    12256 add
    12256 math
    12256 square
    12256 divide
3   $ autoload square; square
```

EXPLANATION

1   The UNIX/Linux ln (link) command lets you give a file alternate names; math and square are the same file. The link count is incremented by one for each link created.

2   A listing shows that all files have the same inode number, meaning they are all one file but can be accessed with different names.

EXPLANATION (CONTINUED)

3   Now, when the square file is autoloaded, the function square has the same name and
    will be invoked. None of the other functions defined in the file can be referenced
    until they, in turn, have been specifically autoloaded by name.

12.9 Trapping Signals

While your program is running, if you press Ctrl-C or Ctrl-\, the program terminates as
soon as the signal arrives. There are times when you would rather not have the program
terminate immediately after the signal arrives. You could arrange to ignore the signal and
keep running, or perform some sort of cleanup operation before actually exiting the
script. The trap command allows you to control the way a program behaves when it
receives a signal.

A signal is defined as an asynchronous message that consists of a number that can be
sent from one process to another, or by the operating system to a process if certain keys
are pressed or if something exceptional happens.[5] The trap command tells the shell to
terminate the command currently in execution upon the receipt of a signal. If the trap
command is followed by commands within single quotes, those commands will be executed upon receipt of a specified signal. Use the command kill -l to get a list of all signals and the numbers corresponding to them.

FORMAT

```
trap 'command; command' signal
```

EXAMPLE 12.59

```
trap 'rm tmp*$$; exit 1' 1 2 15
```

EXPLANATION

When any of the signals 1 (hangup), 2 (interrupt), or 15 (software termination) arrives,
remove all the tmp files and then exit.

If an interrupt comes in while the script is running, the trap command lets you handle
the interrupt signal in several ways. You can let the signal behave normally (default),
ignore the signal, or create a handler function to be called when the signal arrives. See
Table 12.12 for a list of signal numbers and their corresponding names.[6] Type kill -l to
get the output shown in Table 12.12.

---

5. Morris I. Bolsky and David G. Korn, *The New KornShell Command and Programming Language* (Engle-
    wood Cliffs, NJ: Prentice Hall PTR, 1995), p. 327.

6. For a complete discussion of UNIX signals, see W. Richard Stevens, *Advanced Programming in the UNIX
    Environment* (Boston: Addison-Wesley Professional, 1992).

Table 12.12 Signals[a, b]

1) HUP	12) SYS	23) POLL
2) INT	13) PIPE	24) XCPU
3) QUIT	14) ALRM	25) XFSZ
4) ILL	15) TERM	26) VTALRM
5) TRAP	16) URG	27) PROF
6) IOT	17) STOP	28) WINCH
7) EMT	18) TSTP	29) LOST
8) FPE	19) CONT	30) USR1
9) KILL	20) CHLD	31) USR2
10) BUS	21) TTIN	
11) SEGV	22) TTOU	

a. The output of this command may differ slightly with the operating system.

b. For a complete list of UNIX signals and their meanings, go to www.cybermagician.co.uk/technet/unixsignals.htm. For Linux signals, go to www.comptechdoc.org/os/linux/programming/linux_pgsignals.html.

12.9.1 Pseudo or Fake Signals

These three fake signals are not real signals, but are generated by the shell to help debug a program. They are treated like real signals by the trap command and defined in the same way. See Table 12.13 for a list of pseudo signals.

Table 12.13 Korn Shell Fake Trap Signals

Signal	*What It Does*
DEBUG	Executes trap commands after every script command
ERR	Executes trap commands if any command in the script returns a nonzero exit status
0 or EXIT	Executes trap commands if the shell exits

Signal names such as HUP and INT are normally prefixed with SIG, for example, SIGHUP, SIGINT, and so forth. The Korn shell allows you to use symbolic names for the signals, which are the signal names without the SIG prefix, or you can use the numeric value for the signal. See Example 12.60.

12.9.2   Resetting Signals

To reset a signal to its default behavior, the trap command is followed by the signal name or number. Traps set in functions are local to functions; that is, they are not known outside the function where they were set.

EXAMPLE 12.60

```
trap 2   or   trap INT
```

EXPLANATION

Resets the default action for signal 2, SIGINT. The default action is to kill the process when the interrupt key (Ctrl-C) is pressed.

12.9.3   Ignoring Signals

If the trap command is followed by a pair of empty quotes, the signals listed will be ignored by the process.

EXAMPLE 12.61

```
trap " " 1 2   or   trap "" HUP INT
```

EXPLANATION

Signals 1 (SIGHUP) and 2 (SIGINT) will be ignored by the shell process.

12.9.4   Listing Traps

To list all traps and the commands assigned to them, type trap.

EXAMPLE 12.62

```
(The Script)
    #!/bin/ksh
    # Scriptname: trapping
    # Script to illustrate the trap command and signals
    # Can use the signal numbers or ksh abbreviations seen
    # below. Cannot use SIGINT, SIGQUIT, etc.
1   trap 'print "Ctrl-C will not terminate $PROGRAM."' INT
2   trap 'print "Ctrl-\ will not terminate $PROGRAM."' QUIT
3   trap 'print "Ctrl-Z will not terminate $PROGRAM."' TSTP
4   print "Enter any string after the prompt.\
    When you are ready to exit, type \"stop\"."
5   while true
    do
```

EXAMPLE 12.62 (CONTINUED)

```
6        print -n "Go ahead...> "
7        read
8        if [[ $REPLY = [Ss]top ]]
         then
9            break
         fi
10  done
```

```
(The Output)
    $ trapping
4   Enter any string after the prompt.
    When you are ready to exit, type "stop".
6   Go ahead...> this is it^C
1   Ctrl-C will not terminate trapping.
6   Go ahead...> this is it again^Z
3   Ctrl-Z will not terminate trapping.
6   Go ahead...> this is never it^\
2   Ctrl-\ will not terminate trapping.
6   Go ahead...> stop
    $
```

EXPLANATION

1   The first trap catches the INT signal, Ctrl-C. If Ctrl-C is pressed while the program is running, the command enclosed in quotes will be executed. Instead of aborting, the program will print Ctrl-C will not terminate trapping and continue to prompt the user for input.

2   The second trap command will be executed when the user presses Ctrl-\, the QUIT signal. The string Ctrl-\ will not terminate trapping will be displayed and the program will continue to run. This signal, SIGQUIT by default, kills the process and produces a core file.

3   The third trap command will be executed when the user presses Ctrl-Z, the TSTP signal. The string Ctrl-Z will not terminate trapping will be displayed, and the program will continue to run. This signal normally causes the program to be suspended in the background if job control is implemented.

4   The user is prompted for input.

5   The while loop is entered.

6   The string Go ahead...> is printed and the program waits for input (see line 7).

7   The read command assigns user input to the built-in REPLY variable.

8   If the value of REPLY matches Stop or stop, the break command causes the loop to exit and the program will terminate. Entering Stop or stop is the only way we will get out of this program unless it is killed with the kill command.

9   The break command causes the body of the loop to be exited.

10 The done keyword marks the end of the loop.

EXAMPLE 12.63

```
(The Script)
    $ cat trap.err
    #!/bin/ksh
    # This trap checks for any command that exits with a nonzero
    # status and then prints the message.
1   trap 'print "You gave me a non-integer. Try again. "' ERR
2   typeset -i number      # Assignment to number must be integer
3   while true
    do
4       print -n "Enter an integer. "
5       read -r number 2> /dev/null
6       if (( $? == 0 ))      # Was an integer read in?
        then                  # Was the exit status zero?
7           break
        fi
    done
8   trap - ERR               # Unset pseudo trap for ERR
    n=$number
9   if grep ZOMBIE /etc/passwd > /dev/null 2>&1
    then
        :
    else
10      print "\$n is $n. So long"
    fi

(The Output)
    $ trap.err
4   Enter an integer. hello
1   You gave me a non-integer. Try again.
4   Enter an integer. good-bye
1   You gave me a non-integer. Try again.
4   Enter an integer. \\\
1   You gave me a non-integer. Try again.
4   Enter an integer. 5
10  $n is 5. So long.
    $ trap.err
4   Enter an integer. 4.5
10  $n is 4. So long.
```

EXPLANATION

1   The ERR (fake or pseudo) signal will print the message in double quotes any time a command in the program returns a nonzero exit status, that is, fails.

2   The typeset command with the –i option creates an integer variable, number, which can only be assigned integers.

EXPLANATION (CONTINUED)

3   The exit status of the true command is always 0; the body of the while loop is entered.

4   The user is asked to type in an integer.

5   The read command reads user input and assigns it to the number variable. The number must be an integer; if not, an error message will be sent to /dev/null. The -r option to the read command allows you to enter a negative number (starting with the minus sign).

6   If the exit status from the read command is 0, a number was entered, and the if statements will be executed.

7   The break command is executed and the loop exits.

8   The trap for the fake Korn shell signal ERR is unset.

9   When grep fails, it returns a nonzero exit status; if we had not unset the ERR trap, the script would have printed You gave me a non-integer. Try again. So long if the grep failed to find ZOMBIE in the /etc/passwd file.

10 This line is printed if the grep failed. Note that if a floating-point number such as 4.5 is entered, the number is truncated to an integer.

12.9.5   Traps and Functions

If trap is used in a function, the trap and its commands are local to the function.

EXAMPLE   12.64

```
(The Script)
    #!/bin/ksh
1   function trapper {
        print "In trapper"
2       trap 'print "Caught in a trap!"' INT
        print "Got here."
        sleep 25
    }
3   while :
    do
        print "In the main script"
4       trapper   # Call the function
5       print "Still in main"
        sleep 5
        print "Bye"
    done
    ---------------------------------------------------
```

EXAMPLE 12.64 (CONTINUED)

```
(The Output)
$ functrap
In the main script
In trapper
Got here.
^CCaught in a trap!
$
```

EXPLANATION

1 The function `trapper` is defined. It contains the `trap` command.

2 The `trap` command will be executed if Ctrl-C is entered. The `print` command within the `trap` is executed and the program continues execution. Ctrl-C is entered while the `sleep` command is running. Normally, the program will continue to run just after the command where it was interrupted (with the exception of the `sleep` command, which causes the program to abort). The `trap` has no effect on lines starting after 4.

3 In the main part of the script, a `while` loop is started. The colon is a do-nothing command that always returns a zero exit status. The loop will go forever.

4 Once in the loop, the function `trapper` is called.

5 The `trap` command within the `trapper` function will have no effect in this part of the program because the trap is local to the function. If the function exits normally (i.e., ^C is not pressed), execution will continue here. The default behavior for ^C will cause the script to abort if the signal is sent here or to any of the lines that follow.

12.10 Coprocesses

A coprocess is a special two-way pipeline that allows shell scripts to write to the standard input of another command and to read from its standard output. This provides a way to create a new interface for an existing program. The append operator, |&, is placed at the end of the command to initiate the command as a coprocess. Normal redirection and background processing should not be used on coprocesses. The `print` and `read` commands require a -p switch to read from and write to a coprocess. The output must be sent to standard output and have a newline at the end of each message of output. The standard output must be flushed after each message is sent to standard output. You can run multiple coprocesses by using the `exec` command with the >&p or <&p operator. To open file descriptor 4 as a coprocess, you would enter `exec 4>&p`.

EXAMPLE 12.65

```
(The Script)
#!/bin/ksh
# Scriptname: mycalculator
# A simple calculator -- uses the bc command to perform the calculations
# Because the shell performs operations on integers only, this program allows
# you to use floating-point numbers by writing to and reading from the bcprogram.

1    cat << EOF
     ***************************************************
2        WELCOME TO THE CALCULATOR PROGRAM
     **************************************************
3    EOF

4    bc |&                      # Open coprocess

5    while true
     do
6        print "Select the letter for one of the operators below "
7        cat <<- EOF
             a) +
             s) -
             m) *
             d) /
             e) ∧
         EOF
8        read op
9        case $op in
             a) op="+";;
             s) op="-";;
             m) op="*";;
             d) op="/";;
             e) op="∧";;
             *) print "Bad operator"
                    continue;;
         esac
10       print -p scale=3                 # write to the coprocess
11       print "Please enter two numbers: "   # write to standard out
12       read num1 num2                   # read from standard in
13       print -p "$num1" "$op" "$num2"   # write to the coprocess
14       read -p result                   # read from the coprocess
15       print $result
16       print -n "Continue (y/n)? "
17       read answer
18       case $answer in
         [Nn]* )
```

EXAMPLE 12.65 (CONTINUED)

```
19          break;;
        esac
20  done
21  print Good-bye
```

(The Output)
$ **mycalculator**

```
    **************************************************
1        WELCOME TO THE CALCULATOR PROGRAM
    **************************************************
6   Select one of the operators below
7        a) +
         s) -
         m) *
         d) /
         e) ^
    e
11  Please enter two numbers:
    2.3 4
    27.984
16  Continue (y/n)? y
6   Select one of the operators below
7        a) +
         s) -
         m) *
         d) /
         e) ^
    d
11  Please enter two numbers:
    2.1 4.6
    0.456
16  Continue (y/n)? y
6   Select one of the operators below
7        a) +
         s) -
         m) *
         d) /
         e) ^
    m
11  Please enter two numbers:
    4 5
    20
16  Continue (y/n)? n
21  Good-bye
```

EXPLANATION

1   The here document is used to display a title banner.

2   This text is printed as a header to the menu below.

3   EOF is a user-defined terminator, marking the end of the here document.

4   The bc command (desk calculator) is opened as a coprocess. It is executed in the background.

5   A while loop is started. Because the true command always returns a successful exit status of 0, the loop will continue indefinitely until a break or exit is reached.

6   The user is prompted to select an item from a menu to be displayed.

7   Another here document displays a list of math operations the user can choose for the bc program.

8   The read command assigns user input to the variable op.

9   The case command matches for one of the op values and assigns an operator to op.

10 The print command with the -p option pipes output (scale=3) to the coprocess, the bc command. The bc command accepts the print output as input and sets the scale to 3. (The scale defines the number of significant digits to the right of the decimal point in a number that will be displayed by bc.)

11 The user is prompted to enter two numbers.

12 The read command assigns user input to the variables num1 and num2.

13 The print -p command sends the arithmetic expression to the bc coprocess.

14 The shell reads from the bc coprocess (read -p) and assigns the input to the variable result.

15 The result of the calculation ($result) is printed.

16 The user is asked about continuing.

17 The user enters input. It is assigned to the variable answer.

18 The case command evaluates the variable answer.

19 If the user had entered No or no or nope, and so on, the break command would be executed, and the while loop would be terminated with control sent to line 21.

20 The done keyword marks the end of the while loop.

21 This line is printed when the loop terminates.

12.11 Debugging

By turning on the noexec option or using the -n argument to the ksh command, you can check the syntax of your scripts without really executing any of the commands. If there is a syntax error in the script, the shell will report the error. If there are no errors, nothing is displayed.

The most commonly used method for debugging scripts is to turn on the xtrace option or to use the ksh command with the -x option. These options allow an execution trace of your script. Each command from your script is displayed after variable substitution has been performed, and then the command is executed. When a line from your script is displayed, it is preceded with the value of the PS4 prompt, a plus (+) sign. The PS4 prompt can be changed.

With the verbose option turned on, or by invoking the Korn shell with the –v option (ksh –v scriptname), each line of the script will be displayed, just as it was typed in the script, and then executed. See Table 12.14 for debug commands.

Table 12.14   Debug Commands and Options

Command	Function	How It Works
export PS4='$LINENO '	The PS4 prompt by default is a +.	You can reset the prompt. In this example, a line number will be printed for each line.
ksh –x scriptname	Invokes ksh with echo option.	Displays each line of the script after variable substitution and before execution.
ksh –v scriptname	Invokes ksh with verbose option.	Displays each line of the script before execution, just as you typed it.
ksh –n scriptname	Invokes ksh with noexec option.	Interprets but does not execute commands.
set –x or set –o xtrace	Turns on echo option.	Traces execution in a script.
set +x	Turns off echo.	Turns off tracing.
trap 'print $LINENO ' DEBUG	Prints value of $LINENO for each line in the script.	For each script command, the trap action is performed. See format for trap.
trap 'print Bad input' ERR		If a nonzero exit status is returned, the trap is executed.
trap 'print Exiting from $0' EXIT		Prints message when script or function exits.
typeset –ft	Turns on tracing.	Traces execution in a function.

EXAMPLE 12.66

```
(The Script)
    #!/bin/ksh
    # Scriptname: todebug
1   name="Joe Blow"
2   if [[ $name = [Jj]* ]] then
         print Hi $name
    fi
    num=1
3   while (( num < 5 ))
    do
4        (( num=num+1 ))
    done
5   print The grand total is $num
```

```
(The Output)
1   $ ksh -x todebug
2   + name=Joe Blow
    + [[ Joe Blow = [Jj]* ]]
    + print Hi Joe Blow
    Hi Joe Blow
    + num=1        The + is the PS4 prompt
    + let num < 5
    + let num=num+1
    + let num < 5
    + let num=num+1
    + let num < 5
    + let num=num+1
    + let num < 5
    + let num=num+1
    + let num < 5
    + print The grand total is 5
5   The grand total is 5
```

EXPLANATION

1   The Korn shell is invoked with the -x option. Echoing is turned on. Each line of the script will be displayed on the screen, followed by the result of executing that line. Variable substitution is performed. Alternatively, the -x option can be used in the script instead of at the command line (e.g., #!/bin/ksh -x).

2   The lines are preceded by the plus (+) sign, the PS4 prompt.

3   The while loop is entered. It will loop 4 times.

4   The value of num is incremented by by 1.

5   After the while loop exits, this line is printed.

EXAMPLE   12.67

```
(The Script)
    #!/bin/ksh
    # Scriptname: todebug2
1   trap 'print "num=$num on line $LINENO"' DEBUG
    num=1
    while (( num < 5 ))
    do
        (( num=num+1 ))
    done
    print The grand total is $num

(The Output)
    $ todebug2
2   num=1 on line 3
    num=1 on line 4
    num=2 on line 6
    num=2 on line 4
    num=3 on line 6
    num=3 on line 4
    num=4 on line 6
    num=4 on line 4
    num=5 on line 6
    num=5 on line 4
    The grand total is 5
    num=5 on line 8
    num=5 on line 8
```

EXPLANATION

1   LINENO is a special Korn shell variable that holds the number of the current script line. The DEBUG signal, used with the trap command, causes the string enclosed in single quotes to be executed every time a command in the script is executed.

2   As the while loop executes, the value of the variable num and the line of the script are displayed.

12.12 The Command Line

12.12.1 Processing Command-Line Options with getopts

If you are writing scripts that require a number of command-line options, positional parameters are not always most efficient. For example, the UNIX/Linux ls command takes a number of command-line options and arguments. (An option requires a leading dash; an argument does not.) Options can be passed to the program in several ways: ls -laFi, ls -i -a -l -F, ls -ia -F, and so forth. If you have a script that requires arguments, positional parameters might be used to process the arguments individually, such as ls -l -i -F. Each dash option would be stored in $1, $2, and $3, respectively. But, what if the user listed all of the options as one dash option, as in ls -liF? Now the -liF would all be assigned to $1 in the script. The getopts function makes it possible to process command-line options and arguments in the same way they are processed by the ls program.[7] The getopts function will allow the runit program to process its arguments using a variety of combinations.

EXAMPLE 12.68

```
(The Command Line)
1   $ runit -x -n 200 filex
2   $ runit -xn200 filex
3   $ runit -xy
4   $ runit -yx -n 30
5   $ runit -n250 -xy filey

(any other combination of these arguments )
```

EXPLANATION

1   The program runit takes four arguments; x is an option, n is an option requiring a number argument after it, and filex is an argument that stands alone.

2   The program runit combines the options x and n and the number argument 200; filex is also an argument.

3   The program runit combines the x and y options.

4   The program runit combines the y and x options; the n option is passed separately as is the number argument, 30.

5   The program runit combines the n option with the number argument; the x and y options are combined and the filey is separate.

Before getting into all the details of the runit program, we examine the line from the program where getopts is used to see how it processes the arguments. The following is a line from the script called runit:

while getopts :xyn: name

1. x, y, and n are the options.
2. Options typed at the command line begin with either - or +.
3. Any options that do not contain a + or - tell getopts that the option list is at an end.
4. The colon after an option says that the option requires an argument; that is, the -n option requires an argument.

---

7.   See the UNIX or Linux manual for the C library function getopt.

5. The colon before an option list says that if you type an illegal option, getopts will allow the programmer to handle it. For example, in the command runit -p, where -p is not one of the legal options, getopts will tell you so programmatically. The shell does not print an error message.

6. Each time getopts is called, it places the next option it finds, without the dash, in the variable name. (You can use any variable name here.) If there is a plus sign prepended to the option, then it goes into name with the plus sign. If an illegal argument is given, name is assigned a question mark; if a required argument is missing, name is assigned a colon.

7. OPTIND is a special variable that is initialized to one and is incremented each time getopts completes processing a command-line argument to the number of the next argument getopts will process.

8. The OPTARG variable contains the value of a legal argument, or if an illegal option is given, the value of the illegal option is stored in OPTARG.

Sample getopts Scripts.   The following sample scripts illustrate how getopts processes arguments.

EXAMPLE 12.69

```
(The Script)
    #!/bin/ksh
    # Program opts1
    # Using getopts -- First try --
1   while getopts xy options
    do
2   case $options in
3       x) print "you entered -x as an option";;
        y) print "you entered -y as an option";;
    esac
    done
----------------------------------------------------------------
(The Command Line)
4   $ opts1 -x
    you entered -x as an option
5   $ opts1 -xy
    you entered -x as an option
    you entered -y as an option
6   $ opts1 -y
    you entered -y as an option
7   $ opts1 -b
    opts1[3]: getopts: b bad option(s)
8   $ opts1 b
```

EXPLANATION

1   The getopts command is used as a condition for the while command. The valid options for this program are listed after the getopts command; they are x and y. Each option is tested in the body of the loop, one after the other. Each option will be assigned to the variable options, without the leading dash. When there are no longer any arguments to process, getopts will exit with a nonzero status, causing the while loop to terminate.

2   The case command is used to test each of the possible options found in the options variable, either x or y.

3   If x was an option, the string you entered -x as an option is displayed.

4   At the command line, the opts1 script is given an x option, a legal option to be processed by getopts.

5   At the command line, the opts1 script is given an xy option, legal options to be processed by getopts.

6   At the command line, the opts1 script is given a y option, a legal option to be processed by getopts.

7   The opts1 script is given a b option, an illegal option. Getopts sends an error message.

8   An option without a - or + prepended to it is not an option and causes getopts to stop processing arguments.

EXAMPLE   12.70

```
(The Script)
    #!/bin/ksh
    # Program opts2
    # Using getopts -- Second try --
1   while getopts :xy options
    do
2       case $options in
        x) print "you entered -x as an option";;
        y) print "you entered -y as an option";;
3       \?) print $OPTARG is not a valid option 1>&2;;
        esac
    done
    ----------------------------------------------------------------
(The Command Line)
    $ opts2 -x
    you entered -x as an option
    $ opts2 -y
    you entered -y as an option
```

EXAMPLE 12.70 (CONTINUED)

```
        $ opts2 xy
        $ opts2 -xy
        you entered -x as an option
        you entered -y as an option
4       $ opts2 -g
        g is not a valid option
5       $ opts2 -c
        c is not a valid option
```

EXPLANATION

1   The colon preceding the option list prevents the Korn shell from printing an error message for a bad option. However, if the option is a bad option, a question mark will be assigned to the options variable.

2   The case command can be used to test for the question mark, allowing you to print your own error message to standard error.

3   If the options variable is assigned the question mark, this case statement is executed. The question mark is protected with the backslash so that the Korn shell does not see it as a wildcard and try to perform filename substitution.

4   g is not a legal option. The question mark is assigned to the options variable, and OPTARG is assigned the illegal option g.

5   c is not a legal option. The question mark is assigned to the options variable, and OPTARG is assigned the illegal option c.

EXAMPLE 12.71

```
(The Script)
        #!/bin/ksh
        # Program opts3
        # Using getopts -- Third try --
1       while getopts :d options
        do
            case $options in
2           d) print -R "-d is the ON switch";;
3           +d) print -R "+d is the OFF switch";;
            \?) print $OPTARG is not a valid option;;
            esac
        done
    # Need the -R option with print or the shell tries to use -d as a print option
```

EXAMPLE 12.71 (CONTINUED)

```
(The Command Line)
4   $ opts3 -d
    -d is the ON switch
5   $ opts3 +d
    +d is the OFF switch
6   $ opts3 -e
    e is not a valid option
7   $ opts3 e
```

EXPLANATION

1   The while command tests the exit status of getopts; if getopts can successfully process an argument, it returns 0 exit status, and the body of the while loop is entered. The colon prepended to the d option tells getopts not to print an error message if the user enters an invalid option.

2   One of the legal options is –d. If –d is entered as an option, the d (without the dash) is stored in the options variable. (The –R option to the print command allows the first character in the print string to be a dash.)

3   One of the legal options is +d. If +d is entered as an option, the d (with the plus sign) is stored in the options variable.

4   The –d option is a legal option to opts3.

5   The +d option is also a legal option to opts3.

6   The –e option is invalid. A question mark is stored in options if the option is illegal. The illegal argument is stored in OPTARG.

7   The option is prepended with neither a dash nor a plus sign. The getopts command will not process it as an option and returns a nonzero exit status. The while loop is terminated.

EXAMPLE 12.72

```
(The Script)
    #!/bin/ksh
    # Program opts4
    # Using getopts -- Fourth try --
1   alias USAGE='print "usage: opts4 [-x] filename " >&2'
2   while getopts :x: arguments
    do
    case $arguments in
3       x) print "$OPTARG is the name of the argument ";;
4       :) print "Please enter an argument after the -x option" >&2
           USAGE ;;
```

EXAMPLE 12.72 (CONTINUED)

```
5        \?) print "$OPTARG is not a valid option." >&2
             USAGE;;
     esac
6    print "$OPTIND" # The number of the next argument to be processed
     done
```

```
(The Command Line)
7    $ opts4 -x
     Please enter an argument after the -x option
     usage: opts4 [-x] filename
     2
8    $ opts4 -x filex
     filex is the name of the argument
     3
9    $ opts4 -d
     d is not a valid option.
     usage: opts4 [-x] filename
     1
```

EXPLANATION

1   The alias USAGE is assigned the diagnostic error message that will be printed if getopts fails.

2   The while command tests the exit status of getopts; if getopts can successfully process an argument, it returns zero exit status, and the body of the while loop is entered. The colon prepended to the x option tells getopts not to print an error message if the user enters an invalid option. The colon appended to the x option tells getopts that an argument should follow the x option. If the option takes an argument, the argument is stored in the getopts built-in variable, OPTARG.

3   If the x option was given an argument, the argument is stored in the OPTARG variable and will be printed.

4   If an argument was not provided after the x option, a colon is stored in the variable arguments. The appropriate error message is displayed.

5   If an invalid option is entered, the question mark is stored in the variable arguments and an error message is displayed.

6   The special getopts variable, OPTIND, holds the number of the next option to be processed. Its value is always one more than the actual number of command-line arguments.

7   The x option requires an argument. An error message is printed.

8   The name of the argument is filex. The variable OPTARG holds the name of the argument filex.

9   The option d is invalid. The usage message is displayed.

12.13 Security

12.13.1 Privileged Scripts

A script is privileged if the Korn shell is invoked with the -p option. When the privileged option is used and the real UID and/or the real GID are not the same as the effective UID or effective GID, the .profile will not be executed and a system file called etc/suid_profile will be executed instead of the ENV file.

12.13.2 Restricted Shells

When the Korn shell is invoked with the -r option, the shell is restricted. When the shell is restricted, the cd command cannot be used and the SHELL, ENV, and PATH variables cannot be modified or unset; commands cannot be executed if the first character is a backslash; and the redirection operators (>, <, |, >>) are illegal. This option cannot be unset or set with the set command. The command rksh will invoke a restricted shell.

12.14 Built-In Commands

The Korn shell has a number of built-in commands, as shown in Table 12.15.

Table 12.15 Built-In Commands and Their Functions

Command	Function
:	Do-nothing command; returns exit status 0.
. file	The dot command reads and executes a command from file.
break	See "The break Command" on page 699.
continue	See "The continue Command" on page 700.
cd	Changes directory.
echo [args]	Displays arguments.
eval command	Shell scans the command line twice before execution.
exec command	Runs command in place of this shell.
exit [n]	Exit the shell with status n.
export [var]	Makes var known to subshells.

Table 12.15   Built-In Commands and Their Functions (continued)

Command	Function
fc -e [editor] [lnr] first last	Used to edit commands in the history list. If no editor is specified, the value of FCEDIT is used; if FCEDIT is not set, /bin/ed is used. Usually history is aliased to fc -1.

EXAMPLES

fc -1	Lists the last 16 commands on the history list.
fc -e emacs grep	Reads the last grep command into the emacs editor.
fc 25 30	Reads commands 25 through 30 into the editor specified in FCEDIT, by default the ed editor.
fc -e -	Re-executes the last command.
fc -e - Tom=Joe 28	Replaces Tom with Joe in history command 28.
fg	Brings the last background job to the foreground.
fg %n	Brings job number n to the foreground. Type jobs to find the correct job number.

Command	Function
jobs [-1]	Lists the active jobs by number and with the -1 option by PID number.

EXAMPLES

```
$ jobs
[3] + Running      sleep 50&
[1] - Stopped      vi
[2]   Running      sleep%
```

Command	Function
kill [-signal process]	Sends the signal to the PID number or job number of process. See /usr/include/sys/signal.h for a list of signals.

SIGNALS

```
SIGHUP1   /* hangup (disconnect) */
SIGINT 2  /* interrupt */
SIGQUIT 3 /* quit */
SIGILL 4  /* illegal instruction (not reset when caught) */
SIGTRAP 5 /* trace trap (not reset when caught) */
SIGIOT 6  /* IOT instruction */
SIGABRT 6 /* used by abort, replace SIGIOT in the future */
SIGEMT 7  /* EMT instruction */
SIGFPE 8  /* floating-point exception */
SIGKILL 9 /* kill (cannot be caught or ignored) */
SIGBUS 10 /* bus error */
SIGSEGV 11/* segmentation violation */
SIGSYS 12 /* bad argument to system call */
SIGPIPE 13/* write on a pipe with no one to read it */
SIGALRM 14/* alarm clock */
SIGTERM 15/* software termination signal from kill */
```

Table 12.15 Built-In Commands and Their Functions (continued)

Command	Function
kill *(continued)*	SIGURG 16 /* urgent condition on I/O channel */ SIGSTOP 17/* sendable stop signal not from tty */ SIGTSTP 18/* stop signal from tty */ SIGCONT 19/* continue a stopped process */ **EXAMPLES** (To use the kill command and a signal name, strip off the SIG prefix and precede the signal name with a dash.) kill -INT %3 kill -HUP 1256 kill -9 %3 kill %1
getopts	Used in shell scripts to parse command line and check for legal options.
hash	Lists all tracked aliases.
login [username]	
newgrp [arg]	Changes your real group ID to the group ID.
print -[nrRsup]	Replacement for echo. See print.
pwd	Print present working directory.
read [var]	Read line from standard input into variable var.
readonly [var]	Make variable var readonly. Cannot be reset.
return [n]	Exit value given to a function.
set [-aefhknoptuvx- [-o option] [-A arrayname] [arg]]	**EXAMPLES** set Lists all variables and their values. set + Lists all variables without their values. set -o Lists all option settings. set a b c Resets positional parameters $1, $2, $3. set -s Sorts $1, $2, and $3 alphabetically. set -o vi Sets the vi option. set -xv Turns on the xtrace and verbose options for debugging. set -- Unsets all positional parameters. set -- "$x" Sets $1 to the value of x, even if x is -x. set == $x Does pathname expansion on each item in x and then sets the positional parameters to each item. set -A name tom dick harry name[0] is set to tom; name[1] is set to dick; name[2] is set to harry. set +A name joe name[0] is reset to joe, the rest of the array is left alone; name[1] is dick; name[2] is harry.

Table 12.15   Built-In Commands and Their Functions (continued)

Command	Function
set *(continued)*	(To set options, use the –o flag; to unset options, use the +o flag.)
	`set -o ignoreeof`
	Options:
	`allexport` After setting this, exports any variable defined or changed.
	`bgnice` Runs background jobs with a lesser priority; used instead of `nice`.
	`emacs` Sets the `emacs` built-in editor.
	`errexit` The shell exits when a command returns a nonzero exit status.
	`gmacs` Sets the built-in `gmacs` editor.
	`ignoreeof` Ignores the EOF (Ctrl-D) key from terminating the shell. Must use `exit` to exit.
	`keyword` Adds keyword arguments occurring anywhere on the command line to the environment of the shell.
	`markdirs` Puts a trailing backslash on all directory names resulting from filename expansion.
	`monitor` Sets job control.
	`noclobber` Prevents overwriting files using the redirection operator, >. Use >| to force overwrite.
	`noexec` Same as `ksh -n`; reads commands but does not execute them. Used to check for syntax errors in shell scripts.
	`noglob` Disables pathname expansion with `ksh` wildcard metacharacters.
	`nolog` Function definitions will not be stored in the history file.
	`nounset` Displays an error if a variable has not been set.
	`privileged` Turns on privileged mode for setuid programs.
	`trackall` Ksh causes each command to become a tracked alias; automatically turned on for interactive shells.
	`verbose` Echos each line of input to standard error; useful in debugging.
	`vi` Sets the `vi` built-in editor.
	`viraw` Specifies `vi` character at a time input.
	`xtrace` Expands each command and displays it in the PS4 prompt, with variables expanded.
`shift [ n ]`	Shifts positional parameters to the left n times.
`times`	Prints accumulated user and system times for processes run from this shell.
`trap [ arg ] [ n ]`	When shell receives signal n (0, 1, 2, or 15), arg is executed.

Table 12.15   Built-In Commands and Their Functions (continued)

Command	*Function*
type [command]	Prints the type of command; for example, pwd is a built-in shell. In ksh, an alias for whence -v.
typeset [options] [var]	Sets attributes and values for shell variables and functions.
ulimit [options size]	Sets maximum limits on processes.

> **EXAMPLES**
>
> ulimit -a   Display all limits:
> > Time (seconds) unlimited.
> > File (blocks) unlimited.
> > Data (kbytes) 524280.
> > Stack (kbytes) 8192.
> > Memory (kbytes) unlimited.
> > Core dump (blocks) unlimited.
>
> Other Options:
> -c size   Limits core dumps to size blocks.
> -d size   Limits the data size (of executables) to size blocks.
> -f size   Limits the size of files to size blocks (default).
> -m size   Limits the size of physical memory to size K bytes.
> -s size   Limits the size of the stack area to size K bytes.
> -t secs   Limits process execution time to secs seconds.

Command	*Function*
umask [mask]	Without argument, prints out file creation mask for permissions.
umask [octal digits]	User file creation mode mask for owner, group, and others.
unset [name]	Unsets value of variable or function.
wait [pid#n]	Waits for background process with PID number n and report termination status.
whence [command]	Prints information about the command, like ucb whereis.

> **EXAMPLES**
>
> whence -v happy   happy is a function
> whence -v addon   addon is an undefined function
> whence -v ls   ls is a tracked alias for /bin/ls
> whence ls   /bin/ls

12.15 Korn Shell Invocation Arguments

When the Korn shell is involved, it can take options to control its behavior. See Table 12.16.

Table 12.16   Arguments to ksh

Command	*Function*
-a	Automatically exports all variables.
-c cmd	Executes a command string.
-e	Exits when a command returns a nonzero status.
-f	Turns off globbing, the expansion of filename metacharacters.
-h	Causes commands to be treated as tracked aliases.
-i	Sets the interactive mode.
-k	Sets the keyword option. All the key arguments to commands will be made part of the environment.
-m	Causes commands executed in the background to be run in a separate process group, and will continue to run even if Ctrl-C or logout is attempted. Sends a message that the job has terminated when done.
-n	Can be used for debugging. Commands are scanned, but not executed. Can be used with -x and -v options.
-o	Allows options to be set by the names listed in Table 12.15 with the set command.
-p	Turns on privileged mode. Used for running setuid programs.
-r	Sets the restricted mode.
-s	Reads command from stdin, the default.
-t	Causes the shell to exit after executing the first command found in shell input and the -c option is specified.
-u	Any reference to an unset variable is considered an error.
-v	Each line of a script or standard input is printed before any parsing, variable substitution, or other processing is performed. Output is written to standard error. Used for debugging.
-x	Each line of a script or standard input is printed before it is executed. Filename expansion, variable substitution, and command substitution are shown in the output. All output is prepended with the value of the PS4 prompt, a plus sign followed by a space. Lines are written to standard error.

LAB 33: KORN SHELL—GETTING STARTED

1. What shell are you using? How do you know?

2. Do you have a .profile and/or a .kshrc file in your home directory? What is the difference between the .profile and .kshrc? What is the ENV file and how can you invoke it if you make changes in it?

3. What is the default primary prompt? What is the default secondary prompt? Change your primary prompt at the command line so that it contains your login name.

4. What is the purpose of setting each of the following variables?

   a. `set -o ignoreeof`

   b. `set -o noclobber`

   c. `set -o trackall`

   d. `set -o monitor`

   e. `set -o vi`

   Why are these variables set in the ENV file? What is the purpose of the PATH? What are the elements of your PATH variable?

5. What is the difference between a local and an environment variable? How do you list all your variables? How do you list only environment variables? To list all your current option settings, type the following:

   `set -o`

   Which set options are turned on?

6. Create a local variable called myname that contains your full name. Now export the variable. Type the following at the prompt:

   `ksh`

   Was the variable name exported? Type exit to get back to the parent shell. Make the variable name readonly. What is a readonly variable?

7. What are positional parameters normally used for?

   a. Type the following:

   `set apples pears peaches plums`

   Using the positional parameters, print plums. Print apples peaches. Print apples pears peaches plums. Print the number of parameters. Reset the positional parameters to a list of veggies. Print the whole list of veggies. What happened to the fruit list?

   b. Type the following:

   ```
   set --
   print $*
   ```

   What happened?

8. Print the PID of the current shell. Type the following at the prompt:

   ```
   grep $LOGNAME /etc/passwd
   echo $?
   ```

   What does the $? tell you. What does the exit status tell you about the execution of a command?

9. Change both the primary and secondary prompt in your .profile. How do you re-execute the .profile file without logging out and logging back in?

LAB 34: HISTORY

1. What is your HISTSIZE variable set to? What is your HISTFILE variable set to? Check your .kshrc file to see if set -o vi is there. If it has not been set, set it in the .kshrc file and re-execute the file by typing the following:

   ```
   . .kshrc
   ```

2. Type the following commands at the command line:

   ```
   ls
   date
   who
   cal 2 1993
   date +%T
   ```

   Type history or fc -l. What do these commands do? Print your history list in reverse. Print your history list without numbers. Print the current command and the five preceding it. Print everything from the tenth command to the present. Print everything between the most recent ls command to the most recent cal command.

3. Using the r command, re-execute the last command. Re-execute the last command that started with the letter d. Change the cal command year output to 1897. Change the date command +%T argument to find the current hour.

4. If your history is set, press the Esc key at the command line and use the K key to move up through the history list. Change the ls command to ls -alF and re-execute it.

5. Check to see if the FCEDIT variable has been set by typing the env command. If it has not been set, type the following at the command line:

   ```
   export FCEDIT=vi
   ```

   Now type the following at the command line:

   ```
   fc -1 -4
   ```

   What happened?

6. How do you *comment* a line from your history list, so that it will be placed on the list without being executed?

7. At the command line, type the following:

   ```
   touch a1 a2 a3 apples bears balloons a4 a45
   ```

Now using the history Esc sequences, do the following:

   a. Print the first file beginning with a.

   b. Print a list of all files beginning with a.

   c. Print the first file beginning with b.

   d. Print a command and comment it.

8. At the command line, type the following:

```
print a b c d e
```

Using the history Esc underscore command, change the command to the following:

```
print e
```

Using the history Esc underscore command, change the first command to output:

```
print c
```

LAB 35: ALIASES AND FUNCTIONS

1. What command lists all the aliases currently set?

2. What command lists all the tracked aliases?

3. Create aliases for the following commands:

```
date +%T
history -n
ls -alF
rm -i
cp -i
print
```

4. How do you export an alias?

5. Create a function that contains the following commands:

```
ls -F
print -n "The time is"
date +%T
print -n "Your present working directory is"
pwd
```

6. Execute the function.

7. Now create your own functions, using positional parameters to pass arguments.

8. What command lists the functions and their definitions?

9. Try some of the print options.

LAB 36: SHELL METACHARACTERS

1. Create a directory called meta. Cd to that directory. Use touch to create the following files (the touch command creates a new empty file or updates the timestamp on an existing file):

   abc abc1 abc2 abc2191 Abc1 ab2 ab3 ab345 abc29 abc9 abc91 abc21xyz abc2121 noone nobody nothing nowhere

2. Do the following:

   a. List all files that start with a lowercase a.

   b. List all files starting with uppercase A followed by two characters.

   c. List all files that end in a number.

   d. List all files that match one number after abc.

   e. List all files that match nothing or noone.

   f. List all files that match one or more numbers after abc.

   g. List all files that do not contain the pattern abc.

   h. List all files that contain ab followed by a 3 or 4.

   i. List all files starting with a or A, followed by b, and ending in one number.

   j. What is the error message if there is not a match?

LAB 37: TILDE EXPANSION, QUOTES, AND COMMAND SUBSTITUTION

1. Use the tilde to do the following:

   a. Print your home directory.

   b. Print your neighbor's home directory.

   c. Print your previous working directory.

   d. Print your current working directory.

2. What variable holds the value of your present working directory? What variable holds the value of your previous working directory?

3. Use the – to go to your previous working directory.

4. Use the print command to send the following output to the screen. (The word enclosed in < > is a variable name that will be expanded, and words enclosed in [ ] are output of commands that have been executed; i.e., use command substitution.)

   ```
   Hi <LOGNAME> how's your day going?
   "No, <LOGNAME> you can't use the car tonight!", she cried.
   The time is [ Sun Feb 22 13:19:27 PST 2004 ]
   The name of this machine is [ eagle ] and the time is [ 31:19:27 ]
   ```

5. Create a file that contains a list of usernames. Now create a variable called `nlist` that contains the list of usernames, extracted by using command substitution.

   a. Print out the value of the variable. How does command substitution affect the formatting of a list?

   b. Test this by setting a variable to the output of the `ps -eaf` command.

   c. What happened to the formatting?

LAB 38: REDIRECTION

1. Go into the editor and create the following two-line text file called ex6:

```
Last time I went to the beach I found a sea shell.
While in Kansas I found a corn shell.
```

2. Now append this line to your ex6 file:

```
The National Enquirer says someone gave birth to a shell, called the born shell.
```

3. Mail the ex6 file to yourself.

4. Using a pipe, count the number of lines (`wc -l`) in your ex6 file.

5. To list all set options, type the following:

```
set -o
```

Do you have the `noclobber` variable set? If not, type the following:

```
set -o noclobber
```

What happened?

6. Type the following at the command line:

```
cat << FINIS
How are you $LOGNAME
The time is `date`Bye!!
FINIS
```

What printed?

7. Now try this using tabs:

```
cat <<- END
    hello there
    how are you
END
```

What printed?

8. Type the following at the command line:

```
kat file 2> error || print kat failed
```

What happened? Why?

9. Now type the following at the command line:

```
cat zombie 2> errorfile || print cat failed
```

What happened? Why? How does the && operator work? Try your own command to test it.

10. Use the find command to print all files that begin with an a from the root directory down. Put the standard output in a file called foundit and send the errors to /dev/null.

LAB 39: JOB CONTROL

1. At the command line type the following:

```
mail <user>Press Ctrl-z
```

Now type:

```
jobs
```

What is the number in the square brackets?

2. Now type:

```
sleep 300
jobs
bg
```

What does bg do? What do the + and – signs indicate?

3. Kill the mail job using job control.

4. Go into the editor. Type ^Z to stop the job. Now bring the stopped vi job back into the *foreground*. What command did you type?

5. Type the following command:

```
jobs -l
```

What is the output?

6. What is the TMOUT variable used for?

7. How much time was spent by the kernel when executing the following command:

```
(sleep 5 ; ps -eaf )
```

LAB 40: WRITING THE info SHELL SCRIPT

1. Write a program called info. Make sure you make the program executable with the chmod command before you try to execute it.

2. The program should contain comments.

3. The program should do the following when executed:

   a. Output the number of users logged on.

   b. Output the time and date.

c. Output the present working directory.

d. List all directory files in the parent directory.

e. Print out the name of the shell being used.

f. Print a line from the password file containing your login name.

g. Print your user ID.

h. Print the name of this machine.

i. Print your disk usage.

j. Print a calendar for this month.

k. Tell the user good-bye and print the hour in nonmilitary time.

LAB 41: VARIABLE EXPANSION OF SUBSTRINGS

1. Write a script that will do the following:

a. Set a variable called mypath to your home directory.

b. Print the value of mypath.

c. Print just the last element of the path in mypath.

d. Print the first element of the path in mypath.

e. Print all but the last element of the variable mypath.

LAB 42: THE lookup SCRIPT

1. Create a file called datafile if it has not been provided for you on the CD. It will consist of colon-separated fields:

a. First and last name

b. Phone number

c. Address (street, city, state, and ZIP)

d. Birth date (04/12/66)

e. Salary

2. Put ten entries in your file. Write a script called lookup that will do the following:

a. Welcome the user.

b. Print the names and phone numbers for all the users in datafile.

c. Print the number of lines in datafile.

d. Tell the user good-bye.

LAB 43: USING typeset

1. Write a script that will do the following:

   a. Ask the user to type in his or her first and last name.

   b. Store the answers in two variables.

   c. Use the new ksh read command.

2. Use the typeset command to convert the first and last name variables to all lowercase letters.

3. Test to see if the person's name is tom jones. If it is, print Welcome, Tom Jones; if it is not, print, Are you happy today, FIRSTNAME LASTNAME?. (The user's first and last names are converted to uppercase letters.)

4. Have the user type in an answer to the question and use the new ksh test command to see whether the answer is yes or no. If yes, have your script say something nice to him or her, and if no, tell the user to go home and give the current time of day.

5. Rewrite the lookup script.

   a. The script will ask the user if he or she would like to add an entry to datafile.

   b. If the user answers yes or y, ask for the following input:

   ```
   Name
   Phone number
   Address
   Birth date
   Salary
   ```

   A variable for each item will be assigned the user input.

EXAMPLE

```
print -n "What is the name of the person you are adding to the file?"
read name The information will be appended to the datafile.
```

LAB 44: THE if/else CONSTRUCT AND THE let COMMAND

1. Write a script called grades that will ask the user for his or her numeric grade on a test.

   a. The script will test that the grade is within the possible grade range, 0 to 100.

   b. The script will tell the user if he or she got an A, B, C, D, or F.

2. Write a script called calc that will perform the functions of a simple calculator. The script will provide a simple menu:

   ```
   [a] Add
   [s] Subtract
   [m] Multiply
   ```

    [d] Divide
    [r] Remainder

3. The user will choose one of the letters from the menu.

4. The user will then be asked to enter two integers between 0 and 100.

5. If the numbers are out of the range, an error message will be printed and the script will exit.

6. The program will perform the arithmetic on the two integers.

7. The answer will be printed in base 10, 8, and 16.

LAB 45: THE case STATEMENT

1. Write a script timegreet that will do the following:

   a. Provide a comment section at the top of the script, with your name, the date, and the purpose of this program.

   b. Convert the following program using case statements:

   ```
   # The timegreet script by Ellie Quigley
   you=$LOGNAME
   hour=`date | awk '{print substr($4, 1, 2)}'`
   print "The time is: $(date)"
   if (( hour > 0 && $hour < 12 ))
   then
        print "Good morning, $you!"
   elif (( hour == 12 ))
   then
        print "Lunch time!"
   elif (( hour > 12 && $hour < 16 ))
   then
        print "Good afternoon, $you!"
   else
        print "Good night, $you!"
   fi
   ```

2. Rewrite the lookup script, replacing the if/elif construct with the case command. Add one more menu item:

   ```
   1) Add Entry
   2) Delete Entry
   3) Update Entry
   4) View Entry
   5) Exit
   ```

LAB 46: THE select LOOP

1. Write a script that will do the following:

   a. Provide a comment section at the top of the script, with your name, the date, and the purpose of this program.

b. Use the select loop to provide a menu of foods. The output will resemble the following:

```
$ foods
1) steak and potatoes
2) fish and chips
3) soup and salad
Please make a selection. 1
Stick to your ribs
Watch your cholesterol
Enjoy your meal.

$ foods
1) steak and potatoes
2) fish and chips
3) soup and salad
Please make a selection. 2
British are coming
Enjoy your meal.

$ foods
1) steak and potatoes
2) fish and chips
3) soup and salad
Please make a selection. 3
Health foods...
Dieting is so boring.
Enjoy your meal.

$ foods
1) steak and potatoes
2) fish and chips
3) soup and salad
Please make a selection. 5
Not on the menu today!
```

2. Rewrite the lookup script using the select command to create a main menu and a submenu. The menu will resemble the following:

```
1) Add Entry
2) Delete Entry
3) Update Entry
4) View Entry
      a) Name
      b) Phone
      c) Address
      d) Birthday
      e) Salary
5) Exit
```

LAB 47: AUTOLOADING FUNCTIONS

Steps for autoloading a function:

1. Make a directory called myfunctions.

2. Change directory to myfunctions and use the editor to create a file called good-bye.

3. Insert in the good-bye file a function called good-bye, spelled exactly the same as the filename.

4. The good-bye function contains:

```
function good-bye {
print The current time is $(date)
print "The name of this script is $0"
print See you later $1
print Your machine is `uname -n`
}
```

5. Write and quit the editor. You now have a file containing a function with the same name.

6. Go to your home directory. Modify the .kshrc file in the editor by typing the following line:

```
FPATH=$HOME/myfunctions
```

7. Exit the editor, and to execute the .kshrc in the current environment, use the dot command.

8. In the timegreet script you wrote in Lab 45, include the following lines:

```
autoload good-bye
good-bye $LOGNAME
```

9. Run the timegreet script. The good-bye function output will appear.

10. Create functions for each of the menu items in the lookup script. Store the functions in a file called lookup_functions in a directory called myfunctions.

11. Autoload the functions in your lookup script and make the function calls for the corresponding cases.

12. Use the trap command so that if the user enters a menu selection other than an integer value, the trap command will print an error to the screen, and cause the script to ask the user to re-enter the correct data type.

chapter

13

The Interactive
Bash Shell

13.1 Introduction

With an interactive shell, the standard input, output, and error are tied to a terminal. When using the Bourne Again shell (Bash) interactively, you type UNIX/Linux commands at the bash prompt and wait for a response. Bash provides you with a large assortment of built-in commands and command-line shortcuts, such as history, aliases, file and command completion, command-line editing, and many more. Some of the features were present in the standard UNIX Bourne shell and Korn shell, but the GNU project has expanded the shell to include a number of new features as well adding POSIX compliancy. With the release of Bash 2.x, so many features of the UNIX Korn shell and C shell have been included that the bash shell is a fully functional shell at both the interactive and programming level, while upwardly compatible with the standard Bourne shell. For UNIX users, bash offers an alternative to the standard shells, sh, csh, and ksh.[1]

This chapter focuses on how you interact with bash at the command line and how to customize your working environment. You will learn how to take advantage of all shortcuts and built-in features in order to create an efficient and fun working environment. Chapter 14 takes you a step further. Then you will be ready to write bash shell scripts to further tailor the working environment for yourself by automating everyday tasks and developing sophisticated scripts, and if you are an administrator, doing the same not only for yourself but also for whole groups of users.

13.1.1 Versions of bash

The Bourne Again shell is a Capricorn, born on January 10, 1988, fathered by Brian Fox and later adopted by Chet Ramey, who now officially maintains bash, enhances it, and fixes bugs. The first version of bash was 0.99. The current version (as of this writing) is version 2.05. Major enhancements were completed in version 2.0, but some operating

---

1. Although bash is traditionally the default shell for Linux platforms, it now comes bundled with Solaris 8.

753

systems are still using version 1.14.7. All versions are freely available under the GNU public license.[2] There is even bash for Windows! To see what version you are using, use the --version option to bash or print the value of the BASH_VERSION environment variable.

EXAMPLE 13.1

```
(UNIX)
$ bash --version
GNU bash, version 2.05.0(1)-release (sparc-sun-solaris)
Copyright 2000 Free Software Foundation, Inc.

$ echo $BASH_VERSION
2.05.0(1)-release
```

EXAMPLE 13.2

```
(Linux)
$ bash --version
GNU bash, version 2.05.0(1)-release (i386-redhat-linux-gnu)
Copyright 2000 Free Software Foundation, Inc.
```

13.1.2 Startup

If the bash shell is your login shell, it follows a chain of processes before you see a shell prompt. See Figure 13.1.

When the system boots, the first process to run is called init, PID #1. It spawns a getty process. This process opens up the terminal ports, providing a place where standard input comes from and a place where standard output and errors go, and puts a login prompt on your screen. The /bin/login program is then executed. The login program prompts for a password, encrypts and verifies the password, sets up an initial environment, and starts up the login shell, /bin/bash, the last entry in the passwd file. The bash process looks for the system file, /etc/profile, and executes its commands. It then looks in the user's home directory for an initialization file called .bash_profile. After executing commands from .bash_profile,[3] it will execute a command from the user's ENV file, usually called .bashrc, and finally the default dollar sign ($) prompt appears on your screen and the shell waits for commands. (For more on initialization files, see "The Environment" on page 756.)

---

2. To get the latest version of bash, visit www.delorie.com/gnu/.
3. There are a number of different initialization files used by bash; they are discussed on the next pages.

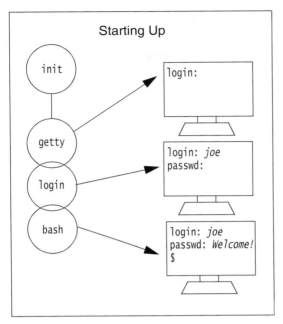

Figure 13.1 Starting the bash shell.

Changing the Shell at the Command Line. If you want to start another shell from the command line temporarily (without changing the /etc/passwd file), just type the name of the shell. For example, if you are currently using the standard Bourne shell and would rather have bash as your shell, you can change the shell at the command line simply by typing bash.

EXAMPLE 13.3

```
1   $ ps
    PID    TTY    TIME   CMD
    1574   pts/6  0:00   sh

2   $ bash
    bash-2.05$

3   bash-2.05$ ps
    PID    TTY    TIME   CMD
    1574   pts/6  0:00   sh
    1576   pts/6  0:00   bash
```

EXPLANATION

1   The output of the ps command shows what processes are running. Currently, sh (the Bourne shell) is running.

2   At the Bourne shell prompt, the user enters bash and starts up the Bourne Again shell. A new prompt appears.

3   At the bash prompt, the ps command is executed. The output shows that two shells are running and the current shell is now bash.

13.2 The Environment

The environment of a process consists of variables, open files, the current working directory, functions, resource limits, signals, and so forth. It defines those features that are inherited from one shell to the next and the configuration for the working environment. The configuration for the user's shell is defined in the shell initialization files.

13.2.1   The Initialization Files

The bash shell has a number of startup files that are sourced. Sourcing a file causes all settings in the file to become part of the current shell; that is, a subshell is not created. (The source command is discussed in "The source or dot Command" on page 773.) The initialization files are sourced depending on the whether the shell is a login shell, an interactive shell (but not the login shell), or a noninteractive shell (a shell script).

When you log on, the .bash_profile in the user's home directory is sourced. It sets the user's aliases and functions and then sets user-specific environment variables and startup scripts.

If the user doesn't have a .bash_profile, but does have a file called .bash_login, that file will be sourced, and if he doesn't have a .bash_login, but does have a .profile, it will be sourced.

The /etc/profile File.   The /etc/profile file is a systemwide initialization file set up by the system administrator to perform tasks when the user logs on. It is executed when bash starts up. It is also available to all Bourne and Korn shell users on the system and normally performs such tasks as checking the mail spooler for new mail and displaying the message of the day from the /etc/motd file. (The following examples will make more sense after you have completed this chapter.)

EXAMPLE 13.4

```
(Sample /etc/profile)
# /etc/profile
# Systemwide environment and startup programs
# Functions and aliases go in /etc/bashrc
1    PATH="$PATH:/usr/X11R6/bin"
2    PS1="[\u@\h \W]\\$ "
```

EXAMPLE 13.4 (CONTINUED)

```
3    ulimit -c 1000000
4    if [ `id -gn` = `id -un` -a `id -u` -gt 14 ]; then
5        umask 002
     else
         umask 022
     fi
6    USER=`id -un`
7    LOGNAME=$USER
8    MAIL="/var/spool/mail/$USER"
9    HOSTNAME=`/bin/hostname`
10   HISTSIZE=1000
11   HISTFILESIZE=1000
12   export PATH PS1 HOSTNAME HISTSIZE HISTFILESIZE USER LOGNAME MAIL
13   for i in /etc/profile.d/*.sh ; do
14       if [ -x $i ]; then
15           . $i
         fi
16   done
17   unset i #
```

EXPLANATION

1 The PATH variable is assigned locations where the shell should search for commands.

2 The primary prompt is assigned. It will be displayed in the shell window as the user's name (\u), the @ symbol, the host machine (\W), and a dollar sign.

3 The ulimit command (a shell built-in command) is set to limit the maximum size of core files created to 1,000,000 bytes. Core files are memory dumps of programs that have crashed, and they take up a lot of disk space.

4 This line reads: If the user's group name is equal to the user's name and the user's ID number is greater than 14 . . . (see line 5)

5 . . . then set the umask to 002. When directories are created they will get 775 permissions and files will get 664 permissions. Otherwise, the umask is set to 022, giving 755 to directories and 644 to files.

6 The USER variable is assigned the username (id -un).

7 The LOGNAME variable is set to the value in $USER.

8 The MAIL variable is assigned the path to the mail spooler where the user's mail is saved.

9 The HOSTNAME variable is assigned the name of the user's host machine.

10 The HISTSIZE variable is set to 1000. HISTSIZE controls the number of history items that are remembered (from the history list stored in the shell's memory) and saved in the history file after the shell exits.

EXPLANATION (CONTINUED)

11 The HISTFILESIZE is set to limit the number of commands stored in the history file to 1000, that is, the history file is truncated after it reaches 1,000 lines. (See "History" on page 785.)

12 These variables are exported so that they will be available in subshells and child processes.

13 For each file (ending in .sh) in the etc/profile.d directory . . . (see line 14)

14 . . . check to see if the file is executable, and if it is . . . (see line 15)

15 . . . execute (source) the file with the dot command. The files in the /etc/profile.d directory (lang.sh and mc.sh, respectively) set the character and font sets and create a function called mc that starts up a visual/browser file manager program called Midnight Commander. To see how the file manager works, type mc at the bash prompt.

16 The done keyword marks the end of the for loop.

17 The variable i is unset, that is, removed from shell's name space. The value of i is whatever was assigned to it while in the for loop, if anything was assigned at all.

The ~/.bash_profile File.   If the ~/.bash_profile is found in the user's home directory, it is sourced after the /etc/profile. If ~/.bash_profile doesn't exist, bash will look for another user-defined file, ~./bash_login, and source it, and if ~./bash_login doesn't exist, it will source the ~/.profile, if it exists. Only one of the three files (~/.bash_profile, ~/.bash_login, or ~/.profile) will be sourced. Bash will also check to see if the user has a .bashrc file and then source it.

EXAMPLE 13.5

```
(Sample .bash_profile)
    # .bash_profile
    # The file is sourced by bash only when the user logs on.

    # Get the aliases and functions
1   if [ -f ~/.bashrc ]; then
2       . ~/.bashrc
    fi

    # User-specific environment and startup programs
3   PATH=$PATH:$HOME/bin
4   ENV=$HOME/.bashrc      # or BASH_ENV=$HOME/.bashrc
5   USERNAME="root"
6   export USERNAME ENV PATH
7   mesg n
8   if [ $TERM = linux ]
    then
        startx    # Start the X Window system
    fi
```

EXPLANATION

1 If there is a file called .bashrc in the user's home directory . . . (see line 2)

2 . . . execute (source) the .bashrc file for the login shell.

3 The PATH variable is appended with a path to the user's bin directory, normally the place where shell scripts are stored.

4 The BASH_ENV[a] (ENV) file is set to the pathname for the .bashrc file, an initialization file that will be sourced for interactive bash shells and scripts only if the BASH_ENV (ENV) variable is set. The .bashrc file contains user-defined aliases and functions.

5 The variable USERNAME is set to root.

6 The variables are exported so that they are available to subshells, and other processes will know about them.

7 The mesg command is executed with the n option, disallowing others to write to the terminal.

8 If the value of the TERM variable is linux, then startx will start the X Window system (the graphical user interface allowing multiple virtual consoles), rather than starting an interactive session in the Linux console window. Because the ~/.bash_profile is only sourced when you log in, the login shell would be the best place to start up your X Windows session.

a. BASH_ENV is used by versions of bash starting at 2.0.

The BASH_ENV (ENV) Variable. Before bash version 2.0, the BASH_ENV file was simply called the ENV file (same as in Korn shell). The BASH_ENV (ENV) variable is set in the ~/.bash_profile. It is assigned the name of a file that will be executed every time an interactive bash shell or bash script is started. The BASH_ENV (ENV) file will contain special bash variables and aliases. The name is conventionally .bashrc, but you can call it anything you want. The BASH_ENV (ENV) file is not processed when the privileged option is on (bash -p or set -o privileged) or the --norc command-line option is used (bash -norc or bash --norc if using bash 2.x+).

The .bashrc File. The BASH_ENV (ENV) variable is assigned (by convention) the name .bashrc. This file is automatically sourced every time a new or interactive bash shell or bash script starts. It contains settings that pertain only to the bash shell.

EXAMPLE 13.6

```
(Sample .bashrc)
# If the .bashrc file exists, it is in the user's home directory.
# It contains aliases (nicknames for commands) and user-defined functions.

# .bashrc
# User-specific aliases and functions
```

EXAMPLE 13.6 (CONTINUED)

```
1    set -o vi
2    set -o noclobber
3    set -o ignoreeof
4    alias rm='rm -i'
     alias cp='cp -i'
     alias mv='mv -i'
5    stty erase ^h
     # Source global definitions
6    if [ -f /etc/bashrc ]; then
          . /etc/bashrc
     fi
7    case "$-" in
8        *i*) echo This is an interactive bash shell
             ;;
9        *)   echo This shell is noninteractive
             ;;
     esac
10   history_control=ignoredups
11   function cd { builtin cd $1; echo $PWD; }
```

EXPLANATION

1   The set command with the –o switch turns on or off special built-in options. (See "The set –o Options" on page 763.) If the switch is –o, a minus sign, the option is turned on, and if a plus sign, the option is turned off. The vi option allows interactive command-line editing. For example, set -o vi turns on interactive command-line editing, whereas set vi +o turns it off. (See Table 13.1 on page 764.)

2   The noclobber option is turned on, which prevents the user from overwriting files when using redirection; for example, sort filex > filex. (See "Standard I/O and Redirection" on page 844.)

3   When exiting a shell, normally you can type ^D (Ctrl-D). With ignoreeof set, you must type exit.

4   The alias for rm, rm -i, causes rm to be interactive (-i), that is, it will ask the user if it's okay to remove files before actually removing them. The alias for the cp command, cp -i, causes the copy to be interactive.

5   The stty command is used to set the terminal backspace key to erase. ^H represents the Backspace key.

6   If a file called /etc/bashrc exists, source it.

7   If the shell is interactive, the special variable, $-, will contain an i. If not, you are probably running a script. The case command evaluates $-.

8   If the value returned from $- matches *i* (i.e., any string containing an i), then the shell prints This is an interactive bash shell.

EXPLANATION (CONTINUED)

9 Otherwise, the shell prints This shell is noninteractive. If you start up a script or a new shell at the prompt, you will be able to tell whether your shell is interactive. It is only here to let you test your understanding of the terms "interactive" and "noninteractive" shell.

10 The history_control setting is used to control how commands are saved in the history file. This line reads: Don't save commands in the history file if they're already there; that is, ignore duplicates.

11 This is a user-defined function. When the user changes directories, the present working directory, PWD, is printed. The function is named cd and contains within its definition the command cd. The special built-in command, called builtin, precedes the cd command within the function definition to prevent the function from going into an infinite recursion; that is, from calling itself indefinitely.

The /etc/bashrc File. Systemwide functions and aliases can be set in the /etc/bashrc file. The primary prompt is often set here.

EXAMPLE 13.7

```
(Sample /etc/bashrc)

    # Systemwide functions and aliases
    # Environment stuff goes in /etc/profile

    # For some unknown reason bash refuses to inherit
    # PS1 in some circumstances that I can't figure out.
    # Putting PS1 here ensures that it gets loaded every time.

1   PS1="[\u@\h \W]\\$ "
2   alias which="type -path"
```

EXPLANATION

1 Systemwide functions and aliases are set here. The primary bash prompt is set to the name of the user (\u), and @ symbol, the host machine (\h), the basename of the current working directory, and a dollar sign. (See Table 13.2 on page 769.) This prompt will appear for all interactive shells.

2 Aliases, nicknames for commands, are usually set in the user's .bashrc file. The alias was preset and is available when bash starts up. You use it when you want to find out where a program resides on disk; that is, what directory it is found in (e.g., which ls will print /bin/ls).

The ~/.profile File.   The .profile file is a user-defined initialization file. It is found
in the user's home directory, and sourced once at login if running sh (Bourne shell).
Because this file is used by the Bourne shell, it should not contain any bash-specific settings. If running bash, .profile will be run if bash cannot find any other of the initialization files listed previously. It allows a user to customize and modify his or her shell
environment. Environment and terminal settings are normally put here, and if a window
application or database application is to be initiated, it is started here.

EXAMPLE   13.8

```
(Sample .profile)
# A login initialization file sourced when running as sh or the #.bash_profile or
# .bash_login are not found.

1    TERM=xterm
2    HOSTNAME=`uname -n`
3    EDITOR=/bin/vi
4    PATH=/bin:/usr/ucb:/usr/bin:/usr/local:/etc:/bin:/usr/bin:.
5    PS1="$HOSTNAME $ > "
6    export TERM HOSTNAME EDITOR PATH PS1
7    stty erase ^h
8    go () { cd $1; PS1=`pwd`; PS1=`basename $PS1`; }
9    trap '$HOME/.logout' EXIT
10   clear
```

EXPLANATION

1   The TERM variable is assigned the value of the terminal type, xterm.

2   Because the uname -n command is enclosed in backquotes, the shell will perform
    command substitution; that is, the output of the command (the name of the host
    machine) will be assigned to the variable HOSTNAME.

3   The EDITOR variable is assigned /bin/vi. Programs such as mail and history will now
    have this variable available when defining an editor.

4   The PATH variable is assigned the directory entries that the shell searches in order
    to find a UNIX/Linux program. If, for example, you type ls, the shell will search
    the PATH until it finds that program in one of the listed directories. If it never finds
    the program, the shell will tell you so.

5   The primary prompt is assigned the value of HOSTNAME, the machine name, and the
    $ and > symbols.

6   All of the variables listed are exported. They will be known by child processes
    started from this shell.

7   The stty command sets terminal options. The Erase key is set to ^H, so that when
    you press the Backspace key, the letter typed preceding the cursor is erased.

8 A function called go is defined. The purpose of this function is to take one argument, a directory name, then cd to that directory and set the primary prompt to the present working directory. The basename command removes all but the last entry of the path. The prompt will show you the current directory.

9 The trap command is a signal-handling command. When you exit the shell, that is, log out, the .logout file will be executed. The .logout file is a user-defined file containing commands that will be executed just before logging out, commands that will clean up temp files, log the time of logout, and so forth.

10 The clear command clears the screen.

The ~/.bash-logout File.   When the user logs out (exits the login shell), if a file called ~/.bash_logout exists, it is sourced. This file normally contains commands to clean up temporary files, truncate the history file, record the time of logout, and perform other housekeeping tasks.

Options to Prevent Startup Files from Being Executed.   If bash is invoked with the --noprofile option (for example, bash --noprofile), then the /etc/profile, ~/.bash_profile, ~/.bash_login, or ~/.profile startup files will not be sourced.

   If invoked with the -p option (e.g., bash -p), bash will not read the user's ~/.profile file.

   If bash is invoked as sh (Bourne shell), it tries to mimic the behavior of the Bourne shell as closely as possible. For a login shell, it attempts to source only /etc/profile and ~/.profile, in that order. The -noprofile option may still be used to disable this behavior. If the shell is invoked as sh, it does not attempt to source any other startup files.

The .inputrc File.   Another default initalization file, .inputrc, is also read when bash starts up. This file, if it exists in the user's home directory, contains variables to customize keystroke behavior and settings that bind strings, macros, and control functions to keys. The names for the key bindings and what they do are found in the Readline library, a library that is used by applications that manipulate text. The bindings are used particularly by the built-in emacs and vi editors when performing command-line editing. (See "Command-Line Editing" on page 793 for more on readline.)

13.2.2 Setting bash Options with the Built-In set and shopt Commands

The set -o Options.   The set command can take options when the -o switch is used. Options allow you to customize the shell environment. They are either on or off, and are normally set in the BASH_ENV (ENV) file. Many of the options for the set command are set with an abbreviated form. For example, set -o noclobber can also be written, set -C. (See Table 13.1.)

Table 13.1   The Built-In set Command Options

Name of Option	Shortcut Switch	What It Does
allexport	-a	Automatically marks new or modified variables for export from the time the option is set, until unset.
braceexpand	-B	Enables brace expansion, and is a default setting.
emacs		For command-line editing, uses the emacs built-in editor, and is a default setting.
errexit	-e	If a command returns a nonzero exit status (fails), exits. Not set when reading initialization files.
histexpand	-H	Enables ! and !! when performing history substitution, and is a default setting.
history		Enables command-line history; on by default.
ignoreeof		Disables EOF (Ctrl-D) from exiting a shell; must type exit. Same as setting shell variable IGNOREEOF=10.
keyword	-k	Places keyword arguments in the environment for a command.
interactive-comments		For interactive shells, a leading # is used to comment out any text remaining on the line.
monitor	-m	Allows job control.
noclobber	-C	Protects files from being overwritten when redirection is used.
noexec	-n	Reads commands, but does not execute them. Used to check the syntax of scripts. Not on when running interactively.
noglob	-d	Disables pathname expansion; that is, turns off wildcards.
notify	-b	Notifies user when background job finishes.
nounset	-u	Displays an error when expanding a variable that has not been set.
onecmd	-t	Exits after reading and executing one command.
physical	-P	If set, does not follow symbolic links when typing cd or pwd. The physical directory is used instead.
posix		Shell behavior is changed if the default operation doesn't match the POSIX standard.
privileged	-p	When set, the shell does not read the .profile or ENV file and shell functions are not inherited from the environment; automatically set for setuid scripts.

Table 13.1 The Built-In set Command Options (continued)

Name of Option	Shortcut Switch	What It Does
verbose	-v	Turns on the verbose mode for debugging.
vi		For command-line editing, uses the vi built-in editor.
xtrace	-x	Turns on the echo mode for debugging.

FORMAT

```
set -o option   # Turns on the option.
set +o option   # Turns off the option.
set -[a-z]   # Abbreviation for an option; the minus turns it on.
set +[a-z]   # Abbreviation for an option; the plus turns it off.
```

EXAMPLE 13.9

```
1    set -o allexport
2    set +o allexport
3    set -a
4    set +a
```

EXPLANATION

1   Sets the allexport option. This option causes all variables to be automatically exported to subshells.

2   Unsets the allexport option. All variables will now be local in the current shell.

3   Sets the allexport option. Same as 1. Not every option has an abbreviation. (See Table 13.1.)

4   Unsets the allexport option. Same as 2.

EXAMPLE 13.10

```
1 $ set -o
  braceexpand        on
  errexit            off
  hashall            on
  histexpand         on
  keyword            off
  monitor            on
  noclobber          off
  noexec             off
  noglob             off
  notify             off
```

EXAMPLE   13.10 (CONTINUED)

```
nounset                 off
onecmd                  off
physical                off
privileged              off
verbose                 off
xtrace                  off
history                 on
ignoreeof               off
interactive-comments    on
posix                   off
emacs                   off
vi                      on

2   $ set -o noclobber
3   $ date > outfile
4   $ ls > outfile
    bash: outfile: Cannot clobber existing file.
5   $ set +o noclobber
6   $ ls > outfile
7   $ set -C
```

EXPLANATION

1   With the -o option, the set command lists all the options currently set or not set.

2   To set an option, the -o option is used. The noclobber option is set. It protects you from overwriting files when using redirection. Without noclobber, the file to the right of the > symbol is truncated if it exists, and created if it doesn't exist.

3   The output of the UNIX/Linux date command is redirected to a file called outfile.

4   This time, the outfile exists. By attempting to redirect the output of ls to outfile, the shell complains that the file already exists. Without noclobber set, it would be clobbered.

5   With the +o option to the set command, noclobber is turned off.

6   This time, trying to overwrite outfile is fine because noclobber is no longer set.

7   Using the -C switch to the set command is an alternate way of turning on noclobber. +C would turn it off.

The shopt Built-In (Version 2.x+).   The shopt (*shell options*) built-in command is used in newer versions of bash as an alternative to the set command. In many ways shopt duplicates the set built-in command, but it adds more options for configuring the shell. See Table 13.27 on page 855 for a list of all the shopt options. In the following example, shopt with the -p option prints all the available options settings. The -u switch indicates an unset option and -s indicates one that is currently set.

EXAMPLE 13.11

```
1   $ shopt -p
    shopt -u cdable_vars
    shopt -u cdspell
    shopt -u checkhash
    shopt -u checkwinsize
    shopt -s cmdhist
    shopt -u dotglob
    shopt -u execfail
    shopt -s expand_aliases
    shopt -u extglob
    shopt -u histreedit
    shopt -u histappend
    shopt -u histverify
    shopt -s hostcomplete
    shopt -u huponexit
    shopt -s interactive_comments
    shopt -u lithist
    shopt -u mailwarn
    shopt -u nocaseglob
    shopt -u nullglob
    shopt -s promptvars
    shopt -u restricted_shell
    shopt -u shift_verbose
    shopt -s sourcepath
2   $ shopt -s cdspell
3   $ shopt -p cdspell
    shopt -s cdspell
4   $ cd /hame
    /home
5   $ pwd
    /home
6   $ cd /ur/lcal/ban
    /usr/local/man
7   $ shopt -u cdspell
8   $ shopt -p cdspell
    shopt -u cdspell
```

EXPLANATION

1   With the -p (print) option, the shopt command lists all settable shell options and their current values, either set (-s) or unset (-u).

2   With the -s option, shopt sets (or turns on) an option. The cdspell option causes the shell to correct minor spelling errors on directory names given as arguments to the cd command. It will correct simple typos, insert missing letters, and even transpose letters if it can.

3   With the -p option and the name of the option, shopt indicates whether the option is set. The option has been set (-s).

EXPLANATION (CONTINUED)

4   In this example, the user tries to cd to his or her home directory, but misspells home. The shell fixes the spelling and hame becomes home. The directory is changed to /home.

5   The output of the pwd command displays the current working directory, showing that the directory was really changed even though the user spelled it wrong.

6   This time the directory name is missing letters and has a misspelling for the last entry, ban. The shell makes a pretty good attempt to spell out the correct pathname by inserting the missing letters, and correcting ban to man. Because the b in ban is the first misspelled character, the shell searches in the directory for an entry that might end with a and n. It finds man.

7   With the -u switch,[a] shopt unsets (or turns off) the option.

8   With the -p switch and the name of the option, shopt indicates whether the option is set. The cdspell option has been unset (-u).

a.   The words *switch* and *option* are interchangeable. They are arguments to a command that contain a leading dash.

13.2.3   The Prompts

When used interactively, the shell prompts you for input. When you see the prompt, you know that you can start typing commands. The bash shell provides four prompts: the primary prompt is a dollar sign ($); the secondary prompt is a right angle bracket symbol (>); the third and fourth prompts, PS3 and PS4, respectively, will be discussed later. The prompts are displayed when the shell is running interactively. You can change these prompts.

The variable PS1 is set to a string containing the primary prompt. Its value, the dollar sign, appears when you log on and waits for user input, normally a UNIX/Linux command. The variable PS2 is the secondary prompt, initially set to the right angle bracket character (>). It appears if you have partially typed a command and then pressed Enter. You can change the primary and secondary prompts.

The Primary Prompt.   The dollar sign (or bash $) is the default primary prompt. You can change your prompt. Normally, prompts are defined in /etc/bashrc or the user initialization file, .bash_profile, or .profile (Bourne shell).

EXAMPLE 13.12

```
1    $ PS1="$(uname -n) > "
2    chargers >
```

EXPLANATION

1   The default primary prompt is a dollar sign (bash $). The PS1 prompt is being reset to the name of the machine[a] (uname -n) and a > symbol.

2   The new prompt is displayed.

a.   The command, uname -n, is executed because it is enclosed in a set of parentheses preceded by a dollar sign. An alternative would be to enclose the command in backquotes. (See "Command Substitution" on page 835.)

Setting the Prompt with Special Escape Sequences. By inserting special backslash/escape sequences into the prompt string, you can customize the prompts. Table 13.2 lists the special sequences.

Table 13.2 Prompt String Settings

Backslash Sequence	What It Evaluates To
\d	The date in Weekday Month Date format (e.g., Tue May 26)
\h	The hostname
\n	Newline
\nnn	The character corresponding to the octal number nnn
\s	The name of the shell, the basename of $0 (the portion following the final slash)
\t	The current time in HH:MM:SS format
\u	The username of the current user
\w	The current working directory
\W	The basename of the current working directory
\#	The command number of this command
\!	The history number of this command
\$	If the effective UID is 0, a #, otherwise a $
\\	Backslash
\[	Begin a sequence of nonprinting characters; could be used to embed a terminal control sequence into the prompt
\]	End a sequence of nonprinting characters

New in bash 2.x+

\a	The ASCII bell character
\e	The ASCII escape character (033)
\H	The hostname
\T	The current time in 12-hour format: HH:MM:SS
\v	The version of bash, e.g., 2.03
\V	The release and pathlevel of bash; e.g., 2.03.0
\@	The current time in 12-hour AM/PM format

EXAMPLE 13.13

```
1    $  PS1="[\u@\h \W]\\$ "
     [ellie@homebound ellie]$
2    $  PS1="\W:\d> "
     ellie:Tue May 18>
```

EXPLANATION

1   You customize the primary bash prompt using special backslash/escape sequences.
    \u evaluates to the user's login name, \h to the host machine, and \W is the base-
    name for the current working directory. There are two backslashes. The first back-
    slash escapes the second backslash, resulting in \$. The dollar sign is protected
    from shell interpretation and thus printed literally.

2   The primary prompt is assigned \W, the escape sequence evaluating to the base-
    name of the current working directory, and \d, the escape sequence evaluating to
    today's date.

The Secondary Prompt.   The PS2 variable is assigned a string called the secondary
prompt. Its value is displayed to standard error, which is the screen by default. This
prompt appears when you have not completed a command or more input is expected.
The default secondary prompt is >.

EXAMPLE 13.14

```
1    $ echo "Hello
2    > there"
3    Hello
     there
4    $

5    $ PS2="----> "
6    $ echo 'Hi
7    ------>
     ------>
     ------> there'
      Hi


     there
     $
```

EXAMPLE 13.14 (CONTINUED)

```
8    $ PS2="\s:PS2 > "
     $ echo 'Hello
     bash:PS2 > what are
     bash:PS2 > you
     bash:PS2 > trying to do?
     bash:PS2 > '
     Hello
     what are
     you
     trying to do?
     $
```

EXPLANATION

1   The double quotes must be matched after the string "Hello.
2   When a newline is entered, the secondary prompt appears. Until the closing double quotes are entered, the secondary prompt will be displayed.
3   The output of the echo command is displayed.
4   The primary prompt is displayed.
5   The secondary prompt is reset.
6   The single quote must be matched after the string 'Hi.
7   When a newline is entered, the new secondary prompt appears. Until the closing single quote is entered, the secondary prompt will be displayed.
8   The PS2 prompt is set to the name of the shell (\s) followed by a string consisting of a colon, PS2 and >, followed by a space.

13.2.4 The Search Path

Bash uses the PATH variable to locate commands typed at the command line. The path is a colon-separated list of directories used by the shell when searching for commands. The default path is system-dependent, and is set by the administrator who installs bash. The path is searched from left to right. The dot at the end of the path represents the current working directory. If the command is not found in any of the directories listed in the path, the shell sends to standard error the message filename: not found. The path is normally set in the .bash_profile if running the bash shell or .profile file if using sh, the Bourne shell.

If the dot is not included in the path and you are executing a command or script from the current working directory, the name of the script must be preceded with a ./, such as ./program_name, so that shell can find the program.

EXAMPLE 13.15

```
(Printing the PATH)
1    $ echo $PATH
     /usr/gnu/bin:/usr/local/bin:/usr/ucb:/bin:/usr/bin:.

(Setting the PATH)
2    $ PATH=$HOME:/usr/ucb:/usr:/usr/bin:/usr/local/bin:
3    $ export PATH
4    $ runit
     bash: runit: command not found
5    $ ./runit
     < program starts running here >
```

EXPLANATION

1   By echoing $PATH, the value of the PATH variable is displayed. The path consists of a list of colon-separated elements and is searched from left to right. The dot at the end of the path represents the user's current working directory.

2   To set the path, a list of colon-separated directories are assigned to the PATH variable. Note that in this path, the dot is not at the end of the path, perhaps as a security measure.

3   By exporting the path, child processes will have access to it. It is not necessary to export the PATH on a separate line: It could be written as follows:
    export PATH=$HOME:/usr/ucb:/bin:., and so on, on the same line.

4   Because the dot is not in the search path, when the runit program is executed in the present working directory, bash can't find it.

5   Because the program name is preceded with a dot and a slash (./), the shell will be able to find it, and execute it, if it is the current working directory.

13.2.5 The hash Command

The hash command controls the internal hash table used by the shell to improve efficiency in searching for commands. Instead of searching the path each time a command is entered, the first time you type a command, the shell uses the search path to find the command, and then stores it in a table in the shell's memory. The next time you use the same command, the shell uses the hash table to find it. This makes it much faster to access a command than having to search the complete path. If you know that you will be using a command often, you can add the command to the hash table. You can also remove commands from the table. The output of the hash command displays the number of times the shell has used the table to find a command (*hits*) and the full pathname of the command. The hash command with the -r option clears the hash table. An argument of -- disables option checking for the rest of the arguments. Hashing is automatically implemented by bash. Although you can turn it off, if there isn't any compelling reason to do so, don't.

EXAMPLE 13.16

(Printing the PATH)

(Command line)
1 **hash**
   hits   command
   1   /usr/bin/mesg
   4   /usr/bin/man
   2   /bin/ls
2 **hash -r**
3 **hash**
   No commands in hash table
4 **hash find**
   hits   command
   0   /usr/bin/find

EXPLANATION

1   The hash command displays the full pathname of commands that have been exe-cuted in this login session. (Built-in commands are not listed.) The number of hits is the number of times the hash table has been used to find the command.

2   The -r option to the hash command erases all remembered locations in the hash table.

3   After the -r option was used in the last command, the hash command reports that there are no commands currently in the table.

4   If you know you are going to use a command often, you can add it to the hash table by giving it as an argument to the hash command. The find command has been added. The table has 0 hits because the command hasn't been used yet.

13.2.6 The source or dot Command

The source command (from the C shell) is a built-in bash command. The dot command, simply a period (from the Bourne shell), is another name for source. Both commands take a script name as an argument. The script will be executed in the environment of the current shell; that is, a child process will not be started. All variables set in the script will become part of the current shell's environment. Likewise, all variables set in the current shell will become part of the script's environment. The source (or dot) command is nor-mally used to re-execute any of the initialization files, such as .bash_profile, .profile, and so on, if they have been modified. For example, if one of the settings, such as the EDITOR or TERM variable, has been changed in the .bash_profile since you logged on, you can use the source command to re-execute commands in the .bash_profile without logging out and then logging back on. A file, such as .bash_profile, or for that matter any shell script, does not need execute permissions to be sourced with either the dot or the source commands.

EXAMPLE 13.17

```
$ source .bash_profile
$ . .bash_profile
```

EXPLANATION

The source or dot command executes the initialization file, .bash_profile, within the context of the current shell. Local and global variables are redefined within this shell. The dot command makes it unnecessary to log out and then log back in again after the file has been modified.[a]

---

a. If the .bash_profile were executed directly as a script, a child shell would be started. Then the variables would be set in the child shell, and when the child shell exited, the parent shell would not have any of the settings available to it.

13.3 The Command Line

After you log on, the bash shell displays its primary prompt, a dollar sign by default. The shell is your command interpreter. When the shell is running interactively, it reads commands from the terminal and breaks the command line into words. A command line consists of one or more words (or tokens), separated by whitespace (blanks and/or tabs), and terminated with a newline, generated by pressing the Enter key. The first word is the command, and subsequent words are the command's arguments. The command may be a UNIX/Linux executable program such as ls or date, a user-defined function, a built-in command such as cd or pwd, or a shell script. The command may contain special characters, called metacharacters, which the shell must interpret while parsing the command line. If a command line is too long, the backslash character, followed by a newline, will allow you to continue typing on the next line. The secondary prompt will appear until the command line is terminated.

13.3.1   The Order of Processing Commands

The first word on the command line is the command to be executed. The command may be a keyword, an alias, a function, a special built-in command or utility, an executable program, or a shell script. The command is executed according to its type in the following order:

1. Aliases
2. Keywords (such as if, function, while, until)
3. Functions
4. Built-in commands
5. Executables and scripts

Special built-in commands and functions are defined within the shell, and therefore are executed from within the context of the current shell, making them much faster in execution. Scripts and executable programs such as ls and date are stored on disk, and the shell, in order to execute them, must first locate them within the directory hierarchy by searching the PATH environment variable; the shell then forks a new shell that executes the script. To find out the type of command you are using—that is, a built-in command, an alias, a function, or an executable—use the built-in type command. (See Example 13.18.)

EXAMPLE 13.18

```
$ type pwd
pwd is a shell builtin
$ type test
test is a shell builtin
$ type clear
clear is /usr/bin/clear
$ type m
m is aliased to 'more'
$ type bc
bc is /usr/bin/bc
$ type if
if is a shell keyword
$ type -path cal
/usr/bin/cal
$ type which
which is aliased to 'type -path'
$ type greetings
greetings is a function
greetings ()
{
     echo "Welcome to my world!";
}
```

13.3.2 Built-In Commands and the help Command

Built-in commands are commands that are part of the internal source code for the shell. They are built-in and readily available to the shell, whereas commands such as date, cal, and finger are compiled binary programs that reside on the disk. There is less overhead in executing a built-in because it involves no disk operations. Built-in commands are executed by the shell before executable programs on disk. Bash has added a new online help system so that you can see all the built-ins, or a description for a particular built-in; help itself is a built-in command. See Table 13.28 on page 857 for a complete list of built-in commands.

EXAMPLE 13.19

```
1   $ help help
    help: help [pattern ...]
    Display helpful information about built-in commands. if PATTERN
    is specified, gives detailed help on all commands matching
    PATTERN, otherwise a list of the built-ins is printed.
2   $ help pw
    pwd: pwd
        Print the current working directory.
```

13.3.3 Changing the Order of Command-Line Processing

Bash provides three built-in commands that can override the order of command-line processing: command, builtin, and enable.

The command built-in eliminates aliases and functions from being looked up in the order of processing. Only built-ins and executables, found in the search path, will be processed.

The builtin command looks up only built-ins, ignoring functions and executables found in the path.

The enable built-in command turns built-ins on and off. By default, built-ins are enabled. Disabling a built-in allows an executable command to be executed without specifying a full pathname, even if it has the same name as a built-in. (In normal processing, bash searches for built-ins before disk executable commands.) Built-ins become disabled by using the -n switch. For example, a classic confusion for new shell programmers is naming a script test. Because test is a built-in command, the shell will try to execute it rather than the user's script (because a built-in is normally executed before any executable program). By typing: enable -n test, the test built-in is disabled, and the user's script will take precedence.

Without options, the enable built-in prints a list of all the built-ins. Each of the following built-ins are described in "Shell Built-In Commands" on page 857.

EXAMPLE 13.20

```
1   $ enable
    enable .
    enable :
    enable [
    enable alias
    enable bg
    enable bind
    enable break
    enable builtin
    enable cd
    enable command
```

EXAMPLE **13.20** (CONTINUED)

```
        enable continue
        enable declare
        enable dirs
          .....
        enable read
        enable readonly
        enable return
        enable set
        enable shift
        enable shopt
          .....
        enable type
        enable typeset
        enable ulimit
        enable umask
        enable unalias
        enable unset
        enable wait

2    enable -n test

3    function cd { builtin cd; echo $PWD; }
```

EXPLANATION

1   The enable built-in, without any options, displays a complete list of all bash shell built-in commands. This example shows just part of that list.

2   With the -n switch, the test built-in command is disabled. Now, you execute your script named test without worrying about the built-in test being executed instead. It's not good practice to name a script by the same name as an operating system command, because if you try to run the same script in another shell, the disabling of built-ins doesn't exist.

3   The function is called cd. The builtin command causes the cd within the function definition to be called instead of the function cd, which would cause an endless recursive loop.

13.3.4 The Exit Status

After a command or program terminates, it returns an exit status to the parent process. The exit status is a number between 0 and 255. By convention, when a program exits, if the status returned is 0, the command was successful in its execution. When the exit status is nonzero, the command failed in some way. If a command is not found by the shell, the exit status returned is 127. If a fatal signal causes the command to terminate, the exit status is 128 plus the value of the signal that caused it to die.

The shell status variable, ?, is set to the value of the exit status of the last command that was executed. Success or failure of a program is determined by the programmer who wrote the program.

EXAMPLE   13.21

```
1    $ grep ellie /etc/passwd
     ellie:MrHJEFd2YpkJY:501:501::/home/ellie:/bin/bash
2    $ echo $?
     0

3    $ grep nicky /etc/passwd
4    $ echo $?
     1

5    $ grep ellie /junk
     grep: /junk: No such file or directory
6    $ echo $?
     2

7    $ grip ellie /etc/passwd
     bash: grip: command not found
8    $ echo $?
     127

9    $ find / -name core ^C     # User presses Ctrl-C
10   $ echo $?
     130
```

EXPLANATION

1   The grep program searches for the pattern ellie in the /etc/passwd file and is successful. The line from /etc/passwd is displayed.

2   The ? variable is set to the exit value of the grep command. Zero indicates successful status.

3   The grep program cannot find user nicky in the /etc/passwd file.

4   The grep program cannot find the pattern; the ? variable return value is nonzero. An exit status of 1 indicates failure.

5   The grep fails because the /junk file cannot be opened. The grep error message is sent to standard error, the screen.

6   If grep cannot find the file, it returns an exit status of 2.

7   The grip command is not found by the shell.

8   Because the command is not found, the exit status, 127, is returned.

9   The find command is interrupted when the SIGINT signal is sent by pressing Ctrl-C. The signal number for Ctrl-C is 2.

10 The status returned from a process that has been killed is 128 + the number of the signal (i.e., 128 + 2).

13.3.5   Multiple Commands at the Command Line

A command line can consist of multiple commands. Each command is separated by a semicolon, and the command line is terminated with a newline. The exit status is that of the last command in the chain of commands.

EXAMPLE 13.22

```
$ ls; pwd; date
```

EXPLANATION

The commands are executed from left to right, one after the other, until the newline is reached.

13.3.6   Command Grouping

Commands may also be grouped so that all of the output is either piped to another command or redirected to a file.

EXAMPLE 13.23

```
$ ( ls; pwd; date ) > outputfile
```

EXPLANATION

The output of each of the commands is sent to the file called outputfile. The spaces inside the parentheses are necessary.

13.3.7   Conditional Execution of Commands

With conditional execution, two command strings are separated by the special metacharacters, double ampersands (&&) and double vertical bars (||). The command on the right of either of these metacharacters will or will not be executed based on the exit condition of the command on the left.

EXAMPLE 13.24

```
$ cc prgm1.c -o prgm1 && prgm1
```

EXPLANATION

If the first command is successful (has a 0 exit status), the command after the && is executed; that is, if the cc program can successfully compile prgm1.c, the resulting executable program, prgm1, will be executed.

EXAMPLE 13.25

```
$ cc prog.c >& err || mail bob < err
```

EXPLANATION

If the first command fails (has a nonzero exit status), the command after the || is executed; that is, if the cc program cannot compile prog.c, the errors are sent to a file called err, and user bob will be mailed the err file.

13.3.8   Commands in the Background

Normally, when you execute a command, it runs in the foreground, and the prompt does not reappear until the command has completed execution. It is not always convenient to wait for the command to complete. When you place an ampersand (&) at the end of the command line, the shell will return the shell prompt immediately and execute the command in the background concurrently. You do not have to wait for one command to finish before starting another. The output from a background job will be sent to the screen as it processes. Therefore, if you intend to run a command in the background, the output of that command might be redirected to a file or piped to another device, such as a printer, so that its output does not interfere with the more recent command that was typed.

The ! variable contains the PID number of the last job put in the background. (See the following section, "Job Control," for more on background processing.)

EXAMPLE 13.26

```
1   $ man sh | lp&
2   [1] 1557
3   $ kill -9 $!
```

EXPLANATION

1   The output of the man command (the manual pages for the UNIX command) is piped to the printer. The ampersand at the end of the command line puts the job in the background.

2   There are two numbers that appear on the screen: the number in square brackets indicates that this is the first job to be placed in the background; the second number is the PID, or the process identification number of this job.

3   The shell prompt appears immediately. While your program is running in the background, the shell is waiting for another command in the foreground. The ! variable evaluates to the PID of the job most recently put in the background. If you get it in time, you will kill this job before it goes to the print queue.

13.4 Job Control

Job control is a powerful feature of the bash shell that allows you to selectively run programs, called jobs, in the background or foreground. A running program is called a process or a job and each process has a process ID number, called the PID. Normally, a command typed at the command line is running in the foreground and will continue until it has finished unless you send a signal by pressing Ctrl-C or Ctrl-\ to terminate it. With job control, you can send a job to the background and let it keep running; you can stop a job by pressing Ctrl-Z, which sends the job to the background and suspends it; you can cause a stopped job to run in the background; you can bring a background job back to the foreground; and you can even kill the jobs you have running in the background or foreground. For a list of job commands, see Table 13.3 on page 782.

13.4.1 Job Control Commands and Options

By default, job control is already set (some older versions of UNIX do not support this feature). If disabled, it can be reset by any one of the following commands:

FORMAT

```
set -m          # set job control in the .bashrc file
set -o monitor  # set job control in the .bashrc file
bash -m -i      # set job control when invoking interactive bash
```

EXAMPLE 13.27

```
1   $ vi
    [1]+  Stopped     vi

2   $ sleep 25&
    [2] 4538

3   $ jobs
    [2]+  Running     sleep 25&
    [1]-  Stopped     vi

4   $ jobs -l
    [2]+ 4538  Running     sleep 25&
    [1]- 4537  Stopped     vi

5   $ jobs %%
    [2]+ 4538  Running     sleep 25&

6   $ fg %1
```

EXAMPLE   13.27 (CONTINUED)

```
7    $ jobs -x echo %1
     4537

8    $ kill %1        # or  kill 4537
     [1]+  Stopped      vi
     Vim: Caught deadly signal TERM
     Vim: Finished.
     [1]+  Exit 1       vi
```

EXPLANATION

1 After the vi editor is invoked, you can press ^Z (Ctrl-Z) to suspend the vi session. The editor will be suspended in the background, and after the message Stopped appears, the shell prompt will appear immediately.

2 The ampersand at the end of the command causes the sleep command, with an argument of 25, to execute in the background. The notation [2] means that this is the second job to be run in the background and the PID of this job is 4538.

3 The jobs command displays the jobs currently in the background.

4 The jobs command with the -l option displays the processes (jobs) running in the background and the PID numbers of those jobs.

5 The %% argument causes jobs to display the most recent command put in the job table.

6 The fg command followed by a percent sign and the job number will bring that numbered job into the foreground. Without a number, fg brings the most recently backgrounded job back into the foreground.

7 The -x option can be used to print just the PID number of the job. %1 refers to the vi session that was stopped in the first example.

8 The kill command sends a TERM signal to the process and kills it. The vi program is killed. You can specify either the job number or the PID number as arguments to the kill command.

Table 13.3 Job Control Commands

Command	Meaning
bg	Starts running the stopped job in the background
fg	Brings a background job to the foreground
jobs	Lists all the jobs running
kill	Sends the kill signal to a specified job
stop	Suspends a background job

Table 13.3 Job Control Commands (continued)

Command	Meaning
stty tostop	Suspends a background job if it sends output to the terminal
wait [n]	Waits for a specified job and returns its exit status; n is a PID or job number
^Z (Ctrl-Z)	Stops (suspends) the job; the prompt appears on the screen

Argument to Jobs Command	Represents
%n	Job number n
%sting	Job name starting with string
%?string	Job name containing string
%%	Current job
%+	Current job
%-	Previous job, before current job
-r	Lists all running jobs
-s	Lists all suspended jobs

New jobs Options. Two new options were added to the jobs command in bash versions 2.x. They are the -r and -s options. The -r option lists all running jobs, and the -s option lists all stopped jobs.

The disown Built-In. The disown built-in command (bash 2.x) removes a specified job from the job table. After the job has been removed, the shell will no longer recognize it as a viable job process and it can only be referenced by its process ID number.

13.5 Command-Line Shortcuts

13.5.1 Command and Filename Completion

To save typing, bash implements command and filename completion, a mechanism that allows you to type part of a command or filename, press the Tab key, and the rest of the word will be completed for you.

If you type the first letters in a command and press the Tab key, bash will attempt to complete the command and execute it. If bash cannot complete the filename or command, because neither exists, the terminal may beep and the cursor will stay at the end of the command. If there is more than one command starting with those characters and you press the Tab key a second time, all commands that start with those characters will be listed.

If there are several files starting with the same letters, bash will complete the shortest name that matches, expand out the filename until the characters differ, and then flash the cursor for you to complete the rest.

EXAMPLE 13.28

```
1   $ ls
    file1 file2 foo foobarckle fumble

2   $ ls fu[tab]        # Expands filename to fumble

3   $ ls fx[tab]        # Terminal beeps, nothing happens

4   $ ls fi[tab]        # Expands to file_  (_ is a cursor)

5   $ ls fi[tab][tab]  # Lists all possibilities
    file1 file2

6   $ ls foob[tab]      # Expands to foobarckle

7   $ da[tab]           # Completes the date command
    date
    Tue Feb 24 18:53:40 PST 2004

8   $ ca[tab][tab]      # Lists all commands starting with ca
    cal    captoinfo  case   cat
```

EXPLANATION

1   All files are listed for the current working directory.

2   After fu is typed, the Tab key is pressed, causing the spelling of the filename to be completed to fumble, and listed.

3   Because none of the files start with fx, the terminal beeps and the cursor remains, but does nothing. (The terminal may not beep if that feature has been disabled.)

4   There are a number of files starting with fi; the filenames are completed until the letters are no longer the same. If another Tab is pressed, all files with that spelling are listed.

5   By pressing two Tabs, a list of all files beginning with file is printed.

6   When the Tab key is pressed, the filename is expanded to foobarckle.

7   When the Tab key is pressed after da, the only command that begins with da is the date command. The command name is expanded and executed.

8   When the Tab key is pressed after ca, nothing happens because more than one command starts with ca. Pressing the Tab key twice lists all commands starting with ca.

13.5.2 History

The history mechanism keeps a history list, a numbered record of the commands that you have typed at the command line. During a login session, the commands you type are stored in the the shell's memory in a history *list* and then appended to the history *file* when you exit. You can recall a command from the history list and re-execute it without retyping the command. The history built-in command displays the history list. The default name for the history file is .bash_history, and it is located in your home directory.

When bash starts accessing the history file, the HISTSIZE variable specifies how many commands can be copied from the history file into the history list. The default size is 500. The HISTFILE variable specifies the name of the command history file (~/.bash_history is the default) where commands are stored. If unset, the command history is not saved when an interactive shell exits.

The history file grows from one login session to the next. The HISTFILESIZE variable controls the maximum number of lines contained in the history file. When this variable is assigned a value, the history file is truncated when it surpasses that number of lines. The default size is 500.

The fc -1 command can be used to display or edit commands in the history list.

Table 13.4 History Variables

Variable	Description
FCEDIT	The pathname of the UNIX/Linux editor that uses the fc command.
HISTCMD	The history number, or index in the history list, of the current command. If HISTCMD is unset, it loses its special properties, even if it is subsequently reset.
HISTCONTROL	If set to a value of ignorespace, lines that begin with a space character are not entered on the history list. If set to a value of ignoredups, lines matching the last history line are not entered. A value of ignoreboth combines the two options. If unset, or if set to any other value than those above, all lines read by the parser are saved on the history list.
HISTFILE	Specifies file in which to store command history. The default value is ~/.bash_history. If unset, the command history is not saved when an interactive shell exits.
HISTFILESIZE	The maximum number of lines contained in the history file. When this variable is assigned a value, the history file is truncated, if necessary, to contain no more than that number of lines. The default value is 500.
HISTIGNORE	A colon-separated list of patterns used to decide which command lines should be saved on the history list. Each pattern is anchored to the beginning of the line and consists of normal shell pattern-matching characters. An & can be used in the pattern causing the history command to ignore duplicates; for example, ty??:& would match for any command line starting with ty followed by two characters, and any duplicates of that command. Those commands would not be placed in the history list.
HISTSIZE	The number of commands to remember in the command history. The default value is 500.

13.5.3   Accessing Commands from the History File

The Arrow Keys.   To access commands from the history file, you can use the arrow keys on the keyboard to move up and down through the history file, and from left to right (see Table 13.5). You can edit any of the lines from the history file by using the standard keys for deleting, updating, backspacing, and so forth. As soon as you have edited the line, pressing the Enter key will cause the command line to be re-executed.

Table 13.5   The Arrow Keys

↑	Up arrow moves up the history list.
↓	Down arrow moves down the history list.
→	Right arrow moves cursor to right on history command.
←	Left arrow moves cursor to left on history command.

The history Built-In Command.   The history built-in command displays the history of commands typed preceded by an event number.

EXAMPLE 13.29

```
    1   $ history
        982   ls
        983   for i in 1 2 3
        984   do
        985   echo $i
        986   done
        987   echo $i
        988   man xterm
        989   adfasdfasdfadfasdfasdfadfasdfasdf
        990   id -gn
        991   id -un
        992   id -u
        993   man id
        994   more /etc/passwd
        995   man ulimit
        996   man bash
        997   man baswh
        998   man bash
        999   history
        1000  history
```

EXPLANATION

1   The built-in history command displays a list of numbered commands from the history list. Any lines listed with an ＊ have been modified.

The fc Command. The fc command, also called the fix command, can be used in two ways: (1) to select commands from the history list, and (2) to edit the commands in either the vi or emacs editor, or for that matter, any editor on your system.

In the first form, fc with the -l option can select specific lines or ranges of lines from the history list. When the -l switch is on, the output goes to the screen. For example, fc -l, the default, prints the last 16 lines from the history list, fc -l 10 selects lines numbered 10 through the end of the list, and fc -l -3 selects the last three lines. The -n switch turns off the numbering of commands in the history list. With this option on, you could select a range of commands and redirect them to a file, which in turn could be executed as a shell script. The -r switch reverses the order of the commands.

The second form of fc is described in "Command-Line Editing" on page 793.

Table 13.6 The fc Command

Argument	Meaning
-e editor	Puts history list into editor
-l n-m	Lists commands in range from n to m
-n	Turns off numbering of history list
-r	Reverses the order of the history list
-s string	Accesses command starting with string

EXAMPLE 13.30

```
1  $ fc -l
    4      ls
    5      history
    6      exit
    7      history
    8      ls
    9      pwd
   10      clear
   11      cal 2000
   12      history
   13      vi file
   14      history
   15      ls -l
   16      date
   17      more file
   18      echo a b c d
   19      cd
   20      history
```

EXAMPLE 13.30 (CONTINUED)

```
 2 $ fc -l -3
   19       cd
   20       history
   21       fc -l
 3 $  fc -ln
         exit
         history
         ls
         pwd
         clear
         cal 2000
         history
         vi file
         history
         ls -l
         date
         more file
         echo a b c d
         cd
         history
         fc -l
         fc -l -3
 4 $ fc -ln -3 > saved
 5 $ more saved
         fc -l
         fc -l -3
         fc -ln
 6 $ fc -l 15
   15       ls -l
   16       date
   17       more file
   18       echo a b c d
   19       cd
   20       history
   21       fc -l
   22       fc -l -3
   23       fc -ln
   24       fc -ln -3 > saved
   25       more saved
   26       history
 7 $ fc -l 15 20
   15       ls -l
   16       date
   17       more file
   18       echo a b c d
   19       cd
   20       history
```

EXPLANATION

1   fc -l selects the last 16 commands from the history list.

2   fc -l -3 selects the last three commands from the history list.

3   fc with the -ln options prints the history list without line numbers.

4   The last three commands, without line numbers, from the history list are redirected to a file called saved.

5   The contents of the file saved are displayed.

6   Commands from the history list, starting at number 15, are listed.

7   Commands numbered 15 through 20 are displayed.

If fc is given the -s option, a string pattern can be used to re-execute a previous command; for example, fc -s rm will cause the most previous line containing the pattern rm to be re-executed. To emulate the Korn shell's redo command, you can create a bash alias called r (e.g., alias r='fc -s') so that if you type r vi at the command line, the last history item containing that pattern will be re-executed; in this case, the vi editor will be started just as it was the last time it started, including any arguments passed.

EXAMPLE   13.31

```
1   $ history
    1   ls
    2   pwd
    3   clear
    4   cal 2000
    5   history
    6   ls -l
    7   date
    8   more file
    9   echo a b c d
2   $ fc -s da
    date
    Thu Jul  15 12:33:25 PST 2004
3   $ alias r="fc -s"
4   $ date +%T
    18:12:32
5   $ r d
    date +%T
    18:13:19
```

EXPLANATION

1   The built-in history command displays the history list.

2   fc with the -s option searches for the last command that began with string da. The date command is found in the history list and is re-executed.

3   An alias (a user-defined nickname) called r is assigned the command fc -s. This means that any time r is typed at the command line, it will be substituted with fc -s.

4   The date command is executed. It will print the current time.

5   The alias is used as a shortcut to the fs -s command. The last command beginning with a d is re-executed.

Re-executing History Commands (Bang! Bang!).   To re-execute a command from the history list, the exclamation point (called bang) is used. If you type two exclamation points, (!!) *bang, bang,* the last command in the history list is re-executed. If you type an exclamation point, followed by a number, the command listed by that number is re-executed. If you type an exclamation point and a letter or string, the last command that started with that letter or string is re-executed. The caret (∧) is also used as a short-cut method for editing the previous command. See Table 13.7 for a complete list of history substitution characters.

Table 13.7   Substitution and History

Event Designator	Meaning
!	Indicates the start of history substitution.
!!	Re-executes the previous command.
!N	Re-executes the Nth command from the history list.
!-N	Re-executes the Nth command back from present command.
!string	Re-executes the last command starting with string.
!?string?	Re-executes the last command containing string.
!?string?%	Re-executes the most recent command-line argument from the history list containing string.
!$	Uses the last argument from the last history command in the current command line.
!! string	Appends string to the previous command and executes.
!N string	Appends string to Nth command in history list and executes.
!N:s/old/new/	In previous Nth command, substitutes the first occurrence of old string with new string.
!N:gs/old/new/	In previous Nth command, globally substitutes old string with new string.

Table 13.7 Substitution and History (continued)

Event Designator	Meaning
^old^new^	In last history command, substitutes old string with new string.
command !N:wn	Executes current command appending an argument (wn) from the Nth previous command. Wn is a number starting at 0, 1, 2, ... designating the number of the word from the previous command; word 0 is the command itself, and 1 is its first argument, etc. (See Example 11.32.)

EXAMPLE 13.32

```
1   $ date
    Mon Jul  12 12:27:35 PST 2004

2   $ !!
    date
    Mon Jul  12 12:28:25 PST 2004

3   $ !106
    date
    Mon Jul  12 12:29:26 PST 2004

4   $ !d
    date
    Mon Jul  12 12:30:09 PST 2004

5   $ dare
    dare: Command not found.

6   $ ^r^t
    date
    Mon Jul  12 12:33:25 PST 2004
```

EXPLANATION

1   The UNIX/Linux date command is executed at the command line. The history list is updated. This is the last command on the list.

2   The !! (bang bang) gets the last command from the history list; the command is re-executed.

3   Command number 106 from the history list is re-executed.

4   The last command on the history list that started with the letter d is re-executed.

5   The command is mistyped. It should be date, not dare.

6   The carets are used to substitute letters from the last command on the history list. The first occurrence of an r is replaced with a t; that is, dare becomes date.

EXAMPLE 13.33

```
1   $ ls  file1 file2 file3
    file1 file2 file3
    $ vi !:1
    vi file1

2   $ ls file1 file2 file
    file1 file2 file3
    $ ls !:2
    ls file2
    file2

3   $ ls file1 file2 file3
    $ ls  !:3
    ls file3
    file3

4   $ echo a b c
    a b c
    $ echo !$
    echo c
    c

5   $ echo a b c
    a b c
    $ echo !^
    echo a
    a

6   % echo a b c
    a b c
    % echo !*
    echo a b c
    a b c

7   % !!:p
    echo a b c
```

EXPLANATION

1   The ls command lists file1, file2, and file3. The history list is updated. The command line is broken into words, starting with word number 0. If the word number is preceded by a colon, that word can be extracted from the history list. The !:1 notation means: get the first argument from the last command on the history list and replace it in the command string. The first argument from the last command is file1. (Word 0 is the command itself.)

2   The !:2 is replaced with the second argument of the last command, file2, and given as an argument to ls. file2 is printed. (file2 is the third word.)

EXPLANATION (CONTINUED)

3   ls !:3 reads: go to the last command on the history list and get the fourth word (words start at 0) and pass it to the ls command as an argument. (file3 is the fourth word.)

4   The bang (!) with the dollar sign ($) refers to the last argument of the last command on the history list. The last argument is c.

5   The caret (∧) represents the first argument after the command. The bang (!) with the ∧ refers to the first argument of the last command on the history list. The first argument of the last command is a.

6   The asterisk (*) represents all arguments after the command. The ! with the * refers to all of the arguments of the last command on the history list.

7   The last command from the history list is printed but not executed. The history list is updated. You could now perform caret substitutions on that line.

13.5.4 Command-Line Editing

The bash shell provides two built-in editors, emacs and vi, that allow you to interactively edit your history list. When you use the editing features at the command line, whether in vi or emacs mode, the readline functions determine which keys will perform certain functions. For example, if using emacs, Ctrl-P allows you to scroll upward in the command-line history, whereas if using vi, the K key moves upward through the history list. Readline also controls the arrow keys, cursor movement, changing, deleting, inserting text, and redoing or undoing corrections. Another feature of readline is the completion feature previously discussed in "Command and Filename Completion" on page 783. This allows you to type part of a command, filename, or variable, and then, by pressing the Tab key, the rest of the word is completed. There are many more features provided by the Readline library designed to help manipulate text at the command line.

    The emacs built-in editor is the default built-in editor and is modeless, whereas the vi built-in editor works in two modes, one to execute commands on lines and the other to enter text. If you use UNIX, you are probably familiar with at least one of these editors. To enable the vi editor, add the set command listed below[4] and put this line in your ~/.bashrc file. To set vi, type what's shown in the following example, at either the prompt or in the ~/.bashrc file.

EXAMPLE 13.34

```
set -o vi
```

EXPLANATION

Sets the built-in vi editor for command-line editing of the history list.

---

4. If the set -o (editor) has not been set, but the EDITOR variable has been set to either emacs or vi, then bash will use that definition.

To switch to the emacs editor, type:

EXAMPLE 13.35

    set -o emacs

EXPLANATION

Sets the built-in emacs editor for command-line editing of the history list.

The vi Built-In Editor.   To edit the history list, go to the command line and press the Esc key. Then press the K key if you want to scroll upward in the history list, and the J key[5] to move downward, just like standard vi motion keys. When you find the command that you want to edit, use the standard keys that you would use in vi for moving left and right, deleting, inserting, and changing text. (See Table 13.8.) After making the edit, press the Enter key. The command will be executed and added to the bottom of the history list.

Table 13.8   vi Commands

Command	Function
Moving Through the History File	
Esc k *or* +	Move up the history list
Esc j *or* –	Move down the history list
G	Move to first line in history file
5G	Move to fifth command in history file for string
/string	Search upward through history file
?	String search downward through history file
Moving Around on a Line	
h	Move left on a line
l	Move right on a line
b	Move backward a word
e *or* w	Move forward a word
^ *or* 0	Move to beginning of first character on the line
$	Move to end of line

---

5. vi is case-sensitive; an uppercase J and a lowercase j are different commands.

Table 13.8   vi Commands (continued)

Command	Function
Editing with vi	
a A	Append text
i I	Insert text
dd dw x	Delete text into a buffer (line, word, or character)
cc C	Change text
u U	Undo
yy Y	Yank (copy a line into buffer)
p P	Put yanked or deleted line down below or above the line
r R	Replace a letter or any amount of text on a line

The emacs Built-In Editor.   If using the emacs built-in editor, like vi, start at the command line. To start moving upward through the history file, press ^P. To move down, press ^N. Use emacs editing commands to change or correct text, then press Enter and the command will be re-executed. See Table 13.9.

Table 13.9   emacs Commands

Command	Function
Ctrl-P	Move up history file
Ctrl-N	Move down history file
Ctrl-B	Move backward one character
Ctrl-R	Search backward for string
Esc B	Move backward one word
Ctrl-F	Move forward one character
Esc F	Move forward one word
Ctrl-A	Move to the beginning of the line
Ctrl-E	Move to the end of the line
Esc <	Move to the first line of the history file
Esc >	Move to the last line of the history file

Table 13.9 emacs Commands (continued)

Command	Function
Editing with emacs	
Ctrl-U	Delete the line
Ctrl-Y	Put the line back
Ctrl-K	Delete from cursor to the end line
Ctrl-D	Delete a letter
Esc D	Delete one word forward
Esc H	Delete one word backward
Esc space	Set a mark at cursor position
Ctrl-X Ctrl-X	Exchange cursor and mark
Ctrl-P Ctrl-Y	Push region from cursor to mark into a buffer (Ctrl-P) and put it down (Ctrl-Y)

FCEDIT and Editing Commands.   If the fc command is given the -e option followed by the name of a UNIX/Linux editor, that editor is invoked containing history commands selected from the history list; for example, fc -e vi -1 -3 will invoke the vi editor, create a temporary file in /tmp, with the last three commands from the history list in the vi buffer. The commands can be edited or commented out. (Preceding the command with a # will comment it.) If the user quits the editor, the commands will all be echoed and executed.[6]

If the editor name is not given, the value of the FCEDIT variable is used (typically set in the initialization files, either bash_profile or .profile), and the value of the EDITOR variable is used if FCEDIT is not set. When editing is complete, and you exit the editor, all of the edited commands are echoed and executed.

---

6. Whether the user saves and quits the editor, or simply quits the editor, the commands will all be executed, unless they are commented or deleted.

EXAMPLE 13.36

```
1   $ FCEDIT=/bin/vi
2   $ pwd
3   $ fc
```
< *Starts up the full screen vi editor with the pwd command on line 1*>

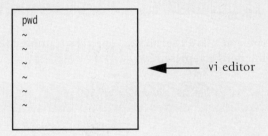

```
pwd
~
~
~
~
~
~
```
vi editor

```
4   $ history
    1 date
    2 ls -l
    3 echo "hello"
    4 pwd

5   $ fc -3 -1      # Start vi, edit, write/quit, and execute
                    # last 3 commands.
```

EXPLANATION

1 The FCEDIT variable can be assigned the pathname for any of the UNIX/Linux text editors you have on your system, such as vi, emacs, and so on. If not set, the vi editor is the default.

2 The pwd command is typed at the command line. It will be placed in the history file.

3 The fc command caused the editor (set in FCEDIT) to be invoked with the last command typed in the editor window. After the user writes and quits the editor, any commands typed there will be executed.

4 The history command lists recently typed commands.

5 The fc command is used to start up the editor with the last three commands from the history file in the editor's buffer.

13.6 Aliases

An alias is a bash user-defined abbreviation for a command. Aliases are useful if a command has a number of options and arguments or the syntax is difficult to remember. Aliases set at the command line are not inherited by subshells. Aliases are normally set in the .bashrc file. Because the .bashrc is executed when a new shell is started, any aliases set there will be reset for the new shell. Aliases may also be passed into shell scripts but will cause potential portability problems unless they are set directly within the script.

13.6.1   Listing Aliases

The alias built-in command lists all set aliases. The alias is printed first, followed by the real command or commands it represents.

EXAMPLE   13.37

```
$ alias
alias co='compress'
alias cp='cp -i'
alias mroe='more'
alias mv='mv -i'
alias ls='ls --colorztty'
alias uc='uncompress'
```

EXPLANATION

The alias command lists the alias (nickname) for the command and the real command the alias represents after the = sign.

13.6.2   Creating Aliases

The alias command is used to create an alias. The first argument is the name of the alias, the nickname for the command. The rest of the line consists of the command or commands that will be executed when the alias is executed. Bash aliases cannot take arguments (see "Defining Functions" on page 841). Multiple commands are separated by a semicolon, and commands containing spaces and metacharacters are surrounded by single quotes.

EXAMPLE   13.38

```
1    $ alias m=more
2    $ alias mroe=more
3    $ alias lF='ls -alF'
4    $ alias r='fc -s'
```

EXPLANATION

1   The nickname for the more command is set to m.
2   The alias for the more command is set to mroe. This is handy if you can't spell.
3   The alias definition is enclosed in quotes because of the whitespace. The alias lF is a nickname for the command ls -alF.
4   The alias r will be used instead of fc -s to recall commands from the history list by a specified pattern; for example, r vi will re-execute the last command in the history list containing the pattern vi.

13.6.3   Deleting Aliases

The unalias command is used to delete an alias. To temporarily turn off an alias, precede the alias name by a backslash.

EXAMPLE 13.39

```
1   $ unalias mroe
2   $ \ls
```

EXPLANATION

1   The unalias command deletes the alias mroe from the list of defined aliases.
2   The alias ls is temporarily turned off for this execution of the command only.

13.7 Manipulating the Directory Stack

If you find that as you work, you cd up and down the directory tree into many of the same directories, you can make it easy to access those directories by pushing them onto a directory stack and manipulating the stack. The pushd built-in command pushes directories onto a stack and the popd command removes them. (See Example 13.40.) The stack is a list of directories with the directory at the left being the most recent directory pushed onto the stack. The directories can be listed with the built-in dirs command.

13.7.1   The dirs Built-In Command

The built-in command dirs, with a -l option, displays the directory stack with each of its directories in full pathname format; without an option, dirs uses a tilde to denote the home directory. With a +n option, dirs displays the nth directory entry counting from the left in the directory list, starting at 0. With the -n option, it does the same thing, but starts at the right-hand side of the directory list with 0.

13.7.2   The pushd and popd Commands

The pushd command, with a directory as an argument, causes the new directory to be added to the directory stack and, at the same time, changes to that directory. If the argument is a +n where n is a number, pushd rotates the stack so that the nth directory from the stack, starting at the left-hand side, is pushed onto the top of the stack. With a -n option, it does the same thing but starts at the right-hand side. Without arguments, pushd exchanges the top two elements of the directory stack, making it easy to switch back and forth between directories.

The popd command removes a directory from the top of the stack, and changes to that directory. With +n, where n is a number, popd removes the nth entry, starting at the left of the list shown by dirs.

EXAMPLE   13.40

```
1    $ pwd
     /home/ellie

     $ pushd ..
     /home ~

     $ pwd
     /home

2    $ pushd           # Swap the two top directories on the stack
     ~ /home

     $ pwd
     /home/ellie

3    $ pushd perlclass
     ~/perlclass  ~  /home

4    $ dirs
     ~/perlclass ~ /home

5    $ dirs -l
     /home/ellie/perlclass /home/ellie  /home

6    $ popd
     ~/home

     $ pwd
     /home/ellie

7    $ popd
     /home

     $ pwd
     /home

8    $ popd
     bash: popd: Directory stack empty.
```

EXPLANATION

1   First the pwd command displays the present working directory, /home/ellie. Next the pushd command with .. as its argument, pushes the parent directory (..) onto the directory stack. The output of pushd indicates that /home is at the top of the directory stack (starting at the left-hand side of the displayed list) and the user's home directory, represented by the tilde character (~) is at the bottom of the stack. pushd also changes the directory to the one that was pushed onto the stack; that is, .., which translates to /home. The new directory is displayed with the second pwd command.

2   The pushd command, without arguments, exchanges the two top directory entries on the stack and changes to the swapped directory; in this example, the directory is switched back to the user's home directory, /home/ellie.

3   The pushd command will push its argument, ~/perlclass, onto the stack, and change to that directory.

4   The built-in dirs command displays the directory stack, with the top level starting at left-hand side of the listing. The tilde expands to the user's home directory.

5   With the -l option, dirs list displays the directory stack with full pathnames instead of using tilde expansion.

6   The popd command removes a directory from the top of the stack, and changes to that directory.

7   The popd command removes another directory from the top of the stack, and changes to that directory.

8   The popd command cannot remove any more directory entries because the stack is empty, and issues an error message saying so.

13.8 Metacharacters (Wildcards)

Metacharacters are special characters used to represent something other than themselves. Shell metacharacters are called *wildcards*. Table 13.10 lists metacharacters and what they do.

Table 13.10   Metacharacters

Metacharacter	Meaning
\	Interprets the following character literally
&	Processes in the background
;	Separates commands
$	Substitutes variables
?	Matches for a single character

Table 13.10 Metacharacters (continued)

Metacharacter	Meaning
[abc]	Matches for one character from a set of characters; for example, a, b, or c
[!abc]	Matches for one character *not* from the set of characters; for example, not a, b, or c
*	Matches for zero or more characters
(cmds)	Executes commands in a subshell
{cmds}	Executes commands in current shell

13.9 Filename Substitution (Globbing)

When evaluating the command line, the shell uses metacharacters to abbreviate filenames or pathnames that match a certain set of characters. The filename substitution metacharacters listed in Table 13.11 are expanded into an alphabetically listed set of filenames. The process of expanding the metacharacter into filenames is also called *filename substitution,* or *globbing.* If a metacharacter is used and there is no filename that matches it, the shell treats the metacharacter as a literal character.

Table 13.11 Shell Metacharacters and Filename Substitution

Metacharacter	Meaning
*	Matches zero or more characters
?	Matches exactly one character
[abc]	Matches one character in the set a, b, or c
[!abc]	Matches one character *not* in the set, not a, b, or c
{a,ile,ax}	Matches for a character or set of characters
[a-z]	Matches for one character in the range from a to z
[!a-z]	Matches one character *not* in the range from a to z
\	Escapes or disables the metacharacter

13.9.1 The Asterisk

The asterisk is a wildcard that matches for zero or more of any characters in a filename.

EXAMPLE 13.41

```
1   $ ls *
    abc abc1 abc122 abc123 abc2 file1 file1.bak file2 file2.bak none
    nonsense nobody nothing nowhere one
2   $ ls *.bak
    file1.bak file2.bak
3   $ echo a*
    ab abc1 abc122 abc123 abc2
```

EXPLANATION

1   The asterisk expands to all of the files in the present working directory. All of the files are passed as arguments to ls and displayed.

2   All files starting with zero or more characters and ending with .bak are matched and listed.

3   All files starting with a, followed by zero or more characters, are matched and passed as arguments to the echo command.

13.9.2   The Question Mark

The question mark represents a single character in a filename. When a filename contains one or more question marks, the shell performs filename substitution by replacing the question mark with the character it matches in the filename.

EXAMPLE 13.42

```
1   $ ls
    abc abc122 abc2 file1.bak file2.bak nonsense nothing one
    abc1 abc123 file1 file2 none noone nowhere
2   $ ls a?c?
    abc1 abc2
3   $ ls ??
    ls: ??: No such file or directory
4   $ echo abc???
    abc122 abc123
5   $ echo ??
    ??
```

EXPLANATION

1   The files in the current directory are listed.

2   Filenames starting with a, followed by a single character, followed by c and a single character, are matched and listed.

3   Filenames containing exactly two characters are listed, if found. Because there are not any two-character files, the question marks are treated as a literal filename. Such a file is not found, and the error message is printed.

EXPLANATION (CONTINUED)

4   Filenames starting with abc and followed by exactly three characters are expanded and displayed by the echo command.

5   There are no files in the directory that contain exactly two characters. The shell treats the question mark as a literal question mark if it cannot find a match.

13.9.3   The Square Brackets

The brackets are used to match filenames containing *one* character in a set or range of characters.

EXAMPLE 13.43

```
1   $ ls
    abc abc122 abc2 file1.bak file2.bak nonsense nothing
    one abc1 abc123 file1 file2 none noone nowhere
2   $ ls abc[123]
    abc1  abc2
3   $ ls abc[1-3]
    abc1  abc2
4   $ ls [a-z][a-z][a-z]
    abc one
5   $ ls [!f-z]???
    abc1  abc2
6   $ ls abc12[23]
    abc122 abc123
```

EXPLANATION

1   All of the files in the present working directory are listed.

2   All filenames containing four characters are matched and listed if the filename starts with abc, followed by 1, 2, or 3. Only one character from the set in the brackets is matched.

3   All filenames containing four characters are matched and listed, if the filename starts with abc and is followed by a number in the range from 1 to 3.

4   All filenames containing three characters are matched and listed, if the filename contains exactly three lowercase alphabetic characters.

5   All filenames containing four characters are listed if the first character is *not* a letter between f and z ([!f-z], followed by three of any characters, where ? represents a single character.

6   Files are listed if the filenames contain abc12 followed by 2 or 3.

13.9.4 Brace Expansion

The curly braces match for any of a list of comma-separated strings. Normally the strings are filenames. Any characters prepended to the opening curly brace are called the *preamble*, and any characters appended to the closing curly brace are called the *postamble*. Both the *preamble* and *postamble* are optional. There can be no unquoted whitespace within the braces.

EXAMPLE 13.44

```
1   $ ls
    a.c b.c abc ab3 ab4 ab5 file1 file2 file3 file4 file5 foo
    faa fumble
2   $ ls f{oo,aa,umble}
    foo faa fumble
3   $ ls a{.c,c,b[3-5]}
    a.c ab3 ab4 ab5
4   $ mkdir /usr/local/src/bash/{old,new,dist,bugs}
5   $ chown root /usr/{ucb/{ex,edit},lib/{ex?.?*,how_ex}}
6   $ echo fo{o, um}*
    fo{o, um}*
7   $ echo {mam,pap,ba}a
    mama papa baa
8   $ echo post{script,office,ure}
    postscript postoffice posture
```

EXPLANATION

1   All the files in the current directory are listed.
2   Files starting with f and followed by the strings oo, aa, or umble are listed. Spaces inside the curly braces will cause the error message Missing }.
3   Files starting with a followed by .c, c, or b3, b4, or b5 are listed. (The square brackets can be used inside the curly braces.)
4   Four new directories will be made in /usr/local/src/bash: old, new, dist, and bugs.
5   Root ownership will be given to files, ex and edit, in directory /usr/ucb and to files named ex followed by one character, a period, and at least one more character, and a file called how_ex in directory /usr/lib.
6   Brace expansion will not occur if there are any unquoted spaces within the braces.
7   Brace expansion does not necessarily always cause expansion of filenames. In this example the postamble a is added to each of the strings within the curly braces and echoed back after the expansion.
8   The preamble is the string post, followed by a comma-separated list enclosed within braces. Brace expansion is performed and the resulting strings are displayed.

13.9.5   Escaping Metacharacters

To use a metacharacter as a literal character, use the backslash to prevent the metacharacter from being interpreted.

EXAMPLE 13.45

```
1   $ ls
    abc file1 youx
2   $ echo How are you?
    How are youx
3   $ echo How are you\?
    How are you?
4   $ echo  When does this line \
    > ever end\?
    When does this line ever end?
```

EXPLANATION
---

1   The files in the present working directory are listed. (Note the file youx.)

2   The shell will perform filename expansion on the ?. Any files in the current directory starting with y-o-u and followed by exactly one character are matched and substituted in the string. The filename youx will be substituted in the string to read How are youx (probably not what you wanted to happen).

3   By preceding the question mark with a backslash, it is escaped, meaning that the shell will not try to interpret it as a wildcard.

4   The newline is escaped by preceding it with a backslash. The secondary prompt is displayed until the string is terminated with a newline. The question mark (?) is escaped to protect it from filename expansion.

13.9.6   Tilde and Hyphen Expansion

The tilde character was adopted by the bash shell (from the C shell) for pathname expansion. The tilde by itself evaluates to the full pathname of the user's home directory.[7] When the tilde is appended with a username, it expands to the full pathname of that user.

When the plus sign follows the tilde, the value of the PWD (present working directory) replaces the tilde. The tilde followed by the hyphen character is replaced with the previous working directory; OLDPWD also refers to the previous working directory.

---

7. The tilde character will not be expanded if enclosed in either double or single quotes.

```
1   $ echo ~
    /home/jody/ellie
2   $ echo ~joe
    /home/joe
3   $ echo ~+
    /home/jody/ellie/perl
4   $ echo ~-
    /home/jody/ellie/prac
5   $ echo $OLDPWD
    /home/jody/ellie/prac
6   $ cd -
    /home/jody/ellie/prac
```

EXPLANATION

1   The tilde evaluates to the full pathname of the user's home directory.
2   The tilde preceding the username evaluates to the full pathname of joe's home directory.
3   The ~+ notation evaluates to the full pathname of the working directory.
4   The ~- notation evaluates to the previous working directory.
5   The OLDPWD variable contains the previous working directory.
6   The hyphen refers to the previous working directory; cd to go to the previous working directory and display the directory.

13.9.7 Controlling Wildcards (Globbing)

If the bash noglob variable is set or if the set command is given a -f option, filename substitution, called *globbing*, is turned off, meaning that all metacharacters represent themselves; they are not used as wildcards. This can be useful when searching for patterns containing metacharacters in programs like grep, sed, or awk. If globbing is not set, all metacharacters must be escaped with a backslash to turn off wildcard interpretation.

The built-in shopt command (bash versions 2.x) also supports options for controlling globbing.

EXAMPLE 13.47

```
1   $ set noglob or set -f
2   $ print * ?? [] ~ $LOGNAME
    * ?? [] /home/jody/ellie ellie
3   $ unset noglob or set +f
4   $ shopt -s dotglob     # Only available in bash versions 2.x
5   $ echo *bash*
    .bash_history .bash_logout .bash_profile .bashrc bashnote
    bashtest
```

EXPLANATION

1 The -f option is given as an argument to the set command. It turns off the special meaning of wildcards used for filename expansion.

2 The filename expansion metacharacters are displayed as themselves without any interpretation. Note that the tilde and the dollar sign are still expanded, because they are not used for filename expansion.

3 If either noglob is unset or the +f option is set, filename metacharacters will be expanded.

4 The shopt built-in allows you to set options for the shell. The dotglob option allows filenames to be matched with globbing metacharacters, even if they start with a dot. Normally the files starting with a dot are invisible and not recognized when performing filename expansion.

5 Because the dotglob option was set in line 4, when the wildcard * is used for filename expansion, the filenames starting with a dot are also expanded if the filename contains the pattern bash.

13.9.8   Extended Filename Globbing (bash 2.x)

Derived from Korn shell pattern matching, bash 2.x has included this extended functionality, allowing regular expression-type syntax (see Table 13.12). The regular expression operators are not recognized unless the extglob option to the shopt command is turned on:

shopt -s extglob

Table 13.12   Extended Pattern Matching

Regular Expression	Meaning
abc?(2|9)1	? matches zero or one occurrences of any pattern in the parentheses. The vertical bar represents an OR condition; for example, either 2 or 9. Matches abc21, abc91, or abc1.
abc*([0-9])	* matches zero or more occurrences of any pattern in the parentheses. Matches abc followed by zero or more digits; for example, abc, abc1234, abc3, abc2, and so on.
abc+([0-9])	+ matches one or more occurrences of any pattern in the parentheses. Matches abc followed by one or more digits; for example, abc3, abc123, and so on.
no@(one|ne)	@ matches exactly one occurrence of any pattern in the parentheses. Matches noone or none.
no!(thing|where)	! matches all strings except those matched by any of the patterns in the parentheses. Matches no, nobody, or noone, but not nothing or nowhere.

EXAMPLE 13.48

```
1   $ shopt -s extglob

2   $ ls
    abc       abc122    f1    f3      nonsense   nothing   one
    abc1      abc2      f2    none    noone      nowhere

3   $ ls abc?(1|2)
    abc       abc1      abc2

4   $ ls abc*([1-5])
    abc       abc1      abc122    abc2

5   $ ls abc+([0-5])
    abc1      abc122    abc2

6   $ ls no@(thing|ne)
    none      nothing

7   $ ls no!(thing)
    none      nonsense  noone     nowhere
```

EXPLANATION

1   The shopt built-in is used to set the extglob (extended globbing) option, allowing bash to recognize extended pattern-matching characters.

2   All the files in the present working directory are listed.

3   Matches filenames starting with abc and followed by *zero characters or one* of either of the patterns in parentheses. Matches abc, abc1, or abc2.

4   Matches filenames starting with abc and followed by *zero or more* numbers between 1 and 5. Matches abc, abc1, abc122, abc123, and abc2.

5   Matches filenames starting with abc and followed by *one or more* numbers between 0 and 5. Matches abc1, abc122, abc123, and abc2.

6   Matches filenames starting with no and followed by thing or ne. Matches nothing or none.

7   Matches filenames starting with no and followed by anything except thing. Matches none, nonsense, noone, and nowhere. The ! means NOT.

13.10 Variables

13.10.1   Types of Variables

There are two types of variables: local and environment. Local variables are known only to the shell in which they were created. Environment variables are available to any child processes spawned from the shell from which they were created. Some variables are created by the user and others are special shell variables.

13.10.2   Naming Conventions

Variable names must begin with an alphabetic or underscore character. The remaining characters can be alphabetic, decimal digits (0 to 9), or an underscore character. Any other characters mark the termination of the variable name. Names are case sensitive. When assigning a value to a variable, do not include any whitespace surrounding the equal sign. To set the variable to null, follow the equal sign with a newline. The simplest format for creating a local variable is to assign a value to a variable in the following format.

FORMAT

```
variable=value
```

EXAMPLE 13.49

```
name=Tommy
```

13.10.3   The declare Built-In

There are two built-in commands, declare and typeset, used to create variables, with options to control the way the variable is set. The typeset command (from Korn shell) is exactly the same as the declare command (bash). The bash documentation says, "The typeset command is supplied for compatibility with the Korn shell; however, it has been deprecated in favor of the declare built-in command."[8] So from this point on we'll use the declare built-in (even though we could just as easily have chosen to use typeset).

Without arguments, declare lists all set variables. Normally read-only variables cannot be reassigned or unset. If read-only variables are created with declare, they *cannot* be unset, but they *can* be reassigned. Integer-type variables can also be assigned with declare.

---

8. Bash Reference Manual: www.delorie.com/gnu/docs/bash/bashref_56.html.

FORMAT

```
declare variable=value
```

EXAMPLE 13.50

```
declare name=Tommy
```

Table 13.13 declare Options

Option	Meaning
-a[a]	Treats variable as an array (i.e., assigns elements)
-f	Lists functions names and definitions
-F[a]	Lists just function names
-i	Makes variables integer types
-r	Makes variables read-only
-x	Exports variable names to subshells

a. -a and -F are implemented only on versions of bash 2.x.

13.10.4 Local Variables and Scope

The scope of a variable refers to where the variable is visible within a program. For the shell, the scope of local variables is confined to the shell in which the variable is created.

When assigning a value, there can be no whitespace surrounding the equal sign. To set the variable to null, the equal sign is followed by a newline.[9]

A dollar sign is used in front of a variable to extract the value stored there.

The local function can be used to create local variables, but this is only used within functions. (See "Defining Functions" on page 841.)

Setting Local Variables.   Local variables can be set by simply assigning a value to a variable name, or by using the declare built-in function as shown in Example 13.51.

---

9. A variable set to a value or to null will be displayed by using the set command, but an unset variable will not.

EXAMPLE 13.51

```
1   $ round=world  or declare round=world
    $ echo $round
    world
2   $ name="Peter Piper"
    $ echo $name
    Peter Piper
3   $ x=
    $ echo $x
4   $ file.bak="$HOME/junk"
    bash: file.bak=/home/jody/ellie/junk: not found
```

EXPLANATION

1   The local variable round is assigned the value world. When the shell encounters the dollar sign preceding a variable name, it performs variable substitution. The value of the variable is displayed. (Don't confuse the prompt $ with the $ used to perform variable substitution.)

2   The local variable name is assigned the value "Peter Piper". The quotes are needed to hide the whitespace so that the shell will not split the string into separate words when it parses the command line. The value of the variable is displayed.

3   The local variable x is not assigned a value. It will be assigned null. The null value, an empty string, is displayed.

4   The period in the variable name is illegal. The only characters allowed in a variable name are numbers, letters, and the underscore. The shell tries to execute the string as a command.

EXAMPLE 13.52

```
1   $ echo $$
    1313
2   $ round=world
    $ echo $round
    world
3   $ bash              # Start a subshell
4   $ echo $$
    1326
5   $ echo $round
6   $ exit              # Exits this shell, returns to parent shell
7   $ echo $$
    1313
8   $ echo $round
    world
```

1   The value of the double dollar sign variable evaluates to the PID of the current shell. The PID of this shell is 1313.

2   The local variable round is assigned the string value world, and the value of the variable is displayed.

3   A new bash shell is started. This is called a *subshell*, or *child shell*.

4   The PID of this shell is 1326. The parent shell's PID is 1313.

5   The local variable round is not defined in this shell. A blank line is printed.

6   The exit command terminates this shell and returns to the parent shell. (Ctrl-D will also exit this shell.)

7   The parent shell returns. Its PID is displayed.

8   The value of the variable round is displayed. It is local to this shell.

Setting Read-Only Variables.   A read-only variable is a special variable that cannot be redefined or unset. If, however, the declare function is used, a read-only variable can be redefined, but not unset.

EXAMPLE 13.53

```
1   $ name=Tom
2   $ readonly name
    $ echo $name
    Tom

3   $ unset name
    bash: unset: name: cannot unset: readonly variable
4   $ name=Joe
    bash: name: readonly variable

5   $ declare -r city='Santa Clara'
6   $ unset city
    bash: unset: city: cannot unset: readonly variable

7   $ declare city='San Francisco'     # What happened here?
    $ echo $city
    San Francisco
```

1   The local variable name is assigned the value Tom.

2   The variable is made read-only.

3   A read-only variable cannot be unset.

4   A read-only variable cannot be redefined.

EXPLANATION (CONTINUED)

5   The `declare` built-in command assigns a read-only variable, `city`, the value `Santa Clara`. Quotes are necessary when assigning a string containing whitespace.

6   Because it is read-only, the variable cannot be unset.

7   When a read-only variable is created with the `declare` command, it cannot be unset, but it can be reassigned.

13.10.5 Environment Variables

Environment variables are available to the shell in which they are created and any subshells or processes spawned from that shell. They are often called global variables to differentiate them from local variables. By convention, environment variables are capitalized. Environment variables are variables that have been exported with the `export` built-in command.

The shell in which a variable is created is called the *parent shell*. If a new shell is started from the parent shell, it is called the *child shell*. Environment variables are passed to any child process started from the shell where the environment variables were created. They are passed from parent to child to grandchild, and so on, but not in the other direction—a child process can create an environment variable, but cannot pass it back to its parent, only to its children.[10] Some of the environment variables, such as `HOME`, `LOGNAME`, `PATH`, and `SHELL`, are set before you log on by the `/bin/login` program. Normally, environment variables are defined and stored in the `.bash_profile` file in the user's home directory. See Table 13.14 for a list of environment variables.

Table 13.14 bash Environment Variables

Variable Name	Meaning
_ (underscore)	The last argument to the previous command.
BASH	Expands to the full pathname used to invoke this instance of bash.
BASH_ENV	Same as ENV but set only in bash.[a]
BASH_VERSINFO	Version information about this version of bash.[a]
BASH_VERSION	Expands to the version number of this instance of bash.
CDPATH	The search path for the cd command. This is a colon-separated list of directories in which the shell looks for destination directories specified by the cd command. A sample value is .:~:/usr.
COLUMNS	If set, defines the width of the edit window for shell edit modes and the select command.

---

10. Like DNA, inheritance goes in one direction only, from parent to child.

Table 13.14   bash Environment Variables (continued)

Variable Name	Meaning
DIRSTACK	The current contents of the directory stack of the bash.[a]
EDITOR	Pathname for a built-in editor: emacs, gmacs, or vi.
ENV	The environment file that is executed every time a new bash shell is started, including a script. Normally the filename assigned to this variable is .bashrc. The value of ENV is subjected to parameter expansion, command substitution, and arithmetic expansion before being interpreted as a pathname.
EUID	Expands to the effective user ID of the current user, initialized at shell startup.
FCEDIT	Default editor name for the fc command.
FIGNORE	A colon-separated list of suffixes to ignore when performing filename completion. A filename whose suffix matches one of the entries in FIGNORE is excluded from the list of matched filenames. A sample value is .o:~.
FORMAT	Used to format the output of the *time* reserved word on a command pipeline.
GLOBIGNORE	A list of files that will be ignored during filename expansion (called globbing).[a]
GROUPS	An array of groups to which the current user belongs.[a]
HISTCMD	The history number, or index in the history list, of the current command. If HISTCMD is unset, it loses its special properties, even if it is subsequently reset.
HISTCONTROL	If set to a value of ignorespace, lines that begin with a space character are not entered on the history list. If set to a value of ignoredups, lines matching the last history line are not entered. A value of ignoreboth combines the two options. If unset, or if set to any other value than those above, all lines read by the parser are saved on the history list.
HISTFILE	Specifies file in which to store command history. The default value is ~/.bash_history. If unset, the command history is not saved when an interactive shell exits.
HISTFILESIZE	The maximum number of lines contained in the history file. When this variable is assigned a value, the history file is truncated, if necessary, to contain no more than that number of lines. The default value is 500.
HISTSIZE	The number of commands to remember in the command history. The default value is 500.
HOME	Home directory; used by cd when no directory is specified.
HOSTFILE	Contains the name of a file in the same format as in /etc/hosts that should be read when the shell needs to complete a hostname. The file may be changed interactively; the next time hostname completion is attempted, bash adds the contents of the new file to the already existing database.

Table 13.14 bash Environment Variables (continued)

Variable Name	Meaning
HOSTTYPE	Automatically set to the type of machine on which bash is executing. The default is system-dependent.
IFS	Internal field separators, normally SPACE, TAB, and NEWLINE, used for field splitting of words resulting from command substitution, lists in loop constructs, and reading input.
IGNOREEOF	Controls the action of the shell on receipt of an EOF character as the sole input. If set, the value is the number of consecutive EOF characters typed as the first characters on an input line before bash exits. If the variable exists but does not have a numeric value, or has no value, the default value is 10. If it does not exist, EOF signifies the end of input to the shell. This is only in effect for interactive shells.
INPUTRC	The filename for the readline startup file, overriding the default of ~./inputrc.
LANG	Used to determine the locale category for any category not specifically selected with a variable starting with LC_.[a]
LC_ALL	Overrides the value of LANG and any other LC_ variable.[a]
LC_COLLATE	Determines the collation order used when sorting the results of pathname expansion and the behavior of range expressions, equivalence classes, and collating sequences when matching pathnames and patterns.[a]
LC_MESSAGES	Determines the locale used to translate double-quoted strings preceded by a $.[a]
LINENO	Each time this parameter is referenced, the shell substitutes a decimal number representing the current sequential line number (starting with 1) within a script or function.
MACHTYPE	Contains a string describing the system on which bash is executing.[a]
MAIL	If this parameter is set to the name of a mail file and the MAILPATH parameter is not set, the shell informs the user of the arrival of mail in the specified file.
MAIL_WARNING	If set, and a file that bash is checking for mail has been accessed since the last time it was checked, the message The mail in [filename where mail is stored] has been read is printed.
MAILCHECK	This parameter specifies how often (in seconds) the shell will check for the arrival of mail in the files specified by the MAILPATH or MAIL parameters. The default value is 600 seconds (10 minutes). If set to zero, the shell will check before issuing each primary prompt.
MAILPATH	A colon-separated list of filenames. If this parameter is set, the shell informs the user of the arrival of mail in any of the specified files. Each filename can be followed by a % and a message that will be printed when the modification time changes. The default message is You have mail.

Table 13.14   bash Environment Variables (continued)

Variable Name	Meaning
OLDPWD	Last working directory.
OPTARG	The value of the last option argument processed by the getopts built-in command.
OPTERR	If set to 1, displays error messages from the getopts built-in.
OPTIND	The index of the next argument to be processed by the getopts built-in command.
OSTYPE	Automatically set to a string that describes the operating system on which bash is executing. The default is system-dependent.
PATH	The search path for commands. It is a colon-separated list of directories in which the shell looks for commands. The default path is system-dependent, and is set by the administrator who installs bash. A common value is /usr/gnu/bin:/usr/local/bin:/usr/ucb:/bin:/usr/bin:.
PIPESTATUS	An array containing a list of exit status values from processes in the most recently executed foreground jobs in a pipeline.
PPID	Process ID of the parent process.
PROMPT_COMMAND	The command assigned to this variable is executed before the primary prompt is displayed.
PS1	Primary prompt string, by default $.
PS2	Secondary prompt string, by default >.
PS3	Selection prompt string used with the select command, by default #?.
PS4	Debug prompt string used when tracing is turned on, by default +. Tracing can be turned on with set -x.
PWD	Present working directory; set by cd.
RANDOM	Each time this parameter is referenced, a random integer is generated. The sequence of random numbers may be initialized by assigning a value to RANDOM. If RANDOM is unset, it loses its special properties, even if it is subsequently reset.
REPLY	Set when read is not supplied arguments.
SECONDS	Each time SECONDS is referenced, the number of seconds since shell invocation is returned. If a value is assigned to SECONDS, the value returned upon subsequent references is the number of seconds since the assignment plus the value assigned. If SECONDS is unset, it loses its special properties, even if it is subsequently reset.

Table 13.14   bash Environment Variables (continued)

Variable Name	Meaning
SHELL	When the shell is invoked, it scans the environment for this name. The shell gives default values to PATH, PS1, PS2, MAILCHECK, and IFS. HOME and MAIL are set by login(1).
SHELLOPTS	Contains a list of enabled shell options, such as braceexpand, hashall, monitor, etc.
SHLVL	Incremented by one each time an instance of bash is started.
TMOUT	Specifies number of seconds to wait for input before exiting.
UID	Expands to the user ID of the current user, initialized at shell startup.

a. Not available in bash versions prior to 2.x.

Setting Environment Variables.   To set environment variables, the export command is used either after assigning a value or when the variable is set. (See Table 13.15.) The declare built-in, given the -x option, will do the same. (Do not use the $ on a variable when exporting it.)

FORMAT

```
export variable=value
variable=value; export variable
declare -x variable=value
```

EXAMPLE 13.54

```
export NAME=john
PS1= '\d:\W:$USER> ' ; export PS1
declare -x TERM=sun
```

Table 13.15   The export Command and Its Options

Option	Value
--	Marks the end of option processing; the remaining parameters are arguments.
-f	Name–value pairs are treated as functions, not variables.
-n	Converts a global (exported) variable to a local variable. The variable will not be exported to child processes.
-p	Displays all the global variables.

EXAMPLE 13.55

```
1   $ export TERM=sun      # or declare -x TERM=sun
2   $ NAME="John Smith"
    $ export NAME
    $ echo $NAME
    John Smith
3   $ echo $$
    319             # pid number for parent shell
4   $ bash          # Start a subshell
5   $ echo $$
    340             # pid number for new shell
6   $ echo $NAME
    John Smith
7   $ declare -x NAME="April Jenner"
    $ echo $NAME
    April Jenner
8   $ exit          # Exit the subshell and go back to parent shell
9   $ echo $$
    319             # pid number for parent shell
10  $ echo $NAME
    John Smith
```

EXPLANATION

1   The TERM variable is assigned sun. The variable is exported at the same time. Now, processes started from this shell will inherit the variable. You can use declare -x to do the same thing.

2   The variable NAME is defined and exported to make it available to subshells started from the shell.

3   The value of this shell's PID is printed.

4   A new bash shell is started. The new shell is called the *child*. The original shell is its *parent*.

5   The PID of the new bash shell is stored in the $$ variable and its value is echoed.

6   The variable, set in the parent shell, was exported to this new shell and is displayed.

7   The built-in declare function is another way to set a variable. With the -x switch, declare marks the variable for export. The variable is reset to April Jenner. It is exported to all subshells, but will not affect the parent shell. Exported values are not propagated upward to the parent shell.

8   This bash child shell is exited.

9   The PID of the parent is displayed again.

10 The variable NAME contains its original value. Variables retain their values when exported from parent to child shell. The child cannot change the value of a variable for its parent.

13.10.6   Unsetting Variables

Both local and environment variables can be unset by using the unset command, unless the variables are set as read-only.

unset name; unset TERM

The unset command removes the variable from the shell's memory.

13.10.7   Printing the Values of Variables

The echo Command.   The built-in echo command prints its arguments to standard output. Echo, with the -e option, allows the use of numerous escape sequences that control the appearance of the output. Table 13.16 lists the echo options and escape sequences.

Table 13.16   echo Options and Escape Sequences

Option	Meaning
-e	Allows interpretation of the escape sequences shown below
-E	Disables the interpretation of these escape characters, even on systems where they are interpreted by default[a]
-n	Suppresses newline at the end of a line of output

Escape Sequence	
\a	Alert (bell)[a]
\b	Backspace
\c	Prints the line without a newline
\f	Form feed
\n	Newline
\r	Return
\t	Tab
\v	Vertical tab
\\	Backslash
\nnn	The character whose ASCII code is nnn (octal)

a. Not available in bash versions prior to 2.x.

When using the escape sequences, don't forget to use the -e switch!

```
1   $ echo The username is $LOGNAME.
    The username is ellie.

2   $ echo -e "\t\tHello there\c"
                Hello there$

3   $ echo -n "Hello there"
    Hello there$
```

1   The echo command prints its arguments to the screen. Variable substitution is performed by the shell before the echo command is executed.
2   The echo command, with the –e option, supports escape sequences similar to those of the C programming language. The $ is the shell prompt.
3   When the –n option is on, the line is printed without the newline. The escape sequences are not supported by this version of echo.

The printf Command.   The GNU version of printf[11] can be used to format printed output. It prints the formatted string in the same way as the C printf function. The format consists of a string that may contain formatting instructions to describe how the printed output will look. The formatting instructions are designated with a % followed by specifiers (diouxXfeEgGcs) where %f would represent a floating-point number and %d would represent a whole (decimal) number.

To see a complete listing of printf specifiers and how to use them, type printf --help at the command-line prompt. To see what version of printf you are using, type printf --version. If you are using bash 2.x, the built-in printf command uses the same format as the executable version in /usr/bin.

```
printf format [argument...]
```

```
printf "%10.2f%5d\n" 10.5  25
```

---

11. On bash versions 2.x, printf is a built-in command.

Table 13.17   Format Specifiers for the `printf` Command

Format Specifier	Value
\"	Double quote
\0NNN	An octal character where NNN represents 0 to 3 digits
\\	Backslash
\a	Alert or beep
\b	Backspace
\c	Produce no further output
\f	Form feed
\n	Newline
\r	Return
\t	Horizontal tab
\v	Vertical tab
\xNNN	Hexadecimal character, where NNN is 1 to 3 digits
%%	A single %
%b	Argument as a string with \ escapes interpreted

EXAMPLE 13.59

```
1   $ printf --version
    printf (GNU sh-utils) 1.16

2   $ type printf
    printf is a shell builtin

3   $ printf "The number is %.2f\n" 100
    The number is 100.00

4   $ printf "%-20s%-15s%10.2f\n" "Jody" "Savage" 28
    Jody                Savage                  28.00

5   $ printf "|%-20s|%-15s|%10.2f|\n" "Jody" "Savage" 28
    Jody                |Savage         |     28.00|

6   $ printf "%s's average was %.1f%%.\n" "Jody" $(( (80+70+90)/3 ))
    Jody's average was 80.0%.
```

EXPLANATION

1   The GNU version of the `printf` command is printed.

2   If using `bash` 2.x, `printf` is a built-in command.

3   The argument 100 is printed as a floating-point number with only 2 places to the right of the decimal point as designated by the specification `%.2f` in the format string. Unlike C, there are no commas separating the arguments.

4   The format string specifies that three conversions will take place: the first one is `%-20s` (a left-justified, 20-character string), next is `%-15s` (a left-justified, 15-character string), and last is `%10.2f` (a right-justified, 10-character floating-point number, one of whose characters is the period and the last two characters are the two numbers to the right of the decimal point). Each argument is formatted in the order of the corresponding `%` signs, so that string Jody corresponds to first `%`, string Savage corresponds to the second `%`, and the number 28 to the last `%` sign.

5   This line is the same as line 4 except vertical bars have been added to demonstrate left and right justification of the strings.

6   The `printf` command formats the string Jody and formats the result of the arithmetic expansion. (See "Arithmetic Expansion" on page 837.) Two percent (`%%`) signs are needed to print one percent sign (`%`).

13.10.8   Variable Expansion Modifiers (Parameter Expansion)

Variables can be tested and modified by using special modifiers. The modifier provides a shortcut conditional test to check if a variable has been set, and then assigns a value to the variable based on the outcome of the test. See Table 13.18 for a list of variable modifiers.

Table 13.18   Variable Modifiers

Modifier	Value
`${variable:-word}`	If `variable` is set and is non-null, substitute its value; otherwise, substitute word.
`${variable:=word}`	If `variable` is set or is non-null, substitute its value; otherwise, set it to word. The value of `variable` is substituted permanently. Positional parameters may not be assigned in this way.
`${variable:+word}`	If `variable` is set and is non-null, substitute word; otherwise, substitute nothing.
`${variable:?word}`	If `variable` is set and is non-null, substitute its value; otherwise, print word and exit from the shell. If word is omitted, the message `parameter null or not set` is printed.
`${variable:offset}`	Gets the substring of the value in `variable` starting at offset, where offset starts at 0 to the end of the string.[a]

Table 13.18 Variable Modifiers (continued)

Modifier	Value
${variable:offset:length}	Gets the substring of the value in variable starting at offset, length characters over.

a. Not available on bash versions prior to 2.0.

Using the colon with any of the modifiers (-, =, +, ?) checks whether the variable is not set or is null; without the colon, a variable set to null is considered to be set.

EXAMPLE 13.60

(Substitute Temporary Default Values)

```
1    $ fruit=peach
2    $ echo ${fruit:-plum}
     peach
3    $ echo ${newfruit:-apple}
     apple
4    $ echo $newfruit
5    $ echo $EDITOR          # More realistic example
6    $ echo ${EDITOR:-/bin/vi}
     /bin/vi
7    $ echo $EDITOR
8    $ name=
     $ echo ${name-Joe}
9    $ echo ${name:-Joe}
     Joe
```

EXPLANATION

1   The variable fruit is assigned the value peach.

2   The special modifier will check to see if the variable fruit has been set. If it has, the value is printed; if not, plum is substituted for fruit and its value is printed.

3   The variable newfruit has not been set. The value apple will be temporarily substituted for newfruit.

4   The setting was only temporary. The variable newfruit is not set.

5   The environment variable EDITOR has not been set.

6   The :- modifier substitutes EDITOR with /bin/vi.

7   The EDITOR was never set. Nothing prints.

8   The variable name is set to null. By not prefixing the modifier with a colon, the variable is considered to be set, even if to null, and the new value Joe is not assigned to name.

9   The colon causes the modifier to check that a variable is either *not* set or is set to null. In either case, the value Joe will be substituted for name.

EXAMPLE 13.61

(Substitute Permanent Default Values)

```
1    $ name=
2    $ echo  ${name:=Peter}
     Peter
3    $ echo $name
     Peter
4    $ echo ${EDITOR:=/bin/vi}
     /bin/vi
5    $ echo $EDITOR
     /bin/vi
```

EXPLANATION

1   The variable name is assigned the null value.

2   The special modifier := will check to see if the variable name has been set. If it has been set, it will not be changed; if it is either null or not set, it will be assigned the value to the right of the equal sign. Peter is assigned to name because the variable is set to null. The setting is permanent.

3   The variable name still contains the value Peter.

4   The value of the variable EDITOR is set to /bin/vi.

5   The value of the variable EDITOR is displayed.

EXAMPLE 13.62

(Substitute Temporary Alternate Value)

```
1    $ foo=grapes
2    $ echo ${foo:+pears}
     pears
3    $ echo $foo
     grapes
     $
```

EXPLANATION

1   The variable foo has been assigned the value grapes.

2   The special modifier :+ will check to see if the variable has been set. If it has been set, pears will temporarily be substituted for foo; if not, null is returned.

3   The variable foo now has its original value.

EXAMPLE 13.63

(Creating Error Messages Based On Default Values)

1   $ echo ${namex:?"namex is undefined"}
    namex: namex is undefined
2   $ echo ${y?}
    y: parameter null or not set

EXPLANATION

1   The :? modifier will check to see if the variable has been set. If not, the string to
    the right of the ? is printed to standard error, after the name of the variable. If in
    a script, the script exits.
2   If a message is not provided after the ?, the shell sends a default message to stan-
    dard error.

EXAMPLE 13.64

(Creating Substring[a])

1   $ var=notebook
2   $ echo ${var:0:4}
    note
3   $ echo ${var:4:4}
    book
4   $ echo ${var:0:2}
    no

a.   Not available in versions of bash prior to 2.x.

EXPLANATION

1   The variable is assigned the value, notebook.
2   The substring of var starts at offset 0, the n in notebook, and has a length of 4 char-
    acters, ending at the e.
3   The substring of var starts at offset 4, the b in notebook, and has a length of 4 char-
    acters, ending at the k.
4   The substring of var starts at offset 0, the n in notebook, and has a length of 2 char-
    acters, ending at the o.

13.10.9 Variable Expansion of Substrings

Pattern-matching arguments are used to strip off certain portions of a string from either the front or end of the string. The most common use for these operators is stripping off pathname elements from the head or tail of the path. See Table 13.19.

Table 13.19 Variable Expansion Substrings[a]

Expression	Function
${variable%pattern}	Matches the *smallest trailing portion* of the value of variable to pattern and removes it.
${variable%%pattern}	Matches the *largest trailing portion* of the value of variable to pattern and removes it.
${variable#pattern}	Matches the *smallest leading portion* of the value of variable to pattern and removes it.
${variable##pattern}	Matches the *largest leading portion* of the value of variable to pattern and removes it.
${#variable}	Substitutes the number of characters in the variable. If * or @, the length is the number of positional parameters.

a. Not available on versions of bash prior to 2.x.

EXAMPLE 13.65

```
1   $ pathname="/usr/bin/local/bin"
2   $ echo ${pathname%/bin*}
    /usr/bin/local
```

EXPLANATION

1   The local variable pathname is assigned /usr/bin/local/bin.

2   The % removes the *smallest trailing portion* of pathname containing the pattern /bin, followed by zero or more characters; that is, it strips off /bin.

EXAMPLE 13.66

```
1   $ pathname="usr/bin/local/bin"
2   $ echo ${pathname%%/bin*}
    /usr
```

EXPLANATION

1   The local variable pathname is assigned /usr/bin/local/bin.

2   The %% removes the *largest trailing portion* of pathname containing the pattern /bin, followed by zero or more characters; that is, it strips off /bin/local/bin.

EXAMPLE 13.67

```
1   $ pathname=/home/lilliput/jake/.bashrc
2   $ echo ${pathname#/home}
    /lilliput/jake/.bashrc
```

EXPLANATION

1   The local variable pathname is assigned /home/lilliput/jake/.bashrc.

2   The # removes the *smallest leading portion* of pathname containing the pattern /home; that is, /home is stripped from the beginning of the path variable.

EXAMPLE 13.68

```
1   $ pathname=/home/lilliput/jake/.bashrc
2   $ echo ${pathname##*/}
    .bashrc
```

EXPLANATION

1   The local variable pathname is assigned /home/lilliput/jake/.bashrc.

2   The ## removes the *largest leading portion* of pathname containing zero or more characters up to and including the last slash; that is, it strips off /home/lilliput/jake from the path variable.

EXAMPLE 13.69

```
1   $ name="Ebenezer Scrooge"
2   $ echo  ${#name}
    16
```

EXPLANATION

1   The variable name is assigned the string Ebenezer Scrooge.

2   The ${#variable} syntax displays the number of characters in the string assigned to the variable name. There are 16 characters in Ebenezer Scrooge.

13.10.10 Positional Parameters

Normally, the special built-in variables, often called positional parameters, are used in shell scripts when passing arguments from the command line, or used in functions to hold the value of arguments passed to the function. The variables are called positional parameters because they are referenced by numbers 1, 2, 3, and so on, representing their respective positions in the parameter list. See Table 13.20.

The name of the shell script is stored in the $0 variable. The positional parameters can be set, reset, and unset with the set command.

Table 13.20 Positional Parameters

Expression	Function
$0	References the name of the current shell script
$1–$9	Positional parameters 1-9
${10}	Positional parameter 10
$#	Evaluates to the number of positional parameters
$*	Evaluates to all the positional parameters
$@	Same as $*, except when double quoted
"$*"	Evaluates to "$1 $2 $3", and so on
"$@"	Evaluates to "$1" "$2" "$3", and so on

EXAMPLE 13.70

```
1   $ set punky tommy bert jody
    $ echo $*              # Prints all the positional parameters
    punky tommy bert jody
2   $ echo $1              # Prints the first position
    punky
3   $ echo $2 $3           # Prints the second and third position
    tommy bert
4   $ echo $#              # Prints the total number of positional parameters
    4
5   $ set a b c d e f g h i j k l m
    $ print $10            # Prints the first positional parameter followed by a 0
    a0
    $ echo ${10} ${11}     # Prints the 10th and 11th positions
    j k
6   $ echo $#
    13
7   $ echo $*
    a b c d e f g h i j k l m
8   $ set file1 file2 file3
    $ echo \$$#
    $3
9   $ eval echo \$$#
    file3
10  $ set --               # Unsets all positional parameters
```

EXPLANATION

1　The set command assigns values to positional parameters. The $* special variable contains all of the parameters set.

2　The value of the first positional parameter, punky, is displayed.

3　The value of the second and third parameters, tommy and bert, are displayed.

4　The $# special variable contains the number of positional parameters currently set.

5　The set command resets all of the positional parameters. The original parameter list is cleared. To print any positional parameters beyond 9, use the curly braces to keep the two digits together. Otherwise, the value of the first positional parameter is printed, followed by the number appended to it.

6　The number of positional parameters is now 13.

7　The values of all the positional parameters are printed.

8　The dollar sign is escaped; $# is the number of arguments. The echo command displays $3, a literal dollar sign followed by the number of positional parameters.

9　The eval command parses the command line a second time before executing the command. The first time parsed by the shell, the print would display $3; the second time, after eval, the print displays the value of $3, file3.

10　The set command with the -- option clears or unsets all positional parameters.

13.10.11　Other Special Variables

The shell has special variables consisting of a single character. The dollar sign preceding the character allows you to access the value stored in the variable. See Table 13.21.

Table 13.21　Special Variables

Variable	Meaning
$	The PID of the shell
-	The sh options currently set
?	The exit value of last executed command
!	The PID of the last job put in the background

EXAMPLE　13.71

```
1   $ echo The pid of this shell is $$
    The pid of this shell is 4725
2   $ echo The options for this shell are $-
    The options for this shell are imh
```

EXAMPLE 13.71 (CONTINUED)

```
3    $ grep dodo /etc/passwd
     $ echo $?
     1
4    $ sleep 25&
     4736
     $ echo $!
     4736
```

EXPLANATION

1   The $ variable holds the value of the PID for this process.

2   The - variable lists all options for this interactive bash shell.

3   The grep command searches for the string dodo in the /etc/passwd file. The ? variable holds the exit status of the last command executed. Because the value returned from grep is 1, grep is assumed to have failed in its search. An exit status of 0 indicates a successful exit.

4   The ! variable holds the PID number of the last command placed in the background. The & appended to the sleep command sends the command to the background.

13.11 Quoting

Quoting is used to protect special metacharacters from interpretation and prevent parameter expansion. There are three methods of quoting: the backslash, single quotes, and double quotes. The characters listed in Table 13.22 are special to the shell and must be quoted.

Table 13.22   Special Metacharacters Requiring Quotes

Metacharacter	Meaning
;	Command separator
&	Background processing
( )	Command grouping; creates a subshell
{ }	Command grouping; does not create a subshell
		Pipe
<	Input redirection
>	Output redirection

Table 13.22   Special Metacharacters Requiring Quotes (continued)

Metacharacter	Meaning
newline	Command termination
space/tab	Word delimiter
$	Variable substitution character
* [ ] ?	Shell metacharacters for filename expansion

Single and double quotes must be matched. Single quotes protect special metacharacters, such as $, *, ?, |, >, and <, from interpretation. Double quotes also protect special metacharacters from being interpreted, but allow variable and command substitution characters (the dollar sign and backquotes) to be processed. Single quotes will protect double quotes and double quotes will protect single quotes.

Unlike the Bourne shell, bash tries to let you know if you have mismatched quotes. If running interactively, a secondary prompt appears when quotes are not matched; if in a shell script, the file is scanned and if the quote is not matched, the shell will attempt to match it with the next available quote. If the shell cannot match it with the next available quote, the program aborts and the message `bash:unexpected EOF while looking for ``"``` appears on the terminal. Quoting can be a real hassle for even the best of shell programmers!

13.11.1   The Backslash

The backslash is used to quote (or escape) a single character from interpretation. The backslash is not interpreted if placed in single quotes. The backslash will protect the dollar sign ($), backquotes (` `), and the backslash from interpretation if enclosed in double quotes.

EXAMPLE 13.72

```
1   $ echo Where are you going\?
    Where are you going?
2   $ echo Start on this line and \
    >  go to the next line.
    Start on this line and go to the next line.
3   $ echo \\
    \
4   $ echo '\\'
    \\
5   $ echo '\$5.00'
    \$5.00
```

EXAMPLE 13.72 (CONTINUED)

```
6  $ echo "\$5.00"
   $5.00
7  $ echo 'Don\'t you need $5.00?'
   >
   >'
   Don\t you need .00?
```

EXPLANATION

1 The backslash prevents the shell from performing filename substitution on the question mark.

2 The backslash escapes the newline, allowing the next line to become part of this line.

3 Because the backslash itself is a special character, it prevents the backslash following it from interpretation.

4 The backslash is not interpreted when enclosed in single quotes.

5 All characters in single quotes are treated literally. The backslash does not serve any purpose here.

6 When enclosed in double quotes, the backslash prevents the dollar sign from being interpreted for variable substitution.

7 The backslash is not interpreted when inside single quotes; therefore, the shell sees three single quotes (the one at the end of the string is not matched). A secondary prompt appears, waiting for a closing single quote. When the shell finally gets the closing quote, it strips out all of the quotes and passes the string on to the echo command. Because the first two quotes were matched, the rest of the string, t you need $5.00?, was not enclosed within any quotes. The shell tried to evaluate $5; it was empty and .00 printed.

13.11.2 Single Quotes

Single quotes must be matched. They protect all metacharacters from interpretation. To print a single quote, it must be enclosed in double quotes or escaped with a backslash.

EXAMPLE 13.73

```
1  $ echo 'hi there
   > how are you?
   > When will this end?
   > When the quote is matched
   > oh'
```

EXAMPLE 13.73 (CONTINUED)

```
        hi there
        how are you?
        When will this end?
        When the quote is matched
        oh
    2   $ echo Don\'t you need '$5.00?'
        Don't you need $5.00?
    3   $ echo 'Mother yelled, "Time to eat!"'
        Mother yelled, "Time to eat!"
```

EXPLANATION

1   The single quote is not matched on the line. The bash shell produces a secondary prompt. It is waiting for the quote to be matched.

2   The single quotes protect all metacharacters from interpretation. The apostrophe in Don't is escaped with a backslash (the backslash protects a single character, rather than a string). Otherwise, it would match the single quote before the $. Then the single quote at the end of the string would not have a mate. The $ and the ? are enclosed in a pair of single quotes, protecting them from shell interpretation, thus treating them as literals.

3   The single quotes protect the double quotes in this string.

13.11.3 Double Quotes

Double quotes must be matched, will allow variable and command substitution, and protect any other special metacharacters from being interpreted by the shell.

EXAMPLE 13.74

```
    1   $ name=Jody
    2   $ echo "Hi $name, I'm glad to meet you!"
        Hi Jody, I'm glad to meet you!
    3   $ echo "Hey $name, the time is $(date)"
        Hey Jody, the time is Wed Jul 14 14:04:11 PST 2004
```

EXPLANATION

1   The variable name is assigned the string Jody.

2   The double quotes surrounding the string will protect all special metacharacters from interpretation, with the exception of $ in $name. Variable substitution is performed within double quotes.

3   Variable substitution and command substitution are both performed when enclosed within double quotes. The variable name is expanded, and the command in parentheses, date, is executed. (See "Command Substitution," next.)

13.12 Command Substitution

Command substitution is used when assigning the output of a command to a variable or when substituting the output of a command within a string. All shells use backquotes to perform command substitution.[12] Bash allows two forms: the older form, where the command(s) is placed within backquotes, and the new Korn-style form, where the command(s) is placed within a set of parentheses preceded by a dollar sign.

Bash performs the expansion by executing the command and returning the standard output of the command, with any trailing newlines deleted. When the old-style backquote form of substitution is used, the backslash retains its literal meaning except when followed by $, `, or \. When using the $(command) form, all characters between the parentheses make up the command; none are treated specially.

Command substitutions may be nested. To nest when using the old form, the inner backquotes must be escaped with backslashes.

FORMAT

```
`UNIX command`    # Old method with backquotes

$(UNIX command)  # New method
```

EXAMPLE 13.75

```
(The Old Way)
1   $ echo "The hour is `date +%H`"
    The hour is 09
2   $ name=`awk -F: '{print $1}' database`
    $ echo $name
    Ebenezer Scrooge
3   $ ls `ls /etc`
    shutdown
4   $ set `date`
5   $ echo $*
    Wed Jul 14 09:35:21 PDT 2004
6   $ echo $2 $6
    Jul 2004
7   $ echo `basename \`pwd\``
    ellie
```

EXPLANATION

1   The output of the date command is substituted into the string.

2   The output of the awk command is assigned to the variable name and displayed.

---

12. The bash shell allows backquotes for command substitution for upward compatibility, but provides an alternate method as well.

EXPLANATION (CONTINUED)

3   The output of the ls command, enclosed in backquotes, is a list of files from the /etc directory. The filenames will be arguments to the first ls command. All files with the same name in /etc in the current directory are listed. (The files that are not matches in this directory will cause an error message, such as ls: `termcap: No such file or directory`.)

4   The set command assigns the output of the date command to positional parameters. Whitespace separates the list of words into its respective parameters.

5   The $* variable holds all of the parameters. The output of the date command was stored in the $* variable. Each parameter is separated by whitespace.

6   The second and sixth parameters are printed.

7   To set the variable dirname to the name (only) of the present working directory, command substitution is nested. The pwd command is executed first, passing the full pathname of the present working directory as an argument to the UNIX command basename. The basename command strips off all but the last element of a pathname. When nesting commands within backquotes, the backquotes for the inner command must be escaped with a backslash.

The bash alternate for using backquotes in command substitution is presented below in Example 13.76.

EXAMPLE 13.76

```
(The New Way)
1   $ d=$(date)
    $ echo $d
    Wed Jul 14 09:35:21 PDT 2004
2   $ lines = $(cat filex)
3   $ echo The time is $(date +%H)
    The time is 09
4   $ machine=$(uname -n)
    $ echo $machine
    jody
5   $ pwd
    /usr/local/bin
    $ dirname="$(basename $(pwd)) "    # Nesting commands
    $ echo $dirname
    bin
6   $ echo $(cal)                      # Newlines are lost
    July 2004 S M Tu W Th F S 1 2 3 4 5 6 7 8 9 10 11 12 13 14 15
    16 17 18 19 20 21 22 23 24 25 26 27 28 29 30 31
```

EXAMPLE 13.76 (CONTINUED)

```
7  $ echo "$(cal)"
        July 2004
     S  M  Tu  W  Th  F  S
                     1  2  3
     4  5   6  7   8  9 10
    11 12  13 14  15 16 17
    18 19  20 21  22 23 24
    25 26  27 28  29 30 31
```

EXPLANATION

1   The date command is enclosed within parentheses. The output of the command is substituted into the expression, then assigned to the variable d, and displayed.

2   The output from the cat command is assigned to the variable lines.

3   Again the date command is enclosed in parentheses. The output of date +%H, the current hour, is substituted for the expression and echoed to the screen.

4   The variable machine is assigned the output of uname -n, the name of the host machine. The value of the machine variable is echoed to the screen.

5   The output of the pwd command (present working directory) is /usr/local/bin. The variable dirname is assigned the output resulting from command substitution where the command substitutions are nested. $(pwd) is the first command substitution to be be performed. The output of the pwd command is substituted in the expression, then the basename program will use the results of that substitution, /usr/local/bin, as its argument, resulting in basename /usr/local/bin.

6   The output of the cal (the current month) command is echoed. The trailing newlines are deleted when command substitution is performed.

7   When you put the whole command substitution expression in double quotes, the trailing newlines are preserved, and calendar looks like it should.

13.13 Arithmetic Expansion

The shell performs arithmetic expansion by evaluating an arithmetic expression and substituting the result. The expression is treated as if it were in double quotes and the expressions may be nested. For a complete discussion of arithmetic operations, and arithmetic evaluations, see "Arithmetic Operators and the let Command" on page 662.

There are two formats for evaluating arithmetic expressions:

FORMAT

```
$[ expression ]
$(( expression ))
```

EXAMPLE 13.77

```
echo $[ 5 + 4 - 2 ]
7
echo $[ 5 + 3 * 2]
11
echo $[(5 + 3) * 2]
16
echo $(( 5 + 4 ))
9
echo $(( 5 / 0 ))
bash: 5/0: division by 0 ( error token is "0")
```

13.14 Order of Expansion

When you are performing the expansion of variables, commands, arithmetic expressions, and pathnames, the shell is programmed to follow a specific order when scanning the command line. Assuming that the variables are not quoted, the processing is performed in the following order:

1. Brace expansion
2. Tilde expansion
3. Parameter expansion
4. Variable substitution
5. Command substitution
6. Arithmetic expansion
7. Word splitting
8. Pathname expansion

13.15 Arrays

Versions of bash 2.x provide for creation of one-dimensional arrays. Arrays allow you to collect a list of words into one variable name, such as a list of numbers, a list of names, or a list of files. Arrays are created with the built-in function declare -a, or can be created on the fly by giving a subscript to a variable name, such as x[0]=5. The index value is an integer starting at 0. There is no maximum size limit on the array, and indices do not have to be ordered numbers, such as, x[0], x[1], x[2], and so on. To extract an element of an array, the syntax is ${arrayname[index]}. If declare is given the -a and -r options, a read-only array is created.

FORMAT

```
declare -a variable_name
variable = ( item1 item2 item3 ... )
```

EXAMPLE 13.78

```
declare -a nums=(45 33 100 65)
declare -ar names    (array is readonly)
names=( Tom  Dick  Harry)
states=( ME  [3]=CA  CT )
x[0]=55
n[4]=100
```

When assigning values to an array, they are automatically started at index 0 and incremented by 1 for each additional element added. You do not have to provide indices in an assignment, and if you do, they do not have to be in order. To unset an array, use the unset command followed by the array name, and to unset one element of the array, use unset and the arrayname[subscript] syntax.

The declare, local, and read-only built-ins also can take the -a option to declare an array. The read command with the -a option is used to read in a list of words from standard input into array elements.

EXAMPLE 13.79

```
1    $ declare -a friends
2    $ friends=(Sheryl Peter Louise)
3    $ echo ${friends[0]}
     Sheryl
4    $ echo ${friends[1]}
     Peter
5    $ echo ${friends[2]}
     Louise
6    $ echo "All the friends are ${friends[*]}"
     All the friends are Sheryl Peter Louise
7    $ echo "The number of elements in the array is ${#friends[*]}"
     The number of elements in the array is 3
8    $ unset friends  or unset ${friends[*]}
```

EXPLANATION

1   The declare built-in command is used to explicitly declare an array, but it is not necessary. Any variable that uses a subscript, such as variable[0], when being assigned a value, will automatically be treated as an array.

2   The array friends is assigned a list of values: Sheryl, Peter, and Louise.

EXPLANATION (CONTINUED)

3   The first element of the friends array is accessed by enclosing the array name and its subscript in curly braces, with an index of 0 used as the value of the subscript. Sheryl is printed.

4   The second element of the friends array is accessed by using the index value of 1.

5   The third element of the friends array is accessed by using the index value of 2.

6   When you place the asterisk within the subscript, all of the elements of the array can be accessed. This line displays all the elements in the friends array.

7   The syntax ${#friends[*]} produces the size of the array (i.e., the number of elements in the array). On the other hand, ${#friends[0]} produces the number of characters in the value of the first element of the array. There are six characters in Sheryl.

8   The unset built-in command deletes the whole array. Just one element of the array can be removed by typing unset friends[1]; this would remove Sheryl.

EXAMPLE 13.80

```
1   $ x[3]=100
    $ echo ${x[*]}
    100
2   $ echo ${x[0]}
3   $ echo ${x[3]}
    100
4   $ states=(ME  [3]=CA  [2]=CT)
    $ echo ${states[*]}
    ME CA CT
5   $ echo ${states[0]}
    ME
6   $ echo ${states[1]}
7   $ echo ${states[2]}
    CT
8   $ echo ${states[3]}
    CA
```

EXPLANATION

1   The third element of the array, x, is being assigned 100. It doesn't matter if the index number is 3, but because the first two elements do not exist yet, the size of the array is only 1. ${x[*]} displays the one element of the array, x.

2   x[0] has no value, and neither do x[1] and x[2].

3   x[3] has a value of 100.

4   The states array is being assigned ME at index 0, CA at index 3, and CT at index 2. In this example, you can see that bash doesn't care at what index you store values, and that the index numbers do not have to be contiguous.

5   The first element of the states array is printed.

6   There is nothing stored in states[1].

7   The third element of the states array, states[2], was assigned CT.

8   The fourth element of the states array, states[3], was assigned CA.

13.16 Functions

Bash functions are used to execute a group of commands with a name within the context of the current shell (a child process is not forked). They are like scripts, only more efficient. Once defined, functions become part of the shell's memory so that when the function is called, the shell does not have to read it in from the disk as it does with a file. Often functions are used to improve the modularity of a script. Once defined, functions can be used again and again. Although functions can be defined at the prompt when running interactively, they are often defined in the user's initialization file, .bash_profile. They must be defined before they are invoked.

13.16.1   Defining Functions

There are two ways to declare a bash function. One way, the old Bourne shell way, is to give the function name followed by a set of empty parentheses, followed by the function definition. The new way (Korn shell way) is to use the function keyword followed by the function name and then the function definition. If using the new way, the parentheses are optional. The function definition is enclosed in curly braces. It consists of commands separated by semicolons. The last command is terminated with a semicolon. Spaces around the curly braces are required. Any arguments passed to the function are treated as positional parameters within the function. The positional parameters in a function are local to the function. The local built-in function allows local variables to be created within the function definition. Functions may also be recursive; that is, they can call themselves an unlimited number of times.

FORMAT

```
function_name () { commands ; commands; }
function function_name { commands ; commands; }
function function_name () { commands ; commands; }
```

EXAMPLE   13.81

```
1    $ function greet { echo "Hello $LOGNAME, today is $(date)"; }
2    $ greet
     Hello ellie, today is Wed Jul 14 14:56:31 PDT  2004
```

EXAMPLE 13.81 (CONTINUED)

```
3   $ greet () { echo "Hello $LOGNAME, today is $(date)"; }
4   $ greet
    Hello ellie, today is Wed Jul 14 15:16:22 PDT  2004
5   $ declare -f
    declare -f greet()
    {
        echo "Hello $LOGNAME, today is $(date)"
    }
6   $ declare -Fᵃ
    declare -f greet
7   $ export -f greet
8   $ bash              # Start subshell
9   $ greet
    Hello ellie, today is Wed Jul 14 17:59:24 PDT  2004
```

a.   Only on bash version 2.x.

EXPLANATION

1   The keyword function is followed by the name of the function, greet. The function definition is surrounded by curly braces. There must be a space after the opening curly brace. Statements on the same line are terminated with a semicolon.

2   When the greet function is invoked, the command(s) enclosed within the curly braces are executed in the context of the current shell.

3   The greet function is defined again using the Bourne shell syntax, the name of the function, followed by an empty set of parentheses, and the function definition.

4   The greet function is invoked again.

5   The declare command with the -f switch lists all functions defined in this shell and their definitions.

6   The declare command with the -F switch lists only function names.

7   The export command with the -f switch makes the function global (i.e., available to subshells).

8   A new bash shell is started.

9   The function is defined for this child shell because it was exported.

EXAMPLE 13.82

```
1   $ function fun {
        echo "The current working directory is $PWD."
        echo "Here is a list of your files: "
        ls
        echo "Today is $(date +%A).";
    }
```

EXAMPLE 13.82 (CONTINUED)

```
2   $ fun
    The current working directory is /home.
    Here is a list of your files:
    abc       abc123    file1.bak    none       nothing    tmp
    abc1      abc2      file2        nonsense   nowhere    touch
    abc122    file1     file2.bak    noone      one
    Today is Wednesday.
3   $ function welcome { echo "Hi $1 and $2"; }
4   $ welcome tom joe
    Hi tom and joe
5   $ set jane anna lizzy
6   $ echo $*
    jane anna lizzy
7   $ welcome johan joe
    hi johan and joe
8   $ echo  $1 $2
    johan joe
9   $ unset -f welcome      # unsets the function
```

EXPLANATION

1   The function fun is named and defined. The keyword function is followed by the function's name and a list of commands enclosed in curly braces. Commands are listed on separate lines; if they are listed on the same line, they must be separated by semicolons. A space is required after the first curly brace or you will get a syntax error. A function must be defined before it can be used.

2   The function behaves just like a script when invoked. Each of the commands in the function definition is executed in turn.

3   There are two positional parameters used in the function welcome. When arguments are given to the function, the positional parameters are assigned those values.

4   The arguments to the function, tom and joe, are assigned to $1 and $2, respectively. The positional parameters in a function are private to the function and will not interfere with any used outside the function.

5   The positional parameters are set at the command line. These variables have nothing to do with the ones set in the function.

6   $* displays the values of the currently set positional parameters.

7   The function welcome is called. The values assigned to the positional parameters are johan and joe.

8   The positional variables assigned at the command line are unaffected by those set in the function.

9   The unset built-in command with the –f switch unsets the function. It is no longer defined.

13.16.2   Listing and Unsetting Functions

To list functions and their definitions, use the `declare` command. In `bash` versions 2.x and above, `declare -F` lists just function names. The function and its definition will appear in the output, along with the exported and local variables. Functions and their definitions are unset with the `unset -f` command.

13.17 Standard I/O and Redirection

When the shell starts up, it inherits three files: `stdin`, `stdout`, and `stderr`. Standard input normally comes from the keyboard. Standard output and standard error normally go to the screen. There are times when you want to read input from a file or send output or errors to a file. This can be accomplished by using I/O redirection. See Table 13.23 for a list of redirection operators.

Table 13.23   Redirection

Redirection Operator	What It Does
`< filename`	Redirects input
`> filename`	Redirects output
`>> filename`	Appends output
`2> filename`	Redirects error
`2>> filename`	Redirects and appends error
`&> filename`	Redirects output and error
`>& filename`	Redirects output and error (preferred way)
`2>&1`	Redirects error to where output is going
`1>&2`	Redirects output to where error is going
`>|`	Overrides `noclobber` when redirecting output
`<> filename`	Uses file as both standard input and output if a device file (from /dev)

EXAMPLE   13.83

```
1   $ tr '[A-Z]' '[a-z]' < myfile    # Redirect input
2   $ ls > lsfile                    # Redirect output
    $ cat lsfile
    dir1
    dir2
    file1
    file2
    file3
```

EXAMPLE 13.83 (CONTINUED)

```
3   $ date >> lsfile                 # Redirect and append otuput
    $ cat lsfile
    dir1
    dir2
    file1
    file2
    file3
    Sun Sept 17 12:57:22 PDT 2004

4   $ cc prog.c 2> errfile           # Redirect error

5   $ find . -name \*.c -print > foundit 2> /dev/null
    # Redirect output to foundit and errors to /dev/null,
    # respectively.

6   $ find . -name \*.c -print >& foundit
    # Redirect both output and errors to foundit.

7   $ find . -name \*.c -print > foundit 2>&1
    # Redirect output to foundit and send errors to where output
    # is going; i.e. foundit

8   $ echo "File needs an argument" 1>&2
    # Send standard output to error
```

EXPLANATION

1   Instead of getting input from the keyboard, standard input is redirected from the file myfile to the UNIX/Linux tr command. All uppercase letters are converted to lowercase.

2   Instead of sending output to the screen, the ls command redirects its output to the file lsfile.

3   The output of the date command is redirected and appended to lsfile.

4   The C program source file prog.c is compiled. If the compile fails, the standard error is redirected to the file errfile. Now you can take your error file to the local guru for an explanation (of sorts)!

5   The find command starts searching in the current working directory for filenames ending in .c, and prints the filenames to a file named foundit. Errors from the find command are sent to /dev/null.

6   The find command starts searching in the current working directory for filenames ending in .c, and prints the filenames to a file named foundit. The errors are also sent to foundit.

7   Same as 6.

8   The echo command sends its message to standard error. Its standard output is merged with standard error.

13.17.1   The exec Command and Redirection

The exec command can be used to replace the current program with a new one without starting a new process. Standard output or input can be changed with the exec command without creating a subshell. (See Table 13.24.) If a file is opened with exec, subsequent read commands will move the file pointer down the file a line at a time until the end of the file. The file must be closed to start reading from the beginning again. However, if using UNIX utilities such as cat and sort, the operating system closes the file after each command has completed.

Table 13.24   The exec Command

Command	What It Does
exec ls	ls executes in place of the shell. When ls is finished, the shell in which it was started does not return.
exec < filea	Opens filea for reading standard input.
exec > filex	Opens filex for writing standard output.
exec 3< datfile	Opens datfile as file descriptor 3 for reading input.
sort <&3	Datfile is sorted.
exec 4>newfile	Opens newfile as file descriptor (fd) 4 for writing.
ls >&4	Output of ls is redirected to newfile.
exec 5<&4	Makes fd 5 a copy of fd 4.
exec 3<&–	Closes fd 3.

EXAMPLE 13.84

```
1   $ exec date
    Thu Oct 14 10:07:34  PDT 2004
    <Login prompt appears if you are in your login shell >
2   $ exec > temp
    $ ls
    $ pwd
    $ echo Hello
3   $ exec > /dev/tty
4   $ echo Hello
    Hello
```

EXPLANATION

1   The exec command executes the date command in the current shell (does not fork a child shell). Because the date command is executed in place of the current shell, when the date command exits, the shell terminates. If a bash shell had been started from the TC shell, the bash shell would exit and the TC shell prompt would appear. If you are in your login shell when you try this, you will be logged out. If you are working interactively in a shell window, the window exits.

2   The exec command opens standard output for the current shell to the temp file. Output from ls, pwd, and echo will no longer go to the screen, but to temp. (See Figure 13.2.)

3   The exec command reopens standard output to the terminal. Now, output will go to the screen as shown in line 4.

4   Standard output has been directed back to the terminal (/dev/tty).

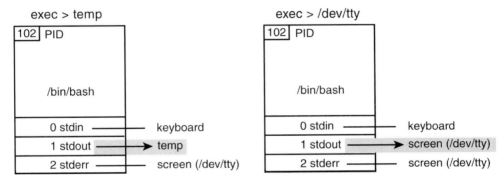

Figure 13.2   The exec command and file descriptors.

EXAMPLE   13.85

```
1   > bash
2   $ cat doit
    pwd
    echo hello
    date
3   $ exec < doit
    /home/homebound/ellie/shell
    hello
    Thu Oct 14 10:07:34  PDT 2004
4   >
```

EXPLANATION

1   From a TC shell prompt, bash is started up. (This is done so that when the exec command exits, the user will not be logged out.)

2   The contents of a file called doit are displayed.

3   The exec command opens standard input to the file called doit. Input is read from the file instead of from the keyboard. The commands from the file doit are executed in place of the current shell. When the last command exits, so does the shell.

4   The bash shell exited when the exec command completed. The TC shell prompt appeared. It was the parent shell. If you had been in your login shell when the exec finished, you would be logged out; if in a window, the window would have disappeared.

EXAMPLE   13.86

```
1   $ exec 3> filex
2   $ who >& 3
3   $ date >& 3
4   $ exec 3>&-
5   $ exec 3<filex
6   $ cat <&3
    ellie     tty1    Jul 21 09:50
    ellie     ttyp1   Jul 21 11:16   (:0.0)
    ellie     ttyp0   Jul 21 16:49   (:0.0)
    Wed Jul 21 17:15:18 PDT 2004
7   $ exec 3<&-
8   $ date >& 3
    date: write error: Bad file descriptor
```

EXPLANATION

1   File descriptor 3 (fd 3) is assigned to filex and opened for redirection of output. See Figure 13.3(a).

2   The output of the who command is sent to fd 3, filex.

3   The output of the date command is sent to fd 3; filex is already opened, so the output is appended to filex.

4   Fd 3 is closed.

5   The exec command opens fd 3 for reading input. Input will be redirected from filex. See Figure 13.3(b).

6   The cat program reads from fd 3, assigned to filex.

7   The exec command closes fd 3. (Actually, the operating system will close the file once end of file is reached.)

8   When attempting to send the output of the date command to fd 3, bash reports an error condition, because fd 3 was previously closed.

exec 3>filex   exec 3<filex

101			102	
/bin/bash			/bin/bash	
0	stdin		0	stdin
1	stdout		1	stdout
2	stderr		2	stderr
3	filex		3	filex

a. opened for writing   b. opened for reading

Figure 13.3 exec and file descriptors.

13.18 Pipes

A *pipe* takes the output from the command on the left-hand side of the pipe symbol and sends it to the input of the command on the right-hand side of the pipe symbol. A pipeline can consist of more than one pipe.

The purpose of the commands in Example 13.87 is to count the number of people logged on (who), save the output of the command in a file (tmp), use the wc -l to count the number of lines in the tmp file (wc -l), and then remove the tmp file (i.e., find the number of people logged on).

EXAMPLE 13.87

```
1    $ who > tmp
2    $ wc -l tmp
     4 tmp
3    $ rm tmp

# Using a pipe saves disk space and time.

4    $ who | wc -l
     4
5    $ du .. | sort -n | sed -n '$p'
     1980   ..
6    $ ( du / | sort -n | sed -n '$p' ) 2> /dev/null
     1057747  /
```

EXPLANATION

1   The output of the who command is redirected to the tmp file.
2   The wc -l command displays the number of lines in tmp.

EXPLANATION (CONTINUED)

3   The tmp file is removed.

4   With the pipe facility, you can perform all three of the preceding steps in one step. The output of the who command is sent to an anonymous kernel buffer; the wc -1 command reads from the buffer and sends its output to the screen. See Figure 13.4.

5   The output of the du command, the number of disk blocks used per directory, starting in the parent directory (..), is piped to the sort command and sorted numerically. It is then piped to the sed command, which prints the last line of the output it receives. See Figure 13.5.

6   The du command (starting in the root directory) will send error messages to stderr (the screen) if it is unable to get into a directory because the permissions have been turned off. When you put the whole command line in a set of parentheses, all the output is sent to the screen, and all the errors are directed to the UNIX/Linux bit bucket, /dev/null.

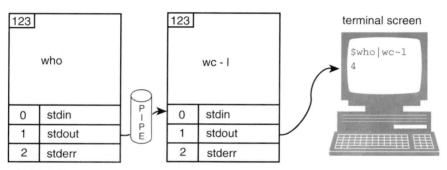

Figure 13.4   The pipe.

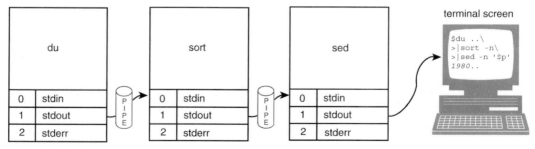

Figure 13.5   Multiple pipes (filter).

13.18.1 The here document and Redirecting Input

The here document is a special form of quoting. It accepts inline text for a program expecting input, such as mail, sort, or cat, until a user-defined terminator is reached. It is often used in shell scripts for creating menus. The command receiving the input is appended with a << symbol, followed by a user-defined word or symbol, and a newline. The next lines of text will be the lines of input to be sent to the command. The input is terminated when the user-defined word or symbol is then placed on a line by itself in the leftmost column (it cannot have spaces surrounding it). The word is used in place of Ctrl-D to stop the program from reading input.

If the terminator is preceded by the <<- operator, leading tabs, and only tabs, may precede the final terminator. The user-defined terminating word or symbol must match exactly from "here" to "here." The following examples illustrate the use of the here document at the command line to demonstrate the syntax. It is much more practical to use them in scripts.

EXAMPLE 13.88

```
1   $ cat << FINISH              ◄─┐    # FINISH is a user-defined terminator
2   > Hello there $LOGNAME         │
3   > The time is $(date +%T).     │
    > I can't wait to see you!!!   │
4   > FINISH                     ◄─┘    # terminator matches first

5   Hello there ellie                   # FINISH on line 1.
    The time is 19:42:12.
    I can't wait to see you!!!
6   $
```

EXPLANATION

1   The UNIX/Linux cat program will accept input until the word FINISH appears on a line by itself.

2   A secondary prompt appears. The following text is input for the cat command. Variable substitution is performed within the here document.

3   Command substitution, $(date +%T), is performed within the here document. Could have also used the older form of command substitution: `date +T`.

4   The user-defined terminator FINISH marks the end of input for the cat program. It cannot have any spaces before or after it and is on a line by itself.

5   The output from the cat program is displayed.

6   The shell prompt reappears.

EXAMPLE 13.89

```
1  $ cat <<- DONE
   >    Hello there
   >        What's up?
   >Bye now The time is `date`.
2  >    DONE
     Hello there
         What's up?
     Bye now The time is Sun Feb 819:48:23 PST 2004.
     $
```

EXPLANATION

1   The cat program accepts input until DONE appears on a line by itself. The <<- operator allows the input and final terminator to be preceded by one or more tabs. Typing this example at the command line may cause problems with the Tab key; the example will work fine, if run from a script.

2   The final matching terminator, DONE, is preceded by a tab. The output of the cat program is displayed on the screen.

13.19 Shell Invocation Options

When the shell is started using the bash command, it can take options to modify its behavior. There are two types of options: single-character options and multicharacter options. The single-character options consist of a single leading dash followed by a single character. The multicharacter options consist of two leading dashes and any number of characters. Multicharacter options must appear before single-character options. An interactive login shell normally starts up with -i (starts an interactive shell), -s (reads from standard input), and -m (enables job control). See Table 13.25.

Table 13.25 Bash 2.x Shell Invocation Options

Option	Meaning
-c string	Commands are read from string. Any arguments after string are assigned to positional parameters, starting at $0.
-D	A list of double quoted strings, preceded by a $, are printed to standard output. These strings are subject to language translation when the current locale is not C or POSIX.
-i	Shell is in the interactive mode. TERM, QUIT, and INTERRUPT are ignored.
-s	Commands are read from standard input and allows the setting of positional parameters.

Table 13.25 Bash 2.x Shell Invocation Options (continued)

Option	Meaning
-r	Starts a restricted shell.
--	Signals the end of options and disables further option processing. Any arguments after -- or - are treated as filenames and arguments.
--dump-strings	Same as -D.
--help	Displays a usage message for a built-in command and exits.
--login	Causes bash to be invoked as a login shell.
--noediting	When bash is running interactively, does not use the Readline library.
--noprofile	When starting up, bash does not read the initialization files: /etc/profile, ~/.bash_profile, ~/.bash_login, or ~/.profile.
--norc	For interactive shells, bash will not read the ~/.bashrc file. Turned on by default, if running shell as sh.
--posix	Changes the behavior of bash to match the POSIX 1003.2 standard, if otherwise it wouldn't.
--quiet	Displays no information at shell startup, the default.
--rcfile file	If bash is interactive, uses this intialization file instead of ~/.bashrc.
--restricted	Starts a restricted shell.
--verbose	Turns on verbose; same as -v.
--version	Displays version information about this bash shell and exits.

13.19.1   The set Command and Options

The set command can be used to turn shell options on and off, as well as for handling command-line arguments. To turn an option on, the dash (-) is prepended to the option; to turn an option off, the plus sign (+) is prepended to the option. See Table 13.26 for a list of set options.

EXAMPLE 13.90

```
1   $ set -f
2   $ echo *
    *
3   $ echo ??
    ??
4   $ set +f
```

EXPLANATION

1   The f option is turned on, disabling filename expansion.

2   The asterisk is not expanded.

3   The question marks are not expanded.

4   The f is turned off; filename expansion is enabled.

Table 13.26   The Built-In set Command Options

Name of Option	Shortcut Switch	What It Does
allexport	-a	Automatically marks new or modified variables for export from the time the option is set until unset.
braceexpand	-B	Enables brace expansion, and is a default setting.
emacs		For command-line editing, uses the emacs built-in editor, and is a default setting.
errexit	-e	If a command returns a nonzero exit status (fails), exits. Not set when reading initialization files.
histexpand	-H	Enables ! and !! when performing history substitution, and is a default setting.
history		Enables command-line history; on by default.
ignoreeof		Disables EOF (Ctrl-D) from exiting a shell; must type exit. Same as setting shell variable, IGNOREEOF=10.
keyword	-k	Places keyword arguments in the environment for a command.
interactive_comments		For interactive shells, a leading # is used to comment out any text remaining on the line.
monitor	-m	Allows job control.
noclobber	-C	Protects files from being overwritten when redirection is used.
noexec	-n	Reads commands, but does not execute them. Used to check the syntax of scripts. Not on when running interactively.
noglob	-d	Disables pathname expansion (i.e., turns off wildcards).
notify	-b	Notifies user when background job finishes.
nounset	-u	Displays an error when expanding a variable that has not been set.

Table 13.26 The Built-In set Command Options (continued)

Name of Option	Shortcut Switch	What It Does
onecmd	-t	Exits after reading and executing one command.
physical	-P	If set, does not follow symbolic links when typing cd or pwd. The physical directory is used instead.
posix		Shell behavior is changed if the default operation doesn't match the POSIX standard.
privileged	-p	When set, the shell does not read the .profile or ENV file and shell functions are not inherited from the environment; automatically set for setuid scripts.
verbose	-v	Turns on the verbose mode for debugging.
vi		For command-line editing, uses the vi built-in editor.
xtrace	-x	Turns on the echo mode for debugging.

13.19.2 The shopt Command and Options

The shopt (bash 2.x) command can also be used to turn shell options on and off.

Table 13.27 The shopt Command Options

Option	Meaning
cdable_vars	If an argument to the cd built-in command is not a directory, it is assumed to be the name of a variable whose value is the directory to change to.
cdspell	Corrects minor errors in the spelling of a directory name in a cd command. The errors checked for are transposed characters, a missing character, and a character too many. If a correction is found, the corrected path is printed, and the command proceeds. Only used by interactive shells.
checkhash	Bash checks that a command found in the hash table exists before trying to execute it. If a hashed command no longer exists, a normal path search is performed.
checkwinsize	Bash checks the window size after each command and, if necessary, updates the values of LINES and COLUMNS.
cmdhist	Bash attempts to save all lines of a multiple-line command in the same history entry. This allows easy re-editing of multiline commands.
dotglob	Bash includes filenames beginning with a dot (.) in the results of filename expansion.

Table 13.27   The shopt Command Options (continued)

Option	Meaning
execfail	A noninteractive shell will not exit if it cannot execute the file specified as an argument to the exec built-in command. An interactive shell does not exit if exec fails.
expand_aliases	Aliases are expanded. Enabled by default.
extglob	The extended pattern-matching features (regular expression metacharacters derived from Korn shell for filename expansion) are enabled.
histappend	The history list is appended to the file named by the value of the HISTFILE variable when the shell exits, rather than overwriting the file.
histreedit	If readline is being used, a user is given the opportunity to re-edit a failed history substitution.
histverify	If set, and readline is being used, the results of history substitution are not immediately passed to the shell parser. Instead, the resulting line is loaded into the readline editing buffer, allowing further modification.
hostcomplete	If set, and readline is being used, bash will attempt to perform hostname completion when a word containing @ is being completed. Enabled by default.
huponexit	If set, bash will send SIGHUP (hangup signal) to all jobs when an interactive login shell exits.
interactive_comments	Allows a word beginning with # to cause that word and all remaining characters on that line to be ignored in an interactive shell. Enabled by default.
lithist	If enabled, and the cmdhist option is enabled, multiline commands are saved to the history with embedded newlines rather than using semicolon separators where possible.
mailwarn	If set, and a file that bash is checking for mail has been accessed since the last time it was checked, the message The mail in mailfile has been read is displayed.
nocaseglob	If set, bash matches filenames in a case-insensitive fashion when performing filename expansion.
nullglob	If set, bash allows filename patterns that match no files to expand to a null string, rather than themselves.
promptvars	If set, prompt strings undergo variable and parameter expansion after being expanded. Enabled by default.

Table 13.27 The shopt Command Options (continued)

Option	Meaning
restricted_shell	The shell sets this option if it is started in restricted mode. The value may not be changed. This is not reset when the startup files are executed, allowing the startup files to discover whether or not a shell is restricted.
shift_verbose	If this is set, the shift built-in prints an error message when the shift count exceeds the number of positional parameters.
sourcepath	If set, the source built-in uses the value of PATH to find the directory containing the file supplied as an argument. Enabled by default.
source	A synonym for dot (.).

13.20 Shell Built-In Commands

The shell has a number of commands that are built-in to its source code. Because the commands are built-in, the shell doesn't have to locate them on disk, making execution much faster. The help feature provided with bash gives you online help for any built-in command. The built-in commands are listed in Table 13.28.

Table 13.28 Built-In Commands

Command	What It Does
:	Do-nothing command; returns exit status zero.
.	Executes program in context of current process; same as source.
. file	The dot command reads and executes command from file.
break	Breaks out of the innermost loop.
break [n]	See "The break Command" on page 919.
alias	Lists and creates "nicknames" for existing commands.
bg	Puts a job in the background.
bind	Display current key and function bindings, or binds keys to a readline function or macro.
builtin [sh-builtin [args]]	Runs a shell built-in, passing it args and returning zero exit status. Useful if a function and built-in have the same name.
cd [arg]	Changes the directory to home if no arg or to value of arg.

Table 13.28 Built-In Commands (continued)

Command	What It Does
command command [arg]	Runs a command even if a function has the same name; i.e., bypasses function lookup.
continue [n]	See "The continue Command" on page 920.
declare [var]	Displays all variables or declares variables with optional attributes.
dirs	Displays a list of currently remembered directories resulting from pushd.
disown	Removes an active job from the job table.
echo [args]	Displays args terminated with a newline.
enable	Enables and disables shell built-in commands.
eval [args]	Reads args as input to the shell and executes the resulting command(s).
exec command	Runs command in place of this shell.
exit [n]	Exits the shell with status n.
export [var]	Makes var known to subshells.
fc	History's fix command for editing history commands.
fg	Puts background job into foreground.
getopts	Parses and processes command-line options.
hash	Controls the internal hash table for quicker searches for commands.
help [command]	Displays helpful info about built-in commands and, if command is specified, detailed help about that built-in command.
history	Displays the history list with line numbers.
jobs	Lists jobs put in the background.
kill [-signal process]	Sends the signal to the PID number or job number of the process. Type at the prompt: kill -l.
getopts	Used in shell scripts to parse command line and check for legal options.
let	Used for evaluating arithmetic expressions and assigning results of arithmetic calculations to variables.
local	Used in functions to restrict the scope of variables to the function.
logout	Exits the login shell.
popd	Removes entries from the directory stack.

Table 13.28   Built-In Commands (continued)

Command	What It Does
pushd	Adds entries to the directory stack.
pwd	Prints present working directory.
read [var]	Reads line from standard input into variable var.
readonly [var]	Makes variable var read-only. Cannot be reset.
return [n]	Returns from a function where n is the exit value given to the return.
set	Sets options and positional parameters. See "The set Command and Positional Parameters" on page 876.
shift [n]	Shifts positional parameters to the left n times.
stop pid	Halts execution of the process number PID.
suspend	Stops execution of the current shell (but not if a login shell).
test	Checks file types and evaluates conditional expressions.
times	Prints accumulated user and system times for processes run from this shell.
trap [arg] [n]	When shell receives signal n (0, 1, 2, or 15), executes arg.
type [command]	Prints the type of command (e.g., pwd is a built-in shell command).
typeset	Same as declare. Sets variables and gives them attributes.
ulimit	Diplays and sets process resource limits.
umask [octal digits]	Sets user file creation mode mask for owner, group, and others.
unalias	Unsets aliases.
unset [name]	Unset value of variable or function.
wait [pid#n]	Waits for background process with PID number n and reports termination status.

LAB 48: bash SHELL—GETTING STARTED

1. What process puts the login prompt on your screen?

2. What process assigns values to HOME, LOGNAME, and PATH?

3. How do you know what shell you are using?

4. What command will allow you to change your login shell?

5. Where is your login shell assigned (what file)?

6. Explain the difference between the /etc/profile and ~/.bash_profile file. Which one is executed first?

7. Edit your .bash_profile file as follows:

   a. Welcome the user.

   b. Add your home directory to the path if it is not there.

   c. Set erase to the Backspace key using stty.

   d. Type source.bash_profile. What is the function of the source command?

8. What is the BASH_ENV file? When is it executed?

9. What is the default primary prompt?

   a. Change the prompt to include the time of day and your home directory.

   b. What is the default secondary prompt? What is its function?

10. Explain the function of each of the following settings:

    a. set -o ignoreeof

    b. set -o noclobber

    c. set -o emacs

    d. set -o vi

11. In what file are the settings in the previous example stored? Why are they stored there?

12. What does shopt -p do? Why use shopt instead of set?

13. What is a built-in command? How can you tell if a command is a built-in or an executable? What is the purpose of the builtin command? The enable command?

14. What would cause the shell to return an exit status of 127?

LAB 49: JOB CONTROL

1. What is the difference between a program and a process? What is a job?

2. What is the PID of your shell?

3. How do you stop a job?

4. What command brings a background job into the foreground?

5. How do you list all running jobs? All stopped jobs?

6. What is the purpose of the kill command?

7. What does jobs -l display? What does kill -l display?

LAB 50: COMMAND COMPLETION, HISTORY, AND ALIASES

1. What is filename completion?

2. What is the name of the file that stores a history of commands entered at the command line?

3. What does the HISTSIZE variable control? What does HISTFILESIZE control?

4. What does "bang, bang" mean?

5. How would you re-execute the last command that started with a v?

6. How would you re-execute the 125th command? How would you print the history list in reverse?

7. How do you set interactive editing to use the vi editor? In what initialization file would you put this setting?

8. What is the fc command?

9. What is the purpose of the Readline library? From what initialization file does it read instructions?

10. What is key binding? How do you find out what keys are bound?

11. What is the universal argument?

12. Create an alias for the following commands:

   a. clear

   b. fc -s

   c. ls --color=tty

   d. kill -l

LAB 51: SHELL METACHARACTERS

1. Make a directory called wildcards. Cd to that directory and type at the prompt:

   touch ab abc a1 a2 a3 a11 a12 ba ba.1 ba.2 filex filey AbC ABC ABc2 abc

   Write and test the command that will do the following:

   a. List all files starting with a.

   b. List all files ending in at least one digit.

   c. List all files starting with a or A.

   d. List all files ending in a period, followed by a digit.

   e. List all files containing just two alphabetic characters.

   f. List three character files where all letters are uppercase.

   g. List files ending in 10, 11, or 12.

   h. List files ending in x or y.

   i. List all files ending in a digit, an uppercase letter, or a lowercase letter.

   j. List all files *not* starting with a b or B.

   k. Remove two character files starting with a or A.

LAB 52: REDIRECTION

1. What are the names of the three file streams associated with your terminal?

2. What is a file descriptor?

3. What command would you use to do the following:

    a. Redirect the output of the ls command to a file called lsfile?

    b. Redirect and append the output of the date command to lsfile?

    c. Redirect the output of the who command to lsfile? What happened?

4. What happens when you type cp all by itself?

5. How do you save the error message from the above example to a file?

6. Use the find command to find all files, starting from the parent directory, of type directory. Save the standard output in a file called found and any errors in a file called found.errs.

7. Take the output of three commands and redirect the output to a file called gottem_all?

8. Use a pipe(s) with the ps and wc commands to find out how many processes you are currently running.

LAB 53: VARIABLES

1. What is a positional parameter? Type at the command line:

    set dogs cats birds fish

    a. How do you list all of the positional parameters?

    b. Which positional parameter is assigned birds?

    c. How do you print the number of positional parameters?

    d. How do you remove all the positional parameters from the shell's memory?

2. What is an environment variable? What is the command used to list them? Create an environment variable called CITY and assign it the value of your hometown. How do you export it?

3. What is a local variable? Set a local variable to your name. Print its value. Unset it.

4. What is the function of declare -i?

5. What does the $$ variable display? What does the $! display?

14

Programming the Bash Shell

14.1 Introduction

When commands are executed from within a file, instead of from the command line, the file is called a shell script and the shell is running noninteractively. When the bash (Bourne Again) shell starts running noninteractively, it looks for the environment variable, BASH_ENV (ENV) and starts up the file (normally .bashrc) assigned as its value. After the BASH_ENV file has been read, the shell will start executing commands in the script.[1]

14.1.1   The Steps in Creating a Shell Script

A shell script is normally written in an editor and consists of commands interspersed with comments. Comments are preceded by a pound sign (#) and consist of text used to document what is going on.

The First Line.   The first line at the top left corner of the script will indicate the program that will be executing the lines in the script. This line, commonly called the *shbang* line, is written as

```
#!/bin/bash
```

The #!, also called the *magic number*, is used by the kernel to identify the program that should be interpreting the lines in the script. This line must be the top line of your script. The bash program can also accept arguments to modify its behavior. See Table 14.8 on page 951 for a list of bash options.

---

1. When bash starts interactively, if the -norc or --norc option is given, the BASH_ENV or ENV file will not be read.

Comments.   *Comments* are lines preceded by a pound sign and can be on a line by themselves or on a line following a script command. They are used to document your script. It is sometimes difficult to understand what the script is supposed to do if it is not commented. Although comments are important, they are often too sparse or not used at all. Try to get used to commenting what you are doing not only for someone else, but also for yourself. Two days from now you may not recall exactly what you were trying to do.

Executable Statements and bash Shell Constructs.   A bash shell program consists of a combination of UNIX/Linux commands, bash shell commands, programming constructs, and comments.

Making the Script Executable.   When you create a file, it is not given the execute permission. You need this permission to run your script. Use the chmod command to turn on the execute permission.

EXAMPLE 14.1

```
1   $ chmod +x myscript
2   $ ls -lF myscript
    -rwxr-xr-x   1 ellie   0 Jul  13:00 myscript*
```

EXPLANATION

1   The chmod command is used to turn on the execute permission for the user, group, and others.

2   The output of the ls command indicates that all users have execute permission on the myscript file. The asterisk at the end of the filename also indicates that this is an executable program.

A Scripting Session.   In the following example, the user will create a script in the editor. After the user saves the file, the execute permissions are turned on, and the script is executed. If there are errors in the program, the shell will respond immediately.

EXAMPLE 14.2

```
(The Script)
1   #!/bin/bash
2   # This is the first Bash shell program of the day.
    # Scriptname: greetings
    # Written by:  Barbara Bashful
3   echo "Hello $LOGNAME, it's nice talking to you."
4   echo "Your present working directory is `pwd`."
    echo "You are working on a machine called `uname -n`."
    echo "Here is a list of your files."
```

EXAMPLE 14.2 (CONTINUED)

```
5    ls    # List files in the present working directory
6    echo  "Bye for now $LOGNAME. The time is `date +%T`!"

(The Command Line)
     $ greetings     # Don't forget to turn turn on x permission!
     bash: ./greetings: Permission denied.
     $ chmod +x greetings
     $ greetings  or  ./greetings
3    Hello barbara, it's nice talking to you.
4    Your present working directory is /home/lion/barbara/prog
     You are working on a machine called lion.
     Here is a list of your files.
5    Afile        cplus    letter    prac
     Answerbook   cprog    library   prac1
     bourne       joke     notes     perl5
6    Bye for now barbara. The time is 18:05:07!
```

EXPLANATION

1   The first line of the script, #!/bin/bash, lets the kernel know what interpreter will execute the lines in this program; in this case, the bash interpreter.

2   The comments are nonexecutable lines preceded by a pound sign. They can be on a line by themselves or appended to a line after a command.

3   After variable substitution is performed by the shell, the echo command displays the line on the screen.

4   After command substitution is performed by the shell, the echo command displays the line on the screen.

5   The ls command is executed. The comment will be ignored by the shell.

6   The echo command displays the string enclosed within double quotes. Variables and command substitution (backquotes) are expanded when placed within double quotes. In this case, the quotes were really not necessary.

14.2 Reading User Input

14.2.1 Variables (Review)

In the last chapter we talked about declaring and unsetting variables. Variables are set local to the current shell or as environment variables. Unless your shell script will invoke another script, variables are normally set as local variables within a script. (See "Variables" on page 810.)

To extract the value from a variable, precede the variable with a dollar sign. You can enclose the variable within double quotes and the dollar sign will be interpreted by the shell for variable expansion. Variable expansion is not performed if the variable is enclosed in single quotes.

EXAMPLE 14.3

```
1   name="John Doe" or declare name="John Doe"   # local variable
2   export NAME="John Doe"    # global variable
3   echo "$name" "$NAME"      # extract the value
```

14.2.2   The read Command

The read command is a built-in command used to read input from the terminal or from a file (see Table 14.1). The read command takes a line of input until a newline is reached. The newline at the end of a line will be translated into a null byte when read. If no names are supplied, the line read is assigned to the special built-in variable REPLY. You can also use the read command to cause a program to stop until the user hits Enter. To see how the read command is most effectively used for reading lines of input from a file, see "Looping Commands" on page 903. The -r option to read causes the backslash/newline pair to be ignored; the backslash is treated as part of the line. The read command has four options to control its behavior: -a, -e, -p, and -r.[2]

Table 14.1   The read Command

Format	Meaning
read answer	Reads a line from standard input and assigns it to the variable answer
read first last	Reads a line from standard input to the first whitespace or newline, putting the first word typed into the variable first and the rest of the line into the variable last
read	Reads a line from standard input and assigns it to the built-in variable REPLY (Bash and Korn shell)
read –a arrayname	Reads a list of words into an array called arrayname[a]
read –e	Used in interactive shells with command-line editing in effect; for example, if editor is vi, vi commands can be used on the input line[a]
read –p prompt	Prints a prompt, waits for input, and stores input in REPLY variable[a]
read –r line	Allows the input to contain a backslash[a]

a. Not implemented on versions of bash prior to 2.0.

---

2. Options -a, -e, and -p are available only in bash versions 2.x.

EXAMPLE   14.4

```
(The Script)
    #!/bin/bash
    # Scriptname: nosy

    echo -e "Are you happy? \c"
1   read answer
    echo "$answer is the right response."
    echo -e "What is your full name? \c"
2   read first middle last
    echo "Hello $first"
    echo -n "Where do you work? "
3   read
4   echo I guess $REPLY keeps you busy!
--------------------------------------------------------a
5   read -p "Enter your job title: "
6   echo "I thought you might be an $REPLY."
7   echo -n "Who are your best friends? "
8   read -a friends
9   echo "Say hi to ${friends[2]}."
--------------------------------------------------------
(The Output)
    $ nosy
    Are you happy? Yes
1   Yes is the right response.
2   What is your full name? Jon Jake Jones
    Hello Jon
3   Where do you work? the Chico Nut Factory
4   I guess the Chico Nut Factory keeps you busy!
5   Enter your job title: Accountant
6   I thought you might be an Accountant.
7,8 Who are your best friends? Melvin Tim Ernesto
9   Say hi to Ernesto.
```

a.   The commands listed below this line are not implemented on versions of bash prior to 2.x.

EXPLANATION

1   The read command accepts a line of user input and assigns the input to the variable answer.

2   The read command accepts input from the user and assigns the first word of input to the variable first, the second word of input to the variable middle, and all the rest of the words up to the end of the line to the variable last.

3   A line is read from standard input and stored in the built-in REPLY variable.

4   The value of the REPLY variable is printed.

EXPLANATION (CONTINUED)

5   With the -p option, the read command produces a prompt, Enter your job title: and stores the line of input in the special built-in REPLY variable.

6   The value of the REPLY variable is displayed in the string.

7   The user is asked to enter input.

8   With the -a option, the read command takes input as an array of words. The array is called friends. The elements read into the array are Melvin, Tim, and Ernesto.

9   The third element of the friends array, Ernesto, is printed. Array indices start at 0.

EXAMPLE 14.5

```
(The Script)
    #!/bin/bash
    # Scriptname: printer_check
    # Script to clear a hung-up printer
1   if [ $LOGNAME != root ]
    then
        echo "Must have root privileges to run this program"
        exit 1
    fi
2   cat << EOF
      Warning: All jobs in the printer queue will be removed.
      Please turn off the printer now. Press return when you
      are ready to continue. Otherwise press Control C.
    EOF
3   read JUNK        # Wait until the user turns off the printer
    echo
4   /etc/rc.d/init.d/lpd stop        # Stop the printer
5   echo -e "\nPlease turn the printer on now."
6   echo "Press Enter to continue"
7   read JUNK                # Stall until the user turns the printer back on
    echo                     # A blank line is printed
8   /etc/rc.d/init.d/lpd start    # Start the printer
```

EXPLANATION

1   Checks to see if user is root. If not, sends an error and exits.

2   Creates a here document. Warning message is displayed on the screen.

3   The read command waits for user input. When the user presses Enter, the variable JUNK accepts whatever is typed. The variable is not used for anything. The read in this case is used to wait until the user turns off the printer, comes back, and presses Enter.

4   The lpd program stops the print daemon.

5   Now it's time to turn the printer back on!

6   The user is asked to press Enter when ready.

7   Whatever the user types is read into the variable JUNK, and when Enter is pressed, the program will resume execution.

8   The lpd program starts the print daemon.

14.3 Arithmetic

14.3.1   Integers (declare and let Commands)

The declare Command.   Variables can be declared as integers with the declare -i command. If you attempt to assign any string value, bash assigns 0 to the variable. Arithmetic can be performed on variables that have been declared as integers. (If the variable has not been declared as an integer, the built-in let command allows arithmetic operations. See "The let Command" on page 873.) If you attempt to assign a floating-point number, bash reports a syntax error. Numbers can also be represented in different bases such as *binary*, *octal*, and *hex*.

EXAMPLE   14.6

```
1   $ declare -i num
2   $ num=hello
    $ echo $num
    0
3   $ num=5 + 5
    bash: +: command not found
4   $ num=5+5
    $ echo $num
    10
5   $ num=4*6
    $ echo $num
    24
6   $ num="4 * 6"
    $ echo $num
    24
7   $ num=6.5
    bash: num: 6.5: syntax error in expression (remainder of expression is ".5")
```

EXPLANATION

1   The declare command with the -i option creates an integer variable num.

2   Trying to assign the string hello to the integer variable num causes the string to be stored as 0.

EXPLANATION (CONTINUED)

3 The whitespace must be quoted or removed unless the `let` command is used.

4 The whitespace is removed and arithmetic is performed.

5 Multiplication is performed and the result assigned to num.

6 The whitespace is quoted so that the multiplication can be performed and to keep the shell from expanding the wildcard (*).

7 Because the variable is set to integer, adding a fractional part causes a bash syntax error.

Listing Integers. The `declare` command with only the `-i` argument will list all preset integers and their values, as shown in the following display.

```
$ declare -i
declare -ir EUID="15"      # effective user id
declare -ir PPID="235"     # parent process id
declare -ir UID="15"       # user id
```

Representing and Using Different Bases. Numbers can be represented in decimal (base 10, the default), octal (base 8), hexadecimal (base 16), and a range from base 2 to 36.

FORMAT

```
variable=base#number-in-that-base
```

EXAMPLE 14.7

```
n=2#101    # Base is 2; number 101 is in base 2
```

EXAMPLE 14.8

```
(The Command Line)
1 $ declare -i x=017
  $ echo $x
  15
2 $ x=2#101
  $ echo $x
  5
3 $ x=8#17
  $ echo $x
  15
4 $ x=16#b
  $ echo $x
  11
```

EXPLANATION

1. The declare function is used to assign an integer variable x the octal value 017. Octal numbers must start with a leading 0. 15, the decimal value of 017, is printed.

2. The variable x is assigned the value of 101 (binary). 2 represents the base, separated by a #, and the number in that base, 101. The value of x is printed as decimal, 5.

3. The variable x is assigned the value of 17 (octal). The value of x is printed as decimal, 15.

4. The variable x is assigned the value of b (hexadecimal). The value of x is decimal 11.

The let Command.   The let command is a bash built-in command that is used to perform integer arithmetic and numeric expression testing. To see what let operators your version of bash supports, type at the prompt:

```
help let
```

A list of the let operators is also found in Table 14.4 on page 884.

EXAMPLE 14.9

```
(The Command Line)
1    $ i=5  or let i=5
2    $ let i=i+1
     $ echo $i
     6
3    $ let "i = i + 2"
     $ echo $i
     8
4    $ let "i+=1"
     $ echo $i
     9
5    $ i=3
6    $ (( i+=4))
     $ echo $i
     7
7    $ (( i=i-2 ))
     $ echo $i
     5
```

EXPLANATION

1. The variable i is assigned the value 5.

2. The let command will add 1 to the value of i. The $ (dollar sign) is not required for variable substitution when performing arithmetic.

3. The quotes are needed if the arguments contain whitespace.

4. The shortcut operator, +=, is used to add 1 to the value of i.

EXPLANATION (CONTINUED)

5   The variable i is assigned the value 3.

6   The double parentheses can be used to replace let.[a] 4 is added and assigned to i.

7   2 is subtracted from i. We could have also written i-=2

a.   Implemented in versions of bash 2.x.

14.3.2   Floating-Point Arithmetic

Bash supports only integer arithmetic, but the bc, awk, and nawk utilities are useful if you need to perform more complex calculations.

EXAMPLE 14.10

```
(The Command Line)
1   $ n=`echo "scale=3; 13 / 2" | bc`
    $ echo $n
    6.500
2   product=`gawk -v x=2.45 -v y=3.123 'BEGIN{printf "%.2f\n",x*y}'`
    $ echo $product
    7.65
```

EXPLANATION

1   The output of the echo command is piped to the bc program. The scale is set to 3, which is the number of significant digits to the right of the decimal point that will be printed. The calculation is to divide 13 by 2. The entire pipeline is enclosed in backquotes. Command substitution will be performed and the output assigned to the variable n.

2   The gawk program gets its values from the argument list passed in at the command line, x=2.45 y=3.123. After the numbers are multiplied, the printf function formats and prints the result with a precision of two places to the right of the decimal point. The output is assigned to the variable product.

14.4 Positional Parameters and Command-Line Arguments

14.4.1   Positional Parameters

Information can be passed into a script via the command line. Each word (separated by whitespace) following the script name is called an argument.

Command-line arguments can be referenced in scripts with positional parameters; for example, $1 for the first argument, $2 for the second argument, $3 for the third argument, and so on. After $9, curly braces are used to keep the number as one number. For example, positional parameter 10 is referenced as ${10}. The $# variable is used to test for the number of parameters, and $* is used to display all of them. Positional parameters can be set or reset with the set command. When the set command is used, any positional parameters previously set are cleared out. See Table 14.2.

Table 14.2 Positional Parameters

Positional Parameter	What It References
$0	References the name of the script
$#	Holds the value of the number of positional parameters
$*	Lists all of the positional parameters
$@	Means the same as $*, except when enclosed in double quotes
"$*"	Expands to a single argument (e.g., "$1 $2 $3")
"$@"	Expands to separate arguments (e.g., "$1" "$2" "$3")
$1 ... ${10}	References individual positional parameters

EXAMPLE 14.11

```
(The Script)
    #!/bin/bash
    # Scriptname: greetings2
    echo "This script is called $0."
1   echo  "$0  $1 and $2"
    echo "The number of positional parameters is $#"
    ----------------------------------------------------------

(The Command Line)
    $ chmod +x greetings2
2   $ greetings2
    This script is called  greetings2.
    greetings  and
    The number of positional parameters is
3   $ greetings2 Tommy
    This script is called greetings2.
    greetings Tommy and
    The number of positional parameters is 1
4   $ greetings2 Tommy Kimberly
    This script is called greetings2.
    greetings Tommy and Kimberly
    The number of positional parameters is 2
```

EXPLANATION

1   In the script greetings2, positional parameter $0 references the script name, $1 the first command-line argument, and $2 the second command-line argument.

2   The greetings2 script is executed without any arguments passed. The output illustrates that the script is called greetings2 ($0 in the script) and that $1 and $2 were never assigned anything; therefore, their values are null and nothing is printed.

3   This time, one argument is passed, Tommy. Tommy is assigned to positional parameter 1.

4   Two arguments are entered, Tommy and Kimberly. Tommy is assigned to $1 and Kimberly is assigned to $2.

14.4.2   The set Command and Positional Parameters

The set command with arguments resets the positional parameters.[3] Once reset, the old parameter list is lost. To unset all of the positional parameters, use set --. $0 is always the name of the script.

EXAMPLE 14.12

```
(The Script)
    #!/bin/bash
    # Scriptname: args
    # Script to test command-line arguments
1   echo The name of this script is $0.
2   echo The arguments are $*.
3   echo The first argument is $1.
4   echo The second argument is $2.
5   echo The number of arguments is $#.
6   oldargs=$*
7   set Jake Nicky Scott      # Reset the positional parameters
8   echo All the positional parameters are $*.
9   echo The number of positional parameters is $#.
10  echo "Good-bye for now, $1."
11  set $(date)               # Reset the positional parameters
12  echo The date is $2 $3, $6.
13  echo "The value of \$oldargs is $oldargs."
14  set $oldargs
15  echo $1 $2 $3
```

---

3. Remember, without arguments, the set command displays all the variables that have been set for this shell, local and exported. With options, the set command turns on and off shell control options such as -x and -v.

EXAMPLE 14.12 (CONTINUED)

```
(The Output)
     $ args a b c d
1    The name of this script is args.
2    The arguments are a b c d.
3    The first argument is a.
4    The second argument is b.
5    The number of arguments is 4.
8    All the positional parameters are Jake Nicky Scott.
9    The number of positional parameters is 3.
10   Good-bye for now, Jake.
12   The date is Mar 25, 2004.
13   The value of $oldargs is a b c d.
15   Wed Mar 25
```

EXPLANATION

1   The name of the script is stored in the $0 variable.

2   $* represents all of the positional parameters.

3   $1 represents the first positional parameter (command-line argument).

4   $2 represents the second positional parameter.

5   $# is the total number of positional parameters (command-line arguments).

6   All positional parameters are saved in a variable called oldargs.

7   The set command allows you to reset the positional parameters, clearing out the old list. Now, $1 is Jake, $2 is Nicky, and $3 is Scott.

8   $* represents all of the parameters, Jake, Nicky, and Scott.

9   $# represents the number of parameters, 3.

10 $1 is Jake.

11 After command substitution is performed (i.e., date is executed), the positional parameters are reset to the output of the date command.

12 The new values of $2, $3, and $6 are displayed.

13 The values saved in oldargs are printed.

14 The set command creates positional parameters from the values stored in oldargs.

15 The first three positional parameters are displayed.

EXAMPLE 14.13

```
(The Script)
     #!/bin/bash
     # Scriptname: checker
     # Script to demonstrate the use of special variable modifiers and arguments
1    name=${1:?"requires an argument" }
     echo Hello $name
```

EXAMPLE 14.13 (CONTINUED)

```
(The Command Line)
2   $ checker
    checker: 1: requires an argument
3   $ checker Sue
    Hello Sue
```

EXPLANATION

1   The special variable modifier :? will check whether $1 has a value. If not, the script exits and the message is printed.

2   The program is executed without an argument. $1 is not assigned a value; an error is displayed.

3   The checker program is given a command-line argument, Sue. In the script, $1 is assigned Sue. The program continues.

How $* and $@ Differ.   The $* and $@ differ only when enclosed in double quotes. When $* is enclosed within double quotes, the parameter list becomes a single string. When $@ is enclosed within double quotes, each of the parameters is quoted; that is, each word is treated as a separate string.

EXAMPLE 14.14

```
1   $ set 'apple pie' pears peaches
2   $ for i in $*
    > do
    > echo $i
    > done
    apple
    pie
    pears
    peaches

3   $ set 'apple pie' pears peaches
4   $ for i in "$*"
    > do
    > echo $i
    > done
    apple pie pears peaches

5   $ set 'apple pie' pears peaches
6   $ for i in $@
    > do
    > echo $i
```

EXAMPLE   14.14 (CONTINUED)

```
> done
apple
pie
pears
peaches

7   $ set 'apple pie' pears peaches
8   $ for i in "$@"        # At last!!
> do
> echo $i
> done
apple pie
pears
peaches
```

EXPLANATION

1   The positional parameters are set.

2   When $* is expanded, the quotes surrounding apple pie are stripped; apple and pie become two separate words. The for loop assigns each of the words, in turn, to the variable i, and then prints the value of i. Each time through the loop, the word on the left is shifted off, and the next word is assigned to the variable i.

3   The positional parameters are set.

4   By enclosing $* in double quotes, the entire parameter list becomes one string, apple pie pears peaches. The entire list is assigned to i as a single word. The loop makes one iteration.

5   The positional parameters are set.

6   Unquoted, $@ and $* behave the same way (see entry 2 of this explanation).

7   The positional parameters are set.

8   By surrounding $@ with double quotes, each of the positional parameters is treated as a quoted string. The list would be apple pie, pears, and peaches. The desired result is finally achieved.

14.5 Conditional Constructs and Flow Control

14.5.1   Exit Status

Conditional commands allow you to perform some task(s) based on whether a condition succeeds or fails. The if command is the simplest form of decision making; the if/else commands allow a two-way decision; and the if/elif/else commands allow a multiway decision.

Bash allows you to test two types of conditions: the success or failure of commands or whether an expression is true or false. In either case, the exit status is always used. An exit status of 0 indicates success or true, and an exit status that is nonzero indicates failure or false. The ? status variable contains a numeric value representing the exit status. To refresh your memory on how exit status works, look at Example 14.15.

EXAMPLE 14.15

```
   (At the Command Line)
 1  $ name=Tom
 2  $ grep "$name"  /etc/passwd
    Tom:8ZKX2F:5102:40:Tom Savage:/home/tom:/bin/sh
 3  $ echo $?
    0                  # Success!
 4  $ name=Fred
 5  $ grep "$name" /etc/passwd
    $ echo $?
    1                  # Failure
```

EXPLANATION

1 The variable name is assigned the string Tom.

2 The grep command will search for string Tom in the passwd file.

3 The ? variable contains the exit status of the last command executed; in this case, the exit status of grep. If grep is successful in finding the string Tom, it will return an exit status of 0. The grep command was successful.

4 The variable name is assigned Fred.

5 The grep command searches for Fred in the passwd file and is unable to find him. The ? variable has a value of 1, indicating that grep failed.

14.5.2   The Built-In test and let Commands

The test Command with Single Brackets.   To evaluate an expression, the built-in test command is commonly used. This command is also linked to the bracket symbol. Either the test command itself can be used, or the expression can be enclosed in a set of single brackets. Shell metacharacter expansion is not performed on expressions evaluated with the simple test command or when square brackets are used. Because word splitting is performed on variables, strings containing whitespace must be quoted. (See Example 14.16.)

The test Command with Double Brackets.   On versions of bash 2.x, double brackets [[ ]] (the built-in compound test command) can be used to evaluate expressions. Word splitting is not performed on variables and pattern matching is done, allowing the expansion of metacharacters. A literal string containing whitespace must be quoted and if a string (with or without whitespace) is to be evaluated as an exact string, rather than part of a pattern, it too must be enclosed in quotes. The logical operators && (AND) and || (OR) replace the -a and -o operators used with the simple test command. (See Example 14.17.)

Table 14.3 The test Command Operators

Test Operator	Tests True If
String Test	
[string1 = string2] [string1==string2]	String1 is equal to String2 (*space surrounding = required*). (Can be used instead of the single = sign on bash versions 2.x.)
[string1 != string2]	String1 is not equal to String2 (*space surrounding != required*).
[string]	String is not null.
[-z string]	Length of string is zero.
[-n string]	Length of string is nonzero.
[-l string]	Length of string (number of characters).
	EXAMPLE test -n $word or [-n $word] test tom = sue or [tom = sue]
Logical Test	
[string1 -a string1]	Both string1 **and** string2 are true.
[string1 -o string2]	Either string1 **or** string2 is true.
[! string1]	**Not** a string1 match.
Logical Test (Compound Test)[a]	
[[pattern1 && pattern2]]	Both pattern1 **and** pattern2 are true.
[[pattern1 || pattern2]]	Either pattern1 **or** pattern2 is true.
[[! pattern]]	**Not** a pattern match.
Integer Test	
[int1 -eq int2]	Int1 is equal to int2.
[int1 -ne int2]	Int1 is not equal to int2.
[int1 -gt int2]	Int1 is greater than int2.
[int1 -ge int2]	Int1 is greater than or equal to int2.

Table 14.3   The test Command Operators (continued)

Test Operator	Tests True If
[int1 -lt int2]	Int1 is less than int2.
[int1 -le int2]	Int1 is less than or equal to int2.

Binary Operators for File Testing

[file1 -nt file2]	True if file1 is newer than file2 (according to modification date).
[file1 -ot file2]	True if file1 is older than file2.
[file1 -ef file2]	True if file1 and file2 have the same device or inode numbers.

a. With the compound test, pattern can contain pattern-matching metacharacters; for exact string testing, pattern2 must be enclosed in quotes.

EXAMPLE 14.16

```
(The test Command)
(At the Command Line)

1   $ name=Tom
2   $ grep "$name" /etc/passwd
3   $ echo $?
4   $ test $name != Tom
5   $ echo $?
    1               # Failure
6   $ [ $name = Tom ]       # Brackets replace the test command
7   $ echo $?
    0
8   $ [ $name = [Tt]?? ]
    $ echo $?
    1
9   $ x=5
    $ y=20
10  $ [ $x -gt $y ]
    $ echo $?
    1
11  $ [ $x -le $y ]
    $ echo $?
    0
```

EXPLANATION

1   The variable name is assigned the string Tom.
2   The grep command will search for string Tom in the passwd file.

EXPLANATION (CONTINUED)

3   The ? variable contains the exit status of the last command executed, in this case, the exit status of grep. If grep is successful in finding the string Tom, it will return an exit status of 0. The grep command was successful.

4   The test command is used to evaluate strings, numbers, and perform file testing. Like all commands, it returns an exit status. If the exit status is 0, the expression is true; if the exit status is 1, the expression evaluates to false. There *must* be spaces surrounding the equal sign. The value of name is tested to see if it is not equal to Tom.

5   The test fails and returns an exit status of 1.

6   The brackets are an alternate notation for the test command. There must be spaces after the first bracket. The expression is tested to see if name evaluates to the string Tom. Bash allows either a single or double equal sign to be used to test for equality of strings.

7   The exit status of the test is 0. The test was successful because name is equal to Tom.

8   The test command does not allow wildcard expansion. Because the question mark is treated as a literal character, the test fails. Tom and [Tt]?? are not equal. The exit status is 1, indicating that the text in line 8 failed.

9   x and y are given numeric values.

10   The test command uses numeric relational operators to test its operands; in this example it tests whether $x is greater than (-gt) $y, and returns 0 exit status if true, 1 if false. (See Table 14.3 on page 881.)

11   Tests if $x less than or equal to (-le) $y, returning 0 exit status if true, 1 if false.

EXAMPLE 14.17

```
(The compound test command)(bash 2.x)

    $ name=Tom; friend=Joseph
1   $ [[ $name == [Tt]om ]]        # Wildcards allowed
    $ echo $?
    0
2   $ [[ $name == [Tt]om && $friend == "Jose" ]]
    $ echo $?
    1
3   $ shopt -s extglob             # Turns on extended pattern matching
4   $ name=Tommy
5   $ [[ $name == [Tt]o+(m)y ]]
    $ echo $?
    0
```

EXPLANATION

1   If using the compound test command, shell metacharacters can be used in string tests. In this example, the expression is tested for string equality where name can match either Tom, tom, tommy, and so forth. If the expression is true, the exit status (?) is 0.

2   The logical operators && (AND) and || (OR) can be used with the compound test. If && is used, both expressions must be true, and if the first expression evaluates as false, no further checking is done. With the || logical operator, only one of the expressions must be true. If the first expression evaluates true, no further checking is done. Note that "Jose" is quoted. If not quoted, the friend variable would be checked to see if it contained the pattern Jose. Jose would match, and so would Joseph. The expression evaluates to false because the second condition is not true. The exit status is 1.

3   Extended pattern matching is turned on with the built-in shopt command.

4   The variable is assigned the value Tommy.

5   In this test, the expression is tested for string equality using the new pattern-matching metacharacters. It tests if name matches a string starting with T or t, followed by an o, one or more m characters, and a y.

The following examples illustrate how the exit status is tested with the built-in test command and the alternate form of test, a set of single brackets [ ]; the compound command, a set of double brackets [[ ]].

The let Command and Arithmetic with Double Parentheses.   Although   the test command can evaluate arithmetic expressions, you may prefer to use the let command with its rich set of C-like operators (bash 2.x). The let command can be represented alternatively by enclosing its expression in a set of double parentheses.

Whether you are using the test command, compound command, or let command, the result of an expression is tested, with zero status indicating success and nonzero status indicating failure. (See Table 14.4.)

Example 14.18 illustrates how the let command uses double parentheses (( )).

Table 14.4   The let Command Operators[a]

Operator	Meaning
-	Unary minus
+	Unary plus
!	Logical NOT
~	Bitwise NOT (negation)

Table 14.4 The `let` Command Operators[a] (continued)

Operator	Meaning
*	Multiply
/	Divide
%	Remainder
+	Add
−	Subtract

`let` Operators Not Implemented Prior to bash 2.x

Operator	Meaning
<<	Bitwise left shift
>>	Bitwise right shift
<= >= < >	Comparison operators
== !=	Equal to and not equal to
&	Bitwise AND
^	Bitwise exclusive OR
|	Bitwise OR
&&	Logical AND
||	Logical OR
= *= /= %= += -= <<= >>= &= ^= |=	Assignment and shortcut assignment

a. See Example 14.18.

EXAMPLE 14.18

```
(The let Command) (bash 2.x)
(At the Command Line)

1    $ x=2
     $ y=3

2    (( x > 2 ))
     echo $?
     1

3    (( x < 2 ))
     echo $?
     0
```

EXAMPLE 14.18 (CONTINUED)

```
4    (( x == 2 && y == 3 ))
     echo $?
     0

5    (( x > 2 || y < 3 ))
     echo $?
     1
```

EXPLANATION

1   x and y are assigned numeric values.

2   The double parentheses replace the let command to evaluate the numeric expression. If x is greater than y, the exit status is 0. Because the condition is not true, the exit status is 1. The ? variable holds the exit status of the last command executed—the (( )) command. Note: To evaluate a variable, the dollar sign is not necessary when the variable is enclosed in (( )).

3   The double parentheses evaluate the expression. If x is less than 2, an exit status of 0 is returned; otherwise, 1 is returned.

4   The compound expression is evaluated. The expression is tested as follows: if x is equal to 2 AND y is equal to 3 (i.e., *both* expressions are true), then an exit status of 0 is returned; otherwise, 1 is returned.

5   The compound expression is evaluated. The expression is tested as follows: if x is greater than 2 OR y is less than 3 (i.e., *one* of the expressions is true), then an exit status of 0 is returned; otherwise, 1 is returned.

14.5.3 The if Command

The simplest form of conditional is the if command. The command (a bash built-in or executable) following the if construct is executed and its exit status is returned. The exit status is usually determined by the programmer who wrote the utility. If the exit status is 0, the command succeeded and the statement(s) after the then keyword are executed. In the C shell, the expression following the if command is a Boolean-type expression as in C. But in the Bash, Bourne, and Korn shells, the statement following the if is a command or group of commands. If the exit status of the command being evaluated is 0, the block of statements after the then is executed until fi is reached. The fi terminates the if block. If the exit status is nonzero, meaning that the command failed in some way, the statement(s) after the then keyword are ignored and control goes to the line directly after the fi statement.

It is important that you know the exit status of the commands being tested. For example, the exit status of grep is reliable in letting you know whether grep found the pattern it was searching for in a file. If grep is successful in its search, it returns a 0 exit status; if not, it returns 1. The sed and awk programs also search for patterns, but they will report a successful exit status regardless of whether they find the pattern. The criterion for success with sed and awk is correct syntax, not functionality.

FORMAT

```
    if command
    then
        command
        command
    fi
```

(Using **test** for numbers and strings -- old format)

```
    if test expression
    then
        command
    fi
```

            or

```
    if [ string/numeric expression ] then
            command
    fi
```

(Using **test** for strings -- new format)

```
    if [[ string expression ]] then
            command
    fi
```

(Using **let** for numbers -- new format)

```
  if (( numeric expression ))
```

EXAMPLE   14.19

```
1    if grep "$name" /etc/passwd > /dev/null 2>&1
2    then
         echo Found $name!
3    fi
```

EXPLANATION

1   The grep command searches for its argument, name, in the /etc/passwd database. Standard output and standard error are redirected to /dev/null, the UNIX bit bucket.

> **EXPLANATION** (CONTINUED)
>
> 2   If the exit status of the grep command is zero, the program goes to the then state-
>   ment and executes commands until fi is reached. Indentation of commands be-
>   tween the then and fi keywords is a convention used to make the program more
>   readable, and hence, easier to debug.
>
> 3   The fi terminates the list of commands following the then statement.

EXAMPLE 14.20

```
1    echo  "Are you o.k. (y/n) ?"
     read answer
2    if [ "$answer" = Y -o "$answer" = y ]
     then
         echo  "Glad to hear it."
3    fi

4    if [ $answer = Y -o "$answer" = y ]
     [: too many arguments


     ---------------------------------------------
5    if [[ $answer == [Yy]* || $answer == Maybe ]]ᵃ
     then
         echo  "Glad to hear it."
     fi

6    shopt -s extglob
7    answer="not really"

8    if [[ $answer = [Nn]o?( way|t really) ]]
     then
          echo "So sorry. "
     fi
```

a.   Lines 5 through 8 are only implemented on versions of bash 2.x.

> **EXPLANATION**
>
> 1   The user is asked the question and told to respond. The read command waits for
>   a response.
>
> 2   The test command, represented by square brackets, is used to test expressions. It
>   returns an exit status of zero if the expression is true and nonzero if the expression
>   is false. If the variable answer evaluates to Y or y, the commands after the then state-
>   ment are executed. (The test command does not allow the use of wildcards when
>   testing expressions, and spaces must surround the square brackets, as well as the
>   = operators. See Table 14.3.) Quoting $answer assures that its value is a single
>   string. The test command will fail if more than one word is tested.

EXPLANATION (CONTINUED)

3   The fi terminates the if on line 2.

4   The test command fails if more than one word appears before the = operator. For example, if the user entered yes, you betcha, the answer variable would evaluate to three words, causing the test to fail. $answer is enclosed in double quotes to prevent the resulting error message shown here.

5   The compound command operators [[ ]] allow the expansion of shell metacharacters in a string expression. The variable does not need quotes surrounding it, even if it contains more than one word, as it did with the old test command. (The double equal sign can be used to replace the single equal sign.)

6   The shopt built-in, if set to extglob, allows expanded parameter expansion. See Table 14.11 on page 955.

7   The answer variable is set to the string "not really".

8   Extended pattern matching is used here. The expression reads: If the value of the answer variable matches a string starting with no or No and if followed by zero or one occurrences of the expression in the parentheses, the expression is true. The expression could be evaluated to no, No, no way, No way, not really, or Not really.

The exit Command and the ? Variable.   The exit command is used to terminate the script and return to the command line. You may want the script to exit if some condition occurs. The argument given to the exit command is a number ranging from 0 to 255. If the program exits with 0 as an argument, the program exited with success. A nonzero argument indicates some kind of failure. The argument given to the exit command is stored in the shell's ? variable.

EXAMPLE   14.21

```
(The Script)
$ cat bigfiles
    # Name: bigfiles
    # Purpose: Use the find command to find any files in the root
    # partition that have not been modified within the past n (any
    # number within 30 days) days and are larger than 20 blocks
    # (512-byte blocks)

1   if (( $# != 2 ))ᵃ             # [ $# -ne 2 ]
    then
          echo  "Usage:    $0 mdays size " 1>&2
          exit 1
2   fi
3   if (( $1 < 0 || $1 > 30 ))ᵇ    # [ $1 -lt 0 -o $1 -gt 30 ]
    then
          echo "mdays is out of range"
          exit 2
4   fi
```

EXAMPLE 14.21 (CONTINUED)

```
5    if (( $2 <= 20 ))        # [ $2 -le 20 ]
     then
          echo "size is out of range"
          exit 3
6    fi
7    find / -xdev -mtime $1 -size +$2

(The Command Line)
$ bigfiles
Usage: bigfiles mdays size

$ echo $?
1
$ bigfiles 400 80
mdays is out of range
$ echo $?
2
$ bigfiles 25 2
size is out of range
$ echo $?
3
$ bigfiles 2 25
(Output of find prints here)
```

a.   Not implemented on versions prior to bash 2.x. On older versions could also be written if let $(($# != 2)).
b.   Same as above. On older versions could also be written if let $(($1 < 0 || $1 > 30).

EXPLANATION

1   The statement reads: If the number of arguments is not equal to 2, print the error
     message and send it to standard error, then exit the script with an exit status of 1.
     Either the built-in test command or the let command can be used to test numeric
     expressions.

2   The fi marks the end of the block of statements after then.

3   The statement reads: If the value of the first positional parameter passed in from
     the command line is less than 0 or greater than 30, then print the message and
     exit with a status of 2. See Table 14.4 on page 884 for numeric operators.

4   The fi ends the if block.

5   The statement reads: If the value of the second positional parameter passed in at
     the command line is less than or equal to 20 (512-byte blocks), then print the
     message and exit with a status of 3.

6   The fi ends the if block.

7   The find command starts its search in the root directory. The -xdev option prevents
     find from searching other partitions. The -mtime option takes a number argument,
     which is the number of days since the file was modified, and the -size option takes
     a number argument, which is the size of the file in 512-byte blocks.

Checking for Null Values.   When checking for null values in a variable, use double quotes to hold the null value or the test command will fail.

EXAMPLE 14.22

```
(The Script)
1   if [ "$name" = "" ]      # Alternative to  [ ! "$name" ]  or  [ -z "$name" ]
    then
          echo The name variable is null
    fi

(From System showmount program, which displays all remotely mounted systems)
2   remotes=$(/usr/sbin/showmount)
    if [ "X${remotes}" != "X" ]
    then
          /usr/sbin/wall ${remotes}
              ...
3   fi
```

EXPLANATION

1   If the name variable evaluates to null, the test is true. The double quotes are used to represent null.

2   The showmount command lists all clients remotely mounted from a host machine. The command will list either one or more clients, or nothing. The variable remotes will either have a value assigned or will be null. The letter X precedes the variable remotes when being tested. If remotes evaluates to null, no clients are remotely logged on and X will be equal to X, causing the program to start execution again on line 3. If the variable has a value, for example, the hostname pluto, the expression would read if Xpluto != X, and the wall command would be executed. (All users on remote machines will be sent a message.) The purpose of using X in the expression is to guarantee that even if the value of remotes is null, there will always be a placeholder on either side of the != operator in the expression.

3   The fi terminates the if.

Nested if Commands.   When if statements are nested, the fi statement always goes with the nearest if statement. Indenting the nested ifs makes it easier to see which if statement goes with which fi statement.

14.5.4   The if/else Command

The if/else commands allow a two-way decision-making process. If the command after the if fails, the commands after the else are executed.

FORMAT

```
if command
then
    command(s)
else
    command(s)
fi
```

EXAMPLE 14.23

```
(The Script)
    #!/bin/bash
    # Scriptname: grepit
1   if grep "$name" /etc/passwd >& /dev/null; then
2       echo Found $name!
3   else
4       echo "Can't find $name."
        exit 1
5   fi
```

EXPLANATION

1   The grep command searches for its argument, name, in the NIS passwd database. Because the user does not need to see the output, standard output and standard error are redirected to /dev/null, the UNIX/Linux bit bucket.

2   If the exit status of the grep command is 0, program control goes to the then statement and executes commands until else is reached.

3   The commands under the else statement are executed if the grep command fails to find $name in the passwd database; that is, the exit status of grep must be nonzero for the commands in the else block to be executed.

4   If the value in $name is not found in the passwd database, this echo statement is executed and the program exits with a value of 1, indicating failure.

5   The fi terminates the if.

EXAMPLE 14.24

```
(The Script)
#!/bin/bash
# Scriptname: idcheck
# purpose:check user id to see if user is root.
# Only root has a uid of 0.
# Format for id output:uid=9496(ellie) gid=40 groups=40
# root's uid=0
```

EXAMPLE   14.24 (CONTINUED)

```
1    id=`id | gawk -F'[=(]' '{print $2}'`     # get user id
     echo your user id is: $id
2    if (( id == 0 ))ᵃ               # [ $id -eq 0 ] (See cd file: idcheck2)
     then
3        echo "you are superuser."
4    else
         echo "you are not superuser."
5    fi

     (The Command Line)
6    $ idcheck
     your user id is: 9496
     you are not superuser.
7    $ su
     Password:
8    # idcheck
     your user id is: 0
     you are superuser
```

a.   Not implemented on versions of bash prior to 2.x.

EXPLANATION

1   The id command is piped to the gawk command. Gawk uses an equal sign and open parenthesis as field separators, extracts the user ID from the output, and assigns the output to the variable id.

2,3,4   If the value of id is equal to 0, then line 3 is executed. If id is not equal to 0, the else statements are executed.

5   The fi marks the end of the if command.

6   The idcheck script is executed by the current user, whose UID is 9496.

7   The su command switches the user to root.

8   The # prompt indicates that the superuser (root) is the new user. The UID for root is 0.

14.5.5   The if/elif/else Command

The if/elif/else commands allow a multiway decision-making process. If the command following the if fails, the command following the elif is tested. If that command succeeds, the commands under its then statement are executed. If the command after the elif fails, the next elif command is checked. If none of the commands succeeds, the else commands are executed. The else block is called the default.

FORMAT

```
if  command
then
     command(s)
elif command
then
     commands(s)
elif command
then
     command(s)
else
     command(s)
fi
```

EXAMPLE 14.25

```
(The Script)
     #!/bin/bash
     # Scriptname: tellme
     # Using the old-style test command

1    echo -n "How old are you? "
     read age
2    if [ $age -lt 0 -o $age -gt 120 ]
     then
          echo  "Welcome to our planet! "
          exit 1
     fi
3    if [ $age -ge 0 -a $age -le 12 ]
     then
          echo "A child is a garden of verses"
     elif [ $age -gt 12 -a $age -le 19 ]
     then
          echo "Rebel without a cause"
     elif [ $age -gt 19 -a  $age -le 29 ]
     then
          echo "You got the world by the tail!!"
     elif [ $age -gt  29 -a  $age -le 39 ]
     then
          echo "Thirty something..."
4    else
          echo "Sorry I asked"
5    fi
```

EXAMPLE 14.25 (CONTINUED)

(The Output)
```
$ tellme
How old are you? 200
Welcome to our planet!

$ tellme
How old are you? 13
Rebel without a cause

$ tellme
How old are you? 55
Sorry I asked
```

```
    #!/bin/bash
    # Using the new (( )) compound let command
    # Scriptname: tellme2

1   echo -n "How old are you? "
    read age
2   if (( age < 0 || age > 120 ))
    then
         echo "Welcome to our planet! "
         exit 1
    fi
3   if ((age >= 0 && age <= 12))
    then
         echo "A child is a garden of verses"
    elif ((age > 12 && age <= 19 ))
    then
        echo "Rebel without a cause"
    elif (( age > 19 &&  age <=  29 ))
    then
         echo "You got the world by the tail!!"
    elif  (( age >  29 &&  age <= 39 ))
    then
         echo "Thirty something..."
4   else
         echo "Sorry I asked"
5   fi
```

EXPLANATION

1   The user is asked for input. The input is assigned to the variable age.

2   A numeric test is performed by the test command. If age is less than 0 or greater than 120, the echo command is executed and the program terminates with an exit status of 1. The interactive shell prompt will appear.

3   A numeric test is performed by the test command. If age is greater than or equal to 0 and less than or equal to 12, the test command returns exit status 0, true, and the statement after the then is executed. Otherwise, program control goes to the elif. If that test is false, the next elif is tested.

4   The else construct is the default. If none of the above statements are true, the else commands will be executed.

5   The fi terminates the initial if statement.

14.5.6   File Testing

Often when you are writing scripts, your script will require that there are certain files available and that those files have specific permissions, are of a certain type, or have other attributes. You will find file testing a necessary part of writing dependable scripts.

Table 14.5   File-Testing Operators

Test Operator	Tests True If
-b filename	Block special file
-c filename	Character special file
-d filename	Directory existence
-e filename	File existence
-f filename	Regular file existence and not a directory
-G filename	True if file exists and is owned by the effective group ID
-g filename	Set-group-ID is set
-k filename	Sticky bit is set
-L filename	File is a symbolic link
-p filename	File is a named pipe
-O filename	File exists and is owned by the effective user ID
-r filename	File is readable
-S filename	File is a socket
-s filename	File is nonzero size
-t fd	True if fd (file descriptor) is opened on a terminal

Table 14.5 File-Testing Operators (continued)

Test Operator	Tests True If
-u filename	Set-user-ID bit is set
-w filename	File is writable
-x filename	File is executable

EXAMPLE 14.26

```
(The Script)
    #!/bin/bash
    # Using the old-style test command [ ] single brackets
    # filename: perm_check
    file=./testing

1   if [ -d $file ]
    then
        echo "$file is a directory"
2   elif [ -f $file ]
    then
3       if [ -r $file -a -w $file -a -x $file ]
        then               # nested if command
            echo "You have read,write,and execute permission on $file."
4       fi
5   else
        echo "$file is neither a file nor a directory. "
6   fi
---------------------------------------------------------------
    #!/bin/bash
    # Using the new compound operator for test [[ ]]ᵃ
    # filename: perm_check2
    file=./testing

1   if [[ -d $file ]]
    then
        echo "$file is a directory"
2   elif [[ -f $file ]]
    then
3       if [[ -r $file && -w $file && -x $file ]]
        then    # nested if command
            echo "You have read,write,and execute permission on $file."
4       fi
```

EXAMPLE 14.26 (CONTINUED)

```
5   else
        echo "$file is neither a file nor a directory. "
6   fi
```

a.   New-style test with compound operators not implemented before bash 2.x.

EXPLANATION

1   If the file testing is a directory, print testing is a directory.
2   If the file testing is not a directory, else if the file is a plain file, then . . .
3   If the file testing is readable and writable, and executable, then . . .
4   The fi terminates the innermost if command.
5   The else commands are executed if lines 1 and 2 are not true.
6   This fi goes with the first if.

14.5.7   The null Command

The null command, represented by a colon, is a built-in, do-nothing command that returns an exit status of 0. It is used as a placeholder after an if command when you have nothing to say, but need a command or the program will produce an error message because a command is required after the then statement. Often the null command is used as an argument to a loop command to make the loop a forever loop.

EXAMPLE 14.27

```
(The Script)
    #!/bin/bash
    # filename: name_grep

1   name=Tom
2   if grep "$name" databasefile >& /dev/null
    then
3       :
4   else
        echo "$1 not found in databasefile"
        exit 1
    fi
```

EXPLANATION

1   The variable name is assigned the string Tom.
2   The if command tests the exit status of the grep command. If Tom is found in data-basefile, the null command (a colon) is executed and does nothing. Both output and errors are redirected to /dev/null.

EXPLANATION (CONTINUED)

3   The colon is the `null` command. It does nothing other than returning a 0 exit status.

4   What we really want to do is print an error message and exit if Tom is *not found*. The commands after the `else` will be executed if the `grep` command fails.

EXAMPLE 14.28

```
(The Command Line)
1   $ DATAFILE=
2   $ : ${DATAFILE:=$HOME/db/datafile}
    $ echo $DATAFILE
    /home/jody/ellie/db/datafile
3   $ : ${DATAFILE:=$HOME/junk}
    $ echo $DATAFILE
    /home/jody/ellie/db/datafile
```

EXPLANATION

1   The variable `DATAFILE` is assigned null.

2   The colon command is a do-nothing command. The modifier (`:=`) returns a value that can be assigned to a variable or used in a test. In this example, the expression is passed as an argument to the do-nothing command. The shell will perform variable substitution; that is, assign the pathname to `DATAFILE` if `DATAFILE` does not already have a value. The variable `DATAFILE` is permanently set.

3   Because the variable has already been set, it will not be reset with the default value provided on the right of the modifier.

EXAMPLE 14.29

```
(The Script)
    #!/bin/bash
    # Scriptname: wholenum
    # Purpose:The expr command tests that the user enters an integer

1   echo "Enter an integer."
    read number
2   if expr "$number" + 0 >& /dev/null
    then
3       :
    else
4       echo "You did not enter an integer value."
        exit 1
5   fi
```

EXPLANATION

1   The user is asked to enter an integer. The number is assigned to the variable number.

2   The expr command evaluates the expression. If addition can be performed, the number is a whole number and expr returns a successful exit status. All output is redirected to the bit bucket /dev/null.

3   If expr is successful, it returns a 0 exit status, and the colon command does nothing.

4   If the expr command fails, it returns a nonzero exit status, the echo command displays the message, and the program exits.

5   The fi ends the if block.

14.5.8   The case Command

The case command is a multiway branching command used as an alternative to if/elif commands. The value of the case variable is matched against value1, value2, and so forth, until a match is found. When a value matches the case variable, the commands following the value are executed until the double semicolons are reached. Then execution starts after the word esac (case spelled backward).

 If the case variable is not matched, the program executes the commands after the *), the default value, until ;; or esac is reached. The *) value functions the same as the else statement in if/else conditionals. The case values allow the use of shell wildcards and the vertical bar (pipe symbol) for ORing two values.

FORMAT

```
case variable in
value1)
     command(s)
     ;;
value2)
     command(s)
     ;;
*)
command(s)
     ;;
esac
```

EXAMPLE 14.30

```
(The Script)
    #!/bin/bash
    # Scriptname: xcolors
```

1   echo -n "Choose a foreground color for your xterm window: "
    read color

EXAMPLE 14.30 (CONTINUED)

```
2    case "$color" in
3    [Bb]l??)
4        xterm -fg blue -fn terminal &
5        ;;
6    [Gg]ree*)
         xterm -fg darkgreen -fn terminal &
         ;;
7    red | orange)              # The vertical bar means "or"
         xterm -fg "$color"  -fn terminal &
         ;;
8    *)
         xterm -fn terminal
         ;;
9    esac
10   echo  "Out of case command"
```

EXPLANATION

1   The user is asked for input. The input is assigned to the variable color.

2   The case command evaluates the expression $color.

3   If the color begins with a B or b, followed by the letter l and any two characters, such as blah, blue, blip, and so on, the case expression matches the first value (the wildcards are shell metacharacters). The value is terminated with a single closed parenthesis. The xterm command sets the foreground color to blue.

4   The statement is executed if the value in line number 3 matches the case expression.

5   The double semicolons are required after the last command in this block of commands. Control branches to line 10 when the semicolons are reached. The script is easier to debug if the semicolons are on their own line.

6   If the case expression matches a G or g, followed by the letters ree and ending in zero or more of any other characters, the xterm command is executed. The double semicolons terminate the block of statements and control branches to line 10.

7   The vertical bar is used as an OR conditional operator. If the case expression matches either red or orange, the xterm command is executed.

8   This is the default value. If none of the above values match the case expression, the commands after the *) are executed.

9   The esac statement terminates the case command.

10 After one of the case values are matched, execution continues here.

Creating Menus with the here document and case Command.   The here document and case command are often used together. The here document is used to create a menu of choices that will be displayed to the screen. The user will be asked to select one of the menu items, and the case command will test against the set of choices to execute the appropriate command.

EXAMPLE 14.31

```
(From the .bash_profile File)
      echo "Select a terminal type:  "
1  cat <<- ENDIT
          1) unix
          2) xterm
          3) sun
2  ENDIT
3  read choice
4  case "$choice" in
5  1)   TERM=unix
          export TERM
          ;;
   2)   TERM=xterm
          export TERM
          ;;
6  3)   TERM=sun
          export TERM
          ;;
7  esac
8  echo "TERM is $TERM."

(The Command Line and Output)
$ . .bash_profile
      Select a terminal type:
      1) unix
      2) xterm
      3) sun
      2                 <-- User input
      TERM is xterm.
```

EXPLANATION

1   If this segment of script is put in the .bash_profile, when you log on, you will be given a chance to select the proper terminal type. The here document is used to display a menu of choices.

2   The user-defined ENDIT terminator marks the end of the here document.

3   The read command stores the user input in the variable TERM.

4   The case command evaluates the variable TERM and compares that value with one of the values preceding the closing parenthesis: 1, 2, or 3.

5   The first value tested is 1. If there is a match, the terminal is set to unix. The TERM variable is exported so that subshells will inherit it.

6   A default value is not required. The TERM variable is normally assigned in /etc/profile at login time. If the choice is 3, the terminal is set to sun.

7   The esac terminates the case command.

8   After the case command has finished, this line is executed.

14.6 Looping Commands

Looping commands are used to execute a command or group of commands a set number of times or until a certain condition is met. The bash shell has three types of loops: for, while, and until.

14.6.1 The for Command

The for looping command is used to execute commands a finite number of times on a list of items. For example, you might use this loop to execute the same commands on a list of files or usernames. The for command is followed by a user-defined variable, the keyword in, and a list of words. The first time in the loop, the first word from the wordlist is assigned to the variable, and then shifted off the list. Once the word is assigned to the variable, the body of the loop is entered, and commands between the do and done keywords are executed. The next time around the loop, the second word is assigned to the variable, and so on. The body of the loop starts at the do keyword and ends at the done keyword. When all of the words in the list have been shifted off, the loop ends and program control continues after the done keyword.

FORMAT

```
for variable in word_list
do
     command(s)
done
```

EXAMPLE 14.32

```
(The Script)
     #!/bin/bash
     # Scriptname: forloop
1    for pal in Tom Dick Harry Joe
2    do
3         echo "Hi $pal"
4    done
5    echo "Out of loop"

(The Output)
Hi Tom
Hi Dick
Hi Harry
Hi Joe
Out of loop
```

EXPLANATION

1   This for loop will iterate through the list of names, Tom, Dick, Harry, and Joe, shifting each one off to the left and assigning its value to the user-defined variable, pal, after it is used. As soon as all of the words are shifted and the wordlist is empty, the loop ends and execution starts after the done keyword. The first time in the loop, the variable pal will be assigned the word Tom. The second time through the loop, pal will be assigned Dick, the next time pal will be assigned Harry, and the last time pal will be assigned Joe.

2   The do keyword is required after the wordlist. If it is used on the same line, the list must be terminated with a semicolon. For example:

    for pal in Tom Dick Harry Joe; do

3   This is the body of the loop. After Tom is assigned to the variable pal, the commands in the body of the loop (i.e., all commands between the do and done keywords) are executed.

4   The done keyword ends the loop. Once the last word in the list (Joe) has been assigned and shifted off, the loop exits, and execution starts at line 2.

5   Control resumes here when the loop exits.

EXAMPLE 14.33

```
(The Command Line)
1   $ cat mylist
    tom
    patty
    ann
    jake


(The Script)
    #!/bin/bash
    # Scriptname: mailer
2   for person in $(cat mylist)     # `cat mylist` command substitution the alternate way
    do
3       mail $person < letter
        echo $person was sent a letter.
4   done
5   echo "The letter has been sent."
```

EXPLANATION

1   The contents of a file called mylist are displayed.

2   Command substitution is performed and the contents of mylist becomes the wordlist. The first time in the loop, tom is assigned to the variable person, then it is shifted off to be replaced with patty, and so forth.

3   In the body of the loop, each user is mailed a copy of a file called letter.

4   The done keyword marks the end of this loop iteration.

5   When all of the users in the list have been sent mail and the loop has exited, this line is executed.

EXAMPLE 14.34

```
(The Script)
    #!/bin/bash
    # Scriptname: backup
    # Purpose: Create backup files and store
    # them in a backup directory.
    #

1   dir=/home/jody/ellie/backupscripts
2   for file in memo[1-5]
    do
3       if [ -f $file ]
        then
            cp $file $dir/$file.bak
            echo "$file is backed up in $dir"
        fi
4   done

(The Output)
memo1 is backed up in /home/jody/ellie/backupscripts
memo2 is backed up in /home/jody/ellie/backupscripts
memo3 is backed up in /home/jody/ellie/backupscripts
memo4 is backed up in /home/jody/ellie/backupscripts
memo5 is backed up in /home/jody/ellie/backupscripts
```

EXPLANATION

1   The variable dir is assigned the directory where the backup scripts are to be stored.

2   The wordlist will consist of all files in the current working directory with names starting with memo and ending with numbers between 1 and 5. Each filename will be assigned, one at time, to the variable file for each iteration of the loop.

3   When the body of the loop is entered, the file will be tested to make sure it exists and is a real file. If so, it will be copied into the directory /home/jody/ellie/backup-scripts with the .bak extension appended to its name.

4   The done marks the end of the loop.

14.6.2 The $* and $@ Variables in Wordlists

When expanded, the $* and $@ are the same unless enclosed in double quotes. $* evaluates to one string, whereas $@ evaluates to a list of separate words.

EXAMPLE 14.35

```
(The Script)
    #!/bin/bash
    # Scriptname: greet
1   for name in $*          # same as for name in $@
2   do
        echo Hi $name
3   done

(The Command Line)
$ greet Dee Bert Lizzy Tommy
Hi Dee
Hi Bert
Hi Lizzy
Hi Tommy
```

EXPLANATION

1   $* and $@ expand to a list of all the positional parameters, in this case, the arguments passed in from the command line: Dee, Bert, Lizzy, and Tommy. Each name in the list will be assigned, in turn, to the variable name in the for loop.
2   The commands in the body of the loop are executed until the list is empty.
3   The done keyword marks the end of the loop body.

EXAMPLE 14.36

```
(The Script)
    #!/bin/bash
    # Scriptname: permx

1   for file          # Empty wordlist
    do
2     if [[ -f $file && ! -x $file ]]
      then
3         chmod +x $file
          echo $file now has execute permission
      fi
    done
```

EXAMPLE 14.36 (CONTINUED)

(The Command Line)
```
4    $ permx *
     addon now has execute permission
     checkon now has execute permission
     doit now has execute permission
```

EXPLANATION

1   If the for loop is not provided with a wordlist, it iterates through the positional parameters. This is the same as for file in $*.

2   The filenames are coming in from the command line. The shell expands the asterisk (*) to all filenames in the current working directory. If the file is a plain file and does not have execute permission, line 3 is executed.

3   Execute permission is added for each file being processed.

4   At the command line, the asterisk will be evaluated by the shell as a wildcard and all files in the current directory will be replaced for the *. The files will be passed as arguments to the permx script.

14.6.3   The while Command

The while command evaluates the command following it and, if its exit status is 0, the commands in the body of the loop (commands between do and done) are executed. When the done keyword is reached, control is returned to the top of the loop and the while command checks the exit status of the command again. Until the exit status of the command being evaluated by the while becomes nonzero, the loop continues. When the exit status reaches nonzero, program execution starts after the done keyword.

FORMAT

```
while command
do
      command(s)
done
```

EXAMPLE 14.37

(The Script)
```
     #!/bin/bash
     # Scriptname: num
1    num=0          # Initialize num
```

EXAMPLE 14.37 (CONTINUED)

```
2    while (( $num < 10 ))ᵃ    # or while [ num -lt 10 ]
     do
          echo  -n "$num "
3         let num+=1              # Increment num
     done
4    echo -e "\nAfter loop exits, continue running here"
```

(The Output)
```
    0 1 2 3 4 5 6 7 8 9
4   After loop exits, continue running here
```

a. Versions of bash 2.x use this form.

EXPLANATION

1   This is the initialization step. The variable num is assigned 0.

2   The while command is followed by the let command. The let command evaluates the arithmetic expression, returning an exit status of 0 (true) if the condition is true (i.e., if the value of num is less than 10, the body of the loop is entered).

3   In the body of the loop, the value of num is incremented by one. If the value of num never changes, the loop would iterate infinitely or until the process is killed.

4   After the loop exits, the echo command (with the -e option) prints a newline and the string.

EXAMPLE 14.38

(The Script)
```
     #!/bin/bash
     # Scriptname: quiz
1    echo "Who was the 2nd U.S. president to be impeached?"
     read answer
2    while [[ "$answer" != "Bill Clinton" ]]
3    do
          echo "Wrong try again!"
4         read answer
5    done
6    echo You got it!
```

(The Output)
Who was the 2nd U.S. president to be impeached? **Ronald Reagan**
Wrong try again!
Who was the 2nd U.S. president to be impeached? **I give up**
Wrong try again!
Who was the 2nd U.S. president to be impeached? **Bill Clinton**
You got it!

EXPLANATION

1   The echo command prompts the user, Who was the 2nd U.S. president to be impeached? The read command waits for input from the user. The input will be stored in the variable answer.

2   The while loop is entered and the test command, the bracket, tests the expression. If the variable answer does not exactly equal the string Bill Clinton, the body of the loop is entered and commands between the do and done are executed.

3   The do keyword is the start of the loop body.

4   The user is asked to re-enter input.

5   The done keyword marks the end of the loop body. Control is returned to the top of the while loop, and the expression is tested again. As long as answer does not evaluate to Bill Clinton, the loop will continue to iterate. When the user enters Bill Clinton, the loop ends. Program control goes to line 6.

6   When the body of the loop ends, control starts here.

EXAMPLE   14.39

```
(The Script)
$ cat sayit
    #!/bin/bash
    # Scriptname: sayit
    echo  Type q to quit.
    go=start
1   while [[ -n "$go" ]]    # Make sure to double quote the variable
    do
2       echo -n I love you.
3       read word
4       if [[ $word == [Qq] ]]
        then        # [ "$word" = q -o "$word" = Q ]  Old style
            echo "I'll always love you!"
                go=
        fi
    done

(The Output)
Type q to quit.
I love you.          <-- When user presses Enter, the program continues
I love you.
I love you.
I love you.
I love you.q
I'll always love you!
$
```

EXPLANATION

1   The command after the `while` is executed and its exit status tested. The `-n` option to the `test` command tests for a non-null string. Because variable go initially has a value, the test is successful, producing a zero exit status. If the variable go is not enclosed in double quotes and the variable is null, the `test` command would complain:

```
go: test: argument expected
```

2   The loop is entered. The string `I love you` is echoed to the screen.

3   The `read` command waits for user input.

4   The expresson is tested. If the user enters a q or Q, the string `I'll always love you!` is displayed, and the variable go is set to null. When the `while` loop is re-entered, the test is unsuccessful because the variable is null. The loop terminates. Control goes to the line after the `done` statement. In this example, the script will terminate because there are no more lines to execute.

14.6.4   The until Command

The `until` command is used like the `while` command, but executes the loop statements only if the command after `until` fails, that is, if the command returns an exit status of nonzero. When the `done` keyword is reached, control is returned to the top of the loop and the `until` command checks the exit status of the command again. Until the exit status of the command being evaluated by `until` becomes 0, the loop continues. When the exit status reaches 0, the loop exits, and program execution starts after the `done` keyword.

FORMAT

```
until command
do
     command(s)
done
```

EXAMPLE 14.40

```
      #!/bin/bash
1     until who | grep linda
2     do
          sleep 5
3     done
      talk linda@dragonwings
```

EXPLANATION

1 The until loop tests the exit status of the last command in the pipeline, grep. The who command lists who is logged on this machine and pipes its output to grep. The grep command will return a 0 exit status (success) only when it finds user linda.

2 If user linda has not logged on, the body of the loop is entered and the program sleeps for five seconds.

3 When linda logs on, the exit status of the grep command will be zero and control will go to the statements following the done keyword.

EXAMPLE 14.41

```
(The Script)
    #!/bin/bash
    # Scriptname: hour

1   hour=0
2   until (( hour > 24 ))
    do
3       case "$hour" in
        [0-9]|1[0-1])echo "Good morning!"
            ;;
        12)  echo "Lunch time."
            ;;
        1[3-7])echo "Siesta time."
            ;;
        *)   echo "Good night."
            ;;
        esac
4       (( hour+=1 ))   # Don't forget to increment the hour
5   done

(The Output)
Good morning!
Good morning!
    ...
Lunch time.
Siesta time.
    ...
Good night.
    ...
```

EXPLANATION

1   The variable hour is initialized to 0.

2   The let command (( )) tests the arithmetic expression for an hour greater than 24. If the hour is not greater than 24, the body of the loop is entered. The until loop is entered if the command following it returns a nonzero exit status. Until the condition is true, the loop continues to iterate.

3   The case command evaluates the hour variable and tests each of the case statements for a match.

4   The hour variable is incremented before control returns to the top of the loop.

5   The done command marks the end of the loop body.

14.6.5   The select Command and Menus

The here document is an easy method for creating menus, but bash introduces another looping mechanism, called the select loop, used primarily for creating menus. A menu of numerically listed items is displayed to standard error. The PS3 prompt is used to prompt the user for input; by default, PS3 is #?. After the PS3 prompt is displayed, the shell waits for user input. The input should be one of the numbers in the menu list. The input is stored in the special shell REPLY variable. The number in the REPLY variable is associated with the string to the right of the parentheses in the list of selections.

The case command is used with the select command to allow the user to make a selection from the menu and, based on that selection, execute commands. The LINES and COLUMNS variables can be used to determine the layout of the menu items displayed on the terminal. (These variables are built into versions of bash 2.x, but are not built into earlier versions; if they have not been defined, you can define and export them in the .bash_profile.) The output is displayed to standard error, each item preceded by a number and closing parenthesis, and the PS3 prompt is displayed at the bottom of the menu. Because the select command is a looping command, it is important to remember to use either the break command to get out of the loop, or the exit command to exit the script.

FORMAT

```
select var in wordlist
do
      command(s)
done
```

EXAMPLE 14.42

```
(The Script)
    #!/bin/bash
    # Scriptname: runit

1   PS3="Select a program to execute: "
2   select program  in 'ls -F' pwd date
3   do
4          $program
5   done

(The Command Line)
Select a program to execute: 2
1) ls -F
2) pwd
3) date
/home/ellie
Select a program to execute: 1
1) ls -F
2) pwd
3) date
12abcrty abc12  doit* progs/  xyz
Select a program to execute: 3
1) ls -F
2) pwd
3) date
Sun Mar 12 13:28:25 PST 2004
```

EXPLANATION

1   The PS3 prompt is assigned the string that will appear below the menu that the select loop displays. This prompt is $# by default and is sent to standard error, the screen.

2   The select loop consists of a variable called program and the three-word list that will be displayed in the menu: ls -F, pwd, and date. The words in this list are UNIX/Linux commands, but they could be any words (e.g., red, green, yellow, or cheese, bread, milk, crackers). If the word has a space, it must be quoted (e.g., 'ls -F')

3   The do keyword starts the body of the select loop.

4   When the user selects numbers in the menu, that number will be equated with the word value to the right of the number after the parentheses. For example, if the user selects number 2, that is associated with pwd and pwd is stored in the program variable. $program evaluates to the executable command, pwd; the command is executed.

5   The done keyword marks the end of the body of statements in the select loop. Control will return to the top of the loop. This loop will continue to execute until the user presses ^C.

EXAMPLE 14.43

```
(The Script)
    #!/bin/bash
    # Scriptname: goodboys

1   PS3="Please choose one of the three boys : "
2   select choice in tom dan guy
3   do
4       case "$choice" in
        tom)
            echo Tom is a cool dude!
5           break;;          # break out of the select loop
6       dan | guy )
            echo Dan and Guy are both wonderful.
            break;;
        *)
7           echo "$REPLY is not one of your choices" 1>&2
            echo "Try again."
            ;;
8       esac
9   done

(The Command Line)
$ goodboys
1) tom
2) dan
3) guy
Please choose one of the three boys : 2
Dan and Guy are both wonderful.
$ goodboys
1) tom
2) dan
3) guy
Please choose one of the three boys : 4
4 is not one of your choices
Try again.
Please choose one of the three boys : 1
Tom is a cool dude!
$
```

EXPLANATION

1   The PS3 prompt will be printed below the menu created by the select loop on line 2.

2   The select loop is entered. It causes the words in its list to be displayed as a numbered menu.

3   The loop body starts here.

EXPLANATION (CONTINUED)

4   The variable choice is assigned the first value on the list, after which the value is
     shifted off the list and the next item will be first.

5   The break statement sends loop control after line 9.

6   If either dan or guy are selected, the following echo command is executed, followed
     by the break command, sending control after line 9.

7   The built-in REPLY variable contains the number of the current list item; that is, 1,
     2, or 3.

8   This marks the end of the case command.

9   The done marks the end of the select loop.

EXAMPLE 14.44

```
(The Script)
    #!/bin/bash
    # Scriptname: ttype
    # Purpose: set the terminal type
    # Author: Andy Admin

1   COLUMNS=60
2   LINES=1
3   PS3="Please enter the terminal type: "
4   select choice in wyse50 vt200 xterm sun
    do
5       case "$REPLY" in
        1)
6           export TERM=$choice
            echo "TERM=$choice"
            break;;              # break out of the select loop
        2 | 3 )
            export TERM=$choice

            echo "TERM=$choice"
            break;;
        4)
            export TERM=$choice
            echo "TERM=$choice"
            break;;
        *)
7           echo -e "$REPLY is not a valid choice. Try again\n" 1>&2
8           REPLY=   # Causes the menu to be redisplayed
            ;;
        esac
9   done
```

```
(The Command Line)
$ ttype
1) wyse50    2) vt200   3) xterm    4) sun
Please enter the terminal type : 4
TERM=sun

$ ttype
1) wyse50    2) vt200   3) xterm    4) sun
Please enter the terminal type : 3
TERM=xterm

$ ttype
1) wyse50    2) vt200   3) xterm    4) sun
Please enter the terminal type : 7
7 is not a valid choice. Try again.

1) wyse50    2) vt200   3) xterm    4) sun
Please enter the terminal type: 2
TERM=vt200
```

EXPLANATION

1   The COLUMNS variable is set to the width of the terminal display in columns for menus created with the select loop. The default is 80.

2   The LINES variable controls the vertical display of the select menu on the terminal. The default is 24 lines. When you change the LINES value to 1, the menu items will be printed on one line, instead of vertically as in the last example.

3   The PS3 prompt is set and will appear below the menu choices.

4   The select loop will print a menu with four selections: wyse50, vt200, xterm, and sun. The variable choice will be assigned one of these values based on the user's response held in the REPLY variable. If REPLY is 1, wyse50 is assigned to choice; if REPLY is 2, vt200 is assigned to choice; if REPLY is 3, xterm is assigned to choice; and if REPLY is 4, sun is assigned to choice.

5   The REPLY variable evaluates to the user's input selection.

6   The terminal type is assigned, exported, and printed.

7   If the user does not enter a number between 1 and 4, he or she will be prompted again. Note that the menu does not appear, just the PS3 prompt.

8   If the REPLY variable is set to null (e.g., REPLY=), the menu will be redisplayed.

9   The end of the select loop.

14.6.6   Looping Control Commands

If some condition occurs, you may want to break out of a loop, return to the top of the loop, or provide a way to stop an infinite loop. The bash shell provides loop control commands to handle these kinds of situations.

The shift Command.   The shift command shifts the parameter list to the left a specified number of times. The shift command without an argument shifts the parameter list once to the left. Once the list is shifted, the parameter is removed permanently. Often, the shift command is used in a while loop when iterating through a list of positional parameters.

FORMAT

```
shift [n]
```

EXAMPLE 14.45

```
(Without a Loop)
(The Script)
    #!/bin/bash
    # Scriptname: shifter
1   set joe mary tom sam
2   shift
3   echo $*
4   set $(date)
5   echo  $*
6   shift 5
7   echo  $*
8   shift 2

(The Output)
3   mary tom sam
5   Thu Mar 18 10:00:12 PST 2004
7   2001
8   shift: shift count must be <= $#
```

EXPLANATION

1   The set command sets the positional parameters. $1 is assigned joe, $2 is assigned mary, $3 is assigned tom, and $4 is assigned sam. $* represents all of the parameters.

2   The shift command shifts the positional parameters to the left; joe is shifted off.

3   The parameter list is printed after the shift.

4   The set command resets the positional parameters to the output of the UNIX date command.

5   The new parameter list is printed.

EXPLANATION (CONTINUED)

6   This time the list is shifted 5 times to the left.

7   The new parameter list is printed.

8   By attempting to shift more times than there are parameters, the shell sends a message to standard error stating that the `shift` command cannot shift off more parameters than it has. $# is the total number of positional parameters. On versions of bash 2.x, no error message occurs.

EXAMPLE 14.46

```
(With a Loop)
(The Script)
    #!/bin/bash
    # Name: doit
    # Purpose: shift through command-line arguments
    # Usage: doit [args]
1   while (( $# > 0 ))
    do
2       echo $*
3       shift
4   done

(The Command Line and Output)
$ doit a b c d e
a b c d e
b c d e
c d e
d e
e
```

EXPLANATION

1   The `while` command tests the numeric expression. If the number of positional parameters ($#) is greater than 0, the body of the loop is entered. The positional parameters are coming from the command line as arguments. There are five.

2   All positional parameters are printed.

3   The parameter list is shifted once to the left.

4   The body of the loop ends here; control returns to the top of the loop. Each time the loop is entered, the `shift` command causes the parameter list to be decreased by one. After the first shift, $# (number of positional parameters) is four. When $# has been decreased to 0, the loop ends.

EXAMPLE 14.47

```
(The Script)
    #!/bin/bash
    # Scriptname: dater
    # Purpose: set positional parameters with the set command
    # and shift through the parameters.

1   set $(date)
2   while (( $# > 0 ))
    do
3        echo $1
4        shift
    done

(The Output)
Wed
Mar
17
19:25:00
PST
2004
```

EXPLANATION

1   The set command takes the output of the date command and assigns the output to positional parameters $1 through $6.
2   The while command tests whether the number of positional parameters ($#) is greater than 0. If true, the body of the loop is entered.
3   The echo command displays the value of $1, the first positional parameter.
4   The shift command shifts the parameter list once to the left. Each time through the loop, the list is shifted until the list is empty. At that time, $# will be zero and the loop terminates.

The break Command.   The built-in break command is used to force immediate exit from a loop, but not from a program. (To leave a program, the exit command is used.) After the break command is executed, control starts after the done keyword. The break command causes an exit from the innermost loop, so if you have nested loops, the break command takes a number as an argument, allowing you to break out of a specific outer loop. If you are nested in three loops, the outermost loop is loop number 3, the next nested loop is loop number 2, and the innermost nested loop is loop number 1. The break is useful for exiting from an infinite loop.

```
break [n]
```

EXAMPLE 14.48

```
  #!/bin/bash
  # Scriptname: loopbreak

1 while true; do
2     echo Are you ready to move on\?
      read answer
3     if [[ "$answer" == [Yy] ]]
      then
4         break ──────────┐
5     else                │
          ....commands...  │
      fi                  │
6 done                    │
7 print "Here we are" ◄───┘
```

1   The true command is a UNIX/Linux command that always exits with 0 status. It is often used to start an infinite loop. It is okay to put the do statement on the same line as the while command, as long as a semicolon separates them. The body of the loop is entered.

2   The user is asked for input. The user's input is assigned to the variable answer.

3   If $answer evaluates to Y or y, control goes to line 4.

4   The break command is executed, the loop is exited, and control goes to line 7. The line Here we are is printed. Until the user answers with a Y or y, the program will continue to ask for input. This could go on forever!

5   If the test fails in line 3, the else commands are executed. When the body of the loop ends at the done keyword, control starts again at the top of the while at line 1.

6   This is the end of the loop body.

7   Control starts here after the break command is executed.

The continue Command.   The continue command returns control to the top of the loop if some condition becomes true. All commands below the continue will be ignored. If nested within a number of loops, the continue command returns control to the innermost loop. If a number is given as its argument, control can then be started at the top of any loop. If you are nested in three loops, the outermost loop is loop number 3, the next nested loop is loop number 2, and the innermost nested loop is loop number 1.[4]

───────────────

4. If the continue command is given a number higher than the number of loops, the loop exits.

FORMAT

continue [n]

EXAMPLE 14.49

```
(The mailing List)
    $ cat mail_list
    ernie
    john
    richard
    melanie
    greg
    robin

(The Script)
    #!/bin/bash
    # Scriptname: mailem
    # Purpose: To send a list
1   for name in $(cat  mail_list)◄
    do
2        if [[ $name == richard ]] ; then
3            continue
        else
4            mail $name < memo
        fi
5   done
```

EXPLANATION

1   After command substitution, $(cat mail_list) or `cat mail_list`, the for loop will iterate through the list of names from the file called mail_list.

2   If the name matches richard, the continue command is executed and control goes back to top of the loop where the loop expression is evaluated. Because richard has already been shifted off the list, the next user, melanie, will be assigned to the variable name. Old style: if ["$name" = richard] ; then

3   The continue command returns control to the top of the loop, skipping any commands in the rest of the loop body.

4   All users in the list, except richard, will be mailed a copy of the file memo.

5   This is the end of the loop body.

Nested Loops and Loop Control. When you are using nested loops, the break and continue commands can be given a numeric, integer argument so that control can go from the inner loop to an outer loop.

EXAMPLE   14.50

```
(The Script)
    #!/bin/bash
    # Scriptname: months
1   for month in Jan Feb Mar Apr May Jun Jul Aug Sep Oct Nov Dec
    do
2       for week in  1 2 3 4
        do
            echo -n "Processing the month of $month. OK? "
            read ans
3           if [ "$ans" = n  -o -z "$ans" ]
            then
4               continue 2
            else
                echo -n "Process week $week of $month? "
                read ans
                if [ "$ans" = n -o -z "$ans"  ]
                then
5               continue
                else
                echo "Now processing week $week of $month."
                sleep 1
                    # Commands go here
                echo  "Done processing..."
                fi
            fi
6       done
7   done
```

```
(The Output)
Processing the month of Jan. OK?
Processing the month of Feb. OK? y
Process week 1 of Feb? y
Now processing  week 1 of Feb.
Done processing...
Processing the month of Feb. OK? y
Process week 2 of Feb? y
Now processing week 2 of Feb.
Done processing...
Processing the month of Feb. OK? n
Processing the month of Mar. OK? n
Processing the month of Apr. OK? n
Processing the month of May. OK? n
```

EXPLANATION

1 The outer for loop is started. The first time in the loop, Jan is assigned to month.

2 The inner for loop starts. The first time in this loop, 1 is assigned to week. The inner loop iterates completely before going back to the outer loop.

3 If the user enters either an n or presses Enter, line 4 is executed.

4 The continue command with an argument of 2 starts control at the top of the second outermost loop. The continue without an argument returns control to the top of the innermost loop.

5 Control is returned to the innermost for loop.

6 This done terminates the innermost loop.

7 This done terminates the outermost loop.

14.6.7 I/O Redirection and Subshells

Input can be piped or redirected to a loop from a file. Output can also be piped or redirected to a file from a loop. The shell starts a subshell to handle I/O redirection and pipes. Any variables defined within the loop will not be known to the rest of the script when the loop terminates.

Redirecting the Output of a Loop to a File.   Output from a bash loop can be sent to a file rather than to the screen. See Example 14.51.

EXAMPLE 14.51

```
(The Command Line)
1    $ cat memo
     abc
     def
     ghi

(The Script)
     #!/bin/bash
     # Program name: numberit
     # Put line numbers on all lines of memo
2    if (( $# < 1 ))
     then
3        echo "Usage: $0 filename " >&2
         exit 1
     fi
4    count=1                        # Initialize count
```

EXAMPLE 14.51 (CONTINUED)

```
5   cat $1 | while read line
    # Input is coming from file provided at command line
    do
6      ((count == 1)) && echo "Processing file $1..." > /dev/tty
7      echo -e "$count\t$line"
8      let count+=1
9   done > tmp$$                    # Output is going to a temporary file
10  mv tmp$$ $1


(The Command Line)
11  $ numberit memo
    Processing file memo...


12  $ cat memo
    1   abc
    2   def
    3   ghi
```

EXPLANATION

1   The contents of file memo are displayed.

2   If the user did not provide a command-line argument when running this script, the number of arguments ($#) will be less than one and the error message appears.

3   The usage message is sent to stderr (>&2) if the number of arguments is less than 1.

4   The count variable is assigned the value 1.

5   The UNIX/Linux cat command displays the contents of the filename stored in $1, and the output is piped to the while loop. The read command is assigned the first line of the file the first time in the loop, the second line of the file the next time through the loop, and so forth. The read command returns a 0 exit status if it is successful in reading input and 1 if it fails.

6   If the value of count is 1, the echo command is executed and its output is sent to /dev/tty, the screen.

7   The echo command prints the value of count, followed by the line in the file.

8   The count is incremented by one.

9   The output of this entire loop, each line of the file in $1, is redirected to the file tmp$$, with the exception of the first line of the file, which is redirected to the terminal, /dev/tty.[a]

10 The tmp file is renamed to the filename assigned to $1.

11 The program is executed. The file to be processed is called memo.

12 The file memo is displayed after the script has finished, demonstrating that line numbers have been prepended to each line.

a. $$ expands to the PID number of the current shell. By appending this number to the filename, the filename is made unique.

Piping the Output of a Loop to a UNIX/Linux Command.   Output can be either piped to another command(s) or redirected to a file.

EXAMPLE   14.52

```
(The Script)
      #!/bin/bash
1     for i in 7 9 2 3 4  5
2     do
            echo $i
3     done | sort -n

(The Output)
2
3
4
5
7
9
```

EXPLANATION

1   The for loop iterates through a list of unsorted numbers.
2   In the body of the loop, the numbers are printed. This output will be piped into the UNIX/Linux sort command, a numerical sort.
3   The pipe is created after the done keyword. The loop is run in a subshell.

14.6.8   Running Loops in the Background

Loops can be executed to run in the background. The program can continue without waiting for the loop to finish processing.

EXAMPLE   14.53

```
(The Script)
      #!/bin/bash
1     for person in bob jim joe sam
      do
2          mail $person < memo
3     done &
```

EXPLANATION

1   The for loop shifts through each of the names in the wordlist: bob, jim, joe, and sam. Each of the names is assigned to the variable person, in turn.
2   In the body of the loop, each person is sent the contents of the memo file.
3   The ampersand at the end of the done keyword causes the loop to be executed in the background. The program will continue to run while the loop is executing.

14.6.9   The IFS and Loops

The shell's internal field separator (IFS) evaluates to spaces, tabs, and the newline character. It is used as a word (token) separator for commands that parse lists of words, such as read, set, and for. It can be reset by the user if a different separator will be used in a list. Before changing its value, it is a good idea to save the original value of the IFS in another variable. Then it is easy to return to its default value, if needed.

EXAMPLE 14.54

```
(The Script )
    #/bin/bash
    # Scriptname: runit2
    # IFS is the internal field separator and defaults to
    # spaces, tabs, and newlines.
    # In this script it is changed to a colon.

1   names=Tom:Dick:Harry:John
2   oldifs="$IFS"               # Save the original value of IFS

3   IFS=":"

4   for persons in $names
    do
5         echo  Hi $persons
    done

6   IFS="$oldifs"               # Reset the IFS to old value

7   set Jill Jane Jolene        # Set positional parameters
8   for girl in $*
    do
9         echo Howdy $girl
    done

(The Output)
5   Hi Tom
    Hi Dick
    Hi Harry
    Hi John
9   Howdy Jill
    Howdy Jane
    Howdy Jolene
```

1   The names variable is set to the string Tom:Dick:Harry:John. Each of the words is separated by a colon.

2   The value of IFS, whitespace, is assigned to another variable, oldifs. Because the value of the IFS is whitespace, it must be quoted to preserve it.

3   The IFS is assigned a colon. Now the colon is used to separate words.

4   After variable substitution, the for loop will iterate through each of the names, using the colon as the internal field separator between the words.

5   Each of the names in the wordlist is displayed.

6   The IFS is reassigned its original value stored in oldifs.

7   The positional parameters are set. $1 is assigned Jill, $2 is assigned Jane, and $3 is assigned Jolene.

8   $* evaluates to all the positional parameters, Jill, Jane, and Jolene. The for loop assigns each of the names to the girl variable, in turn, through each iteration of the loop.

9   Each of the names in the parameter list is displayed.

14.7 Functions

Functions were introduced to the Bourne shell in AT&T's UNIX SystemVR2 and have been enhanced in the Bourne Again shell. A function is a name for a command or group of commands. Functions are used to modularize your program and make it more efficient. They are executed in context of the current shell. In other words, a child process is not spawned as it is when running an executable program such as ls. You may even store functions in another file and load them into your script when you are ready to use them.

Here is a review of some of the important rules about using functions.

1. The shell determines whether you are using an alias, a function, a built-in command, or an executable program (or script) found on the disk. It looks for aliases first, then functions, built-in commands, and executables last.

2. A function must be defined before it is used.

3. The function runs in the current environment; it shares variables with the script that invoked it, and lets you pass arguments by assigning them as positional parameters. Local variables can be created within a function by using the local function.

4. If you use the exit command in a function, you exit the entire script. If you exit the function, you return to where the script left off when the function was invoked.

5. The return statement in a function returns the exit status of the last command executed within the function or the value of the argument given.

6. Functions can be exported to subshells with the export -f built-in command.

7. To list functions and definitions, use the `declare -f` command. To list just function names, use `declare -F`.[5]

8. Traps, like variables, are global within functions. They are shared by both the script and the functions invoked in the script. If a trap is defined in a function, it is also shared by the script. This could have unwanted side effects.

9. If functions are stored in another file, they can be loaded into the current script with the `source` or dot command.

10. Functions can be recursive; that is, they can call themselves. There is no limit imposed for the number of recursive calls.

FORMAT

```
function function_name { commands ; commands; }
```

EXAMPLE 14.55

```
function dir { echo "Directories: ";ls -l|awk '/^d/ {print $NF}'; }
```

EXPLANATION

The keyword `function` is followed by the name of the function `dir`. (Sometimes empty parentheses follow the function name, but they are not necessary.) The commands within the curly braces will be executed when `dir` is typed. The purpose of the function is to list only the subdirectories below the present working directory. The spaces surrounding the first curly brace are required.

14.7.1 Unsetting Functions

To remove a function from memory, use the `unset` command.

FORMAT

```
unset -f function_name
```

14.7.2 Exporting Functions

Functions may be exported so that subshells know about them.

FORMAT

```
export -f function_name
```

---

5. Only on bash versions 2.x.

14.7.3 Function Arguments and the Return Value

Because the function is executed within the current shell, the variables will be known to both the function and the shell. Any changes made to your environment in the function will also be made to the shell.

Arguments.   Arguments can be passed to functions by using positional parameters. The positional parameters are private to the function; that is, arguments to the function will not affect any positional parameters used outside the function. See Example 14.56.

The Built-In local Function.   To create local variables that are private to the function and will disappear after the function exits, use the built-in local function. See Example 14.57.

The Built-In return Function.   The return command can be used to exit the function and return control to the program at the place where the function was invoked. (Remember, if you use exit anywhere in your script, including within a function, the script terminates.) The return value of a function is really just the value of the exit status of the last command in the script, unless you give a specific argument to the return command. If a value is assigned to the return command, that value is stored in the ? variable and can hold an integer value between 0 and 256. Because the return command is limited to returning only an integer between 0 and 256, you can use command substitution to capture the output of a function. Place the entire function in parentheses preceded by a $ (e.g., $(function_name)), or traditional backquotes to capture and assign the output to a variable just as you would if getting the output of a UNIX command.

EXAMPLE 14.56

```
(Passing Arguments)
(The Script)
    #!/bin/bash
    # Scriptname: checker
    # Purpose: Demonstrate function and arguments

1   function Usage { echo "error: $*" 2>&1; exit 1; }

2   if (( $# != 2 ))
    then
3       Usage "$0: requires two arguments"
    fi
4   if [[ ! ( -r $1 && -w $1 ) ]]
    then
5       Usage "$1: not readable and writable"
    fi
6   echo The arguments are: $*
  < Program continues here >
```

EXAMPLE 14.56 (CONTINUED)

```
(The Command Line and Output)
$ checker
error: checker: requires two arguments
$ checker file1 file2
error: file1: not readable and writable
$ checker filex file2
The arguments are filex file2
```

EXPLANATION

1   The function called Usage is defined. It will be used to send an error message to
    standard error (the screen). Its arguments consist of any string of characters
    sent when the function is called. The arguments are stored in $*, the special vari-
    able that contains all positional parameters. Within a function, positional pa-
    rameters are local and have no effect on those positional parameters used out-
    side the function.

2   If the number of arguments being passed into the script from the command line
    does not equal 2, the program branches to line 3.

3   When the Usage function is called, the string $0: requires two arguments is passed to
    the function and stored in the $* varable. The echo statement will then send the
    message to standard error and the script will exit with an exit status of 1 to indi-
    cate that something went wrong.[a]

4, 5   If the first argument coming into the program from the command line is not the
       name of a readable and writable file, the Usage function will be called with $1: not
       readable and writable as its argument.

6   The arguments coming into the script from the command line are stored in $*.
    This has no effect on the $* in the function.

a. With the old test form, the expression is written if [! \(-r $1 -a -w $1 \)].

EXAMPLE 14.57

```
(Using the return Command)
(The Script)
    #!/bin/bash
    # Scriptname: do_increment
1   increment () {
2      local sum;    # sum is known only in this function
3      let "sum=$1 + 1"
4      return $sum   # Return the value of sum to the script
    }
5   echo -n "The sum is "
```

EXAMPLE 14.57 (CONTINUED)

```
6    increment 5     # Call function increment; pass 5 as a
                     # parameter; 5 becomes $1 for the increment function
7    echo $?         # The return value is stored in $?
8    echo  $sum      # The variable "sum" is not known here
```

```
(The Output)
4,6 The sum is 6
8
```

EXPLANATION

1   The function called increment is defined.

2   The built-in local function makes variable sum local (private) to this function. It will not exist outside the function. When the function exits, it will be removed.

3   When the function is called, the value of the first argument, $1, will be incremented by one and the result assigned to sum.

4   The return built-in command, when given an argument, returns to the main script after the line where the function was invoked. It stores its argument in the ? variable.

5   The string is echoed to the screen.

6   The increment function is called with an argument of 5.

7   When the function returns, its exit status is stored in the ? variable. The exit status is the exit value of the last command executed in the function unless an explicit argument is used in the return statement. The argument for return must be an integer between 0 and 255.

8   Although the sum was defined in the function increment, it is local in scope, and therefore also not known outside the function. Nothing is printed.

EXAMPLE 14.58

```
(Using Command Substitution)
(The Script)
     #!/bin/bash
     # Scriptname: do_square
1    function square {
        local sq      # sq is local to the function
        let "sq=$1 * $1"
        echo "Number to be squared is $1."
2       echo "The result is $sq "
     }
```

EXAMPLE   14.58 (CONTINUED)

```
3    echo "Give me a number to square. "
     read number
4    value_returned=$(square $number)      # Command substitution
5    echo   "$value_returned"
```

(The Command Line and Output)
```
    $ do_square
3    Give me a number to square.
    10
5    Number to be squared is 10.
     The result is 100
```

EXPLANATION

1   The function called square is defined. Its purpose, when called, is to multiply its argument, $1, times itself.

2   The result of squaring the number is printed.

3   The user is asked for input. This is the line where the program starts executing.

4   The function square is called with a number (input from the user) as its argument. Command substitution is performed because the function is enclosed in parentheses preceded by a $. The output of the function, both of its echo statements, is assigned to the variable value_returned.

5   The value returned from the command substitution is printed.

14.7.4   Functions and the source (or dot) Command

Storing Functions.   Functions are often defined in the .profile file so that when you log in, they will be defined. Functions can be exported, and they can be stored in a file. Then when you need the function, the source or dot command is used with the name of the file to activate the definitions of the functions within it.

EXAMPLE   14.59

```
1    $ cat myfunctions
2    function go() {
         cd $HOME/bin/prog
         PS1='`pwd` > '
         ls
     }
3    function greetings() { echo "Hi $1! Welcome to my world." ; }
4    $ source myfunctions
5    $ greetings george
     Hi george! Welcome to my world.
```

EXPLANATION

1 The file myfunctions is displayed. It contains two function definitions.

2 The first function defined is called go. It sets the primary prompt to the present working directory.

3 The second function defined is called greetings. It will greet the name of the user passed in as an argument.

4 The source or dot command loads the contents of the file myfunctions into the shell's memory. Now both functions are defined for this shell.

5 The greetings function is invoked and executed.

EXAMPLE 14.60

(The dbfunctions file shown below contains functions to be used by the main program. See cd for complete script.)

```
1   $ cat dbfunctions
2   function addon () {        # Function defined in file dbfunctions
3       while true
        do
            echo "Adding information "
            echo "Type the full name of employee "
            read name
            echo "Type address for employee "
            read address
            echo "Type start date for employee (4/10/88 ) :"
            read startdate
            echo $name:$address:$startdate
            echo -n "Is this correct? "
            read ans
            case "$ans" in
            [Yy]*)
                echo "Adding info..."
                echo $name:$address:$startdate>>datafile
                sort -u datafile -o datafile
                echo -n "Do you want to go back to the main menu? "
                read ans
                if [[ $ans == [Yy] ]]
                then
4                   return      # Return to calling program
                else
```

EXAMPLE   14.60 (CONTINUED)

```
5                continue    # Go to the top of the loop
                 fi
                 ;;
            *)
            echo "Do you want to try again? "
            read answer
            case "$answer" in
            [Yy]*) continue;;
            *) exit;;
            esac
                 ;;
        esac
    done
6    }    # End of function definition


------------------------------------------------------------
(The Command Line)
7    $ more mainprog
     #!/bin/bash
     # Scriptname: mainprog
     # This is the main script that will call the function, addon

     datafile=$HOME/bourne/datafile
8    source dbfunctions      # The file is loaded into memory
         if [ ! -e $datafile ]
     then
         echo "$(basename $datafile) does not exist" >&2
         exit 1
     fi
9        echo "Select one: "
         cat <<EOF
            [1] Add info
            [2] Delete info
            [3] Update info
            [4] Exit
         EOF
         read choice
         case $choice in
10           1)   addon      # Calling the addon function
                  ;;
             2)   delete     # Calling the delete function
                  ;;
             3)   update
                  ;;
```

EXAMPLE   14.60 (CONTINUED)

```
          4)
                echo Bye
                exit 0
                ;;
          *)    echo Bad choice
                exit 2
                ;;
      esac
      echo Returned from function call
      echo The name is $name
      # Variable set in the function are known in this shell.
   done
```

EXPLANATION

1   The dbfunctions file is displayed.

2   The addon function is defined. Its function is to add new information to datafile.

3   A while loop is entered. It will loop forever unless a loop control statement such as break or continue is included in the body of the loop.

4   The return command sends control back to the calling program where the function was called.

5   Control is returned to the top of the while loop.

6   The closing curly brace ends the function definition.

7   This is the main script. The function addon will be used in this script.

8   The source command loads the file dbfunctions into the program's memory. Now the function addon is defined for this script and available for use. It is as though you had just defined the function right here in the script.

9   A menu is displayed with the here document. The user is asked to select a menu item.

10 The addon function is invoked.

14.8 Trapping Signals

While your program is running, if you press Ctrl-C or Ctrl-\, your program terminates as soon as the signal arrives. There are times when you would rather not have the program terminate immediately after the signal arrives. You could arrange to ignore the signal and keep running or perform some sort of cleanup operation before actually exiting the script. The trap command allows you to control the way a program behaves when it receives a signal.

A *signal* is defined as an asynchronous message that consists of a number that can be sent from one process to another, or by the operating system to a process if certain keys are pressed or if something exceptional happens.[6] The trap command tells the shell to terminate the command currently in execution upon the receipt of a signal. If the trap command is followed by commands within quotes, the command string will be executed upon receipt of a specified signal. The shell reads the command string twice, once when the trap is set, and again when the signal arrives. If the command string is surrounded by double quotes, all variable and command substitution will be performed when the trap is set the first time. If single quotes enclose the command string, variable and command substitution do not take place until the signal is detected and the trap is executed.

Use the command kill -l or trap -l to get a list of all signals. Table 14.6 provides a list of signal numbers and their corresponding names. The most commonly used signals for trap are 1) SIGHUP (hangup), 2) SIGINT (interrupt), 3) SIGQUIT (quit), and 4) SIGTERM (exit).

FORMAT

```
trap 'command; command' signal-number
trap 'command; command' signal-name
```

EXAMPLE 14.61

```
trap 'rm tmp*; exit 1'  0 1 2 15
trap 'rm tmp*; exit 1'  EXIT HUP INT TERM
```

EXPLANATION

When any of the signals 1 (hangup), 2 (interrupt), or 15 (software termination) arrives, remove all the tmp files and exit.

Table 14.6   Signal Numbers and Signals[a]

1) SIGHUP	9) SIGKILL	17) SIGCHLD	25) SIGXFSZ
2) SIGINT	10) SIGUSR1	18) SIGCONT	26) SIGVTALRM
3) SIGQUIT	11) SIGSEGV	19) SIGSTOP	27) SIGPROF
4) SIGILL	12) SIGUSR2	20) SIGTSTP	28) SIGWINCH
5) SIGTRAP	13) SIGPIPE	21) SIGTTIN	29) SIGIO
6) SIGABRT	14) SIGALRM	22) SIGTTOU	30) SIGPWR
7) SIGBUS	15) SIGTERM	23) SIGURG	
8) SIGFPE	16) SIGSTKFLT	24) SIGXCPU	

a. For a complete list of UNIX signals and their meanings, go to www.cybermagician.co.uk/technet/unixsignals.htm. For Linux signals, go to www.comptechdoc.org/os/linux/programming/linux_pgsignals.html.

---

6. Morris I. Bolsky and David G. Korn, *The New KornShell Command and Programming Language* (Englewood Cliffs, NJ: Prentice Hall PTR, 1995), p. 327.

If an interrupt comes in while the script is running, the trap command lets you handle the interrupt signal in several ways. You can let the signal behave normally (default), ignore the signal, or create a handler function to be called when the signal arrives.

Signal names such as HUP and INT are normally prefixed with SIG, for example, SIGHUP, SIGINT, and so forth.[7] The bash shell allows you to use symbolic names for the signals, which are the signal names without the SIG prefix, or you can use the numeric value for the signal. See Table 14.6. A pseudo signal name EXIT, or the number 0, will cause the trap to be executed when the shell exits.

14.8.1 Resetting Signals

To reset a signal to its default behavior, the trap command is followed by the signal name or number. Traps set in functions are recognized by the shell that invoked the function, once the function has been called. Any traps set outside the function are also recognized with the function.

EXAMPLE 14.62

```
trap INT
```

EXPLANATION

Resets the default action for signal 2, SIGINT. The default action is to kill the process when the interrupt key (Ctrl-C) is pressed.

EXAMPLE 14.63

```
trap 2
```

EXPLANATION

Resets the default action for signal 2, SIGINT, which is used to kill a process (i.e., Ctrl-C).

EXAMPLE 14.64

```
trap 'trap 2' 2
```

EXPLANATION

Sets the default action for signal 2 (SIGINT) to execute the command string within quotes when the signal arrives. The user must press Ctrl-C twice to terminate the program. The first trap catches the signal, and the second trap resets the trap back to its default action, which is to kill the process.

---

7. SIGKILL, number 9, often called a "sure kill," is not trappable.

14.8.2   Ignoring Signals

If the trap command is followed by a pair of empty quotes, the signals listed will be
ignored by the process.

EXAMPLE 14.65

```
trap " " 1 2   or    trap "" HUP INT
```

EXPLANATION

Signals 1 (SIGHUP) and 2 (SIGINT) will be ignored by the shell process.

14.8.3   Listing Traps

To list all traps and the commands assigned to them, type trap.

EXAMPLE 14.66

```
(At the command line)
1   $ trap 'echo "Caught ya!; exit"' 2
2   $ trap
    trap -- 'echo "Caught ya!; exit 1"' SIGINT
3   $ trap -
```

EXPLANATION

1   The trap command is set to exit on signal 2 (Ctrl-C).

2   The trap command without an argument lists all set traps.

3   If the argument is a dash, all signals are reset to their original values, that is, what-
     ever they were when the shell started up.

EXAMPLE 14.67

```
(The Script)
    #!/bin/bash
    # Scriptname: trapping
    # Script to illustrate the trap command and signals
    # Can use the signal numbers or bash abbreviations seen
    # below. Cannot use SIGINT, SIGQUIT, etc.
1   trap 'echo "Ctrl-C will not terminate $0."'  INT
2   trap 'echo "Ctrl-\\ will not terminate $0."'  QUIT
3   trap 'echo "Ctrl-Z will not terminate $0."'  TSTP
4   echo  "Enter any string after the prompt.
    When you are ready to exit, type \"stop\"."
```

EXAMPLE 14.67 (CONTINUED)

```
5   while true
    do
6       echo -n "Go ahead...> "
7       read
8       if [[ $REPLY == [Ss]top ]]
        then
9           break
        fi
10  done
```

(The Output)
4   *Enter any string after the prompt.*
    When you are ready to exit, type "stop".
6   *Go ahead...>* **this is it**^C
1   *Ctrl-C will not terminate trapping.*
6   *Go ahead...>* **this is it again**^Z
3   *Ctrl-Z will not terminate trapping.*
6   *Go ahead...>* **this is never it**/^\
2   *Ctrl-\\ will not terminate trapping.*
6   *Go ahead...>* **stop**
    $

EXPLANATION

1   The first trap catches the INT signal, Ctrl-C. If Ctrl-C is pressed while the program is running, the command enclosed in quotes will be executed. Instead of aborting, the program will print Ctrl-C will not terminate trapping and continue to prompt the user for input.

2   The second trap command will be executed when the user presses Ctrl-\, the QUIT signal. The string Ctrl-\\ will not terminate trapping will be displayed and the program will continue to run. This signal, SIGQUIT by default, kills the process and produces a core file.

3   The third trap command will be executed when the user presses Ctrl-Z, the TSTP signal. The string Ctrl-Z will not terminate trapping will be displayed, and the program will continue to run. This signal normally causes the program to be suspended in the background if job control is implemented.

4   The user is prompted for input.

5   The while loop is entered.

6   The string Go ahead...> is printed and the program waits for input (see read on the next line).

7   The read command assigns user input to the built-in REPLY variable.

EXPLANATION (CONTINUED)

8 If the value of REPLY matches Stop or stop, the break command causes the loop to exit and the program will terminate. Entering Stop or stop is the only way we will get out of this program unless it is killed with the kill command.

9 The break command causes the body of the loop to be exited.

10 The done keyword marks the end of the loop.

14.8.4   Traps and Functions

If you use a trap to handle a signal in a function, it will affect the entire script, once the function is called. The trap is global to the script. In the following example, the trap is set to ignore the interrupt key, ^C. This script had to be killed with the kill command to stop the looping. It demonstrates potential undesirable side effects when using traps in functions.

EXAMPLE   14.68

```
(The Script)
      #!/bin/bash
1     function trapper () {
           echo "In trapper"
2          trap 'echo "Caught in a trap!"' INT
           # Once set, this trap affects the entire script. Anytime
           # ^C is entered, the script will ignore it.
      }
3     while :
      do
           echo "In the main script"
4          trapper
5          echo "Still in main"
6          echo "The pid is $$"
           sleep 5
7     done

(The Output)
In the main script
In trapper
Still in main
The pid is 4267
Caught in a trap!          # User presses ^C
```

EXAMPLE 14.68 (CONTINUED)

```
In the main script
In trapper
Still in main
The pid is 4267
Caught in a trap!        # User just pressed Ctrl-C
In the main script
```

EXPLANATION

1   The trapper function is defined. All variables and traps set in the function are global to the script.

2   The trap command will ignore INT, signal 2, the interrupt key (^C). If ^C is pressed, the message Caught in a trap! is printed, and the script continues forever. The script can be killed with the kill command or Ctrl-\.

3   The main script starts a forever loop.

4   The function trapper is called.

5   When the function returns, execution starts here.

6   The PID will be displayed. Later you can use this number to kill the process from another terminal. For example, if the PID is 4267, the kill 4267 will terminate this process.

7   The program pauses (sleeps) for 5 seconds.

14.9 Debugging

By using the -n option to the bash command, you can check the syntax of your scripts without really executing any of the commands. If there is a syntax error in the script, the shell will report the error. If there are no errors, nothing is displayed.

The most commonly used method for debugging scripts is the set command with the -x option, or bash invoked with the -x option and the script name. See Table 14.7 for a list of debugging options. These options allow an execution trace of your script. Each command from your script is displayed after substitution has been performed, and then the command is executed. When a line from your script is displayed, it is preceded with a plus (+) sign.

With the verbose option turned on, or by invoking the shell with the -v option (bash -v scriptname), each line of the script will be displayed just as it was typed in the script, and then executed. (See Chapter 15, "Debugging Shell Scripts," on page 967 for details.)

Table 14.7   Debugging Options

Command	Option	What It Does
bash -x scriptname	Echo option	Displays each line of script after variable substitutions and before execution.
bash -v scriptname	Verbose option	Displays each line of script before execution, just as you typed it.
bash -n scriptname	Noexec option	Interprets but does not execute commands.
set -x	Turns on echo	Traces execution in a script.
set +x	Turns off echo	Turns off tracing.

EXAMPLE 14.69

```
(The Script)
    #!/bin/bash
    # Scriptname: todebug

1   name="Joe Shmoe"
    if [[ $name == "Joe Blow" ]]
    then
        printf "Hello $name\n"
    fi

    declare -i num=1
    while (( num < 5 ))
    do
        let num+=1
    done
    printf "The total is %d\n", $num

(The Output)
2 bash -x todebug
+ name=Joe Shmoe
+ [[ Joe Shmoe == \J\o\e\ \B\l\o\w ]]
+ declare -i num=1
+ (( num < 5 ))
+ let num+=1
+ (( num < 5 ))
+ let num+=1
+ (( num < 5 ))
+ let num+=1
```

EXAMPLE 14.69 (CONTINUED)

```
+ (( num < 5 ))
+ let num+=1
+ (( num < 5 ))
+ printf 'The total is %d\n,' 5
The total is 5
```

EXPLANATION

1   The script is called todebug. You can watch the script run with the -x switch turned on. Each iteration of the loop is displayed and the values of variables are printed as they are set and when they change.

2   Bash is invoked with the -x option. Echoing is turned on. Each line of the script will be displayed to the screen prepended with a plus sign (+). Variable substitution is performed before the line is displayed. The result of the execution of the command appears after the line has been displayed.

14.10 The Command Line

14.10.1   Processing Command-Line Options with getopts

If you are writing scripts that require a number of command-line options, positional parameters are not always the most efficient. For example, the UNIX ls command takes a number of command-line options and arguments. (An option requires a leading dash; an argument does not.) Options can be passed to the program in several ways: ls -laFi, ls -i -a -l -F, ls -ia -F, and so forth. If you have a script that requires arguments, positional parameters might be used to process the arguments individually, such as ls -l -i -F. Each dash option would be stored in $1, $2, and $3, respectively. But, what if the user listed all of the options as one dash option, as in ls -liF? Now the -liF would all be assigned to $1 in the script. The getopts function makes it possible to process command-line options and arguments in the same way they are processed by the ls program.[8] The getopts function will allow the runit program to process its arguments using any variety of combinations.

EXAMPLE 14.70

```
(The Command Line )
1    $ runit -x -n  200 filex
2    $ runit -xn200 filex
3    $ runit -xy
```

---

8. See the UNIX/Linux manual pages (Section 3) for the C library function getopt.

EXAMPLE 14.70 (CONTINUED)

```
4   $ runit -yx -n 30
5   $ runit -n250 -xy filey
( any other combination of these arguments )
```

EXPLANATION

1   The program runit takes four arguments: x is an option, n is an option requiring a number argument after it, and filex is an argument that stands alone.
2   The program runit combines the options x and n and the number argument 200; filex is also an argument.
3   The program runit is invoked with the x and y options combined.
4   The program runit is invoked with the y and x options combined; the n option is passed separately, as is the number argument, 30.
5   The program runit is invoked with the n option combined with the number argument, the x and y options are combined, and the filey is separate.

Before getting into all the details of the runit program, we examine the line from the program where getopts is used to see how it processes the arguments.

EXAMPLE 14.71

```
(A line from the script called runit)
while getopts :xyn: name
```

EXPLANATION

x, y, and n are the options. In this example the first option is preceded by a colon. This tells getopts to use silent error reporting. If there is a colon after one of the options, the option expects an argument separated from it by whitespace. An argument is a word that does not begin with a dash. -n requires an argument.

Any options typed at the command line must begin with a dash.

Any options that do not contain a dash tell getopts that the option list has ended.

Each time getopts is called, it places the next option value it finds in the variable name. (You can use any variable name here.) If an illegal argument is given, name is assigned a question mark.

Sample getopts Scripts.   The following examples illustrate how getopts processes arguments.

EXAMPLE 14.72

```
(The Script)
    #!/bin/bash
    # Program: opts1
    # Using getopts -- First try --

1   while getopts xy options
    do
2       case $options in
3       x) echo "you entered -x as an option";;
        y) echo "you entered -y as an option";;
        esac
    done

(The Command Line)
4   $ opts1 -x
    you entered -x as an option
5   $ opts1 -xy
    you entered -x as an option
    you entered -y as an option
6   $ opts1 -y
    you entered -y as an option
7   $ opts1 -b
    opts1:   illegal option -- b
8   $ opts1 b
```

EXPLANATION

1   The getopts command is used as a condition for the while command. The valid options for this program are listed after the getopts command; they are x and y. Each option is tested in the body of the loop, one after the other. Each option will be assigned to the variable options, without the leading dash. When there are no longer any arguments to process, getopts will exit with a nonzero status, causing the while loop to terminate.

2   The case command is used to test each of the possible options found in the options variable, either x or y.

3   If x was an option, the string you entered -x as an option is displayed.

4   At the command line, the opts1 script is given an x option, a legal option to be processed by getopts.

5   At the command line, the opts1 script is given an xy option; x and y are legal options to be processed by getopts.

6   At the command line, the opts1 script is given a y option, a legal option to be processed by getopts.

EXPLANATION (CONTINUED)

7   The opts1 script is given a b option, an illegal option. Getopts sends an error message to stderr.

8   An option without a dash prepended to it is not an option and causes getopts to stop processing arguments.

EXAMPLE   14.73

```
(The Script)
    #!/bin/bash
    # Program: opts2
    # Using getopts -- Second try --
```

1   `while getopts xy options 2> /dev/null`
     `do`
2   `    case $options in`
     `    x) echo "you entered -x as an option";;`
     `    y) echo "you entered -y as an option";;`
3   `    \?) echo "Only -x and -y are valid options"  1>&2;;`
     `    esac`
     `done`

```
(The Command Line)
    $ opts2 -x
    you entered -x as an option
    $ opts2 -y
    you entered -y as an option
    $ opts2 xy
    $ opts2 -xy
    you entered -x as an option
    you entered -y as an option
```
4   `    $ opts2 -g`
     `    Only -x and -y are valid options`
5   `    $ opts2 -c`
     `    Only -x and -y are valid options`

EXPLANATION

1   If there is an error message from getopts, it is redirected to /dev/null.

2   If the option is a bad option, a question mark will be assigned to the options variable. The case command can be used to test for the question mark, allowing you to print your own error message to standard error.

EXPLANATION (continued)

3   If the options variable is assigned the question mark, the case statement is executed. The question mark is protected with the backslash so that the shell does not see it as a wildcard and try to perform filename substitution.

4   g is not a legal option. A question mark is assigned to the variable options and the error message is displayed.

5   c is not a legal option. A question mark is assigned to the variable options and the error message is displayed.

Special getopts Variables. The getopts function provides two variables to help keep track of arguments: OPTIND and OPTARG. OPTIND is a special variable that is initialized to one and is incremented each time getopts completes processing a command-line argument to the number of the next argument getopts will process. The OPTARG variable contains the value of a legal argument. See Examples 14.74 and 14.75.

EXAMPLE 14.74

```
(The Script)
    #!/bin/bash
    # Program: opts3
    # Using getopts -- Third try --

1   while getopts dq: options
    do
            case $options in
2               d) echo "-d is a valid switch ";;
3               q) echo "The argument for -q is $OPTARG";;
                \?) echo "Usage:opts3 -dq filename ... " 1>&2;;
            esac
    done

(The Command Line)
4   $ opts3 -d
    -d is a valid switch
5   $ opts3 -q  foo
    The argument for -q is foo
6   $ opts3 -q
    Usage:opts3 -dq filename ...
7   $ opts3 -e
    Usage:opts3 -dq filename ...
8   $ opts3 e
```

EXPLANATION

1   The while command tests the exit status of getopts; if getopts can successfully process an argument, it returns 0 exit status, and the body of the while loop is entered. The colon appended to the argument list means that the q option requires an argument. The argument will be stored in the special variable, OPTARG.

2   One of the legal options is d. If d is entered as an option, the d (without the dash) is stored in the options variable.

3   One of the legal options is q. The q option requires an argument. There must be a space between the q option and its argument. If q is entered as an option followed by an argument, the q, without the dash, is stored in the options variable and the argument is stored in the OPTARG variable. If an argument does not follow the q option, the question mark is stored in the variable options.

4   The d option is a legal option to opts3.

5   The q option with an argument is also a legal option to opts3.

6   The q option without an argument is an error.

7   The e option is invalid. A question mark is stored in the options variable if the option is illegal.

8   The option is prepended with neither a dash nor a plus sign. The getopts command will not process it as an option and returns a nonzero exit status. The while loop is terminated.

EXAMPLE 14.75

```
(The Script)
#!/bin/bash
# Program: opts4
# Using getopts -- Fourth try --

1    while getopts xyz: arguments 2>/dev/null
     do
          case $arguments  in
2         x) echo "you entered -x as an option .";;
          y) echo "you entered -y as an option." ;;
3         z) echo "you entered -z as an option."
             echo "\$OPTARG is $OPTARG.";;
4         \?) echo "Usage opts4 [-xy] [-z  argument]"
             exit 1;;
          esac
     done
5    echo "The number of arguments passed was $(( $OPTIND - 1 ))"
```

EXAMPLE 14.75 (CONTINUED)

(The Command Line)
```
$ opts4 -xyz foo
```
You entered -x as an option.
You entered -y as an option.
You entered -z as an option.
$OPTARG is foo.
The number of arguments passed was 2.

```
$ opts4 -x -y -z  boo
```
You entered -x as an option.
You entered -y as an option.
You entered -z as an option.
$OPTARG is boo.
The number of arguments passed was 4.

```
$ opts4 -d
```
Usage: opts4 [-xy] [-z argument]

EXPLANATION

1   The while command tests the exit status of getopts; if getopts can successfully process an argument, it returns 0 exit status, and the body of the while loop is entered. The colon appended to the z option tells getopts that an argument must follow the -z option. If the option takes an argument, the argument is stored in the getopts built-in variable OPTARG.

2   If x is given as an option, it is stored in the variable arguments.

3   If z is given as an option with an argument, the argument is stored in the built-in variable OPTARG.

4   If an invalid option is entered, the question mark is stored in the variable arguments and an error message is displayed.

5   The special getopts variable OPTIND holds the number of the next option to be processed. Its value is always one more than the actual number of command-line arguments.

14.10.2   The eval Command and Parsing the Command Line

The eval command evaluates a command line, performs all shell substitutions, and then executes the command line. It is used when normal parsing of the command line is not flexible enough for what we want to do.

EXAMPLE 14.76

```
1   $ set a b c d
2   $ echo The last argument is \$$#
3   The last argument is $4

4   $ eval echo The last argument is \$$#
    The last argument is d

5   $ set -x
    $ eval echo The last argument is \$$#
    + eval echo the last argument is '$4'
    ++ echo the last argument is d
    The last argument is d
```

EXPLANATION

1   Four positional parameters are set.

2   The desired result is to print the value of the last positional parameter. The \$ will print a literal dollar sign. The $# evaluates to 4, the number of positional parameters. After the shell evaluates the $#, it does not parse the line again to get the value of $4.

3   $4 is printed instead of the last argument.

4   After the shell performs variable substitution, the eval command performs the variable substitution and then executes the echo command.

5   Turn on the echoing to watch the order of parsing.

EXAMPLE 14.77

```
(From Shutdown Program)
1   eval `/usr/bin/id | /usr/bin/sed 's/[^a-z0-9=].*//'`
2   if [ "${uid:=0}" -ne 0 ]
    then
3       echo $0: Only root can run $0
        exit 2
    fi
```

EXPLANATION

1   This is a tricky one. The id program's output is sent to sed to extract the uid part of the string. The output for id is

```
uid=9496(ellie) gid=40 groups=40
uid=0(root) gid=1(daemon) groups=1(daemon)
```

The sed regular expression reads: Starting at the beginning of the string, find any character that is not a letter, number, or an equal sign and remove that character and all characters following it. The result is to substitute everything from the first opening parenthesis to the end of the line with nothing. What is left is either uid=9496 or uid=0.

After eval evaluates the command line, it then executes the resulting command: uid=9496 or uid=0.

For example, if the user's ID is root, the command executed would be uid=0. This creates a local variable in the shell called uid and assigns 0 to it.

2   The value of the uid variable is tested for 0, using command modifiers.

3   If the uid is not 0, the echo command displays the script name ($0) and the message.

14.11 bash **Options**

14.11.1   Shell Invocation Options

When the shell is started using the bash command, it can take options to modify its behavior. There are two types of options: single-character options and multicharacter options. The single-character options consist of a single leading dash followed by a single character. The multicharacter options consist of two leading dashes and any number of characters. Multicharacter options must appear before single-character options. An interactive login shell normally starts up with -i (start an interactive shell), -s (read from standard input), and -m (enable job control). See Table 14.8.

Table 14.8   bash 2.x Shell Invocation Options

Option	Meaning
-c string	Commands are read from string. Any arguments after string are assigned to positional parameters, starting at $0.
-D	A list of double-quoted strings, preceded by a $, are printed to standard output. These strings are subject to language translation when the current locale is not C or POSIX. The -n option is implied; no commands will be executed.
-i	Shell is in the interactive mode. TERM, QUIT, and INTERRUPT are ignored.
-s	Commands are read from standard input and allow the setting of positional parameters.
-r	Starts a restricted shell.

Table 14.8   bash 2.x Shell Invocation Options (continued)

Option	Meaning
--	Signals the end of options and disables further option processing. Any arguments after -- or - are treated as filenames and arguments.
--dump-strings	Same as -D.
--help	Displays a usage message for a built-in command and exits.
--login	Causes bash to be invoked as a login shell.
--noediting	When bash is running interactively, does not use the Readline library.
--noprofile	When starting up, bash does not read the initialization files /etc/profile, ~/.bash_profile, ~/.bash_login, or ~/.profile.
--norc	For interactive shells, bash will not read the ~/.bashrc file. Turned on by default, if running shell as sh.
--posix	Changes the behavior of bash to match the POSIX 1003.2 standard, if otherwise it wouldn't.
--quiet	Displays no information at shell startup, the default.
--rcfile file	If bash is interactive, uses this intialization file instead of ~/.bashrc.
--restricted	Starts a restricted shell.
--verbose	Turns on verbose; same as -v.
--version	Displays version information about this bash shell and exits.

Table 14.9   bash (Versions Prior to 2.x) Shell Invocation Options

Option	Meaning
-c string	Commands are read from string. Any arguments after string are assigned to positional parameters, starting at $0.
-D	A list of double-quoted strings, preceded by a $, are printed to standard output. These strings are subject to language translation when the current locale is not C or POSIX. The -n option is implied; no commands will be executed.
-i	Shell is in the interactive mode. TERM, QUIT, and INTERRUPT are ignored.
-s	Commands are read from standard input and allows the setting of positional parameters.
-r	Starts a restricted shell.
-	Signals the end of options and disables further option processing. Any arguments after -- or - are treated as filenames and arguments.

Table 14.9   bash (Versions Prior to 2.x) Shell Invocation Options (continued)

Option	*Meaning*
-login	Causes bash to be invoked as a login shell.
-nobraceexpansion	Curly brace expansion is turned off.
-nolineediting	When bash is running interactively, does not use the Readline library.
-noprofile	When starting up, bash does not read the initialization files /etc/profile, ~/.bash_profile, ~/.bash_login, or ~/.profile.
-posix	Changes the behavior of bash to match the POSIX standard, if otherwise it wouldn't.
-quiet	Displays no information at shell startup, the default.
-rcfile file	If bash is interactive, uses this intialization file instead of ~/.bashrc.
-verbose	Turns on verbose; same as -v.
-version	Displays version information about this bash shell and exits.

14.11.2   The set Command and Options

The set command can be used to turn shell options on and off, as well as for handling command-line arguments. To turn an option on, the dash (-) is prepended to the option; to turn an option off, the plus sign (+) is prepended to the option. See Table 14.10 for a list of set options.

EXAMPLE 14.78

```
1    $ set -f
2    $ echo *
     *
3    $ echo ??
     ??
4    $ set +f
```

EXPLANATION

1   The f option is turned on, disabling filename expansion.
2   The asterisk is not expanded.
3   The question marks are not expanded.
4   The f is turned off; filename expansion is enabled.

Table 14.10 The Built-In set Command Options

Name of Option	Shortcut Switch	What It Does
allexport	-a	Automatically marks new or modified variables for export from the time the option is set until unset.
braceexpand	-B	Enables brace expansion, and is a default setting.[a]
emacs		For command-line editing, uses the emacs built-in editor, and is a default setting.
errexit	-e	If a command returns a nonzero exit status (fails), exits. Not set when reading initialization files.
histexpand	-H	Enables ! and !! when performing history substitution, and is a default setting.[a]
history		Enables command-line history; on by default.[a]
ignoreeof		Disables EOF (Ctrl-D) from exiting a shell; must type exit. Same as setting shell variable, IGNOREEOF=10.
keyword	-k	Places keyword arguments in the environment for a command.[a]
interactive-comments		For interactive shells, a leading # is used to comment out any text remaining on the line.
monitor	-m	Allows job control.
noclobber	-C	Protects files from being overwritten when redirection is used.
noexec	-n	Reads commands, but does not execute them. Used to check the syntax of scripts. Not on when running interactively.
noglob	-d	Disables pathname expansion (i.e., turns off wildcards).
notify	-b	Notifies user when background job finishes.
nounset	-u	Displays an error when expanding a variable that has not been set.
onecmd	-t	Exits after reading and executing one command.[a]
physical	-P	If set, does not follow symbolic links when typing cd or pwd. The physical directory is used instead.
posix		Shell behavior is changed if the default operation doesn't match the POSIX standard.
privileged	-p	When set, the shell does not read the .profile or ENV file and shell functions are not inherited from the environment; automatically set for setuid scripts.

Table 14.10   The Built-In set Command Options (continued)

Name of Option	Shortcut Switch	What It Does
posix		Changes the default behavior to POSIX 1003.2.
verbose	-v	Turns on the verbose mode for debugging.
vi		For command-line editing, uses the vi built-in editor.
xtrace	-x	Turns on the echo mode for debugging.

a. Option applies only to versions of bash 2.x.

14.11.3   The shopt Command and Options

The shopt (bash 2.x) command can also be used to turn shell options on and off. See Table 14.11.

Table 14.11   The shopt Command Options

Option	Meaning
cdable_vars	If an argument to the cd built-in command is not a directory, it is assumed to be the name of a variable whose value is the directory to change to.
cdspell	Corrects minor errors in the spelling of a directory name in a cd command. The errors checked for are transposed characters, a missing character, and a character too many. If a correction is found, the corrected path is printed, and the command proceeds. Only used by interactive shells.
checkhash	Bash checks that a command found in the hash table exists before trying to execute it. If a hashed command no longer exists, a normal path search is performed.
checkwinsize	Bash checks the window size after each command and, if necessary, updates the values of LINES and COLUMNS.
cmdhist	Bash attempts to save all lines of a multiple-line command in the same history entry. This allows easy re-editing of multiline commands.
dotglob	Bash includes filenames beginning with a dot (.) in the results of filename expansion.
execfail	A noninteractive shell will not exit if it cannot execute the file specified as an argument to the exec built-in command. An interactive shell does not exit if exec fails.
expand_aliases	Aliases are expanded. Enabled by default.

Table 14.11   The shopt Command Options (continued)

Option	*Meaning*
extglob	The extended pattern matching features (regular expression metacharacters derived from Korn shell for filename expansion) are enabled.
histappend	The history list is appended to the file named by the value of the HISTFILE variable when the shell exits, rather than overwriting the file.
histreedit	If readline is being used, a user is given the opportunity to re-edit a failed history substitution.
histverify	If set, and readline is being used, the results of history substitution are not immediately passed to the shell parser. Instead, the resulting line is loaded into the readline editing buffer, allowing further modification.
hostcomplete	If set, and readline is being used, bash will attempt to perform hostname completion when a word containing an @ is being completed. Enabled by default.
huponexit	If set, bash will send SIGHUP (hangup signal) to all jobs when an interactive login shell exits.
interactive_comments	Allows a word beginning with # to cause that word and all remaining characters on that line to be ignored in an interactive shell. Enabled by default.
lithist	If enabled, and the cmdhist option is enabled, multiline commands are saved to the history with embedded newlines rather than using semicolon separators where possible.
mailwarn	If set, and a file that bash is checking for mail has been accessed since the last time it was checked, the message The mail in mailfile has been read is displayed.
nocaseglob	If set, bash matches filenames in a case-insensitive fashion when performing filename expansion.
nullglob	If set, bash allows filename patterns that match no files to expand to a null string, rather than themselves.
promptvars	If set, prompt strings undergo variable and parameter expansion after being expanded. Enabled by default.
restricted_shell	The shell sets this option if it is started in restricted mode. The value may not be changed. This is not reset when the startup files are executed, allowing the startup files to discover whether or not a shell is restricted.
shift_verbose	If this is set, the shift built-in prints an error message when the shift count exceeds the number of positional parameters.

Table 14.11 The shopt Command Options (continued)

Option	Meaning
sourcepath	If set, the source built-in uses the value of PATH to find the directory containing the file supplied as an argument. Enabled by default.
source	A synonym for dot (.).

14.12 Shell Built-In Commands

The shell has a number of commands that are built into its source code. Because the commands are built-in, the shell doesn't have to locate them on disk, making execution much faster. The help feature provided with bash gives you online help for any built-in command. The built-in commands are listed in Table 14.12.

Table 14.12 Built-In Commands

Command	What It Does
.	Executes program in context of current process; same as source.
. file	The dot command reads and executes command from file.
:	Do-nothing command; returns 0 exit status.
alias	Lists and creates "nicknames" for existing commands.
bg	Puts a job in the background.
bind	Displays current key and function bindings, or binds keys to a readline function or macro.[a]
break	Breaks out of the innermost loop.
break [n]	See "The break Command" on page 919.
builtin [sh-builtin [args]]	Runs a shell built-in, passing it args, and returning 0 exit status. Useful if a function and built-in have the same name.[a]
cd [arg]	Changes the directory to home if no arg or to value of arg.
command command [arg]	Runs a command even if a function has the same name (i.e., bypasses function lookup).[a]
continue [n]	See "The continue Command" on page 920.
declare [var]	Displays all variables or declares variables with optional attributes.[a]
dirs	Displays a list of currently remembered directories resulting from pushd.

Table 14.12   Built-In Commands (continued)

Command	*What It Does*
disown	Removes an active job from the job table.
echo [args]	Displays args terminated with a newline.
enable	Enables and disables shell built-in commands.[a]
eval [args]	Reads args as input to the shell and executes the resulting command(s).
exec command	Runs command in place of this shell.
exit [n]	Exits the shell with status n.
export [var]	Makes var known to subshells.
fc	History's fix command for editing history commands.
fg	Puts background job into foreground.
getopts	Parses and processes command-line options.
hash	Controls the internal hash table for quicker searches for commands.
help [command]	Displays helpful info about built-in commands and, if command is specified, detailed help about that built-in command.[a]
history	Displays the history list with line numbers.
jobs	Lists jobs put in the background.
kill [-signal process]	Sends the signal to the PID number or job number of the process. Type kill -l for a list of signals.
let	Used for evaluating arithmetic expressions and assigning results of arithmetic calculations to variables.
local	Used in functions to restrict the scope of variables to the function.
logout	Exits the login shell.
popd	Removes entries from the directory stack.
pushd	Adds entries to the directory stack.
pwd	Prints present working directory.
read [var]	Reads line from standard input into variable var.
readonly [var]	Makes variable var read-only. Cannot be reset.
return [n]	Returns from a function where n is the exit value given to the return.

Table 14.12   Built-In Commands (continued)

Command	What It Does
set	Sets options and positional parameters. See Table 14.2 on page 875.
shift [n]	Shifts positional parameters to the left n times.
stop pid	Halts execution of the process number PID.
suspend	Stops execution of the current shell (but not if a login shell).
test	Checks file types and evaluates conditional expressions.
times	Prints accumulated user and system times for processes run from this shell.
trap [arg] [n]	When shell receives signal n (0, 1, 2, or 15), executes arg.
type [command]	Prints the type of command (e.g., pwd is a built-in shell command).
typeset	Same as declare. Sets variables and gives them attributes.
ulimit	Displays and sets process resource limits.
umask [octal digits]	Sets user file creation mode mask for owner, group, and others.
unalias	Unsets aliases.
unset [name]	Unsets value of variable or function.
wait [pid#n]	Waits for background process with PID number n and reports termination status.

a. Option applies to bash 2.x and later.

LAB 54: bash SHELL—FIRST SCRIPT

1. Write a script called greetme that will do the following:

   a. Contain a comment section with your name, the name of this script, and the purpose of this script.

   b. Greet the user.

   c. Print the date and the time.

   d. Print a calendar for this month.

   e. Print the name of your machine.

   f. Print the name and release of this operating system (cat /etc/motd).

   g. Print a list of all files in your parent directory.

   h. Print all the processes root is running.

    i. Print the value of the TERM, PATH, and HOME variables.

    j. Print your disk usage (du).

    k. Use the id command to print your group ID.

    l. Print Please, could you loan me $50.00?

    m. Tell the user Good-bye and the current hour (see *man* pages for the date command).

2. Make sure your script is executable.

```
chmod +x greetme
```

What was the first line of your script? Why do you need this line?

LAB 55: COMMAND-LINE ARGUMENTS

1. Write a script called rename that will take two arguments: the first argument is the name of the original file and the second argument is the new name for the file.

   If the user does not provide two arguments, a usage message will appear on the screen and the script will exit. Here is an example of how the script works:

```
$ rename
Usage: rename oldfilename newfilename
$


$ rename file1 file2
file1 has been renamed file2
Here is a listing of the directory:
a file2
b file.bak
```

2. The following find command (SunOS) will list all files in the root partition that are larger than 100K and that have been modified in the last week. (Check your *man* pages for the correct find syntax on your system.)

```
find / -xdev -mtime -7 -size +200 -print
```

3. Write a script called bigfiles that will take two arguments: one will be the mtime and one the size value. An appropriate error message will be sent to stderr if the user does not provide two arguments.

4. If you have time, write a script called vib that creates backup files for vi. The backup files will have the extension .bak appended to the original name.

LAB 56: GETTING USER INPUT

1. Write a script called nosy that will do the following:

    a. Ask the user's full name—first, last, and middle name.

    b. Greet the user by his or her first name.

    c. Ask the user's year of birth and calculate his or her age (use expr).

   d. Ask the user's login name and print his or her user ID (from /etc/passwd).

   e. Tell the user his or her home directory.

   f. Show the user the processes he or she is running.

   g. Tell the user the day of the week, and the current time in nonmilitary time. The output should resemble

      `The day of the week is Tuesday and the current time is 04:07:38 PM.`

2. Create a text file called datafile (unless this file has already been provided for you). Each entry consists of fields separated by colons. The fields are as follows:

   a. First and last name

   b. Phone number

   c. Address

   d. Birth date

   e. Salary

3. Create a script called lookup that will do the following:

   a. Contain a comment section with the script name, your name, the date, and the reason for writing this script. The reason for writing this script is to display datafile in sorted order.

   b. Sort datafile by last names.

   c. Show the user the contents of datafile.

   d. Tell the user the number of entries in the file.

4. Try the -x and -v options for debugging your script. How did you use these commands? How do they differ?

LAB 57: CONDITIONAL STATEMENTS

1. Write a script called checking that will do the following:

   a. Take a command-line argument, a user's login name.

   b. Test to see if a command-line argument was provided.

   c. Check to see if the user is in the /etc/passwd file. If so, will print

      `Found <user> in the /etc/passwd file.`

      Otherwise, will print
      `No such user on our system.`

2. In the lookup script from Lab 56, ask the user if he or she would like to add an entry to datafile. If the answer is yes or y:

a. Prompt the user for a new name, phone number, address, birth date, and salary. Each item will be stored in a separate variable. You will provide the colons between the fields and append the information to the datafile.

b. Sort the file by last names. Tell the user you added the entry, and show him or her the line preceded by the line number.

LAB 58: CONDITIONALS AND FILE TESTING

1. Rewrite the checking script from Lab 57. After checking whether the named user is in the /etc/passwd file, the program will check to see if the user is logged on. If so, the program will print all the processes that are running; otherwise it will tell the user

   <user> is not logged on.

2. Use the let command to evaluate a set of grades. The script will ask the user for his or her numeric grade on an examination. (Use declare -i.) The script will test that the grade is within the allowable range between 0 and 100. If not, the program will exit. If the grade is within the range, the user's letter grade will be displayed (e.g., You received an A. Excellent!). The range is as follows:

   A (90–100)   B (80–89)   C (70–79)   D (60–69)   F (Below 60)

3. The lookup script from Lab 57 depends on datafile in order to run. In the lookup script, check to see if the datafile exists and if it is readable and writable. Add a menu to the lookup script to resemble the following:

   ```
   [1] Add entry
   [2] Delete entry
   [3] View entry
   [4] Exit
   ```

   You already have the Add entry part of the script written. The Add entry routine should now include code that will check to see if the name is already in the datafile and if it is, tell the user so. If the name is not there, add the new entry.

   Now write the code for the Delete entry, View entry, and Exit functions.

   The Delete part of the script should first check to see if the entry exists before trying to remove it. If it does, notify the user; otherwise, remove the entry and tell the user you removed it. On exit, make sure that you use a digit to represent the appropriate exit status.

   How do you check the exit status from the command line?

LAB 59: THE case STATEMENT

1. The ps command is different on BSD (Berkeley UNIX), System 5 (AT&T UNIX), and Linux. On System 5, the command to list all processes is

   ps -ef

   On BSD UNIX, the command is

   ps aux

On Linux, the command is

```
ps -aux
```

Write a program called systype that will check for a number of different system types. The cases to test for will be

AIX
Darwin (Mac OS X)
Free BSD
HP-UX
IRIX
Linux
OS
OSF1
SCO
SunOS (Solaris/SunOS)
ULTRIX

Solaris, HP-UX, SCO, and IRIX are AT&T-type systems. The rest are BSD-ish.

The version of UNIX you are using will be printed to stdout. The system name can be found with the uname -s command or from the /etc/motd file.

2. Write a script called timegreet that will do the following:

   a. Provide a comment section at the top of the script, with your name, the date, and the purpose of the program.

   b. Convert the following program to use the case command rather than if/elif.

```bash
#!/bin/bash
# Comment section
you=$LOGNAME
hour=$( date +%H )
echo "The time is: $( date +%T )"
if (( hour > 0 && hour < 12 ))
then
    echo "Good morning, $you!"
elif (( hour == 12 ))
then
    echo "Lunch time!"
elif (( hour > 12 && hour < 16 ))
then
    echo "Good afternoon, $you!"
else
    echo "Good night, $you. Sweet dreams."
fi
```

LAB 60: LOOPS

Select one of the following:

1. Write a program called mchecker to check for new mail and write a message to the screen if new mail has arrived.

   a. The program will get the size of the mail spool file for the user. (The spool files are found in /usr/mail/$LOGNAME on AT&T systems; /usr/spool/mail/$USER on BSD and UCB systems; and /var/spool/mail/$USER on Linux. Use the find command if you cannot locate the file.) The script will execute in a continuous loop, once every 30 seconds. Each time the loop executes, it will compare the size of the mail spool file with its size from the previous loop. If the new size is greater than the old size, a message will be printed on your screen, saying Username, You have new mail.

   The size of a file can be found by looking at the output from ls -l, wc -c or from the find command.

2. Write a script that will do the following:

   a. Provide a comment section at the top of the script, with your name, the date, and the purpose of the program.

   b. Use the select loop to produce a menu of foods.

   c. Produce output to resemble the following:

```
1)  steak and potatoes
2)  fish and chips
3) soup and salad
Please make a selection. 1
Stick to your ribs.
Watch your cholesterol.
Enjoy your meal.
1)  steak and potatoes
2)  fish and chips
3) soup and salad
Please make a selection. 2
British are coming!
Enjoy your meal.
1)  steak and potatoes
2) fish and chips
3) soup and salad
Please make a selection. 3
Health foods...
Dieting is so boring.
Enjoy your meal.
```

3. Write a program called dusage that will mail a list of users, one at a time, a listing of the number of blocks they are currently using. The list of users will be in a file called potential_hogs. One of the users listed in the potential_hogs file will be admin.

   a. Use file testing to check that the potential_hogs file exists and is readable.

   b. A loop will be used to iterate through the list of users. Only those users who are using over 500 blocks will be sent mail. The user admin will be skipped over (i.e., he or she does not get a mail message). The mail message will be stored in a here document in your dusage script.

   c. Keep a list of the names of each person who received mail. Do this by creating a log file. After everyone on the list has been sent mail, print the number of people who received mail and a list of their names.

LAB 61: FUNCTIONS

1. Rewrite the systype program from Lab 59 as a function that returns the name of the system. Use this function to determine what options you will use with the ps command in the checking program.

   The ps command to list all processes on AT&T UNIX is

   ps -ef

   On UNIX/BSD UNIX/Linux, the command is

   ps -aux or ps aux[9]

2. Write a function called cleanup that will remove all temporary files and exit the script. If the interrupt or hangup signal is sent while the program is running, the trap command will call the cleanup function.

3. Use a here document to add a new menu item to the lookup script to resemble the following:

   ```
   [1] Add entry
   [2] Delete entry
   [3] Change entry
   [4] View entry
   [5] Exit
   ```

   Write a function to handle each of the items in the menu. After the user has selected a valid entry, and the function has completed, ask if the user would like to see the menu again. If an invalid entry is entered, the program should print

   Invalid entry, try again.

   and the menu will be redisplayed.

---

9. Using the leading dash with UNIX will produce a warning. See the *man* page. Without the leading dash, Linux displays only user's processes.

4. Create a submenu under View entry in the lookup script. The user will be asked if he or she would like to view specific information for a selected individual:

   a) Phone
   b) Address
   c) Birth date
   d) Salary

5. Use the trap command in a script to perform a cleanup operation if the interrupt signal is sent while the program is running.

chapter
15

Debugging
Shell Scripts

15.1 Introduction

Programmers often spend more time debugging programs than writing them. Because many shell programs perform tasks that can affect the entire operating system, making sure those scripts perform properly is imperative. Whether you are a user or a system administrator writing scripts to automate simple or complex tasks, you want your script to do what you want it to do, and not cause weird and unexpected surprises even after all the syntax errors have been weeded out. The expression "If it ain't broke, don't fix it" is often ignored when you are thinking of ways to "improve" a script that is already working. Perhaps you think your script should be a little more user-friendly, might need some cosmetic surgery, or a little more error checking. Or you might even be cleaning up some other programmer's code. So, you put the script back in the editor, type, type, type, exit the editor, and run the program. Whoops! It's broken! @<!@%5#!>!! This chapter aims to provide an invaluable tool for finding, fixing, and understanding many types of errors that cause shell scripts to misbehave and leave you frustrated, wasting a lot of time that you probably don't have.

15.2 Style Issues

Although it is not required, style can make all the difference in how quickly you find bugs in your program. Here are some simple guidelines:

- Put *comments* in your program so that you and others know what you are trying to do. A cute little trick today may be an time-consuming enigma tomorrow.
- *Define variables* with meaningful names and put them at the top of the program to help detect *spelling errors* and *null values*. Names like foo1, foo2, and foo3 really don't say much. Check that you are not using *reserved words* and pay attention to *case sensitivity*.

- Whenever you use a conditional or looping command, *indent* the statement block that follows, at least one tab stop. If conditions or loops are nested, indent further. *Align ending keywords* with conditional and looping commands such as if and endif, if and fi, while, done, and so on. (See "Missing Keywords" on page 976 and "Indentation" on page 976.)
- Use the echo command in areas where you keep getting a syntax error, or turn on the *echoing* and *verbose switches* to trace your program's execution. (See "Tracing with Shell Options and the set Command" on page 1009.)
- *Logic errors* can be a source for hidden glitches in your program, even if the program runs without error. Know your *operators*. They vary from shell to shell and are often a cause for a logic error.
- Make your program *robust*—check for all possibilities of human error, such as bad input, insufficient arguments, nonexistent files, and the like. (See "Logic Errors and Robustness" on page 1001.)
- Keep things short and simple when testing. For example, if you are using a function, test the *syntax*, and then try it with a small script to see if you are getting what you want.
- Know your operating system *commands*. Because most statements consist of UNIX/Linux commands, go to the command line and try the command before using it in a script if you are not sure about how it behaves. Do you understand its *exit code*, how *variables* are being interpreted, how to use *quotes* properly, how to *redirect output and errors*?
- Last, if you are a system administrator, test your script carefully before taking it to the system level. An unexpected error could bring a whole system to its knees.

The following guidelines will help you with all of these issues and give you a list of the most common syntax errors for each shell, what caused it, and how to fix it.

15.3 Types of Errors

There are several types of errors you will experience in shell programs: runtime errors, logical errors, and errors that could have been prevented by making the program robust. Runtime errors occur when the script starts running and encounters the use of a bad script name, permission issues, path problems, or syntactical errors such as mismatched quotes or mispelled words. The shell will report some diagnostic message if you have this type of error and normally abort the program. Logical errors are are often harder to find, because they are not obvious, and involve problems in the way in which the program was constructed, such as using the wrong operator in an expression, not knowing the exit status of a command, or using faulty logic in branching or looping statements. Other errors involve lack of robustness, that is, errors that could have been avoided with proper error checking, such as not anticipating bad user input or insufficient arguments, and so forth.

15.3.1 Runtime Errors

Runtime errors occur when the script starts running and encounters use of a bad script name, permission issues, path problems, or syntactical errors, such as mismatched quotes or mispelled words.

15.3.2 Naming Conventions

When you type a command at the shell prompt, the shell searches the UNIX/Linux path to find that command. When you type your script name at the prompt, it is treated as any other command—the shell searches the path to find it. But suppose you name a script with the same name as some other UNIX command. Suppose, for example, you name your program "ls". Which ls will be executed? It depends on which ls is found in the path first, and most likely the UNIX command will be executed instead of your script. Although it seems obvious to avoid calling your script ls or cat, it is less obvious with more obscure commands such as test or script. For example, because the UNIX test command produces no output, realizing that a naming problem exists can be tricky. The UNIX script command starts up another interactive shell, which copies your session at the terminal into a typescript file. It is not obvious that another shell has started running and may take some time before you realize something is really wrong. So avoid using test and script as filenames just as you would avoid using cat or ls.

One way to see if you have named a script after a UNIX/Linux command is to use the which command. It will show you the path where the named program is found. See Example 15.1. You can also start the script with a leading ./; then the script will run in your current working directory.

EXAMPLE 15.1

```
1   $ cat test
    #! /bin/sh
    echo "She sells C shells on the C shore"
2   $ test
    $ (no output)
3   $ echo $PATH
    /usr/bin:/bin:/usr/local/bin:/usr/X11R6/bin:/home/ellie/bin:.
4   $ which test
    /usr/bin/test
5   $ mv test mytest
6   $ mytest
    She sells C shells on the C shore
```

EXPLANATION

1   Notice that the script name is test, which is also a UNIX/Linux command name.

2   When the user tries to run the script, called test, the UNIX/Linux command runs instead. The UNIX test command produces no output.

EXPLANATION (CONTINUED)

3   The user's search path is displayed. The first path that will be searched is /usr/bin. The dot at the end of the path represents the user's current working directory.

4   The which command locates the test command and displays its full pathname. The UNIX/Linux test command is in /usr/bin/test.

5, 6 If the script called test is given a unique name, and not a UNIX/Linux command name, it should run as expected. The test script is renamed mytest.

15.3.3   Insufficient Permissions

Ordinary files do not have execute permission. If a script is run directly from the command line, it must have execute permission turned on, or the shell will tell you that you have insufficient permission. Scripts are made executable with the chmod command.

EXAMPLE 15.2

```
1   $ mytest
    sh: ./mytest: Permission denied.
2   $ ls -l mytest
    -rw-rw-r-- 1  ellie    ellie     23 Jan  22   12:37    mytest
3   $ chmod +x mytest    # or chmod 755 mytest
4   $ ls -l mytest
    -rwxrwxr-x 1  ellie    ellie     23 Jan  22   12:37    mytest
5   $ mytest
    She sells C shells on the C shore
```

EXPLANATION

1   When the script is executed, an error message is displayed indicating that the script does not have the proper permission to run.

2   The ls -l command shows that the script does not have execute permission for anyone, including the owner of the script.

3   The chmod command adds execute permission (+x) for everyone. Now the script should run.

4   The ls -l command displays the new permissions. Execute permission is turned on.

5   The script executes as expected.

15.3.4   Path Problems

As we mentioned before, when you type the name of a shell script on the command line, the shell will check the directories listed in the search PATH variable to locate your script. If the dot directory is listed in the path, the shell will look in the current working directory for your script. If the script is there, it will be executed. However, if the dot is *not* in your path, you will receive an error message: Command not found. To enable the shell to locate your script, you can add the dot (.) directory to your PATH. However, if you have a superuser account (an account with UID of 0), it is recommended, for security reasons, that you do *not* include a dot in the search path. There are two alternative solutions if you choose not to put the dot in your PATH variable:

1. Explicitly indicate the location of your script by preceding the script name with ./ (e.g., ./mytest).
2. Precede the script name with the name of the invoking shell (e.g., csh mytest or bash mytest).

When the script name is given as an argument to the shell, the shell automatically checks the current directory for the script name.

EXAMPLE 15.3

```
1   $ cat mytest
    #!/bin/sh
    echo "Users may wish to include the . directory in their PATH"
2   $ echo $PATH
    /usr/bin:/bin:/usr/local/bin:/usr/X11R6/bin:/home/ellie/bin:
3   $ mytest
    not found
4   $ ./mytest      # this is one possible solution
    Users may wish to include the . directory in their PATH
5   $ PATH=$PATH:. # this solution should only be used by non-root
    $ export PATH  # bash, sh, ksh set PATH this way
    % setenv PATH ${PATH}:.   # csh/tcsh set path this way
6   $ mytest
    Users may wish to include the . directory in their PATH
```

EXPLANATION

1   The Bourne shell script is displayed. It is located in the user's current working directory.
2   The PATH variable does not contain a dot, which represents the current working directory.
3   The shell cannot locate the mytest script.
4   The shell is now able to locate the script because the directory (the .) is included with the script name.
5   The PATH is updated to include the current directory. The first syntax can be used for sh/ksh/bash shells, the second for csh/tcsh.
6   The script now runs correctly.

15.3.5 The Shbang Line

When you create a script, the first line of the script is normally the *shbang* (#!) line. When the script is started, the UNIX kernel examines the first line of the file to determine what type of program is to be executed. The path that follows the shbang notation (#!) is the location of the shell that will be invoked to interpret this script. The #! characters must be the first two characters in the file for this feature to operate properly. If you have a blank line or blank space at the top of your file, this feature will be ignored and the line will be interpreted as an ordinary comment line.

EXAMPLE 15.4

```
(The Script)
1
2    #!/bin/csh
     # Scriptname: shbang.test
3    setenv MYVAR 18
     echo "The value of MYVAR is $MYVAR"

(The Output)
     ./shbang.test: line 3: setenv: command not found
     The value of MYVAR is

(The Script)
4    #!/bin/csh
     setenv MYVAR 18
     echo "The value of MYVAR is $MYVAR"

(The Output)
     The value of MYVAR is 18
```

EXPLANATION

1   Notice that this script has a blank line at the top. Also note that the script was written for the C shell. The setenv command on line 3 will not work in the Bourne, Korn, or Bash shells.

2, 3 Because the #! line is not the first line of the script, the script will be executed by the user's login shell. If the login shell is ksh, the Korn shell will execute the script; if bash, the Bash shell will execute the script. If, however, the user's login shell is C shell, this script will be executed by the Bourne shell. The error message is displayed because the Bourne shell doesn't understand the setenv command.

4   The script now runs correctly because the #! notation has been entered on the top line. The kernel will recognize the #! and start up the shell listed in the path that follows. Because the shell is /bin/csh, the C shell will be the interpreter for this script (provided that the execute permissions are turned on). The setenv command is understood by the C shell.

EXAMPLE 15.5

```
1   #! /bin/chs
    echo "Watch out for typing errors on the #! line"
2   $ ./mytest
    mytest: Command not found.

---------------------------------------

3   #! /bin/csh
    echo "Watch out for typing errors on the #! line"
4   ./mytest
    Watch out for typing errors on the #! line
```

EXPLANATION

1   The shbang line has a typing error in the shell name. The shell should be /bin/csh instead of /bin/chs. Misspelling on the shbang line is a very common error!

2   Because of the typing error, the kernel looks for the /bin/chs program, causing the Command not found error message. This message can be misleading, causing you to think that the script itself or a command typed in the script cannot be found. If the only error you get is Command not found, first check the shbang line for spelling.

3   The spelling of the shell is corrected on the shbang line.

4   The script now runs correctly.

15.3.6 Sneaky Aliases

An *alias* is an abbreviation or an alternative name for a command. Aliases are not supported by the Bourne shell. Aliases are usually put in an initialization file and used as shortcuts at the command line, but are not readily used in shell scripts. However, they may find their way into a script if the user's .cshrc or .kshrc defines an alias and does not limit the aliases to interactive shell sessions.

EXAMPLE 15.6

```
(In the .cshrc File)
1   alias ls 'ls -aF'

(At the shell prompt)
2   $ ls
    ./        a         c         t1        t3
    ../       b         t*        t2        tester*

(The Script)
    #!/bin/csh
3   foreach i ( `ls` )
4       echo $i
    end
```

EXAMPLE 15.6 (CONTINUED)

```
(Output)
 ./
 ../
 a
 b
 c
 t t1 t2 t3 tester    <-- What happened here?
 t1
 t2
 t3
 tester


 ----------------Possible Fix------------------------

 5   #!/bin/csh -f      <-- Add the -f option to the shbang line
 6   unalias ls         <-- turn off the alias
```

EXPLANATION

1   In the user's .cshrc initialization file, an alias has been defined. Normally the .cshrc file is started up any time you invoke a C shell, including a C shell script. Many generic .cshrc files define aliases after the expression:

```
if ( $?prompt ) then
   < aliases listed here >
endif
```

This means: If you are running an interactive shell, that is, a shell that produces a prompt, then you can use the aliases. Because shell scripts are noninteractive and do not have a prompt, they would not able to use the aliases. (Often aliases are also stored in a file called .aliases and are sourced in the .cshrc file, .kshrc file, .bashrc file, or .tcshrc file.)

2   When the user types ls at the prompt, the alias is used. It causes ls -aF to be executed. The -F switch lists files with a * appended to executable files, a / appended to directories, and an @ appended to symbolic links. The -a switch causes invisible files to be printed (i.e., those files starting with a period).

3   In the shell script, the ls command is executed in the foreach expression. The shell will evaluate the alias, causing the ls -aF command to list the files in the format described above, something the unsuspecting programmer may not realize. Each executable file is appended with a *, which the shell will treat as a globbing meta-character and start matching on filenames. Because the file called t is an executable file, it will be listed as t*, causing the shell to match all files starting with a t.

4   All the files are listed using the alias.

5   One solution to this problem is to add the -f option to /bin/csh in the shbang line. Often called a fast startup, the -f switch tells the shell *not* to load the .cshrc file when it starts the script. For ksh the shbang line would be #!/bin/ksh -p and for bash it would be #!/bin/bash --noprofile.

15.4 Probable Causes for Syntax Errors

15.4.1   Undefined and Misspelled Variables

As you know, the shells do not require variables to be declared. When a variable name is used in a program, the variable is created automatically. Although this may seem more convenient than having to declare every variable explicitly, there is an unfortunate consequence: An inadvertent spelling error might introduce an extra variable that you had no intention of creating. And because UNIX/Linux is case sensitive, even changing from uppercase to lowercase can cause a program to fail.

When setting a variable in the C/TC shells, the set command is used, and the = sign must be surrounded with space (or no space at all). The set command in bash, sh, and ksh is used to set shell options or create positional parameters, but is not used to define variables. Space is not allowed on either side of the = sign. When switching from one shell to another, it is easy to forget when to use set and when to use or not use spaces.

The C and TC shells will tell you when you are using an undefined variable. The Bourne, Bash, and Korn shells display a blank line, unless you request error checking with the set -u or the shell's -u invocation option. The -u option flags any variables that have not been defined, called *unbound variables*.

In the Bourne, Korn, and Bash shells, a variable is set as follows:

```
x=5
name=John
friend="John Doe"
empty=    or empty=""
```

To check for undefined variables:

```
set -u
echo "Hi $firstname"

(Output)
ksh: firstname: parameter not set
```

In the C and TC shells:

```
set x = 5
set name = John
set friend = "John Doe"
set empty = ""
```

The shell checks for undefined variables:

```
echo "Hi $firstname"
```

```
(Output)
firstname: Undefined variable
```

EXAMPLE 15.7

```
    #!/bin/tcsh
1   set friend1 = "George"
    set friend2 = "Jake"
    set friend4 = "Danny"
2   echo "Welcome $friend3 "
```

```
(Output)
3   friend3: Undefined variable.
```

EXPLANATION

1   Three variables are set. When variables are so similar in thier names, it is easy to mistype one of them later in the program.

2   The variable friend3 was never defined.

3   The C and TC shells send an error to let you know that you have an undefined variable. The Bourne, Korn, and Bash shells leave a blank line.

15.4.2 Incomplete Programming Statements

Missing Keywords.   When using a programming statement such as an if statement or while loop, you may accidentally omit part of the statement. For example, you may forget to complete your while loop with the done keyword. Whenever you see an error message concerning unexpected end of file, or if the message points to the line number one past the last (e.g., your script contains 10 lines and the error message refers to line 11), you should check for incomplete programming statements.

Indentation.   An easy way to ensure that if/else, while/do/done, case statements, and other contructs are complete is to indent the block of statements under each test expression (at least one tab stop), and move the terminating keyword (done, end, endsw, etc.) to line up with the conditional or looping command that it terminates. This is an extremely helpful technique when these constructs are nested.

In sh, bash, ksh: In csh, tcsh:

```
if [ expression ]                  if ( expression ) then
  then                                 statement
     statement                         statement
     statement                       endif
  fi
```

if/endif Errors.   See the following format for the correct way to set up your if/endif construct with tab stops.

FORMAT

In Bourne, Korn, and Bash shells:

```
# Without indentation
if [ $ch = "a" ]     # Use indentation
then
echo $ch
if [ $ch = "b" ]     <-- Missing 'then'
echo $ch
else
echo $ch
fi
         <-- Missing 'fi' for first 'if'
--------------------------Fix--------------------------
# With indentation
if [ $ch = "a" ]
then
    echo $ch
    if [ $ch = "b" ]
    then
        echo $ch
    else    # 'else' goes with nearest 'if'
        echo $ch
    fi
fi
```

In C and TC shells:

```
if ( $ch == "a" )      <-- Missing 'then'
    echo $ch
    if ( $ch == "b" ) then
        echo $ch
else
    echo $ch
endif
        <-- Missing 'endif' for first 'if'
```

FORMAT (CONTINUED)

```
--------------------------Fix--------------------------
if ( $ch == "a" ) then
    echo $ch
    if ( $ch == "b" ) then
        echo $ch
    else
        echo $ch
    endif
endif
```

case and switch Errors.   There are a number of bugs often found in case and switch commands. The variable that is being tested should be in double quotes if the variable value consists of more than one word. Relational, logical, and equality operators are not allowed in the case constants.

FORMAT

Case statements for the Bourne, Korn, and Bash shells:

```
case $color in          <-- Variable should be quoted
blue)
    statements
    statements          <-- Missing ;;
red || orange)          <-- Logical || not allowed
    statements
      ;;
*)  statements
      ;;
                        <-- Missing esac
----------------------The Fix---------------------------
case "$color" in
blue )
    statement
    statement
      ;;
red | orange )
    statements
      ;;
*)
    statements
      ;;
esac
```

FORMAT (CONTINUED)

Switch statements for C and TC shells:

```
switch ($color)           <-- Variable should be quoted
case blue:
   statements
   statements             <-- Missing breaksw
case red || orange:       <-- Logical operator not allowed
   statements
   breaksw
default:
   statements
   breaksw
                          <-- Missing endsw
-----------------------The Fix-------------------------------
switch ("$color")
case blue:
   statements
   statements
   breaksw
case red:
case orange:
   statements
   breaksw
default:
   statements
   breaksw
endsw
```

Looping Errors.   A looping error occurs when the syntax of a for, foreach, while, or until loop is incorrect, most commonly when one of the keywords used to terminate the looping block is omitted, such as do, done, or end.

FORMAT

Bourne shell:

```
while  [ $n -lt 10 ]      <-- Missing do keyword
   echo $n
   n=`expr $n + 1`
done

while  [ $n -lt 10 ]
do
   echo $n
   n=`expr $n + 1`
                          <-- Missing done keyword
```

FORMAT (CONTINUED)

```
----------------------The Fix---------------------------------
 while  [ $n -lt 10 ]
do
    echo $n
    n=`expr $n + 1`
done
```

Loops for Bash and Korn shells:

```
while  (( $n <= 10 ))        <-- Missing do keyword
    echo $n
    (( n+=1 ))
done

while  (( $n <= 10 ))
do
    echo $n
    (( n+=1 ))
                             <-- Missing done keyword
----------------------The Fix---------------------------------
while  (( $n <= 10 ))
do
    echo $n
    (( n+=1 ))
done
```

Loops for the C and TC shells:

```
while ( $n <= 10 )
    echo $n
    @n+=1              <-- Missing space after the @ symbol
                       <-- Missing end keyword
foreach ( a b c )      <-- Missing variable after foreach
    echo $char
end
----------------------The Fix---------------------------------
while ( $n <= 10 )
    echo $n
    @ n+=1
end

foreach char ( a b c )
    echo $char
end
```

Operator Errors.   The shells use different operators for manipulating strings and numbers. The Bourne shell uses the test command (see *man* test) and its operators for comparing numbers and strings. Although these operators will work with Korn and Bash shells, normally they are not used. Instead, the Korn and Bash shells provide a set of C-like operators to handle arithmetic with the let command (( )) and string operators to be used with the new test command [[ ]]. But the Korn shell does not use the double == sign for equality, whereas the Bash shell does.

The C and TC shells also provide a set of C-like operators for comparing numbers and strings, and use the == for both numbers and strings. Confusing? If you are porting shell scripts, it might be a good idea to check the operators for each shell. They are provided in tables for each shell in this book. (See Appendix B.) The following examples illustrate some of the operators for each shell.

FORMAT

Bourne shell:

```
Numeric testing
    if [ $n -lt 10 ]
    if [ $n -gt $y ]
    if [ $n -eq 6 ]
    if [ $n -ne 6
String testing
    if [ "$name" = "John" ]
    if [ "$name" != "John" ]
```

Korn shell:

```
Numeric testing
    if (( n < 10 ))
    if (( n >  y ))
    if (( n == 6 ))
    if (( n != 6 ))
String testing
    if [[ $name = "John" ]]
    if [[ $name != "John" ]]
```

Bash shell:

```
Numeric testing
    if (( n < 10 ))
    if (( n >  y ))
    if (( n == 6 ))
    if (( n != 6 ))
String testing
    if [[ $n == "John" ]]
    if [[ $n != "John" ]]
```

FORMAT (CONTINUED)

C and TC shells:

```
Numeric testing
   if ( $n < 10 )
   if ( $n >  $y )
   if ( n == 6 ))
   if ( n != 6 )

String testing
   if ( "$name" == "John" )
   if ( "$name" != "John" )
```

Misusing an Operator.   The following examples illustrate the most common causes of misused operators.

EXAMPLE   15.8

```
(sh)
1    n=5; name="Tom"
2    if [ $n > 0 ]     # Should be: if [ $n -gt 0 ]
     then
3    if [ $n == 5 ]    # Should be: if [ $n -eq 5 ]
     then
4    n++   # Should be: n=`expr $n + 1`
5    if [ "$name" == "Tom" ]     # Should be: if [ $name = "Tom" ]

(csh/tcsh)
     set n = 5; set name = "Tom"
6    if ( $n =< 5 ) then         # Should be: if ( $n <= 5 ) then
7    if ( $n == 5 && < 6 ) then  # Should be: if ( $n == 5 && $n < 6)
8    if ( $name == [Tt]om ) then # Should be: if ($name =~ [Tt]om )

(ksh)
     name="Tom"
     n=5
9    if [ $name == [Tt]om ]      # Should be: if [[ $name == [Tt]om ]]ᵃ
10   [[ n+=5 ]]  # Should be: (( n+=5 ))
```

---

a.   On versions of ksh newer than ksh88, the == is okay; earlier version must use a single = sign.

EXPLANATION

1   In the Bourne shell, the variable n is assigned 5.

2   The [bracket is a symbol for the test command. The test command does not use > for greater than, but instead, uses -gt for the relational operator.

EXPLANATION (CONTINUED)

3   The double equal sign is not a valid equality operator for the test command. The operator that should be used is -eq.

4   The Bourne shell does not support arithmetic operations.

5   The test command does not use == for equality testing; it uses a single = for string testing and -eq for numeric testing.

6   The csh/tcsh relational operator should be <=. Misusing relational operators causes a syntax error in all shells.

7   The expression on the right-hand side of the logical && is incomplete.

8   The csh/tcsh shells use =~ when evaluating strings containing wildcards. The error in this example would be No match.

9   The single bracket type of testing does not support the == sign. Bash and ksh use the [[test command to test expressions containing wildcards. The double equal sign, rather than the single equal sign, is used for testing string equality. (Only versions of ksh newer than ksh88 support the == sign. Earlier versions require the single = for string testing.)

10   The [[test command is used with string expressions; the ((let command is used for numeric expressions.

Quoting Errors. Misused quotes are such a common cause for error in shell scripts that a whole section has been devoted to quoting. (See "What You Should Know About Quotes" on page 985.) Quotes are often called the "bane of shell programmers" or the "quotes from hell." There are three types of quotes: single quotes, double quotes, and backquotes. Single and double quotes surround strings of text to protect certain characters from interpretation, whereas backquotes are used for command substitution. Although we have discussed quotes in previous chapters, the next few sections will focus on how to use them properly to avoid errors.

Quoting Metacharacters. A problem directly related to quoting is the misuse of metacharacters. We've already discussed two kinds of metacharacters: shell metacharacters and regular expression metacharacters used with vi, grep, sed, awk, and utility programs other than the shell. (See Chapter 3, "Regular Expressions and Pattern Matching," on page 67.) Unquoted metacharacters will be interpreted by the shell to mean file matching, and unquoted regular expression metacharacters may cause programs like grep, sed, and nawk to break down. In the following example, the * is used by grep to represent zero or more of the letter "b" and the * is used by the shell to match all filenames starting with an "f". The shell always evaluates the command line before executing the command. Because grep's * is not quoted, the shell will try to evaluate it, causing an error.

```
grep ab*c  f*
```

To fix the problem, quotes are used:

```
grep 'ab*c'  f*
```

Now when the shell parses the command line, it will not evaluate the characters within the quotes.

Quotes must be matched. Most shells will send an error message when they realize that there are unmatched quotes. The Bourne shell, on the other hand, parses an entire script file before reporting a problem, which is usually "unexpected end of file," hardly a big help when the same error message is displayed for a number of other problems.

In order to really achieve expertise in shell scripting, it is imperative to get a good understanding of the quoting mechanism.

EXAMPLE 15.9

```
#! /bin/csh
1   echo I don't understand you.    # Unmatched single quote

    (Output)
2   Unmatched '
-----------------------------------------
    #! /bin/csh
3   echo Gotta light?   # Unprotected wildcard

(Output)
4   echo: No match
---------------------------------
    #!/bin/csh
5   set name = "Steve"
6   echo 'Hello $name.'     # Variable not interpreted

(Output)
Hello $name
```

EXPLANATION

1   Quotes must be matched. The single quote in don't causes an error. To fix the problem, the string can be enclosed in double quotes or the single quote can be preceded by a backslash, as don\'t.

2   The C shell displays its error message for a mismatched single quote.

3   The shell metacharacter, ?, is used to match for single character filenames. There is not a file in the directory spelled light and followed by a single character.

4   The C shell complains that there is No match for that metacharacter. To fix the problem, the string should be enclosed in either single or double quotes or the question mark should be preceded by a backslash, as 'Gotta light?' or light\?

5   The string "Steve" is assigned to a variable.

6   The string is enclosed in single quotes. The characters within the single quotes are treated literally (i.e., the variable will not be interpreted). To fix the problem, the string should be enclosed in double qutoes or no quotes at all, as "Hello $name."

What You Should Know About Quotes.   Quotes are so inherently part of shell scripting that this section is provided to clarify their use in all the shells. If you are regularly getting quoting syntax errors, study this section to be sure you know how to use them, especially if your script contains commands like grep, sed, and awk.

The Backslash

1. Precedes a character and escapes that character
2. Same as putting single quotes around one character

Single Quotes

1. Must be matched
2. Protect all metacharacters from interpretation except the following:
   a. Itself
   b. Exclamation point (csh only)
   c. Backslash

Table 15.1   Proper Single Quoting Examples

C/TC Shells	Bourne/Bash Shells	Korn Shell
echo '$*&><?' *$*&><?*	echo '$*&!><?' *$*&!><?*	print '$*&!><?' *$*&!><?*
(C) echo 'I need $5.00\!' *I need $5.00!* (TC) echo 'I need $5.00!'	echo 'I need $5.00!' *I need $5.00!*	print 'I need $5.00!'
echo 'She cried, "Help"' *She cried, "Help"*	echo 'She cried,"Help"' *She cried, "Help"*	print 'She cried, "Help"' *She cried, "Help"*
echo '\\\\' \\\\	echo '\\\\' (Bourne) \\ (Bash) \\\\	print '\\\\' \\

Double Quotes

1. Must be matched
2. Protect all metacharacters from interpretation except the following:
   a. Itself
   b. Exclamation point (csh only)
   c. $ used for variable substitution
   d. ` ` Backquotes for command substitution

Table 15.2 Proper Double Quoting Examples

C Shell	Bourne Shell	Korn Shell
echo "Hello $LOGNAME\!"	echo "Hello $LOGNAME!"	print "Hello $LOGNAME!"
echo "I don't care"	echo "I don't care"	print "I don't care"
echo "The date is `date`"	echo "The date is `date`"	print "The date is $(date)"
echo "\\\\"	echo "\\\\"	print "\\\\"
\\\\	\	\

Backquotes

Backquotes are used in shell programs for command substitution. They are unrelated to single and double quotes, but often the source of problems. For example, when copying a shell script, if the backquotes are replaced with single quotes (merely by misreading the code), the program will no longer work.[1]

EXAMPLE 15.10

```
#!/bin/sh
1    now=`date`
2    echo Today is $now
3    echo "You have `ls|wc -l` files in this directory"
4    echo 'You have `ls|wc -l` files in this directory'

(Output)
2    Today is Mon Jul 5 10:24:06 PST 2004
3    You have 33 files in this directory
4    You have `ls|wc -l` files in this directory
```

EXPLANATION

1   The variable now is assigned to the output of the UNIX/Linux date command. (For the T/TC shell: set now = `date`.) The backquotes cause command substitution. The backquote is normally found under the tilde (~) on your keyboard.

2   The value of variable now is displayed with the current date.

3   The backquotes surround a UNIX/Linux pipe. The output of ls is piped to wc -l. The result is to count the number of files listed in this directory. Double quotes around the string will not interfere with command substitution. The output is embedded in the string and printed.

4   By enclosing the string in single quotes, the backquotes are not interpreted, but treated as literal characters.

---

1. In the production of this type of book, it is very easy to mistake backquotes for single quotes!

Combining Quotes

Combining quotes can be a major trick. This next section will guide you through the steps for successfull quoting. We will demonstrate how to embed a shell variable in the awk command line and have the shell expand the variable without interfering with awk's field designators, $1 and $2.

Setting the Shell Variable

```
name="Jacob Savage"     (Bourne and Korn shells)
set name = "Jacob Savage"  (C shell)

(The line from the datafile)
Jacob Savage:408-298-7732:934 La Barbara Dr. , San Jose, CA:02/27/78:500000

(The nawk command line)
nawk -F: '$1 ~ /^'"$name"'/{print $2}'  datafile

(Output)
408-298-7732
```

Try this example:

1. Test your knowledge of the UNIX/Linux command at the command line before plugging in any shell variables.

   ```
   nawk -F: '$1 ~ /^Jacob Savage/{print $2}' filename

   (Output)
   408-298-7732
   ```

2. Plug in the shell variable without changing anything else. Leave all quotes as they were.

   ```
   nawk -F: '$1 ~ /^$name/{print $2}' datafile
   ```

   Starting at the left-hand side of the awk command leave the first quote as is; right before the shell dollar sign in $name, place another single quote. Now the first quote is matched and all text within these two quotes is protected from shell interference. The variable is exposed. Now put another single quote right after the e in $name. This starts another matched set of single quotes ending after awk's closing curly brace. Everything within this set of quotes is also protected from shell interpretation.

   ```
   nawk -F: '$1 ~ /^'$name'/{print $2}' datafile
   ```

3. Enclose the shell variable in a set of double quotes. This allows the variable to be expanded but the value of the variable will be treated as single string if it contains whitespace. The whitespace must be protected so that the command line is parsed properly.

```
nawk -F: '$1 ~ /^'"$name"'/{print $2}'  datafile
```

Count the number of quotes. There should be an even number of single quotes and an even number of double quotes.

Here's another example:

```
oldname="Ellie Main"
newname="Eleanor Quigley"
```

1. Make sure the command works.

```
nawk -F: '/^Ellie Main/{$1="Eleanor Quigley"; print $0}' datafile
```

2. Plug in the variables.

```
nawk -F: '/^$oldname/{$1="$newname"; print $0}' datafile
```

3. Play the quoting game. Starting at the first single quote at the left, move across the line until you come to the variable $oldname and place another single quote just before the dollar sign. Put another single quote right after the last letter in the variable name.

   Now move to the right and place another single quote right before the dollar sign in $newname. Put another single quote after the last character in $newname.

```
nawk -F: '/^'$oldname'/{$1="'$newname'"; print $0}' datafile
```

4. Count the number of single quotes. If the number of single quotes is an even number, each quote has a matching quote. If not, you have forgotten a step.

5. Enclose each of the shell variables in double quotes. The double quotes are placed snugly around the shell variable.

```
nawk -F: '/^'"$oldname"'/{$1="'"$newname"'"; print $0}' datafile
```

Problems with the here document. The here document, used primarily for creating menus in shell scripts, is often a source of error. The problem is usually found with the user-defined terminator that ends the here document. There can be no space around the terminator. All shells are strict about this rule, although the Bourne, Bash, and Korn shells allow you to use tabs under certain conditions. See the following example.

EXAMPLE 15.11

```
#! /bin/ksh
        print "Do you want to see the menu?"
        read answer
        if [[ $answer = y ]]
        then
1           cat << EOF           <-- No space after user-defined terminator
            1) Steak and eggs
            2) Fruit and yogurt
            3) Pie and icecream
2           EOF                  <-- User-defined terminator cannot
                                     have spaces surrounding it
            print "Pick one "
            read choice
            case "$choice" in
                1) print "Cholesterol"
                    ;;
                2) print "Dieter"
                    ;;
                3) print "Sweet tooth"
                    ;;
            esac
        else
            print "Later alligator!"
        fi
```

```
(Output)
file: line 6: here document 'EOF' unclosed
or
file: line 6: syntax error: unexpected end of file (bash)
```

EXPLANATION

1   This is the start of a here document. The cat command is followed by << and a user-defined terminator, in this case, EOF. The lines following the terminator are used as input to the cat command, producing a menu of choices on the screen. The input stops when the terminator is reached on line 2.

EXPLANATION (CONTINUED)

2   The terminator on line 2 must exactly match the one on line 1 or the here document will not end. In addition, the final terminator cannot be surrounded by any space. The well-meaning programmer tried to indent the script for better readability, but, in this case indenting the EOF on line 2 causes a syntax error. The solution is to move the terminating EOF to the far left-hand margin and make sure there is no space surrounding it. The bash/ksh/sh shells allow one other fix, which is to put a dash after the << symbol: cat <<- EOF. This allows you to use tabs (and only tabs) to indent the final terminator on line 2.

File-Testing Errors.   If you are using external files in a script, it is best to check certain properties of the files before using them, such as their existence, whether they are readable or writable, have any data, are a symbolic link, and so forth. The file tests are quite similar for each shell, but the test for file existence varies. For example, the C, TC, and Bash shells use the -e switch to check if a file exists, the Korn shell uses the -a switch, and the Bourne shell uses the -f switch. With the exception of the TC shell, the file-testing switches cannot be bound together, such as -rw for read and write. Instead a single file-testing switch precedes the filename. An example of a C shell test for a readable, writable, and executable file would be if (-r filename && -w filename && -x filename). An example for a TC shell test would be if (-rwx filename).

Checking for File Existence in the Five Shells

The following error message was generated before file testing was performed in a script. The file called db did not exist.

grep: db: cannot open [No such file or directory]

The following example demonstrates how to fix this problem for each of the five shells.

EXAMPLE   15.12

```
(csh/tcsh)
set filedb = db
if ( ! -e $filedb ) then
  echo "$filedb does not exist"
  exit 1
endif

(sh)
filedb=db
if [ ! -f $filedb ]
then
  echo "$filedb does not exist"
  exit 1
fi
```

EXAMPLE 15.12 (CONTINUED)

```
(ksh)
filedb=db
if [[ ! -a $filedb ]]
then
  print "$filedb does not exist"
  exit 1
fi

(bash)
filedb=db
if [[ ! -e $filedb ]]
then
  echo "$filedb does not exist"
  exit 1
fi
```

15.4.3   Common Error Messages from the Big 5 Shells

There are a number of different types of syntax errors that will be reported by the shell when you run a script. Each shell reports these errors by sending a message to standard error, and the messages vary from shell to shell. The C shell, for example, is very verbose, and reports errors such as unmatched quotes and undefined variables on the same line where the error occurred, whereas the Bourne shell error messages are sparse and quite cryptic. It is often very hard to debug a Bourne shell script because the error is not reported at all until the script has been completely parsed, and when you get the error message, it may not tell you anything to help you understand your erring ways.

Because each of the shells has its own style of error reporting, Tables 15.3 through 15.6 illustrate the most common syntax errors, the probable cause, what the error message means, and a simple fix.

Common C/TC Shell Error Messages. Table 15.3 lists commonly found C shell error messages. Because the TC shell mimics the the C shell errors so closely, the chart serves to address both shells.

Table 15.3 Common C/TC Shell Error Messages

Error Message	What Caused It	What It Means	How to Fix It
": Event not found.	echo "Wow!"	The exclamation mark (history character) must be escaped. Quotes will not protect it.	echo "Wow\!"
@: Badly formed number	set n = 5.6; @ n++; @ n = 3+4	Arithmetic can be performed only on whole numbers and there must be space surrounding arithmetic operators.	set n = 5; @ n++; @ n = 3 + 4
@n++: Command not found	@n++	The @ sign must be followed by a space.	@ n++
Ambiguous.	`date`	The backquotes are used for command substitution when the output of a command is being assigned to a variable or is part of a string. If the command is on a line by itself, it should not be enclosed in backquotes. Tcsh will give the error Fri: Command not found.	echo The date is `date` or set d = `date`
Bad : modifier in $ (f).	echo $cwd:f	The :f is an invalid pathname expansion modifier.	echo $cwd:t or $cwd:h etc.
Badly placed ()'s.	echo (abc)	The parentheses are used to start a subshell. The whole command should be placed in () or the string should be quoted.	(echo abc) or echo "(abc)"
echo: No match.	echo How are you?	The question mark is a shell metacharacter used in filename expansion. It represents one character in a filename. The shell will match for a file named you followed by a single character. Because there isn't a file by that name, the error No match is displayed.	echo "How are you?" or echo 'How are you?' or echo How are you\?

Table 15.3 Common C/TC Shell Error Messages (continued)

Error Message	What Caused It	What It Means	How to Fix It
filex: File exists.	sort filex > temp	The noclobber variable has been set and the temp file exists. noclobber will not let you overwrite an existing file.	sort filex > temp1 (use a different file for output) or unset noclobber or sort filex >! temp (override noclobber)
fruit: Subscript out of range	echo $fruit[3]	The array fruit does not have three elements.	set fruit = (apples pears plums)
if : Empty if	if ($x > $y)	The if expression is incomplete. The then is missing.	if ($x > $y) then
if : Expression Syntax	if ($x = $y) then	The if equality operator should be ==.	if ($x == $y) then
if : Expression Syntax	set name = "Joe Doe" if ($name == "Joe Doe") then	The variable name on the left-hand side of the == sign should be double quoted.	if ("$name" == "Joe Doe") then
if: Expression syntax.	if (grep john filex) then	When evaluating a command, curly braces should surround the command, not parentheses.	if { grep john filex } then
Invalid null command	echo "hi" &> temp	The redirection operator is backwards. Should be >&.	echo "hi" >& temp
Missing }.	if {grep john filex} then	The curly braces must be surrounded by space.	if { grep john filex } then
set: Syntax error	set name= "Tom"	The equal sign must have space on either side, or no space at all.	set name = "Tom" or set name="Tom"
set: Syntax error	set name.1 = "Tom"	A period is not a valid character in a variable name.	set name1 = "Tom"
set: Syntax error	set file-text = "fool"	The dash is an illegal character in the variable name.	set file_text = "fool"
shift: No more words	shift fruit	The shift command removes the leftmost word in an array. The error is caused because the array, fruit, has no more word elements. You cannot shift an empty array.	set fruit = (apples pears plums)

then: then/endif not found.	if ($x > $y) then
	 statements
	 statements
		The if expression is incomplete. The endif is missing.	if ($x > $y) then
			 statements
			 endif

Table 15.3 Common C/TC Shell Error Messages (continued)

Error Message	What Caused It	What It Means	How to Fix It
Too many ('s	`if ( $x == $y && ( $x != 3 ) then`	The expression has unbalanced parentheses. Either add one to the right-hand side or remove the (after the &&.	`if ( $x == $y && ( $x != 3 )) then` or `if ( $x == $y && $x != 3 ) then`
top: label not found.	`goto top`	The goto command is looking for a label called top that should be on a line by itself somewhere in the program. Either that, or the label is there but is spelled differently.	`top:` `goto top`
Undefined variable	`echo $name`	The variable name has never been set.	`set name; set name = "John"; set name = ""`
Unmatched ".	`echo She said, "Hello`	The double quote must be matched on the same line.	`echo 'She said, "Hello"'`
Unmatched '.	`echo I don't care`	The single quote must be matched on the same line.	`echo "I don't care"` or `echo I don\'t care`
while: Expression syntax.	`while ( $n =< 5 )`	The wrong operator was used. It should be <=.	`while ( $n <= 5 )`

Common Bourne Shell Error Messages.

Table 15.4 lists commonly found Bourne shell error messages.

Table 15.4 Common Bourne Shell Error Messages

Error Message	What Caused It	What It Means	How to Fix It
./file: line 5: syntax error near unexpected token blue)	`color="blue"` `case $color`	The case command is missing the in keyword.	`case $color in`
[Blank line] The shell produces a blank line, no error message.	`echo $name`	The variable doesn't exist or is empty.	`name="some value";`
[ellie]: not found	`if [$USER = "ellie"] ; then`	There must be a space after the [.	`if [ $USER = "ellie" ] ; then`
answer: not found	`answer = "yes"`	There cannot be any space on either side of the equal sign.	`answer="yes"`

Table 15.4 Common Bourne Shell Error Messages (continued)

Error Message	What Caused It	What It Means	How to Fix It
cannot shift	shift 2	The shift built-in command is used to shift positional parameters to the left. If there are not at least two positional parameters, the shift will fail.	set apples pears peaches; shift 2 (apples and pears will be shifted from the list)
name: is read only	name="Tom"; readonly name; name="Dan"	The variable was set to be a readonly variable. It cannot be redefined or unset.	name2="Dan" or exit shell
name: parameter not set	echo $name	set -u has been set. With this option to the set command, undefined variables are flagged.	name="some value";
name.1=Tom: not found	name.1="Tom"	A period is not valid in a variable name.	name1="Tom"
syntax error at line 7 'fi' unexpected	if [$USER = "ellie"] echo "hi" fi	There must be then after the expression.	if [$USER = "ellie"] then echo "hi" fi
syntax error: `{'	fun() {echo "hi";}	There should be space surrounding the curly braces in the definition for the function, fun().	fun() { echo "hi"; }

syntax error: 'done' unexpected	while [$n < 5]
	    statements
	 done
		The while is missing the do keyword.	while [$n -lt 5]
			 do
			    statements
			 done

syntax error: 'fi' unexpected"	if [$USER = "ellie"] then	The then should be on the next line or preceded by a semicolon.	if [$USER = "ellie"] then or if [$USER = "ellie"]; then
test: argument expected	if [25 >= 24] ; then	The >= is not a valid test operator. Should be -ge.	if [25 -ge 24]; then
test: unknown operator	if [grep $USER /etc/passwd] ; then	The grep command should not be surrounded by square brackets or any other symbols. The brackets are used only when testing expressions. The [is a test operator.	if grep $USER /etc/passwd ; then

Table 15.4 Common Bourne Shell Error Messages (continued)

Error Message	What Caused It	What It Means	How to Fix It
test: unknown operator Doe	name="John Doe"; if [$name = Joe]	The variable, name, should be double quoted in the test expression. There can be only one string on the left-hand side of the = operator unless it is quoted.	if ["$name" = Joe]
trap: bad trap	trap 'rm tmp*' 500	The number 500 is an illegal signal. Normally signals 2 or 3 will be trapped in a shell script. 2 is for Ctrl-C and 3 is for Ctrl-\. Both signals cause the program named after the trap command to be terminated.	trap 'rm tmp*' 2
unexpected EOF or unexpected end of file	echo "hi	The double quote is unmatched in the script. The Bourne shell will search until the end of the file for the matching quote. You may not receive an error message, but program output will be unexpected. The unexpected EOF error will occur if the case or looping commands are not ended with their respective keywords, esac and done.	echo "hi"

Common Korn Shell Error Messages.

Table 15.5 lists commonly found Korn shell error messages.

Table 15.5 Common Korn Shell Error Messages

Error Message	What Caused It	What It Means	How to Fix It
./file: line 5: syntax error near unexpected token blue)	case $color blue) ...	The case command is missing the in keyword in a script.	case "$color" in blue) ...
.filename: line2:syntax error at line 6: ")" unexpected .	case $color in blue) echo "blue" red) echo "red" ;; esac	The first case statement is not terminated with ;; after echo "blue".	case $color in blue) echo "blue" ;; red) echo "red" ;; esac

Table 15.5 Common Korn Shell Error Messages (continued)

Error Message	What Caused It	What It Means	How to Fix It
[Blank line]	echo $name or echo ${fruit[5]}	The variable doesn't exist or is empty.	name="some value"
file: line2: syntax error at line 6: 'done' unexpected	while (($n < 5)) statements done	The while is missing the do keyword.	while ((n < 5)) do statements done
file: syntax error at line 3: '"' unmatched	print I don't care	The single quote is unmatched in the script. It should be preceded by a backslash or enclosed in double quotes.	echo I don\'t care or echo "I don't care"
file: syntax error at line 3: '""' unmatched	print She said "Hello	The double quote is unmatched in the script.	print She said "Hello"

ksh: [: Doe: unknown operator	name="John Doe"
	 if [$name = Joe]; then
		The variable, name, should be double quoted in the test expression. There can be only one string on the left-hand side of the = test operator unless it is quoted. The other alternative is to use the compound test operator [[ ]]. Words will not be split when using this operator.	if ["$name" = Joe]; then
			 or
			 if [[$name = Joe]]; then

ksh: [ellie: not found	if [$USER = "ellie"] ; then
	 if [[$USER = "ellie"]] ; then
		There must be a space after the [or [[.	if [$USER = "ellie"] ; then
			 or
			 if [[$USER = "ellie"]] ; then

ksh: apples: bad number	set -A fruit apples pears peaches; shift fruit	The shift built-in command cannot shift an array. It is used only to shift positional parameters.	set apples pears peaches; shift
-ksh: file.txt=foo1: not found	file.txt="foo1"	The variable cannot have a period in its name.	file_txt="foo1"
ksh: filex: file already exists.	sort filex > temp	The noclobber variable has been set and the temp file exists. noclobber will not let you overwrite an existing file.	sort filex > temp1 (use a different file for output) or set +o noclobber or sort filex > temp (override noclobber)

Table 15.5 Common Korn Shell Error Messages (continued)

Error Message	What Caused It	What It Means	How to Fix It
ksh: fred: unknown test operator	if [grep fred /etc/passwd] ; then	The grep command should not be surrounded by square brackets or any other symbols. The brackets are used only when testing expressions. The [is a test operator.	if grep fred /etc/passwd ; then
ksh: name: not found	name = "Tom"	There cannot be any space on either side of the equal sign.	name="Tom"
ksh: shift: bad number	shift 2	The shift built-in command is used to shift positional parameters to the left. If there are not at least two positional parameters, the shift will fail.	set apples pears peaches; shift 2 (apples and pears will be shifted from the list)
ksh: syntax error: '{echo' not expected	function fun {echo "hi"}	There should be space surrounding the curly braces in the definition for the function fun() and a semicolon to terminate the function statement.	function fun { echo "hi"; }
ksh: syntax error: 'Doe' unexpected	if [[$name = John Doe]]	Word splitting is not performed on the variable on the left-hand side of the =, but the string on the right-hand side must be quoted.	if [[$name = "John Doe"]]
ksh: syntax error: 'fi' unexpected"	if [$USER = "ellie] then	The then should be on the next line or preceded by a semicolon.	if [$USER = "ellie"] then or if [$USER = "ellie"] ; then
ksh: syntax error: 'then' unexpected	if ((n==5 && (n>3 || n<7))	The parentheses enclosing the second expression are not matched.	if ((n==5 && (n>3 || n<7)))
ksh: trap: 500: bad trap[a]	trap 'rm tmp*' 500	The number 500 is an illegal signal. Normally signals 2 or 3 will be trapped in a shell script. 2 is for Ctrl-C and 3 is for Ctrl-\. Both signals cause the program named after the trap command to be terminated.	trap 'rm tmp*' 2

a. This error occurs with public domain Korn shell, but Korn shell 88 (Solaris) produces no output.

Common Bash Error Messages. Table 15.6 lists commonly found Bash shell error messages.

Table 15.6 Common Bash Shell Error Messages

Error Message	What Caused It	What It Means	How to Fix It
bash: syntax error: '" unexpected EOF while looking for matching '"	echo I don't care	The single quote is unmatched in the script.	echo "I don't care"
bash: syntax error: '"' unexpected EOF while looking for matching '"	print She said "Hello	The double quote is unmatched in the script.	print She said "Hello"
[Blank line] No error message, no output	echo $name or echo ${fruit[5]}	The variable doesn't exist or is empty.	name="some value" or use set -u to catch any variables that have not been sent. The message ksh: name: parameter not set will be sent to stderr.
bash: name: command not found	name = "Tom"	There cannot be any space on either side of the equal sign.	name="Tom"
bash: 6.5: syntax error in expression (error token is ".5")	declare -i num; num=6.5	Only integer values can be assigned to variable num.	num=6

bash: [ellie: command not found	if [$USER = "ellie"] ; then
	or
	if [[$USER = "ellie"]] ; then
		There must be a space after the [or [[.	if [$USER = "ellie"] ; then
			or
			if [[$USER = "ellie"]] ; then

bash: syntax error near unexpected token 'fi'	if [$USER = "ellie"] then	The then should be on the next line or preceded by a semicolon.	if [$USER = "ellie"] ; then or if [$USER = "ellie"] then
bash: syntax error in conditional expression	if [[$name = John Doe]] ; then	Word splitting is not performed on the variable on the left-hand side of the =, but the string on the right-hand side must be quoted.	if [[$name == "John Doe"]] ; then
[: fred: binary operator expected	if [grep fred /etc/passwd] ; then	The grep command should not be surrounded by square brackets or any other symbols. The brackets are used only when testing expressions. The [is a test operator.	if grep fred /etc/passwd ; then

Table 15.6 Common Bash Shell Error Messages (continued)

Error Message	What Caused It	What It Means	How to Fix It
./file: line 5: syntax error near unexpected token blue)	`color="blue"` `case $color`	The case command is missing the in keyword.	`case $color in`

.filename: line2:syntax error at line 6: ")" unexpected.	`case $color in`
	`  blue)`
	`    echo "blue"`
	`  red)`
	`    echo "red"`
	`    ;;`
	`esac`
		The case statement is not terminated with ;; after echo "blue".	`case $color in`
			`  blue)`
			`    echo "blue"`
			`    ;;`
			`  red)`
			`    echo "red"`
			`    ;;`
			`esac`

bash: shift: bad non-numeric arg 'fruit'	`declare -a fruit=(apples pears peaches);` `shift fruit`	The shift built-in command cannot shift an array. It is used only to shift positional parameters.	`set apples pears peaches; shift`

[: too many arguments	`name="John Doe";`
	`if [ $name = Joe ]`
		The variable name should be double quoted in the test expression. There can be only one string on the left-hand side of the = test operator unless it is quoted. The other alternative is to use the compound test operator [[ ]]. Words will not be split when using this operator.	`if [ "$name" = Joe ]`
			or
			`if [[ $name == Joe ]]`

bash: syntax error near unexpected token '{echo'	`function fun {echo "hi"}`	There should be space surrounding the curly braces in the definition for the function fun() and a semicolon to terminate the function statement.	`function fun { echo "hi"; }`

bash: filex: cannot overwrite existing file	`sort filex > temp`	The noclobber variable has been set and the temp file exists. noclobber will not let you overwrite an existing file.	`sort filex > temp1`
			(use a different file for output)
			or
			`set -o noclobber` or `sort filex >|`
			`temp`
			(override noclobber)

bash: trap: 500: not a signal specification	`trap 'rm tmp*' 500`	The number 500 is an illegal signal. Normally signals 2 or 3 will be trapped in a shell script. 2 is for Ctrl-C and 3 is for Ctrl-\. Both signals cause the program named after the trap command to be terminated.	`trap 'rm tmp*' 2`

15.4.4   Logic Errors and Robustness

Logic errors are hard to find because they do not necessarily cause an error message to be displayed, but cause the program to behave in an unexpected way. Such errors might be the misuse of a relational, equality, or logical operator, branching incorrectly in a set of nested conditional statements, or going into an infinite loop. Robustness refers to errors that should have been spotted if sufficient error checking had been performed, such as checking for bad user input, insufficient arguments, or null values in variables.

Logical Operator Errors.   Example 15.13 shows a logical operator error and a possible fix for it.

EXAMPLE   15.13

```
  #!/bin/csh
1 echo -n "Enter -n your grade: "
  set grade = $<
2 if ( $grade < 0 && $grade > 100 ) then
3     echo Illegal grade.    # This line will never be executed
      exit 1
  endif
4 echo "This line will always be executed."
```

```
(Output)
Enter your grade: -44
This line will always be executed.

Enter your grade: 234
This line will always be executed.
Enter your grade
```

```
------------------Possible Fix----------------

if ( $grade < 0 || $grade > 100 ) then
```

EXPLANATION

1   The user is asked for input. The input is assigned to the variable grade.

2   With the logical AND (&&) both expressions must be true in order to enter the if block on line 3. If both expressions are true, the user would have to have entered a grade that is both lower than 0 and also greater than 100. How could that be possible? The || OR operator should be used. Then only one of the conditions must be true.

3   This line will never be printed.

4   Because line 2 will never be true, this statement will always be executed.

Relational Operator Errors.   Example 15.14 shows a relational operator error and a possible fix for it.

EXAMPLE 15.14

```
        #!/bin/csh
        echo -n "Please enter your age "
        set age = $<

  1     if ( $age > 12 && $age < 19 ) then
            echo A teenager              # What if you enter 20?
  2     else if ( $age > 20 && $age < 30 ) then
            echo A young adult
  3     else if ( $age >= 30 ) then      # What if the user enters 125?
            echo Moving on in years
        else
  4         echo "Invalid input"
        endif


(Output)
Please enter your age  20
Invalid input

Please enter your age  125
Moving on in years


------------------Possible Fix----------------

if ( $age > 12 && $age <= 19 ) then
    echo A teenager
else if ( $age >= 20 && $age < 30 ) then
    echo A young adult
else if ( $age >= 30  && $age < 90 ) then
    echo Moving on in years
else if ( $age <=12 ) then
    echo still a kid
else
    echo "Invalid input"
endif
```

EXPLANATION

1   This expression tests for an age between 13 and 18. To check for ages between 13 and 20, the right-hand expression can be changed in two ways: ($age <= 19) to include 19, or ($age < 20).

2   If the age is 19, the program will always go to line 3. This expression tests for ages between 21 and 29. We need to include 20 in this expression. If the user enters 19 or 20, the program prints Invalid input.

EXPLANATION (CONTINUED)

3   This expression tests for any age older than 29. There is no range here. Unless the user can be infinitely old, the expression needs to include the outside range.

4   Invalid inputs are 19, 20, and any number below 13.

Branching Errors.   Example 15.15 shows a branching error and a possible fix for it.

EXAMPLE   15.15

```
1    set ch = "c"
2    if ( $ch == "a" ) then
3        echo $ch
4        if ( $ch == "b" ) then       # This "if" is never evaluated
             echo $ch
5    else
6        echo $ch
7    endif
8    endif

(Output)
<no output>

------------------Possible Fix----------------

set ch = "c"
if ( $ch == "a" ) then
    echo $ch
else if ( $ch == "b" ) then
        echo $ch
else
    echo $ch
endif
```

EXPLANATION

1   The variable ch is assigned the letter c.

2   If the value of $ch is an a, then lines 3 to 5 are executed.

3   If the value of $ch is an a, the value of $ch is printed, and the program continues with the nested if on line 4. This statement will never get executed unless $ch was an a.

4   If the value of $ch were an a, then it could not be a b and line 6 would be executed.

5   This else should be indented so that it is placed under the inner if. The else goes with the innermost if on line 4.

6   This line will be executed only if $ch is an a.

7   This endif goes with the innermost if on line 4.

8   This endif goes with the outer if on line 2.

Exit Status with an if Conditional.   When the if command is evaluating the success or failure of a command, it checks the exit status of that command. If the exit status is 0, the command was successful and if nonzero the command failed in some way. If you are not sure of what exit status a command returns, you should check before using it, or your program may not perform as expected. Consider the following example. The awk, sed, and grep commands are all able to use regular expressions for searches in a pattern, but grep is the only one of the three commands that reports a nonzero exit status if it cannot find the search pattern. The sed and awk programs will return 0, whether the pattern is found or not. Therefore, neither of these programs would be of any use after an if condition, because the condition would always be true.

EXAMPLE   15.16

```
    #!/bin/sh
1   name="Fred Fardbuckle"
2   if grep "$name" db > /dev/null 2>&1
    then
3        echo Found $name
    else
4        echo "Didn't find $name"        # Fred is not in the db file
    fi
5   if awk "/$name/" db > /dev/null 2>&1
    then
6        echo Found $name
    else
         echo "Didn't find $name"
    fi
7   if sed -n "/$name/p" db > /dev/null 2>&1
    then
8        echo Found $name
    else
         echo "Didn't find $name"
    fi


(Output)
4   grep: Didn't find Fred Fardbuckle
6   awk: Found Fred Fardbuckle
8   sed: Found Fred Fardbuckle


-----------------------Possible Fix-------------------------

Check the exit status of the command before using it.

    awk "/$name/" db
    echo $? (bash, sh, ksh)
    echo $status (tcsh, csh, bash)
```

EXPLANATION

Here we see that awk, nawk, and gawk always return an exit status of 0, unless the command statements are incorrect. grep returns an exit status of 0 if its search is successful, and a nonzero integer if it cannot find the pattern in the file or if the file does not exist.

Lacking Robustness.   A program is robust if it can handle illegal input and other unexpected situations in a reasonable way. For example, if a program is expecting numeric data, then it must be able to check to see if that's what it got, and print an error message and ignore the bad input. Another example of robustness would be if the script is going to extract data from an external file, but the external file doesn't exist or does not have read permissions. The robust program would use file testing to check for the existence of the file before trying to read from it.

Example 15.17 shows how to check for null input.

EXAMPLE 15.17

```
#!/bin/csh
# Program should check for null input -- T and TC shells

1    echo -n "Enter your name: "
        set name = $<        # If user enters nothing, program will hang
2    if { grep "$name" db >& /dev/null } then
        echo Found name
     endif


(Output)
Enter your name:  Ellie
Found name

Enter your name:
     <program prints every line in the file Found name>

---------------------Possible Fix-------------------------------------

     echo -n "Enter your name: "
     set name = $<     # If user enters nothing, program will hang
3    while ( $name == "" )
        echo "Error: you did not enter anything."
        echo -n "Please enter your name"
        set name = $<
     end
        <program continues here>
```

EXPLANATION

1   The user is asked for input. If he or she presses the Enter key, the variable, name, will be set to null.

EXPLANATION (CONTINUED)

2   The first time the program runs, the user types something and grep searches in the file for that pattern. The next time, the user presses the Enter key. The variable is set to null, causing the the grep program to search for null. Every line will be printed. Because the errors and output are sent to /dev/null, it is not obvious why the grep is printing the contents of the entire file.

3   The loop tests for a null value in the variable name. The loop will continue until the user enters something other than pressing Enter. For ksh, bash, and sh, use the correct syntax for a while loop (e.g., while [$name = " "] or while [[$name = " "]]). See specific character for syntax.

Examples 15.18 and 15.19 show how to check for insufficient arguments.

EXAMPLE   15.18

```
    #!/bin/sh
    # Script: renames a file -- Bourne shell

1   if [ $# -lt 2 ]      # Argument checking
2   then
        echo "Usage: $0 file1 file2 " 1>&2
        exit 1
    fi
3   if [ -f $1 ]         # Check for file existence
    then
        mv $1 $2         # Rename file1
        echo $1 has been renamed to $2
    else
        echo "$1 doesn't exist"
        exit 2
    fi


(Output)
$ ./rename file1
Usage: mytest file1 file2
```

EXPLANATION

1   If the number of positional parameters (arguments) is less than 2 . . .

2   . . . the error message is sent to standard error and the program exits. The exit status will be 1, indicating a problem with the program.

3   The program continues if sufficient arguments are passed in from the command line. Check correct syntax to convert this program to ksh or bash.

EXAMPLE 15.19

```
#!/bin/csh
# Script: renames a file -- C/TC shells

1   if ( $#argv < 2 ) then          # Argument checking
2       echo "Usage: $0 file1 file2 "
3       exit 1
    endif
    if ( -e $1 ) then               # Check for file existence
        mv $1 $2                    # Rename file1
        echo $1 has been renamed to $2
    else
        echo "$1 doesn't exist"
        exit 2
    endif

(Output)
% ./rename file1
Usage: mytest file1 file2
```

Examples 15.20 and 15.21 show how to check for numeric input.

EXAMPLE 15.20

```
(The Script)
    $ cat trap.err
    #!/bin/ksh
    # This trap checks for any command that exits with a nonzero
    # status and then prints the message -- Korn shell

1   trap 'print "You gave me a non-integer. Try again. "' ERR
2   typeset -i number      # Assignment to number must be integer
3   while true
    do
4       print -n "Enter an integer. "
5       read -r number 2> /dev/null
6       if (( $? == 0 ))      # Was an integer read in?
        then                  # Was the exit status zero?
7           break
        fi
    done
8   trap - ERR            # Unset pseudo trap for ERR
    n=$number
```

EXAMPLE 15.20 (CONTINUED)

```
9    if grep ZOMBIE /etc/passwd > /dev/null 2>&1
     then
         :
     else
10       print "\$n is $n. So long"
     fi
```

(The Command Line and Output)
```
     $ trap.err
4    Enter an integer. hello
1    You gave me a non-integer. Try again.
4    Enter an integer. good-bye
1    You gave me a non-integer. Try again.
4    Enter an integer. \\\
1    You gave me a non-integer. Try again.
4    Enter an integer. 5
10   $n is 5. So long.


     $ trap.err
4    Enter an integer. 4.5
10   $n is 4. So long.
```

EXAMPLE 15.21

(The Script)
```
     #!/bin/bash
1    # Scriptname: wholenum
     # Purpose:The expr command tests that the user enters an integer -- Bash shell

     echo "Enter an integer."
     read number
2    if expr "$number" + 0 >& /dev/null
     then
3        :
     else
4        echo "You did not enter an integer value."
         exit 1
5    fi
```

15.5 Tracing with Shell Options and the set Command

15.5.1   Debugging Bourne Shell Scripts

Bourne Shell Debugging Options.   By using the -n option to the sh command, you can check the sytnax of your scripts without really executing any of the commands. If there is a syntax error in the script, the shell will report the error. If there are no errors, nothing is displayed.

The most commonly used method for debugging scripts is to use the set command with the -x option (set -x), or to use the -x option as an argument to the sh command (sh -x) followed by the script name. See Table 15.7 for a list of debugging options. These options allow an execution trace of your script. Each command from the script is displayed after substitution has been performed, and then the command is executed. When a line from your script is displayed, it is preceded with a plus (+) sign.

With the verbose option (set -v) turned on, or by invoking the Bourne shell with the -v option (sh -v), each line of the script will be displayed just as it was typed in the script, and then executed.

Table 15.7   Bourne Shell Debugging Options

Command	*Option*	*What It Does*
sh -x scriptname	Echo option	Displays each line of script after variable substitutions and before execution.
sh -v scriptname	Verbose option	Displays each line of script before execution, just as you typed it.
sh -n scriptname	Noexec option	Interprets but does not execute commands.
set -u	Unbound variables	Flags variables that have not been set.
set -x	Turns on echo	Traces execution in a script.
set +x	Turns off echo	Turns off tracing.

The set command allows you to turn echoing on or off in a script in order to debug a portion of the script, not the whole program.

FORMAT

```
set -x     # turns echoing on
    <program statements go here>
set +x     # turns echoing off
```

EXAMPLE 15.22

```
(The Script)
$ cat todebug
    #!/bin/sh
1   # Scriptname: todebug
    name="Joe Blow"
    if [ "$name" = "Joe Blow" ]
    then
        echo "Hi $name"
    fi

    num=1
    while [ $num -lt 5 ]
    do
        num=`expr $num + 1`
    done
    echo The grand total is $num

(The Output)
2   $ sh -x todebug
    + name=Joe Blow
    + [ Joe Blow = Joe Blow ]
    + echo Hi Joe Blow

    Hi Joe Blow
    num=1
    + [ 1 -lt 5 ]
    + expr 1 + 1
    num=2
    + [ 2 -lt 5 ]
    + expr 2 + 1
    num=3
    + [ 3 -lt 5 ]
    + expr 3 + 1
     num=4
    + [ 4 -lt 5 ]
    + expr 4 + 1
     num=5
    + [ 5 -lt 5 ]
    + echo The grand total is 5
    The grand total is 5
```

EXPLANATION

1   The script is called todebug. You can watch the script run with the -x switch turned
    on. Each iteration of the loop is displayed and the values of variables are printed
    as they are set and when they change.

EXPLANATION (CONTINUED)

2   The sh command starts the Bourne shell with the -x option. Echoing is turned on. Each line of the script will be displayed to the screen prepended with a plus sign (+). Variable substitution is performed before the line is displayed. The result of the execution of the command appears after the line has been displayed.

15.5.2   Debugging C/TC Shell Scripts

C shell scripts often fail because of some simple syntax error or logic error. Options to the csh command are provided to help you debug your programs. See Table 15.8.

Table 15.8   echo (-x) and verbose (-v)

As Options to csh (Works the Same in tcsh)	
csh -x scriptname	Display each line of script after variable substitution and before execution.
csh -v scriptname	Display each line of script before execution, just as you typed it.
csh -n scriptname	Interpret but do not execute commands.
As Arguments to the set Command	
set echo	Display each line of script after variable substitution and before execution.
set verbose	Display each line of script before execution, just as you typed it.
As the First Line in a Script	
#!/bin/csh -xv	Turns on both echo and verbose. These options can be invoked separately or combined with other csh/tcsh invocation arguments.

EXAMPLE 15.23

(The -v and -x Options)

```
1   % cat practice
    #!/bin/csh
    echo Hello $LOGNAME
    echo The date is `date`
    echo Your home shell is $SHELL
    echo Good-bye $LOGNAME
```

EXAMPLE 15.23 (CONTINUED)

```
2   % csh -v practice
    echo Hello $LOGNAME
    Hello ellie
    echo The date is `date`
    The date is Sun May 23 12:24:07 PDT  2004
    echo Your login shell is $SHELL
    Your login shell is /bin/csh
    echo Good-bye $LOGNAME
    Good-bye ellie

3   % csh -x practice
    echo Hello ellie
    Hello ellie
    echo The date is `date`
    date
    The date is Sun May 23 12:24:15 PDT  2004
    echo Your login shell is /bin/csh
    Your login shell is /bin/csh
    echo Good-bye ellie
    Good-bye ellie
```

EXPLANATION

1   The contents of the C shell script are displayed. Variable and command substitution lines are included so that you can see how echo and verbose differ.

2   The -v option to the csh command causes the verbose feature to be enabled. Each line of the script is displayed as it was typed in the script, and then the line is executed.

3   The -x option to the csh command enables echoing. Each line of the script is displayed after variable and command substitution are performed, and then the line is executed. Because this feature allows you to examine what is being replaced as a result of command and variable substitution, it is used more often than the verbose option.

EXAMPLE 15.24

```
(Echo)
1   % cat practice
    #!/bin/csh
    echo Hello $LOGNAME
    echo The date is `date`
    set echo
    echo Your home shell is $SHELL
    unset echo
    echo Good-bye $LOGNAME
```

EXAMPLE 15.24 (CONTINUED)

```
% chmod +x practice
```

2   **% practice**
Hello ellie
The date is Sun May 26 12:25:16 PDT 2004
--> *echo Your login shell is /bin/csh*
--> *Your login shell is /bin/csh*
--> *unset echo*
Good-bye ellie

EXPLANATION

1   The echo option is set and unset within the script. This enables you to debug certain sections of your script where you have run into a bottleneck, rather than echoing each line of the entire script.

2   The --> marks where the echoing was turned on. Each line is printed after variable and command substitution and then executed.

EXAMPLE 15.25

(Verbose)
1   **% cat practice**
#!/bin/csh
echo Hello $LOGNAME
echo The date is `date`
set verbose
echo Your home shell is $SHELL
unset verbose
echo Good-bye $LOGNAME

2   **% practice**
Hello ellie
The date is Sun May 23 12:30:09 PDT 2001
--> *echo Your login shell is $SHELL*
--> *Your login shell is /bin/csh*
--> *unset verbose*
Good-bye ellie

EXPLANATION

1   The verbose option is set and unset within the script.

2   The --> marks where verbose was turned on. The lines are printed just as they were typed in the script and then executed.

15.5.3 Debugging Korn Shell Scripts

By turning on the noexec option or using the -n argument to the ksh command, you can check the syntax of your scripts without really executing any of the commands. If there is a syntax error in the script, the shell will report the error. If there are no errors, nothing is displayed.

The most commonly used method for debugging scripts is to turn on the xtrace option or to use the ksh command with the -x option. These options allow an execution trace of your script. Each command from your script is displayed after variable substitution has been performed, and then the command is executed. When a line from your script is displayed, it is preceded with the value of the PS4 prompt, a plus (+) sign. The PS4 prompt can be changed.

With the verbose option turned on, or by invoking the Korn shell with the -v option (ksh -v scriptname), each line of the script will be displayed, just as it was typed in the script, and then executed. See Table 15.9 for debug commands.

Table 15.9 Korn Shell Debugging Commands and Options

Command	*Function/How It Works*
export PS4='$LINENO '	The PS4 prompt by default is a +. You can reset the prompt. In this example, a line number will be printed for each line.
ksh -n scriptname	Invokes ksh with noexec option. Interprets but does not execute commands.
ksh -u scriptname	Checks for unset variables. Displays an error when expanding a variable that has not been set.
ksh -v scriptname	Invokes ksh with verbose option. Displays each line of the script before execution, just as you typed it.
ksh -x scriptname	Invokes ksh with echo option. Displays each line of the script after variable substitution and before execution.
set +x	Turns off echo. Turns off tracing.
set -x or set -o xtrace	Turns on echo option. Traces execution in a script.
trap 'print $LINENO ' DEBUG	For each script command, the trap action is performed. See format for trap. Prints value of $LINENO for each line in the script.
trap 'print Bad input' ERR	If a nonzero exit status is returned, the trap is executed.
trap 'print Exiting from $0' EXIT	Prints message when script or function exits.
typeset -ft	Turns on tracing. Traces execution in a function.

EXAMPLE   15.26

```
(The Script)
    #!/bin/ksh
    # Scriptname: todebug
1   name="Joe Blow"
2   if [[ $name = [Jj]* ]] then
         print Hi $name
    fi
    num=1
3   while (( num < 5 ))
    do
4        (( num=num+1 ))
    done
5   print The grand total is $num

(The Command Line and Output)
1   $ ksh -x todebug
2   + name=Joe Blow
    + [[ Joe Blow = [Jj]* ]]
    + print Hi Joe Blow
    Hi Joe Blow
    + num=1                    # The + is the PS4 prompt
    + let num < 5
    + let num=num+1
    + let num < 5
    + let num=num+1
    + let num < 5
    + let num=num+1
    + let num < 5
    + let num=num+1
    + let num < 5
    + print The grand total is 5
    The grand total is 5
```

EXPLANATION

1   The Korn shell is invoked with the -x option. Echoing is turned on. Each line of the script will be displayed on the screen, followed by the result of executing that line. Variable substitution is performed. Alternatively, the -x option can be used in the script instead of at the command line (i.e., #!/bin/ksh -x).

2   The lines are preceded by the plus (+) sign, the PS4 prompt.

3   The while loop is entered. It will loop 4 times.

4   The value of num is incremented by by 1.

5   After the while loop exits, this line is printed.

EXAMPLE 15.27

```
(The Script)
    #!/bin/ksh
    # Scriptname: todebug2
1   trap 'print "num=$num on line $LINENO"' DEBUG
    num=1
    while (( num < 5 ))
    do
        (( num=num+1 ))
    done
    print The grand total is $num

(The Output)
2   num=1 on line 3
    num=1 on line 4
    num=2 on line 6
    num=2 on line 4
    num=3 on line 6
    num=3 on line 4
    num=4 on line 6
    num=4 on line 4
    num=5 on line 6
    num=5 on line 4
    The grand total is 5
    num=5 on line 8
    num=5 on line 8
```

EXPLANATION

1. LINENO is a special Korn shell variable that holds the number of the current script line. The DEBUG signal, used with the trap command, causes the string enclosed in single quotes to be executed every time a command in the script is executed.

2. As the while loop executes, the value of the variable num and the line of the script are displayed.

15.5.4 Debugging Bash Scripts

By using the -n option to the bash command, you can check the syntax of your scripts without really executing any of the commands. If there is a syntax error in the script, the shell will report the error. If there are no errors, nothing is displayed.

The most commonly used method for debugging scripts is the set command with the -x option, or bash invoked with the -x option and the script name. See Table 15.10 for a list of debugging options. These options allow an execution trace of your script. Each command from your script is displayed after substitution has been performed, and then the command is executed. When a line from your script is displayed, it is preceded with a plus (+) sign.

With the verbose option turned on, or by invoking the shell with the -v option (bash -v scriptname), each line of the script will be displayed just as it was typed in the script, and then executed.

Table 15.10   Bash Debugging Options

Command	Option	What It Does
bash -x scriptname	Echo option	Displays each line of script after variable substitutions and before execution.
bash -v scriptname	Verbose option	Displays each line of script before execution, just as you typed it.
bash -n scriptname	Noexec option	Interprets but does not execute commands.
set -x	Turns on echo	Traces execution in a script.
set +x	Turns off echo	Turns off tracing.

Bash Invocation Options.   When the shell is started using the bash command, it can take options to modify its behavior. There are two types of options: single-character options and multicharacter options. The single-character options consist of a single leading dash followed by a single character. The multicharacter options consist of two leading dashes and any number of characters. Multicharacter options must appear before single-character options. An interactive login shell normally starts up with -i (start an interactive shell), -s (read from standard input), and -m (enable job control). See Table 15.11.

Table 15.11   Additional bash Options to Assist in Debugging

Option	Meaning
-i	Shell is in the interactive mode. TERM, QUIT, and INTERRUPT are ignored.
-r	Starts a restricted shell.
--	Signals the end of options and disables further option processing. Any arguments after -- or - are treated as filenames and arguments.
--help	Displays a usage message for a built-in command and exits.
--noprofile	When starting up, bash does not read the initialization files:/etc/profile, ~/.bash_profile, ~/.bash_login, or ~/.profile.
--norc	For interactive shells, bash will not read the ~/.bashrc file. Turned on by default, if running shell as sh.

Table 15.11 Additional bash Options to Assist in Debugging (continued)

Option	Meaning
--posix	Changes the behavior of bash to match the POSIX 1003.2 standard, if otherwise it wouldn't.
--quiet	Displays no information at shell startup, the default.
--rcfile file	If bash is interactive, uses this intialization file instead of ~/.bashrc.
--restricted	Starts a restricted shell.
--verbose	Turns on verbose; same as -v.
--version	Displays version information about this bash shell and exit.

The set Command and Options. The set command can be used to turn shell options on and off, as well as for handling command-line arguments. To turn an option on, the dash (-) is prepended to the option; to turn an option off, the plus sign (+) is prepended to the option.

Table 15.12 The Built-In set Command Options

Name of Option	Shortcut Switch	What It Does
allexport	-a	Automatically marks new or modified variables for export from the time the option is set until unset.
braceexpand	-B	Enables brace expansion, and is a default setting.[a]
emacs		For command-line editing, uses the emacs built-in editor, and is a default setting.
errexit	-e	If a command returns a nonzero exit status (fails), exits. Not set when reading initialization files.
histexpand	-H	Enables ! and !! when performing history substitution, and is a default setting.[a]
history		Enables command-line history; on by default.[a]
ignoreeof		Disables EOF (Ctrl-D) from exiting a shell; must type exit. Same as setting shell variable, IGNOREEOF=10.
keyword	-k	Places keyword arguments in the environment for a command.[a]

Table 15.12   The Built-In set Command Options (continued)

Name of Option	Shortcut Switch	What It Does
interactive-comments		For interactive shells, a leading # is used to comment out any text remaining on the line.
monitor	-m	Allows job control.
noclobber	-C	Protects files from being overwritten when redirection is used.
noexec	-n	Reads commands, but does not execute them. Used to check the syntax of scripts. Not on when running interactively.
noglob	-d	Disables pathname expansion (i.e., turns off wildcards).
notify	-b	Notifies user when background job finishes.
nounset	-u	Displays an error when expanding a variable that has not been set.
onecmd	-t	Exits after reading and executing one command.[a]
physical	-P	If set, does not follow symbolic links when typing cd or pwd. The physical directory is used instead.
posix		Shell behavior is changed if the default operation doesn't match the POSIX standard.
privileged	-p	When set, the shell does not read the .profile or ENV file and shell functions are not inherited from the environment; automatically set for setuid scripts.
verbose	-v	Turns on the verbose mode for debugging.
vi		For command-line editing, uses the vi built-in editor.
xtrace	-x	Turns on the echo mode for debugging.

a. Option applies only to versions of bash 2.x.

The shopt Command and Options. The shopt (bash 2.x) command can also be used to turn shell options on and off.

Table 15.13 The shopt Command Options

Option	Meaning
cdable_vars	If an argument to the cd built-in command is not a directory, it is assumed to be the name of a variable whose value is the directory to change to.
cdspell	Corrects minor errors in the spelling of a directory name in a cd command. The errors checked for are transposed characters, a missing character, and a character too many. If a correction is found, the corrected path is printed, and the command proceeds. Only used by interactive shells.
checkhash	Bash checks that a command found in the hash table exists before trying to execute it. If a hashed command no longer exists, a normal path search is performed.
checkwinsize	Bash checks the window size after each command and, if necessary, updates the values of LINES and COLUMNS.
cmdhist	Bash attempts to save all lines of a multiple-line command in the same history entry. This allows easy re-editing of multiline commands.
dotglob	Bash includes filenames beginning with a dot (.) in the results of filename expansion.
execfail	A noninteractive shell will not exit if it cannot execute the file specified as an argument to the exec built-in command. An interactive shell does not exit if exec fails.
expand_aliases	Aliases are expanded. Enabled by default.
extglob	The extended pattern matching features (regular expression metacharacters derived from Korn shell for filename expansion) are enabled.
histappend	The history list is appended to the file named by the value of the HISTFILE variable when the shell exits, rather than overwriting the file.
histreedit	If readline is being used, a user is given the opportunity to re-edit a failed history substitution.
histverify	If set, and readline is being used, the results of history substitution are not immediately passed to the shell parser. Instead, the resulting line is loaded into the readline editing buffer, allowing further modification.
hostcomplete	If set, and readline is being used, bash will attempt to perform hostname completion when a word containing an @ is being completed. Enabled by default.

Table 15.13 The shopt Command Options (continued)

Option	Meaning
huponexit	If set, bash will send SIGHUP (hangup signal) to all jobs when an interactive login shell exits.
interactive_comments	Allows a word beginning with # to cause that word and all remaining characters on that line to be ignored in an interactive shell. Enabled by default.
lithist	If enabled, and the cmdhist option is enabled, multiline commands are saved to the history with embedded newlines rather than using semicolon separators where possible.
mailwarn	If set, and a file that bash is checking for mail has been accessed since the last time it was checked, the message The mail in mailfile has been read is displayed.
nocaseglob	If set, bash matches filenames in a case-insensitive fashion when performing filename expansion.
nullglob	If set, bash allows filename patterns that match no files to expand to a null string, rather than themselves.
promptvars	If set, prompt strings undergo variable and parameter expansion after being expanded. Enabled by default.
restricted_shell	The shell sets this option if it is started in restricted mode. The value may not be changed. This is not reset when the startup files are executed, allowing the startup files to discover whether or not a shell is restricted.
shift_verbose	If this is set, the shift built-in prints an error message when the shift count exceeds the number of positional parameters.
sourcepath	If set, the source built-in uses the value of PATH to find the directory containing the file supplied as an argument. Enabled by default.
source	A synonym for dot (.).

15.6 Summary

Now that we have covered the major UNIX and Linux shells, you can start reading, writing, and maintaining scripts. Remember, a lot of time is spent debugging scripts. So often, you'll have a successful script, but you'll want to make it better. So, back in the editor you'll go make a few changes, try to run the program, and whoops! It's broken! With what you've learned in this chapter, you'll be able to keep these surprises to a minimum. If you are a system administrator and want to learn more about how the shells interact with the system, the next chapter will shed some light on topics that typically apply to the way the shells are used for system administration.

16

The System
Administrator and the Shell

Written by Susan Barr

16.1 Introduction

System administrators are in charge of tasks that require expertise beyond the user level, such as modifying boot scripts, adding users, fixing installation software, monitoring processes, mounting filesystems, backups, and much more. Because many of the system tasks have been automated with shell scripts, the system administrator requires knowledge of shell programming so that he or she can read and modify existing scripts, and create new scripts when the need arises. This chapter is not meant to be a definitive guide to system administration, but rather a look at system administration in respect to the UNIX/Linux shell. It will cover topics such as running shell scripts as root, system boot scripts, shell initialization scripts, and how to write portable shell scripts. Examples will be provided from specific UNIX/Linux versions that will run on a majority of systems. You will need to consult the documentation for your specific release for more specific information.

If you are familiar with system administration, you may find that the information in this chapter fills a gap in your knowledge. If you are new to system administration, you will gain an understanding of shell topics often not used by unprivileged users.

16.2 The Superuser

A newbie to UNIX or Linux forgets his or her password and asks a colleague what to do. A typical response would be "You can't fix it yourself, unless you're root. Go find a superuser." Before looking into the details of running scripts as a superuser (also called *root* user), you should make sure you understand what the term *superuser* means. UNIX/Linux systems come with two types of user accounts, regular and superuser. Regular accounts have access only to the files and processes they own or that give them specific permissions, such as *group* and *other*. Superuser accounts, on the other hand, have access to all the files and processes on the system. Superusers can modify, copy, remove, examine, change permissions, and delete files owned by other users without having specific permissions to do so; they can kill processes without being the process owner. They are omnipotent and have no restrictions. The most common superuser account is called root. Many machines also have additional superuser accounts. You can identify a superuser account by running the id command or by looking at the prompt. If the output of the id command displays a user identification number (uid) of 0, or the shell prompt is a pound sign (#), then the account belongs to a superuser. The terms superuser and root are often used interchangeably.

EXAMPLE   16.1

```
1   # id
    uid=0(root) gid=0(root) groups=0(root)
2   # ls -l /tmp
    total 1
    drwxr-xr-x    2 root      root          72 Feb 10 23:29 .
    drwxr-xr-x   26 root      root         680 Feb 10 23:28 ..
    -r--------    1 ellie     users          0 Feb 10 23:29 myfile
3   # cat myfile
    This is my file.
```

EXPLANATION

1   First, notice that the prompt is a pound sign (#). Superuser accounts traditionally use this prompt. When the id command is run, the output shows a uid number of 0, which means that this is a superuser account. (The uid number is your account number, listed in the third field of /etc/passwd file on your machine.) The output also shows a login name of root. Although root is commonly the name of the account, it is technically the uid number of 0 that gives you superuser access; it doesn't matter whether the account is named root or something else.

2   The ls command displays a file called myfile in the /tmp directory owned by user ellie. User ellie is the only user who has permission to read the file. All other permissions are all turned off.

3   Because this is a superuser account, the file contents can be displayed without having read access to the file.

16.3 Becoming a Superuser with the su Command

The su (switch user) command allows you to become another user without logging off. The su command can take as its argument the name of another user, and if you know that user's password, a new shell will be started owned by the username you specified, allowing you to gain the privileges of that user temporarily. If you do not specify a username, the *su* command defaults to root, and will ask for a password. If you use a dash (-) option after the su command (with or without the username), the new shell will inherit the environment of the specified user, including variables such as SHELL, HOME, and PATH.

Traditionally, when a system administrator wants to run some commands that require root privileges, he or she logs onto an unprivileged account first, and then uses the su command to switch to superuser. A new root-owned shell will be started, and after running privileged commands (presumably to fix a problem that the user can't handle), the superuser will exit from the root shell and return to the account of the unprivileged user.

EXAMPLE 16.2

```
1   $ id  # or use whoami instead
    uid=501(ellie) gid=100(users) groups=100(users)
2   $ echo $PATH
    /usr/local/bin:/usr/bin:/bin:/usr/X11R6/bin:.
3   $ su
    Password:
4   # id
    uid=0(root) gid=0(root) groups=0(root)
5   # echo $PATH
    /usr/local/bin:/usr/bin:/bin:/usr/X11R6/bin:.
6   # exit
    exit
7   $ su -
    Password:
8   # id
    uid=0(root) gid=0(root) groups=0(root)
9   # echo $PATH
    /usr/sbin:/bin:/usr/bin:/sbin:/usr/X11R6/bin
```

EXPLANATION

1   The id command shows that ellie is the current user.

2   The PATH variable for user ellie is displayed.

3   The su command is run to switch user to root. Note that a password must be provided.

4   The prompt has changed to a pound sign (#). This almost always signifies a superuser account. The id command is run, showing that the current shell has root permissions.

5   When the value of the PATH variable is displayed, it shows the same value as before. This is because the plain su command (without the dash) was used to become root. Plain su does not change the value of the PATH variable.

6   Exit is run to terminate the shell created by the su command.

7   The prompt changes back to a dollar sign because the previous command terminated the root-owned shell. The su command is run, this time including the dash option.

8   The id command verifies that root is the current user.

9   Because this shell was run using the dash option to the su command, the PATH value from the root account was used. When the value of the PATH variable is echoed, it shows root's path.

If you use the su command to gain root privileges, you should use the dash (-) option to obtain the root environment, especially the root PATH. The example below shows the su command being run with and without the dash option. Notice that without the dash, the wrong version of the useradd command is run.

EXAMPLE 16.3

```
1   $ id
    uid=501(ellie) gid=100(users) groups=100(users)
2   $ echo $PATH
    /usr/local/bin:/usr/bin:/bin:/usr/X11R6/bin:.
3   $ su
    password:
4   # echo $PATH
    /usr/local/bin:/usr/bin:/bin:/usr/X11R6/bin:.
5   # cd /tmp
6   # ls -l useradd
    -rwxr-xr-x 1 ellie group 65 Feb 12 11:56 useradd
7   # ls -l /usr/sbin/useradd
    -rwxr-xr-x   1 root      root        57348 Mar 17  2003
    /usr/sbin/useradd
8   # useradd newguy
    this is the useradd script in the /tmp directory
9   # tail -1 /etc/passwd
    ellie:x:501:100::/home/ellie:/bin/bash
    # exit
10  $ su -
    password:
11  # useradd newguy
12  # tail -1 /etc/passwd
    newguy:x:502:100::/home/newguy:/bin/bash
13  # exit
```

EXPLANATION

1   The id command is run and shows that this shell is owned by the user ellie, a non-superuser account.

2   The PATH variable is displayed, showing that it does contain the . directory but does not contain the /usr/sbin directory.

3   The su command is run, starting a new shell owned by root.

4   The PATH variable is displayed, showing that it has not changed.

5   The cd command is run to make /tmp the current directory.

6   The ls command shows that a program called useradd exists in the current directory, which is the /tmp directory. This program will almost certainly not exist on your system. This program happens to be in the /tmp directory on this particular system.

EXPLANATION (CONTINUED)

7 This ls command shows that there is also a useradd program in the /usr/sbin directory. The version in /usr/sbin is the normal useradd command that the administrator uses to create a new account.

8 The useradd command is run. The shell runs the copy of useradd in the current directory because of the . (dot) in the PATH. This was not the intention; the useradd command from the /usr/sbin directory was meant to be run instead. As a result of this error, the newguy account was never added.

9 The current root-owned shell is terminated with the exit command.

10 The su command is run again, this time using the dash option. The su command will use root's PATH instead of the PATH from the nonprivileged account when it creates the new shell (the shell created by the su command).

11 The useradd command is executed again. The shell will use root's PATH to find the command, and useradd from the /usr/sbin directory will be executed. The useradd command will add a new line to the end of the /etc/passwd file to create this account.

12 The tail command is used to display the last line of the /etc/passwd file. You can see that the newguy account has been added.

13 The root-owned shell is exited. This is a good practice—root shells should be terminated when the superuser has finished running commands that require root access. If the superuser forgets to exit the root shell, it is wide open to anyone who uses the account. Not a good idea!

16.3.1 Running Scripts As Root

Running a script from a root account (superuser) requires a slightly different technique than running a script as a regular user. Traditionally, root accounts have a different value for the PATH variable than that in nonprivileged accounts. The PATH for root usually consists of directories containing system commands. For example, the /usr/sbin directory is usually part of root's PATH, but not part of the PATH for a nonroot account. In order to prevent root from accidentally running a program in the current directory, root's PATH variable does not usually contain the current directory, called the dot directory and represented by a period.

Running a Script in the Current Directory. Because the . (dot) is not part of root's PATH, scripts will not run when invoked in the normal manner by typing the script name by itself at the command line. When you run a script as root, you should precede the script with the name of the invoking shell.

EXAMPLE 16.4

```
1   # cat myscript
    #! /bin/sh
    echo this is my script
2   # echo $PATH
    /usr/sbin:/bin:/usr/bin:/sbin:/usr/X11R6/bin
3   # myscript
    bash: myscript: command not found
4   # /bin/sh myscript
```

EXPLANATION

1   The contents of the shell script, myscript, are displayed. The first line of this script indicates that it was written for the /bin/sh program, which is the Bourne shell.

2   The value of the PATH variable is displayed. Notice that the PATH does not contain the dot (.) directory.

3   This command fails because the PATH does not include the . (dot) directory.

4   This command succeeds because the script name is passed as an argument to the shell, /bin/sh. By invoking the shell in this way, the PATH variable is not used to locate the script; instead the shell will check the current working directory to see if the script is there.

Another way to execute a script or any other command in the current working directory is to precede the program with a ./ to indicate that the program is in the current working directory.

EXAMPLE 16.5

```
1   # cd /usr/local/bin
2   # myprog
    -bash: myprog: command not found
3   # ./myprog
    this is my program
```

EXPLANATION

1   The current directory is changed to /usr/local/bin.

2   This directory contains a program called myprog. An attempt to run the program, myprog, does not succeed. Without a . in the PATH, the shell cannot locate the program.

3   After specifying the location of myprog (the . directory), the command runs successfully.

16.3.2 Scripts That Run As Root (setuid Programs)

Whoever runs a setuid program temporarily becomes the owner of that program and has the same permissions as the owner. Although most setuid programs are set to root, they can be set to any user. If a setuid program is set to root, when an unprivileged user runs such a program, he or she temporarily becomes root. This is kind of a Cinderella story because when the program exits, the user goes back to his or her lowly station in life and loses all root privileges. The passwd program is a good example of a setuid program. When you change your password, you temporarily become root, but only during the execution of the passwd program. That is why you are able to change your password without going to a system administrator for help. If you couldn't run as root, you would not be allowed to access the /etc/passwd (or /etc/shadow) file, which normally is off-limits to regular users. To identify a setuid program, use the ls -l command. The x (execute) permission will be replaced with an s if the program is a setuid program.

EXAMPLE 16.6

```
1   $ ls -l /bin/passwd
    -r-sr-sr-x   1 root      sys        21964 Apr  6  2002 /bin/passwd
2   $ ls -l /etc/shadow
    -r--------   1 root      sys         4775 May  5 13:33 /etc/shadow
```

EXPLANATION

1 The output of ls -l shows that this setuid program will run as root. The letter s replaces the x (execution bit) in the permissions field.
2 The /etc/shadow file, where passwords are stored (Solaris), shows that this is a root-owned file, and only root can read it.

Shell programs can be written as setuid programs and are a serious security threat if they are not monitored by a system administrator. If a shell script is a setuid program (to root), the shell spawned is a root-owned shell and commands executed from the script are run as root. Why would a shell script need to be a setuid program? If a file such as a database or log file contains information that should not be accessible to regular users, the permissions on that file should be turned off for everyone except the owner. If a script needs to access the file, and it is executed by a nonprivileged user, the error Permission denied will be displayed and the script will fail. If the script is a setuid script, the person running the script can take on the identity of the owner of the file and get access to the data in the file. Not all shells allow scripts setuid to root permission, and even if the shell allows it, the operating system may not. For example, Bash does not support setuid scripts, whereas Korn shell has a privileged mode (-p) used to run setuid scripts, only if allowed by the operating system. The following steps set up a setuid program for a C/TC shell script.

1. In the script, the first line is

   ```
   #!/bin/csh -feb
   ```

   The -feb options:
   - -f   fast start up; don't execute .cshrc
   - -e   abort immediately if interrupted
   - -b   this is a setuid script

2. Next, change the permissions on the script so that it can run as a setuid program:

   ```
   % chmod 4755 script_name
              or
   % chmod +srx script_name
   % ls -l
   -rwsr-xr-x   2 ellie          512 Oct 10 17:18 script_name
   ```

Because of the security risks involved with setuid programs, most systems will allow the administrator to disable setuid and setgid programs for individual filesytems. The UNIX find command can also be used to locate programs that are setuid to root:

```
# find / -user root -perm -4000 | more
```

Within a shell script, you can check for files that are setuid programs with the file-testing operators available for all shells. For example, Korn and Bash shells, the test would be:

```
if [[ -u filename ]] ; then
```

for C/TC shell:

```
if { test -u filename } then
```

and for Bourne shell:

```
if test -u filename; then
```

or

```
if [ -u filename ]; then
```

16.4 Boot Scripts

During a system boot, shell scripts are run to perform tasks such as starting daemons and network services, starting database engines, mounting disks, and so on. They are also run during system shutdown. These scripts are known as boot scripts, startup and shutdown scripts, init scripts, or run control scripts, depending on which documentation you are reading and to whom you are talking. They are frequently called *boot scripts*, and that term will be used to refer to these scripts for the rest of the chapter. On almost all UNIX/Linux systems, the boot scripts are written in Bourne or Bash shells. A UNIX installation will come with a starter set of boot scripts so that administrators are not required to write the scripts themselves, but they should be able to debug and modify scripts when required.

For those familiar with the differences between System V and BSD-style UNIX systems, this section will focus on the System V-style boot scripts, mainly because they are the most commonly used.

16.4.1   A Little Terminology

Throughout this text, we have used the terms such as the kernel, init, processes, PIDs, deamons, and initialization scripts in relation to the shell. This section provides some further clarification of these terms as they relate to the boot-up process and the scripts that are started during system initialization.

The Kernel and init.   When the system boots, the UNIX/Linux kernel is loaded from disk. It is the program that manages the operating system from boot-up to shutdown. Initially it initializes device drivers, starts the swapper, and mounts the root filesystem (/). The kernel then creates the first process, called init, the parent of all processes, with a PID (process identification number) number 1. When init starts, it reads from an initialization file called /etc/inittab. This file defines what processes to start during boot-up as well as during normal operation, supervises logins on serial ports, and defines run levels to determine what processes or groups of processes should be started.

What Is a Run Level?   A run level, also called a system state, determines which set of processes are currently available on a system. Usually there are eight run levels: 0–6 and s or S. The run levels fit into three general categories: halted, single-user, and multiuser. In the halted system state, UNIX is not running—it is halted. Moving to a halted state shuts down the system. Run level 0 is a halted state. On some versions of UNIX, notably Solaris, run level 5 is also a halted state and unlike run level 0, the machine is automatically powered off after UNIX is halted. The single-user run level is either S or 1. In single-user mode, the system console is opened, and only root is logged on. (See "Single-User Mode" on page 1033.) The multiuser run levels are 2–5. The multiuser mode allows users to log into the system. The run level numbers for multiuser vary quite a bit from one version of UNIX/Linux to another. To complicate things even more, there may be more than one multiuser run level on a particular system. For example, under SuSE Linux, run levels 2 and 5 are both multiuser levels. Level 2 allows users to log in, but they will log into a text-only, single-screen session. Level 5 allows login, and additional processes are started including window managers such as KDE (the K Desktop Environment). As superuser, you can change to a different run level with the init (or telinit) command. For example init 0 would move the system into run level 0, thus shutting it down.

The run level numbers can be frustrating since each vendor has a different definition of what the run levels will do. The only consistent values seem to be 0 for halted and 2 and 3 for multiuser. The `who -r` command lists the current run level. See Table 16.1.

Table 16.1   Run Levels

Run Level	What It Signifies
Solaris	
S, s	Single-user mode. Filesystems required for basic system operation are mounted.
0	Halt.
1	System administrator mode. All local filesystems are mounted. Small set of essential system processes are running. Also a single-user mode.
2	Put the system in multiuser mode. All multiuser environment terminal processes and daemons are spawned.
3	Extend multiuser mode by making local resources available over the network.
4	Is available to be defined as an alternative multiuser environment configuration. It is not necessary for system operation and is usually not used.
5	Shut the machine down so that it is safe to remove the power. Have the machine remove power, if possible.
6	Reboot.
a, b, c	Process only those /etc/inittab entries having the a, b, or c run level set. These are pseudo-states, which may be defined to run certain commands, but which do not cause the current run level to change.
Q, q	Re-examine /etc/inittab.
HP-UX	
0	System is completely shut down.
1, s, S	Single-user mode. All system services and daemons are terminated and all filesystems are unmounted.
2	Multiuser mode, except NFS is not enabled.
3, 4	Multiuser mode. NFS is enabled.
4	Multiuser mode with NFS and HP's desktop.
6	Reboot.

Table 16.1 Run Levels (continued)

Run Level	What It Signifies
OpenBSD	
−1	Permanently insecure mode—always run system in level 0 mode.
0	Insecure mode—All devices may be read or written subject to permissions.
1	Secure mode—disks for mounted filesystems, /dev/mem, and /dev/kmem are read-only.
2	Highly secure mode—same as secure mode, plus disks are always read-only whether mounted or not and the settimeofday system call can only advance the time.
Linux	
0	Halt the system.
1	Single-user mode.
2, 3	Multiuser modes. Usually identical. Level 2 or 3 is default.
4	Unused.
5	Multiuser with graphical environment (X Windows).
6	Reboot the system.

EXAMPLE 16.7

```
$ who -r
.    run-level 3  Mar 18 14:24    3      0  S
```

EXPLANATION

The who -r command displays the current run level of the init process, which in this case is run level 3, multiuser mode (Solaris).

Single-User Mode.   In the single-user states, UNIX is running, but users cannot log in. Either init 1 or init s will bring your system into a single-user state. The only interaction with the system is through a root-owned shell that is started automatically on a particular window or workstation. Single-user states are for maintenance and not all system processes will be started. For example, networking and database processes will usually not be running. Generally, the system administrator will change the machine to a single-user state to fix a serious software problem, install software, or perform any other task where logged in users might see a partially functioning system (and be confused) or might interfere with system performance (e.g., you don't want users to access files while you're trying to upgrade the operating system).

Boot Scripts.　Each of the run levels defined on a system should contain a directory of scripts that are run for a particular run level. These scripts manage such services as `mail`, `cron`, network services, `lpd`, and more. The directory name reflects the run level: The `rc5.d` directory contains scripts for run level 5, the `rc3.d` directory contains scripts for run level 3, and so on. These directories are located in different places depending upon your UNIX/Linux version. For example, the scripts for run level 3 are usually stored in one of the following directories: `/etc/rc3.d`, `/sbin/rc3.d`, `/etc/init.d/rc3.d`, or `/etc/rc.d/rc3.d`. Once you find the correct directory, almost all versions of UNIX/Linux use the same general scheme for the names of the scripts within those directories. The script names start with one of the letters S or K, followed by a number, and then a name describing what the script does. The scripts take an argument of either `start` or `stop`. A `start` argument asks the script to start services; a `stop` argument asks it to shut down services. If a script name starts with an S, that script will be run with a `start` argument. If the script name starts with a K, the script is run with a `stop` argument. The K scripts are useful when the system is brought to a lower run level, stopping processes, as the machine is brought down. The scripts are run in the order they are listed with the `ls` command.

EXAMPLE　16.8

```
$ cd rc3.d
$ ls
README          S34dhcp      S77dmi       S89sshd      s15nfs.server
S13kdc.master   S50apache    S80mipagent  S90samba     s99idled
S14kdc          S52imq       S81volmgt    S99fixkde
S16boot.server  S76snmpdx    S84appserv   S99snpslmd
```

EXPLANATION

This example was taken from a system running Solaris 5.9. The contents of the `rc3.d` directory (run level 3) are displayed. Check the documentation on your system.

EXAMPLE　16.9

```
$ cd rc3.d
$ ls
K00linuxconf  K25squid      K55routed    K92iptables      S55sshd
K03rhusd      K28ams        K61dap       K95kudzu         S56rawdevices
K05anacron    K30mcserv     K65identd    K95reconfig ig   S56xinetd
K05innd       K30sendmail   K65kadmin    K96irda          S60lpd
       <not all output is shown>
```

EXPLANATION

This example was taken from a system running Red Hat Linux. The partial contents of the `rc3.d` directory (run level 3) are displayed. Check the documentation on your system.

What Is a Daemon?   A daemon[1] is a process that runs in the background and performs one or more tasks on a user's behalf. For example, the printer daemon, lpsched, sends files one at a time to a printer. If the lpsched daemon is not running on systems that use it for printing, then files will not be sent to the printer. A Web server, such as Apache, is a daemon; it stays dormant until it is asked for a Web page. The cron (called crond on some systems) program is also a daemon. It checks the cron instruction files (called crontab files) once a minute to see if it is time to run any commands specified there. When the correct time comes, the cron daemon automatically runs the program specified in the crontab file. For a complete discussion on the cron utility, see "An Example Boot Script—The cron Utility," below. Many daemon programs, such as cron, are started during the boot process and run the whole time the system is booted. Other daemons, such as telnet, are under the control of a master daemon and are only started when they are needed (the master daemon does need to run all the time).

16.4.2   An Example Boot Script—The cron Utility

In this section, we will look at a sample boot script from Red Hat Linux. This script starts the cron daemon during the system boot. The script can also be run manually to control the daemon. The cron boot script is a good example because it is relatively easy to understand and the cron program exists on virtually every UNIX version. Before we look at the boot script for cron, it's helpful to know what cron does. The cron utility allows root and other users to schedule system commands, shell scripts, programs, and more to run at preset times. The user does not need to be present to interact with the system; cron will run commands from the user's crontab file, a file that contains a table specifying a list of commands and specified dates and times when the commands should be executed. The following example shows that the Solaris cron daemon is running as root.

EXAMPLE   16.10

```
$ ps -ef | grep cron | grep -v grep
root    202    1 0   Mar 18 ?      0:03 /usr/sbin/cron
```

Red Hat Linux starts the *crond* daemon at boot-up.

```
$ ps aux  | grep cron | grep -v grep
root    436 0.0  0.5 1552 700    ?     S  06:13  0:0   crond
```

Creating a cron Instruction File (crontab File).   The cron daemon reads the crontab files that have been submitted by system users. Each line in the crontab file consists of six fields separated by spaces. The first five fields tell the cron daemon when to run the

---

1. The term comes from Greek mythology, where daemons were guardian spirits, not to be confused with a demon, associated with a devil.

command that is contained in the sixth field. The values in the first five fields are: minutes (00–59), hours of the day (00–23), day of the month (1–31) and months of the year (1–12), and weekday (0–6). The sixth field is the command that will be executed at the time specified in the first five fields. See Table 16.2.

Table 16.2 Crontab Field Values

Field	Values
minute	00 to 59
hour	00 to 23
day	1 to 31
month	1 to 12
weekday	0 to 6, where 0 = Sunday (Linux uses sun, mon, etc.)

The first five fields can also use any one of the following formats.

- An asterisk (*) matches all values for that field.
- A single integer matches that exact value.
- A comma-separated list of integers (e.g., 1,3,5) to match one of the listed values. A range of integers separated by a dash (e.g., 4-6) matches values within the range.

The sample below shows a crontab file submitted to cron using the crontab command.

EXAMPLE 16.11

```
1    # crontab -l > instructions
2    # vi instructions
     .
     (There might or might not be lines at the top of this file.
      You can ignore any lines except the one added below.)
3    25 1 * * * /root/checkpercent
4    #  crontab instructions
5    #  crontab -l
     .
     (There may not be lines above the entry that was added in item 3.)
     .
     25 1 * * * /root/checkpercent
```

EXPLANATION

1   The output of the crontab -l command is redirected to the file named instructions. In this example, because there were not any commands listed in the crontab file, the instructions file will contain only some comments generated by the crontab command.

2   The instructions file is edited using vi. This file may or may not contain any lines to start. It depends on your version of UNIX/Linux and whether or not root has previously entered instructions for cron.

3   A new instruction is added to the bottom of the file. This instruction tells cron to run the /root/checkpercent script at 1:25 a.m., every day of every month. Detailed information on specifying the time in this file (the time is indicated by the numbers and asterisks at the beginning of the line) can be found in the crontab *man* page.

4   The crontab command is used to submit the instructions file to cron.

5   The crontab -l command causes cron to display the current set of instructions for the current user, in this case the root user. This verifies that cron has accepted the file from the previous command.

The cron Boot Script.   Before we look at the contents of the cron boot script, let's look at the layout of boot scripts in general. The following example displays a partial list of boot scripts for run level 5 on a Red Hat system. Although most other UNIX versions have a similar layout for their boot scripts, some, such as Darwin in Mac OS X, are quite different.

Below is a truncated listing of the directory containing the boot scripts for run level 5 under Red Hat Linux.

EXAMPLE 16.12

```
1   # pwd
    /etc/rc5.d
2   # ls
    .        K20nfs     K45named     S55sshd       S90crond
    ..       K35smb     S12syslog    S80sendmail
3   # ls -l /etc/rc5.d/*cron*
    lrwxrwxrwx 1 root 15   Oct 13 21:19 /etc/rc5.d/S90crond ->
    ../init.d/crond
4   # ls -l /etc/init.d/cron*
    -rwxr-xr-x 1 root 1316 Feb 19 2004 /etc/init.d/crond
```

EXPLANATION

1   The current directory is /etc/rc5.d, the boot script directory for run level 5 (Red Hat Linux).

2   The listing shows that some script names begin with S and some begin with K.

3   This script starts the cron daemon because the filename starts with an S. If the script name had started with a K, the script would stop the cron daemon. The output shows that the file is actually a link—the letter l in front of the file permissions indicates a link. The -> characters point to the linked file, crond, located in the /etc/init.d directory.

4   Each script in the run-level directory is normally a link to a master copy in the /etc/init.d directory.

5   This is a listing for the master copy of the boot script for cron. Notice that the master copies don't start with S or K and don't contain numbers in their names. There are frequently multiple links to the master scripts from the boot directories, and only the link names will contain numbers. This master script can be used to either start or stop the cron daemon. We'll look at the script in detail in the next section.

The cron boot script, called crond, can be run manually to start or stop the cron daemon. On some releases, it can also be used to check the status or restart cron. Other releases allow additional arguments. Traditionally, boot scripts are run by preceding the script name with the shell for which the script was written, followed by the name of the script. The examples below run the master copy of the crond script from the /etc/init.d directory. Because they are linked, you could accomplish the same thing by running the /etc/rc5.d/crond script instead.

EXAMPLE 16.13

```
1    # cd /etc/init.d
2    # ls crond
     crond
3    # sh crond stop
     Stopping crond:    [OK]
4    # sh crond start
     Starting crond:    [OK]
5    # sh crond restart
     Stopping crond:    [OK]
     Starting crond:    [OK]
```

EXPLANATION

1   The cd command is used to change to the /etc/init.d directory, which contains the master copies of the boot scripts.

2   The ls command verifies that the cron boot script exists.

3   The crond script is run with the stop argument to stop the cron daemon. The script is run by preceding the script name with the shell for which it was written because root is the current user.

4   The script is run again, this time starting the cron daemon.

5   The script is run a third time. This time the daemon will be stopped, then started again.

Below is a simplified version of the boot script for the cron daemon from Red Hat Linux. This script sources another script called functions, which defines daemon and killproc for the script. The daemon function takes a daemon name as an argument. It attempts to start that daemon and will return a success or failure code depending on what happened.

EXAMPLE   16.14

```
#! /bin/bash
# crond Start/Stop the cron clock daemon.
#
# chkconfig: 2345 90 60
# description: cron is a standard UNIX program that runs
# user-specified programs at periodic scheduled times.
# config: /etc/crontab
# pidfile: /var/run/crond.pid

# Source function library.
1    . /etc/init.d/functions
2    RETVAL=0 ; prog="crond"
3    start() {
4        echo -n $"Starting $prog: "
5        daemon crond
6        RETVAL=$?
7        echo
8        [ $RETVAL -eq 0 ] && touch /var/lock/subsys/crond
9        return RETVAL
     }
10   stop() {
11       echo -n $"Stopping $prog: "
12       killproc crond
13       RETVAL=$?
14       echo
15       [ $RETVAL -eq 0 ] && rm -f /var/lock/subsys/crond
         return RETVAL
     }
16   restart() {  stop ; start }
17   case "$1" in
18       start)   start            ;;
19       stop)    stop             ;;
```

EXAMPLE 16.14 (CONTINUED)

```
20      restart) restart        ;;
21      *)       echo $"Usage: $0 {start|stop|restart}"
        exit 1          ;;
    esac
```

EXPLANATION

1   A script called `functions` is sourced to make functions defined there available to this script.

2   The RETVAL variable (which holds the function return value) is initialized to 0 and the prog variable is initialized to crond.

3   This line begins the definition for the `start()` function.

4   A message is displayed saying that the cron daemon is starting.

5   The daemon function is called with crond as its argument. (The function was defined in the `functions` script sourced at the beginning of the script.) The function attempts to start the crond daemon and returns a value of success (0) or failure (1).

6   The RETVAL variable is assigned the value of the status variable ?. It contains the value returned by the daemon() function. This value is used by the operating system to print an OK or FAILED message to the screen during the boot process.

7   The echo command prints a blank line to the screen.

8   If the return value indicates success (0 mean success) then a lock file for the cron daemon, /var/lock/subsys/crond, is created with the touch command.

9   The RETVAL variable is returned from the function.

10   This line begins the definition for the stop() function.

11   A message is displayed saying that the cron daemon is being stopped.

12   This calls the killproc() function, which is defined in the functions script sourced on line 1. It sends an argument of crond to this function. The function attempts to stop the daemon process and sends a return value based on its success or failure.

13   The RETVAL variable is assigned the value returned by the killproc() function, which is stored in $?.

14   A blank line is printed.

15   If the return value indicates success, the lock file for the cron daemon, /var/lock/subsys/crond, is deleted.

16   This defines the restart() function, which stops then starts the cron daemon.

17   The case command evaluates $1 and holds the value of the first argument sent to this script, either start or stop.

18   If the value of $1 is start, then the start() function is run.

19   If the value of $1 is stop, then the stop() function is run.

20   If the value of $1 is restart, then the restart() function is run.

21   Otherwise, a usage message is printed and the script will exit with status 1, failure.

16.4.3 Writing a Portable Script

System administrators often write shell scripts that work on multiple UNIX versions. Because commands change from UNIX to UNIX, your script will need to determine the UNIX version on which it is being run. This can be done using the uname command. Listed below are some popular versions of UNIX and the output of the uname command from each version. To create a script that will port to these different UNIX versions, your script should check the uname output and modify commands accordingly.

UNIX Version:	**uname Output:**
AIX	AIX
FreeBSD	FreeBSD
HP-UX	HP-UX
IRIX	IRIX
Linux	Linux
Mac OS X	Darwin
NetBSD	NetBSD
OpenBSD	OpenBSD
SCO OpenServer 5	SCO_SV
Solaris	SunOS

A case command is commonly used to check for the operating system you are using. Example 16.15 checks for Linux (any brand), HP-UX, Solaris, FreeBSD, and Mac OS X UNIX.

EXAMPLE 16.15

```
1    uname_out=`uname`
2    case "$uname_out" in
3    HP-UX)  echo "You are running HP-UX"
        ;;
4    SunOS) echo "You are running Solaris"
        ;;
     FreeBSD) echo "You are running FreeBSD"
        ;;
     Linux) echo "You are running Linux"
        ;;
     Darwin) echo "You are running Mac OS X"
        ;;
5       *)  echo "Sorry, $uname_out UNIX "
            echo "is not supported by this script"
        ;;
6    esac
```

EXPLANATION

1 The variable uname_out is assigned the output of the uname command. This assigns the name of the current version of UNIX to the variable.

2 The case statement will evaluate the uname_out variable.

3 If the uname_out variable evaluates to HP-UX, this is Hewlett-Packard's version of UNIX and You are running HP-UX will be printed.

4 If uname_out evaluates to SunOS, the message is printed. The case statement checks for other versions of UNIX in subsequent statements.

5 If uname_out contains a value not listed in the above choices, then it will match the default pattern, an asterisk. In this case, a generic message is printed telling the user that the operating system is not supported by this script.

6 The case statement is ended using the esac statement.

Example 16.16 is a sample script to tell the administrator when any of a machine's filesystems are getting full. This script does not check for all versions of UNIX, although you can modify the script for any version of UNIX. The sample script changes the form of the df command to accommodate four types of UNIX.

EXAMPLE 16.16

```
# cat /root/checkpercent
1    #! /bin/sh
2    rm $HOME/df_output $HOME/message 2> /dev/null
3    uname_out=`uname`
4    case "$uname_out" in
5        HP-UX)
6            bdf | awk  '{print $5,$6}' | awk -F% '$1>90 {print $0}' \
                                    > $HOME/df_output
         ;;
7        SunOS)
8            df -k | awk '{print $5,$6}' | awk -F% '$1>90 {print $0}' \
                                    > $HOME/df_output
         ;;
9        Linux)
10           df | awk '{print $5,$6}' | awk -F% '$1>90 {print $0}' \
                                    > $HOME/df_output
         ;;
11       Darwin)
12           df | awk '{print $5,$6}' | awk -F% '$1>90 {print $0}' \
                                    > $HOME/df_output
         ;;
```

EXAMPLE 16.16 (CONTINUED)

```
13       *)
         echo "Sorry, $uname_out UNIX not supported by this script"

         ;;
    esac

14  if [ -s $HOME/df_output ]
    then
15  echo "** WARNING **" > $HOME/message
    echo "The following file systems are filling up." >> $HOME/message
    echo "You may want to look into the situation." >> $HOME/message
    cat $HOME/df_output >> $HOME/message
16  cat $HOME/message
17  echo "This warning message is stored in the file $HOME/message"
    echo "You should create a copy of the file now if you would"
    echo "like to save this message."
    fi
18  rm $HOME/df_output
```

EXPLANATION

1   The shell name is /bin/sh. On some systems, /bin/sh is Bourne, on others it is bash, or the POSIX shell—all of these shells are compatible with the Bourne shell. To make sure this is a portable script, use Bourne shell syntax.

2   This command will remove the $HOME/df_output and $HOME/message files if they exist. Any error messages generated by this command are discarded by redirecting them to the /dev/null file. Removing the files is a precaution—if either of these files exist, they might cause a problem with this script. Remember that $HOME is a variable that stores a user's home directory, so $HOME/message indicates a file called message in the home directory of the person running the script. $HOME/df_output indicates a file called df_output in the user's home directory.

3   The output of the uname command is assigned to a variable called uname_out. As in the previous example, note that this command is using backward single quotes (backquotes) and not regular single quotes.

4   This case statement evaluates the variable, uname_out, which contains the name of the operating system.

5   If the variable evaluates to HP-UX , the case statement on line 6 is executed.

6   The HP-UX version of the df command, bdf, is run. The output of the bdf command is piped through awk to select fields 5 and 6, which are the percent full and the filesystem name. These two values are then piped through a second awk, which will print lines that have a percent full of greater than 90. (The $0 prints the whole line as long as the first field is greater than 90.) The output is then stored in the $HOME/df_output file.

7   If this is a Sun system . . .

8   . . . then run the Solaris version of the df command, df -k. The rest of the command is the same as the HP-UX version.

9   If this is a Linux system . . .

10   . . . then the plain df command is run for Linux. The rest of the command is the same as the HP-UX version.

11   If this is an OS X system . . .

12   . . . the df command is run. Notice that this is the same command used for Linux. These two could be combined into one case statement.

13   If the variable uname_out contains any other value, the error message shown is printed.

14   This if statement checks to see if the file $HOME/df_output contains any text. This true/false test results in a true value if the file $HOME/df_output contains any text and a false value if the file is empty or does not exist. If the $HOME/df_output file does exist . . .

15   . . . then a message is generated and stored in the $HOME/message file. The three echo commands print a warning message and then the $HOME/df_output file is appended to the $HOME/message file.

16   The contents of the $HOME/message file are displayed. This will display the warning message with a list of full filesystems.

17   The script prints a reminder that the information is in the $HOME/message file.

18   The $HOME/df_output is removed because it is no longer needed.

16.4.4   User-Specific Initialization Files

When user accounts are initially created, the administrator normally places login files, such as .profile and .login, in the user's home directory. The administrator must understand the syntax of the shells in order to write a version of these files that will be suitable for their users.

Each shell has one or more initialization files that can be placed in a user's home directory. As administrator, you may wish to place a starter copy of these initialization files in your user's home directory when it is first created. Most versions of UNIX help you automate this process through the /etc/skel directory, although sometimes the directory name is slightly different. When creating a new account using the useradd command, all files from /etc/skel are copied to a user's home directory.

EXAMPLE 16.17

```
1   # ls -a /etc/skel
    . .. .profile .cshrc
2   # useradd -m newguy1
3   # ls -a /home/newguy1
    . .. .profile .cshrc
```

EXAMPLE 16.17 (CONTINUED)

```
4  # useradd newguy2
5  # ls -a /home/newguy2
   ls: /home/newguy2: No such file or directory
```

EXPLANATION

1 This particular /etc/skel directory contains the two files, .profile and .cshrc.

2 The -m option tells useradd to create the home directory for the new account. By default the directory will be /home/newguy1. The useradd program automatically copies the files from /etc/skel. Both .profile and .cshrc will be copied to /home/newguy1.

3 The ls command verifies that the /home/newguy1 directory contains the .profile and .cshrc files.

4 Without the -m option, the useradd command does not create a home directory for this account. The /etc/skel files are not copied.

5 The ls command shows that newguy2 does not have a home directory.

Possible Files for /etc/skel. You should put a set of starter initialization files in the home directory of a new user when you create his or her home directory. A chart of the initialization files used by the five major UNIX shells is listed in Table 16.3. You might want to create a generic version of all of these files and place them in the /etc/skel directory. These files will be copied into a user's home directory whenever a new account is created, giving the user a starter copy of the initialization files needed for his or her login shell. See the other chapters for individual shells for more details on the initialization files.

Table 16.3 Initialization Files Used by the Five Shells

	Bourne	**Bash**	**Korn**	**C**	**TC**
.profile	✔	✔	✔		
.kshrc			✔		
.bash_profile		✔			
.bash_login		✔			
.bashrc		✔			
.bash_logout		✔			
.login				✔	✔
.cshrc				✔	✔
.tcshrc					✔
.logout				✔	✔

16.4.5   System-Wide Initialization Files

The system administrator is responsible for maintaining a set of system-wide initialization files used by various login shells. The administrator will often perform tasks such as setting an initial value for the PATH and MANPATH variables in these files. For a login shell, /etc/profile is the system-wide intialization file for the Bourne, Korn, and Bash shells and /etc/.cshrc or /etc/csh.login are system-wide initialization files for the C and TC shells (filenames vary on different systems). See Table 16.4. Most UNIX installations come with a starter set of these files that can be customized for a particular system.

Table 16.4   System-Wide Initialization Files

Shell	Filename	Versions Implemented On	Notes
/bin/sh	/etc/profile	Most versions	Run at login only.
	/etc/profile.local	SuSE Linux	Run at login only in addition to /etc/profile. Used for local settings. The SuSE /etc/profile contains a comment asking you not to modify /etc/profile, but instead to modify /etc/profile.local.
	/etc/login.conf	FreeBSD	Run at login only.
/bin/ksh	/etc/profile	Most versions	Run at login only.
	/etc/profile.local	SuSE Linux	Run at login only in addition to /etc/profile. Used for local settings. The SuSE /etc/profile contains a comment asking you not to modify /etc/profile, but instead to modify /etc/profile.local.
/bin/bash	/etc/profile	Most versions	Run at login only.
	/etc/profile.local	SuSE Linux	Run at login only in addition to /etc/profile. Used for local settings. The SuSE /etc/profile contains a comment asking you not to modify /etc/profile, but instead to modify /etc/profile.local.
	/etc/bash.bashrc	SuSE Linux	Run each shell invocation.
	/etc/bashrc	Some versions of Linux	Run when bash is started manually. If this script isn't run automatically by your UNIX version, you can call it from the user's local .bashrc file. See "/etc/bashrc" on page 1049 for details on how to do this.

Table 16.4   System-Wide Initialization Files (continued)

Shell	Filename	Versions Implemented On	Notes
/bin/csh	/etc/csh.login	Linux, FreeBSD, HP-UX,	Same for tcsh.
		OS X	Run at login only.
	/etc/.login	Solaris	Run at login only.
	/etc/csh.cshrc	Linux, FreeBSD, OS X	Run for each shell invocation.
	/etc/.cshrc	Solaris	Run by tcsh, but not by csh, each time a tcsh is run.

In addition to the system initialization files, the local initialization files are also run when a user logs in. If, for example, a user logs into the TC shell on a Red Hat system, the files listed below will be sourced in the order listed. The first two files are system files and the last two files are local files. The value of the HOME environment variable is the path of the user's home directory.

```
/etc/csh.cshrc
/etc/csh.login
$HOME/.tcshrc
$HOME/.login
```

/etc/profile.   The /etc/profile file contains commands that are automatically run when a user logs into a system using the Bourne, Bash, or Korn shell. A starter copy of /etc/profile will be provided during the installation process. This file is normally modified by the system administrator to accomodate the needs of a particular system.

EXAMPLE 16.18

```
# cat /etc/profile
# System-wide environment and startup programs, for login setup
# Functions and aliases go in /etc/bashrc

1    pathmunge () {
2        if ! echo $PATH | /bin/egrep -q "(^|:)$1($|:)" ; then
3            if [ "$2" = "after" ] ; then
4                PATH=$PATH:$1
             else
5                PATH=$1:$PATH
             fi
         fi
```

EXAMPLE   16.18 (CONTINUED)

```
6    }
     # Path manipulation
7    if [ `id -u` = 0 ]; then
8         pathmunge /sbin
9         pathmunge /usr/sbin
10        pathmunge /usr/local/sbin
          fi
11   pathmunge /usr/X11R6/bin after
12   unset pathmunge
     # No core files by default
13   ulimit -S -c 0 > /dev/null 2>&1

14   USER="`id -un`"
15   LOGNAME=$USER
16   MAIL="/var/spool/mail/$USER"
17   HOSTNAME=`/bin/hostname`
18   HISTSIZE=1000

19   if [ -z "$INPUTRC" -a ! -f "$HOME/.inputrc" ]; then
          INPUTRC=/etc/inputrc
     fi
20   export PATH USER LOGNAME MAIL HOSTNAME HISTSIZE INPUTRC
21   for i in /etc/profile.d/*.sh ; do
22        if [ -r "$i" ]; then
23             . $i
          fi
     done
     unset i
```

EXPLANATION

1   Starts the definition for the function called pathmunge(). This function takes a directory name as an argument. Its purpose is to prepend the directory, given as an argument, to the PATH variable. The function can optionally take a second argument of after, which will append the directory to the PATH. Note that the function definition simply places the code for pathmunge() into memory; the function will not be activated until it is called.

2   Checks to see if the directory to be added is already in the user's PATH.

3   Checks to see if the optional argument after was included in the function call.

4   Adds the directory (the first argument to the pathmunge function) to the beginning of the PATH. This line is only executed if the optional argument after was not included in the function call.

5   Adds the directory (the first argument to the pathmunge function) to the end of the PATH. This line is only executed if the optional argument after was included in the function call.

EXPLANATION (CONTINUED)

6   Ends the pathmunge definition.

7   If the user's UID equals 0 (in other words, if he or she is a superuser), then . . .

8   . . . calls the pathmunge() function, which adds the /sbin directory to the PATH.

9   Adds the /usr/sbin directory to the PATH.

10   Adds the /usr/local/sbin directory to the PATH.

11   Adds the /usr/X11R6/bin directory to the end of the PATH. Because this line is not inside the if statement, it will always be executed.

12   Removes the pathmunge() function definition from memory.

13   Sets the maximum coredump size to 0—this effectively stops the user from generating coredump files.

14   Sets the USER variable to the user's login name.

15   Sets the LOGNAME variable to the same value as USER.

16   Sets the MAIL variable to the user's incoming mailbox file.

17   Sets the HOSTNAME variable to this system's hostname.

18   Sets the history list size to a maximum of 1,000 commands.

19   If the INPUTRC variable has no value and $HOME/.inputrc does not exist, then sets the INPUTRC variable to /etc/inputrc.

20   Exports all variables set in this script.

21   This for loop will cycle through all the files in the /etc/profile.d directory.

22   If the user has read permission on the file currently being processed by the for loop . . .

23   . . . then source the file.

/etc/bashrc.   The /etc/bashrc file is used on some UNIX releases, such as Red Hat Linux, to run bash commands whenever a bash shell is run. This file should contain settings that are not passed automatically to child processes, such as command aliases.

EXAMPLE 16.19

```
1   $ cat /etc/bashrc
2   alias ls="ls -F"
3   alias grep="grep -i"
```

EXPLANATION

1   The contents of the /etc/bashrc file are displayed.

2   An alias for the ls command is defined as ls -F. When ls is typed, ls -F will be executed, modifying the display of ls.

3   An alias for the grep command is defined as grep -i. When the grep command is used, it will be case insensitive.

If you wish to use /etc/bashrc and your UNIX doesn't source it automatically, you can include it in the user's personal .bashrc file in his or her home directory.

EXAMPLE   16.20

```
1    $ cat .bashrc
2    if [ -f /etc/bashrc ]
         then
3          . /etc/bashrc
     fi
4    alias dir=ls
```

EXPLANATION

1   The .bashrc file, found in the user's home directory, is sourced.

2   If the /etc/bashrc file exists and is a regular file, then go to line 3. Some machines run /etc/bashrc automatically; on those machines this if statement will not be required.

3   The dot command sources the /etc/bashrc file (runs the commands from the file in context of the current shell process; i.e., does not create a child process).

4   An alias for the dir command is defined. Notice that this is a personal alias created by the user in his .bashrc file.

/etc/csh.login.   The /etc/csh.login file is sourced by the C and TC shells during the login process. Example 16.21 is an /etc/csh.login file from a Red Hat Linux system. Like the .login file, this file is run at login time by the login shell, and not by any child shells spawned thereafter. It is used to set environment variables for the shell and any other commands that will be executed by the login shell.

EXAMPLE   16.21

```
     # cat /etc/csh.login
     # System-wide environment and startup programs, for login setup
1    if ($?PATH) then
2        setenv PATH "${PATH}:/usr/X11R6/bin"
     else
3        setenv PATH "/bin:/usr/bin:/usr/local/bin:/usr/X11R6/bin"
     endif

4    limit coredumpsize unlimited

5    setenv HOSTNAME `/bin/hostname`
6    set history=1000

7    if ( -f $HOME/.inputrc ) then
8        setenv INPUTRC /etc/inputrc
     endif
```

EXAMPLE   16.21 (CONTINUED)

```
9    if ( $?tcsh ) then
10       bindkey "^[[3~" delete-char
     endif
```

EXPLANATION

1   If the PATH variable has been set, the ? evaluates to true.

2   /usr/X11R6/bin is added to the PATH environment variable.

3   Otherwise, the PATH is assigned an initial value of /bin:/usr/bin:/usr/local/bin:/usr/X11R6/bin.

4   The limit command restricts an upper limit on the size of a coredump.

5   The HOSTNAME variable is assigned the output of the hostname command, the system's hostname.

6   The history list size is set to a maximum of 1,000 commands.

7   The .inputrc file sets editing modes, key bindings, and so forth for the Readline library. This line checks to see if $HOME/.inputrc exists.

8   If $HOME/.inputrc does exist, then set the INPUTRC variable to /etc/inputrc.

9   If tcsh is the current shell, ? will return true, and line 10 will be executed.

10   The bindkey command sets an escape sequence for the Delete key used in command-line editing.

/etc/csh.cshrc.   The /etc/csh.cshrc file is sourced by the C and TC shells whenever they are run. C and TC shells can be started at login time (if it has been specified as a user's login shell) when running a C or TC shell script, or when opening a shell window that runs the C or TC shell. The example /etc/csh.cshrc file given below is from a Red Hat Linux system. The /etc/csh.cshrc file should include items that are not exported to child processes, such as setting a umask or setting the prompt. Note that in the C and TC shell the prompt variable is local, which means it will not be passed to child processes.

EXAMPLE   16.22

```
     # cat /etc/csh.cshrc
1    umask 022
2    if ($?prompt) then
3        if ($?tcsh) then
4            set prompt='[%n@%m %c]$ '
         else
5            set prompt=\[`id -nu`@`hostname -s`\]\$\
         endif
     endif
```

EXAMPLE 16.22 (CONTINUED)

```
6     if ( -d /etc/profile.d ) then
7         set nonomatch
8         foreach i ( /etc/profile.d/*.csh )
9             if ( -r $i ) then
10                source $i
              endif
          end
11        unset i nonomatch
      endif
```

EXPLANATION

1   Sets the umask to 022, which will block write permissions from being set on permissions for the group and others on newly created files.

2   The ? is used to check if the prompt variable has a value. If it does, then this is an interactive shell.

3   The ? is used to see if the tcsh variable has a value. This variable is set only if we are in the tcsh; it is not set in the C shell.

4   If this is a TC shell, then the prompt is set to the username (%n), followed by an @ symbol, followed by the host name (%h), followed by the current directory (%c).

5   If this is a C shell, then the prompt is set to the username (the output of the id -nu command), followed by an @ symbol, followed by the hostname (the output of the hostname -s command), followed by a dollar sign.

6   If the /etc/profile.d directory exists, then go to line 7.

7   The nonomatch is set to suppress any error messages produced if a shell wildcard doesn't match a filename. This setting is in effect until the unset command is run.

8   This foreach loop will cycle through any files in the /etc/profile.d directory whose name ends in .csh, assigning each name, in turn, to the variable i. Notice that if *.csh does not match any of the filenames in the /etc/profile.d directory, an error message, No match, would normally be displayed. Because of the nonomatch setting, this will not happen.

9   If the user running this script has read permission on the file, whose name is currently stored in the variable i, then go to line 10.

10 The file is sourced.

11 The nonomatch variable is unset. This means that error messages will again be displayed if a shell wildcard doesn't match any filenames. The i variable is also unset, which removes its value from memory. Shell scripts that are run in the regular manner, that is, by typing the script name in at the command line, are run in a subshell, making it uneccessary to unset variables because when the script exits, the subshell also exits, and the variables will be removed from memory automatically. Because this script is sourced, a subshell is not created, and the variables will remain in the memory of the current shell. Because they are no longer needed, the variables should be unset.

16.5 **Summary**

As a system administrator you are the superuser and supreme in your power. Like a god, you can create or destroy systems with just a few keystrokes. For such responsibility, a little knowledge is a dangerous thing. Understanding how the shell works and how to read, write, and modify shell scripts is crucial to your job, not only for automating everyday tasks, but for keeping the environment safe and clean for those users who depend on you. Shell scripts are run from the time the system boots to when it shuts down. They are used for system initialization, monitoring processes, installing software, checking disk usage, scheduling tasks, and so on. Beyond system chores, much of your time will be devoted to managing user accounts that start with a login shell, run initialization scripts, execute commands in a shell, and exit when the shell exits. This book was written to help all types of UNIX/Linux users understand how the major shells work and how to read and write scripts. This chapter was added to outline some of the shell scripts that pertain to system administration and how they interact with the system and its users. There are many topics that are not relevant here, but are important in the overall subject of system administration. You may find the following list of resources helpful.

Nemeth, E., Snyder, G., Seebass, S., Hein, T. R., *UNIX System Administration Handbook*, *3rd Ed.*, Upper Saddle River, NJ: Prentice Hall PTR, 2000. ISBN: 0131510517.

Nemeth, E., Snyder, G., Hein, T. R., *Linux Administration Handbook*, Upper Saddle River, NJ: Prentice Hall PTR, 2002. ISBN: 0130084662.

Gagné, M., *Linux System Administration: A User's Guide*, Boston: Addison-Wesley, 2001. ISBN: 0201719347.

Sobell, M. G., *A Practical Guide to Red Hat Linux: Fedora Core and Red Hat Enterprise Linux, 2nd Ed.,* Pearson Education, 2004. ISBN: 0131470248.

See also www.ugu.com, Unix Guru Universe: The Official Home Page for Unix System Administrators.

Useful UNIX/Linux Utilities
for Shell Programmers

apropos—searches the whatis database for strings

    apropos keyword ...

apropos searches a set of database files (see directory /usr/man/whatis) containing short descriptions of system commands for keywords and displays the result on the standard output. Same as man -k.

EXAMPLE A.1

```
1 $ apropos bash
   bash (1)                - GNU Bourne-Again SHell

2 $ man -k tcsh
   tsh (1)                 - C shell with filename completionand command-line editing
```

EXPLANATION

1   apropos searches for the keyword bash and prints a short description of what it is.

2   man -k behaves the same as apropos.

arch—prints the machine architecture (see uname -m)

    arch

On current Linux systems, arch prints things such as i386, i486, i586, alpha, sparc, arm, m68k, mips, or ppc.

EXAMPLE A.2

```
$ arch
i386
```

at, batch—executes commands at a later time

```
at [-csm] [-f script] [-qqueue] time [date] [+ increment]
at -l [ job...]
at -r job...
batch
```

at and batch read commands from standard input to be executed at a later time. at allows you to specify when the commands should be executed, whereas jobs queued with batch will execute when system load level permits. Executes commands read from stdin or a file at some later time. Unless redirected, the output is mailed to the user.

EXAMPLE A.3

```
1    at 6:30am Dec 12 < program
2    at noon tomorrow < program
3    at 1945 pm August 9 < program
4    at now + 3 hours < program
5    at 8:30am Jan 4 < program
6    at -r 83883555320.a
```

EXPLANATION

1   At 6:30 in the morning on December 12, start the job.

2   At noon tomorrow start the job.

3   At 7:45 in the evening on August 9, start the job.

4   In three hours start the job.

5   At 8:30 in the morning on January 4, start the job.

6   Removes previously scheduled job 83883555320.a.

awk—pattern scanning and processing language

```
awk [ -fprogram-file ] [ -Fc ] [ prog ] [ parameters ] [ filename...]
```

awk scans each input filename for lines that match any of a set of patterns specified in prog.

EXAMPLE A.4

```
1    awk '{print $1, $2}' file
2    awk '/John/{print $3, $4}' file
3    awk -F: '{print $3}' /etc/passwd
4    date | awk '{print $6}'
```

EXPLANATION

1   Prints the first two fields of file where fields are separated by whitespace.

2   Prints fields 3 and 4 if the pattern John is found.

3   Using a colon as the field separator, prints the third field of the /etc/passwd file.

4   Sends the output of the date command to awk and prints the sixth field.

banner—makes posters

banner prints its arguments (each up to 10 characters long) in large letters on the standard output.

EXAMPLE A.5

```
banner Happy Birthday
```

EXPLANATION

Displays in banner format the string Happy Birthday.

basename—with a directory name delivers portions of the pathname

```
basename string [ suffix ]
dirname string
```

basename deletes any prefix ending in / (forward slash) and the suffix (if present in string) from string, and prints the result on the standard output.

EXAMPLE A.6

```
1    basename /usr/local/bin
2    scriptname="`basename $0`"
```

EXPLANATION

1   Strips off the prefix /usr/local/ and displays bin.
2   Assigns just the name of the script, $0, to the variable scriptname.

bash—GNU Bourne Again Shell

```
bash [options] [file[arguments]]
sh [options] [file[arguments]]
```

bash is Copyright © 1989, 1991 by the Free Software Foundation, Inc. bash is a sh-compatible command language interpreter that executes commands read from the standard input or from a file. bash also incorporates useful features from the Korn and C shells (ksh and csh).

bc—processes precision arithmetic

```
bc [ -c ] [ -l ] [ filename...]
```

bc is an interactive processor for a language that resembles C, but provides unlimited precision arithmetic. It takes input from any files given, then reads the standard input.

EXAMPLE A.7

```
1    bc << EOF
     scale=3
     4.5 + 5.6 / 3
     EOF
     Output : 6.366
     -----------------------------
2    bc
     ibase=2
     5
     101 (Output)
     20
     10100 (Output
     ^D
```

EXPLANATION

1   This is a here document. From the first EOF to the last EOF input is given to the bc command. The scale specifies the number of digits to the right of the decimal point. The result of the calculation is displayed on the screen.

2   The number base is 2. The number is converted to binary (AT&T only).

bdiff—compares two big files

bdiff compares two files that are too large for diff.

cal—displays a calendar

```
cal [ [ month ] year ]
```

cal prints a calendar for the specified year. If a month is also specified, a calendar just for that month is printed. If neither is specified, a calendar for the present month is printed.

EXAMPLE A.8

```
1    cal 1997
2    cal 5 1978
```

EXPLANATION

1   Prints the calendar year 1997.

2   Prints the month of May for 1978.

cat—concatenates and displays files

```
cat [ -bnsuvet ] filename...
```

cat reads each filename in sequence and writes it on the standard output. If no input file is given, or if the argument - is encountered, cat reads from the standard input file.

EXAMPLE A.9

```
1    cat /etc/passwd
2    cat -n file1 file2 >> file3
```

EXPLANATION

1   Displays the contents of the /etc/passwd file.

2   Concatenates file1 and file2 and appends output to file3. The -n switch causes each line to be numbered.

chfn—changes the finger information

```
chfn  [ -f full-name ] [ -o office ] [ -poffice-phone ]
      [ -h home-phone ] [ -u ] [ -v ] [ username ]
```

chfn is used to change your finger information. This information is stored in the /etc/passwd file, and is displayed by the finger program. The Linux finger command will display four pieces of information that can be changed by chfn: your real name, your work room and phone, and your home phone.

chmod—changes the permissions mode of a file

```
chmod [ -fR ] mode filename...
chmod [ugoa ]{ + | - | = }[ rwxlsStTugo] filename...
```

chmod changes or assigns the mode of a file. The mode of a file specifies its permissions and other attributes. The mode may be absolute or symbolic.

EXAMPLE A.10

```
1    chmod +x script.file
2    chmod u+x,g-x file
3    chmod 755 *
```

EXPLANATION

1   Turns on execute permission for user, group, and others on script.file.

2   Turns on execute permission for user, and removes it from group on file.

3   Turns on read, write, and execute for the user, read and execute for the group, and read and execute for others on all files in the current working directory. The value is octal (111 101 101).
```
rwxxr-xr-x
```

chown—changes owner of file

```
chown [ -fhR ] owner filename ...
```

chown changes the owner of the files to owner. The owner may be either a decimal user ID or a login name found in /etc/passwd file. Only the owner of a file (or the superuser) may change the owner of that file.

EXAMPLE A.11

```
1    chown john filex
2    chown -R ellie ellie
```

EXPLANATION

1   Changes the user ID of filex to john.
2   Recursively changes the ownership to ellie for all files in the ellie directory.

chsh—changes your login shell

```
chsh [ -s shell ] [ -l ] [ -u ] [ -v ] [ username ]
```

chsh is used to change your login shell. If a shell is not given on the command line, chsh prompts for one. All valid shells are listed in the /etc/shells file.

-s, --shell	Specifies your login shell.
-l, --list-shells	Prints the list of shells listed in /etc/shells and exits.
-u, --help	Prints a usage message and exits.
-v, --version	Prints version information and exits.

EXAMPLE A.12

```
1 $ chsh -l
/bin/bash
/bin/sh
/bin/ash
/bin/bsh
/bin/tcsh
/bin/csh
/bin/ksh
/bin/zsh


2 $ chsh
Changing shell for ellie.
New shell [/bin/sh] tcsh
chsh: shell ust be a full pathname.
```

EXPLANATION

   1   Lists all available shells on this Linux system.

   2   Asks the user to type in the full pathname for a new login shell. Fails unless a full pathname, such as /bin/tcsh, is given.

clear—clears the terminal screen

cmp—compares two files

       cmp [-l] [-s] filename1 filename2

The two files are compared. cmp makes no comment if the files are the same; if they differ, it announces the byte and line numbers at which the first difference occurred.

EXAMPLE A.13

    cmp file.new file.old

EXPLANATION

If the files differ, the character number and the line number are displayed.

compress—compress, uncompress, zcat compress, uncompress files, or display expanded files

       compress [-cfv] [-b bits] [filename...]
       uncompress [-cv] [filename...]
       zcat [filename...]

compress reduces the size of the named files using adaptive Lempel-Ziv coding. Whenever possible, each file is replaced by one with a .Z extension. The ownership modes, access time, and modification time will stay the same. If no files are specified, the standard input is compressed to the standard output.

EXAMPLE A.14

   1   compress -v book
       book:Compression:35.07% -- replaced with book.Z
   2   ls
       book.Z

EXPLANATION

   1   Compresses the book into a file called book.Z and displays the percentage that the file was compressed and its new name.

cp—copies files

cp [-i] [-p] [-r] [filename ...] target

The cp command copies filename to another target, which is either a file or directory. The filename and target cannot have the same name. If the target is not a directory, only one file may be specified before it; if it is a directory, more than one file may be specified. If target does not exist, cp creates a file named target. If target exists and is not a directory, its contents are overwritten. If target is a directory, the file(s) are copied to that directory.

EXAMPLE A.15

```
1   cp file1 file2
2   cp chapter1 book
3   cp -r desktop /usr/bin/tester
```

EXPLANATION

1   Copies the contents of file1 to file2.
2   Copies the contents of chapter1 to the book directory. In the book directory, chapter1 has its original name.
3   Recursively copies the entire desktop directory into /usr/bin/tester.

cpio—copies file archives in and out

```
cpio -i [ bBcdfkmrsStuvV6 ] [ -C bufsize ] [ -E filename ]
   [ -H header ] [ -I filename [ -M message ] ] [ -R id ]    [ pattern ... ]
cpio -o [ aABcLvV ] [ -C bufsize ] [ -H header ]
   [ -O filename [ -M message ] ]
cpio -p [ adlLmuvV ] [ -R id ] directory
```

cpio copies file archives according to the modifiers given, usually for backup to a tape or directory.

EXAMPLE A.16

```
find . -depth -print | cpio -pdmv /home/john/tmp
```

EXPLANATION

Starting at the current directory, find descends the directory hierarchy, printing each entry of the directory even if the directory does not have write permission, and sends the filenames to cpio to be copied into the john/tmp directory in the /home partition.

cron—the clock daemon

cron executes commands at specified dates and times. Regularly scheduled jobs can be specified in the /etc/crontab file. In order to use cron, one of the following must be true: (1) you are superuser; (2) you are regular user, but your user ID is listed in the

/etc/cron.allow file; (3) you are regular user, but your system contains a file /etc/cron.deny, which is empty.

crypt—encodes or decodes a file

```
crypt [ password ]
```

crypt encrypts and decrypts the contents of a file. The password is a key that selects a type of transformation.

cut—removes selected fields or characters from each line of a file

```
cut -clist [ filename ... ]
cut -flist [ -dc ] [ -s ] [ filename ... ]
```

The cut command cuts out columns or characters from a line of a file; if no files are given, uses standard input. The -d option specifies the field delimiter. The default delimiter is a tab.

EXAMPLE A.17

```
1   cut -d: -f1,3 /etc/passwd
2   cut -d: -f1-5 /etc/passwd
3   cut -c1-3,8-12 /etc/passwd
4   date | cut -c1-3
```

EXPLANATION

1   Using the colon as a field delimiter, displays fields 1 and 3 of the /etc/passwd file.

2   Using the colon as a field separator, displays fields 1 through 5 of the etc/passwd file.

3   Cuts and displays characters 1 through 3 and 8 through 12 of each line from the /etc/passwd file.

4   Sends the output of the date command as input to cut. The first three characters are printed.

---

date—displays the date and time or sets the date

```
[ -u ] [ -a [ - ] sss.fff ] [ yymmddhhmm [ .ss ] ] [+format ]
```

Without arguments, the date command displays the date and time. If the command-line argument starts with a plus sign, the rest of the argument is used to format the output. If a percent sign is used, the next character is a formatting character to extract a particular part of the date, such as just the year or weekday. To set the date, the command-line argument is expressed in digits representing the year, month, day, hours, and minutes.

EXAMPLE A.18

```
1    date +%T
2    date +20%y
3    date "+It is now %m/%d /%y"
```

EXPLANATION

1   Displays the time as 20:25:51.
2   Displays 2096.
3   Displays It is now 07/25/96.

dd—converts a file while copying it

```
dd [--help] [--version] [if=file] [of=file][ibs=bytes] [obs=bytes]
   [bs=bytes] [cbs=bytes] [skip=blocks] [seek=blocks] [count=blocks]
   [conv={ascii,ebcdic,ibm,block,unblock,lcase,ucase,swab,noerror,notrunc, sync}]
```

Copies a file from one place to another, most commonly to and from tape drives or from different operating systems.

EXAMPLE A.19

```
1    $ dd --help
2    $ dd if=inputfile of=outputfile conv=ucase
```

EXPLANATION

1   Prints all options and flags with a short description of each.
2   Converts all characters in inputfile to uppercase and sends output to outputfile.

diff—compares two files for differences

```
[-bitw] [-c | -Cn]
```

Compares two files and displays the differences on a line-by-line basis. Also displays commands that you would use with the ed editor to make changes.

EXAMPLE A.20

```
diff file1 file2
1c1
< hello there
---
> Hello there.
2a3
> I'm fine.
```

EXPLANATION

Shows how each line of `file1` and `file2` differs. The first file is represented by the < symbol, and the second file by the > symbol. Each line is preceded by an `ed` command indicating the editing command that would be used to make the files the same.

dos, xdos, dosexec, dosdebug—a Linux DOS emulator that runs MS-DOS and MS-DOS programs under Linux

(See Linux man page for a complete description. It's long . . .)

df—summarizes free disk space

```
df [-aikPv] [-t  fstype] [-x fstype] [--all][--inodes][--type=fstype]
    [--exclude-type=fstype][--kilobytes] [--portability] [--print-type]
    [--help] [--version] [filename...]
```

The `df` command shows information about the filesystem on which each file resides, or all filesystems by default.

EXAMPLE A.21

```
df
Filesystem          1024-blocks  Used Available Capacity
Mounted on
/dev/hda5            1787100 1115587   579141    66%   /
```

du—summarizes disk usage

```
du [-arskod] [name ...]
```

The `du` command reports the number of 512-byte blocks contained in all files and (recursively) directories within each directory and file specified.

EXAMPLE A.22

```
1    du -s /desktop
2    du -a
```

EXPLANATION

1   Displays a summary of the block usage for all the files in /desktop and its subdirectories.

2   Displays block usage for each file in this directory and subdirectories.

echo—echoes arguments

```
echo [ argument ] ...
echo [ -n ] [ argument ]
```

echo writes its arguments separated by blanks and terminated by a newline on the standard output.

<u>System V echo options</u>:

\b	backspace
\c	suppress newline
\f	form feed
\n	newline
\r	return
\t	tab
\v	vertical tab
\\	backslash
\0n	n is a 1, 2, or 3, octal value

egrep—searches a file for a pattern using full regular expressions

```
egrep [ -bchilnsv ] [ -e special-expression ][ -f filename ]
[ strings ] [ filename ... ]
```

egrep (expression grep) searches files for a pattern of characters and prints all lines that contain that pattern. egrep uses full regular expressions (expressions with string values that use the full set of alphanumeric and special characters) to match the patterns.

EXAMPLE A.23

```
1   egrep 'Tom|John' datafile
2   egrep '^ [A-Z]+' file
```

EXPLANATION

1   Displays all lines in datafile containing the pattern either Tom or John.
2   Displays all lines starting with one or more uppercase letters.

expr—evaluates arguments as an expression

```
expr arguments
```

The arguments are taken as an expression. After evaluation, the result is written to the standard output. The terms of the expression must be separated by blanks. Characters special to the shell must be escaped. Used in Bourne shell scripts for performing simple arithmetic operations.

EXAMPLE A.24

```
1   expr 5 + 4
2   expr 5 \* 3
3   num=0
    num=`expr $num + 1`
```

EXPLANATION

1   Prints the sum of 5 + 4

2   Prints the result of 5 * 3. The asterisk is protected from shell expansion.

3   After assigning 0 to variable num, the expr command adds 1 to num and result is assigned to num.

fgrep—searches a file for a character string

```
fgrep [ -bchilnsvx ] [ -e special string ]
[ -f filename ] [ strings ] [ filename ... ]
```

fgrep (fast grep) searches files for a character string and prints all lines that contain that string. fgrep is different from grep and egrep because it interprets regular expression metacharacters as literals.

EXAMPLE A.25

```
1   fgrep '***' *
2   fgrep '[ ] * ? $' filex
```

EXPLANATION

1   Displays any line containing three asterisks from each file in the present directory. All characters are treated as themselves (i.e., metacharacters are not special).

2   Displays any lines in filex containing the string enclosed in quotes.

file—determines the type of a file by looking at its contents

```
file [[ -f ffile ] [ -cl ] [ -m mfile ] filename...
```

file performs a series of tests on each filename in an attempt to determine what it contains. If the contents of the file appear to be ASCII text, file examines the first 512 bytes and tries to guess its language.

EXAMPLE A.26

```
1   file bin/ls
    /bin/ls: sparc pure dynamically linked executable
2   file go
    go:     executable shell script
3   file junk
    junk:   English text
```

1   `ls` is a binary file dynamically linked when executed.
2   `go` is an executable shell script.
3   `junk` is a file containing ASCII text.

find—finds files

```
find path-name-list expression
```

find recursively descends the directory hierarchy for each pathname in the pathname list (i.e., one or more pathnames) seeking files that match options. The first argument is the path where the search starts. The rest of the arguments specify some criteria by which to find the files, such as name, size, owner, permissions, and so on. Check the UNIX manual pages for different syntax.

EXAMPLE A.27

```
1    find . -name \*.c -print
2    find .. -type f -print
3    find . -type d -print
4    find / -size 0 - exec rm "{}" \;
5    find ~ -perm 644 -print
6    find . -type f -size +500c -atime +21 -ok rm -f "{}" \;
7    find . -name core -print 2> /dev/null    (Bourne and Korn Shells)
     ( find . -name core -print > /dev/tty ) >& /dev/null   (C shell)
8    find / -user ellie xdev -print
9    find ~ -atime +31 -exec mv {} /old/{} \; -print
```

EXPLANATION

1   Starting at the present working directory (dot), finds all files ending in `.c` and prints the full pathname of the files.

2   Starting at the parent directory (dot dot), finds all files of type `file` (i.e., files that are not directories).

3   Starting at the present directory (dot), finds all directory files.

4   Starting at the root directory, finds all files of size 0 and removes them. The {} are used as a placeholder for the name of each file as it is found.

5   Starting at the user's home directory ~ (Korn and C shells), finds all files that have permissions 644 (read and write for the owner, and read permission for the group and others).

6   Starting at the present working directory, finds files that are over 500 bytes and have not been accessed in the last 21 days and asks if it is okay to remove them.

7   Starting at the present working directory, finds and displays all files named `core` and sends errors to /dev/null, the UNIX bit bucket.

8   Prints all files on the root partition that belong to user `ellie`.

9   Moves files that are older than 31 days into a directory, `/old`, and prints the files as it moves them.

`finger`—displays information about local and remote users

```
finger [ -bfhilmpqsw ] [ username... ]
finger [-l] username@hostname...
```

By default, the `finger` command displays information about each logged-in user, including login name, full name, terminal name (prepended with an ∗ if write permission is denied), idle time, login time, and location if known.

`fmt`—simple text formatters

```
fmt [ -c ] [ -s ] [ -w width | -width ] [ inputfile... ]
```

`fmt` is a simple text formatter that fills and joins lines to produce output lines of (up to) the number of characters specified in the -w width option. The default width is 72. `fmt` concatenates the input files listed as arguments. If none are given, `fmt` formats text from the standard input.

EXAMPLE A.28

```
fmt -c -w45 letter
```

EXPLANATION

Formats `letter`. The -c switch preserves the indentation of the first two lines within the paragraph and aligns the left margin of each subsequent line with that of the second line. The -w switch fills the output line of up to 45 columns.

`fold`—folds long lines

```
fold [ -w width | -width ] [ filename ... ]
```

Folds the contents of the specified filenames, or the standard input if no files are specified, breaking the lines to have maximum width. The default for width is 80. Width should be a multiple of 8 if tabs are present, or the tabs should be expanded.

`ftp`—file transfer program

```
ftp [ -dgintv ] [ hostname ]
```

The `ftp` command is the user interface to the Internet standard File Transfer Protocol (FTP). `ftp` transfers files to and from a remote network site. The file transfer program is not limited to UNIX machines.

EXAMPLE A.29

```
1   ftp ftp.uu.net
2   ftp -n 127.150.28.56
```

EXPLANATION

1   ftp to the machine ftp.uu.net, a large repository run by the UUNET service that handles e-mail and net news for UNIX systems.

2   Opens a connection to the machine at 127.45.4.1 and does not attempt to auto-login.

---

free—displays amount of free and used memory in the system

```
free [-b | -k | -m] [-o] [-s delay ] [-t] [-V]
```

free displays the total amount of free and used physical and swap memory in the system, as well as the shared memory and buffers used by the kernel.

EXAMPLE A.30

```
% free
              total      used       free     shared   buffers  cached
Mem:          64148      54528      9620     45632    3460     29056
-/+ buffers/cache:       22012      42136
Swap:         96352          0      96352
```

---

fuser—identifies processes using files or sockets

```
fuser [-a|-s] [-n space] [-signal] [-kmuv] name ...[-] [-n space]
    [-signal] [-kmuv] name ...
fuser -1
fuser -V
```

The fuser command displays the PIDs of processes using the specified file or filesystems. In the default display mode, each filename is followed by a letter denoting the type of access.

EXAMPLE A.31

```
% fuser --help
usage: fuser [ -a | -q ] [ -n space ] [ -signal ] [ -kmuv ]
filename ... [ - ] [ -n space ] [ -signal ] [ -kmuv ] name
...
       fuser -1
       fuser -V
    -a        display unused files too
    -k        kill processes accessing that file
```

EXAMPLE A.31 (CONTINUED)

```
    -1        list signal names
    -m        mounted FS
    -n        space  search in the specified name space (file, udp, or tcp)
    -s        silent operation
    -signal   send signal instead of SIGKILL
    -u        display user ids
    -v        verbose output
    -V        display version information
    -         reset options

udp/tcp names: [local_port][,[rmt_host][,[rmt_port]]]
```

gawk—pattern scanning and processing language

```
gawk [ POSIX or GNU style options ] -f program-file [-- ] file ...
gawk [ POSIX or GNU style options ] [ -- ]program-text file ...
```

gawk is the GNU Project's implementation of the awk programming language. It conforms to the definition of the language in the POSIX 1003.2 Command Language And Utilities Standard. This version in turn is based on the description in *The AWK Programming Language*, by Aho, Kernighan, and Weinberger, with the additional features found in the System V Release 4 version of UNIX awk. gawk also provides more recent Bell Labs awk extensions, and some GNU-specific extensions.

gcc, g++—GNU project C and C++ Compiler (v2.7)

```
gcc [ option | filename ]...
g++ [ option | filename ]...
```

getopt(s)—parses command-line options

The getopts command supersedes getopt. getopts is used to break up options in command lines for easy parsing by shell procedures and to check for legal options.

grep—searches a file for a pattern

```
grep [ -bchilnsvw ] limited-regular-expression [ filename ... ]
```

grep searches files for a pattern and prints all lines that contain that pattern. Uses regular expression metacharacters to match the patterns. egrep has an extended set of metacharacters.

EXAMPLE A.32

```
1   grep Tom file1 file2 file3
2   grep -in '^tom savage' *
```

EXPLANATION

1   Grep displays all lines in file1, file2, and file3 that contain the pattern Tom.

2   Grep displays all lines with line numbers from the files in the current working directory that contain tom savage if tom savage is at the beginning of the line, ignoring case.

groups—prints group membership of user

```
groups [ user... ]
```

The command groups prints on standard output the groups to which you or the optionally specified user belong.

gzip, gunzip, zcat—compresses or expands files

```
gzip [ -acdfhlLnNrtvV19 ] [-S suffix] [ name ... ]
gunzip [ -acfhlLnNrtvV ] [-S suffix] [ name ... ]
zcat [ -fhLV ] [ name ... ]
```

gzip reduces the size of the named files using Lempel-Ziv encoding (LZ77). Whenever possible, each file is replaced by one with the extension .GZ, while keeping the same ownership modes, access, and modification times.

head—outputs the first ten lines of a file(s)

```
head [-c N[bkm]] [-n N] [-qv] [--bytes=N[bkm]] [--lines=N] [--quiet]
    [--silent] [--verbose] [--help] [--version] [file...]
head [-Nbcklmqv] [file...]
```

head displays the first ten lines of each file to standard output. With more than one file, it precedes each file with a header giving the filename. With no file, or when file is -, reads from standard input.

host—prints information about specified hosts or zones in DNS

```
host [l]  [-v]  [-w]  [-r]  [-d]  [-t querytype]  [a]  host [server]
```

The host command prints information about specified Internet hosts. It gets its information from a set of interconnected servers spread across the country. By default, it converts between hostnames and IP addresses. With the -a or -t switch, all information is printed.

id—prints the username, user ID, group name, and group ID

```
/usr/bin/id [ -a ]
```

id displays your user ID, username, group ID, and group name. If your real ID and your effective IDs do not match, both are printed.

jsh—the standard, job control shell

```
jsh [ -acefhiknprstuvx ] [ argument...]
```

The command jsh is an interface to the standard Bourne shell that provides all of the functionality of the Bourne shell and enables job control.

kill—sends a signal to terminate one or more processes

```
kill  [
```

kill sends a signal to terminate one or more process IDs.

killall—kills processes by name

less—opposite of more

```
less -?
less --help
less -V
less --version
less [-[+]aBcCdeEfgGiImMnNqQrsSuUVwX][-b bufs] [-h lines] [-j line]
    [-k keyfile][-{oO} logfile] [-p pattern] [-P prompt] [-t tag]
    [-T tagsfile] [-x tab] [-y lines] [-[z] lines] [+[+]cmd] [--]
    [filename]...
```

less is a program similar to more, but which allows backward movement in the file as well as forward movement. Also, less does not have to read the entire input file before starting, so with large input files it starts up faster than text editors like vi. less uses ter-mcal (or terminfo on some systems), so it can run on a variety of terminals. There is even limited support for hardcopy terminals.

line—reads one line

line copies one line (up to a newline) from the standard input and writes it on the standard output. It returns an exit code of 1 on EOF and always prints at least a newline. It is often used within shell files to read from the user's terminal.

ln—creates hard links to files

```
ln [options] source [dest]
ln [options] source... directory
Options:
[-bdfinsvF] [-S  backup-suffix] [-V {numbered,existing,simple}]
[--version-control={numbered,existing,simple}] [--backup]
[--directory] [--force][--interactive] [--no-dereference] [--symbolic]
[--verbose] [--suffix=backup-suffix] [--help] [--version]
```

If the last argument names an existing directory, ln links each other given file into a file with the same name in that directory. If only one file is given, it links that file into the current directory. Otherwise, if only two files are given, it links the first onto the second. It is an error if the last argument is not a directory and more than two files are given. Symbolic links are used if crossing a partition.

OPTIONS:

-b, --backup	Makes backups of files that are about to be removed.
-d, -F, --directory	Allows the superuser to make hard links to directories.
-f, --force	Removes existing destination files.
i, --interactive	Prompts whether to remove existing destination files.
-n, --no-dereference	When the specified destination is a symbolic link to a directory, attempts to replace the symbolic link rather than dereferencing it to create a link in the directory to which it points. This option is most useful in conjunction with --force.
-s, --symbolic	Makes symbolic links instead of hard links.
-v, --verbose	Prints the name of each file before linking it.
--help	Prints a usage message on standard output; exits successfully.
--version	Prints version information on standard output; exits successfully.
-S, --suffix backup-suffix	The suffix used for making simple backup files can be set with the SIMPLE_BACKUP_SUFFIX environment variable, which can be overridden by this option. If neither of those is given, the default is ~, as it is in emacs.
-V, --version-control {numbered,existing,simple}	The type of backups made can be set with the VERSION_CONTROL environment variable.

EXAMPLE A.33

```
1   ls -l
    total 2
    drwxrwsr-x   2 ellie    root           1024 Jan 19 18:34 dir
    -rw-rw-r--   1 ellie    root             16 Jan 19 18:34 filex
2   % ln filex dir
3   % cd dir
4   % ls -l
    total 1
    -rw-rw-r--   2 ellie    root             16 Jan 19 18:34 filex
```

EXPLANATION

1   The output of the ls command displays a long listing for a directory called dir and a file called filex. The number of links on a directory is always at least two, one for the directory itself, and one for its parent. The number of links for a file is always at least one, one to link it to the directory where it was created. When you remove a file, its link count drops to zero.

2   The ln command creates a hard link. fllex is now linked to the directory, dir, as well as the current directory. A link does not create a new file. It simply gives an existing file an additional name or directory where it can be found. If you remove one of the links, you'll still have one left. Any changes made to one of the linked files, results in changes to the other, because they are the same file.

3   Change to the directory where filex was linked.

4   The link count for filex is 2. It is the same file but can now be accessed in this directory as well as the parent directory.

logname—**gets the name of the user running the process**

look—**displays lines beginning with a given string**

```
look [-dfa] [-t termchar] string [file]
```

look displays any lines in a file that contain a string as a prefix. As look performs a binary search, the lines in the file must be sorted. If a file is not specified, the file /usr/dict/words is used, only alphanumeric characters are compared, and the case of alphabetic characters is ignored.

OPTIONS:

-d	Dictionary character set and order; i.e., only alphanumeric characters are compared.
-f	Ignores the case of alphabetic characters.
-a	Uses the alternate dictionary /usr/dict/web2.
-t	Specifies a string termination character; i.e., only the characters in string up to and including the first occurrence of the termination character are compared.

The look utility exits 0 if one or more lines were found and displayed, 1 if no lines were found, and >1 if an error occurred.

EXAMPLE A.34

```
1   % look sunb
    sunbeam
    sunbeams
    Sunbelt
    sunbonnet
    sunburn
    sunburnt
2   % look karen sorted.datebook
3   % look Karen sorted.datebook
    Karen Evich:284-758-2857:23 Edgecliff Place, Lincoln, NB
    92086:7/25/53:85100
    Karen Evich:284-758-2867:23 Edgecliff Place, Lincoln, NB
    92743:11/3/35:58200
    Karen Evich:284-758-2867:23 Edgecliff Place, Lincoln, NB
    92743:11/3/35:58200
4   % look -f karen sorted.datebook
    Karen Evich:284-758-2857:23 Edgecliff Place, Lincoln, NB
    92086:7/25/53:85100
    Karen Evich:284-758-2867:23 Edgecliff Place, Lincoln, NB
    92743:11/3/35:58200
    Karen Evich:284-758-2867:23 Edgecliff Place, Lincoln, NB
    92743:11/3/35:58200
```

EXPLANATION

1   look displays all lines in /usr/dict/words that start with the string sunb, assuming /usr/dict/words is in the current directory.

2   look cannot find a line that starts with karen in a file called sorted.datebook. (The file must be sorted or look will not find anything.)

3   look displays all lines with lines starting with the string, Karen, in file, sorted.date-book.

4   The -f option folds upper and lowercase in the search string (i.e., turns off case-sensitivity).

lp—sends output to a printer (AT&T)

```
lp [ -cmsw ] [ -ddest ] [ -number ] [ -ooption ] [ -ttitle ] filename ...
cancel [ ids ] [ printers ]
```

lp, cancel sends or cancels requests to a lineprinter.

EXAMPLE A.35

```
1   lp -n5 filea fileb
2   lp -dShakespeare filex
```

EXPLANATION

1   Send five copies of filea and fileb to the printer.
2   Specify Shakespeare as the printer where filex will be printed.

lpr—sends output to a printer (UCB)

```
lpr [ -Pprinter ] [ -#copies ] [ -Cclass ] [ -Jjob ]
   [ -Ttitle ] [ -i [ indent ] ] [ -1234font ] [ -wcols ]
   [ -r ] [ -m ] [ -h ] [ -s ] [ -filter-option ] [ filename ... ]
```

lpr creates a printer job in a spooling area for subsequent printing as facilities become available. Each printer job consists of a control job and one or more data files.

EXAMPLE A.36

```
1   lpr -#5 filea fileb
2   lpr -PShakespeare filex
```

EXPLANATION

1   Sends five copies of filea and fileb to the printer.
2   Specifies Shakespeare as the printer where filex will be printed.

lpstat—prints information about the status of the LP print service (AT&T)

lpq—prints information about the status of the printer (UCB)

ls—lists contents of directory

```
ls [ -abcCdfFgilLmnopqrRstux1 ] [ names ]
```

For each directory argument, ls lists the contents of the directory; for each file argument, ls repeats its name and any other information requested. The output is sorted alphabetically by default. When no argument is given, the current directory is listed.

EXAMPLE A.37

```
1   ls -alF
2   ls -d a*
3   ls -i
```

EXPLANATION

1   The -a lists invisible files (those files beginning with a dot), the -l is a long listing showing attributes of the file, the -F puts a slash at the end of directory filenames, an * at the end of executable script names, and an @ symbol at the end of symbolically linked files.

EXPLANATION (CONTINUED)

2   If the argument to the -d switch is a directory, only the name of the directory is displayed, not its contents.

3   The -i switch causes each filename to be preceded by its inode number.

mail, rmail—reads mail or sends mail to users

```
Sending mail
    mail [ -tw ] [ -m message_type ] recipient...
    rmail [ -tw ] [ -m message_type ] recipient...
Reading mail
    mail [ -ehpPqr ] [ -f filename ]
Forwarding mail
    mail -F recipient...
Debugging
    mail [ -x debug_level ] [ other_mail_options ] recipient...
    mail [ -T mailsurr_file ] recipient...
```

A recipient is usually a username recognized by login. When recipients are named, mail assumes a message is being sent. It reads from the standard input up to an end-of-file (Ctrl-D), or if reading from a terminal, until it reads a line consisting of just a period. When either of those indicators is received, mail adds the letter to the mailfile for each recipient.

mailx—interactive message processing system

```
mailx [ -deHiInNUvV ] [ -f [ filename|+folder ]]
    [ -T filename ] [ -u user ] [ recipient... ]
mailx [ -dFinUv ] [ -h number ] [ -r address ][ -s subject ] recipient...
```

The mail utilities listed above provide an interactive interface for sending, receiving, and manipulating mail messages. Basic Networking Utilities must be installed for some of the features to work. Incoming mail is stored in a file called mailbox, and after it is read, is sent to a file called mbox.

make—maintains, updates, and regenerates groups of related programs and files

```
make [ -f makefile ] ... [ -d ] [ -dd ] [ -D ]
[ -DD ] [ -e ] [ -i ] [ -k ] [ -n ] [ -p ] [ -P ]
[ -q ] [ -r ] [ -s ] [ -S ] [ -t ] [ target ... ]
[ macro=value ... ]
```

make updates files according to commands listed in a description file, and if the target file is newer than the dependency file of the same name, make will update the target file.

man—formats and displays the online manual pages

```
man [-acdfhktwW] [-m system] [-p string] [-C config_file] [-M path]
    [-P pager] [-S section_list] [section] name...
```

manpath—determines user's search path for man pages

```
man [-acdfhkKtwW] [-m system] [-p string][-C config_file][-M path]
    [-P pager] [-S section_list][section] name  ...
```

man formats and displays the online manual pages. This version knows about the MAN-PATH and (MAN)PAGER environment variables, so you can have your own set(s) of personal man pages and choose whatever program you like to display the formatted pages. If section is specified, man only looks in that section of the manual.

mesg—permits or denies messages resulting from the write command

```
mesg [ -n ] [ -y ]
```

mesg with argument -n forbids messages via write by revoking nonuser write permission on the user's terminal. mesg with argument -y reinstates permission. All by itself, mesg reports the current state without changing it.

mkdir—creates a directory

```
mkdir [ -p ] dirname ...
```

more—browses or pages through a text file

```
more [ -cdflrsuw ] [ -lines ] [ +linenumber ] [ +/pattern ] [ filename ... ]
page [ -cdflrsuw ] [ -lines ] [ +linenumber ] [ +/pattern ] [ filename ... ]
```

more is a filter that displays the contents of a text file on the terminal, one screenful at a time. It normally pauses after each screenful, and prints –More– at the bottom of the screen.

mtools—utilities to access DOS disks in UNIX

mtools is a public domain collection of tools to allow UNIX systems to manipulate MS-DOS files read, write, and move around files on an MS-DOS file system (typically a floppy disk). Where reasonable, each program attempts to emulate the MS-DOS equivalent command. However, unnecessary restrictions and oddities of DOS are not emulated. For instance, it is possible to move subdirectories from one subdirectory to another. mtools can be found at the following places (and their mirrors):

http://mtools.ltnb.lu/mtools/mtools-3.9.1.tar.gz

ftp://www.tux.org/pub/knaff/mtools/mtools-3.9.1.tar.gz

ftp://sunsite.unc.edu/pub/Linux/utils/disk-management/mtools-3.9.1.tar.gz

mv—moves or renames files

    mv [-f] [-i] filename1 [filename2 ...] target

The mv command moves a source filename to a target filename. The filename and the target may not have the same name. If target is not a directory, only one file may be specified before it; if it is a directory, more than one file may be specified. If target does not exist, mv creates a file named target. If target exists and is not a directory, its contents are overwritten. If target is a directory, the file(s) are moved to that directory.

EXAMPLE   A.38

    1   mv file1 newname
    2   mv -i test1 test2 train

EXPLANATION

1   Renames file1 to newname. If newname exists its contents are overwritten.
2   Moves files test1 and test2 to the train directory. The -i switch is for interactive mode, meaning it asks before moving the files.

---

nawk—pattern scanning and processing language

    nawk [-F re] [-v var=value] ['prog'] [filename ...]
    nawk [-F re] [-v var=value] [-f progfile][filename ...]

nawk scans each input filename for lines that match any of a set of patterns. The command string must be enclosed in single quotes (') to protect it from the shell. Awk programs consist of a set of pattern/action statements used to filter specific information from a file, pipe, or stdin.

newgrp—logs into a new group

    newgrp [-] [group]

newgrp logs a user into a new group by changing a user's real and effective group ID. The user remains logged in and the current directory is unchanged. The execution of newgrp always replaces the current shell with a new shell, even if the command terminates with an error (unknown group).

news—prints news items

    news [-a] [-n] [-s] [items]

news is used to keep the user informed of current events. By convention, these events are described by files in the directory /var/news. When invoked without arguments, news prints the contents of all current files in /var/news, most recent first, with each preceded by an appropriate header.

nice—runs a command at low priority

    nice [-increment] command [arguments]

/usr/bin/nice executes a command with a lower CPU scheduling priority. The invoking process (generally the user's shell) must be in the time-sharing scheduling class. The command is executed in the time-sharing class. An increment of 10 is the default. The increment value must be in a range between 1 and 19, unless you are the superuser. Also a csh built-in.

nohup—makes commands immune to hangups and quits

    /usr/bin/nohup command [arguments]

There are three distinct versions of nohup. nohup is built into the C shell and is an executable program available in /usr/bin/nohup when using the Bourne shell. The Bourne shell version of nohup executes commands such that they are immune to HUP (hangup) and TERM (terminate) signals. If the standard output is a terminal, it is redirected to the file nohup.out. The standard error is redirected to follow the standard output. The priority is incremented by five. nohup should be invoked from the shell with & in order to prevent it from responding to interrupts or input from the next user.

EXAMPLE A.39

    nohup lookup &

EXPLANATION

The lookup program will run in the background and continue to run until it has completed, even if the user logs off. Any output generated goes to a file in the current directory called nohup.out.

od—octal dump

    od [-bcCDdFfOoSsvXx] [filename] [[+] offset [.] [b]]

od displays a filename in one or more formats, as selected by the first argument. If the first argument is missing, -o is default (e.g., the file can be displayed in bytes octal, ASCII, decimal, hex, etc.).

pack, pcat, unpack—compresses and expands files

    pack [-] [-f] name ...
    pcat name ...
    unpack name ...

pack compresses files. Wherever possible (and useful), each input file name is replaced by a packed file name.z with the same access modes, access and modified dates, and owner as those of name. Typically, text files are reduced to 60–75% of their original size.

pcat does for packed files what cat does for ordinary files, except that pcat cannot be used as a filter. The specified files are unpacked and written to the standard output. Thus, to view a packed file named name.z, use pcat name.z or just pcat name. unpack expands files created by pack.

passwd—changes the login password and password attributes

```
passwd [ name ]
passwd [ -d | -l ] [ -f ] [ -n min ] [ -w warn ][ -x max ] name
passwd -s [ -a ]
passwd -s [ name ]
```

The passwd command changes the password or lists password attributes associated with the user's login name. Additionally, privileged users may use passwd to install or change passwords and attributes associated with any login name.

paste—merges same lines of several files or subsequent lines of one file

```
paste filename1 filename2...
paste -d list filename1 filename2...
paste -s [ -d list ] filename1 filename2...
```

paste concatenates corresponding lines of the given input files filename1, filename2, and so on. It treats each file as a column or columns of a table and pastes them together horizontally (see cut).

EXAMPLE A.40

```
1   ls | paste - - -
2   paste -s -d"\t\n" testfile1 testfile2
3   paste file1 file2
```

EXPLANATION

1   Files are listed in three columns and glued together with a tab.

2   Combines a pair of lines into a single line using a tab and newline as the delimiter (i.e., the first pair of lines are glued with a tab; the next pair are glued by a newline, the next pair by a tab, etc.). The -s switch causes subsequent lines from testfile1 to be pasted first and then subsequent lines from testfile2.

3   A line from file1 is pasted to a line from file2, glued together by a tab so that the file lines appear as two columns.

pcat—(see pack)

pine—a Program for Internet News and E-mail

```
pine [ options ] [ address, address ]
pinef [ options ] [ address, address ]
```

pine is a screen-oriented message-handling tool. In its default configuration, pine offers an intentionally limited set of functions geared toward the novice user, but it also has a growing list of options and "power-user" and personal-preference features. pinef is a variant of pine that uses function keys rather than mnemonic single-letter commands. pine's basic feature set includes: View, Save, Export, Delete, Print, Reply, and Forward messages.

pg—displays files one page at a time

```
pg [ -number ] [ -p string ] [ -cefnrs ] [ +linenumber ]
    [ +/pattern/ ] [ filename ... ]
```

The pg command is a filter that allows you to page through filenames one screenful at a time on a terminal. If no filename is specified or if it encounters the filename -, pg reads from standard input. Each screenful is followed by a prompt. If the user types a return, another page is displayed. It allows you to back up and review something that has already passed. (See more.)

pr—prints files

```
pr [[-columns] [-wwidth] [-a]] [-eck] [-ick] [-drtfp]
    [+page] [-nck] [-ooffset] [-llength] [-sseparator]
    [-    hheader] [-F] [filename ...]
pr [[-m] [-wwidth]] [-eck] [-ick] [-drtfp] [+page] [-nck]
    [-ooffset] [-llength] [-sseparator] [-hheader] [-F]
    [filename1 filename2 ...]
```

The pr command formats and prints the contents of a file according to different format options. By default, the listing is sent to stdout and is separated into pages, each headed by the page number, the date and time that the file was last modified, and the name of the file. If no options are specified, the default file format is 66 lines with a five-line header and five-line trailer.

EXAMPLE A.41

```
pr -2dh "TITLE" file1 file2
```

EXPLANATION

Prints two columns double-sided with header "TITLE" for file1 and file2.

ping—reports if a remote system is reachable and alive

```
ping [-dfnqrvR] [-c count] [-i wait] [-l preload] [-p pattern]
    [-s packetsize]
```

ping sends ICMP ECHO_REQUEST packets to a host machine and waits for a response to tell you if the host or gateway is reachable and alive. It is used to track down network connectivity problems. If ping does not receive any reply packets at all it will exit with code

1. On error it exits with code 2. Otherwise it exits with code 0. This makes it possible to use the exit code to see if a host is alive or not.

This program is intended for use in network testing, measurement, and management. Because of the load it can impose on the network, it is unwise to use ping during normal operations or from automated scripts.

ps—reports process status

```
ps [ -acdefjl ] [ -g grplist ] [ -p proclist ]
    [ -s sidlist ] [ -t term ] [ -u uidlist ]
```

ps prints information about active processes. Without options, ps prints information about processes associated with the controlling terminal. The output contains only the process ID, terminal identifier, cumulative execution time, and the command name. Otherwise, the information that is displayed is controlled by the options. The ps options are not the same for AT&T and Berkeley type versions of UNIX.

EXAMPLE A.42

```
1    ps -aux | grep '^linda'      # ucb
2    ps -ef | grep '^ *linda'     # at&t
```

EXPLANATION

1   Prints all processes running and pipes the output to the grep program, and printing only those processes owned by user linda, where linda is at the beginning of each line. (UCB version)

2   Same as the first example, only the AT&T version.

---

pstree—displays a tree of processes

```
pstree [-a] [-c] [-h] [-l] [-n] [-p] [-u] [-G|-U][pid|user]
pstree -V
```

pstree shows running processes as a tree. The tree is rooted at either pid or init if pid is omitted. If a username is specified, all process trees rooted at processes owned by that user are shown. pstree visually merges identical branches by putting them in square brackets and prefixing them with the repetition count, for example:

```
init-+-getty
     |-getty
     |-getty
     '-getty
```

becomes

```
init---4*[getty]
```

pwd—displays the present working directory name

quota—displays users' disk usage and limits

```
quota [ -guvv | q ]
quota [ -uvv | q ] user
quota [ -gvv | q ] group
```

quota displays users' disk usage and limits. By default, only the user quotas are printed.

-g   Prints group quotas for the group of which the user is a member.

-u   An optional flag, equivalent to the default.

-v   Displays quotas on file systems where no storage is allocated.

-q   Prints a more terse message, containing only information on filesystems where usage is over quota.

rcp—remote file copy

```
rcp [ -p ] filename1 filename2
rcp [ -pr ] filename...directory
```

The rcp command copies files between machines in the following form:

```
remotehostname:path
user@hostname:file
user@hostname.domainname:file
```

EXAMPLE A.43

```
1    rcp dolphin:filename /tmp/newfilename
2    rcp filename broncos:newfilename
```

EXPLANATION

1   Copies filename from remote machine dolphin to /tmp/newfilename on this machine.

2   Copies filename from this machine to remote machine broncos and names it newfilename.

rdate—gets the date and time via the network

```
rdate [-p] [-s] [host...]
```

rdate uses TCP to retrieve the current time of another machine using the protocol described in RFC 868. With the -p option, rdate prints the time retrieved from the remote machines. This is the default mode. With the -s option, rdate sets the local system time from the time retrieved from the remote machine. Only the superuser can reset the time. The time for each system is returned in ctime(3) format.

EXAMPLE A.44

```
1    rdate homebound atlantis
(Output)
[homebound]    Tue Jan 18 20:35:41 2000
[atlantis]     Tue Jan 18 20:36:19 2000
```

rgrep—a recursive, highlighting grep program

```
rgrep [ options] pattern [file] ......
```

rgrep, unlike grep and egrep, can recursively descend directories. The traditional way of performing this kind of search on UNIX systems utilizes the find command in conjunction with grep. Using rgrep results in much better performance. See also xargs command.

COMMAND-LINE OPTIONS:

-?	Additional help (use -? to avoid shell expansion on some systems).
-c	Count matches.
-h	Highlight match (ANSI-compatible terminal assumed).
-H	Output match instead of entire line containing match.
-i	Ignore case.
-l	List filename only.
-n	Print line number of match.
-F	Follow links.
-r	Recursively scan through directory tree.
-N	Do NOT perform a recursive search.
-R pat	Like -r except that only those files matching pat are checked.
-v	Print only lines that do NOT match the specified pattern.
-x ext	Check only files with extension given by ext.
-D	Print all directories that would be searched. This option is for debugging purposes only. No file is grepped with this option.
-W len	Lines are len characters long (not newline terminated).

SUPPORTED REGULAR EXPRESSIONS:

.	Matches any character except newline.
\d	Matches any digit.
\e	Matches ESC char.
*	Matches zero or more occurrences of previous RE.
+	Matches one or more occurrences of previous RE.
?	Matches zero or one occurrence of previous RE.
^	Matches beginning of line.
$	Matches end of line.
[...]	Matches any single character between brackets. For example, [-02468] matches - or any even digit, and [-0-9a-z] matches - and any digit between 0 and 9 as well as letters a through z.
\{ ...\}	Used for repetition; e.g., x\{9\} matches nine x characters
\(...\)	Used for backreferencing. Pattern in \(...\) is tagged and saved. Starting at the left-hand side of the regular expression, allowed up to nine tags. To restore saved pattern, \1, \2 ... \9 are used.
\2 \1, =, ..., \9	Matches match specified by nth \(... \) expression. For example, \([\t][a-zA-Z]+\)\1[\t] matches any word repeated consecutively.

EXAMPLE A.45

```
1    rgrep -n -R '*.c' '^int'
2    rgrep -n -xc '^int'
```

EXPLANATION

1   Look in all files with a "c" extension in current directory and all its subdirectories looking for matches of "int" at the beginning of a line, printing the line containing the match with its line number.

2   Look in all files with a ".c" extension, printing the line beginning with "int" and preceded with its line number. (Same as above.)

rlogin—remote login

```
rlogin [ -L ] [ -8 ] [ -ec ] [ -l username ] hostname
```

rlogin establishes a remote login session from your terminal to the remote machine named hostname. Hostnames are listed in the host's database, which may be contained in the /etc/hosts file, the Network Information Service (NIS) hosts map, the Internet domain name server, or a combination of these. Each host has one official name (the first name in the database entry), and, optionally, one or more nicknames. Either official hostnames or nicknames may be specified in hostname. A list of trusted hostnames can be stored in the machine's file /etc/hosts.equiv.

rm—removes files from directories

```
rm [-f] [-i] filename...
rm -r [-f] [-i] dirname...[filename...]
```

rm removes the entries for one or more files from a directory if the file has write permission. If filename is a symbolic link, the link will be removed, but the file or directory to which it refers will not be deleted. A user does not need write permission on a symbolic link to remove it, provided he or she has write permissions in the directory.

EXAMPLE A.46

```
1    rm file1 file2
2    rm -i *
3    rm -rf dir
```

EXPLANATION

1   Removes file1 and file2 from the directory.
2   Removes all files in the present working directory, but asks first if it is okay.
3   Recursively removes all files and directories below dir and ignores error messages.

---

rmdir—removes a directory

```
rmdir [-p] [-s] dirname...
```

Removes a directory if it is empty. With -p, parent directories are also removed.

rsh—starts a remote shell

```
rsh [ -n ] [ -l username ] hostname command
rsh hostname [ -n ] [ -l username ] command
```

rsh connects to the specified hostname and executes the specified command. rsh copies its standard input to the remote command, the standard output of the remote command to its standard output, and the standard error of the remote command to its standard error. Interrupt, quit, and terminate signals are propagated to the remote command; rsh normally terminates when the remote command does. If a command is not given, then rsh logs you on to the remote host using rlogin.

EXAMPLE A.47

```
1    rsh bluebird ps -ef
2    rsh -l john owl ls; echo $PATH;cat .profile
```

EXPLANATION

1   Connects to machine bluebird and displays all processes running on that machine.

2   Goes to the remote machine owl as user john and executes all three commands.

ruptime—shows the host status of local machines

    ruptime [-alrtu]

ruptime gives a status line–like uptime for each machine on the local network; these are formed from packets broadcast by each host on the network once a minute. Machines for which no status report has been received for five minutes are shown as being down. Normally, the listing is sorted by hostname, but this order can be changed by specifying one of ruptime's options.

rwho—who is logged in on local machines

    rwho [-a]

The rwho command produces output similar to who, but for all machines on your network. However, it does not work through gateways and host must have the directory /var/spool/rwho as well as the rwho daemon running. If no report has been received from a machine for five minutes, rwho assumes the machine is down, and does not report users last known to be logged into that machine. If a user has not typed to the system for a minute or more, rwho reports this idle time. If a user has not typed to the system for an hour or more, the user is omitted from the output of rwho, unless the -a flag is given.

script—creates a typescript of a terminal session

    script [-a] [filename]

script makes a typescript of everything printed on your terminal. The typescript is written to a filename. If no filename is given, the typescript is saved in the file called typescript. The script ends when the shell exits or when Ctrl-D is typed.

EXAMPLE A.48

    1   script
    2   script myfile

EXPLANATION

1   Starts up a script session in a new shell. Everything displayed on the terminal is stored in a file called typescript. Must press ^d or exit to end the session.

2   Starts up a script session in a new shell, storing everything displayed on the terminal in myfile. Must press ^d or exit to end the session.

sed—streamlined editor

```
sed [-n] [-e script] [-f sfilename] [filename ...]
```

sed copies the named filename (standard input default) to the standard output, edited according to a script or command. Does not change the original file.

EXAMPLE A.49

```
1   sed 's/Elizabeth/Lizzy/g' file
2   sed '/Dork/d' file
3   sed -n '15,20p' file
```

EXPLANATION

1   Substitute all occurrences of Elizabeth with Lizzy in file and display on the terminal screen.

2   Remove all lines containing Dork and print the remaining lines on the screen.

3   Print only lines 15 through 20.

size—prints section sizes in bytes of object files

```
size [ -f ] [ -F ] [ -n ] [ -o ] [ -V ] [ -x ] filename...
```

The size command produces segment or section size information in bytes for each loaded section in ELF or COFF object files. size prints out the size of the text, data, and bss (uninitialized data) segments (or sections) and their total.

sleep—suspends execution for some number of seconds

```
sleep time
```

sleep suspends execution for time seconds. It is used to execute a command after a certain amount of time.

EXAMPLE A.50

```
1   (sleep 105; command)&
2   (In Script)
    while true
    do
          command
          sleep 60
    done
```

EXPLANATION

1   After 105 seconds, command is executed. Prompt returns immediately.

2   Enters loop; executes command and sleeps for a minute before entering the loop again.

sort—sorts and/or merges files

```
sort [ -cmu ] [ -ooutput ] [ -T directory ] [ -ykmem ]
    [ -dfiMnr ] [ -btx ] [ +pos1 [ -pos2 ]] [ filename...]
```

The sort command sorts (ASCII) lines of all the named files together and writes the result on the standard output. Comparisons are based on one or more sort keys extracted from each line of input. By default, there is one sort key, the entire input line, and ordering is lexicographic by bytes in machine collating sequence.

EXAMPLE A.51

```
1    sort filename
2    sort -u filename
3    sort -r filename
4    sort +1 -2 filename
5    sort -2n filename
6    sort -t: +2n -3 filename
7    sort -f filename
8    sort -b +1 filename
```

EXPLANATION

1 Sorts the lines alphabetically.

2 Sorts out duplicate entries.

3 Sorts in reverse.

4 Sorts starting on field 1 (fields are separated by whitespace and start at field 0), stopping at field 2 rather than sorting to the end of the line.

5 Sorts the third field numerically.

6 Sorts numerically starting at field 2 and stopping at field 3, with the colon designated as the field separator (-t:).

7 Sorts folding in uppercase and lowercase letters.

8 Sorts starting at field 1, removing leading blanks.

spell—finds spelling errors

```
spell [ -blvx ] [ -d hlist ] [ -s hstop ] [ +local_file ] [ filename]...
```

spell collects words from the named filenames and looks them up in a spelling list. Words that neither occur among nor are derivable from (by applying certain inflections, prefixes, and/or suffixes) words in the spelling list are printed on the standard output. If no filenames are named, words are collected from the standard input.

split—splits a file into pieces

```
split [ -n ] [ filename [ name ] ]
```

split reads `filename` and writes it in `n` line pieces into a set of output files. The first output file is named with aa appended, and so on lexicographically, up to zz (a maximum of 676 files). The maximum length of `name` is 2 characters less than the maximum file-name length allowed by the filesystem. See statvfs. If no output name is given, x is used as the default. (Output files will be called xaa, xab, etc.)

EXAMPLE A.52

```
1   split -500 filea
2   split -1000 fileb out
```

EXPLANATION

1   Splits `filea` into 500-line files. Files are named xaa, xab, xac, and so on.

2   Splits `fileb` into 1,000-line files named out.aa, out.ab, and so on.

---

strings—finds any printable strings in an object or binary file

strings [-a] [-o] [-number] [filename...]

The strings command looks for ASCII strings in a binary file. A string is any sequence of four or more printing characters ending with a newline or a null character. strings is useful for identifying random object files and many other things.

EXAMPLE A.53

```
strings /bin/nawk | head -2
```

EXPLANATION

Prints any ASCII text in the first two lines of the binary executable /bin/nawk.

---

stty—sets the options for a terminal

stty [-a] [-g] [modes]

stty sets certain terminal I/O options for the device that is the current standard input; without arguments, it reports the settings of certain options.

EXAMPLE A.54

```
1   stty erase <Press backspace key> or ^h
2   stty -echo; read secretword; stty echo
3   stty -a (AT&T) or stty -everything (BSD)
```

EXPLANATION

1   Sets the Backspace key to erase.

2   Turns off echoing; waits for user input; turns echoing back on.

3   Lists all possible options to stty.

su—become superuser or another user

```
su [ - ] [ username [ arg ... ] ]
```

su allows one to become another user without logging off. The default username is root (superuser). To use su, the appropriate password must be supplied (unless the invoker is already root). If the password is correct, su creates a new shell process that has the real and effective user ID, group IDs, and supplementary group list set to those of the specified username. The new shell will be the shell specified in the shell field of username's password file entry. If no shell is specified, sh (Bourne shell) is used. To return to normal user ID privileges, type Ctrl-D to exit the new shell. The - option specifies a complete login.

sum—calculates a checksum for a file

sync—updates the superblock and sends changed blocks to disk

tabs—sets tab stops on a terminal

tail—displays the tail end of a file

```
tail +[-number [ lbc ] [ f ] [ filename ]
tail +[-number [ l ] [ rf ] [ filename ]
```

When a plus sign precedes the number, tail displays blocks, characters, or lines counting from the beginning of the file. If a hyphen precedes the number, tail counts from the end of the file.

EXAMPLE A.55

```
1    tail +50 filex
2    tail -20 filex
3    tail filex
```

EXPLANATION

1   Displays contents of filex starting at line 50.
2   Displays the last 20 lines of filex.
3   Displays the last 10 lines of filex.

---

talk—allows you to talk to another user

```
talk username [ ttyname ]
```

talk is a visual communications program that copies lines from your terminal to that of another user.

EXAMPLE A.56

```
talk joe@cowboys
```

EXPLANATION

Opens a request to talk to user joe on a machine called cowboys.

---

tar—stores and retrieves files from an archive file, normally a tape device

```
tar [ - ] c|r|t|u|x [ bBefFhilmopvwX0134778 ] [ tarfile ]
[ blocksize ] [ exclude-file ] [ -I include-file ]
filename1 filename2 . . . -C directory filenameN …
```

EXAMPLE A.57

```
1    tar cvf /dev/diskette
2    tar tvf /dev/fd0
3    tar xvf /dev/fd0
```

EXPLANATION

1   Sends all files under the present working directory to tape at device /dev/diskette, and prints the files that are being sent.
2   Displays the table of contents of what is on tape device /dev/fd0.
3   Extracts all files from tape and prints which files were extracted.

---

tee—replicates the standard output

```
tee [ -ai ] [ filename ]
```

tee copies the standard input to the standard output and one or more files, as in ls|tee outfile. Output goes to screen and to outfile.

EXAMPLE A.58

```
date | tee nowfile
```

EXPLANATION

The output of the date command is displayed on the screen and also stored in nowfile.

---

telnet—communicates with a remote host

EXAMPLE A.59

```
telnet necom.com
```

EXPLANATION

Opens a session with the remote host necom.com.

test—evaluates an expression

test evaluates an expression and returns an exit status indicating that the expression is either true (0) or false (not zero). Used primarily by Bourne and Korn shell for string, numeric, and file testing. The C shell has most of the tests built-in.

EXAMPLE A.60

```
1    test 5 gt 6
2    echo $? ( Bourne and Korn shells)
     (Output is 1, meaning the result of the test is not true.)
```

EXPLANATION

1   The test command performs an integer test to see if 5 is greater than 6.

2   The $? variable contains the exit status of the last command. If a nonzero status is reported, the test results are not true; if the return status is 0, the the test result is true.

---

time—displays a summary of time used by this shell and its children

timex—times a command; reports process data and system activity

timex [-o] [-p [-fhkmrt]] [-s] command

The given command is executed; the elapsed time, user time, and system time spent in execution are reported in seconds. Optionally, process accounting data for the command and all its children can be listed or summarized, and total system activity during the execution interval can be reported. The output of timex is written on standard error.

top—displays top CPU processes

top [-] [d delay] [q] [c] [S] [s] [i]

top provides an ongoing look at the CPU's activity in real time and a listing of the most CPU-intensive tasks.

touch—updates access time and/or modification time of a file

touch [-amc] [mmddhhmm [yy]] filename...

touch causes the access and modification times of each argument to be updated. The filename is created if it does not exist. If no time is specified the current time is used.

EXAMPLE A.61

```
touch a b c
```

EXPLANATION

Three files, a, b, and c are created. If any of them already exist, the modification time-stamp on the files is updated.

---

tput—initializes a terminal or queries the terminfo database

```
tput [ -Ttype ] capname [ parms...]
tput [ -Ttype ] init
tput [ -Ttype ] reset
tput [ -Ttype ] longname
tput -S <<
```

tput uses the terminfo database to make the values of terminal-dependent capabilities and information available to the shell (see sh), to initialize or reset the terminal, or return the long name of the requested terminal type.

EXAMPLE A.62

```
1    tput longname
2    bold=`tput smso`
     unbold=`tput rmso`
     echo "${bold}Enter your id: ${offbold}\c"
```

EXPLANATION

1   Displays a long name for the terminal from the terminfo database.
2   Sets the shell variable bold to turn on the highlighting of displayed text. Then sets the shell variable unbold to return to normal text display. The line Enter your id: is highlighted in black with white letters. Further text is displayed normally.

---

tr—translates characters

```
tr [ -cds ] [ string1 [ string2 ] ]
```

tr copies the standard input to the standard output with substitution or deletion of selected characters. Input characters found in string1 are mapped into the corresponding characters of string2. The forward slash can be used with an octal digit to represent the ASCII code. When string2 (with any repetitions of characters) contains fewer characters than string1, characters in string1 with no corresponding character in string2 are not translated. Octal values for characters may be used when preceded with a backslash:

\11	Tab
\12	Newline
\042	Single quote
\047	Double quote

EXAMPLE A.63

```
1    tr 'A' 'B' < filex
2    tr '[A-Z]' '[a-z]' < filex
3    tr -d ' ' < filex
```

EXAMPLE A.63 (CONTINUED)

```
4    tr -s '\11' '\11' < filex
5    tr -s ':' ' ' < filex
6    tr '\047' '\042'
```

EXPLANATION

1   Translates As to Bs in filex.

2   Translates all uppercase letters to lowercase letters.

3   Deletes all spaces from filex.

4   Replaces (squeezes) multiple tabs with single tabs in filex.

5   Squeezes multiple colons into single spaces in filex.

6   Translates double quotes to single quotes in text coming from standard input.

true—provides successful exit status

true does nothing, successfully, meaning that it always returns a 0 exit status, indicating success. Used in Bourne and Korn shell programs as a command to start an infinite loop.

```
while true
do
     command
done
```

tsort—topological sort

```
/usr/ccs/bin/tsort [filename]
```

The tsort command produces, on the standard output, an ordered list of items consistent with a partial ordering of items mentioned in the input filename. If no filename is specified, the standard input is understood. The input consists of pairs of items (nonempty strings) separated by blanks. Pairs of different items indicate ordering. Pairs of identical items indicate presence, but not ordering.

tty—gets the name of the terminal

```
tty [ -l ] [ -s ]
```

tty prints the pathname of the user's terminal.

umask—sets file-creation mode mask for permissions

```
umask [ ooo ]
```

The user file-creation mode mask is set to 000. The three octal digits refer to read/write/execute permissions for owner, group, and other, respectively. The value of each specified digit is subtracted from the corresponding "digit" specified by the system for the creation of a file. For example, umask 022 removes write permission for group and other (files normally created with mode 777 become mode 755; files created with mode 666 become mode 644). If 000 is omitted, the current value of the mask is printed. umask is recognized and executed by the shell.

EXAMPLE A.64

```
1    umask
2    umask 027
```

EXPLANATION

1   Displays the current file permission mask.

2   The directory permissions, 777, minus the umask 027 is 750. The file permissions, 666, minus the umask 027 is 640. When created, directories and files will be assigned the permissions created by umask.

---

uname—prints name of current machine

```
uname [ -amnprsv ]
uname [ -S system_name ]
```

uname prints information about the current system on the standard output. If no options are specified, uname prints the current operating system's name. The options print selected information returned by uname and/or sysinfo.

EXAMPLE A.65

```
1    uname -n
2    uname -a
```

EXPLANATION

1   Prints the name of the host machine.

2   Prints the machine hardware name, network nodename, operating system release number, the operating system name, and the operating system version—same as -m, -n, -r, -s, and -v.

---

uncompress—restores files to their original state after they have been compressed using the compress command

```
uncompress [ -cFv ] [ file . . . ]
```

EXAMPLE A.66

```
uncompress file.Z
```

EXPLANATION

Restores file.Z back to its original state (i.e., what it was before being compressed).

uniq—reports on duplicate lines in a file

```
uniq [ [ -u ] [ -d ] [ -c ] [ +n ] [ -n ] ] [ input [ output ] ]
```

uniq reads the input file, comparing adjacent lines. In the normal case, the second and succeeding copies of repeated lines are removed; the remainder is written on the output file. Input and output should always be different.

EXAMPLE A.67

```
1    uniq file1 file2
2    uniq -d -2 file3
```

EXPLANATION

1   Removes duplicate adjacent lines from file1 and puts output in file2.
2   Displays the duplicate lines where the duplicate starts at third field.

units—converts quantities expressed in standard scales to other scales

units converts quantities expressed in various standard scales to their equivalents in other scales. It works interactively in this fashion:

```
You have: inch
You want: cm
    * 2.540000e+00
    / 3.937008e-01
```

unpack—expands files created by pack

unpack expands files created by pack. For each filename specified in the command, a search is made for a file called name.z (or just name, if name ends in .z). If this file appears to be a packed file, it is replaced by its expanded version. The new file has the .z suffix stripped from its name, and has the same access modes, access and modification dates, and owner as those of the packed file.

uucp—copies files to another system, UNIX-to-UNIX system copy

```
uucp [ -c | -C ] [ -d | -f ] [ -ggrade ] [ -j ] [ -m ] [ -nuser ] [ -r ]
[ -sfile ] [ -xdebug_level ] source-file destination-file
```

uucp copies files named by the source-file arguments to the destination-file argument.

uuencode, uudecode—encodes a binary file into ASCII text in order to send it through e-mail, or converts it back into its original form

```
uuencode [ source-file ] file-label
uudecode [ encoded-file ]
```

uuencode converts a binary file into an ASCII-encoded representation that can be sent using mail. The label argument specifies the output filename to use when decoding. If no file is given, stdin is encoded. uudecode reads an encoded file, strips off any leading and trailing lines added by mailer programs, and re-creates the original binary data with the filename and the mode and owner specified in the header. The encoded file is an ordinary ASCII text file; it can be edited by any text editor. But it is best only to change the mode or file label in the header to avoid corrupting the decoded binary.

EXAMPLE A.68

```
1    uuencode mybinfile decodedname > uumybinfile.tosend
2    uudecode uumybinfile.tosend
```

EXPLANATION

1   The first argument, mybinfile, is the existing file to be encoded. The second argument is the name to be used for the uudecoded file, after mailing the file, and uumybinfile.tosend is the file that is sent through the mail.

2   This decodes the uuencoded file and creates a filename as given as the second argument to uuencode.

wc—counts lines, words, and characters

```
wc [ -lwc ] [ filename ... ]
```

wc counts lines, words, and characters in a file or in the standard input if no filename is given. A word is a string of characters delimited by a space, tab, or newline.

EXAMPLE A.69

```
1    wc filex
2    who | wc -l
3    wc -l filex
```

EXPLANATION

1   Prints the number of lines, words, and characters in filex.

2   The output of the who command is piped to wc, displaying the number of lines counted.

3   Prints the number of lines in filex.

what—extracts SCCS version information from a file by printing information found after the @(#) pattern

```
what [ -s] filename
```

what searches each filename for the occurrence of the pattern @(#), which the SCCS get command substitutes for the %Z% keyword, and prints what follows up to a " >, newline, \, or null character.

which—locates a command and displays its pathname or alias (UCB)

> which [filename]

which takes a list of names and looks for the files that would be executed had the names been given as commands. Each argument is expanded if it is aliased, and searched for along the user's path. Both aliases and path are taken from the user's .cshrc file. Only .cshrc file is used.

whereis—locates the binary, source, and manual page files for a command (UCB)

> whereis [-bmsu] [-BMS directory ... -f] filename

who—displays who is logged on the system

write—writes a message to another user

> write username [ttyname]

write copies lines from your terminal to another user's terminal.

xargs—constructs an argument list(s) and executes a command

> xargs [flags] [command [initial-arguments]]

xargs allows you to transfer contents of files into a command line and dynamically build command lines.

EXAMPLE A.70

```
1    ls $1 | xargs -i -t mv $1/{} $2/{}
2    ls | xargs -p -l rm -rf
```

EXPLANATION

1. Moves all files from directory $1 to directory $2, and echos each mv command just before executing.
2. Prompts (-p) the user which files are to be removed one at a time and removes each one.

zcat—uncompresses a compressed file to standard output; Same as uncompress -c

> zcat [file . . .]

EXAMPLE A.71

```
zcat book.doc.Z | more
```

EXPLANATION

Uncompresses book.doc.Z and pipes the output to more.

zipinfo—lists detailed information about a ZIP archive

`zipinfo [-12smlvhMtTz] file[.zip][file(s)...] [-x xfile(s) ...]`

zipinfo lists technical information about files in a ZIP archive, most commonly found on MS-DOS systems. Such information includes file access permissions, encryption status, type of compression, version and operating system or file system of compressing program, and the like. The default behavior (with no options) is to list single-line entries for each file in the archive, with header and trailer lines providing summary information for the entire archive. The format is a cross between UNIX ls -l and unzip -v output.

zmore—file perusal filter for crt viewing of compressed text

`zmore [ name ... ]`

zmore is a filter which allows examination of compressed or plain text files one screenful at a time on a soft-copy terminal. zmore works on files compressed with compress, pack, or gzip,and also on uncompressed files. If a file does not exist, zmore looks for a file of the same name with the addition of a .gz, .z, or .Z suffix. Behaves like the more command, printing a screenful at a time.

appendix B

Comparison of the Shells

B.1 The Shells Compared

Feature	Bourne	C	TC	Korn	Bash
Aliases	no	yes	yes	yes	yes
Advanced Pattern Matching	no	no	no	yes	yes
Command-Line Editing	no	no	yes	yes*	yes
Directory Stacks (pushd, popd)	no	yes	yes	no	yes
Filename Completion	no	yes*	yes	yes	yes
Functions	yes	no	no	yes	yes
History	no	yes	yes	yes	yes
Job Control	no	yes	yes	yes	yes
Key Binding	no	no	yes	no	yes
Prompt Formatting	no	no	yes	no	yes
Spelling Correction	no	no	yes*	no	yes†

* not a default setting; must be set by the user.
† cdspell is a shopt option set to correct minor spelling errors in directory names when cd is used.

B.2   tcsh versus csh

The TC shell (tcsh) is an enhanced version of the Berkeley C shell (csh). Listed here are some of the new features.

- An enhanced history mechanism
- A built-in command line editor (emacs or vi) for editing the command line
- Formatting the prompts
- A spelling correction facility and special prompts for spelling correction and looping
- Enhanced and programmed word completion for completing commands, filenames, variables, user names, etc.
- Ability to create and modify key bindings
- Automatic, periodic, and timed events (scheduled events, special aliases, automatic logout, terminal locking, etc.)
- New built-in commands (hup, ls -F, newgrp, printenv, which, where, etc.)
- New built-in variables (gid, loginsh, oid, shlvl, tty, uid, version, HOST, REMOTEHOST, VENDOR, OSTYPE, MACHTYPE)
- Read-only variables
- Better bug reporting facility

B.3   bash versus sh

The Bourne Again (bash) shell has the following features not found in the traditional Bourne shell (sh).

- Formatting the prompts
- History (csh style)
- Aliases
- A built-in command line editor (emacs or vi) for editing the command line
- Directory manipulation with pushd and popd
- Csh-type job control to stop or run jobs in the background, bring them to the foreground, etc. with command such as bg, fg, Ctrl-Z, etc.
- Tilde, brace, and parameter expansion
- Key bindings to customize key sequences
- Advanced pattern matching
- Arrays
- The select loop (from Korn shell)
- Many new built-in commands

Feature	C/TC	Bourne	Bash	Korn
Variables:				
Assigning values to local variables	set x = 5	x=5	x=5	x=5
Assigning variable attributes			declare or typeset	typeset
Assigning values to environment variables	setenv NAME Bob	NAME='Bob'; export NAME	export NAME='Bob'	export NAME='Bob'
Read-Only Variables:				
Accessing variables	echo $NAME set var = net echo ${var}work *network*	echo $NAME var=net echo ${var}work *network*	echo $NAME var=net echo ${var}work *network*	echo $NAME or print $NAME var=net print ${var}work *network*
Number of characters	echo %%var (tcsh only)	N/A	${#var}	${#var}
Special Variables:				
PID of the process	$$	$$	$$	$$
Exit status	$status, $?	$?	$?	$?
Last background job	$! (tcsh only)	$!	$!	$!
Arrays:				
Assigning arrays	set x = (a b c)	N/A	y[0]='a'; y[2]='b'; y[2]='c' fruit=(apples pears peaches plums)	y[0]='a'; y[1]='b'; y[2]='c' set –A fruit apples pears plums
Accessing array elements	echo $x[1] $x[2]	N/A	echo ${y[0]} ${y[1]}	print ${y[1]}
All elements	echo $x or $x[*]	N/A	echo ${y[*]}, ${fruit[0]}	print ${y[*]}, ${fruit[0]}
No. of elements	echo $#x	N/A	echo ${#y[*]}	print ${#y[*]}

Feature	C/TC	Bourne	Bash	Korn
Command Substitution:				
Assigning output of command to variable	set d = `date`	d=`date`	d=$(date) *or* d=`date`	d=$(date) *or* d=`date`
Accessing values	echo $d echo $d[1], $d[2], ... echo $#d	echo $d	echo $d	print $d
Command Line Arguments (Positional Parameters):				
Accessing	$argv[1], $argv[2] *or* $1, $2 ...	$1, $2 ... $9	$1, $2, ... ${10} ...	$1, $2, ... ${10} ...
Setting positional parameters	N/A	set a b c set `date` echo $1 $2 ...	set a b c set `date` *or* set $(date) echo $1 $2 ...	set a b c set `date` *or* set $(date) print $1 $2 ...
No. of command line arguments	$#argv $# (tcsh)	$#	$#	$#
No. of characters in $arg[number]	$%1, $%2, (tcsh)	N/A	N/A	N/A
Metacharacters for Filename Expansion:				
Matches for:				
Single character	?	?	?	?
Zero or more characters	*	*	*	*
One character from a set	[abc]	[abc]	[abc]	[abc]
One character from a range of characters in a set	[a-c]	[a-c]	[a-c]	[a-c]

Feature	C/TC	Bourne	Bash	Korn
Metacharacters for Filename Expansion (continued):				
One character not in the set	N/A (csh) [^abc] (tcsh)	[!abc]	[!abc]	[!abc]
? matches zero or one occurrences of any pattern in the parentheses. The vertical bar represents an OR condition; e.g., either 2 or 9. Matches abc21, abc91, or abc1.			abc?(2|9)1	abc?(2|9)1
Filenames not matching a pattern	^pattern (tcsh)			
I/O Redirection and Pipes:				
Command output redirected to a file	cmd > file	cmd > file	cmd > file	cmd > file
Command output redirected and appended to a file	cmd >> file	cmd >> file	cmd >> file	cmd >> file
Command input redirected from a file	cmd < file	cmd < file	cmd < file	cmd < file
Command errors redirected to a file	(cmd > /dev/tty)>&errors	cmd 2>errors	cmd 2> file	cmd 2> errors
Output and errors redirected to a file	cmd >& file	cmd > file 2>&1	cmd >& file *or* cmd &> file *or* cmd > file 2>&1	cmd > file 2>&1

Feature	C/TC	Bourne	Bash	Korn
I/O Redirection and Pipes (continued):				
Assign output and ignore clobber	`cmd >| file`	N/A	`cmd >| file`	`cmd >| file`

here document	`cmd << EOF`
	`input`
	`EOF`
		`cmd << EOF`
		`input`
		`EOF`
			`cmd << EOF`
			`input`
			`EOF`
				`cmd << EOF`
				`input`
				`EOF`

Pipe output of one command to input of another command	`cmd	cmd`	`cmd	cmd`	`cmd	cmd`	`cmd	cmd`
Pipe output and error to a command	`cmd |& cmd`	N/A	N/A	(See coprocesses)
Coprocess	N/A	N/A	N/A	`command |&`
Conditional statement	`cmd && cmd` `cmd || cmd`	`cmd && cmd` `cmd || cmd`	`cmd && cmd` `cmd || cmd`	`cmd && cmd` `cmd || cmd`
Reading from the Keyboard:				

Read a line of input and store into variable(s)	`set var = $<`
	`set var = 'line'`
		`read var`
		`read var1 var2...`
			`read var`
			`read var1 var2...`
			`read`
			`read -p prompt`
			`read -a arrayname`
				`read var`
				`read var1 var2...`
				`read`
				`read var?"Enter value"`

Arithmetic:				
Perform calculation	`@ var = 5 + 1`	`` var=`expr 5 + 1` ``	`(( var = 5 + 1 ))` `let var=5+1`	`(( var = 5 + 1 ))` `let var=5+1`

Feature	C/TC	Bourne	Bash	Korn
Tilde Expansion:				
Represent home directory of user	~username	N/A	~username	~username
Represent home directory	~	N/A	~	~
Represent present working directory	N/A	N/A	~+	~+
Represent previous working directory	N/A	N/A	~-	~-
Aliases:				
Create an alias	alias m more	N/A	alias m=more	alias m=more
List aliases	alias	N/A	alias, alias -p	alias, alias -t
Remove an alias	unalias m	N/A	unalias m	unalias m
History:				
Set history	set history = 25	N/A	automatic or HISTSIZE=25	automatic or HISTSIZE=25
Display numbered history list	history		history, fc -l	history, fc -l
Display portion of list selected by number	history 5		history 5	history 5 10 history -5
Re-execute a command	!! (last command) !5 (5th command) !v (last command starting with v)		!! (last command) !5 (5th command) !v (last command starting with v)	r (last command) r5 (5th command) r v (last command starting with v)
Set interactive editor	N/A (csh) bindkey -v or bindkey -e (tcsh)	N/A	set -o vi set -o emacs	set -o vi set -o emacs

Feature	C/TC	Bourne	Bash	Korn
Signals:				
Command	onintr	trap	trap	trap
Initialization Files:				
Executed at login	.login	.profile	.bash_profile	.profile
Executed every time the shell is invoked	.cshrc	N/A	BASH_ENV=.bashrc (or other filename) (bash 2.x) ENV=.bashrc	ENV=.kshrc (or other filename)
Functions:				
Define a function	N/A	`fun() { commands; }`	`function fun { commands; }`	`function fun { commands; }`
Call a function	N/A	`fun` `fun param1 param2 ...`	`fun` `fun param1 param2 ...`	`fun` `fun param1 param2 ...`

Programming Constructs:

if conditional

C/TC:
```
if ( expression ) then
    commands
endif

if { ( command ) } then
    commands
endif
```

Bourne:
```
if [ expression ]
then
    commands
fi

if command
then
    commands
fi
```

Bash:
```
if [[ string expression ]]
then
    commands
fi

if (( numeric expression ))
then
    commands
fi
```

Korn:
```
if [[ string expression ]]
then
    commands
fi

if (( numeric expression ))
then
    commands
fi
```

if/else conditional

C/TC:
```
if ( expression ) then
    commands
else
    commands
endif
```

Bourne:
```
if command
then
    commands
else
    commands
fi
...
```

Bash:
```
if command
then
    commands
else
    commands
fi
...
```

Korn:
```
if command
then
    commands
else
    commands
fi
...
```

Feature	C/TC	Bourne	Bash	Korn
Programming Constructs (continued):				

if/else/elseif conditional	`if (expression) then`
	`    commands`
	`else if (expression) then`
	`    commands`
	`else`
	`    commands`
	`endif`
		`if command`
		`then`
		`    commands`
		`elif command`
		`then`
		`    commands`
		`else`
		`    commands`
		`fi`
			`if command`
			`then`
			`    commands`
			`elif command`
			`then`
			`    commands`
			`else`
			`    commands`
			`fi`
				`if command`
				`then`
				`    commands`
				`elif command`
				`then`
				`    commands`
				`else`
				`    commands`
				`fi`

goto	`goto label`
	`...`
	`label:`
		N/A	N/A	N/A

switch and case	`switch ("$value")`
	`case pattern1:`
	`    commands`
	`    breaksw`
	`case pattern2:`
	`    commands`
	`    breaksw`
	`default:`
	`    commands`
	`    breaksw`
	`endsw`
		`case "$value" in`
		`pattern1) commands`
		`    ;;`
		`pattern2) commands`
		`    ;;`
		`*) commands`
		`    ;;`
		`esac`
			`case "$value" in`
			`pattern1) commands`
			`    ;;`
			`pattern2) commands`
			`    ;;`
			`*) commands`
			`    ;;`
			`esac`
				`case "$value" in`
				`pattern1) commands`
				`    ;;`
				`pattern2) commands`
				`    ;;`
				`*) commands`
				`    ;;`
				`esac`

Loops:				

while	`while (expression)`
	`    commands`
	`end`
		`while command`
		`do`
		`    command`
		`done`
			`while command`
			`do`
			`    command`
			`done`
				`while command`
				`do`
				`    commands`
				`done`

for/foreach	`foreach var (wordlist)`
	`    commands`
	`end`
		`for var in wordlist`
		`do`
		`    commands`
		`done`
			`for var in wordlist`
			`do`
			`    commands`
			`done`
				`for var in wordlist`
				`do`
				`    commands`
				`done`

Feature	C/TC	Bourne	Bash	Korn
Loops (continued):				

until	N/A	until command
		do
		  commands
		done
			until command
			do
			  commands
			done
				until command
				do
				  commands
				done

repeat	repeat 3 "echo hello" *hello* *hello* *hello*	N/A	N/A	N/A

select	N/A	N/A	PS3="Please select a menu item"
			select var in wordlist
			do
			  commands
			done
				PS3="Please select a menu item"
				select var in wordlist
				do
				  commands
				done

Index

informIT

YOUR GUIDE TO IT REFERENCE

Articles

Keep your edge with thousands of free articles, in-depth features, interviews, and IT reference recommendations – all written by experts you know and trust.

Online Books

Answers in an instant from **InformIT Online Book's** 600+ fully searchable on line books. For a limited time, you can get your first 14 days **free**.

POWERED BY

Safari
TECH BOOKS ONLINE

Catalog

Review online sample chapters, author biographies and customer rankings and choose exactly the right book from a selection of over 5,000 titles.

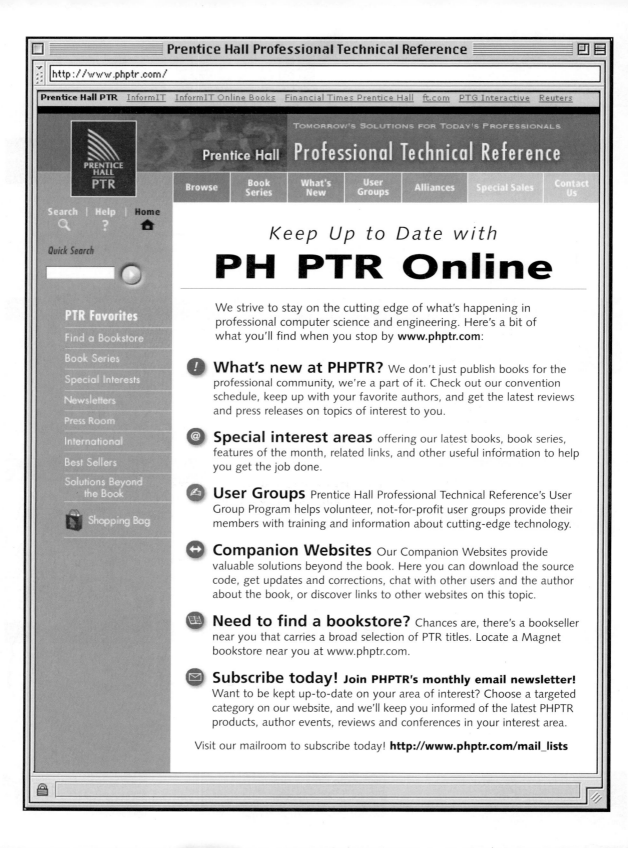

TOMORROW'S SOLUTIONS FOR TODAY'S PROFESSIONALS

Prentice Hall **Professional Technical Reference**

| Browse | Book Series | What's New | User Groups | Alliances | Special Sales | Contact Us |

Search | Help | Home

Quick Search

PTR Favorites

Find a Bookstore

Book Series

Special Interests

Newsletters

Press Room

International

Best Sellers

Solutions Beyond the Book

Shopping Bag

Keep Up to Date with
PH PTR Online

We strive to stay on the cutting edge of what's happening in professional computer science and engineering. Here's a bit of what you'll find when you stop by **www.phptr.com**:

What's new at PHPTR? We don't just publish books for the professional community, we're a part of it. Check out our convention schedule, keep up with your favorite authors, and get the latest reviews and press releases on topics of interest to you.

Special interest areas offering our latest books, book series, features of the month, related links, and other useful information to help you get the job done.

User Groups Prentice Hall Professional Technical Reference's User Group Program helps volunteer, not-for-profit user groups provide their members with training and information about cutting-edge technology.

Companion Websites Our Companion Websites provide valuable solutions beyond the book. Here you can download the source code, get updates and corrections, chat with other users and the author about the book, or discover links to other websites on this topic.

Need to find a bookstore? Chances are, there's a bookseller near you that carries a broad selection of PTR titles. Locate a Magnet bookstore near you at www.phptr.com.

Subscribe today! Join PHPTR's monthly email newsletter! Want to be kept up-to-date on your area of interest? Choose a targeted category on our website, and we'll keep you informed of the latest PHPTR products, author events, reviews and conferences in your interest area.

Visit our mailroom to subscribe today! **http://www.phptr.com/mail_lists**

CD-ROM Warranty

Prentice Hall PTR warrants the enclosed CD-ROM to be free of defects in materials and faulty workmanship under normal use for a period of ninety days after purchase (when purchased new). If a defect is discovered in the CD-ROM during this warranty period, a replacement CD-ROM can be obtained at no charge by sending the defective CD-ROM, postage prepaid, with proof of purchase to:

Disc Exchange
Pearson Technology Group
75 Arlington Street, Suite 300
Boston, MA 02116
Email: AWPro@aw.com

Prentice Hall PTR makes no warranty or representation, either expressed or implied, with respect to this software, its quality, performance, merchantability, or fitness for a particular purpose. In no event will Prentice Hall, its distributors, or dealers be liable for direct, indirect, special, incidental, or consequential damages arising out of the use or inability to use the software. The exclusion of implied warranties is not permitted in some states. Therefore, the above exclusion may not apply to you. This warranty provides you with specific legal rights. There may be other rights that you may have that vary from state to state. The contents of this CD-ROM are intended for personal use only.

More information and updates are available at:
http://www.phptr.com/

About the CD-ROM

Script files and datafiles are contained in separate directories for each appropriate chapter.

The script names and datafile names are the same as in the book.

NOTE: Some of the early scripts send mail to a specified list of persons, so you may choose not to run these scripts (or you may want to change the list to just include your own e-mail address to ensure it works okay).

For example, to run Example 2.6, just change directory to chap02 and run "example02.06" from the command line. (You may need to run "chmod +x example02.06" after copying it to your hard disk to ensure that it has execute permission. If so, you'll have to do this for every script file.) The script "example02.06" requires a datafile named "guests" which is provided in the same chap02 directory.

EXAMPLE DIRECTORIES WITH SUBDIRECTORIES

Some chapters have so many examples that the example files are separated into subdirectories by example number. For example, Chapter10 contains subdirectories named:

    Ex_10.02-10.14
    Ex_10.15-10.26
    Ex_10.27-10.29
    Ex_10.32-10.49

To run Example 10.23 you would need to go to the directory named chap10/Ex_10.15-10.26.

MINOR SCRIPT CHANGES

Lastly, a few of the scripts in the book ask for a datafile to be in a certain directory. The CD version of each of these scripts has been changed to look for the datafile in the same directory as the script. This minor change was made to enable each script to run immediately without further modification.

For instance, Example 2.6 in the book has a line: `set guestfile = ~/shell/guests`

The CD version of the script has been changed to: `set guestfile = ./guests`

HAPPY SHELLING!!